The Promise of America

The Promise of America

Shane Borrowman
University of Nevada, Reno

Edward M. White
University of Arizona

PEARSON
Longman

New York   San Francisco   Boston
London   Toronto   Sydney   Tokyo   Singapore   Madrid
Mexico City   Munich   Paris   Cape Town   Hong Kong   Montreal

Acquisitions Editor: Lauren A. Finn
Development Manager: Mary Ellen Curley
Development Editor: Janice Wiggins-Clarke
Senior Marketing Manager: Sandra McGuire
Senior Supplements Editor: Donna Campion
Project Coordination, Text Design, and Electronic Page Makeup: Pre-Press Company, Inc.
Cover Design/Manager: John Callahan
Cover Designer: Maria Ilardi
Cover Photo: Punchstock/Banana Stock, Punchstock/Creatas Images,
    Punchstock/Media Images
Photo Researcher: Julie Tesser
Senior Manufacturing Buyer: Dennis J. Para
Printer and Binder: R. R. Donnelley and Sons
Cover Printer: Phoenix Color Corporation

For permission to use copyrighted material, grateful acknowledgment is made to the
copyright holders on pp. 771–776, which are hereby made part of this copyright page.

Library of Congress Cataloging-in-Publication Data

The promise of America / [edited by] Shane Borrowman and Edward White. -- 1st ed.
    p. cm.
  Includes index.
  ISBN 0-321-35471-0
  1. United States--History--Sources.   2. United States--Politics and government--Sources.
3. Speeches, addresses, etc., American.   4. English language--Rhetoric--Study
and teaching.   I. Borrowman, Shane.   II. White, Edward M. (Edward Michael), 1933–
  E173.P95 2007
  973--dc22
                                                                    2006027263

Library of Congress Control Number: 2006027263

Please visit us at www.ablongman.com

ISBN 0-321-35471-0

1 2 3 4 5 6 7 8 9 10—DOC—09 08 07 06

CONTENTS

7 America's Promises   638

Appendix I   753

PREFACE FOR INSTRUCTORS

About The Promise of America

A Web search of the term "American dream" yields intriguing findings. The 158 million search results include such oddball entries as a Clydesdale horse; a Crosby, Stills, Nash & Young album; and a pizza house chain, along with such mainstream hits as real estate companies with properties for sale in every state, nonprofit groups concerned with land ownership, sermons by the Reverend Martin Luther King, Jr., and speeches by President Ronald Reagan. In a nutshell, this search encapsulates the issues discussed in *The Promise of America*. That is, the American dream, with its millions of dimensions, is based on a set of promises built into the idea of America itself, the world's oldest continuing democracy but still a young and developing nation.

Designed for first-year writing and critical thinking courses, *The Promise of America* is built around a wide variety of readings that discuss ways in which the American promises of freedom, opportunity, and equality are realized in whole, in part, or not at all. Arguing from a range of political and philosophical positions, these readings define the reality of America and its promises—both to Americans, citizens and noncitizens, and to the world beyond its borders. While these readings include foundational American documents, such as the Declaration of Independence, texts that redefine the nation and its purpose are also included—from President Lyndon Johnson's speech on "The Great Society" and Cesar Chavez's eulogy for Martin Luther King, Jr. to Barbara Ehrenreich's consideration of the value of work and Mike Rose's consideration of equal access to education in America. Taken together, the readings in *The Promise of America* provide both historical depth and a contemporary edge, allowing students to question their own ideas and beliefs about American culture while, simultaneously, expanding the base of knowledge on which these thoughts and attitudes are built.

Furthermore, *The Promise of America* views America as a work in progress; to understand that progress we need to examine where America has been, where it is now, and where it may be going in the future. Focusing on a variety of topics including social equality, education, the media, health,

employment, and success, the readings that follow look at the partial fulfillment of these promises not as a betrayal but as movement toward the
extremely difficult but ultimately attainable goal of freedom, opportunity, and
equality for all people, as articulated in America's foundational documents and
pursued for more than 200 years. Some of the readings in this book register
more impatience than others that this goal remains distant. The perspectives
presented in *The Promise of America* embody neither blind cynicism nor
unbridled optimism. Seeing only good or bad in *any* subject makes no sense,
intellectually. The complex issues discussed in this text—such as the unequal
access Americans have to health care—are far too complex to be viewed only
in absolutes of success or failure and such a view would likely only serve to
reinforce whatever beliefs a reader already holds. Instead of an intellectual
binary built around nebulous concepts of "good" and "bad," then, *The Promise
of America* attempts to deal with components of the American dream as it is
lived by Americans—to consider the reality rather than the mythology.

There is also a personal dimension to this avoidance of both willful cynicism and unreasoning optimism that matters greatly to us: As Americans
who are, to speak of our separate lived experiences together, the children of
immigrants and of military veterans, children who are first-generation
college graduates, we could not and would not let such an imbalance in our
text exist—either by implication or by choice. We have ourselves experienced
too much of the best America has offered to be cynical about its promise.

America simply isn't a promise broken. America is a promise always in
the process of being kept, a promise made that is, in the words of poet Robert
Service, "a debt unpaid." America is a promise made in its foundational documents and reaffirmed and redefined by its citizens—native and naturalized—
in every generation. To allude to Robert Frost, once Poet Laureate, America is
a promise that the nation must still travel miles to keep.

Many metaphorical miles have already been traveled to keep the
promise of America. The texts that follow all serve as markers along the way.

The Goal of The Promise of America

The goal of *The Promise of America* is to provide instructors with thought-
provoking readings and pedagogy to help students become more effective
writers and critical thinkers. To that end, the book includes a wide range of
readings on seven crucial topics: social equality and the right to vote, education, the American news media, health care, employment, civil liberty, and
America's role in the world. Useful pedagogy designed to help students
hone their critical thinking, reading, and writing is woven throughout the
book. Additionally, each chapter of the book provides students and instructors with a solid foundation with which to examine an issue. Chapter

introductions focus specifically on single, broad issues within American culture, such as the promise of a free press, providing a general overview of the issue and connections to contemporary concerns. Two types of reading selections appear most frequently within each chapter: (1) expository essays of varying length (including multiple textual forms such as magazine articles and newspaper editorials) and (2) speeches by individuals prominent in a given debate, from Neil Postman and Steve Powers on the bias in the modern press to Condoleezza Rice on diplomacy and democracy in the "long War on Terror." Each chapter also includes a series of in-depth questions (before and after each reading) that help students think about the issue and perspective presented. A series of visual texts, including both photographs and political cartoons, are also included in each chapter, along with questions for discussion and writing prompts. While thematic threads connect the chapters to one another, the chapters are designed to function on their own without relying on other sections of the book. Because they each have their own introduction, chapters are internally coherent rather than mutually dependent.

One of the most vexing issues in teaching writing emerges from the scholarship demonstrating that learning how to write is most powerful and enduring when it happens indirectly. That is, a student may learn a good bit *about* sentence and paragraph structure by studying other people's writing and linguistic patterns. *Writing* clear sentences and coherent paragraphs is another matter. For that learning to occur there is no substitute for actual student writing on a topic the student cares about, responded to with insight by the teacher. That's when we become an ally of the student, helping him or her convince the reader about something that matters, rather than an enemy imposing rules that may not seem to relate to what the student seeks to do.

For this reason, reading plays an important part in any writing course, particularly reading that embodies problems to be discussed, not just answers to be repeated. As you look through the Table of Contents of *The Promise of America*, you will notice many readings on topics of central importance for Americans, grouped so that differing points of view can be well represented. The readings provide ample material for classroom discussion, whatever the political assumptions students—or teachers—may bring with them.

In more than 80 reading selections, with publication dates ranging from 1776 to 2006, *The Promise of America* covers:

- the promise that all Constitutional rights, especially the right to vote and thus have a voice, are denied to no citizens based upon gender, race, etc.;
- the promise that access to information that is not censored by a governmental agency will allow those same citizens to exercise their right to vote in an informed way;

- the promise that education serves as a leveler, giving everyone access to power, comfort, and some measure of stability and safety;
- the promise that health care, a basic, fundamental requirement of human happiness, will be available to all, citizens and noncitizens, the well-to-do and the welfare recipients alike;
- the promise that work, like education, provides a path to a future better than the past;
- the promise that all laws apply in the same measure to all Americans;
- and the promise that these inalienable human rights are the birthright of all people, both within and beyond America's shores.

In the end, the promise of America is a promise of equality for all people—a promise built upon the fundamental belief that all people are created equal.

Regardless of the order in which instructors choose to approach the readings, the interconnected nature of these texts will be clear. Chapter One addresses the promise of American social justice, especially realized in debates over the right to vote. Chapter Two explores the promise of education as a leveler—and the failure of that promise when education acts primarily to reinforce existing inequalities. Chapter Three looks at the promise of a free press expressed in the First Amendment, while Chapter Four deals with the causes and consequences of a health-care system to which Americans have unequal access. Chapter Five explores the promise that an inevitable outcome of hard work is success and socioeconomic stability. Chapter Six continues this focus on systems of justice and injustice—in this case, as the chapter's readings focus on equality before the law. Like Chapter One, Chapter Seven focuses on issues of social justice, expanding the debate outwards to consider the promise of America to Americans and to the world.

Features

The Promise of America includes a wide wide variety of features to help students strengthen their writing and critical thinking skills. These features include:

An Introductory Chapter on Critical Reading, Writing, and Thinking

The Promise of America opens with an overview of the processes of critical reading, critical writing, and critical thinking. Because this textbook is designed to be read either front to back or according to instructor needs, the introduction functions as a stand-alone chapter and is not anchored in the readings presented in later chapters. Readings discuss issues of American safety and stability, issues also addressed in the accompanying visuals, and a sample response serves to model how students may apply the critical thinking/reading/writing concepts as they work through this textbook.

Prereading Questions

Every reading in *The Promise of America* begins with a question that asks students to consider the issue that will be raised in the following text in relation to their own experiences. These questions can be used either to spark discussion or as prompts for writing assignments.

Post-Reading Questions

While each reading in *The Promise of America* is led by a prereading question, each is also followed by a series of questions in several categories. These question sets begin with comprehension questions, which are never quite as simple as they appear to be, and progress to more challenging tasks. "Textual Questions" are followed by "Rhetorical Questions," both focused on the way the writing of the text at hand conveys its meaning. "Intertextual Questions" push students to think of the texts in relation to one another, sometimes within and sometimes across chapters, while "Thinking Beyond the Text" questions trace the arc of each reading beyond the book entirely. Questions "For Writing and Discussion" will bring students' research and writing tasks back into the classroom, asking them to organize their information, synthesize it, and present it in verbal or textual forms.

Headnotes

An editorial headnote appears before each reading, providing biographical information about each writer or speaker, publication information or (in the case of speeches) details about the context and audience for the speech, and general comments on either the issue raised within the following text or on the text itself. The information in these headnotes links logically with the questions that follow each reading, particularly those "Textual Questions" and "Rhetorical Questions" that concern issues of credibility and timeliness.

Focal Point Sections

Each chapter is accompanied by a set of photographs and cartoons, all chosen for their connections to both the readings in their respective chapters and to the general focus of the chapters. The questions that accompany each photograph in these Critical Lens sections guide students as they interpret what the images mean in their historical and contemporary contexts.

☙

Supplements

An Instructor's Manual

The *Instructor's Manual* provides additional contextual information regarding both chapters of the book and individual readings, along with commentary that addresses the question sets after each reading and suggestions for individual/group activities within the classroom. Its greatest strength, however, is its focus upon incorporating service learning into a class using *The Promise of America*. Instructors comfortable with service learning as a component of their classes will find the suggestions here useful, as will composition teachers who have never asked their students to do such work. It seems natural to ask students to explore the extent to which these promises have been realized in their own communities and to use their abilities to further the realization of the promises.

MyCompLab (www.mycomplab.com)

A dynamic and comprehensive Web site that will engage students as it helps them to learn, MyCompLab provides market-leading online resources for grammar, writing, and research—all in one easy-to-use place. Here are some of the highlights:

- **Writing resources:** Exchange (online peer review tool); visual analysis instruction and exercises; video tutorials on the writing process; activities (100 activities, many video- and image-based); and model documents.
- **Research resources:** citation diagnostics and exercises (MLA and APA); ResearchNavigator (access to searchable databases of credible sources and access to Autocite, a bibilography-maker); avoiding plagiarism and evaluating sources tutorials; and video tutorials on stages of the research process.
- **Grammar resources:** diagnostics; common error video tutorials; ExerciseZone (over 4,600 self-grading practice exercises, including sentence and paragraph editing); and ESL ExerciseZone.
- **Other resources:** Students using MyCompLab receive complimentary access to **Longman's English Tutor Center.** Instructors who order a MyCompLab package for their course can receive a complimentary subscription to **MyDropBox,** a leading online plagiarism detection service.

MyCompLab is available in four versions: Web site with Grade Tracker, CourseCompass, Blackboard, and WebCT. Please contact your local Allyn & Bacon/Longman representative for more information.

The features and overall structure of *The Promise of America,* along with the materials available online and in the *Instructor's Manual,* will help you use this text effectively. In the end, you will, of course, use these materials in ways appropriate to your institution, your class population, your course goals, and your own teaching style. You will come up with a balance of class time between discussion of the readings and attention to the writing, as students move through drafts toward more finished work. As you use the book, rest confident that these are topics of immense importance, given that they concern matters directly affecting the lives of your students—from the lived reality of civil liberties in post-9/11 America to the ongoing spread—or contraction—of various forms of democracy across the world. These issues, explored here from a wide variety of perspectives, are likely to resonate with your students long after the course is over.

ACKNOWLEDGMENTS

We owe great debts to those individuals who made *The Promise of America* a reality. For their thoughtful commentary and suggestions on this book from proposal through polished form, we thank the following instructors: Michael J. Anzelone, Nassau Community College; Andrea Beaudin, Southern Connecticut State University; Lynda Behan, Ohio State University at Marion; Kirk Branch, Montana State University; Tamara Ponzo Brattoli, Joliet Junior College; Lisa Day-Lindsey, Eastern Kentucky University; Steven Elmore, Mt. San Antonio College; Kathy Fedorko, Middlesex County College; Laura Fine, Clark Atlanta University; Lindsay Lewan, Arapahoe Community College; Eunice Madison, Purdue University Calumet; Connie Mictlicki, Governors State University; Sherilyn Moody-Bouwhuis, Utah State University; Roxanne Munch, Joliet Junior College; Julie Nash, University of Massachusetts Lowell; Donna Niday, Iowa State University; Hector Perez, University of the Incarnate Word; Elizabeth Rich, Saginaw Valley State University; Kelly Ritter, Southern Connecticut State University; Kathleen J. Ryan, West Virginia University; Douglas Trevor, University of Iowa; Collin T. Wansor, Seton Hill University; and Bronwyn T. Williams, University of Lousiville.

For their hours of research, writing, and revision—sometimes under very tight deadlines—we thank Andy Bourelle and Sarah Perrault, whose enthusiasm and professionalism are reflected in the headnotes that precede each reading. For her hours of photocopying and manuscript preparation, we thank Marcia Kmetz.

While we began this project with Eben Ludlow, whose guidance was invaluable as this book took shape, we especially thank Lauren Finn for her passion and proficiency. Additionally thanks are due to Janice Wiggins-Clarke, whose energy and support carried this project through its last miles. This would have been a lesser book without their input.

Shane Borrowman, *University of Nevada, Reno*
Edward M. White, *University of Arizona*

INTRODUCTION

On the Promises of America

The United States of America, the oldest constitutional republic in the world, is a nation founded upon a logical fallacy, promises both general and specific, and slippery semantics—all three visible in the nation's founding document.

The U.S. Constitution, ratified by the States in 1787, begins with a logical fallacy and ends with a promise. The preamble to the Constitution is among the first government documents that schoolchildren memorize—through the Saturday-morning efforts of *Schoolhouse Rock* if not through the efforts of their teachers:

> We the people of the United States, in Order to form a more perfect Union, establish Justice, insure domestic Tranquility, provide for the common defence, promote the general Welfare, and secure the Blessings of Liberty to ourselves and our Posterity, do ordain and establish this Constitution for the United States of America.

The problem of logic appears in the thirteenth and fourteenth words: *more perfect*. Perfection is an absolute. If something is perfect, then another thing cannot be *more* perfect. Perfection is an absolute state, a condition that simply is or is not. The promise of America exists within the preamble's elaboration on that logical fallacy.

The Constitution of the United States served, at the time of its writing, as a formal rejection of old ways of organizing human institutions—a rejection of monarchy, the rule of a king or queen; theocracy, the rule of the church; and oligarchy, the rule of the few over the many. It was a rejection of any rigidly hierarchical view of the world wherein some individuals were, through birth or wealth, ranked above all other members of a society. It was a formal declaration of intent, an elaboration of ideas articulated in the years leading up to the American Revolution and in the Declaration of Independence, that all "men" are equal.

Yet even at the moment of its signing, the U.S. Constitution was a promise unevenly kept. Women were excluded both semantically, as the reference above to the Declaration of Independence demonstrates, and politically. Women were, at the moment of the nation's creation, not given the right to vote—one of the most fundamental rights of any citizen in a democratic governmental structure from the ancient Greek *polis* to the present day. The right to vote is the fundamental marker of one's existence

1

in the nation; it is the right to "count," to matter, to stand (at least potentially and without fear of punishment or retribution) with like-minded individuals and together attempt to effect change. It is a right denied to women from the very beginning, a right that continued to be denied (or unevenly granted) until the early twentieth century. Like women, minorities, particularly both enslaved and free African Americans, were denied their "equal" rights, including the right to vote—and were formally counted as less-than-equal to a "whole" citizen when the distribution of members of the House of Representatives was made.

But in the more than two centuries since its creation, the U.S. Constitution has been revised to make the promise of America a promise that applies to all Americans. In the post–Civil War era, it was revised to make all men free and equal. Some six decades later it was revised again to extend equality—signified by the right to vote—to women. Less than a generation later it was further revised in an attempt to truly grant the right to vote to women and men of color. The list of revisions and emendations could continue—and could include not only all of the formal revisions, written in the text of the Constitutional Amendments, but also in the legal decisions that continue to guide the application of these principles and the interpretation of the formal laws to which they have led.

Still, even more than two centuries after the Constitution articulated the promises of America, they are unevenly kept—to women, to minorities, to the economically disadvantaged, to the physically challenged, to the very young, and the most elderly of citizens. The promises of America apply to all citizens but are unevenly and unequally kept to all citizens.

In Chapter 1, we ask you to consider the promises of America as they are made in the nation's foundational documents and then interpreted and reinterpreted throughout time. Specifically, we focus on the all-important right to vote and the tumultuous history of this promise, with its attendant promise of equality, throughout the past centuries—as the power of "men" who are created equal becomes, over time and through painful national growth, the power of all men and women to be equal in society and to have an equal say in how their society is governed.

Chapter 2 focuses on the promise of free, equal education for all Americans. In this country, education is defined, implicitly if not explicitly, as a great leveler. Every citizen—every child—has the right to an education that is equal to that of every other child. Thus the playing field is, according to this promise, equal and fair—giving every child the same chances in American life. Further, the promise of education is directly related to the promise of the vote, since the Constitution asserts that democracy relies on "the consent of the governed" and an uninformed consent is no consent at all. Without the promise of education, the promise of the vote is empty.

The focus of Chapter 3 is on the Constitutional promise of a free press: free access to information that is vital and necessary to each citizen's ability to function *as* a citizen of the American nation, a promise fully as important as the promise of equal education. An informed citizenry is a mandatory component of a republican democracy in which all citizens have equal power, and an informed citizenry is only possible through the workings of a free press—a news media structure in which truth can be told with neither bias nor fear of retribution by society's most powerful members.

The promise of health, the focus of Chapter 4, is an American promise made implicitly in the preamble to the Constitution, where one of the goals behind the founding of the nation is to "promote the general Welfare." The value of keeping this promise, made implicitly in 1787, to all Americans is impossible to overestimate. Within America's borders, the percentage of citizens without insurance to cover basic health care continues to grow. According to the U.S. Census Bureau, in 1987 only 12.9 percent of U.S. citizens were without health insurance, yet by 2004 that number had increased to 15.7 percent (meaning that as many as 45.8 million people in the United States lacked insurance to cover their health-care needs in 2004). As the population of the United States ages and more and more citizens lose health insurance coverage, the burden of supporting public health falls on local and national agencies, private and governmental. And these agencies struggle beneath the burden, causing prices of basic coverage to rise, hospitals to close, and the gulf between the quality of life and life expectancy of those citizens who have access to health care and those who do not to widen. Beyond America, many nations exist on the constant edge of collapse because of the deprivations of disease, especially AIDS.

Chapter 5, like Chapter 4, focuses on the making and keeping of an implicit rather than explicit promise, a promise that has been known almost from the moment of this nation's founding as the American Dream: The promise that hard work will equal success—both for the individual and for his/her posterity. "In America," argues the promise of this dream, "every generation does a little bit better."

The readings in Chapter 6 consider the promise of equality of all citizens before the law, primarily in the latter half of the twentieth century and in the early years of the third millennium—including the promise of property ownership free from the threat of governmental seizure (the latter an explicit promise made in and then revised out of the Declaration of Independence, where the original wording of the promise was concerned with citizens' life, liberty, and *property*—rather than their life, liberty, and pursuit of happiness).

Chapter 7 focuses on the promises of America in the new millennium—promises to its citizens and to the citizens of the world. It considers how promises made in the closing decades of the eighteenth century and remade into the twenty-first century are—or are not—realized both within and beyond America's shores.

A final word on the readings that comprise this book: While Chapter 1 provides a great deal of historical depth within a narrow range of issues (primarily the single issue of the right to vote with its attendant issues of equality), the chapters that follow make no attempt to provide this same level of historical depth. Instead, a wide range of issues is considered within each chapter, with recently published readings—from Chapter 2's focus on multiple issues within the promise of education to Chapter 7's focus on the issues facing America today, both at home and abroad. It is a tip-of-the-iceberg approach, with individual readings providing only a glimpse into various American promises that have been made, kept, and/or broken. These readings, which are of varying length and complexity, are meant to provoke you—to provoke thought, discussion, and writing. They are worth reading in their own individual right, but read against one another, they provide a multifaceted view of the promise of America as it has been realized (and left unrealized) for more than two centuries.

On Reading and Writing Critically

The purpose of the book you hold in your hands is not to argue that America is an unrealized ideal, not to argue that the truths of the American Dream are lies, not to argue that America is a myth that breaks down in reality, not to argue pessimistically and cynically that America is a promise that has been consistently (if not completely) broken. Nor is the book designed to applaud the promises that have been made, implicitly and explicitly, and to create the illusion that they all have been kept. We see the book as deeply patriotic in the sense that America is and has always been a work in progress that needs careful attention, criticism, and praise to keep it progressing toward fulfillment of its promise. Indeed, that kind of critical thinking about the promise of America is related to its very promise: that an educated and informed citizenry, crucial to the essence of democracy, will be vigilant and responsible.

Instead of asking you either to accept or reject the views expressed in the readings throughout each of the following chapters, we ask you to read each critically—with a pencil or pen in hand and with serious enough concentration on the text so you are fully aware of what the author is saying and not saying. Resist the temptation to read casually, as might be appropriate for light magazine reading, passively dragging the eyes across the page; such reading can be a waking equivalent of sleep rather than an active consideration of the ideas being expressed and the values behind them. Critical reading is engaged reading, reading that asks questions of the text being examined. The questions that a critical reader asks of the text as he/she reads can be broken into three types: textual, structural, and rhetorical.

Reading at the Textual Level

As readers, this is where we spend the bulk of our time. This is reading for content, reading for information, reading for pleasure. We read the information on the side of a cereal box to see how much calcium our breakfast provides; we read a short story, poem, or play simply for the pleasure of the story, the pleasure of the play with language. When we read at the textual level, the level of comprehension, we ask ourselves a single, direct question: "What is this text about?" Put another way, a more blunt way, critical reading at the textual level asks "What's the point?"

When we read at the textual level, however, we can be too focused on getting something out of the text to bother giving attention to how that information is presented, yet considering the structure of the text is one of the most basic and important aspects to which a reader and writer can attend. Structural issues include not only the surface level of the page—the grammar and mechanics of the text—but also the arrangement of its parts, from word choice to sentence length and style to paragraph cohesion to sections of the whole. At the structural level, we consider the parts of the whole and the links between those parts, from the transitions between paragraphs to the connections, stated or implied, between a specific piece of the text and its main point. Reading at this more complex textual level, we think more like writers than readers, asking ourselves "How is this text constructed?"

Reading at the Rhetorical Level

Reading at the rhetorical level involves asking questions of more complexity—questions about the writer or speaker, questions about the audience of the text or speech, questions about the time and place of the speaking event or of the text's publication. To read rhetorically, we must question the writer/speaker's intentions, values, beliefs, purposes: "What does this writer/speaker believe—and want me to believe—to be true?" Rhetorical reading also includes paying attention to the writer or speaker's intended audience: "Was this text/speech crafted for me, for someone with my beliefs, values, and knowledge base, or was it constructed for someone else?" Put another way, we may ask, "Is the argument supported by evidence that is persuasive to me?" This kind of reading also asks you to imagine that the writer is entirely correct and what that might mean; then you consider that the writer might be quite wrong and what that might suggest.

In short, the difference between reading at the textual and rhetorical levels and more passive kinds of reading depends on your level of activity while you read. The readings in this book, in common with reading generally called for in college, ask you to be an active reader, not just a passive recipient of information or entertainment. Since the focus of the book is

The promise of America, you will want to ask yourself questions about each author's take on that issue: "What image of America does each writer/speaker craft?" or "How does each writer/speaker define America and what are the effects of that definition?"

But such engaged, critical, question-based reading is not the end of the job this book is asking you to do.

Reading Intertextually

No writing exists in isolation. Every writer/speaker represented in this collection crafted his/her message at a specific moment in time, for a specific audience, and for specific purposes. All of them represent different views on the promises of America—and their views both complement and compete with one another. As you move from one essay to the next, you will notice that the different authors present different ways of looking at and evaluating the promise of America. Not until you place different views side by side and work to understand their similarities and differences can you feel comfortable that you have understood individual essays.

Thinking Beyond the Text

Questions about the textual, structural, and rhetorical levels will follow each of the readings in this book, as will questions that ask you to think intertextually, but we're going to ask you to take your questions and their answers even further beyond the text. When you read at this level, ask yourself conditional questions built around "if/then" thinking: "If this is true, then what does it mean?" Or "If this is true, then for whom is it true—or most true?" Or "If this is not true, how might I demonstrate that most convincingly?" Often, you will want to test the views and recommendations of the essays by your own experience: "Does this evidence accord with what I think I know or with what I have experienced?" Or "What would happen to me and my family if this writer/speaker's recommendations were put in place?" Or "Does the writer/speaker's vision of America and its promise relate to what I have come to see as important?"

In the end, your task as you read different perspectives on a topic is not to decide who is "right" or which writer agrees most with your preconceptions. Eventually, of course, you are bound to make some judgments about the essays, but you will want to delay those judgments until you have done the kind of careful, active reading we have been talking about here. At this point, after you have read critically at both the textual and rhetorical levels of the text, you are ready to take the last step in understanding and evaluating the reading: writing.

Reading for Writing

Writing is a way of making our thoughts and opinions on various issues visible—to others and to ourselves. Thinking through our own beliefs and assumptions about what is true is the first step in either changing those ideas or reaffirming them. As you write the essays to the topics printed after the readings or to other topics selected by your instructor, you draw upon your reading, your personal experience with the promise of America, and your developing ideas in order to articulate your own thoughts on these complex and important matters. Among the promises of America is the promise that educated Americans will think deeply about the promises made and kept—or not yet kept or never to be kept—and contribute to the continuing dialogue.

The ongoing American dialogue can be entered in many ways, from talking to our family about the issues raised on the nightly news to donating our money and time to a political organization to arguing with our neighbors about an upcoming election. We can paint murals that reflect our views, design Web sites that gather and disseminate information we believe to be true, and march in protest against causes we believe to be unjust.

But one of the most common ways to enter this dialogue, and perhaps the most traditional way, is through writing. We write letters to the editor of our local or campus newspaper, arguing our side of an issue; we write e-mail to our friends and colleagues in which we assert and support our beliefs; we may even write articles for local, regional, or national publications, arguing for our beliefs or against the beliefs of someone else.

Writing such as this is all around us, and it affects every aspect of our lives as citizens.

In this text, we ask that you consider the opinions expressed in the readings—consider them on their own merits, in relation to one another, and in relation to your own lived experience. As you read at the textual and rhetorical levels and consider the questions listed above, your answers to those questions will form the basis of your writing. To illustrate the kind of critical engagement with texts that this book calls for, consider the following text, President Jimmy Carter's 1979 speech "Energy Problems: The Erosion of Confidence," and the brief student responses that follow. (Like all of the readings in this book, President Carter's speech is preceded by a Prereading Question and followed by questions about the textual, rhetorical, and other levels. Unlike the other readings in this book, a student response to one question also appears after the text of Carter's speech, along with a brief discussion of the strong and weak features of the response.)

JIMMY CARTER

Born in Plains, Georgia, in 1924, Jimmy Carter was a naval officer, peanut farmer, U.S. senator, and governor before becoming the 39th president of the United States in 1977. In the last years of his administration, initial successes Carter had with foreign policy were overshadowed by controversial decisions. Carter directed the United States to boycott the 1980 Moscow Summer Olympic Games after the USSR invaded Afghanistan, and during the Iran hostage crisis, when Iranian students took 55 hostages at the U.S. embassy in Tehran, Carter authorized a military rescue that failed. During Carter's presidency, inflation rose each year, and the nation faced an energy crisis, with high fuel prices and short supplies. Republican challenger Ronald Reagan decisively defeated Carter, a Democrat, in the 1980 election. After his presidency, Carter became involved in Habitat for Humanity, a nonprofit organization helping people build and finance new homes, and has written several books of poetry and nonfiction. He also has been active in international human rights efforts, serving as a mediator in North Korea, Bosnia, Cuba, and elsewhere. Carter was awarded the Nobel Peace Prize in 2002 for, in the words of the prize committee, "decades of untiring effort to find peaceful solutions to international conflicts, to advance democracy and human rights, and to promote economic and social development."

"Energy Problems: The Erosion of Confidence" was a nationally televised speech given on July 15, 1979. Carter had previously addressed the nation about its energy crisis four times, speaking at length about his plans to solve the problem. On this date, however, Carter began the speech by addressing what he saw as a more dire issue: a crisis of Americans' confidence that threatened "to destroy the social and political fabric of America." While Carter also outlined his plan for solving the nation's energy woes, his concerns about America's future have had a longer-lasting effect and are remembered and referred to much more.

Energy Problems

The Erosion of Confidence

☙ **Prereading Question**

List the men who have been President of the United States during your lifetime. Select one and describe one or more crises that faced the nation during his years as president. What steps did the president take to reassure the nation during this time/these times of crisis?

Delivered to the Nation, Washington, D.C., July 15, 1979

This is a special night for me. Exactly three years ago, on July 15, 1976, I accepted the nomination of my party to run for President of the United States. I promised to you a President who is not isolated from the people, who feels your pain and shares your dreams and who draws his strength and his wisdom from you.

During the past three years, I've spoken to you on many occasions about national concerns: the energy crisis, reorganizing the Government, our nation's economy and issues of war, and especially peace. But over those years the subjects of the speeches, the talks and the press conferences have become increasingly narrow, focused more and more on what the isolated world of Washington thinks is important.

Gradually you've heard more and more about what the Government thinks, or what the Government should be doing and less and less about our nation's hopes, our dreams, and our vision of the future.

Ten days ago I had plans to speak to you again about a very important subject—energy. For the fifth time I would have described the urgency of the problem and laid out a series of legislative recommendations to the Congress, but as I was preparing to speak I began to ask myself the same question that I now know has been troubling many of you: Why have we not been able to get together as a nation to resolve our serious energy problems?

It's clear that the true problems of our nation are much deeper—deeper than gasoline lines or energy shortages. Deeper, even, than inflation or recession. And I realize more than ever that as President I need your help, so I decided to reach out and to listen to the voices of America. I invited to Camp David people from almost every segment of our society: business and labor; teachers and preachers: governors, mayors and private citizens.

And then I left Camp David to listen to other Americans. Men and women like you. It has been an extraordinary 10 days and I want to share with you what I heard.

First of all, I got a lot of personal advice. Let me quote a few of the typical comments that I wrote down.

This from a Southern Governor: "Mr. President, you're not leading this nation, you're just managing the Government."

"You don't see the people enough anymore."

"Some of your Cabinet members don't seem loyal. There's not enough discipline among your disciples."

"Don't talk to us about politics or the mechanics of government, but about an understanding of our common good."

"Mr. President, we're in trouble. Talk to us about blood and sweat and tears. If you lead, Mr. President, we will follow."

Many people talked about themselves and about the condition of our nation. This from a young woman in Pennsylvania: "I feel so far from government. I feel like ordinary people are excluded from political power." And this from a young Chicano: "Some of us have suffered from recession all our lives. Some people have wasted energy but others haven't had anything to waste." And this from a religious leader: "No material shortage can touch the important things like God's love for us or our love for one another."

And I like this one particularly from a black woman who happens to be the Mayor of a small Mississippi town: "The big shots are not the only ones who are important. Remember, you can't sell anything on Wall Street unless someone digs it up somewhere else first."

This kind of summarized a lot of other statements: "Mr. President, we are confronted with a moral and a spiritual crisis."

Several of our discussions were on energy, and I have a notebook full of comments and advice. I'll read just a few.

"We can't go on consuming 40 percent more energy than we produce. When we import oil, we are also importing inflation plus unemployment. We've got to use what we have. The Middle East has only 5 percent of the world's energy, but the United States has 24 percent."

And this is one of the most vivid statements: "Our neck is stretched over the fence and OPEC has a knife."

"There will be other cartels and other shortages. American wisdom and courage right now can set a path to follow in the future."

This was a good one: "Be bold, Mr. President. We may make mistakes, but we are ready to experiment."

And this one from a labor leader got to the heart of it: "The real issue is freedom. We must deal with the energy problem on a war footing."

And the last one I'll read: "When we enter the moral equivalent of war, Mr. President, don't issue us beebee guns."

These 10 days confirmed my belief in the decency and the strength and the wisdom of the American people, but it also bore out some of my long-standing concerns about our nation's underlying problems. I know, of course, being President, that Government actions and legislation can be very important.

That's why I've worked hard to put my campaign promises into law, and I have to admit with just mixed success. But after listening to the American people I have been reminded again that all the legislatures in the world can't fix what's wrong with America.

So I want to speak to you tonight about a subject even more serious than energy or inflation. I want to talk to you right now about a fundamental threat to American democracy.

I do not mean our political and civil liberties. They will endure. And I do not refer to the outward strength of America—the nation that is at peace tonight everywhere in the world with unmatched economic power and military might. The threat is nearly invisible in ordinary ways. It is a crisis of confidence. It is a crisis that strikes at the very heart and soul and spirit of our national will.

We can see this crisis in the growing doubt about the meaning of our own lives and in the loss of a unity of purpose for our nation.

The erosion of our confidence in the future is threatening to destroy the social and the political fabric of America. The confidence that we have always had as a people is not simply some romantic dream or a proverb in a dusty book that we read just on the Fourth of July. It is the idea which founded our nation and which has guided our development as a people. Confidence in the future has supported everything else—public institutions and private enterprise, our own families and the very Constitution of the United States. Confidence has defined our course and has served as a link between generations.

We've always believed in something called progress. We've always had a faith that the days of our children would be better than our own.

Our people are losing that faith. Not only in Government itself, but in their ability as citizens to serve as the ultimate rulers and shapers of our democracy. As a people, we know our past and we are proud of it. Our progress has been part of the living history of America, even the world. We always believed that we were part of a great movement of humanity itself called democracy, involved in the search for freedom. And that belief has always strengthened us in our purpose. But just as we are losing our confidence in the future, we are also beginning to close the door on our past.

In a nation that was proud of hard work, strong families, close-knit communities and our faith in God, too many of us now tend to worship self-indulgence and consumption. Human identity is no longer defined by what one does but by what one owns.

But we've discovered that owning things and consuming things does not satisfy our longing for meaning.

We've learned that piling up material goods cannot fill the emptiness of lives which have no confidence or purpose. The symptoms of this crisis of the American spirit are all around us. For the first time in the history of our country a majority of our people believe that the next five years will be worse than the past five years. Two-thirds of our people do not even vote. The productivity of American workers is actually dropping and the willingness of Americans to save for the future has fallen below that of all other people in the Western world.

As you know there is a growing disrespect for Government and for churches and for schools, the news media and other institutions. This is not a message of happiness or reassurance but it is the truth. And it is a warning. These changes did not happen overnight. They've come upon us gradually over the last generation. Years that were filled with shocks and tragedy.

We were sure that ours was a nation of the ballot, not of the bullet, until the murders of John Kennedy and Robert Kennedy and Martin Luther King Jr. We were taught that our armies were always invincible and our causes were always just only to suffer the agony of Vietnam. We respected the Presidency as a place of honor until the shock of Watergate. We remember when the phrase "sound as a dollar" was an expression of absolute dependability until 10 years of inflation began to shrink our dollar and our savings. We believed that our nation's resources were limitless until 1973, when we had to face a growing dependence on foreign oil.

These wounds are still very deep. They have never been healed.

Looking for a way out of this crisis, our people have turned to the Federal Government and found it isolated from the mainstream of our nation's life. Washington, D.C., has become an island. The gap between our citizens and our Government has never been so wide. The people are looking for honest answers, not easy answers, clear leadership, not false claims and evasiveness and politics as usual. What you see too often in Washington and elsewhere around the country is a system of government that seems incapable of action.

You see a Congress twisted and pulled in every direction by hundreds of well-financed and powerful special interests. You see every extreme position defended to the last vote, almost to the last breath, by one unyielding group or another.

You often see a balanced and a fair approach that demands sacrifice, a little sacrifice from everyone abandoned like an orphan without support and without friends.

Often you see paralysis and stagnation and drift. You don't like it.

And neither do I.

What can we do? First of all, we must face the truth and then we can change our course. We simply must have faith in each other. Faith in our ability to govern ourselves and faith in the future of this nation. Restoring that faith and that confidence to America is now the most important task we face.

It is a true challenge of this generation of Americans. One of the visitors to Camp David last week put it this way: We've got to stop crying and start sweating; stop talking and start walking; stop cursing and start praying. The strength we need will not come from the White House but from every house in America.

We know the strength of America. We are strong. We can regain our unity. We can regain our confidence. We are the heirs of generations who survived threats much more powerful and awesome than those that challenge us now.

Our fathers and mothers were strong men and women who shaped the new society during the Great Depression, who fought world wars and who carved out a new charter of peace for the world. We ourselves are the same Americans who just 10 years ago put a man on the moon. We are the generation that dedicated our society to the pursuit of human rights and equality.

And we are the generation that will win the war on the energy problem, and in that process rebuild the unity and confidence of America. We are at a turning point in our history. There are two paths to choose. One is a path I've warned about tonight—the path that leads to fragmentation and self-interest. Down that road lies a mistaken idea of freedom.

The right to grasp for ourselves some advantage over others. That path would be one of constant conflict between narrow interests ending in chaos and immobility. It is a certain route to failure.

All the traditions of our past, all the lessons of our heritage, all the promises of our future point to another path: the path of common purpose and the restoration of American values. That path leads to true freedom for our nation and ourselves. We can take the first steps down that path as we begin to solve our energy problem. Energy will be the immediate test of our ability to unite this nation.

And it can also be the standard around which we rally. On the battle-field of energy we can win for our nation a new confidence, and we can seize control again of our common destiny.

In little more than two decades we've gone from a position of energy independence to one in which almost half the oil we use comes from foreign countries at prices that are going through the roof. Our excessive dependence on OPEC has already taken a tremendous toll on our economy and our people. This is the direct cause of the long lines that have made millions of you spend aggravating hours waiting for gasoline. It's a cause of the increased inflation and unemployment that we now face.

This intolerable dependence on foreign oil threatens our economic independence and the very security of our nation.

The energy crisis is real. It is worldwide. It is a clear and present danger to our nation. These are facts and we simply must face them. What I have to say to you now about energy is simple and vitally important.

Point 1: I am tonight setting a clear goal for the energy policy of the United States. Beginning this moment, this nation will never use more foreign oil than we did in 1977. Never. From now on every new addition to our demand for energy will be met from our own production and our own conservation.

The generation-long growth in our dependence on foreign oil will be stopped dead in its tracks right now.

And then reverse as we move to the 1980's. For I am tonight setting the further goal of cutting our dependence on foreign oil by one-half by the end of the next decade—a saving of over four and a half million barrels of imported oil per day.

Point 2: To insure that we meet these targets, I will use my Presidential authority to set import quotas. I am announcing tonight that for 1979 and 1980 I will forbid the entry into this country of one drop of foreign oil more than these goals allow. These quotas will insure a reduction in imports even below the ambitious levels we set at the recent Tokyo summit.

Point 3: To give us energy security, I am asking for the most massive peacetime commitment of funds and resources in our nation's history to develop America's own alternative sources of fuel from coal, from oil shale, from plant products for gasohol, from unconventional gas, from the sun. I propose the creation of an Energy Security Corporation to lead this effort to replace $2\frac{1}{2}$ million barrels of imported oil per day by 1990. The corporation will issue up to $5 billion in energy bonds, and I especially want them to be in small denominations so that average Americans can invest directly in America's energy security.

Just as a similar synthetic rubber corporation helped us win World War II, so will we mobilize American determination and ability to win the energy war. Moreover, I will soon submit legislation to Congress calling for the creation of this nation's first solar bank, which will help us achieve the crucial goal of 20 percent of our energy coming from solar power by the year 2000.

These efforts will cost money, a lot of money. And that is why Congress must enact the windfall profits tax without delay. It will be money well spent. Unlike the billions of dollars we shift to foreign countries to pay for foreign oil, these funds will be paid by Americans to Americans. These funds will go to fight, not to increase, inflation and unemployment.

Point 4: I'm asking Congress to mandate—to require as a matter of law—that our nation's utility companies cut their massive use of oil by 50 percent within the next decade and switch to other fuels, especially coal, our most abundant energy source.

Point 5: To make absolutely certain that nothing stands in the way of achieving these goals, I will urge Congress to create an energy mobilization board which, like the War Production Board in World War II, will have the responsibility and authority to cut through the red tape, the delay and the endless roadblocks to completing key energy projects.

We will protect our environment. But when this nation critically needs a refinery or pipeline, we will build it.

Point 6: I'm proposing a bold conservation program to involve every state, county and city, and every average American in our energy battle. This effort will permit you to build conservation into your homes and your lives at a cost you can afford. I ask Congress to give me authority for mandatory conservation and for standby gasoline rationing.

To further conserve energy, I'm proposing tonight an extra $10 billion over the next decade to strengthen our public transportation systems. And I'm asking you, for your good and your nation's security, to take no unnecessary trips, to use car pools or public transportation whenever you can, to park your car one extra day per week, to obey the speed limit and to set your thermostats to save fuel. Every act of energy conservation like this is more than just common sense. I tell you it is an act of patriotism.

Our nation must be fair to the poorest among us so we will increase aid to needy Americans to cope with rising energy prices.

We often think of conservation only in terms of sacrifice. In fact it is the most painless and immediate way of rebuilding our nation's strength. Every gallon of oil each one of us saves is a new form of production that gives us more freedom, more confidence, that much more control over our own lives so that solutions of our energy crisis can also help us to conquer the crisis of the spirit in our country. It can rekindle our sense of unity, our confidence in the future, and give our nation and all of us individually a new sense of purpose.

You know we can do it. We have the natural resources. We have more oil in our shale alone than several Saudi Arabias. We have more coal than any nation on earth. We have the world's highest level of technology. We have the most skilled work force, with innovative genius.

And I firmly believe we have the national will to win this war.

I do not promise you that this struggle for freedom will be easy. I do not promise a quick way out of our nation's problems when the truth is that the only way out is an all-out effort. What I do promise you is that I will lead our fight, and I will enforce fairness in our struggle and I will insure honesty. And above all, I will act. We can manage the short-term shortages more effectively—and we will. But there are not short-term solutions to our long-range problems.

There is simply no way to avoid sacrifice. Twelve hours from now I will speak again, in Kansas City, to expand and to explain further our energy program. Just as a search for solutions to our energy shortages has now led us to a new awareness of our nation's deeper problems, so our willingness to work for those solutions in energy can strengthen us to attack those deeper problems.

I will continue to travel this country to hear the people of America. You can help me to develop a national agenda for the 1980's. I will listen and I will act. We will act together.

These were the promises I made three years ago and I intend to keep them. Little by little we can and we must rebuild our confidence. We can spend until we empty our treasury and we may summon all the wonders of science, but we can succeed only if we tap our greatest resources: America's people, America's values and America's confidence.

I have seen the strength of America in the inexhaustible resources of our people. In the days to come let us renew that strength in the struggle for an energy-secure nation.

In closing, let me say this: I will do my best, but I will not do it alone. Let your voice be heard. Whenever you have a chance, say something good about our country. With God's help and for the sake of our nation, it is time for us to join hands in America.

Let us commit ourselves together to a rebirth of the American spirit. Working together with our common faith, we cannot fail.

Thank you and good night.

Textual Questions

1. How does President Carter blend his own voice with the voices of "people from almost every segment of our society"? What effect does this blending have on his speech? Does including other voices support President Carter's own voice or mute it?

2. How and where does President Carter link the specific problems of the energy crisis facing America to moral, ethical, social, and spiritual issues challenging the nation?

3. Where is the thesis statement in President Carter's argument? How does he first build to this thesis and then elaborate upon it?

Rhetorical Questions

4. According to President Carter, what is the "fundamental threat to American democracy"? How does he explain this threat—and how effective and persuasive is his explanation?

5. How is America in 1979 a product of its recent past? How persuasive is this argument about causation—about the problems of the present being caused by the traumas of the past?

6. Beginning in paragraph 37, President Carter constructs a problem and its solution. How effective is this argument? How does the speech build to this problem-solution section, and how does it develop from it?

Thinking Beyond the Text

7. According to President Carter, the problems facing America are problems about a lack of unity and a lost sense of purpose—rather than problems with energy and inflation. Do you accept or reject this

description of these problems? That is, are the loss of unity and the lack of purpose the real problems facing America, or are these characterizations simply rhetorical doublespeak?

8. In 1979, President Carter argued that "In a nation that was proud of hard work, strong families, close-knit communities and our faith in God, too many of us now tend to worship self-indulgence and consumption. Human identity is no longer defined by what one does but by what one owns." If this analysis of America was true then, do you believe that it is still true today? Or do you doubt the accuracy of this analysis—then or now?

Student Response to Question #8: Jimmy Carter delivered this speech in 1979, seven years before I was born. But the America he describes, the America that existed in the year my parents married, is the same America I live in as an adult. I'm a fulltime student, but I also work fulltime at a local bookstore. This is the only way I can afford my education, even though a scholarship covers the bulk of my tuition. I value hard work, but I wonder if I'm missing something—working full time and still sliding into student loan debt. I'll have an education when I'm done, but I wont' have anything else. Just a used car and a student loan payment and, if I'm lucky, a job. If Americans still define themselves by what they own—as Carter says they "tend" to do in 1979—then I'm nothing. I simply won't believe that that's true. America is better than that. Americans are better than that. We are a consumer culture. No question. After the terrorist attacks of 9/11, President Bush told us to show the terrorists we weren't beaten—to go out and shop. But that's what makes our economy function. We shop. We spend. We buy. But we also give. Americans are generous people, once something kicks us out of our daily grind. Last night on *60 Minutes*, for example, there was a report about thirteen paramedics from New York City who, after the earthquake in Pakistan [in 2005], flew to one of the devastated regions and stayed to help. They did this without any aid from the government or from a charity group, and they're still doing it. So Americans are more than the sum of the things they own.

This is a well-developed and coherent response to this question, and it's one worth emulating. The student begins by anchoring her discussion in both her own life and President Carter's 1979 speech. She then moves on from the text, moving from her own thoughts about her life to a wider consideration of American consumer culture and, ultimately, concludes with a cogent example. She neither agrees with Carter's points wholeheartedly nor rejects them completely. Instead, she explains the shade of gray that is the truth as she sees it: Americans are self-indulgent and defined by what they buy, but they're also much more.

For Writing & Discussion

9. According to President Carter, in 1979, "For the first time in the history of our country a majority of our people believe that the next five years will be worse than the past five years." In what ways is America today confronted by the same problems—economic, social, or political conditions—as America in 1979? Focus on one problem described by President Carter, and, in a short essay, argue that this same issue still is/is not confronting America.

GEORGE W. BUSH

Born in New Haven, Connecticut, in 1946, George W. Bush is the eldest son of former President George H. W. Bush. The junior Bush, a Republican like his father, was raised in Texas and worked in the oil industry, helped manage his father's 1988 presidential campaign, and was a managing partner of the Texas Rangers baseball team before being elected governor of Texas in 1994 and then president of the United States in 2000. On September 11, 2001, the World Trade Center in New York City was destroyed by terrorist attacks. Consequently, Bush directed the United States in raids in Afghanistan to route forces believed responsible for the attacks. The raids were considered successful but failed to result in the capture of Osama bin Laden, the Islamic militant heading al-Qaeda and believed to be the mastermind behind the September 11th attacks. In 2002, Bush directed the nation's military attention to Iraq, demanding that the nation turn over weapons of mass destruction it was allegedly developing. U.S. forces invaded Iraq in March 2003 and were soon in control of the major cities; however, fighting continues as the United States works toward establishing a new Iraqi government. No weapons of mass destruction were found. Bush won a second term in 2004, defeating Democratic challenger John Kerry.

The speech "We Have Seen the State of Our Union" was delivered before Congress and televised nationally on September 20, 2001, just days after terrorists hijacked and crashed jetliners into the two 110-story twin towers of the World Trade Center, killing more than 2,700 people and injuring more than 7,000, and into the Pentagon building outside Washington, D.C. Patriotism swelled after the attacks, and in his speech, the president lauded the American people for their resolve while pledging to use the country's armed forces in a "war on terror."

We Have Seen the State of Our Union

ↇ **Prereading Question**

Where were you on September 11, 2001, and what were you doing when you learned about the terrorist attacks? How did you respond, physically, emotionally, and mentally? How did your responses change over the following days, weeks, and months? How do you feel now when you think of that day in September?

Delivered to a Joint Session of Congress and the American People, Washington, D.C., September 20, 2001

Mr. Speaker, Mr. President pro tempore. Members of Congress, and fellow Americans: In the normal course of events, presidents come to this chamber to report on the state of the Union. Tonight, no such report is needed. It has already been delivered by the American people.

We have seen it in the courage of passengers, who rushed terrorists to save others on the ground—passengers like an exceptional man named Todd Beamer. Please help me to welcome his wife, Lisa Beamer, here tonight.

We have seen the state of our Union in the endurance of rescuers, working past exhaustion. We have seen the unfurling of flags, the lighting of candles, the giving of blood, the saying of prayers—in English, Hebrew, and Arabic. We have seen the decency of a loving and giving people, who have made the grief of strangers their own.

My fellow citizens, for the last nine days, the entire world has seen for itself the state of our Union—and it is strong.

Tonight we are a country awakened to danger and called to defend freedom. Our grief has turned to anger, and anger to resolution. Whether we bring our enemies to justice, or bring justice to our enemies, justice will be done.

I thank the Congress for its leadership at such an important time. All of America was touched on the evening of the tragedy to see Republicans and Democrats, joined together on the steps of this Capitol, singing "God Bless America." And you did more than sing, you acted, by delivering forty billion dollars to rebuild our communities and meet the needs of our military.

Speaker Hastert and Minority Leader Gephardt—Majority Leader Daschle and Senator Lott—I thank you for your friendship and your leadership and your service to our country.

And on behalf of the American people, I thank the world for its outpouring of support. America will never forget the sounds of our National Anthem playing at Buckingham Palace, and on the streets of Paris, and at

Berlin's Brandenburg Gate. We will not forget South Korean children gathering to pray outside our embassy in Seoul, or the prayers of sympathy offered at a mosque in Cairo. We will not forget moments of silence and days of mourning in Australia and Africa and Latin America.

Nor will we forget the citizens of eighty other nations who died with our own. Dozens of Pakistanis. More than 130 Israelis. More than 250 citizens of India. Men and women from El Salvador, Iran, Mexico, and Japan. And hundreds of British citizens. America has no truer friend than great Britain. Once again, we are joined together in a great cause. The British Prime Minister has crossed an ocean to show his unity of purpose with America, and tonight we welcome Tony Blair.

On September the eleventh, enemies of freedom committed an act of war against our country. Americans have known wars—but for the past 136 years, they have been wars on foreign soil, except for one Sunday in 1941. Americans have known the casualties of war—but not at the center of a great city on a peaceful morning. Americans have known surprise attacks—but never before on thousands of civilians. All of this was brought upon us in a single day—and night fell on a different world, a world where freedom itself is under attack.

Americans have many questions tonight. Americans are asking:

Who attacked our country?

The evidence we have gathered all points to a collection of loosely affiliated terrorist organizations known as al-Qaida. They are the same murderers indicted for bombing American embassies in Tanzania and Kenya, and responsible for the bombing of the U.S.S. Cole.

Al-Qaida is to terror what the mafia is to crime. But its goal is not making money; its goal is remaking the world—and imposing its radical beliefs on people everywhere.

The terrorists practice a fringe form of Islamic extremism that has been rejected by Muslim scholars and the vast majority of Muslim clerics—a fringe movement that perverts the peaceful teachings of Islam. The terrorists' directive commands them to kill Christians and Jews, to kill all Americans, and make no distinctions among military and civilians, including women and children.

This group and its leader—a person named Usama bin Ladin—are linked to many other organizations in different countries, including the Egyptian Islamic Jihad and the Islamic Movement of Uzbekistan.

There are thousands of these terrorists in more than sixty countries. They are recruited from their own nations and neighborhoods, and brought to camps in places like Afghanistan where they are trained in the tactics of terror. They are sent back to their homes or sent to hide in countries around the world to plot evil and destruction.

The leadership of al-Qaida has great influence in Afghanistan, and supports the Taliban regime in controlling most of that country.

In Afghanistan, we see al-Qaida's vision for the world.

Afghanistan's people have been brutalized—many are starving and many have fled. Women are not allowed to attend school. You can be jailed for owning a television. Religion can be practiced only as their leaders dictate. A man can be jailed in Afghanistan if his beard is not long enough.

The United States respects the people of Afghanistan—after all, we are currently its largest source of humanitarian aid—but we condemn the Taliban regime. It is not only repressing its own people, it is threatening people everywhere by sponsoring and sheltering and supplying terrorists. By aiding and abetting murder, the Taliban regime is committing murder. And tonight, the United States of America makes the following demands on the Taliban:

Deliver to United States authorities all the leaders of al-Qaida who hide in your land.

Release all foreign nationals—including American citizens—you have unjustly imprisoned, and protect foreign journalists, diplomats, and aid workers in your country.

Close immediately and permanently every terrorist training camp in Afghanistan and hand over every terrorist, and every person in their support structure, to appropriate authorities.

Give the United States full access to terrorist training camps, so we can make sure they are no longer operating.

These demands are not open to negotiation or discussion. The Taliban must act and act immediately. They will hand over the terrorists, or they will share in their fate.

I also want to speak tonight directly to Muslims throughout the world: We respect your faith. It is practiced freely by many millions of Americans, and by millions more in countries that America counts as friends. Its teachings are good and peaceful, and those who commit evil in the name of Allah blaspheme the name of Allah. The terrorists are traitors to their own faith, trying, in effect, to hijack Islam itself. The enemy of America is not our many Muslim friends; it is not our many Arab friends. Our enemy is a radical network of terrorists, and every government that supports them.

Our war on terror begins with al-Qaida, but it does not end there. It will not end until every terrorist group of global reach has been found, stopped, and defeated.

Americans are asking: Why do they hate us?

They hate what we see right here in this chamber—a democratically elected government. Their leaders are self-appointed. They hate our freedoms—our freedom of religion, our freedom of speech, our freedom to vote and assemble and disagree with each other.

They want to overthrow existing governments in many Muslim countries, such as Egypt, Saudi Arabia, and Jordan. They want to drive Israel out of the Middle East. They want to drive Christians and Jews out of vast regions of Asia and Africa.

These terrorists kill not merely to end lives, but to disrupt and end a way of life. With every atrocity, they hope that America grows fearful, retreating from the world and forsaking our friends. They stand against us, because we stand in their way.

We are not deceived by their pretenses to piety. We have seen their kind before. They are the heirs of all the murderous ideologies of the twentieth century. By sacrificing human life to serve their radical visions—by abandoning every value except the will to power—they follow in the path of fascism, and Nazism, and totalitarianism. And they will follow that path all the way, to where it ends: in history's unmarked grave of discarded lies.

Americans are asking: How will we fight and win this war?

We will direct every resource at our command—every means of diplomacy, every tool of intelligence, every instrument of law enforcement, every financial influence, and every necessary weapon of war—to the disruption and defeat of the global terror network.

This war will not be like the war against Iraq a decade ago, with its decisive liberation of territory and its swift conclusion. It will not look like the air war above Kosovo two years ago, where no ground troops were used and not a single American was lost in combat.

Our response involves far more than instant retaliation and isolated strikes. Americans should not expect one battle, but a lengthy campaign, unlike any other we have seen. It may include dramatic strikes, visible on television, and covert operations, secret even in success. We will starve terrorists of funding, turn them one against another, drive them from place to place, until there is no refuge or rest. And we will pursue nations that provide aid or safe haven to terrorism. Every nation, in every region, now has a decision to make. Either you are with us, or you are with the terrorists. From this day forward, any nation that continues to harbor or support terrorism will be regarded by the United States as a hostile regime.

Our nation has been put on notice: We are not immune from attack. We will take defensive measures against terrorism to protect Americans.

Today, dozens of federal departments and agencies, as well as state and local governments, have responsibilities affecting homeland security. These efforts must be coordinated at the highest level. So tonight I announce the creation of a Cabinet-level position reporting directly to me—the Office of Homeland Security.

These measures are essential. But the only way to defeat terrorism as a threat to our way of life is to stop it, eliminate it, and destroy it where it grows.

Many will be involved in this effort, from FBI agents to intelligence operatives to the reservists we have called to active duty. All deserve our thanks, and all have our prayers. And tonight, a few miles from the damaged Pentagon, I have a message for our military: Be ready. I have called the armed forces to alert, and there is a reason. The hour is coming when America will act, and you will make us proud.

This is not, however, just America's fight. And what is at stake is not just America's freedom. This is the world's fight. This is civilization's fight. This is the fight of all who believe in progress and pluralism, tolerance and freedom.

We ask every nation to join us. We will ask, and we will need, the help of police forces, intelligence services, and banking systems around the world. The United States is grateful that many nations and many international organizations have already responded—with sympathy and with support. Nations from Latin America, to Asia, to Africa, to Europe, to the Islamic world. Perhaps the NATO Charter reflects best the attitude of the world: an attack on one is an attack on all.

The civilized world is rallying to America's side. They understand that if this terror goes unpunished, their own cities, their own citizens may be next. Terror, unanswered, can not only bring down buildings, it can threaten the stability of legitimate governments. And we will not allow it.

Americans are asking: What is expected of us?

I ask you to live your lives and hug your children. I know many citizens have fears tonight, and I ask you to be calm and resolute, even in the face of a continuing threat.

I ask you to uphold the values of America, and remember why so many have come here. We are in a fight for our principles, and our first responsibility is to live by them. No one should be singled out for unfair treatment or unkind words because of their ethnic background or religious faith.

I ask you to continue to support the victims of this tragedy with your contributions. Those who want to give can go to a central source of information, libertyunites.org, to find the names of groups providing direct help in New York, Pennsylvania, and Virginia.

The thousands of FBI agents who are now at work in this investigation may need your cooperation, and I ask you to give it.

I ask for your patience, with the delays and inconveniences that may accompany tighter security—and for your patience in what will be a long struggle.

I ask your continued participation and confidence in the American economy. Terrorists attacked a symbol of American prosperity. They did not touch its source. America is successful because of the hard work, and creativity, and enterprise of our people. These were the true strengths of our economy before September eleventh, and they are our strengths today.

Finally, please continue praying for the victims of terror and their families, for those in uniform, and for our great country. Prayer has comforted us in sorrow, and will help strengthen us for the journey ahead.

Tonight I thank my fellow Americans for what you have already done and for what you will do. And ladies and gentlemen of the Congress, I thank you, their representatives, for what you have already done, and for what we will do together.

Tonight, we face new and sudden national challenges. We will come together to improve air safety, to dramatically expand the number of air marshals on domestic flights, and take new measures to prevent hijacking. We will come together to promote stability and keep our airlines flying with direct assistance during this emergency.

We will come together to give law enforcement the additional tools it needs to track down terror here at home. We will come together to strengthen our intelligence capabilities to know the plans of terrorists before they act, and find them before they strike.

We will come together to take active steps that strengthen America's economy, and put our people back to work.

Tonight we welcome here two leaders who embody the extraordinary spirit of all New Yorkers: Governor George Pataki, and Mayor Rudy Giuliani. As a symbol of America's resolve, my administration will work with the Congress, and these two leaders, to show the world that we will rebuild New York City.

After all that has just passed—all the lives taken, and all the possibilities and hopes that died with them—it is natural to wonder if America's future is one of fear. Some speak of an age of terror. I know there are struggles ahead, and dangers to face. But this country will define our times, not be defined by them. As long as the United States of America is determined and strong, this will not be an age of terror; this will be an age of liberty, here and across the world.

Great harm has been done to us. We have suffered great loss. And in our grief and anger we have found our mission and our moment. Freedom and fear are at war. The advance of human freedom—the great achievement of our time, and the great hope of every time—now depends on us. Our nation—this generation—will lift a dark threat of violence from our people and our future. We will rally the world to this cause, by our efforts and by our courage. We will not tire, we will not falter, and we will not fail.

It is my hope that in the months and years ahead, life will return almost to normal. We'll go back to our lives and routines, and that is good. Even grief recedes with time and grace. But our resolve must not pass. Each of us will remember what happened that day, and to whom it happened. We will remember the moment the news came—where we were and what we were doing. Some will remember an image of a fire, or a story of rescue. Some will carry memories of a face and a voice gone forever.

And I will carry this. It is the police shield of a man named George Howard, who died at the World Trade Center trying to save others. It was given to me by his mom, Arlene, as a proud memorial to her son. This is my reminder of lives that ended, and a task that does not end.

I will not forget this wound to our country, or those who inflicted it. I will not yield—I will not rest—I will not relent in waging this struggle for the freedom and security of the American people.

The course of this conflict is not known, yet its outcome is certain. Freedom and fear, justice and cruelty, have always been at war, and we know that God is not neutral between them.

Fellow citizens, we will meet violence with patient justice—assured of the rightness of our cause, and confident of the victories to come. In all that lies before us, may God grant us wisdom, and may He watch over the United States of America. Thank you.

Textual Questions

1. How do the first three paragraphs build to the thesis statement in paragraph 4? How is the thesis statement in paragraph 4 developed in the rest of the text?

2. In paragraph 5, President Bush sets forth a chain of causation: the events of 9/11 caused grief, grief has caused anger, and anger is leading to resolution. Resolution involves justice, he argues, for America's enemies. What else does this resolution include?

3. In paragraphs 2, 3, 8, and 9, President Bush uses repetition. What does he repeat in each of these paragraphs and why? Where else does he use repetition and for what effect does he use it?

Rhetorical Questions

4. What portions of this text are tailored specifically for a grieving, angry American audience, and what message do they communicate to this audience? What portions of this text are designed to speak to a non-American audience? What messages do these pieces of the text send?

5. How and where does President Bush use examples from 9/11 and from America's past to construct his argument about appropriate actions in the War on Terror?

6. What examples, comparisons, and so on, does President Bush use to define and explain who al-Qaida is and what it wants—considering that most Americans had never heard of this terrorist organization until September of 2001?

Intertextual Questions

7. President Carter is speaking, as he says, during a time of peace abroad; President Bush is clearly speaking during the opening days of a time of war. What does each man do differently to define the problems facing America given this enormous difference in the situation in which he is speaking?

8. In "Energy Problems: The Erosion of Confidence," how does President Carter define the problems facing America at home and abroad? In "We Have Seen the State of Our Union," how does President Bush define the problems facing America both at home and abroad? How are their descriptions of these problems similar to/different from one another?

Thinking Beyond the Text

9. Do you believe or doubt that President Bush's response to the events of 9/11, as outlined in this speech, were reasonable and just? How would you use events since September of 2001 to support your evaluation of Bush's response?

10. Do you believe or doubt that the War on Terror itself can end with al-Qaida and other terrorist groups of "global reach" in "history's unmarked grave"? That is, can the War on Terror be won or is it, by definition, unwinable and unending?

For Writing & Discussion

11. In as much detail as possible, describe the moment where you learned about the terrorist attacks of 9/11. Where were you? What were you doing? Who were you with? What did you think and feel—and how did these thoughts and feelings change in the hours, days, weeks, and months that followed?

FOCAL POINT
Exploring Images of The Promise of America

FOCAL POINT

Exploring Images of The Promise of America

Questions

1. President Bush chose multiple settings from which to address the nation about the terrorists attacks of September 11, 2001. He delivered his speech "We Have Seen the State of Our Union" before Congress, but also spoke to the nation amongst the rubble of the World Trade Center (page 27, top). Why did he choose such different settings? What purposes would speaking at Ground Zero serve? Examine the various elements of the photo closely. What does Bush's physical position amongst the rubble suggest? What is the message sent to viewers of this photograph?

2. What thoughts come to mind when you look at this photo of emergency workers at Ground Zero (page 27, bottom)? What effect is caused by the human figures in the foreground and the mountains of rubble in the background? How is the message in this photograph similar to the message in the photograph of President Bush speaking at Ground Zero? How is the message of this photograph different?

3. This photograph from 1979 (page 28, bottom), shows automobiles lined up to receive their "ration" of gasoline—in the first act of fuel rationing in the United States since World War II. What does this photo say about the state of the American Union in 1979? How does this photo support and/or refute the message delivered by President Jimmy Carter in "Energy Problems: Erosion of Confidence"?

4. Consider the image of gas prices in May of 2006 on page 29. What assumptions can you make about the effects of rising gas prices on consumers based on the prices visible in the photo—the sign with gasoline prices and the price for this sale? Why might the photographer have chosen to feature a young woman? Would the message of the photograph change if she were of another race? If she were elderly? Explain in detail.

5. What message is being sent by the cartoon on page 28? Name four elements of the cartoon that support the message. Does this cartoon address the gas rationing of 1979 and issues of gasoline prices today? How?

∞ 1 ∞

THE PROMISE OF
SOCIAL EQUALITY &
THE RIGHT TO VOTE

In the introduction to this textbook, we argued that the United States was, from the moment of its creation, a rejection of old ways of organizing the world, a rejection of monarchy, theocracy, oligarchy, and any other system in which the rights of powerful individuals at the top of the social and economic hierarchies were greater than the rights of those without power and/or wealth. America was conceived as a formal rejection of these undemocratic ways of organizing human institutions, a rejection of rigidly hierarchical views of the world wherein, to paraphrase George Orwell from *Animal Farm*, all people were equal but some people were more equal than others. America was a formal declaration that all "men" are equal. From the very beginning, though, the promise of America was a promise unevenly kept. Women were excluded both grammatically and politically; they were not given the right to vote, the most fundamental right in a republican democracy—the unquestioned right to voice an opinion about who should lead and how the nation should be run. Like women, minorities, particularly both enslaved and free African Americans, were also denied their equal rights—and were even counted as less-than-equal when the distribution of members of the House of Representatives was made.

In the more than two centuries since its creation, the U.S. Constitution has been revised. It has been revised to make the promise of America a promise that applies to all Americans. But it is still a promise that is unevenly kept—to women, to minorities, to the economically disadvantaged. These changes in the U.S. Constitution were not thought up by lawmakers in consultation with experts or scholars, however. The changes made, changes that extended the promise of equality in America to larger and larger groups of people, came about because such changes were the will of the people themselves. In the readings that follow, these are the voices you will hear, the voices expressing the will of various groups throughout American history, voices calling for change.

Chapter 1 opens with the works of George Mason and Thomas Jefferson, two texts that are the ultimate expression of the promise of America to its citizens: All people are created equal, have equal opportunities in a free nation, and deserve equal treatment before the law. Equality is an ideal, though, a promise made but only sometimes kept, a debt only partially paid in more than two hundred and twenty-five years, an abstraction as difficult to define concretely as is "perfection." The readings in this chapter are expressions of the American promise and arguments about its unequal and ongoing fulfillment.

The readings that follow Mason and Jefferson sometimes question the nature of America's promise, but they also reaffirm it: Only in a free nation can the citizens of that nation argue, peacefully, about the very nature of their freedom, their citizenship, the justice of their government's actions at home and abroad. Elizabeth Cady Stanton, Susan B. Anthony, and Shirley Chisholm argue for equal rights for women; Martin Luther King, Jr. and Lyndon B. Johnson argue for equal rights for African Americans; Frederick Douglass and Hillary Rodham Clinton argue that the rights of African Americans and of women are comparable to the fight for equality waged by other groups of people, including Native Americans, Asian Americans, and all other citizens of the United States—and of the other nations of the world.

All of these readings make similar arguments, focused especially on the generalization "freedom" and the specific right to vote. Because of the nature of this focus, only some of the voices of Americans are represented in these arguments about the promise of America. White men earned the right to vote with the founding of the nation. African American men were granted the right to vote in 1866 (by the Fourteenth Amendment to the U.S. Constitution). Women, Black and white, were granted the right to vote in 1920 by the Nineteenth Amendment. The readings in this chapter reflect the struggle of these latter two groups.

As you read the essays and speeches that follow, consider the connections that bind them: How do the arguments presented in each build upon one another in ways both productive and filled with tension? How is the promise of America defined, explicitly or implicitly, by each speaker or writer? How is the promise of America defined in the time and space *between* these essays and speeches? And who is left out?

G E O R G E   M A S O N

The Virginia Declaration of Rights

Born in Fairfax, Virginia, George Mason (1725–1792) was an early American political leader. An affluent plantation owner, Mason was an early opponent of British colonial policy. As a member of the Virginia Constitutional Convention of 1776, Mason wrote

"The Virginia Declaration of Rights." He was also a member of the Constitutional Convention at Philadephia in 1787 and was active in drafting the U.S. Constitution. However, he refused to sign the Constitution because he objected to its authors' failure to include a bill of rights. The list of human rights he advocated, however, became the basis for the first ten amendments to the Constitution, known as the Bill of Rights.

Mason's highly influential "The Virginia Declaration of Rights" was adopted by the Virginia Constitutional Convention on June 12, 1776. Several other colonies copied from Mason's piece in their own declarations of rights. Thomas Jefferson also drew upon the statement when drafting the first part of "The Declaration of Independence."

THOMAS JEFFERSON

The Declaration of Independence

A scientist, architect, philosopher, and statesman, Thomas Jefferson (1743–1826) was a foundational figure in American politics. Although never known as an elegant public speaker, Jefferson earned a reputation for his writing and played an important role in drafting some of the country's most famous historic documents. In the 1780s, Jefferson drafted a plan for the country's decimal-based monetary system as well as a plan that, while not adopted initially, served as the basis for the Ordinance of 1787, which outlined a system of government for the northern states. He was not present for the adoption of the Constitution but endorsed the need for a stronger central government and, especially, the addition of the Bill of Rights. Jefferson served as the minister to France and secretary of state, and he was elected vice president in 1776 (at the time, the runner-up in the presidential race was awarded the position) and the third U.S. president in 1800.

Jefferson is best remembered as the principal author of "The Declaration of Independence," perhaps the most important American historical document. Although a few changes were made by John Adams, Benjamin Franklin, and Congress, the document was essentially drafted by Jefferson. In writing that "all men are created equal," Jefferson was influenced by English and French political theorists, such as John Locke and Jean Jacques Rousseau. On July 4, 1776,

56 members of the second Continental Congress signed "The Declaration of Independence," which justified the American Revolution against England. Its combination of general principles, abstract theory of government, and list of grievances against England's King George III make it an enduring and influential political document.

∞ Prereading Question

Searching online, find a copy of John Trumbull's painting Declaration of Independence. *What image of America's founding does this painting give to its viewers? Does it matter that, instead of being painted around the time the actual declaration was signed, the painting was not commissioned until 1817 and was not displayed at the Capitol until 1826?*

The Virginia Declaration of Rights

A Declaration of Rights made by the representatives of the good people of Virginia, assembled in full and free convention which rights do pertain to them and their posterity, as the basis and foundation of government.

Section 1. That all men are by nature equally free and independent and have certain inherent rights, of which, when they enter into a state of society, they cannot, by any compact, deprive or divest their posterity; namely, the enjoyment of life and liberty, with the means of acquiring and possessing property, and pursuing and obtaining happiness and safety.

Section 2. That all power is vested in, and consequently derived from, the people; that magistrates are their trustees and servants and at all times amenable to them.

Section 3. That government is, or ought to be, instituted for the common benefit, protection, and security of the people, nation, or community; of all the various modes and forms of government, that is best which is capable of producing the greatest degree of happiness and safety and is most effectually secured against the danger of maladministration. And that, when any government shall be found inadequate or contrary to these purposes, a majority of the community has an indubitable, inalienable, and indefeasible right to reform, alter, or abolish it, in such manner as shall be judged most conducive to the public weal.

Section 4. That no man, or set of men, is entitled to exclusive or separate emoluments or privileges from the community, but in consideration of public services; which, nor being descendible, neither ought the offices of magistrate, legislator, or judge to be hereditary.

Section 5. That the legislative and executive powers of the state should be separate and distinct from the judiciary; and that the members of the two first may be restrained from oppression, by feeling and participating the burdens of the people, they should, at fixed periods, be reduced to a private station, return into that body from which they were originally taken, and the vacancies be supplied by frequent, certain, and regular elections, in which all, or any part, of the former members, to be again eligible, or ineligible, as the laws shall direct.

Section 6. That elections of members to serve as representatives of the people, in assembly ought to be free; and that all men, having sufficient evidence of permanent common interest with, and attachment to, the community, have the right of suffrage and cannot be taxed or deprived of their property for public uses without their own consent or that of their representatives so elected, nor bound by any law to which they have not, in like manner, assembled for the public good.

Section 7. That all power of suspending laws, or the execution of laws, by any authority, without consent of the representatives of the people, is injurious to their rights and ought not to be exercised.

Section 8. That in all capital or criminal prosecutions a man has a right to demand the cause and nature of his accusation, to be confronted with the accusers and witnesses, to call for evidence in his favor, and to a speedy trial by an impartial jury of twelve men of his vicinage, without whose unanimous consent he cannot be found guilty; nor can he be compelled to give evidence against himself; that no man be deprived of his liberty except by the law of the land or the judgment of his peers.

Section 9. That excessive bail ought not to be required, nor excessive fines imposed, nor cruel and unusual punishments inflicted.

Section 10. That general warrants, whereby an officer or messenger may be commanded to search suspected places without evidence of a fact committed, or to seize any person or persons not named, or whose offense is not particularly described and supported by evidence, are grievous and oppressive and ought not to be granted.

Section 11. That in controversies respecting property, and in suits between man and man, the ancient trial by jury is preferable to any other and ought to be held sacred.

Section 12. That the freedom of the press is one of the great bulwarks of liberty, and can never be restrained but by despotic governments.

Section 13. That a well-regulated militia, composed of the body of the people, trained to arms, is the proper, natural, and safe defense of a free state; that standing armies, in time of peace, should be avoided as danger-ous to liberty; and that in all cases the military should be under strict subordination to, and governed by, the civil power.

Section 14. That the people have a right to uniform government; and, there-fore, that no government separate from or independent of the government of Virginia ought to be erected or established within the limits thereof.

Section 15. That no free government, or the blessings of liberty, can be preserved to any people but by a firm adherence to justice, moderation, temperance, frugality, and virtue and by frequent recurrence to fundamen-tal principles.

Section 16. That religion, or the duty which we owe to our Creator, and the manner of discharging it, can be directed only by reason and conviction, not by force or violence; and therefore all men are equally entitled to the free exercise of religion, according to the dictates of conscience; and that it is the mutual duty of all to practise Christian forbearance, love, and charity toward each other.

The Declaration of Independence

A Transcription

In Congress, July 4, 1776.

The unanimous Declaration of the thirteen united States of America,

When in the Course of human events, it becomes necessary for one people to dissolve the political bands which have connected them with another, and to assume among the powers of the earth, the separate and equal station to which the Laws of Nature and of Nature's God entitle them, a decent respect to the opinions of mankind requires that they should declare the causes which impel them to the separation.

We hold these truths to be self-evident, that all men are created equal, that they are endowed by their Creator with certain unalienable Rights, that among these are Life, Liberty and the pursuit of Happiness.—That to secure these rights, Governments are instituted among Men, deriving their just powers from the consent of the governed,—That whenever any Form of Government becomes destructive of these ends, it is the Right of the People to alter or to abolish it, and to institute new Government, laying its foundation on such principles and organizing its powers in such form, as to them shall seem most likely to effect their Safety and

Happiness. Prudence, indeed, will dictate that Governments long estab-lished should not be changed for light and transient causes; and accord-ingly all experience hath shewn, that mankind are more disposed to suffer, while evils are sufferable, than to right themselves by abolishing the forms to which they are accustomed. But when a long train of abuses and usurpations, pursuing invariably the same Object evinces a design to reduce them under absolute Despotism, it is their right, it is their duty, to throw off such Government, and to provide new Guards for their future security.—Such has been the patient sufferance of these Colonies; and such is now the necessity which constrains them to alter their former Systems of Government. The history of the present King of Great Britain is a history of repeated injuries and usurpations, all having in direct object the establishment of an absolute Tyranny over these States. To prove this, let Facts be submitted to a candid world.

He has refused his Assent to Laws, the most wholesome and necessary for the public good.

He has forbidden his Governors to pass Laws of immediate and pressing importance, unless suspended in their operation till his Assent should be obtained; and when so suspended, he has utterly neglected to attend to them.

He has refused to pass other Laws for the accommodation of large districts of people, unless those people would relinquish the right of Representation in the Legislature, a right inestimable to them and formidable to tyrants only.

He has called together legislative bodies at places unusual, uncomfort-able, and distant from the depository of their public Records, for the sole purpose of fatiguing them into compliance with his measures.

He has dissolved Representative Houses repeatedly, for opposing with manly firmness his invasions on the rights of the people.

He has refused for a long time, after such dissolutions, to cause others to be elected; whereby the Legislative powers, incapable of Annihi-lation, have returned to the People at large for their exercise; the State remaining in the mean time exposed to all the dangers of invasion from without, and convulsions within.

He has endeavoured to prevent the population of these States; for that purpose obstructing the Laws for Naturalization of Foreigners; refusing to pass others to encourage their migrations hither, and raising the conditions of new Appropriations of Lands.

He has obstructed the Administration of Justice, by refusing his Assent to Laws for establishing Judiciary powers.

He has made Judges dependent on his Will alone, for the tenure of their offices, and the amount and payment of their salaries.

He has erected a multitude of New Offices, and sent hither swarms of Officers to harrass our people, and eat out their substance.

He has kept among us, in times of peace, Standing Armies without the Consent of our legislatures.

He has affected to render the Military independent of and superior to the Civil power.

He has combined with others to subject us to a jurisdiction foreign to our constitution, and unacknowledged by our laws; giving his Assent to their Acts of pretended Legislation:

For Quartering large bodies of armed troops among us:

For protecting them, by a mock Trial, from punishment for any Murders which they should commit on the Inhabitants of these States:

For cutting off our Trade with all parts of the world:

For imposing Taxes on us without our Consent:

For depriving us in many cases, of the benefits of Trial by Jury:

For transporting us beyond Seas to be tried for pretended offences:

For abolishing the free System of English Laws in a neighbouring Province, establishing therein an Arbitrary government, and enlarging its Boundaries so as to render it at once an example and fit instrument for introducing the same absolute rule into these Colonies:

For taking away our Charters, abolishing our most valuable Laws, and altering fundamentally the Forms of our Governments:

For suspending our own Legislatures, and declaring themselves invested with power to legislate for us in all cases whatsoever.

He has abdicated Government here, by declaring us out of his Protection and waging War against us.

He has plundered our seas, ravaged our Coasts, burnt our towns, and destroyed the lives of our people.

He is at this time transporting large Armies of foreign Mercenaries to compleat the works of death, desolation and tyranny, already begun with circumstances of Cruelty & perfidy scarcely paralleled in the most barbarous ages, and totally unworthy the Head of a civilized nation.

He has constrained our fellow Citizens taken Captive on the high Seas to bear Arms against their Country, to become the executioners of their friends and Brethren, or to fall themselves by their Hands.

He has excited domestic insurrections amongst us, and has endeavoured to bring on the inhabitants of our frontiers, the merciless Indian Savages, whose known rule of warfare, is an undistinguished destruction of all ages, sexes and conditions.

In every stage of these Oppressions We have Petitioned for Redress in the most humble terms: Our repeated Petitions have been answered only by repeated injury. A Prince whose character is thus marked by every act which may define a Tyrant, is unfit to be the ruler of a free people.

Nor have We been wanting in attentions to our Brittish brethren. We have warned them from time to time of attempts by their legislature to extend an unwarrantable jurisdiction over us. We have reminded them of the circumstances of our emigration and settlement here. We have appealed to their native justice and magnanimity, and we have conjured them by the ties of our common kindred to disavow these usurpations, which, would inevitably interrupt our connections and correspondence. They too have been deaf to the voice of justice and of consanguinity. We must, therefore, acquiesce in the necessity, which denounces our Separation, and hold them, as we hold the rest of mankind, Enemies in War, in Peace Friends.

We, therefore, the Representatives of the united States of America, in General Congress, Assembled, appealing to the Supreme Judge of the world for the rectitude of our intentions, do, in the Name, and by Authority of the good People of these Colonies, solemnly publish and declare, That these United Colonies are, and of Right ought to be Free and Independent States; that they are Absolved from all Allegiance to the British Crown, and that all political connection between them and the State of Great Britain, is and ought to be totally dissolved; and that as Free and Independent States, they have full Power to levy War, conclude Peace, contract Alliances, establish Commerce, and to do all other Acts and Things which Independent States may of right do. And for the support of this Declaration, with a firm reliance on the protection of divine Providence, we mutually pledge to each other our Lives, our Fortunes and our sacred Honor.

The 56 signatures on the Declaration appear in the positions indicated:

Georgia:
Button Gwinnett
Lyman Hall
George Walton

North Carolina:
William Hooper
Joseph Hewes
John Penn

South Carolina:
Edward Rutledge
Thomas Heyward, Jr.
Thomas Lynch, Jr.
Arthur Middleton

Massachusetts:
John Hancock

Maryland:
Samuel Chase
William Paca
Thomas Stone
Charles Carroll of Carrollton

Virginia:
George Wythe
Richard Henry Lee
Thomas Jefferson
Benjamin Harrison
Thomas Nelson, Jr.
Francis Lightfoot Lee
Carter Braxton

Pennsylvania:
  Robert Morris
  Benjamin Rush
  Benjamin Franklin
  John Morton
  George Clymer
  James Smith
  George Taylor
  James Wilson
  George Ross

Delaware:
  Caesar Rodney
  George Read
  Thomas McKean

New York:
  William Floyd
  Philip Livingston
  Francis Lewis
  Lewis Morris

New Jersey:
  Richard Stockton
  John Witherspoon
  Francis Hopkinson

  John Hart
  Abraham Clark

New Hampshire:
  Josiah Bartlett
  William Whipple

Massachusetts:
  Samuel Adams
  John Adams
  Robert Treat Paine
  Elbridge Gerry

Rhode Island:
  Stephen Hopkins
  William Ellery

Connecticut:
  Roger Sherman
  Samuel Huntington
  William Williams
  Oliver Wolcott

New Hampshire:
  Matthew Thornton

Textual Questions

1. In what ways are the first two paragraphs of "The Declaration of Independence" similar to the ideas expressed in "The Virginia Declaration of Rights"?

2. Which rights are expressed in "The Virginia Declaration" that are not expressed in "The Declaration of Independence"?

3. How does Jefferson, in "The Declaration of Independence," build to his list of "Facts" about King George III? How effectively constructed is Jefferson's list of indictments?

Rhetorical Questions

4. Where, how, and for what purpose does each author invoke religion? What tone does this invocation set in each document?

5. As an expression of the basic rights that define the American citizen, which document is most effective and persuasive? Why?

6. Does Jefferson's indictment of King George III strengthen or weaken his argument about human rights, in comparison to Mason's declaration?

Intertextual Questions

7. How is the invocation of religion in "The Virginia Declaration of Rights" and the Bill of Rights similar to the use of religious references in President Carter's "Energy Problems: Erosion of Confidence" and President Bush's "We Have Seen the State of Our Union"?

8. Both "The Virginia Declaration of Rights" and the Bill of Rights make clear the promise of American citizenship. How does the promise of America articulated in these two documents compare to the reality of America as described by Martin Luther King Jr.?

Thinking Beyond the Text

9. While "The Virginia Declaration of Rights" is focused solely upon the rights of "the good people of Virginia," "The Declaration of Independence" both expresses the rights of U.S. citizens and indicts King George III. Given this secondary focus of "The Declaration of Independence," which document do you believe is a better expression of the promise of America? Why?

10. Select one signer of "The Declaration of Independence" and research his life. Aside from establishing his age, economic status, familial background, religious beliefs, and estate, ask yourself this: What kind of man was he? What did he believe and why? Considering what you know about this signer after you conclude your research, do you believe or doubt his support for the ideas expressed in "The Declaration of Independence" itself?

For Writing & Discussion

11. Critically read the Bill of Rights in the appendix of this book. In a short essay, compare the language used in "The Virginia Declaration of Rights" to the Bill of Rights. How are the two similar? How are they different?

ELIZABETH CADY STANTON

In the mid-1800s, women were denied the same rights as men, and, among other disparities, they were not allowed to vote, run for public office, or go to college. Elizabeth Cady Stanton (1815–1902) was an early leader of the women's suffrage movement. She, along with Lucretia Mott and others, organized the first women's rights convention in Seneca Falls, New York, in 1848, a cornerstone event in the women's rights movement. Afterward, Stanton was president of the National Women's Suffrage Association for more than 20 years and co-editor of *Revolution*, an early feminist magazine, from 1868–1870. Along with Susan B. Anthony and Matilda Joslyn Gage, she compiled the first three volumes of *History of Women Suffrage*, published from 1881 to 1886, and wrote *Eighty Years and More*, published in 1898.

"The Declaration of Sentiments and Resolutions" was adopted on July 19, 1848, at the Seneca Falls convention. Drawing on Thomas Jefferson's "The Declaration of Independence," the statement lists grievances suffered by women and was signed by both women and men attending the convention. The only resolution not unanimously adopted was the ninth, which demanded the right to vote, because some attendees felt they should strive for rights that seemed more realistic. Stanton, however, argued that the power to choose elected officials and make laws would help secure the remainder of the rights called for in the document, and it passed by a small majority. The convention and "The Declaration of Sentiments and Rights" were controversial at the time and are now considered the start of the women's rights movement.

Declaration of Sentiments and Resolutions

Prereading Question

Consider the place of women in American society. In what ways are women equal to men? In what ways—legally or illegally—are women unequal to men? Why does such inequality continue to exist—despite the law or because of it?

When, in the course of human events, it becomes necessary for one portion of the family of man to assume among the people of the earth a position different from that which they have hitherto occupied, but one to which the laws of nature and of nature's God entitle them, a decent respect to the opinions of mankind requires that they should declare the causes that impel them to such a course.

We hold these truths to be self-evident: that all men and women are created equal; that they are endowed by their Creator with certain inalienable rights; that among these are life, liberty, and the pursuit of happiness; that to secure these rights governments are instituted, deriving their just powers from the consent of the governed. Whenever any form of government becomes destructive of these ends, it is the right of those who suffer from it to refuse allegiance to it, and to insist upon the institution of a new government, laying its foundation on such principles, and organizing its powers in such form, as to them shall seem most likely to effect their safety and happiness. Prudence, indeed, will dictate that governments long established should not be changed for light and transient causes; and accordingly all experience hath shown that mankind are more disposed to suffer, while evils are sufferable, than to right themselves by abolishing the forms to which they were accustomed. But when a long train of abuses and usurpations, pursuing invariably the same object, evinces a design to reduce them under absolute despotism, it is their duty to throw off such government, and to provide new guards for their future security. Such has been the patient sufferance of the women under this government, and such is now the necessity which constrains them to demand the equal station to which they are entitled.

The history of mankind is a history of repeated injuries and usurpations on the part of man toward woman, having in direct object the establishment of an absolute tyranny over her. To prove this, let facts be submitted to a candid world.

He has never permitted her to exercise her inalienable right to the elective franchise.

He has compelled her to submit to laws, in the formation of which she had no voice.

He has withheld from her rights which are given to the most ignorant and degraded men—both natives and foreigners.

Having deprived her of this first right of a citizen, the elective franchise, thereby leaving her without representation in the halls of legislation, he has oppressed her on all sides.

He has made her, if married, in the eye of the law, civilly dead.

He has taken from her all right in property, even to the wages she earns.

He has made her, morally, an irresponsible being, as she can commit many crimes with impunity, provided they be done in the presence of her husband. In the covenant of marriage, she is compelled to promise obedience to her husband, he becoming, to all intents and purposes, her master—the law giving him power to deprive her of her liberty, and to administer chastisement.

He has so framed the laws of divorce, as to what shall be the proper causes, and in case of separation, to whom the guardianship of the children shall be given, as to be wholly regardless of the happiness of women—the law, in all cases, going upon a false supposition of the supremacy of man, and giving all power into his hands.

After depriving her of all rights as a married woman, if single, and the owner of property, he has taxed her to support a government which recognizes her only when her property can be profitable to it.

He has monopolized nearly all the profitable employments, and from those she is permitted to follow, she receives but a scanty remuneration. He closes against her all the avenues to wealth and distinction which he considers most honorable to himself. As a teacher of theology, medicine, or law, she is not known.

He has denied her the facilities for obtaining a thorough education, all colleges being closed against her.

He allows her in Church, as well as State, but a subordinate position, claiming Apostolic authority for her exclusion from the ministry, and, with some exceptions, from any public participation in the affairs of the Church.

He has created a false public sentiment by giving to the world a different code of morals for men and women, by which moral delinquencies which exclude women from society, are not only tolerated, but deemed of little account in man.

He has usurped the prerogative of Jehovah himself, claiming it as his right to assign for her a sphere of action, when that belongs to her conscience and to her God.

He has endeavored, in every way that he could, to destroy her confidence in her own powers, to lessen her self-respect, and to make her willing to lead a dependent and abject life.

Now, in view of this entire disfranchisement of one-half the people of this country, their social and religious degradation—in view of the unjust laws above mentioned, and because women do feel themselves aggrieved, oppressed, and fraudulently deprived of their most sacred rights, we insist that they have immediate admission to all the rights and privileges which belong to them as citizens of the United States.

In entering upon the great work before us, we anticipate no small amount of misconception, misrepresentation, and ridicule; but we shall use every instrumentality within our power to effect our object. We shall employ agents, circulate tracts, petition the State and National legislatures, and endeavor to enlist the pulpit and the press in our behalf. We hope this Convention will be followed by a series of Conventions embracing every part of the country.

[The following resolutions were discussed by Lucretia Mott, Thomas and Mary Ann McClintock, Amy Post, Catharine A. F. Stebbins, and others, and were adopted:]

Whereas, The great precept of nature is conceded to be, that "man shall pursue his own true and substantial happiness." Blackstone in his Commentaries remarks, that this law of Nature being coeval with mankind, and dictated by God himself, is of course superior in obligation to any other. It is binding over all the globe, in all countries and at all times; no human laws are of any validity if contrary to this, and such of them as are valid, derive all their force, and all their validity, and all their authority, mediately and immediately, from this original; therefore,

Resolved, That such laws as conflict, in any way, with the true and substantial happiness of woman, are contrary to the great precept of nature and of no validity, for this is "superior in obligation to any other."

Resolved, That all laws which prevent woman from occupying such a station in society as her conscience shall dictate, or which place her in a position inferior to that of man, are contrary to the great precept of nature, and therefore of no force or authority.

Resolved, That woman is man's equal—was intended to be so by the Creator, and the highest good of the race demands that she should be recognized as such.

Resolved, That the women of this country ought to be enlightened in regard to the laws under which they live, that they may no longer publish their degradation by declaring themselves satisfied with their present position, nor their ignorance, by asserting that they have all the rights they want.

Resolved, That inasmuch as man, while claiming for himself intellectual superiority, does accord to woman moral superiority, it is pre-eminently his duty to encourage her to speak and teach, as she has an opportunity, in all religious assemblies.

Resolved, That the same amount of virtue, delicacy, and refinement of behavior that is required of woman in the social state, should also be required of man, and the same transgressions should be visited with equal severity on both man and woman.

Resolved, That the objection of indelicacy and impropriety, which is so often brought against woman when she addresses a public audience, comes with a very ill-grace from those who encourage, by their attendance, her appearance on the stage, in the concert, or in feats of the circus.

Resolved, That woman has too long rested satisfied in the circumscribed limits which corrupt customs and a perverted application of the Scriptures have marked out for her, and that it is time she should move in the enlarged sphere which her great Creator has assigned her.

Resolved, That it is the duty of the women of this country to secure to themselves their sacred right to the elective franchise.

Resolved, That the equality of human rights results necessarily from the fact of the identity of the race in capabilities and responsibilities.

Resolved, therefore, That, being invested by the Creator with the same capabilities, and the same consciousness of responsibility for their exercise, it is demonstrably the right and duty of woman, equally with man, to promote every righteous cause by every righteous means; and especially in regard to the great subjects of morals and religion, it is self-evidently her right to participate with her brother in teaching them, both in private and in public, by writing and by speaking, by any instrumentalities proper to be used, and in any assemblies proper to be held; and this being a self-evident truth growing out of the divinely implanted principles of human nature, any custom or authority adverse to it, whether modern or wearing the hoary sanction of antiquity, is to be regarded as a self-evident falsehood, and at war with mankind.

[At the last session Lucretia Mott offered and spoke to the following resolution:]

Resolved, That the speedy success of our cause depends upon the zealous and untiring efforts of both men and women, for the overthrow of the monopoly of the pulpit, and for the securing to woman an equal participation with men in the various trades, professions, and commerce.

Textual Questions

1. Why does Stanton write this argument as a "Declaration"? What effect does this choice of title have both on her argument and on her audience?

2. Who is the "we" to whom Stanton addresses her speech? What in the text defines this "we"?

3. Who is the "he" in Stanton's argument and how is "he" defined?

Rhetorical Questions

4. How does Stanton begin generally and build to a specific indictment/list of grievances? Why would she organize her argument in such a way? Is this organization effective or ineffective?

5. Does Stanton's argument build effectively and persuasively to her resolutions? Which of these resolutions is most/least effectively worded?

6. Consider Stanton's resolutions. How do you think her original audience would have reacted to them? What evidence do you have for what you say?

Intertextual Questions

7. What effect does Stanton's modeling of the "Declaration of Sentiments and Resolutions" on the "Virginia Declaration of Rights" and the "Declaration of Independence" have? What effects might she have hoped for this modeling to have on her argument?

8. To what degree do you find more recent statements about the rights of women (Shirley Chisholm's, beginning on page 98) drawing on Stanton's text, continuing the intellectual tradition of this argument? Give specific examples.

Thinking Beyond the Text

9. In the "Declaration of Independence," Thomas Jefferson crafts an indictment of King George III for his treatment of the American colonies; in the "Declaration of Sentiments and Resolutions," Elizabeth Cady Stanton indicts men for their treatment of women. Do you believe that these indictments, one clearly modeled upon the other, are truly parallel? Does this modeling give credibility to Stanton's argument or detract from it?

10. As she indicts men, Stanton lists very specific grievances against them. Do you believe that the situation of women in America now, more than 150 years after Stanton made her "Declaration," is significantly different? In what ways do you believe that the place of women in American society is better? In what ways do you doubt that women are treated better than they were in Stanton's time?

For Writing & Discussion

11. Research the rights—in political, social, and economic terms—of women in America in the late 1840s. Pick one topic from your research and, in a short essay, compare and contrast the rights of women in Stanton's time to the rights of women in the present.

ROGER BROOKE TANEY

Roger Brooke Taney (1777–1864) was appointed to the U.S. Supreme Court in 1836 after previously working as U.S. Attorney General under President Andrew Jackson. Taney, born into a wealthy slave-owning family of tobacco farmers, supported slavery laws, and during the Civil War, President Abraham Lincoln viewed Taney as a nemesis. At the time of his death, there was considerable antipathy toward Taney; however, appreciation for his contributions to constitutional law has gradually grown.

The *Dred Scott v. Sandford* case was argued before the Supreme Court in 1856 and 1857. In 1834, Scott, a slave, was taken by his master from the slave state Missouri to a territory where slavery was prohibited by the Missouri Compromise. The two returned to Missouri four years later. When Scott's owner died, Scott sued the man's widow, saying that residence in a free territory secured his freedom. Scott won in a lower court; however, the Missouri Supreme Court reversed the decision—and its own precedents. The case ended up before the U.S. Supreme Court, where Taney delivered the court's opinion that Scott, as a slave, did not have the rights of other citizens and could not sue in federal court. Further, the court ruled that the Missouri Compromise was unconstitutional and that Congress could not stop citizens from taking slaves—as private property—into free territories. Southerners lauded the decision; in the north, however, the decision inflamed the ire of slavery opponents. The decision may have had a role in the election of Lincoln in 1860.

Dred Scott v. Sandford

☙ Prereading Question

In his novel Animal Farm, *George Orwell writes that "All animals are equal, but some animals are more equal than others." How does this allegorical statement about animals describe modern American society? Who is more equal than whom?*

Dred Scott v. Sandford (1857)

Chief Justice Taney delivered the opinion of the Court.

The question is simply this: Can a negro, whose ancestors were imported into this country, and sold as slaves, become a member of the political community formed and brought into existence by the Constitution of the United States, and as such become entitled to all the rights, and privileges, and immunities, guarantied by that instrument to the citizen? One of which rights is the privilege of suing in a court of the United States in the cases specified in the constitution . . .

The words "people of the United States" and "citizens" are synonymous terms, and mean the same thing. They both describe the political body who, according to our republican institutions, form the sovereignty, and who hold the power and conduct the government through their representatives. They are what we familiarly call the "sovereign people," and every citizen is one of this people, and a constituent member of this sovereignty. The question before us is, whether the class of persons described in the plea in abatement compose a portion of this people, and are constituent members of this sovereignty? We think they are not, and that they are not included, and were not intended to be included, under the word "citizens" in the constitution, and can therefore claim none of the rights and privileges which that instrument provides for and secures to citizens of the United States. On the contrary, they were at that time considered as a subordinate and inferior class of beings, who had been subjugated by the dominant race, and, whether emancipated or not, yet remained subject to their authority, and had no rights or privileges but such as those who held the power and the government might choose to grant them.

It is not the province of the court to decide upon the justice or injustice, the policy or impolicy, of these laws. The decision of that question belonged to the political or law-making power; to those who formed the sovereignty and framed the constitution. The duty of the court is, to interpret the instrument they have framed, with the best lights we can obtain on the subject, and to administer it as we find it, according to its true intent and meaning when it was adopted.

In discussing this question, we must not confound the rights of citizenship which a State may confer within its own limits, and the rights of citizenship as a member of the Union. It does not by any means follow, because he has all the rights and privileges of a citizen of a State, that he must be a citizen of the United States. He may have all of the rights and privileges of the citizen of a State, and yet not be entitled to the rights and privileges of a citizen in any other State. For, previous to the adoption of the constitution of the United States, every State had the undoubted right to confer on whomsoever it pleased the character of citizen, and to endow him with all its rights. But this character of course was confirmed to the boundaries of the State, and gave him no rights or privileges in other States beyond those secured to him by the laws of nations and the comity of States. Nor have the several States surrendered the power of conferring these rights and privileges by adopting the constitution of the United States . . .

It is very clear, therefore, that no State can, by any act or law of its own, passed since the adoption of the constitution, introduce a new member into the political community created by the constitution of the United States. It cannot make him a member of this community by making him a member of its own. And for the same reason it cannot introduce any person, or description of persons, who were not intended to be embraced in this new political family, which the constitution brought into existence, but were intended to be excluded from it.

The question then arises, whether the provisions of the constitution, in relation to the personal rights and privileges to which the citizen of a State should be entitled, embraced the negro African race, at that time in this country, or who might afterwards be imported, who had then or should afterwards be made free in any State; and to put it in the power of a single State to make him a citizen of the United States, and endue him with the full rights of citizenship in every other State without their consent? Does the constitution of the United States act upon him whenever he shall be made free under the laws of a State, and raised there to the rank of a citizen, and immediately clothe him with all the privileges of a citizen in every other State, and in its own courts?

The court think the affirmative of these propositions cannot be maintained. And if it cannot, the plaintiff in error could not be a citizen of the State of Missouri, within the meaning of the constitution of the United States, and, consequently, was not entitled to sue in its courts.

It is true, every person, and every class and description of persons, who were at the time of the adoption of the constitution recognized as citizens in the several States, became also citizens of this new political body; but none other; it was formed by them, and for them and their posterity, but for no one else. And the personal rights and privileges guaranteed to citizens of this new sovereignty were intended to embrace those only who were then members of the several State communities, or who should afterwards by birthright or otherwise become members, according to the provisions of the constitution and the principles on which it was founded. It was the union of those who were at that time members of distinct and separate political communities into one political family, whose power, for certain specified purposes, was to extend over the whole territory of the United States. And it gave to each citizen rights and privileges outside of his State which he did not before possess, and placed him in every other State upon a perfect equality with its own citizens as to rights of person and rights of property; it made him a citizen of the United States . . .

In the opinion of the court, the legislation and histories of the times, and the language used in the declaration of independence, show, that neither the class of persons who had been imported as slaves, nor their descendants, whether they had become free or not, were then acknowledged as a part of the people, nor intended to be included in the general words used in that memorable instrument . . .

It is too clear for dispute, that the enslaved African race were not intended to be included, and formed no part of the people who framed and adopted this declaration; for if the language, as understood in that day, would embrace them, the conduct of the distinguished men who framed the declaration of independence would have been utterly and flagrantly inconsistent with the principles they asserted; and instead of the sympathy of mankind, to which they so confidently appealed, they would have deserved and received universal rebuke and reprobation . . .

But there are two clauses in the constitution which point directly and specifically to the negro race as a separate class of persons, and show clearly that they were not regarded as a portion of the people or citizens of the government then formed.

One of these clauses reserves to each of the thirteen States the right to import slaves until the year 1808, if it thinks proper . . . And by the other provision the States pledge themselves to each other to maintain the right of property of the master, by delivering up to him any slave who may have escaped from his service, and be found within their respective territories . . .

The only two provisions which point to them and include them, treat them as property, and make it the duty of the government to protect it; no other power, in relation to this race, is to be found in the constitution; and as it is a government of special, delegated powers, no authority beyond these two provisions can be constitutionally exercised. The government of the United States had no right to interfere for any other purpose but that of protecting the rights of the owner, leaving it altogether with the several States to deal with this race, whether emancipated or not, as each State may think justice, humanity, and the interests and safety of society, require. The States evidently intended to reserve this power exclusively to themselves . . .

Upon a full and careful consideration of the subject, the court is of opinion, that, upon the facts stated . . . Dred Scott was not a citizen of Missouri within the meaning of the constitution of the United States, and not entitled as such to sue in its courts; and, consequently, that the circuit court had no jurisdiction of the case, and that the judgment on the plea in abatement is erroneous . . .

We proceed . . . to inquire whether the facts relied on by the plaintiff entitled him to his freedom . . .

The act of Congress, upon which the plaintiff relies, declares that slavery and involuntary servitude, except as a punishment for crime, shall be forever prohibited in all that part of the territory ceded by France, under the name of Louisiana, which lies north of thirty-six degrees thirty minutes north latitude and not included within the limits of Missouri. And the difficulty which meets us at the threshold of this part of the inquiry is whether Congress was authorized to pass this law under any of the powers granted to it by the Constitution; for, if the authority is not given by that instrument, it is the duty of this Court to declare it void and inoperative and incapable of conferring freedom upon anyone who is held as a slave under the laws of any one of the states.

The counsel for the plaintiff has laid much stress upon that article in the Constitution which confers on Congress the power "to dispose of and make all needful rules and regulations respecting the territory or other property belonging to the United States"; but, in the judgment of the Court, that provision has no bearing on the present controversy, and the power there given, whatever it may be, is confined, and was intended to be confined, to the territory which at that time belonged to, or was claimed by, the United States and was within their boundaries as settled by the treaty with Great Britain and can have no influence upon a territory afterward acquired from a foreign government. It was a special provision for a known and particular territory, and to meet a present emergency, and nothing more . . .

We do not mean, however, to question the power of Congress in this respect. The power to expand the territory of the United States by the admission of new states is plainly given; and in the construction of this power by all the departments of the government, it has been held to authorize the acquisition of territory, not fit for admission at the time, but to be admitted as soon as its population and situation would entitle it to admission . . .

It may be safely assumed that citizens of the United States who migrate to a territory belonging to the people of the United States cannot be ruled as mere colonists, dependent upon the will of the general government, and to be governed by any laws it may think proper to impose. The principle upon which our governments rest, and upon which alone they continue to exist, is the union of states, sovereign and independent within their own limits in their internal and domestic concerns, and bound together as one people by a general government, possessing certain enumerated and restricted powers, delegated to it by the people of the several states, and exercising supreme authority within the scope of the powers granted to it, throughout the dominion of the United States. A power, therefore, in the general government to obtain and hold colonies and dependent territories, over which they might legislate without restriction, would be inconsistent with its own existence in its present form. Whatever it acquires, it acquires for the benefit of the people of the several states who created it. It is their trustee acting for them and charged with the duty of promoting the interests of the whole people of the Union in the exercise of the powers specifically granted . . .

But the power of Congress over the person or property of a citizen can never be a mere discretionary power under our Constitution and form of government. The powers of the government and the rights and privileges of the citizen are regulated and plainly defined by the Constitution itself. And, when the territory becomes a part of the United States, the federal government enters into possession in the character impressed upon it by those who created it. It enters upon it with its powers over the citizen strictly defined and limited by the Constitution, from which it derives its own existence, and by virtue of which alone it continues to exist and act as a government and sovereignty. It has no power of any kind beyond it; and it cannot, when it enters a territory of the United States, put off its character and assume discretionary or despotic powers which the Constitution has denied to it. It cannot create for itself a new character separated from the citizens of the United States and the duties it owes them under the provisions of the Constitution. The territory, being a part of the United States, the government and the citizen both enter it under the authority of the Constitution, with their respective rights defined and marked out; and the federal government can exercise no power over his person or property, beyond what that instrument confers, nor lawfully deny any right which it has reserved . . .

These powers, and others, in relation to rights of person, which it is not necessary here to enumerate, are, in express and positive terms, denied to the general government; and the rights of private property have been guarded with equal care. Thus the rights of property are united with the rights of person and placed on the same ground by the Fifth Amendment to the Constitution, which provides that no person shall be deprived of life, liberty, and property without due process of law. And an act of Congress which deprives a citizen of the United States of his liberty or property, without due process of law, merely because he came himself or brought his property into a particular territory of the United States, and who had committed no offense against the laws, could hardly be dignified with the name of due process of law . . .

It seems, however, to be supposed that there is a difference between property in a slave and other property and that different rules may be applied to it in expounding the Constitution of the United States. And the laws and usages of nations, and the writings of eminent jurists upon the relation of master and slave and their mutual rights and duties, and the powers which governments may exercise over it, have been dwelt upon in the argument.

But, in considering the question before us, it must be borne in mind that there is no law of nations standing between the people of the United States and their government and interfering with their relation to each other. The powers of the government and the rights of the citizen under it are positive and practical regulations plainly written down. The people of the United States have delegated to it certain enumerated powers and forbidden it to exercise others. It has no power over the person or property of a citizen but what the citizens of the United States have granted. And no laws or usages of other nations, or reasoning of statesmen or jurists upon the relations of master and slave, can enlarge the powers of the government or take from the citizens the rights they have reserved. And if the Constitution recognizes the right of property of the master in a slave, and makes no distinction between that description of property and other property owned by a citizen, no tribunal, acting under the authority of the United States, whether it be legislative, executive, or judicial, has a right to draw such a distinction or deny to it the benefit of the provisions and guaranties which have been provided for the protection of private property against the encroachments of the government.

Now, as we have already said in an earlier part of this opinion, upon a different point, the right of property in a slave is distinctly and expressly affirmed in the Constitution. The right to traffic in it, like an ordinary article of merchandise and property, was guaranteed to the citizens of the United States, in every state that might desire it, for twenty years. And the government in express terms is pledged to protect it in all future time if the slave escapes from his owner. That is done in plain words—too plain to be misunderstood. And no word can be found in the Constitution which gives Congress a greater power over slave property or which entitles property of that kind to less protection than property of any other description. The only power conferred is the power coupled with the duty of guarding and protecting the owner in his rights.

Upon these considerations it is the opinion of the Court that the act of Congress which prohibited a citizen from holding and owning property of this kind in the territory of the United States north of the line therein mentioned is not warranted by the Constitution and is therefore void; and that neither Dred Scott himself, nor any of his family, were made free by being carried into this territory; even if they had been carried there by the owner with the intention of becoming a permanent resident.

Textual Questions

1. Taney argues that "people of the United States" is a term synonymous with "citizens" of the United States. How does this definition support the ultimate decision that African Americans are neither people nor citizens?

2. How does Taney limit the scope of his argument—and the scope of the Court's purpose and authority? Why?

3. How does Taney construct his argument from the explanation of the question before the court to the delivery of its answer? Into what sections can the argument naturally be broken, and which of these sections is most persuasive?

Rhetorical Questions

4. While this Opinion of the Court was written by Chief Justice Taney, a later Chief Justice, Charles Evans Hughes, referred to the Dred Scott decision as a "self-inflicted wound." Why, metaphorically, refer to this not only as a wound but as one self-inflicted?

5. How are the rights of the States defined by Taney, and how do these rights become part of the argument that African Americans are property rather than people? How and why does Taney draw a distinction between the rights of the States and the rights of the government of the Union itself?

6. How does Taney use his reading of the U.S. Constitution to build his argument? How persuasive—even if abhorrent—is this reading within his argument? Why?

Intertextual Questions

7. Figuratively, the Dred Scott decision completely refutes the claim Jefferson makes in the "Declaration of Independence" that "all men are created equal," yet Taney constructs his argument in such a way that, literally, there is no contradiction. How?

8. In what ways do Taney's arguments about power and property echo Mason's arguments in "The Virginia Declaration of Rights"?

Thinking Beyond the Text

9. Do you believe that Taney's conflation of "people" with "citizens" is still true in America today? Are there still people in America who are—symbolically if not literally—treated as property rather than people?

10. Which four provisions/clauses does Taney draw upon from the U.S. Constitution to make his argument? Do you believe, as Taney does, that a literal reading of these provisions/clauses both excludes African Americans from the body politic and defines them as property?

For Writing & Discussion

11. Taney argues that the right to own and traffic in slaves is plainly writ-
    ten in the U.S. Constitution, words "too plain to be misunderstood." If
    this same standard of plainness were applied to Jefferson's "Declara-
    tion of Independence," would the institution of slavery even be
    allowed to have existed in America?

ABRAHAM LINCOLN

Born into a poverty-stricken family, Abraham Lincoln (1809–1865)
worked in various jobs—mill manager, village postmaster, sur-
veyor, and rail splitter—before venturing into politics. He served
in the Illiniois State Legislature and Congress before becoming
president in 1860. As a result of the anti-slavery candidate's
victory, seven states seceded from the country by the time of
Lincoln's inauguration, leading to the beginning of the Civil War
in 1861. After four years of bloodshed, the Union Army was victo-
rious. Lincoln advocated an attitude of forgiveness toward the
South; however, before getting a chance to work toward recon-
structing the nation after the war, he was shot and killed by actor
John Wilkes Booth in 1865. He is now seen as a man of vision and
a symbol of American democracy.

Lincoln delivered "The Gettysburg Address" on November 19,
1863, at the dedication of the Gettysburg National Cemetery at the
site of one of the bloodiest battles of the war. The battle was a
turning point, destroying the South's offensive strategy and forcing it to fight defensively until surrendering in 1865. Nearly 50,000
people died during the three days of fighting. Lincoln's brief
address followed a two-hour speech by Edward Everett, one of the
most famous orators of the time. In newspaper reports, Everett's
speech was lauded and given prominence. Everett, however, sent a
note to Lincoln the day after the dedication, saying, "I wish that
I could flatter myself that I had come as near to the central idea
of the occasion in two hours as you did in two minutes." "The
Gettysburg Address" has become one of the most famous and
most quoted American speeches.

The Gettysburg Address

∾ Prereading Question

Before the Civil War, Americans tended to speak of their nation in the grammatical plural: "The United States of America are allied with England and France." After the Civil War, the nation became a grammatically singular unit: "The United States of America is allied with England and France." How does this difference in the way of referring to the nation itself reflect a very different way of thinking about America?

Transcript of the "Nicolay Draft" of the Gettysburg Address

Four score and seven years ago our fathers brought forth, upon this continent, a new nation, conceived in liberty, and dedicated to the proposition that "all men are created equal."

Now we are engaged in a great civil war, testing whether that nation, or any nation so conceived, and so dedicated, can long endure. We are met on a great battle field of that war. We have come to dedicate a portion of it, as a final resting place for those who died here, that the nation might live. This we may, in all propriety do. But, in a larger sense, we can not dedicate—we can not consecrate—we can not hallow, this ground—The brave men, living and dead, who struggled here, have hallowed it, far above our poor power to add or detract. The world will little note, nor long remember what we say here; while it can never forget what they did here.

It is rather for us, the living, we here be dedicated to the great task remaining before us—that, from these honored dead we take increased devotion to that cause for which they here, gave the last full measure of devotion—that we here highly resolve these dead shall not have died in vain; that the nation, shall have a new birth of freedom, and that government of the people by the people for the people, shall not perish from the earth.

Transcript of the "Hay Draft" of the Gettysburg Address

Four score and seven years ago our fathers brought forth, upon this continent, a new nation, conceived in Liberty, and dedicated to the proposition that all men are created equal.

Now we are engaged in a great civil war, testing whether that nation, or any nation, so conceived, and so dedicated, can long endure. We are met here on a great battlefield of that war. We have come to dedicate a portion of it as a final resting place for those who here gave their lives that that nation might live. It is altogether fitting and proper that we should do this.

But in a larger sense we can not dedicate—we can not consecrate—we can not hallow this ground. The brave men, living and dead, who struggled, here, have consecrated it far above our poor power to add or detract. The world will little note, nor long remember, what we say here, but can never forget what they did here. It is for us, the living, rather to be dedicated here to the unfinished work which they have, thus far, so nobly carried on. It is rather for us to be here dedicated to the great task remaining before us—that from these honored dead we take increased devotion to that cause for which they here gave the last full measure of devotion—that we here highly resolve that these dead shall not have died in vain; that this nation shall have a new birth of freedom; and that this government of the people, by the people, for the people, shall not perish from the earth.

Textual Questions

1. Consider both the Nicolay draft and the Hay draft. What differences exist, textually, between the two drafts of this speech?

2. How does President Lincoln use repetition to enhance his points?

3. What, for President Lincoln, is the basic reason for waging the Civil War? For ending it? What does Lincoln mean by "a new birth of freedom"?

Rhetorical Questions

4. Which version of this speech, the Nicolay draft or the Hay draft, is most effectively worded? Why?

5. Given the short length of this speech, what makes it such a famous, enduring feature of American history?

6. Which features of this speech clearly indicate that it is a funeral oration, a speech delivered to honor the sacrifices of those now dead?

Intertextual Questions

7. How is President Lincoln's "Gettysburg Address" indebted to both the U.S. Constitution and the "Declaration of Independence"? In what ways does it differ, in terms of the ideas expressed, from these texts?

8. How is the tone of President Lincoln's "Gettysburg Address" similar to/different from the tone of President Bush's "We Have Seen the State of Our Union"? Which ideas about America—expressed in very different times and places—are the same?

Thinking Beyond the Text

9. In what ways does the "Gettysburg Address" build on and update Jefferson's "Declaration of Independence"? How might this speech affect perceptions of the purpose of the Civil War itself in ways favorable to President Lincoln and the cause of the Union?

10. Following the Civil War, many of the ideals of the "Gettysbury Address" were ignored, in both the South and the North. Some would say that they are still being ignored. Are such statements of ideals only empty appeals to emotion, or do they have other value?

For Writing & Discussion

11. Searching online and in your campus library, find at least three different oral readings of "The Gettysburg Address." (Many readings exist, both professional and amateur, including readings by legendary singer Johnny Cash and popular actor Sam Waterson.) Compare and contrast two of these readings. In a short essay, describe each reading and explain which seems most effective to you and why.

FREDERICK DOUGLASS

The son of a black slave and an unknown white father, Frederick Douglass (c. 1817–1895) escaped from slavery in 1838 and went on to campaign for the end of slavery and publish three versions of his autobiography. In the books, he described his experiences as a slave, a fugitive, and a free black man during and after the American Civil War. Known as a great orator, Douglass traveled to anti-slavery meetings and spoke about his experiences. He started and edited a series of newspapers championing the rights of free blacks and slaves from 1847 to 1863. In the years after the Civil War, Douglass campaigned for full civil rights for blacks and worked toward the passage of the Thirteenth, Fourteenth, and Fifteenth Amendments, which banned slavery, made all people born in the United States citizens, and prohibited racial discrimination in voting. Born Frederick Augustus Bailey, he changed his name to Douglass—the name of the character in the poem "The Lady of the Lake" by Sir Walter Scott—after he was free.

Douglass's "Appeal to Congress for Impartial Suffrage" was published in *Atlantic Monthly* in January 1867, less than three years after the end of the Civil War. The Fifteenth Amendment, which guaranteed civil rights and suffrage to citizens, including former slaves, was ratified in 1870.

Appeal to Congress for Impartial Suffrage

∾ Prereading Question

The right to vote is a fundamental one in any democracy—direct or republican—and has been since ancient times. Given that voting is among the only legitimate ways in which the citizens of a nation can express their will, why is voter turnout in America, especially among the young, so low?

January 1867

A very limited statement of the argument for impartial suffrage, and for including the negro in the body politic, would require more space than can be reasonably asked here. It is supported by reasons as broad as the nature of man, and as numerous as the wants of society. Man is the only government-making animal in the world. His right to a participation in the production and operation of government is an inference from his nature, as direct and self-evident as is his right to acquire property or education. It is no less a crime against the manhood of a man, to declare that he shall not share in the making and directing of the government under which he lives, than to say that he shall not acquire property and education. The fundamental and unanswerable argument in favor of the enfranchisement of the negro is found in the undisputed fact of his manhood. He is a man, and by every fact and argument by which any man can sustain his right to vote, the negro can sustain his right equally. It is plain that, if the right belongs to any, it belongs to all. The doctrine that some men have no rights that others are bound to respect, is a doctrine which we must banish as we have banished slavery, from which it emanated. If black men have no rights in the eyes of white men, of course the whites can have none in the eyes of the blacks. The result is a war of races, and the annihilation of all proper human relations.

But suffrage for the negro, while easily sustained upon abstract principles, demands consideration upon what are recognized as the urgent necessities of the case. It is a measure of relief,—a shield to break the force of a blow already descending with violence, and render it harmless. The work of destruction has already been set in motion all over the South. Peace to the country has literally meant war to the loyal men of the South, white and black; and negro suffrage is the measure to arrest and put an end to that dreadful strife.

Something then, not by way of argument, (for that has been done by Charles Sumner, Thaddeus Stevens, Wendell Phillips, Gerrit Smith, and other able men,) but rather of statement and appeal.

For better or for worse, (as in some of the old marriage ceremonies) the negroes are evidently a permanent part of the American population. They are too numerous and useful to be colonized, and too enduring and self-perpetuating to disappear by natural causes. Here they are, four millions of them, and, for weal or for woe, here they must remain. Their history is parallel to that of the country; but while the history of the latter has been cheerful and bright with blessings, theirs has been heavy and dark with agonies and curses. What O'Connell said of the history of Ireland may with greater truth be said of the negro's. It may be "traced like a wounded man through a crowd, by the blood." Yet the negroes have marvellously survived all the exterminating forces of slavery, and have emerged at the end of two hundred and fifty years of bondage, not morose, misanthropic, and revengeful, but cheerful, hopeful, and forgiving. They now stand before Congress and the country, not complaining of the past, but simply asking for a better future. The spectacle of these dusky millions thus imploring, not demanding, is touching; and if American statesmen could be moved by a simple appeal to the nobler elements of human nature, if they had not fallen, seemingly, into the incurable habit of weighing and measuring every proposition of reform by some standard of profit and loss, doing wrong from choice, and right only from necessity or some urgent demand of human selfishness, it would be enough to plead for the negroes on the score of past services and sufferings. But no such appeal shall be relied on here. Hardships, services, sufferings, and sacrifices are all waived. It is true that they came to the relief of the country at the hour of its extremest need. It is true that, in many of the rebellious States, they were almost the only reliable friends the nation had throughout the whole tremendous war. It is true that, notwithstanding their alleged ignorance, they were wiser than their masters, and knew enough to be loyal, while those masters only knew enough to be rebels and traitors. It is true that they fought side by side in the loyal cause with our gallant and patriotic white soldiers, and that, but for their help,—divided as the loyal States were,—the Rebels might have succeeded in breaking up the Union, thereby entailing border wars and troubles of unknown duration and incalculable calamity. All this and more is true of these loyal negroes. Many daring exploits will be told to their credit. Impartial history will paint them as men who deserved well of their country. It will tell how they forded and swam rivers, with what consummate address they evaded the sharp-eyed Rebel pickets, how they toiled in the darkness of night through the tangled marshes of briers and thorns, barefooted and weary, running the risk of losing their lives, to warn our generals of Rebel schemes to surprise and destroy our loyal army. It will tell how these poor people, whose rights we still despised, behaved to our wounded soldiers, when found cold, hungry, and bleeding on the deserted battle-field; how they assisted our escaping prisoners from Andersonville, Belle Isle, Castle Thunder, and elsewhere, sharing with them their wretched crusts, and otherwise affording them aid and comfort; how they promptly responded to the trumpet call for their services, fighting against a foe that denied them the rights of civilized warfare, and for a government which was without the courage to assert those rights and avenge their violation in their behalf; with what gallantry they flung themselves upon Rebel fortifications, meeting death as fearlessly as any other troops in the service. But upon none of these things is reliance placed. These facts speak to the better dispositions of the human heart; but they seem of little weight with the opponents of impartial suffrage.

It is true that a strong plea for equal suffrage might be addressed to the national sense of honor. Something, too, might be said of national gratitude. A nation might well hesitate before the temptation to betray its allies. There is something immeasurably mean, to say nothing of the cruelty, in placing the loyal negroes of the South under the political power of their Rebel masters. To make peace with our enemies is all well enough; but to prefer our enemies and sacrifice our friends,—to exalt our enemies and cast down our friends,—to clothe our enemies, who sought the destruction of the government, with all political power, and leave our friends powerless in their hands,—is an act which need not be characterized here. We asked the negroes to espouse our cause, to be our friends, to fight for us, and against their masters; and now, after they have done all that we asked them to do,—helped us to conquer their masters, and thereby directed toward themselves the furious hate of the vanquished,—it is proposed in some quarters to turn them over to the political control of the common enemy of the government and of the negro. But of this let nothing be said in this place. Waiving humanity, national honor, the claims of gratitude, the precious satisfaction arising from deeds of charity and justice to the weak and defenceless,—the appeal for impartial suffrage addresses itself with great pertinency to the darkest, coldest, and flintiest side of the human heart, and would wring righteousness from the unfeeling calculations of human selfishness.

For in respect to this grand measure it is the good fortune of the negro that enlightened selfishness, not less than justice, fights on his side. National interest and national duty, if elsewhere separated, are firmly united here. The American people can, perhaps, afford to brave the censure of surrounding nations for the manifest injustice and meanness of excluding its faithful black soldiers from the ballot-box, but it cannot afford to allow the moral and mental energies of rapidly increasing millions to be consigned to hopeless degradation.

Strong as we are, we need the energy that slumbers in the black man's arm to make us stronger. We want no longer any heavy-footed, melancholy service from the negro. We want the cheerful activity of the quickened manhood of these sable millions. Nor can we afford to endure the moral blight which the existence of a degraded and hated class must necessarily inflict upon any people among whom such a class may exist. Exclude the negroes as a class from political rights,—teach them that the high and manly privilege of suffrage is to be enjoyed by white citizens only,—that they may bear the burdens of the state, but that they are to have no part in its direction or its honors,—and you at once deprive them of one of the main incentives to manly character and patriotic devotion to the interests of the government; in a word, you stamp them as a degraded caste,—you teach them to despise themselves, and all others to despise them. Men are so constituted that they largely derive their ideas of their abilities and their possibilities from the settled judgments of their fellow-men, and especially from such as they read in the institutions under which they live. If these bless them, they are blest indeed; but if these blast them, they are blasted indeed. Give the negro the elective franchise, and you give him at once a powerful motive for all noble exertion, and make him a man among men. A character is demanded of him, and here as elsewhere demand favors supply. It is nothing against this reasoning that all men who vote are not good men or good citizens. It is enough that the possession and exercise of the elective franchise is in itself an appeal to the nobler elements of manhood, and imposes education as essential to the safety of society.

To appreciate the full force of this argument, it must be observed, that disfranchisement in a republican government based upon the idea of human equality and universal suffrage, is a very different thing from disfranchisement in governments based upon the idea of the divine right of kings, or the entire subjugation of the masses. Masses of men can take care of themselves. Besides, the disabilities imposed upon all are necessarily without that bitter and stinging element of invidiousness which attaches to disfranchisement in a republic. What is common to all works no special sense of degradation to any. But in a country like ours, where men of all nations, kindred, and tongues are freely enfranchised, and allowed to vote, to say to the negro, You shall not vote, is to deal his manhood a staggering blow, and to burn into his soul a bitter and goading sense of wrong, or else work in him a stupid indifference to all the elements of a manly character. As a nation, we cannot afford to have amongst us either this indifference and stupidity, or that burning sense of wrong. These sable millions are too powerful to be allowed to remain either indifferent or discontented. Enfranchise them, and they become self-respecting and country-loving citizens. Disfranchise them, and the mark of Cain is set upon them less mercifully than upon the first murderer, for no man was to hurt him. But this mark of inferiority—all the more palpable because of a difference of color—not only dooms the negro to be a vagabond, but makes him the prey of insult and outrage everywhere. While nothing may be urged here as to the past services of the negro, it is quite within the line of this appeal to remind the nation of the possibility that a time may come when the services of the negro may be a second time required. History is said to repeat itself, and, if so, having wanted the negro once, we may want him again. Can that statesmanship be wise which would leave the negro good ground to hesitate, when the exigencies of the country required his prompt assistance? Can that be sound statesmanship which leaves millions of men in gloomy discontent, and possibly in a state of alienation in the day of national trouble? Was not the nation stronger when two hundred thousand sable soldiers were hurled against the Rebel fortifications, than it would have been without them? Arming the negro was an urgent military necessity three years ago,—are we sure that another quite as pressing may not await us? Casting aside all thought of justice and magnanimity, is it wise to impose upon the negro all the burdens involved in sustaining government against foes within and foes without, to make him equal sharer in all sacrifices for the public good, to tax him in peace and conscript him in war, and then coldly exclude him from the ballot-box?

Look across the sea. Is Ireland, in her present condition, fretful, discontented, compelled to support an establishment in which she does not believe, and which the vast majority of her people abhor, a source of power or of weakness to Great Britain? Is not Austria wise in removing all ground of complaint against her on the part of Hungary? And does not the Emperor of Russia act wisely, as well as generously, when he not only breaks up the bondage of the serf, but extends him all the advantages of Russian citizenship? Is the present movement in England in favor of manhood suffrage—for the purpose of bringing four millions of British subjects into full sympathy and co-operation with the British government—a wise and humane movement, or otherwise? Is the existence of a rebellious element in our borders—which New Orleans, Memphis, and Texas show to be only disarmed, but at heart as malignant as ever, only waiting for an opportunity to reassert itself with fire and sword—a reason for leaving four millions of the nation's truest friends with just cause of complaint against the Federal government? If the doctrine that taxation should go hand in hand with representation can be appealed to in behalf of recent traitors and rebels, may it not properly be asserted in behalf of a people who have ever been loyal and faithful to the government? The answers to these questions are too obvious to require statement. Disguise it as we may, we are still a divided nation. The Rebel States have still an anti-national policy. Massachusetts and South Carolina may draw tears from the eyes of our tender-hearted President by walking arm in arm into his Philadelphia Convention, but a citizen of Massachusetts is still an alien in the Palmetto State. There is that, all over the South, which frightens Yankee industry, capital, and skill from its borders. We have crushed the Rebellion, but not its hopes or its malign purposes. The South fought for perfect and permanent control over the Southern laborer. It was a war of the rich against the poor. They who waged it had no objection to the government, while they could use it as a means of confirming their power over the laborer. They fought the government, not because they hated the government as such, but because they found it, as they thought, in the way between them and their one grand purpose of rendering permanent and indestructible their authority and power over the Southern laborer. Though the battle is for the present lost, the hope of gaining this object still exists, and pervades the whole South with a feverish excitement. We have thus far only gained a Union without unity, marriage without love, victory without peace. The hope of gaining by politics what they lost by the sword, is the secret of all this Southern unrest; and that hope must be extinguished before national ideas and objects can take full possession of the Southern mind. There is but one safe and constitutional way to banish that mischievous hope from the South, and that is by lifting the laborer beyond the unfriendly political designs of his former master. Give the negro the elective franchise, and you at once destroy the purely sectional policy, and wheel the Southern States into line with national interests and national objects. The last and shrewdest turn of Southern politics is a recognition of the necessity of getting into Congress immediately, and at any price. The South will comply with any conditions but suffrage for the negro. It will swallow all the unconstitutional test oaths, repeal all the ordinances of Secession, repudiate the Rebel debt, promise to pay the debt incurred in conquering its people, pass all the constitutional amendments, if only it can have the negro left under its political control. The proposition is as modest as that made on the mountain: "All these things will I give unto thee if thou wilt fall down and worship me."

But why are the Southerners so willing to make these sacrifices? The answer plainly is, they see in this policy the only hope of saving something of their old sectional peculiarities and power. Once firmly seated in Congress, their alliance with Northern Democrats re-established, their States restored to their former position inside the Union, they can easily find means of keeping the Federal government entirely too busy with other important matters to pay much attention to the local affairs of the Southern States. Under the potent shield of State Rights, the game would be in their own hands. Does any sane man doubt for a moment that the men who followed Jefferson Davis through the late terrible Rebellion, often marching barefooted and hungry, naked and penniless, and who now only profess an enforced loyalty, would plunge this country into a foreign war to-day, if they could thereby gain their coveted independence, and their still more coveted mastery over the negroes? Plainly enough, the peace not less than the prosperity of this country is involved in the great measure of impartial suffrage. King Cotton is deposed, but only deposed, and is ready to-day to reassert all his ancient pretensions upon the first favorable opportunity. Foreign countries abound with his agents. They are able, vigilant, devoted. The young men of the South burn with the desire to regain what they call the lost cause; the women are noisily malignant towards the Federal government. In fact, all the elements of treason and rebellion are there under the thinnest disguise which necessity can impose.

What, then, is the work before Congress? It is to save the people of the South from themselves, and the nation from detriment on their account. Congress must supplant the evident sectional tendencies of the South by national dispositions and tendencies. It must cause national ideas and objects to take the lead and control the politics of those States. It must cease to recognize the old slave-masters as the only competent persons to rule the South. In a word, it must enfranchise the negro, and by means of the loyal negroes and the loyal white men of the South build up a national party there, and in time bridge the chasm between North and South, so that our country may have a common liberty and a common civilization. The new wine must be put into new bottles. The lamb may not be trusted with the wolf. Loyalty is hardly safe with traitors.

Statesmen of America! beware what you do. The ploughshare of rebellion has gone through the land beam-deep. The soil is in readiness, and the seed-time has come. Nations, not less than individuals, reap as they sow. The dreadful calamities of the past few years came not by accident, nor unbidden, from the ground. You shudder to-day at the harvest of blood sown in the spring-time of the Republic by your patriot fathers. The principle of slavery, which they tolerated under the erroneous impression that it would soon die out, became at last the dominant principle and power at the South. It early mastered the Constitution, became superior to the Union, and enthroned itself above the law.

Freedom of speech and of the press it slowly but successfully banished from the South, dictated its own code of honor and manners to the nation, brandished the bludgeon and the bowie-knife over Congressional debate, sapped the foundations of loyalty, dried up the springs of patriotism, blotted out the testimonies of the fathers against oppression, padlocked the pulpit, expelled liberty from its literature, invented nonsensical theories about master-races and slave-races of men, and in due season produced a Rebellion fierce, foul, and bloody.

This evil principle again seeks admission into our body politic. It comes now in shape of a denial of political rights to four million loyal colored people. The South does not now ask for slavery. It only asks for a large degraded caste, which shall have no political rights. This ends the case.

Statesmen, beware what you do. The destiny of unborn and unnumbered generations is in your hands. Will you repeat the mistake of your fathers, who sinned ignorantly? or will you profit by the blood-bought wisdom all round you, and forever expel every vestige of the old abomination from our national borders? As you members of the Thirty-ninth Congress decide, will the country be peaceful, united, and happy, or troubled, divided, and miserable.

Textual Questions

1. In his introduction, to what does Douglass compare the right to vote? How accurate are his comparisons?

2. What choices does Douglass make—even at the word level—to craft his message as a plea rather than a demand? What effect do these "soft" choices have upon his argument?

3. How does Douglass use the American Civil War to support his argument about impartial suffrage for African Americans? How does this build into an argument about allies and traitors, friends and rebels?

Rhetorical Questions

4. Douglass argues that African Americans "stand before Congress and the country, not complaining of the past, but simply asking for a better future." How does Douglass use the events of the past to build to this declaration without contradicting himself? Why might he speak of the past as he does?

5. What comparisons does Douglass draw between the United States and other nations of the world? To what use does he put these comparisons?

6. How are good business, American honor, and ideas about manhood central to Douglass' argument? How effectively do these aspects of Douglass' argument build upon one another?

Intertextual Questions

7. In what ways are Douglass' arguments for equal rights for African Americans similar to/different from Stanton's arguments (earlier in this chapter) about equal rights for women?

8. In his argument, how does Douglass echo Thomas Jefferson's "Declaration of Independence" and the preamble to the U.S. Constitution (earlier in this chapter and in the appendix, respectively)? How effective are these allusions?

Thinking Beyond the Text

9. While Douglass focuses most directly on the right to vote that was, then, denied to African Americans, he also refers to other rights that are unequally held by groups of Americans. Do you believe that groups of Americans, including African Americans, still have unequal access to these other rights?

10. Throughout American history, the right to vote has been denied to some groups—the poor and illiterate, African Americans, Hispanics, women, those under 18 years of age. Why do you believe this to be true? What power struggle causes the existence of universal suffrage for American citizens to be constantly challenged?

For Writing & Discussion

11. Research the events of the 2000 presidential election in the state of Florida. In what ways is it alleged that African Americans were denied their right to vote? In a short essay, explain one of these allegations.

SOJOURNER TRUTH

Sojourner Truth (c. 1797–1883) was born into slavery in New York. When the state abolished slavery in 1827, she gained her freedom. However, when one of her sons was illegally sold into slavery in Alabama, she sued and won to get him back. She worked as a cook, maid, and laundress before becoming convinced she heard heavenly voices. She changed her name to Sojourner Truth and became a traveling preacher. Truth was active in slave emancipation and women's rights issues. Although illiterate her entire life, she was known as a skillful public speaker.

Truth delivered "Address to the First Annual Meeting of the American Equal Rights Association" on May 9, 1867. The American Civil War had ended, and politicians were working on the details of a series of amendments to give former slaves equal rights. At this time, the women's movement was fighting to gain equal rights for women as well. The Equal Rights Association existed from 1866 to 1869, with the goal of working to "secure equal rights to all American citizens, especially the right of suffrage, irrespective of race, color, or sex."

Address to the First Annual Meeting of the American Equal Rights Association

∾ Prereading Question

Literally, slavery—one individual keeping another in physical bondage—is illegal in America. Does such slavery still exist, though? If so, then how and where? What other forms of slavery exist—economic, emotional, etc.?

May 9, 1867

My friends, I am rejoiced that you are glad, but I don't know how you will feel when I get through. I come from another field—the country of the slave. They have got their liberty—so much good luck to have slavery partly destroyed; not entirely. I want it root and branch destroyed. Then we will all be free indeed. I feel that if I have to answer for the deeds done in my body just as much as a man, I have a right to have just as much as a man. There is a great stir about colored men getting their rights, but not a word about the colored women; and if colored men get their rights, and not colored women theirs, you see the colored men will be masters over the women, and it will be just as bad as it was before. So I am for keeping the thing going while things are stirring; because if we wait till it is still, it will take a great while to got it going again. White women are a great deal smarter, and know more than colored women, while colored women do not know scarcely anything. They go out washing, which is about as high as a colored woman gets, and their men go about idle, strutting up and down; and when the women come home, they ask for their money and take it all, and then scold because there is no food. I want you to consider on that, chil'n I call you chil'n; you are somebody's chil'n and I am old enough to be mother of all that is here. I want women to have their rights. In the courts women have no right, no voice; nobody speaks for them. I wish woman to have her voice there among the pettifoggers. If it is not a fit place for women, it is unfit for men to be there.

I am above eighty years old; it is about time for me to be going. I have been forty years a slave and forty years free, and would be here forty years more to have equal rights for all. I suppose I am kept here because something remains for me to do, I suppose I am yet to help to break the chain. I have done a great deal of work; as much as a man, but did not get so much pay. I used to work in the field and bind grain, keeping up with the cradler; but men doing no more, got twice as much pay; so with the German women. They work in the field and do as much work, but do not got the pay. We do as much, we eat as much, we want as much. I suppose I am about the only colored woman that goes about to speak for the rights of the colored women. I want to keep the thing stirring, now that the ice is cracked. What we want is a little money. You men know that you get as much again as women when you write, or for what you do. When we get our rights we shall not have to come to you for money, for then we shall have money enough in our own pockets; and may be you will ask us for money. But help us now until we get it. It is a good consolation to know that when we have got this battle once fought we shall not be coming to you any more. You have been having our rights so long, that you think, like a slave-holder, that you own us. I know that it is hard for one who has held the reins for so long to give up; it cuts like a knife. It will feel all the better when it closes up again. I have been in Washington about three years, seeing about these colored people. Now colored men have the right to vote. There ought to be equal rights now more than ever, since colored people have got their freedom. I am going to talk several times while I am here; so now I will do a little singing. I have not heard any singing since I came here.

Accordingly, suiting the action to the word, Sojourner sang, "We are going home." "There, children," said she, "in heaven we shall rest from all our labors; first do all we have to do here. There I am determined to go, not to stop short of that beautiful place, and I do not mean to stop till I get there, and meet you there, too."

Textual Questions

1. What metaphor does Truth use to speak of the destruction of slavery? How effective is it?

2. For women, according to Truth, how is the fight for the black man's right to vote reaffirming the powerless place of women in American society?

3. How does Truth describe her own past? Why?

Rhetorical Questions

4. How does Truth use the binaries of men/women, black/white to construct her argument about equality for all people? How effective are these arguments?

5. Where and why does Truth refer to her age? What do these references do for her argument?

6. How does Truth use money/pay in her argument? Why? What purpose does the use of this specific item serve?

Intertextual Questions

7. How does Truth weave together the arguments of both Frederick Douglass and Elizabeth Cady Stanton (both in this chapter)?

8. How does Truth's argument about women's suffrage compare to that of Stanton (earlier in this chapter)? Which is more effective and why?

Thinking Beyond the Text

9. Do you believe that the struggle for equal rights links all marginalized groups, as Truth does? Or is every struggle for equality a separate struggle by separate groups for their own gain?

10. Research the legal rights of women in the late 1860s. Is Truth's description of the powerlessness of women in court an accurate one for the time?

For Writing & Discussion

11. Truth refers to unequal pay several times. Research this issue in modern America: For every dollar a man makes, how much does a modern woman earn? How does this unequal earning compare to earnings 25 years ago? Fifty years ago? Describe the results of your research in a short essay.

SUSAN B. ANTHONY

At the age of 17, when she worked as a teacher, Susan Brownell Anthony (1820–1906) fought for equal pay for women teachers, co-education, and college training for girls. She met Elizabeth Cady Stanton in 1851, and thereafter the two were known as the leaders of the women's rights movement, working integrally to organize the National Women Suffrage Association and later the National American Woman Suffrage Association. She lectured about women's rights throughout the United States and Europe, and, with Stanton and Matilda Joslyn Gage, she compiled volumes one through three of the *History of Women Suffrage*. Anthony acknowledged Stanton as founder of the women's rights movement; Anthony's legacy lies in her singular goal of fighting for women's suffrage, as well as her perseverance in rallying people of both sexes to her cause. The U.S. Mint issued the Susan B. Anthony dollar coin in 1979 to honor her.

Anthony gave the speech "On Women's Right to Vote" after being arrested in 1872 for voting. She led a group of women to the polls in Rochester, New York and was consequently tried, convicted, and fined $100. The women's rights movement rallied behind her cause, and the case ultimately made it to the U.S. Supreme Court, which ruled against her. She refused to pay.

On Women's Right to Vote

∾ Prereading Question

The United States is defined as a republican democracy—a system in which the people elect the leaders who then speak for them in the halls of power. But can the United States legitimately be described as an aristocracy? An oligarchy? A meritocracy?

Friends and fellow citizens: I stand before you tonight under indictment for the alleged crime of having voted at the last presidential election, without having a lawful right to vote. It shall be my work this evening to prove to you that in thus voting, I not only committed no crime, but, instead, simply exercised my citizen's rights, guaranteed to me and all United States citizens by the National Constitution, beyond the power of any state to deny.

The preamble of the Federal Constitution says:

> We, the people of the United States, in order to form a more perfect union, establish justice, insure domestic tranquillity, provide for the common defense, promote the general welfare, and secure the blessings of liberty to ourselves and our posterity, do ordain and establish this Constitution for the United States of America.

It was we, the people; not we, the white male citizens; nor yet we, the male citizens; but we, the whole people, who formed the Union. And we formed it, not to give the blessings of liberty, but to secure them; not to the half of ourselves and the half of our posterity, but to the whole people— women as well as men. And it is a downright mockery to talk to women of their enjoyment of the blessings of liberty while they are denied the use of the only means of securing them provided by this democratic-republican government—the ballot.

For any state to make sex a qualification that must ever result in the disfranchisement of one entire half of the people, is to pass a bill of attainder, or, an ex post facto law, and is therefore a violation of the supreme law of the land. By it the blessings of liberty are forever withheld from women and their female posterity.

To them this government has no just powers derived from the consent of the governed. To them this government is not a democracy. It is not a republic. It is an odious aristocracy; a hateful oligarchy of sex; the most hateful aristocracy ever established on the face of the globe; an oligarchy of wealth, where the rich govern the poor. An oligarchy of learning, where the educated govern the ignorant, or even an oligarchy of race, where the Saxon rules the African, might be endured; but this oligarchy of sex, which makes father, brothers, husband, sons, the oligarchs over the mother and sisters, the wife and daughters, of every household— which ordains all men sovereigns, all women subjects, carries dissension, discord, and rebellion into every home of the nation. Webster, Worcester, and Bouvier all define a citizen to be a person in the United States, entitled to vote and hold office.

The only question left to be settled now is: Are women persons? And I hardly believe any of our opponents will have the hardihood to say they are not. Being persons, then, women are citizens; and no state has a right to make any law, or to enforce any old law, that shall abridge their privileges or immunities. Hence, every discrimination against women in the constitutions and laws of the several states is today null and void, precisely as is every one against Negroes.

Textual Questions

1. Why does Anthony begin her address by referring to "fellow citizens" and explaining that she stands accused of a crime?

2. How does Anthony use the preamble to the U.S. Constitution to argue that, in voting, she committed no crime?

3. What terms are important to the argument Anthony makes in her final paragraph? How do these terms build upon one another to advance a specific line of argument about women and the right to vote?

Rhetorical Questions

4. How does Anthony take a legal issue—a woman's right to vote—and make it personal, not only for her and for women in general but for all people in the American nation?

5. What image of herself does Anthony construct in her argument? How does she construct this image, and how effective or ineffective is it?

6. How does Anthony use the opposition between state power and federal power to advance her argument?

Intertextual Questions

7. How does Anthony's definition of the term *citizen* argue against the definition of this term used by Chief Justice Taney in the Dred Scott decision (in this chapter)?

8. How does Anthony's concluding paragraph echo the arguments made by Chief Justice Taney in the Dred Scott decision (in this chapter)?

Thinking Beyond the Text

9. If, legally, the right to vote can be limited—based upon age, for example—then do you believe that it can be limited to only a specific group—such as white men? Such a limit may seem abhorrent, but is the *possibility* of such a limit a legitimate reading of the U.S. Constitution, where the right to vote is very specifically limited to persons 18 years or older?

10. Considering how hard African Americans and women fought to win the right to vote, why do you believe that fewer than half of the citizens of the United States vote in presidential elections?

For Writing & Discussion

11. Research the percentage of citizens within a given group—African Americans, Hispanics, women, or others—that voted in the most recent presidential election. In an essay, present the results of your research, including the definition of the group being considered, and speculate about why members of this group might choose *not* to exercise on of the most fundamental rights granted in America—the right to vote.

EMMA GOLDMAN

Born in Lithuania, Emma Goldman (1869–1940) emigrated to Rochester, New York in 1886. After a few years working in clothing factories, she became active in the anarchist movement in 1869. She was well known for her writing and speeches, and she was lionized by feminists as an iconic rebel. Goldman was imprisoned in 1893 for inciting a riot, in 1916 for publicly advocating birth control, and again in 1917 for obstructing the draft. She and Alexander Berkman published the anarchist paper *Mother Earth*, and in 1919 the two were deported to Russia. She left the country in the 1920s after witnessing the Russian Revolution. She was later allowed to return to the United States on a lecture tour in 1934 on the condition that she wouldn't publicly discuss politics.

"What Is Patriotism?" was first delivered in 1908 in San Francisco. Arguing against the "patriotic lie," the speech was reprinted numerous times in *Mother Earth*, Goldman's collected works, and other publications.

What Is Patriotism?

∽ Prereading Question

How do you define patriotism? Who are your examples of patriotic Americans? What actions are unpatriotic?

Men and Women:

What is patriotism? Is it love of one's birthplace, the place of childhood's recollections and hopes, dreams and aspirations? Is it the place where, in child-like naivete, we would watch the passing clouds, and wonder why we, too, could not float so swiftly? The place where we would count the milliard glittering stars, terror-stricken lest each one "an eye should be," piercing the very depths of our little souls? Is it the place where we would listen to the music of the birds and long to have wings to fly, even as they, to distant lands? Or is it the place where we would sit on Mother's knee, enraptured by tales of great deeds and conquests? In short, is it love for the spot, every inch representing dear and precious recollections of a happy, joyous and playful childhood?

If that were patriotism, few American men of today would be called upon to be patriotic, since the place of play has been turned into factory, mill, and mine, while deepening sounds of machinery have replaced the music of the birds. No longer can we hear the tales of great deeds, for the stories our mothers tell today are but those of sorrow, tears and grief.

What, then, is patriotism? "Patriotism, sir, is the last resort of scoundrels," said Dr. [Samuel] Johnson. Leo Tolstoy, the greatest anti-patriot of our time, defines patriotism as the principle that will justify the training of wholesale murderers; a trade that requires better equipment in the exercise of man-killing than the making of such necessities as shoes, clothing, and houses; a trade that guarantees better returns and greater glory than that of the honest workingman . . .

Indeed, conceit, arrogance and egotism are the essentials of patriotism. Let me illustrate. Patriotism assumes that our globe is divided into little spots, each one surrounded by an iron gate. Those who have had the fortune of being born on some particular spot consider themselves nobler, better, grander, more intelligent than those living beings inhabiting any other spot. It is, therefore, the duty of everyone living on that chosen spot to fight, kill and die in the attempt to impose his superiority upon all the others. The inhabitants of the other spots reason in like manner, of course, with the result that from early infancy the mind of the child is provided with blood-curdling stories about the Germans, the French, the Italians, Russians, etc. When the child has reached manhood he is thoroughly saturated with the belief that he is chosen by the Lord himself to defend his country against the attack or invasion of any foreigner. It is for that purpose that we are clamoring for a greater army and navy, more battleships and ammunition . . .

An army and navy represent the people's toys. To make them more attractive and acceptable, hundreds and thousands of dollars are being spent for the display of toys. That was the purpose of the American government in equipping a fleet and sending it along the Pacific coast, that every American citizen should be made to feel the pride and glory of the United States.

The city of San Francisco spent one hundred thousand dollars for the entertainment of the fleet; Los Angeles, sixty thousand; Seattle and Tacoma, about one hundred thousand . . . Yes, two hundred and sixty thousand dollars were spent on fireworks, theater parties, and revelries, at a time when men, women, and children through the breadth and length of the country were starving in the streets; when thousands of unemployed were ready to sell their labor at any price.

What could not have been accomplished with such an enormous sum? But instead of bread and shelter, the children of those cities were taken to see the fleet, that it may remain, as one newspaper said, "a lasting memory for the child."

A wonderful thing to remember, is it not? The implements of civilized slaughter. If the mind of the child is poisoned with such memories, what hope is there for a true realization of human brotherhood?

We Americans claim to be a peace-loving people. We hate bloodshed; we are opposed to violence. Yet we go into spasms of joy over the possibility of projecting dynamite bombs from flying machines upon helpless citizens. We are ready to hang, electrocute, or lynch anyone, who, from economic necessity, will risk his own life in the attempt upon that of some industrial magnate. Yet our hearts swell with pride at the thought that America is becoming the most powerful nation on earth, and that she will eventually plant her iron foot on the necks of all other nations.

Such is the logic of patriotism.

. . . Thinking men and women the world over are beginning to realize that patriotism is too narrow and limited a conception to meet the necessities of our time. The centralization of power has brought into being an international feeling of solidarity among the oppressed nations of the world; a solidarity which represents a greater harmony of interests between the workingman of America and his brothers abroad than between the American miner and his exploiting compatriot; a solidarity which fears not foreign invasion, because it is bringing all the workers to the point when they will say to their masters, "Go and do your own killing. We have done it long enough for you."

. . . The proletariat of Europe has realized the great force of that solidarity and has, as a result, inaugurated a war against patriotism and its bloody specter, militarism. Thousands of men fill the prisons of France, Germany, Russia and the Scandinavian countries because they dared to defy the ancient superstition . . .

America will have to follow suit. The spirit of militarism has already permeated all walks of life. Indeed, I am convinced that militarism is a greater danger here than anywhere else, because of the many bribes capitalism holds out to those whom it wishes to destroy . . .

The beginning has already been made in the schools . . . Children are trained in military tactics, the glory of military achievements extolled in the curriculum, and the youthful mind perverted to suit the government. Further, the youth of the country is appealed to in glaring posters to join the Army and the Navy. "A fine chance to see the world!" cries the governmental huckster. Thus innocent boys are morally shanghaied into patriotism, and the military Moloch strides conquering through the nation . . .

When we have undermined the patriotic lie, we shall have cleared the path for the great structure where all shall be united into a universal brotherhood—a truly free society.

Textual Questions

1. Goldman opens her speech with a series of seven questions. Is this list effective because of the accumulation of questions? Or it ineffective because of the accumulation of questions without attendant answers?

2. How does Goldman's second paragraph reverse the tone set in her first paragraph? Why?

3. How, according to Goldman, are "conceit, arrogance, and egotism" the "essentials of patriotism"? What imagery does Goldman use to illustrate her definition of patriotism? How effective is this imagery?

Rhetorical Questions

4. Why does Goldman refer to Johnson and Tolstoy's definitions of patriotism in her own argument? How does each of these men define patriotism, and how are their definitions different from/similar to Goldman's own?

5. Why does Goldman define the military as a "toy"? Within her argument, how is the logic of this definition explained?

6. According to Goldman, what is the "logic of patriotism"? How does this compare to "the patriotic lie"? How is Goldman's argument about war and peace a reflection of her time—a time of peace nearly a decade before U.S. entry into the War to End All Wars?

Intertextual Questions

7. In what ways does Goldman's definition of patriotism stand in opposition to the implicit definition of patriotism used by President Bush in "We Have Seen the State of Our Union"?

8. How would Goldman react to the logic of President Bush's arguments about the War on Terror as they are articulated in "We Have Seen the State of Our Union"?

Thinking Beyond the Text

9. Do you believe that, in modern America, Goldman's definition of patriotism is accurate? Or is her definition the very height of negativity and cynicism?

10. Is patriotism, as Goldman defines it, necessary for the survival of most any nation? Is it particularly necessary for the survival of the American nation?

For Writing & Discussion

11. In what ways does Goldman's definition of patriotism and description of the American military's mission echo in the protests against the Vietnam War, the Gulf Wars, and the War on Terror?

FRANKLIN DELANO ROOSEVELT

Franklin Delano Roosevelt (1882–1945) began his political career in 1910 when he was elected to the New York state senate. By 1920, he was the vice presidential nominee for Democratic hopeful James M. Cox; however, the duo was overwhelmingly defeated by Warren Harding and Calvin Coolidge. The next year, Roosevelt was stricken with poliomyelitis, which paralyzed him from his waist down. He was later able to gain partial use of his legs, but he was crippled for life. Undeterred, he returned to politics and was elected governor of New York in 1928. Four years later, he was elected president of the United States and was subsequently reelected three times, an unprecedented feat. During his tenure he instituted numerous government programs to counter the effects of the Great Depression and saw the country through most of World War II. He died of a cerebral hemorrhage less than a month before Germany surrendered; his successor Harry S. Truman led the country in the concluding months of the war with Japan. While Roosevelt has detractors, there's no question that his presidency had an enormous impact on the nation's development in the twentieth century.

"The Four Freedoms" was part of a longer speech Roosevelt delivered to Congress on January 6, 1941. With the specter of World War II looming over the country, Roosevelt asked citizens to work to produce supplies for the democratic countries of Europe, pay higher taxes, and make other sacrifices. His closing, in which he outlined "four essential human freedoms," became an often-quoted description of America's vision of liberty. After the war concluded, the four freedoms were used in drafting the charter for the United Nations.

The Four Freedoms: Address to Congress

∾ Prereading Question

What basic freedoms are promised to all Americans—promised, in fact, to all people in America, regardless of citizenship? Think, for example, of someone accused of a crime, U.S. citizen or not. What basic rights does that person possess?

January 6, 1941

In the future days, which we seek to make secure, we look forward to a world founded upon four essential human freedoms.

The first is freedom of speech and expression—everywhere in the world.

The second is freedom of every person to worship God in his own way—everywhere in the world.

The third is freedom from want—which, translated into world terms, means economic understandings which will secure to every nation a healthy peacetime life for its inhabitants—everywhere in the world.

The fourth is freedom from fear—which, translated into world terms, means a world-wide reduction of armaments to such a point and in such a thorough fashion that no nation will be in a position to commit an act of physical aggression against any neighbor—anywhere in the world.

That is no vision of a distant millennium. It is a definite basis for a kind of world attainable in our own time and generation. That kind of world is the very antithesis of the so-called new order of tyranny which the dictators seek to create with the crash of a bomb.

To that new order we oppose the greater conception—the moral order. A good society is able to face schemes of world domination and foreign revolutions alike without fear.

Since the beginning of our American history, we have been engaged in change—in a perpetual peaceful revolution—a revolution which goes on steadily, quietly adjusting itself to changing conditions—without the concentration camp or the quick-lime in the ditch. The world order which we seek is the cooperation of free countries, working together in a friendly, civilized society.

This nation has placed its destiny in the hands and heads and hearts of its millions of free men and women; and its faith in freedom under the guidance of God. Freedom means the supremacy of human rights everywhere. Our support goes to those who struggle to gain those rights or keep them. Our strength is our unity of purpose.

To that high concept there can be no end save victory.

Textual Questions

1. What is FDR's vision of the future, a future "attainable in our own time and generation"?

2. Why does FDR list his four freedoms with almost no elaboration? How does this brief list set up the second half of this text?

3. What is the "high purpose" of the American people, according to FDR? How does he construct this definition?

Rhetorical Questions

4. Is brevity the virtue of this speech, adding to its power? Or is the brevity of this speech its downfall, limiting or nullifying whatever rhetorical power it may have had?

5. While he lists neither America's enemies nor America's allies, FDR still makes references to both. How?

6. How does FDR's introduction dovetail with his conclusion? What single line of argument about the future do the two pieces of this text make?

Intertextual Questions

7. In what ways does President Bush, in "We Have Seen the State of Our Union," make the same argument that FDR makes in "The Four Freedoms"? How is the argument in FDR's "The Four Freedoms" similar to/different from President Reagan's argument in "We Have Made a Difference" (pages 104–110)?

8. How does FDR in "The Four Freedoms" echo the arguments of Mason in the "Virginia Declaration" and Jefferson's arguments in the "Declaration of Independence" (at the beginning of this chapter)?

Thinking Beyond the Text

9. Do FDR's four freedoms represent beliefs still held by Americans—beliefs about the world both nationally and internationally? Or do these four freedoms no longer make sense in a world at war with terror?

10. FDR argues that, from the beginning of its existence, America has "been engaged in change—in a perpetual peaceful revolution." Is his characterization of American history accurate, or do you doubt the pacific and pastoral view of the past that he constructs?

For Writing & Discussion

11. Research the global situation in January of 1941, 11 months and one day before the Japanese attack on Pearl Harbor and America's formal entrance into the Second World War. Who was at war with whom in January, and what was America's relationship to these other nations? In an essay, explain how the international situation in early 1941 led to FDR delivering this address to Congress.

JOHN F. KENNEDY

John F. Kennedy (1917–1963) was a naval commander in World War II and a Massachusetts congressman before being elected president of the United States in 1960. Defeating Richard Nixon by a narrow margin, Kennedy, at 43, became the youngest person ever elected to the post. Soon after the inauguration, he kicked off his "New Frontier" domestic program, which included tax reform, action to further civil rights, aid for education, and acceleration of the space program. However, Congress did not pass many of his domestic reform proposals. In 1962, U.S. reconnaissance planes spotted missile bases in Cuba, and Kennedy ordered a blockade of the country and insisted the armaments be removed, leading to several days of tension when the world seemed on the brink of nuclear war before Cuba and the Soviet Union complied. Kennedy was praised for his stance during the crisis. Also during his presidency, Kennedy increased military involvement in South Vietnam, initiated the Peace Corps, and won praise as a civil rights activist by ordering the use of federal troops to quell problems caused by forced school desegregation. Kennedy was shot and killed on November 22, 1963, while riding in a motorcade in Dallas, Texas. The commission created to investigate the assassination found that

Lee Harvey Oswald committed the murder. While his legend has been lessened somewhat over time, he is remembered as a youthful, determinedly idealistic president who strove to make great changes.

This speech was delivered at Kennedy's inauguration on January 20, 1961. At the time, Cold War tensions were increasing, and political divisions in America had begun to harden, as Kennedy's narrow margin of victory showed. In his speech, he called for a new generation of Americans to make their place in the world.

Ask Not What Your Country Can Do for You

∾ Prereading Question

Consider the value Americans place on giving, on supporting one another (and citizens of other nations) in times of need—on September 11, 2001; after the tsunami that devastated parts of southeast Asia in December of 2004; in the wake of Hurricane Katrina in 2005. To what degree do you see Americans as a giving, charitable people? Or is the public display of giving in part self-interested as well?

January 20, 1961

Vice President Johnson, Mr. Speaker, Mr. Chief Justice, President Eisenhower, Vice President Nixon, President Truman, reverend clergy, fellow citizens, we observe today not a victory of party, but a celebration of freedom—symbolizing an end, as well as a beginning—signifying renewal, as well as change. For I have sworn before you and Almighty God the same solemn oath our forebears prescribed nearly a century and three quarters ago.

The world is very different now. For man holds in his mortal hands the power to abolish all forms of human poverty and all forms of human life. And yet the same revolutionary beliefs for which our forebears fought are still at issue around the globe—the belief that the rights of man come not from the generosity of the state, but from the hand of God.

We dare not forget today that we are the heirs of that first revolution. Let the word go forth from this time and place, to friend and foe alike, that the torch has been passed to a new generation of Americans, born in this century, tempered by war, disciplined by a hard and bitter peace, proud of our ancient heritage and unwilling to witness or permit the slow undoing of those human rights to which this Nation has always been committed, and to which we are committed today at home and around the world.

Let every nation know, whether it wishes us well or ill, that we shall pay any price, bear any burden, meet any hardship, support any friend, oppose any foe, to assure the survival and the success of liberty.

This much we pledge and more.

To those old allies whose cultural and spiritual origins we share, we pledge the loyalty of faithful friends. United, there is little we cannot do in a host of cooperative ventures. Divided, there is little we can do—for we dare not meet a powerful challenge at odds and split asunder.

To those new States whom we welcome to the ranks of the free, we pledge our word that one form of colonial control shall not have passed away merely to be replaced by a far more iron tyranny. We shall not always expect to find them supporting our view. But we shall always hope to find them strongly supporting their own freedom—and to remember that, in the past, those who foolishly sought power by riding the back of the tiger ended up inside.

To those peoples in the huts and villages across the globe struggling to break the bonds of mass misery, we pledge our best efforts to help them help themselves, for whatever period is required, not because the Communists may be doing it, not because we seek their votes, but because it is right. If a free society cannot help the many who are poor, it cannot save the few who are rich.

To our sister republics south of our border, we offer a special pledge—to convert our good words into good deeds in a new alliance for progress—to assist free men and free governments in casting off the chains of poverty. But this peaceful revolution of hope cannot become the prey of hostile powers. Let all our neighbors know that we shall join with them to oppose aggression or subversion anywhere in the Americas. And let every other power know that this Hemisphere intends to remain the master of its own house.

To that world assembly of sovereign states, the United Nations, our last best hope in an age where the instruments of war have far outpaced the instruments of peace, we renew our pledge of support—to prevent it from becoming merely a forum for invective—to strengthen its shield of the new and the weak and to enlarge the area in which its writ may run.

Finally, to those nations who would make themselves our adversary, we offer not a pledge but a request—that both sides begin anew the quest for peace, before the dark powers of destruction unleashed by science engulf all humanity in planned or accidental self-destruction.

We dare not tempt them with weakness. For only when our arms are sufficient beyond doubt can we be certain beyond doubt that they will never be employed.

But neither can two great and powerful groups of nations take comfort from our present course—both sides overburdened by the cost of modern weapons, both rightly alarmed by the steady spread of the deadly atom, yet both racing to alter that uncertain balance of terror that stays the hand of mankind's final war.

So let us begin anew, remembering on both sides that civility is not a sign of weakness, and sincerity is always subject to proof. Let us never negotiate out of fear. But let us never fear to negotiate.

Let both sides explore what problems unite us instead of belaboring those problems which divide us. Let both sides, for the first time, formulate serious and precise proposals for the inspection and control of arms and bring the absolute power to destroy other nations under the absolute control of all nations.

Let both sides seek to invoke the wonders of science instead of its terrors. Together let us explore the stars, conquer the deserts, eradicate disease, tap the ocean depths, and encourage the arts and commerce.

Let both sides unite to heed in all corners of the earth the command of Isaiah—to "undo the heavy burdens . . . and let the oppressed go free."

And if a beachhead of cooperation may push back the jungle of suspicion, let both sides join in creating a new endeavor, not a new balance of power, but a new world of law, where the strong are just and the weak secure and the peace preserved.

All this will not be finished in the first 100 days. Nor will it be finished in the first 1,000 days, nor in the life of this administration, nor even perhaps in our lifetime on this planet. But let us begin.

In your hands, my fellow citizens, more than mine, will rest the final success or failure of our course. Since this country was founded, each generation of Americans has been summoned to give testimony to its national loyalty. The graves of young Americans who answered the call to service surround the globe.

Now the trumpet summons us again—not as a call to bear arms, though arms we need—not as a call to battle, though embattled we are—but a call to bear the burden of a long twilight struggle, year in and year out, "rejoicing in hope, patient in tribulation"—a struggle against the common enemies of man: tyranny, poverty, disease, and war itself.

Can we forge against these enemies a grand and global alliance, North and South, East and West, that can assure a more fruitful life for all mankind? Will you join in that historic effort?

In the long history of the world, only a few generations have been granted the role of defending freedom in its hour of maximum danger. I do not shrink from this responsibility—I welcome it. I do not believe that any of us would exchange places with any other people or any other generation. The energy, the faith, the devotion which we bring to this endeavor will light our country and all who serve it—and the glow from that fire can truly light the world.

And so, my fellow Americans: ask not what your country can do for you—ask what you can do for your country.

My fellow citizens of the world: ask not what America will do for you, but what together we can do for the freedom of man.

Finally, whether you are citizens of America or citizens of the world, ask of us here the same high standards of strength and sacrifice which we ask of you. With a good conscience our only sure reward, with history the final judge of our deeds, let us go forth to lead the land we love, asking His blessing and His help, but knowing that here on earth God's work must truly be our own.

Textual Questions

1. JFK opens his address with the statement that "The world is very different now." Why? What changes have occurred/are occurring in America, at this point, since President Eisenhower took office in January of 1953?

2. How does JFK address his speech to the various nations of the Earth—old and new, free and enslaved? How does he tailor his message to each?

3. Where does JFK most clearly articulate his vision of America at home? Of America in the larger world?

Rhetorical Questions

4. How can JFK's speech be seen as a speech about social justice, both at home and abroad? Which sections of his speech specifically concern themselves with this topic?

5. How/where does JFK use repetition to emphasize some of his points? Which of these uses is most effective?

6. Mark the passages where JFK refers to either his generation of Americans or American history. What purpose does each of these references serve in his argument about America's actions as the nation moves forward? Why appeal to both the current generation and to history?

Intertextual Questions

7. How does JFK's message to the world, beginning in paragraph 3, compare to President Bush's arguments in "We Have Seen the State of Our Union" (in the introduction to this book)?

8. According to JFK, who/what are the "common enemies of man"? How do these "common enemies" compare to those in FDR's "Four Freedoms" (earlier in this chapter)?

Thinking Beyond the Text

9. In his inaugural address, JFK makes references to America's enemies, just as President Bush does in "We Have Seen the State of Our Union." Do you believe that such warnings are effective in curbing violence? Or are they simply a rhetorical show of force, bark without (necessarily) any bite?

10. JFK's inaugural address is considered to be a masterpiece of inspirational rhetoric, a call for a new generation to make its way in the world—to make this world a better place for everyone, in America and beyond. Is this a call to which modern Americans would respond, or do you believe that such inspiration to selflessness is a thing of the past?

For Writing & Discussion

11. Research the relationship between the United States and the USSR in 1961. In an essay, explain which portions of JFK's address were, in the context of the Cold War, a warning to the Soviets. How do such warnings then compare with recent warnings presidents have given to other nations—such as President George W. Bush's warnings in 2003 (and on) to Iran and North Korea regarding their nuclear programs?

MARTIN LUTHER KING, JR.

Born in Atlanta, Georgia, Martin Luther King, Jr. (1929–1968) became an ordained minister by age 18 and a doctor of theology by 26. Minister of a Baptist church in Montgomery, Alabama, he led a boycott of segregated bus lines in the mid-1950s and went on to organize the Southern Christian Leadership Conference, an organization of black churches aligned to challenge racial segregation. Advocating nonviolent protests, King was arrested several times in the 1950s and 1960s, believing people had a moral responsibility to disobey unjust laws. Lauded for his inspirational public speaking and personal commitment, King was recognized as the leader of the civil rights movement. He was awarded the Nobel Peace Prize in 1964. By the mid-1960s, however, his status as the unquestioned black civil rights leader started to wane as other black leaders argued that King's nonviolent approach and moral idealism weren't effective. King was assassinated by a sniper in 1968 in Memphis, Tennessee, and news of his death caused shock and outrage throughout the nation and world. James Earl Ray, an escaped convict and lifelong criminal, admitted to the murder. Since his death, King has come to symbolize nonviolent civil rights activism, and his influence has expanded worldwide.

His "I Have a Dream" speech was delivered in Washington, D.C., on August 28, 1963, before more than 200,000 people. King and other black leaders organized a march on Washington, a massive civil rights protest. The march built on previous demonstrations and helped lead to the Civil Rights Act of 1964, which banned both segregation in public buildings and discrimination in education and employment.

I Have a Dream

∾ Prereading Question

The 1960s were a time of great change in America, socially, politically, militarily, and technologically. Why, in such a time of change, would a civil rights leader such as Martin Luther King, Jr. be secretly investigated by the Federal Bureau of Investigation?

Delivered August 28, 1963, at the Lincoln Memorial, Washington, D.C.

I am happy to join with you today in what will go down in history as the greatest demonstration for freedom in the history of our nation.

Five score years ago, a great American, in whose symbolic shadow we stand today, signed the Emancipation Proclamation. This momentous decree came as a great beacon light of hope to millions of Negro slaves who had been seared in the flames of withering injustice. It came as a joyous daybreak to end the long night of their captivity.

But one hundred years later, the Negro still is not free. One hundred years later, the life of the Negro is still sadly crippled by the manacles of segregation and the chains of discrimination. One hundred years later, the Negro lives on a lonely island of poverty in the midst of a vast ocean of material prosperity. One hundred years later, the Negro is still languished in the corners of American society and finds himself an exile in his own land. And so we've come here today to dramatize a shameful condition.

In a sense we've come to our nation's capital to cash a check. When the architects of our republic wrote the magnificent words of the Constitution and the Declaration of Independence, they were signing a promissory note to which every American was to fall heir. This note was a promise that all men, yes, black men as well as white men, would be guaranteed the "unalienable Rights" of "Life, Liberty and the pursuit of Happiness." It is obvious today that America has defaulted on this promissory note, insofar as her citizens of color are concerned. Instead of honoring this sacred obligation, America has given the Negro people a bad check, a check which has come back marked "insufficient funds."

But we refuse to believe that the bank of justice is bankrupt. We refuse to believe that there are insufficient funds in the great vaults of opportunity of this nation. And so, we've come to cash this check, a check that will give us upon demand the riches of freedom and the security of justice.

We have also come to this hallowed spot to remind America of the fierce urgency of Now. This is no time to engage in the luxury of cooling off or to take the tranquilizing drug of gradualism. Now is the time to make real the promises of democracy. Now is the time to rise from the dark and desolate valley of segregation to the sunlit path of racial justice. Now is the time to lift our nation from the quicksands of racial injustice to the solid rock of brotherhood. Now is the time to make justice a reality for all of God's children.

It would be fatal for the nation to overlook the urgency of the moment. This sweltering summer of the Negro's legitimate discontent will not pass until there is an invigorating autumn of freedom and equality. Nineteen sixty-three is not an end, but a beginning. And those who hope that the Negro needed to blow off steam and will now be content will have a rude awakening if the nation returns to business as usual. And there will be neither rest nor tranquility in America until the Negro is granted his citizenship rights. The whirlwinds of revolt will continue to shake the foundations of our nation until the bright day of justice emerges.

But there is something that I must say to my people, who stand on the warm threshold which leads into the palace of justice: In the process of gaining our rightful place, we must not be guilty of wrongful deeds. Let us not seek to satisfy our thirst for freedom by drinking from the cup of bitterness and hatred. We must forever conduct our struggle on the high plane of dignity and discipline. We must not allow our creative protest to degenerate into physical violence. Again and again, we must rise to the majestic heights of meeting physical force with soul force.

The marvelous new militancy which has engulfed the Negro community must not lead us to a distrust of all white people, for many of our white brothers, as evidenced by their presence here today, have come to realize that their destiny is tied up with our destiny. And they have come to realize that their freedom is inextricably bound to our freedom.

We cannot walk alone.

And as we walk, we must make the pledge that we shall always march ahead.

We cannot turn back.

There are those who are asking the devotees of civil rights, "When will you be satisfied?" We can never be satisfied as long as the Negro is the victim of the unspeakable horrors of police brutality. We can never be satisfied as long as our bodies, heavy with the fatigue of travel, cannot gain lodging in the motels of the highways and the hotels of the cities. We cannot be satisfied as long as the Negro's basic mobility is from a smaller ghetto to a larger one. We can never be satisfied as long as our children are stripped of their self-hood and robbed of their dignity by a sign stating: "For Whites Only." We cannot be satisfied as long as a Negro in Mississippi cannot vote and a Negro in New York believes he has nothing for which to vote. No, no, we are not satisfied, and we will not be satisfied until "justice rolls down like waters, and righteousness like a mighty stream."

I am not unmindful that some of you have come here out of great trials and tribulations. Some of you have come fresh from narrow jail cells. And some of you have come from areas where your quest—quest for freedom left you battered by the storms of persecution and staggered by the winds of police brutality. You have been the veterans of creative suffering. Continue to work with the faith that unearned suffering is redemptive. Go back to Mississippi, go back to Alabama, go back to South Carolina, go back to Georgia, go back to Louisiana, go back to the slums and ghettos of our northern cities, knowing that somehow this situation can and will be changed.

Let us not wallow in the valley of despair, I say to you today, my friends.

And so even though we face the difficulties of today and tomorrow, I still have a dream. It is a dream deeply rooted in the American dream.

I have a dream that one day this nation will rise up and live out the true meaning of its creed: "We hold these truths to be self-evident, that all men are created equal."

I have a dream that one day on the red hills of Georgia, the sons of former slaves and the sons of former slave owners will be able to sit down together at the table of brotherhood.

I have a dream that one day even the state of Mississippi, a state sweltering with the heat of injustice, sweltering with the heat of oppression, will be transformed into an oasis of freedom and justice.

I have a dream that my four little children will one day live in a nation where they will not be judged by the color of their skin but by the content of their character.

I have a *dream* today!

I have a dream that one day, down in Alabama, with its vicious racists, with its governor having his lips dripping with the words of "interposition" and "nullification"—one day right there in Alabama little black boys and black girls will be able to join hands with little white boys and white girls as sisters and brothers.

I have a *dream* today!

I have a dream that one day every valley shall be exalted, and every hill and mountain shall be made low, the rough places will be made plain, and the crooked places will be made straight; "and the glory of the Lord shall be revealed and all flesh shall see it together."

This is our hope, and this is the faith that I go back to the South with.

With this faith, we will be able to hew out of the mountain of despair a stone of hope. With this faith, we will be able to transform the jangling discords of our nation into a beautiful symphony of brotherhood. With this faith, we will be able to work together, to pray together, to struggle together, to go to jail together, to stand up for freedom together, knowing that we will be free one day.

And this will be the day—this will be the day when all of God's children will be able to sing with new meaning:

> My country 'tis of thee, sweet
>   land of liberty, of thee I sing.
> Land where my fathers died,
>   land of the Pilgrim's pride,
> From every mountainside, let
>   freedom ring!

And if America is to be a great nation, this must become true.

> And so let freedom ring from the prodigious hilltops of New Hampshire.
>   Let freedom ring from the mighty mountains of New York.
> Let freedom ring from the heightening Alleghenies of Pennsylvania.
>   Let freedom ring from the snow-capped Rockies of Colorado.
> Let freedom ring from the curvaceous slopes of California.
>   But not only that:

> Let freedom ring from Stone Mountain of Georgia.
>   Let freedom ring from Lookout Mountain of Tennessee.
> Let freedom ring from every hill and molehill of Mississippi.
>   From every mountainside, let freedom ring.

And when this happens, when we allow freedom [to] ring, when we let it ring from every village and every hamlet, from every state and every city, we will be able to speed up that day when *all* of God's children, black men and white men, Jews and Gentiles, Protestants and Catholics, will be able to join hands and sing in the words of the old Negro spiritual:

> Free at last! Free at last!
> Thank God Almighty, we are free at last!

Textual Questions

1. How, in the opening of his speech, does MLK refer to President Abraham Lincoln both directly and indirectly?

2. What banking imagery does MLK use to describe the condition of African Americans and the promise of America to them?

3. According to MLK, what will the cashed check deliver to African Americans?

Rhetorical Questions

4. How does MLK construct his argument so that it will appeal to members of different religions, racial groups, and socio-economic classes?

5. Where and how does MLK refer to both the events of the past and of the present as he constructs his argument about equality and African Americans?

6. For MLK, the image of the check waiting to be cashed, the image of the bad check, was at the heart of this speech—not the repetition of the declaration "I have a dream." Why is this repetition so powerful that it, rather than the uncashed/bad check, has come to characterize—and give title to—this speech?

Intertextual Questions

7. In what ways is MLK's appeal to African Americans and those who support equal rights similar to JFK's appeal to all Americans of this same generation (earlier in this chapter)? How does MLK's presentation of the plight of African Americans compare/contrast to Stanton's description (earlier in this chapter) of the marginalized status of women?

8. In 1867, Frederick Douglass appealed to Congress for impartial suffrage for African American men. In 1961, MLK appealed to America for equal treatment of all African Americans. How are their appeals (both printed earlier in this chapter)—separated by nearly a century—similar to one another? How are they different? Explain your answer to both questions in an essay.

Thinking Beyond the Text

9. Research the social status of African Americans in 1961, paying special attention to the existence of Jim Crow laws and the politicians, such as George Wallace, who supported them. Considering this mountain of discrimination, do you believe that MLK's actions, along with those of the other civil rights activists, could have ended institutionalized discrimination? Or was something more required, such as President Lyndon Johnson's package of Great Society initiatives?

10. MLK makes numerous attempts to address all Americans in his speech. How successful has his appeal been for people you know well? Think of some incidents or conversations to support your position.

For Writing & Discussion

11. Watch a video presentation of this speech—either on a VCR tape, DVD, or online. In an essay, compare and contrast your reactions to the speech while reading it to your reactions while listening to/viewing it.

LYNDON B. JOHNSON

Lyndon B. Johnson (1908–1973) served in both the U.S. House of Representatives and Senate for years before becoming John F. Kennedy's vice presidential running mate in 1960. After Kennedy's assassination on November 22, 1963, Johnson was sworn in as president and vowed to carry out Kennedy's programs. Congress quickly passed two significant Kennedy-supported measures: an $11 billion tax cut and the Civil Rights Act of 1964, the largest piece of civil rights legislation passed since the Reconstruction years following the American Civil War. Johnson was elected in 1964 in a landslide over Senator Barry Goldwater and continued to press Congress to pass Great Society legislation, with considerable success. However, these achievements were overshadowed by Johnson's decision to escalate military involvement in Vietnam. During his tenure, American forces increased in Vietnam from 20,000 to 500,000. By the time Johnson chose not to run again in 1968, the nation was harshly divided over the war.

In the speech "The Great Society," delivered May 22, 1964, at the University of Michigan, Johnson described his plans to solve pressing problems facing America. His domestic program, thereafter dubbed the Great Society, turned into the largest burst of legislative activity since President Franklin D. Roosevelt's New Deal. Several of the measures were successful—including improvements to fight poverty, improve education, and provide affordable medical care—but his domestic policies began to lose support and funding as the escalating Vietnam War became the dominant issue of the era.

The Great Society

∽ Prereading Question

Despite his commitment to ending legalized discrimination against African Americans, President Johnson is not remembered by most Americans as a great proponent of civil rights. Why? What parallels do you see between this dilemma of President Johnson and that of President George W. Bush?

May 22, 1964

President Hatcher, Governor Romney, Senators McNamara and Hart, Congressmen Header and Staebler, and other members of the fine Michigan delegation, members of the graduating class, my fellow Americans:

It is a great pleasure to be here today. This university has been coeducational since 1870, but I do not believe it was on the basis of your accomplishments that a Detroit high school girl said, "In choosing a college, you first have to decide whether you want a coeducational school or an educational school."

Well, we can find both here at Michigan, although perhaps at different hours. I came out here today very anxious to meet the Michigan student whose father told a friend of mine that his son's education had been a real value. It stopped his mother from bragging about him.

I have come today from the turmoil of your Capital to the tranquility of your campus to speak about the future of your country.

The purpose of protecting the life of our Nation and preserving the liberty of our citizens is to pursue the happiness of our people. Our success in that pursuit is the test of our success as a Nation.

For a century we labored to settle and to subdue a continent. For half a century we called upon unbounded invention and untiring industry to create an order of plenty for all of our people.

The challenge of the next half century is whether we have the wisdom to use that wealth to enrich and elevate our national life, and to advance the quality of our American civilization.

Your imagination, your initiative, and your indignation will determine whether we build a society where progress is the servant of our needs, or a society where old values and new visions are buried under unbridled growth. For in your time we have the opportunity to move not only toward the rich society and the powerful society, but upward to the Great Society.

The Great Society rests on abundance and liberty for all. It demands an end to poverty and racial injustice, to which we are totally committed in our time. But that is just the beginning.

The Great Society is a place where every child can find knowledge to enrich his mind and to enlarge his talents. It is a place where leisure is a welcome chance to build and reflect, not a feared cause of boredom and restlessness. It is a place where the city of man serves not only the needs of the body and the demands of commerce but the desire for beauty and the hunger for community.

It is a place where man can renew contact with nature. It is a place which honors creation for its own sake and for what it adds to the under-standing of the race. It is a place where men are more concerned with the quality of their goals than the quantity of their goods.

But most of all, the Great Society is not a safe harbor, a resting place, a final objective, a finished work. It is a challenge constantly renewed, beckoning us toward a destiny where the meaning of our lives matches the marvelous products of our labor.

So I want to talk to you today about three places where we begin to build the Great Society—in our cities, in our countryside, and in our classrooms.

Many of you will live to see the day, perhaps 50 years from now, when there will be 400 million Americans—four-fifths of them in urban areas. In the remainder of this century urban population will double, city land will double, and we will have to build homes, highways, and facilities equal to all those built since this country was first settled. So in the next 40 years we must rebuild the entire urban United States.

Aristotle said: "Men come together in cities in order to live, but they remain together in order to live the good life." It is harder and harder to live the good life in American cities today. The catalog of ills is long: there is the decay of the centers and the despoiling of the suburbs. There is not enough housing for our people or transportation for our traffic. Open land is vanishing and old landmarks are violated.

Worst of all, expansion is eroding the precious and time honored val-ues of community with neighbors and communion with nature. The loss of these values breeds loneliness and boredom and indifference.

Our society will never be great until our cities are great. Today the frontier of imagination and innovation is inside those cities and not beyond their borders. New experiments are already going on. It will be the task of your generation to make the American city a place where future generations will come, not only to live but to live the good life.

I understand that if I stayed here tonight I would see that Michigan students are really doing their best to live the good life.

This is the place where the Peace Corps was started. It is inspiring to see how all of you, while you are in this country, are trying so hard to live at the level of the people.

A second place where we begin to build the Great Society is in our countryside. We have always prided ourselves on being not only America the strong and America the free, but America the beautiful. Today that beauty is in danger. The water we drink, the food we eat, the very air that we breathe, are threatened with pollution. Our parks are overcrowded, our seashores overburdened. Green fields and dense forests are disappearing.

A few years ago we were greatly concerned about the "Ugly American." Today we must act to prevent an ugly America.

For once the battle is lost, once our natural splendor is destroyed, it can never be recaptured. And once man can no longer walk with beauty or wonder at nature his spirit will wither and his sustenance be wasted. A third place to build the Great Society is in the classrooms of America. There your children's lives will be shaped. Our society will not be great until every young mind is set free to scan the farthest reaches of thought and imagination. We are still far from that goal.

Today, 8 million adult Americans, more than the entire population of Michigan, have not finished 5 years of school. Nearly 20 million have not finished 8 years of school. Nearly 54 million—more than one-quarter of all America—have not even finished high school.

Each year more than 100,000 high school graduates, with proved ability, do not enter college because they cannot afford it. And if we cannot educate today's youth, what will we do in 1970 when elementary school enrollment will be 5 million greater than 1960? And high school enrollment will rise by 5 million. College enrollment will increase by more than 3 million.

In many places, classrooms are overcrowded and curricula are outdated. Most of our qualified teachers are underpaid, and many of our paid teachers are unqualified. So we must give every child a place to sit and a teacher to learn from. Poverty must not be a bar to learning, and learning must offer an escape from poverty. But more classrooms and more teachers are not enough. We must seek an educational system which grows in excellence as it grows in size. This means better training for our teachers. It means preparing youth to enjoy their hours of leisure as well as their hours of labor. It means exploring new techniques of teaching, to find new ways to stimulate the love of learning and the capacity for creation.

These are three of the central issues of the Great Society. While our Government has many programs directed at those issues, I do not pretend that we have the full answer to those problems.

But I do promise this: We are going to assemble the best thought and the broadest knowledge from all over the world to find those answers for America. I intend to establish working groups to prepare a series of White House conferences and meetings—on the cities, on natural beauty, on the quality of education, and on other emerging challenges. And from these meetings and from this inspiration and from these studies we will begin to set our course toward the Great Society.

The solution to these problems does not rest on a massive program in Washington, nor can it rely solely on the strained resources of local authority. They require us to create new concepts of cooperation, a creative federalism, between the National Capital and the leaders of local communities.

Woodrow Wilson once wrote: "Every man sent out from his university should be a man of his Nation as well as a man of his time."

Within your lifetime powerful forces, already loosed, will take us toward a way of life beyond the realm of our experience, almost beyond the bounds of our imagination.

For better or for worse, your generation has been appointed by history to deal with those problems and to lead America toward a new age. You have the chance never before afforded to any people in any age. You can help build a society where the demands of morality, and the needs of the spirit, can be realized in the life of the Nation.

So, will you join in the battle to give every citizen the full equality which God enjoins and the law requires, whatever his belief, or race, or the color of his skin? Will you join in the battle to give every citizen an escape from the crushing weight of poverty?

Will you join in the battle to make it possible for all nations to live in enduring peace as neighbors and not as mortal enemies?

Will you join in the battle to build the Great Society, to prove that our material progress is only the foundation on which we will build a richer life of mind and spirit?

There are those timid souls who say this battle cannot be won; that we are condemned to a soulless wealth. I do not agree. We have the power to shape the civilization that we want. But we need your will, your labor, your hearts, if we are to build that kind of society.

Those who came to this land sought to build more than just a new country.

They sought a new world. So I have come here today to your campus to say that you can make their vision our reality. So let us from this moment begin our work so that in the future men will look back and say: It was then, after a long and weary way, that man turned the exploits of his genius to the full enrichment of his life.

Thank you. Goodbye.

Textual Questions

1. How, in his introduction, does LBJ allude to the preamble to the U.S. Constitution? Later in his speech, how does he further develop this connection?

2. Why and how many times does LBJ repeat "It is a place" in the section of his speech in which he describes/defines the Great Society? What is the effect of this repetition?

3. How does LBJ use Aristotle to construct his argument about the Great Society? Why use a philosopher from the fourth century BCE to make

an argument about America as it approaches the end of the twentieth century CE?

Rhetorical Questions

4. How does LBJ use the past to launch his argument about America's proper course in the future? Within his speech, how does LBJ define the Great Society that he sees?

5. In what ways is LBJ's Great Society argument a culmination of the struggle for equality for both women and African Americans? Who else is included in LBJ's vision and not in these others?

6. What are the three central issues of the Great Society and how does LBJ define/describe each of them?

Intertextual Questions

7. In what ways is LBJ's speech a call to action for a generation? How does it compare with the call made by JFK only 3 years before? How does it compare with the other calls to action in this chapter, particularly those by Stanton and Douglass (all in this chapter)?

8. How does LBJ define/describe the Great Society that he sees in America's future? How does this vision compare/contrast to President Ronald Reagan's vision of America as a City on a Hill (pages 104–110)?

Thinking Beyond the Text

9. According to LBJ, the future is broken into a simple binary, a binary based upon the choices to be made by the members of his audience. Either Americans will build a nation where "progress is the servant of our needs" or a nation where "old values and new visions are buried under unbridled growth." Is this an accurate description—or a reductive, simplistic binary built only to serve a rhetorical need of the moment?

10. In the years between 1964 and now, has LBJ's Great Society come to pass? Has progress been made? Do you doubt that LBJ's vision of America can ever truly come into existence as he defines it?

For Writing & Discussion

11. Research social and economic conditions in America in 1963, when LBJ became president, and in 1969, when LBJ chose not to seek reelection. In an essay, show how these two times, 1963 and 1969, were similar in some ways and different in others. If your space and time are limited,

you may decide to focus your essay on a specific group of Americans, such as the poor, the wealthy, women, migrant workers, or the like.

SHIRLEY CHISHOLM

A Democrat from New York, Shirley Chisholm (1924–2005) became the first black woman to serve in the U.S. House of Representatives when she was elected in 1968. She served seven terms in Congress and gained national attention advocating women's rights, abortion reform, and an end to the Vietnam War. She made an unsuccessful bid for the 1972 Democratic presidential nomination. She wrote about her life and political efforts in the books *Unbought and Unbossed* and *The Good Fight*.

Chisholm delivered this speech to Congress on August 10, 1970. Congress had considered various versions of such a bill since 1920 when women were first granted the right to vote. The Equal Rights Amendment asked for all forms of discrimination based on sex to be illegal. The proposed constitutional amendment eventually was passed by both houses of Congress in 1972. The ERA did not make it into the Constitution, however, because not enough states agreed to pass the amendment by its 10-year deadline in 1982.

For the Equal Rights Amendment

◌ Prereading Question

Consider the ways in which some group was discriminated against at your high school—particularly a group that was considered unpopular, a group comprised of outcasts. In what ways was this group discriminated against by other groups of students? How was the ongoing discrimination against this group justified—covertly if not overtly?

August 10, 1970

Mr. Speaker, House Joint Resolution 264, before us today, which provides for equality under the law for both men and women, represents one of the most clear-cut opportunities we are likely to have to declare our faith in the principles that shaped our Constitution. It provides a legal basis for attack on the most subtle, most pervasive, and most institutionalized form of prejudice that exists. Discrimination against women, solely on the basis of their sex, is so widespread that is seems to many persons normal, natural and right.

Legal expression of prejudice on the grounds of religious or political belief has become a minor problem in our society. Prejudice on the basis of race is, at least, under systematic attack. There is reason for optimism that it will start to die with the present, older generation. It is time we act to assure full equality of opportunity to those citizens who, although in a majority, suffer the restrictions that are commonly imposed on minorities, to women.

The argument that this amendment will not solve the problem of sex discrimination is not relevant. If the argument were used against a civil rights bill, as it has been used in the past, the prejudice that lies behind it would be embarrassing. Of course laws will not eliminate prejudice from the hearts of human beings. But that is no reason to allow prejudice to continue to be enshrined in our laws—to perpetuate injustice through inaction.

The amendment is necessary to clarify countless ambiguities and inconsistencies in our legal system. For instance, the Constitution guarantees due process of law, in the Fifth and Fourteenth amendments. But the applicability of due process of sex distinctions is not clear. Women are excluded from some state colleges and universities. In some states, restrictions are placed on a married woman who engages in an independent business. Women may not be chosen for some juries. Women even receive heavier criminal penalties than men who commit the same crime. What would the legal effects of the equal rights amendment really be? The equal rights amendment would govern only the relationship between the state and its citizens—not relationships between private citizens. The amendment would be largely self-executing, that is, and Federal or state laws in conflict would be ineffective one year after date of ratification without further action by the Congress or state legislatures.

Opponents of the amendment claim its ratification would throw the law into a state of confusion and would result in much litigation to establish its meaning. This objection overlooks the influence of legislative history in determining intent and the recent activities of many groups preparing for legislative changes in this direction.

State labor laws applying only to women, such as those limiting hours of work and weights to be lifted would become inoperative unless the legislature amended them to apply to men. As of early 1970 most states would have some laws that would be affected. However, changes are being made so rapidly as a result of title VII of the Civil Rights Act of 1964, it is likely that by the time the equal rights amendment would become effective; no conflicting state laws would remain.

In any event, there has for years been great controversy as to the usefulness to women of these state labor laws. There has never been any doubt that they worked a hardship on women who need or want to work overtime and on women who need or want better paying jobs, and there has been no persuasive evidence as to how many women benefit from the archaic policy of the laws. After the Delaware hours law was repealed in 1966, there were no complaints from women to any of the state agencies that might have been approached.

Jury service laws not making women equally liable for jury service would have [to be] revised. The selective service law would have to include women, but women would not be required to serve in the Armed Forces where they are not fitted any more than men are required to serve. Military service, while a great responsibility, is not without benefits, particularly for young men with limited education or training.

Since October 1966, 246,000 young men who did not meet the normal mental or physical requirements have been given opportunities for training and correcting physical problems. This opportunity is not open to their sisters. Only girls who have completed high school and meet high standards on the educational test can volunteer. Ratification of the amendment would not permit application of higher standards to women.

Survivorship benefits would be available to husbands of female workers on the same basis as to wives of male workers. The Social Security Act and the civil service and military service retirement acts are in conflict. Public schools and universities could not be limited to one sex and could not apply different admission standards to men and women. Laws requiring longer prison sentences for women than men would be invalid, and equal opportunities for rehabilitation and vocational training would have to be provided in public correctional institutions. Different ages of majority based on sex would have to be harmonized. Federal, state, and other governmental bodies would be obligated to follow nondiscriminatory practices in all aspects of employment, including public school teachers and State university and college faculties.

What would be the economic effects of the equal rights amendment? Direct economic effects would be minor. If any labor laws applying only to women still remained, their amendment or repeal would provide opportunity for women in better-paying jobs in manufacturing. More opportunities in public vocational and graduate schools for women would also tend to open up opportunities in better jobs for women.

Indirect effects could be much greater. The focusing of public attention on the gross legal, economic, and social discrimination against women by hearings and debates in the Federal and state legislatures would result in changes in attitude of parents, educators, and employers that would bring about substantial economic changes in the long run.

Sex prejudice cuts both ways. Men are oppressed by the requirements of the Selective Service Act, by enforced legal guardianship of minors, and by alimony laws. Each sex, I believe, should be liable when necessary to serve and defend this country. Each has a responsibility for the support of children.

There are objections raised to wiping out laws protecting women workers. No one would condone exploitation. But what does sex have to do with it? Working conditions and hours that are harmful to women are harmful to men; wages that are unfair for women are unfair for men. Laws setting employment limitations on the basis of sex are irrational, and the proof of this is their inconsistency from state to state. The physical characteristics of men and women are not fixed, but cover two wide spans that have a great deal of overlap. It is obvious, I think, that a robust woman could be more fit for physical labor than a weak man. The choice of occupation would be determined by individual capabilities, and the rewards for equal works should be equal.

This is what it comes down to: artificial distinctions between persons must be wiped out of the law. Legal discrimination between the sexes is, in almost every instance, founded on outmoded views of society and the pre-scientific beliefs about psychology and physiology. It is time to sweep away these relics of the past and set further generations free of them. Federal agencies and institutions responsible for the enforcement of equal opportunity laws need the authority of a Constitutional amendment. The 1964 Civil Rights Act and the 1963 Equal Pay Act are not enough; they are limited in their coverage—for instance, one excludes teachers, and the other leaves out administrative and professional women. The Equal Employment Opportunity Commission has not proven to be an adequate device, with its power limited to investigation, conciliation, and recommendation to the Justice Department. In its cases involving sexual discrimination, it has failed in more than one-half. The Justice Department has been even less effective. It has intervened in only one case involving discrimination on the basis of sex, and this was on a procedural point. In a second case, in which both sexual and racial discrimination were alleged, the racial bias charge was given far greater weight.

Evidence of discrimination on the basis of sex should hardly have to be cited here. It is in the Labor Department's employment and salary figures for anyone who is still in doubt. Its elimination will involve so many changes in our state and Federal laws that, without the authority and impetus of this proposed amendment, it will perhaps take another 194 years. We cannot be parties to continuing a delay. The time is clearly now to put this House on record for the fullest expression of that equality of opportunity which our founding fathers professed. They professed it, but they did not assure it to their daughters, as they tried to do for their sons.

The Constitution they wrote was designed to protect the rights of white, male citizens. As there were no black Founding Fathers, there were no founding mothers—a great pity, on both counts. It is not too late to complete the work they left undone. Today, here, we should start to do so.

In closing I would like to make one point. Social and psychological effects will be initially more important than legal or economic results. As Leo Kanowitz has pointed out:

> Rules of law that treat of the sexes per se inevitably produce far-reaching effects upon social, psychological and economic aspects of male-female relations beyond the limited confines of legislative chambers and courtrooms. As long as organized legal systems, at once the most respected and most feared of social institutions, continue to differentiate sharply, in treatment or in words, between men and women on the basis of irrelevant and artificially created distinctions, the likelihood of men and women coming to regard one another primarily as fellow human beings and only secondarily as representatives of another sex will continue to be remote. When men and women are prevented from recognizing one another's essential humanity by sexual prejudices, nourished by legal as well as social institutions, society as a whole remains less than it could otherwise become.

Textual Questions

1. Which arguments, according to Chisholm, are relevant or irrelevant? How does she build her argument through consideration of each?

2. How does Chisholm acknowledge and address each argument her opposition would make?

3. What specific examples does Chisholm use to illustrate her argument that equality for women is entirely feasible, workable, and right—despite any initial difficulties in enacting/revising the applicable laws?

Rhetorical Questions

4. How does Chisholm support her contention that discrimination against women is "so widespread that it seems to many persons normal, natural, and right"? How effective is her support? Have you ever been surprised to find that something you felt was "normal, natural, and right" was seen by someone else as prejudiced?

5. Chisholm attempts to anticipate and nullify the arguments against House Resolution 264. How does she do this—and how successful is she?

6. How, according to Chisholm, are both men and women oppressed by sex-based discrimination? Why might Chisholm choose to end her speech with a quotation from Leo Kanowitz rather than ending with her own words? Does the quotation from Kranowitz strengthen or weaken her argument?

Intertextual Questions

7. Searching online, find the full text of House Resolution 264 from August of 1970. Is Chisholm's characterization of this Resolution fair and accurate?

8. How do Chisholm's arguments about women's rights echo those made by Elizabeth Cady Stanton and Hillary Clinton (both in this chapter)? How do Chisholm's arguments compare and contrast with those made by Frederick Douglass regarding the rights of African Americans (earlier in this chapter)?

Thinking Beyond the Text

9. How does Chisholm describe the battle against discrimination against women as *the* battle that must be fought by her generation, and why does she believe that victory is attainable?

10. Do you believe that equality—true, complete equality in every aspect of civil, social, and political life—is ever achievable by women in America? Why or why not?

For Writing & Discussion

11. Research the history of the Equal Rights Amendment. Why has this amendment never passed into law, even though similar amendments have passed to ensure the rights of other groups of Americans? Explain your answer in a short essay.

RONALD REAGAN

Although never a major star, Ronald Reagan (1911–2004) was an actor in 50 films before becoming governor of California and later the 40th president of the United States. A longtime Democrat, Reagan changed to the Republican Party in 1962, two years before running for governor. He was elected president in 1980, defeating incumbent Jimmy Carter, and he was reelected by a landslide in 1984 over Walter Mondale. Domestically, the U.S. economy experienced modest growth in the Reagan years. At the same time, the president took a hard-line stance against the Soviet Union and oversaw the largest peacetime escalation of military expenditures in American history. However, his tax cuts and military spending more than doubled the size of the national debt. While very popular through most of his tenure, Reagan's final years were tarnished by the Iran-Contra

Affair, which involved accusations of illegal use of funds for an arms-for-hostages deal with Iran, although Reagan denied involvement.

Reagan delivered this speech on January 11, 1988, at the end of his two terms in office. Reagan's presidency was influential in many ways. He changed the way presidents interact with the public by his increased use of television and other media. He has been credited by many for the dissolution of the Soviet Union and the end of the Cold War. And he succeeded in increasing the popularity of conservative politics in a time when liberalism had been more mainstream. Critics argue that the Soviet Union collapsed for other reasons and that swapping arms for hostages rewarded terrorists and fueled attacks against the United States. At the time of his death in 2004, however, Reagan was considered one of the most popular presidents in history.

President's Farewell Address to the People
We Have Made a Difference

∾ **Prereading Question**

Interview someone who was at least 10 years old in 1980. What memories does he/she have of President Reagan? How did he/she feel about him during his presidency? How does he/she feel about him now, long after his presidency ended and years after his death?

Delivered to the American People, Washington D.C., January 11, 1989

My fellow Americans, this is the 34th time I'll speak to you from the Oval Office, and the last. We have been together eight years now, and soon it will be time for me to go. But before I do, I wanted to share some thoughts, some of which I have been saving for a long time.

It has been the honor of my life to be your President. So many of you have written the past few weeks to say thanks, but I could say as much to you. Nancy and I are grateful for the opportunity you gave us to serve.

One of the things about the Presidency is that you're always somewhat apart. You spend a lot of time going by too fast in a car someone else is driving, and seeing the people through tinted glass—the parents holding up a child, and the wave you saw too late and couldn't return. And so many times I wanted to stop, and reach out from behind the glass, and connect. And maybe I can do a little of that tonight.

People ask how I feel about leaving, and the fact is parting is "such sweet sorrow." The sweet part is California, and the ranch, and freedom. The sorrow? The goodbyes, of course, and leaving this beautiful place.

You know, down the hall and up the stairs from this office is the part of the White House where the President and his family live. There are a few favorite windows I have up there that I like to stand and look out of early in the morning. The view is over the grounds here to the Washington Monument, and then the Mall, and the Jefferson Memorial. But on mornings when the humidity is low, you can see past the Jefferson to the river, the Potomac, and the Virginia shore. Someone said that's the view Lincoln had when he saw the smoke rising from the battle of Bull Run. I see more prosaic things: the grass on the banks, the morning traffic as people make their way to work, now and then a sailboat on the river.

I have been thinking a bit at that window. I've been reflecting on what the past eight years have meant, and mean. And the image that comes to mind like a refrain is a nautical one—a small story about a big ship, and a refugee, and a sailor.

It was back in the early Eighties, at the height of the boat people, and the sailor was hard at work on the carrier Midway, which was patrolling the South China Sea. The sailor, like most American servicemen, was young, smart and fiercely observant. The crew spied on the horizon a leaky little boat and crammed inside were refugees from Indochina hoping to get to America. The Midway sent a small launch to bring them to the ship, and safety. As the refugees made their way through the choppy seas, one spied the sailor on deck, and stood up and called out to him. He yelled, "Hello, American sailor. Hello, Freedom Man."

A small moment with a big meaning, a moment the sailor, who wrote it in a letter, couldn't get out of his mind. And when I saw it, neither could I.

Because that's what it was to be an American in the 1980s; we stood, again, for freedom. I know we always have but in the past few years the world—again, and in a way, we ourselves rediscovered it.

It has been quite a journey this decade, and we held together through some stormy seas. And at the end, together, we are reaching our destination.

The fact is, from Grenada to the Washington and Moscow Summits, from the recession of '81 to '82, to the expansion that began in late '82 and continues to this day, we've made a difference.

The way I see it, there were two great triumphs, two things that I'm proudest of. One is the economic recovery, in which the people of America created—and filled—19 million new jobs. The other is the recovery of our morale: America is respected again in the world, and looked to for leadership.

Something that happened to me a few years ago reflects some of this. It was back in 1981, and I was attending my first big economic summit, which was held that year in Canada. The meeting place rotates among the member countries. The opening meeting was a formal dinner for the heads of government of the seven industrialized nations. I sat there like the new kid in school and listened, and it was all Francois this and Helmut that. They dropped titles and spoke to one another on a first name basis. At one point I sort of leaned and said, "My name's Ron."

In that same year, we began the actions we felt would ignite an economic comeback: cut taxes and regulation, started to cut spending. Soon the recovery began.

Two years later, another economic summit, with pretty much the same cast. At the big opening meeting, we all got together, and all of a sudden just for a moment I saw that everyone was looking at me. Then one of them broke the silence. "Tell us about the American miracle," he said.

Back in 1980, when I was running for President, it was all so different. Some pundits said our programs would result in catastrophe. Our views on foreign affairs would cause war, our plans for the economy would cause inflation to soar and bring about economic collapse. I even remember one highly respected economist saying, back in 1982, that "The engines of economic growth have shut down here and across the globe and they are likely to stay that way for years to come."

Well, he—and the other "opinion leaders"—were wrong. The fact is, what they called "radical" was really "right"; What they called "dangerous" was just "desperately needed."

And in all of that time I won a nickname—"The Great Communicator." But I never thought it was my style or the words I used that made a difference—it was the content. I wasn't a great communicator, but I communicated great things, and they didn't spring full bloom from my brow, they came from the heart of a great nation—from our experience, our wisdom, and our belief in principles that have guided us for two centuries.

They call it The Reagan Revolution, and I'll accept that, but for me it always seemed more like The Great Rediscovery: a rediscovery of our values and our common sense.

Common sense told us that when you put a big tax on something, the people will produce less of it. So we cut the people's tax rates, and the people produced more than ever before. The economy bloomed like a plant that had been cut back and could now grow quicker and stronger. Our economic program brought about the longest peacetime expansion in our history: real family income up, the poverty rate down, entrepreneurship booming and an explosion in research and new technology. We are exporting more than ever because American industry became more competitive, and at the same time we summoned the national will to knock down protectionist walls abroad instead of erecting them at home.

Common sense also told us that to preserve the peace we'd have to become strong again after years of weakness and confusion. So we rebuilt our defenses—and this New Year we toasted the new peacefulness around the globe. Not only have the superpowers actually begun to reduce their stockpiles of nuclear weapons—and hope for even more progress is bright—but the regional conflicts that rock the globe are also beginning to cease. The Persian Gulf is no longer a war zone, the Soviets are leaving Afghanistan, the Vietnamese are preparing to pull out of Cambodia and an American-mediated accord will soon send 50,000 Cuban troops home from Angola.

The lesson of all this was, of course, that because we are a great nation, our challenges seem complex. It will always be this way. But as long as we remember our first principles and believe in ourselves, the future will always be ours.

And something else we learned: once you begin a great movement, there's no telling where it will end. We meant to change a nation, and instead, we changed a world.

Countries across the globe are turning to free markets and free speech—and turning away from ideologies of the past. For them, the Great Rediscovery of the 1980's has been that, lo and behold, the moral way of government is the practical way of government. Democracy, the profoundly good, is also the profoundly productive.

When you've got to the point where you can celebrate the anniversaries of your 39th birthday you can sit back sometimes, review your life and see it flowing before you. For me, there was a fork in the river, and it was right in the middle of my life.

I never meant to go into politics: it wasn't my intention when I was young. But I was raised to believe you had to pay your way for the blessings bestowed on you. I was happy with my career in the entertainment world, but I ultimately went into politics because I wanted to protect something precious.

Ours was the first revolution in the history of mankind that truly reversed the course of government, and with three little words: "We the people."

"We the people" tell the Government what to do, it doesn't tell us. "We the people" are the driver—the Government is the car. And we decide where it should go, and by what route, and how fast. Almost all the world's constitutions are documents in which government tell the people what their privileges are. Our Constitution is a document in which "We the people" tell the Government what it is allowed to do. "We the people" are free.

This belief has been the underlying basis for everything I have tried to do these past eight years.

But back in the 1960's, when I began, it seemed to me that we had begun reversing the order of things—that through more and more rules and regulations and confiscatory taxes, the Government was taking more of our money, more of our options, and more of our freedom. I went into politics in part to put up my hand and say, "Stop!" I was a citizen-politician, and it seemed the right thing for a citizen to do.

I think we have stopped a lot of what needed stopping. And I hope we have once again reminded people that man is not free unless government is limited. There's a clear cause and effect here that is as neat and predictable as a law of physics: as government expands, liberty contracts.

Nothing is less free than pure communism, and yet we have, the past few years, forged a satisfying new closeness with the Soviet Union. I've been asked if this isn't a gamble, and my answer is no, because we're basing our actions not on words but deeds.

The detente of the 1970's was based not on actions but promises. They'd promise to treat their own people and the people of the world better, but the gulag was still the gulag, and the state was still expansionist, and they still waged proxy wars in Africa, Asia, and Latin America.

This time, so far, it's different: President Gorbachev has brought about some internal democratic reforms and begun the withdrawal from Afghanistan. He has also freed prisoners whose names I've given him every time we've met.

But life has a way of reminding you of big things through small incidents. Once, during the heady days of the Moscow Summit, Nancy and I decided to break off from the entourage one afternoon to visit the shops on Arbat Street, a little street just off Moscow's main shopping area.

Even though our visit was a surprise, every Russian there immediately recognized us, and called out our names and reached for our hands. We were just about swept away by the warmth—you could almost feel the possibilities in all that joy. But within seconds, a K.G.B. detail pushed their way toward us and began pushing and shoving the people in the crowd. It was an interesting moment. It reminded me that while the man on the street in the Soviet Union yearns for peace, the Government is Communist—those that run it are Communists—and that means we and they view such issues as freedom and human rights very differently.

We must keep up our guard—but we must also continue to work together to lessen and eliminate tension and mistrust.

My view is that President Gorbachev is different from previous Soviet leaders. I think he knows some of the things wrong with his society and is trying to fix them, we wish him well. And we'll continue to work to make sure that the Soviet Union that eventually emerges from this process is a less threatening one.

What it all boils down to is this: I want the new closeness to continue. And it will be long as we make it clear that we will continue to act in a certain way as long as they continue to act in a helpful manner. If and when they don't—at first pull your punches. If they persist, pull the plug.

It's still trust—but verify.

It's still play—but cut the cards.

It's still watch closely—and don't be afraid to see what you see.

I've been asked if I have any regrets. I do.

The deficit is one. I've been talking a great deal about that lately, but tonight isn't for arguments, and I'm going to hold my tongue.

But an observation: I've had my share of victories in the Congress, but what few people noticed is that I never won anything you didn't win for me. They never saw my troops; they never saw Reagan's Regiments, the American people. You won every battle with every call you made and letter you wrote demanding action.

Well, action is still needed. If we're to finish the job, Reagan's Regiments will have to become the Bush Brigades. Soon he'll be the chief, and he'll need you every bit as much as I did.

Finally, there is a great tradition of warnings in Presidential farewells, and I've got one that's been on my mind for some time.

But oddly enough it starts with one of the things I'm proudest of the past eight years; the resurgence of national pride that I called "the new patriotism." This national feeling is good, but it won't count for much, and it won't last unless it's grounded in thoughtfulness and knowledge.

An informed patriotism is what we want. And are we doing a good enough job teaching our children what America is and what she represents in the long history of the world?

Those of us who are over 35 or so years of age grew up in a different America. We were taught, very directly, what it means to be an American, and we absorbed almost in the air a love of country and an appreciation of its institutions. If you didn't get these things from your family you got them from the neighborhood, from the father down the street who fought in Korea or the family who lost someone at Anzio. Or you could get a sense of patriotism from school. And if all else failed, you could get a sense of patriotism from the popular culture. The movies celebrated democratic values and implicitly reinforced the idea that America was special. TV was like that, too, through the mid Sixties.

But now we're about to enter the Nineties, and some things have changed. Younger parents aren't sure that an unambivalent appreciation of America is the right thing to teach modern children. And as for those who create the popular culture, well-grounded patriotism is no longer the style.

Our spirit is back, but we haven't reinstitutionalized it. We've got to do a better job of getting across that America is freedom—freedom of speech, freedom of religion, freedom of enterprise—and freedom is special and rare. It's fragile, it needs protection.

We've got to teach history based not on what's in fashion but what's important: Why the Pilgrims came here, who Jimmy Doolittle was, and what those 30 seconds over Tokyo meant. You know, four years ago on the 40th anniversary of D-Day, I read a letter from a young woman writing to her late father, who'd fought on Omaha Beach. Her name was Lisa Zanatta Henn, and she said, we will always remember, we will never forget what the boys of Normandy did. Well, let's help her keep her word.

If we forget what we did, we won't know who we are. I'm warning of an eradication of the American memory that could result, ultimately, in an erosion of the American spirit.

Let's start with some basics—more attention to American history and a greater emphasis on civic ritual. And let me offer lesson No. 1 about America: All great change in America begins at the dinner table. So tomorrow night in the kitchen I hope the talking begins. And children, if your parents haven't been teaching you what it means to be an American—let them know and nail them on it. That would be a very American thing to do.

And that's about all I have to say tonight. Except for one thing.

The past few days when I've been at the window upstairs, I've thought a bit of the shining "city upon a hill." The phrase comes from John Winthrop, who wrote it to describe the America he imagined. What he imagined was important, because he was an early Pilgrim—an early "Freedom Man." He journeyed here on what today we'd call a little wooden boat; and, like the other pilgrims, he was looking for a home that would be free.

I've spoken of the shining city all my political life, but I don't know if I ever quite communicated what I saw when I said it. But in my mind, it was a tall proud city built on rocks stronger than oceans, wind swept, God blessed, and teeming with people of all kinds living in harmony and peace—a city with free ports that hummed with commerce and creativity, and if there had to be city walls, the walls had doors, and the doors were open to anyone with the will and the heart to get here.

That's how I saw it, and see it still.

And how stands the city on this winter night? More prosperous, more secure and happier than it was eight years ago. But more than that: after 200 years, two centuries, she still stands strong and true on the granite ridge, and her glow has held steady no matter what storm.

And she's still a beacon, still a magnet for all who must have freedom, for all the pilgrims from all the lost places who are hurtling through darkness, toward home. We've done our part. And as I "walk off into the city streets," a final word to the men and women of the Reagan Revolution—the men and women across America who for eight years did the work that brought America back:

My friends, we did it. We weren't just marking time, we made a difference. We made the city stronger—we made the city freer—and we left her in good hands.

All in all, not bad. Not bad at all.

And so, goodbye.

God bless you. And God bless the United States of America.

Textual Questions

1. How does President Reagan make his final address to the American people a personal communication from the president to each citizen—as well as a summative, positive declaration of the accomplishments of the previous eight years. Of what two things is President Reagan most proud? How does he define/describe each of them?

2. How does President Reagan define "The American Miracle" and "The Reagan Revolution"? What other terms' definitions are key to his argument about the accomplishments of the past four years?

3. With what warning does President Reagan leave the American people? How does he define the terms that are key to this warning?

Rhetorical Questions

4. How does President Reagan use the story of "a big ship, and a refugee, and a sailor" to encapsulate and advance his argument?

5. How does President Reagan use concrete examples to illustrate general concepts? Which of these illustrations is most effective?

6. Why does President Reagan's argument about his eight years in office build to a discussion of relations between the United States and the USSR? What regrets does President Reagan have about his time in office? How does he describe each?

Intertextual Questions

7. How does President Reagan in "We Have Made a Difference" repeat the arguments of President Franklin D. Roosevelt in "The Four Freedoms" (earlier in this chapter)?

8. How does the vision of America presented by President Reagan compare and contrast to the visions of America set forth by Presidents Kennedy, Johnson, Carter, and Bush (in this chapter and in the introduction)?

Thinking Beyond the Text

9. As President Reagan describes the situation in the world beyond America's borders, he speaks of strength at home and peace abroad. Based upon your knowledge of America's actions in the 1980s—and your knowledge of events in the years since President Reagan left office—do you think his characterization of America's position in the world was true then or is still true now?

10. President Reagan equates democracy with morality; he also equates democracy with productivity. Thus democracy is both a moral and productive form of human government. What are the strengths and weaknesses of this argument?

For Writing & Discussion

11. Searching online, at http://livingroomcandidate.movingimage.us/index.php, find two of President Reagan's campaign commercials from 1984: "The Bear" and "Prouder, Stronger, Better" (also known as

"Morning in America"). What is the message of each of these commercials? How, in his farewell address, does President Reagan implicitly and explicitly argue that the goals set forth in these two advertisements have been achieved? Explain your answers to these questions in an essay.

HILLARY RODHAM CLINTON

Born in 1947 in Chicago, Hillary Rodham earned a bachelor's degree from Wellesley College and a law degree at Yale Law School, where she met her husband, Bill Clinton. Hillary Rodham Clinton worked as a lawyer and law professor before her husband was elected president in 1992. As First Lady, she was both lauded for having her own successful career and criticized for not taking a more traditional role of First Lady. She traveled extensively as First Lady, promoting women's rights. While her husband was still in office, she ran for and won a seat in the U.S. Senate. Her election to the Senate while First Lady was a first in history, and the senator and former First Lady has come to be a powerful symbol of the changing role of women in America.

In 1995, Hillary Rodham Clinton attended the United Nation's Fourth World Conference on Women in Beijing, China, where she delivered this speech. The conference drew in 17,000 participants from 189 countries to address issues of women's rights around the globe.

Women's Rights Are Human Rights

∽ Prereading Question

In the more than two centuries since its founding, how has the United States worked to extend its definition of freedom to other nations of the world? Where has this mission been most or least successful, in your opinion?

September 5, 1995

Thank you very much Gertrude Mongella, for your dedicated work that has brought us to this point.

Distinguished delegates and guests, I would like to thank the Secretary General of the United Nations for inviting me to be part of this important

United Nations Fourth World Conference on Women. This is truly a celebration—a celebration of the contributions women make in every aspect of life: in the home, on the job, in the community, as mothers, wives, sisters, daughters, learners, workers, citizens and leaders.

It is also a coming together, much the way women come together every day in every country.

We come together in fields and in factories. In village markets and supermarkets. In living rooms and board rooms.

Whether it is while playing with our children in the park, or washing clothes in a river, or taking a break at the office water cooler, we come together and talk about our aspirations and concerns. And time and again, our talk turns to our children and our families.

However different we may appear, there is far more that unites us than divides us. We share a common future. And we are here to find common ground so that we may help bring new dignity and respect to women and girls all over the world—and in so doing, bring new strength and stability to families as well.

By gathering in Beijing, we are focusing world attention on issues that matter most in the lives of women and their families: access to education, health care, jobs, and credit, the chance to enjoy basic legal and human rights and to participate fully in the political life of their countries.

There are some who question the reason for this conference. Let them listen to the voices of women in their homes, neighborhoods, and workplaces.

There are some who wonder whether the lives of women and girls matter to economic and political progress around the globe. . . . Let them look at the women gathered here and at Hairou*. . . . the homemakers, nurses, teachers, lawyers, policymakers, and women who run their own businesses.

It is conferences like this that compel governments and peoples everywhere to listen, look and face the world's most pressing problems.

Wasn't it after the women's conference in Nairobi ten years ago that the world focused for the first time on the crisis of domestic violence?

Earlier today, I participated in a World Health Organization forum. In that forum we talked about where government officials, NGOs, and individual citizens are working on ways to address the health problems of women and girls.

Tomorrow, I will attend a gathering of the United Nations Development Fund for Women. There, the discussion will focus on local—and highly successful—programs that give hard-working women access to credit so they can improve their own lives and the lives of their families.

What we are learning around the world is that, if women are healthy and educated, their families will flourish. If women are free from violence, their families will flourish. If women have a chance to work and earn as full and equal partners in society, their families will flourish.

---

*A similar conference being held concurrently about 30 miles away from Peking.

And when families flourish, communities and nations will flourish.

That is why every woman, every man, every child, every family, and every nation on our planet does have a stake in the discussion that takes place here.

Over the past 25 years, I have worked persistently on issues relating to women, children and families. Over the past two-and-a-half years, I have had the opportunity to learn more about the challenges facing women in my own country and around the world.

I have met new mothers in Indonesia, who come together regularly in their village to discuss nutrition, family planning, and baby care.

I have met working parents in Denmark who talk about the comfort they feel in knowing that their children can be cared for in creative, safe, and nurturing after-school centers.

I have met women in South Africa who helped lead the struggle to end apartheid and are now helping build a new democracy.

I have met with the leading women of my own hemisphere who are working every day to promote literacy and better health care for the children in their countries.

I have met women in India and Bangladesh who are taking out small loans to buy milk cows, rickshaws, thread and other materials to create a livelihood for themselves and their families.

I have met doctors and nurses in Belarus and Ukraine who are trying to keep children alive in the aftermath of Chernobyl.

The great challenge of this conference is to give voice to women everywhere whose experiences go unnoticed, whose words go unheard.

Women comprise more than half the world's population. Women are 70% percent of the world's poor, and two-thirds of those who are not taught to read and write.

Women are the primary caretakers for most of the world's children and elderly. Yet much of the work we do is not valued—not by economists, not by historians, not by popular culture, not by government leaders.

At this very moment, as we sit here, women around the world are giving birth, raising children, cooking meals, washing clothes, cleaning houses, planting crops, working on assembly lines, running companies, and running countries.

Women also are dying from diseases that should have been prevented or treated; they are watching their children succumb to malnutrition caused by poverty and economic deprivation; they are being denied the right to go to school by their own fathers and brothers; they are being forced into prostitution, and they are being barred from the bank lending office and banned from the ballot box.

Those of us who have the opportunity to be here have the responsibility to speak for those who could not.

As an American, I want to speak up for women in my own country—women who are raising children on the minimum wage, women who can't afford health care or child care, women whose lives are threatened by violence, including violence in their own homes.

I want to speak up for mothers who are fighting for good schools, safe neighborhoods, clean air and clean airwaves . . .

. . . for older women, some of them widows, who have raised their families and now find that their skills and life experiences are not valued in the workplace

. . . for women who are working all night as nurses, hotel clerks, and fast food chefs so that they can be at home during the day with their kids

. . . and for women everywhere who simply don't have time to do everything they are called upon to do each day.

Speaking to you today, I speak for them, just as each of us speaks for women around the world who are denied the chance to go to school, or see a doctor, or own property, or have a say about the direction of their lives, simply because they are women.

The truth is that most women around the world work both inside and outside the home, usually by necessity.

We need to understand that there is no one formula for how women should lead their lives.

That is why we must respect the choices that each woman makes for herself and her family. Every woman deserves the chance to realize her God-given potential.

We also must recognize that women will never gain full dignity until their human rights are respected and protected.

Our goals for this conference, to strengthen families and societies by empowering women to take greater control over their own destinies, cannot be fully achieved unless all governments—here and around the world—accept their responsibility to protect and promote internationally recognized human rights.

The international community has long acknowledged—and recently affirmed at Vienna—that both women and men are entitled to a range of protections and personal freedoms, from the right of personal security to the right to determine freely the number and spacing of the children they bear.

No one should be forced to remain silent for fear of religious or political persecution, arrest, abuse or torture.

Tragically, women are most often the ones whose human rights are violated.

Even in the late 20th century, the rape of women continues to be used as an instrument of armed conflict. Women and children make up a large majority of the world's refugees. And when women are excluded from the political process, they become even more vulnerable to abuse.

I believe that, on the eve of a new millennium, it is time to break our silence. It is time for us to say here in Beijing, and the world to hear, that it is no longer acceptable to discuss women's rights as separate from human rights.

These abuses have continued because, for too long, the history of women has been a history of silence. Even today, there are those who are trying to silence our words.

The voices of this conference and of the women at Hairou must be heard loud and clear:

It is a violation of human rights when babies are denied food, or drowned, or suffocated, or their spines broken, simply because they are born girls.

It is a violation of human rights when women and girls are sold into the slavery of prostitution.

It is a violation of human rights when women are doused with gasoline, set on fire and burned to death because their marriage dowries are deemed too small.

It is a violation of human rights when individual women are raped in their own communities and when thousands of women are subjected to rape as a tactic or prize of war.

It is a violation of human rights when a leading cause of death worldwide among women ages 14 to 44 is the violence they are subjected to in their own homes by their own relatives.

It is a violation of human rights when young girls are brutalized by the painful and degrading practice of genital mutilation.

It is a violation of human rights when women are denied the right to plan their own families, and that includes being forced to have abortions or being sterilized against their will.

If there is one message that echoes forth from this conference, let it be that human rights are women's rights. . . . And women's rights are human rights, once and for all.

Let us not forget that among those rights are the right to speak freely. And the right to be heard.

Women must enjoy the right to participate fully in the social and political lives of their countries if we want freedom and democracy to thrive and endure.

It is indefensible that many women in non-governmental organizations who wished to participate in this conference have not been able to attend—or have been prohibited from fully taking part.

Let me be clear. Freedom means the right of people to assemble, organize, and debate openly. It means respecting the views of those who may disagree with the views of their governments.

Textual Questions

1. How does Clinton craft her speech to direct it at all women in all nations? According to Clinton, which issues matter most to women worldwide? How does she describe each?

2. What, within Clinton's argument, causes families to flourish? How effective are her arguments about each cause?

3. What violations of women's rights does Clinton list? How does she define/describe each?

Rhetorical Questions

4. Clinton repeats "I have met" numerous times. Is this an effective or ineffective repetition? Why? How well does Clinton's repetition of "I have met" dovetail with her repetition of "It is a violation"? What effect do these two sections of the speech have—both on the speech as a whole and on one another?

5. What does Clinton want of her audience? What call to action does she make?

6. Although Clinton's speech is clearly rooted in a specific moment in time and place—the United Nations Fourth World Conference on Women in Beijing, China—how is the argument crafted in such a way to make it applicable in all times and places?

Intertextual Questions

7. Clinton argues that the rights of women are inextricably bound to the rights of all people. How is this argument similar to/different from that advanced by Sojourner Truth almost 130 years earlier? How is it similar to/different from the arguments of Elizabeth Cady Stanton and Susan B. Anthony (all in this chapter)?

8. At the end of her speech, Clinton speaks of many violations of the rights of women. In what ways are the rights of which she speaks echoes of those rights enumerated in the works of Mason and Jefferson (at the beginning of this chapter)?

Thinking Beyond the Text

9. Do you agree with Clinton's argument that the rights of women are the same as the rights of all people in all places—that women's rights are human rights—or do you see women's rights as special and different from men's rights?

10. Clinton argues that "the rape of women continues to be used as an instrument of armed conflict." To what twentieth-century conflicts might she refer? Do you believe that, even now, rape is still a weapon of war?

For Writing & Discussion

11. Research the United Nations' other Conferences on Women. Where have they been held and what have been their foci? In an essay, examine one issue raised at one conference and reflect on how this issue is or is not still one of importance to women across the world.

FOCAL POINT

Exploring Images of The Promise of Social Equality and the Right to Vote

FOCAL POINT

Exploring Images of The Promise of Social Equality and the Right to Vote

Questions

1. How does the photograph from the 1968 Democratic National Convention on page 118 (top), portray the protestor and soldiers? Based

on the way in which the protestor is positioned, are viewers sympathetic to him? How do you think Americans in 1968 reacted to this image? How might Americans react to this photo today?

2. Consider the message delivered by Martin Luther King, Jr., in the selection, "I Have a Dream." How does the crowd in the background of the photograph on page 118 (bottom) support and/or refute the message of his speech?

3. In this picture of a small part of the Franklin Delano Roosevelt Memorial in Washington, D.C. (page 119, top), what details of the bronze statue catch your eye and why? What aspects of the statue suggest a specific time in American history? When? Why might this statue of a man listening to the radio be included as part of a memorial to a U.S. President?

4. The women in the photograph on page 119 (bottom) are celebrating the passage of the Nineteenth Amendment to the U.S. Constitution—granting women the right to vote throughout the United States. What elements of this photograph address America's past and future? Why do you think all of the celebrants are white? Does the racial background of the women in the photograph change the way in which people today might view this photograph? How?

5. What argument is the cartoon on page 120 making about elections in America in 1999? Can its message be applied to any elections? Why? Why is the hand placing money in the ballot box that of a Caucasian dressed in a business suit coat and wearing a cufflink? How is this element of the cartoon part of the argument?

∾ 2 ∾

THE PROMISE OF EDUCATION

Education is the bedrock of the promise of America. In one sense, everyone knows that the more education an individual has, the better the job will be that he/she can get; the better the job, the better the salary; the better the salary, the better the life. As always, what everyone knows is partly right and partly wrong. Not only is the easy correlation between education and good salaries often wrong—think of well-educated teachers or clergy, for instance—but there is plenty of evidence suggesting that big salaries do not always lead to satisfying lives. Reality is much more complex. Yet, in general, education does lead to the better and more rewarding jobs in every society. Every parent's desire to see children go to college is based on this deeply felt knowledge. The promise of America was keenly felt by the founders of America as the country was being formed and led to early establishment and support of public schools and public colleges as key elements in the effort to open economic and cultural opportunity to all Americans.

But at a still deeper level, education has been important for more than economic reasons. Democratic government, as our founding documents remind us, depends on the "consent of the governed," and an uninformed consent is no consent at all. For political democracy to function, an educated population must be willing and able to give informed consent to candidates and to public policies.

The promise of education, then, not only included the obvious economic and social benefits but also the qualities of citizenship, including character, learning, and culture. Such great promises were almost bound to fail, particularly as democratic theory argued that all residents of America were entitled to them, in some form or another. Never before had a country made such promises for its entire population. To be sure, the promise has been carried out very slowly. Before the Civil War, in many slave states, teaching slaves to read or write was a serious crime. And even today the gulf between the educational opportunities for the wealthy and the poor is very wide. According to the most recent data from the U.S. Census Bureau, in 2003 almost 23 percent of the U.S. population was enrolled in college—the same percentage enrolled in high school during this same time period. And of the population aged 25 years or older, 34 percent of people had either an associates degree, bachelor's degree, or graduate/professional degree—while 20 percent of this same age group had some college experience but no degree to show for their efforts. Such massive, widespread access to education, secondary and post-secondary, is unprecedented, not only in America but in the entire developed world.

Considering the prevalence of education among Americans and the prominence of education in the American dream, it should be no surprise that reforms and panaceas for education have proliferated. The many successes of American education have sometimes been hard to discern through all the complaints and proposals for changes that will surely (in the eyes of the proposer) make everything better in a flash. As you read the following essays on education, you will encounter a good sampling of personal experiences of success and failure, of bright and not so bright proposals for reform, and descriptions of educational programs at various levels for different kinds of students. Through all the essays runs a continuing question: In the light of education's promise for all Americans, how can we make that promise more fully available and of higher quality?

MIKE ROSE

Mike Rose is an education professor at the University of California, Los Angeles. He says on his UCLA Web site that he is "interested in thinking and learning and the various methods we use to study, foster, and write about them." Rose has written several books, including *The Mind at Work: Valuing the Intelligence of the American Worker*, which explores the thinking processes of skilled workers; *Possible Lives: The Promise of Public Education in America*, which chronicles a four-year project looking at teaching methods; and *Lives on the Boundary: The Struggles and Achievements of America's Underprepared*, in which he describes his own educational struggles.

"Our Schools and Our Children" is the first chapter of *Lives on the Boundary*. The book chronicles Rose's experiences in school when a test-score mix-up placed him on a vocational track rather than a college-prep track. The book also focuses on Rose's experiences as a teacher working with underprivileged students who are "on the boundary."

Our Schools and Our Children

❧ **Prereading Question**

Historically, how are education and social class linked in America? How is this link being strengthened or weakened in modern America?

Her name is Laura, and she was born in the poor section of Tijuana, the Mexican border city directly south of San Diego. Her father was a food vendor, and her memories of him and his chipped white cart come back to her in easy recollection: the odor of frying meat, the feel of tortillas damp with grease, and the serpentine path across the city; rolling the cart through dust, watching her father smile and haggle and curse—hawking burritos and sugar water to old women with armloads of blouses and figurines, to blond American teenagers, wild with freedom, drunk and loud and brawny. She came to the United States when she was six, and by dint of remarkable effort—on her parents' part and hers—she now sits in classes at UCLA among those blond apparitions.

She has signed up for and dropped the course I'm teaching, remedial English, *four* times during this, her freshman year: twice in the summer before she officially started, once in each of the quarters preceding this one. This is her fifth try. She is with me in my office, and she is scared to death: "I get in there, and everything seems okay. But as soon as we start writing, I freeze up. I'm a crummy writer, I know it. I know I'm gonna make lots of mistakes and look stupid. I panic. And I stop coming."

The Middle Ages envisioned the goddess of grammar, Grammatica, as an old woman. In one later incarnation, she is depicted as severe, with a scalpel and a large pair of pincers. Her right hand, which is by her side, grasps a bird by its neck, its mouth open as if in a gasp or a squawk. All this was emblematic, meant as a memory aid for the budding grammarian. But, Lord, how fitting the choices of emblem were—the living thing being strangled, beak open but silent, muted by the goddess Grammatica. And the scalpel, the pincers, are reminders to the teacher to be vigilant for error, to cut it out with the coldest tool. Laura has never seen the obscure book that holds my illustration of Grammatica, but she knows the goddess intimately, the squinting figure who breathes up to her side whenever she sits down to write.

It is the first week of fall quarter, and I am observing a section of English A, UCLA's most basic writing course, the course that students and many professors have come to call "bonehead." English A students vex universities like UCLA. By the various criteria the institutions use, the students deserve admission—have earned their way—but they are considered marginal, "high risk" or "at risk" in current administrative parlance. "The truly illiterate among us," was how one dean described them.

Dr. Gunner is a particularly gifted teacher of English A. She refuses to see her students as marginal and has, with a colleague, developed a writing course on topics in Western intellectual history. As I watch her, she is introducing her class to the first item on her syllabus, classical mythology. She has situated the Golden Age of Athens on a time line on the blackboard, and she is encouraging her students to tell her what they already know about Greek culture. Someone mentions Aristotle; someone else says "Oedipus Rex . . . and the Oedipus complex." "Who wrote about the Oedipus complex?" asks Dr. Gunner. "Freud," offers a soft voice from the end of the table.

One boy is slouched down in his chair, wearing a baseball cap, the bill turned backward. Two or three others are leaning forward: One is resting his head on his folded arms and looking sideways at Dr. Gunner. A girl by me has set out neatly in front of her two pencils, an eraser, a tiny stapler, and a pencil sharpener encased in a little plastic egg. Talismans, I think. Magical objects. The girl sitting next to her is somber and watches the teacher suspiciously. At the end of the table two other girls sit up straight and watch Dr. Gunner walk back and forth in front of the board. One plays with her bracelet. "Narcissus," says Dr. Gunner. "Narcissus. Who was Narcissus?" "A guy who fell in love with himself," says the boy with his head on his arms.

The hour goes on, the class warms up, students let down their defenses, discussion drifts back and forth along the time line. Someone asks about a book he read in high school called *The Stranger*. Another knows that *renaissance* "means rebirth in the French language." Socrates and Plato get mentioned, as do Mars and Apollo. Dr. Gunner's first name is Eugenia; she writes it on the board and asks the class what Greek word it looks like: "Gene," says the girl with the sharpener and stapler. A halting "genetics" comes from the wary girl. "Eugenia, eugen . . . ," says the boy with the baseball cap, shifting in his chair. "Hey, that means something like race or good race." "Race control," says the boy with his head on his arms.

These are the truly illiterate among us.

It hits you most forcefully at lunchtime: the affluence of the place, the attention to dress and carriage, but the size, too—vast and impersonal, a labyrinth of corridors and classrooms and libraries; you're also struck by the wild intersection of cultures, spectacular diversity, compressed by a thousand social forces. I'm sitting under a canopy of purple jacarandas with Bobby, for Bobby is in a jam. Students are rushing to food lines or dormitories or sororities, running for elevators or taking stairs two at a time. Others "blow it off" and relax, mingling in twos and threes. Fifties fashion is everywhere: baggy pants, thin ties, crew cuts, retro ponytails—but so are incipient Yuppiedom and cautious punk, and this month's incarnation of the nuevo wavo. Palm trees sway on the backs of countless cotton shirts. A fellow who looks Pakistani zooms by on a skateboard. A Korean boy whose accent is still very strong introduces himself as Skip. Two Middle Eastern girls walk by in miniskirts and heels. Sometimes I think I'm teaching in a film by Ridley Scott.

I first met Bobby when he enrolled in a summer program I had developed for underprepared students. I was visiting the American social history course we offered, listening to the lecturer discuss the role of working women in the late-nineteenth-century mercantile economy. It was an organized, nicely paced presentation. The professor provided a broad overview of the issues and paused to dwell on particularly revealing cases, reading from editorials of the time and from a rich collection of letters written by those women. I was sitting in the back, watching the eighty or so students, trying to get a sense of their involvement, when I noticed this young man down the aisle to my left. He was watching the professor intently. His notebook was open in front of him. His pen was poised. But he wasn't writing. Nothing. I'd look back during the hour: still attentive but still no notes. I caught up with him after class—he knew me from our orientation—and asked how he liked the lecture. "Interesting," he said. So I asked him why he wasn't taking any notes. "Oh, well, 'cause the teacher was just talking about people and reading letters and such. She didn't cover anything important."

For Bobby, and for lots of other freshmen in lots of other colleges, history is a chronicle. History is dates and facts: Who invaded whom? When? With how many men? And Bobby could memorize this sort of thing like a demon. But *social* history, the history of moods and movements and ordinary people's lives, left Bobby without a clue. He was a star in his inner-city school, and he developed a set of expectations about subjects like history (history is lists of facts) and had appropriated a powerful strategy that fit his expectations (he memorized the lists). Social history was as unfamiliar to him as a Bahamian folktale.

So I sit under the jacarandas with Bobby. His girlfriend joins us. She is having a rough time, too. Both have been at UCLA for about three months now. They completed the summer program, and they are now in the fourth week of fall term. Bobby is talking animatedly about his linguistics course. It is all diagrams and mathematics and glottal stops. It was not what he expected from a course about the study of language. "They're asking me to do things I don't know how to do. All the time. Sometimes I sit in the library and wonder if I'm gonna make it. I mean I don't know, I really don't know." He pauses, looks out across the food lines, looks back at me. He gestures to himself and his girlfriend: "We don't belong at UCLA, do we?"

Students are everywhere. A girl squeals "Vanessa!" and runs over to hug a friend. A big guy with a backpack cuts into the food line. I shift down the bench to make room for a girl with a knee brace. Palm trees swaying on cotton shirts, Pakistanis on skateboards. History woven from letters, language converted to mathematics. A young man who never failed, failing. It's easy to forget what a strange place this is.

The back-to-basics movement got a lot of press, fueled as it was by fears of growing illiteracy and cultural demise. The movement raked in all sorts of evidence of decline: test scores, snippets of misspelled prose, enrollments in remedial courses in our finest schools. Guardians of culture were called on to pronounce and diagnose, and they did. Poets, historians, philologists, and literary scholars were ominously cited in *Newsweek*'s highly influential article, "Why Johnny Can't Write." Among the many, many children, adolescents, and young adults who became the focus of this national panic were college freshmen like Laura, Bobby, and the members of Eugenia Gunner's English A. People with low SATs; people who wrote poorly. The back-to-basics advocates suggested—and many university faculty members solemnly agreed—that what was needed here was a return to the fundamentals: drills on parts of speech, grammar, rules of punctuation, spelling, usage. All of that. Diagraming sentences too. We've gotten soft. Images of the stern grammarian were resurrected from a misty past: gray, pointer in hand, rows of boys and girls, orderly as syntax, reflected in the flat lenses of his spectacles.

The more things change, the more they remain the same. In 1841 the president of Brown complained that "students frequently enter college almost wholly unacquainted with English grammar." In the mid-1870s, Harvard professor Adams Sherman Hill assessed the writing of students after four years at America's oldest college: "Every year Harvard graduates a certain number of men—some of them high scholars—whose manuscripts would disgrace a boy of twelve." In 1896, *The Nation* ran an article entitled "The Growing Illiteracy of American Boys," which reported on another Harvard study. The authors of this one lamented the spending of "much time, energy, and money" teaching students "what they ought to have learnt already." There was "no conceivable justification," noted a rankled professor named Goodwin, to use precious revenues "in an attempt to enlighten the Egyptian darkness in which no small portion of Harvard's undergraduates were sitting." In 1898 the University of California instituted the Subject A Examination (the forerunner of the writing test that landed Laura, Bobby, and Dr. Gunner's crew in English A) and was soon designating about 30 to 40 percent of those who took it as not proficient in English, a percentage that has remained fairly stable to this day. Another development was this: In 1906 an educational researcher named Franklyn Hoyt conducted the first empirical study to determine if traditional instruction in grammar would improve the quality of writing. His results were not encouraging. Neither were the majority of the results of such studies carried out over the next eighty years. Whatever that stern grammarian was doing to his charges, it didn't seem to affect large numbers of them, historically or experimentally. There is one thing, though, we can say with certainty: He wasn't teaching the earlier incarnations of Laura, Bobby, and most of those in English A. Women, immigrants, children of the working class, blacks, and Latinos occupied but a few of the desks at Brown, Harvard, and the other elite colleges. Those disgraceful students were males from the upper crust.

Statistics are often used to demonstrate educational decay, but let's consider our literacy crisis through the perspective provided by another set of numbers. In 1890, 6.7 percent of America's fourteen- to seventeen-year-olds were attending high school; by 1978 that number had risen to 94.1 percent. In 1890, 3.5 percent of all seventeen-year-olds graduated from high school; by 1970 the number was 75.6 percent. In the 1930s "functional literacy" was defined by the Civilian Conservation Corps as a state of having three or more years of schooling; during World War II the army set the fourth grade as a standard; in 1947 the Census Bureau defined functional illiterates as those having fewer than five years of schooling; in 1952 the bureau raised the criterion to the sixth grade; by 1960 the Office of Education was setting the eighth grade as a benchmark; and by the late 1970s some authorities were suggesting that completion of high school should be the defining criterion of functional literacy. In the United States just over 75 percent of our young people complete high school; in Sweden 45 to 50 percent complete the gymnasium (grades 11 to 12); in the Federal Republic of Germany about 15 percent are enrolled in the *Oberprima* (grade 13). In 1900 about 4 percent of American eighteen- to twenty-two-year-olds attended college; by the late 1960s, 50 percent of eighteen- to nineteen-year-olds were entering some form of postsecondary education. Is this an educational system on the decline, or is it a system attempting to honor—through wrenching change—the many demands of a pluralistic democracy?

It would be an act of hollow and evil optimism to downplay the problems of American schools—the way they're structured and financed, the unevenness of their curricula, the low status of their teachers, their dreary record with the poor and disenfranchised. But what a curious thing it is that when we do criticize our schools, we tend to frame our indictments in terms of decline, a harsh, laced-with-doom assault stripped of the historical and social realities of American education—of its struggle to broaden rather than narrow access, of the increasing social as well as cognitive demands made on it, of our complex, ever-changing definitions of what it means to be literate and what a citizenry should know. How worthy of reflection it is that our policy is driven so often by a yearning for a mythic past or by apples-and-oranges comparisons to countries, past or present, less diverse and less educationally accessible than ours.

"The schools," write social historians David Cohen and Barbara Neufeld, "are a great theater in which we play out [the] conflicts in the culture." And it's our cultural fears—of internal decay, of loss of order, of diminishment—that weave into our assessments of literacy and scholastic achievement. The fact is that the literacy crisis has been with us for some time, that our schools have always been populated with students who don't meet some academic standard. It seems that whenever we let ourselves realize that, we do so with a hard or fearful heart. We figure that things were once different, that we've lost something, that somehow a virulent intellectual blight has spread among us. So we look to a past—one that never existed—for the effective, no-nonsense pedagogy we assume that past must have had. We half find and half create a curriculum and deploy it in a way that blinds us to the true difficulties and inequities in the ways we educate our children. Our purpose, finally, is to root out disease—and, too often, to punish. We write reductive prescriptions for excellence—that seductive, sentimental buzzword—and we are doing it in the late eighties with a flourish. What gets lost in all this are the real needs of children and adults working to make written language their own.

Every day in our schools and colleges, young people confront reading and writing tasks that seem hard or unusual, that confuse them, that they fail. But if you can get close enough to their failure, you'll find knowledge that the assignment didn't tap, ineffective rules and strategies that have a logic of their own; you'll find clues, as well, to the complex ties between literacy and culture, to the tremendous difficulties our children face as they attempt to find their places in the American educational system. Some, like Laura, are struck dumb by the fear of making a mistake; others, like Bobby, feel estranged because familiar cognitive landscapes have shifted, because once-effective strategies have been rendered obsolete; and still others are like the young men and women in Dr. Gunner's classroom: They know more than their tests reveal but haven't been taught how to weave that knowledge into coherent patterns. For Laura, Bobby, and the others the pronouncement of deficiency came late, but for many it comes as early as the first grade. Kids find themselves sitting on the threatening boundaries of the classroom. Marginal. Designated as "slow learners" or "remedial" or, eventually, "vocational."

I started this book as an account of my own journey from the high school vocational track up through the latticework of the American university. At first I tried brief sketches: a description of the storefront commerce that surrounded my house in South Los Angeles, a reminiscence about language lessons in grammar school and the teachers I had in Voc. Ed., some thoughts on my first disorienting year in college. But as I wrote, the landscapes and inhabitants of the sketches began to intersect with other places, other people: schools I had worked in, children and adults I had taught. It seemed fruitful to articulate, to probe and carefully render the overlay of my scholastic past and my working present. The sketches grew into a book that, of necessity, mixed genres. Autobiography, case study, commentary—it was all of a piece.

This is not to say that I see my life as an emblem. Representative men are often overblown characters; they end up distorting their own lives and reducing the complexity of the lives they claim to represent. But there are some things about my early life, I see now, that are reflected in other working-class lives I've encountered: the isolation of neighborhoods, information poverty, the limited means of protecting children from family disaster, the predominance of such disaster, the resilience of imagination, the intellectual curiosity and literate enticements that remain hidden from the schools, the feelings of scholastic inadequacy, the dislocations that come from crossing educational boundaries. This book begins, then, with autobiography—with my parents' immigration, my neighborhood, and my classrooms—but moves outward to communities beyond mine, to new encounters with schooling, to struggles to participate in the life of the mind. Those who are the focus of our national panic reveal themselves here, and what we see and hear is, simultaneously, cause for anger and cause for great hope.

Textual Questions

1. Look closely at the title of this chapter, the opening of Rose's *Lives on the Boundary*. Who is the "our" of the title? How do you know this? Are you comfortable being included this way?

2. Paragraph 9 reads: "These are the truly illiterate among us." Why does Rose say this, after showing how much the students actually know? What is he implying about the "us"? To what degree is the "us" responsible for making UCLA a "strange" place where certain kinds of students "don't belong"?

3. Rose concludes by telling us that the working-class students he writes about and represents himself are "cause for anger and cause for great hope." Where does he show causes for anger? For hope? What is the promise of America for these students "sitting on the threatening boundaries of the classroom"?

Rhetorical Questions

4. Rose mixes his and his parents' personal stories with those of many students, all of them looking for the American dream. Amidst all the stories of failed dreams, his own story remains dominant. How does this way of using narrative support his underlying argument about the lives on "the threatening boundaries" of our society?

5. Rose also mixes many facts, figures, and historical dates in with the narratives. Locate a few of these and show how he combines narrative and data as evidence for his argument. How effective is this mixing?

6. Rose was mistakenly placed in the vocational track when his records were mixed up with another Rose, and that experience leads into the next chapter of his book (though not included here). What do you know about tracking in high school? Is it a good idea?

Intertextual Questions

7. Thomas Jefferson linked education to democracy by writing that government derives its just powers from "the consent of the governed." Since an uninformed consent is no consent at all, an educated population is crucial, according to this view, for democracy to function. Most of the statements in Chapter 1 of this book assume this view, though not all of them do. Select two of those statements and consider their ideals in terms of schools that you know or have read about. What practical suggestions can you make to improve the education of voters? Or should there be restrictions of some kind on who should be allowed to vote?

8. Compare what Rose says here about the "back to basics movement" with what bell hooks says in the following essay about attitudes in the black community to education. What are some of the perceived dangers, as well as the obvious advantages, of education?

Thinking Beyond the Text

9. Do you believe that conditions in the vocational track were as grim as Rose portrayed them in his 1989 book? Have they always been that bad? Are they better today?

10. Rose suggests that schools by themselves can't overcome social conditions to provide opportunity for kids such as the ones he describes. Is that so? What would a school need to do to offer a realistic chance for the American Dream to all students?

For Writing & Discussion

11. Does Rose undermine his argument by presenting himself as someone who made it through the discouraging conditions he describes to become a professor and a writer? After all, if he could do it, why couldn't the others? To what degree is success for the children of working-class Americans a matter of individual effort?

bell hooks

Given the name Gloria Watkins by her parents when she was born in 1952, bell hooks (with lowercase "b" and "h") changed her name to honor her great-grandmother, Bell Hooks, whom she described as a sharp-tongued woman who was not afraid to speak her mind. hooks has worked as a professor at numerous universities and has written extensively about race, gender, and politics. Her first publication was a poetry chapbook titled *And There We Wept* (1978), and her first book of theory was *Ain't I a Woman: Black Women and Feminism* (1981), which takes its title from Sojourner Truth's famous speech given at the 1851 Women's Rights Convention. hooks has since published numerous books, including memoirs, children's stories and books of social theory.

"Pedagogy and Political Commitment: A Comment" is a chapter in her book *Talking Back: Thinking Feminist, Thinking Black* (1989). In the 23 essays that comprise the book, hooks writes about teaching women's literature and writing autobiographically, as well as addressing such touchy issues as domestic violence, racist feminists, and black homophobia.

Pedagogy and Political Commitment: A Comment

Prereading Question

List as many of the teachers from your pre-university education as possible, from preschool through high school graduation. Which teachers do you remember best and why? Which teacher's methods of instruction made you most comfortable as a student? Why? Which teacher's methods of instruction made you most uncomfortable and why?

Education is a political issue for exploited and oppressed people. The history of slavery in the United States shows that black people regarded education—book learning, reading, and writing—as a political necessity. Struggle to resist white supremacy and racist attacks informed black attitudes toward education. Without the capacity to read and write, to think critically and analytically, the liberated slave would remain forever bound, dependent on the will of the oppressor. No aspect of black liberation struggled in the United States has been as charged with revolutionary fervor as the effort to gain access to education at all levels.

From slavery to the present, education has been revered in black communities, yet it has also been suspect. Education represented a means of radical resistance but it also led to caste/class divisions between the educated and the uneducated, as it meant the learned black person could more easily adopt the values and attitudes of the oppressor. Education could help one assimilate. If one could not become the white oppressor, one could at least speak and think like him or her, and in some cases the educated black person assumed the role of mediator—explaining uneducated black folks to white folks.

Given this history, many black parents have encouraged children to acquire an education while simultaneously warning us about the danger of education. One very real danger, as many black parents traditionally perceived it, was that the learned black person might lose touch with the concrete reality of everyday black experience. Books and ideas were important but not important enough to become barriers between the individual and community participation. Education was considered to have the potential to alienate one from community and awareness of our collective circumstance as black people. In my family, it was constantly emphasized that too much book learning could lead to madness. Among everyday black folks, madness was deemed to be any loss of one's ability to communicate effectively with others, one's ability to cope with practical affairs.

These ambivalent attitudes toward education have made it difficult for black students to adapt and succeed in educational settings. Many of us have found that to succeed at the very education we had been encouraged to seek would be most easily accomplished if we separated ourselves from the experience of black folk, the underprivileged experience of the black underclass that was our grounding reality. This ambivalent stance toward education has had a tremendous impact on my psyche. Within the working-class black community where I grew up, I learned to be suspicious of education and suspicious of white folks. I went for my formative educational years to all-black schools. In those schools, I learned about the reality of white people but also about the reality of black people, about our history. We were taught in those schools to be proud of ourselves as black people and to work for the uplift of our race.

Experiencing as I did an educational environment structured to meet our needs as black people, we were deeply affected when those schools ceased to exist and we were compelled to attend white schools instead. At the white school, we were no longer people with a history, a culture. We did not exist as anything other than primitives and slaves. School was no longer the place where one learned how to use education as a means to resist white-supremacist oppression. Small wonder that I spent my last few years of high school depressed about education, feeling as though we had suffered a grave loss, that the direction had shifted, the goals had changed. We were no longer taught by people who spoke our language, who understood our culture; we were taught by strangers. And further, we were dependent on those strangers for evaluation, for approval. We learned not to challenge their racism since they had power over us. Although we were told at home that we were not to openly challenge whites, we were also told not to learn to think like them.

Within this atmosphere of ambivalence toward education, I, who had been dubbed smart, was uncertain about whether or not I wanted to go to college. School was an oppressive drag. Yet the fate of smart black women had already been decided; we would be schoolteachers. At the private, mostly white women's college where I spent my first year, I was an outsider. Determined to stay grounded in the reality of southern black culture, I kept myself aloof from the social practices of the white women with whom I lived and studied. They, in their turn, perceived me as hostile and alien. I, who had always been a member of a community, was now a loner. One of my white teachers suggested to me that the alienation I experienced was caused by being at a school that was not intellectually challenging, that I should go to Stanford where she had gone.

My undergraduate years at Stanford were difficult ones. Not only did I feel myself alienated from the white people who were my peers and teachers, but I met black people who were different, who did not think the way I did about black culture or black life—who seemed in some ways as strange to me as white people. I had known black people from different classes in my hometown, but we still experienced much the same reality, shared similar world views. It was different at Stanford. I was in an environment where black people's class backgrounds and their values were radically different than my own.

To overcome my feelings of isolation, I bonded with workers, with black women who labored as maids, as secretaries. With them I felt at home. During holiday break, I would stay in their homes. Yet being with them was not the same as being home. In their houses I was an honored guest, someone to be looked up to, because I was getting a college education. My undergraduate years at Stanford were spent struggling to find meaning and significance in education. I had to succeed. I could not let my family or the race down. And so I graduated in English. I had become an English major for the same reason that hundreds of students of all races become English majors: I like to read. Yet I did not fully understand that the study of literature in English departments would really mean the study of works by white males.

It was disheartening for me and other non-white students to face the extent to which education in the university was not the site of openness and intellectual challenge we had longed for. We hated the racism, the sexism, the domination. I began to have grave doubts about the future.

Why was I working to be an academic if I did not see people in that environment who were opposing domination? Even those very few concerned professors who endeavored to make courses interesting, to create a learning atmosphere, rarely acknowledged destructive and oppressive aspects of authoritarian rule in and outside the classroom. Whether one took courses from professors with feminist politics or marxist politics, their presentations of self in the classroom never differed from the norm. This was especially so with marxist professors. I asked one of these professors, a white male, how he could expect students to take his politics seriously as a radical alternative to a capitalist structure if we found marxist professors to be even more oppressively authoritarian than other professors. Everyone seemed reluctant to talk about the fact that professors who advocated radical politics rarely allowed their critique of domination and oppression to influence teaching strategies. The absence of any model of a professor who was combining a radical politic opposing domination with practice of that politic in the classroom made me feel wary about my ability to do differently. When I first began to teach, I tried not to emulate my professors in any way. I devised different strategies and approaches that I felt were more in keeping with my politics. Reading the work of Paulo Freire greatly influenced my sense that much was possible in the classroom setting, that one did not simply need to conform.

In the introduction to a conversation with Paulo Freire published in *idac*, emphasis is placed on an educative process that is not based on an authoritarian, dominating model where knowledge is transferred from a powerful professor to a powerless student. Education, it was suggested, could be a space for the development of critical consciousness, where there could be dialogue and mutual growth of both student and professor:

> If we accept education in this richer and more dynamic sense of acquiring a critical capacity and intervention in reality, we immediately know that there is no such thing as neutral education. All education has an intention, a goal, which can only be political. Either it mystifies reality by rendering it impenetrable and obscure—which leads people to a blind march through incomprehensible labyrinths—or it unmasks the economic and social structures which are determining the relationships of exploitation and oppression among persons, knocking down labyrinths and allowing people to walk their own road. So we find ourselves confronted with a clear option: to educate for liberation or to educate for domination.

In retrospect, it seems that my most radical professors were still educating for domination. And I wondered if this was so because we could not imagine how to educate for liberation in the corporate university. In Freire's case, he speaks as a white man of privilege who stands and acts in solidarity with oppressed and exploited groups, especially in their efforts to establish literacy programs that emphasize education for critical consciousness. In my case, as a black woman from a working-class background, I stand and act as a member of an oppressed, exploited group who has managed to acquire a degree of privilege. While I choose to educate for liberation, the site of my work has been within the walls of universities peopled largely by privileged white students and a few non-white students. Within those walls, I have tried to teach literature and Women's Studies courses in a way that does not reinforce structures of domination: imperialism, racism, sexism, and class exploitation.

I do not pretend that my approach is politically neutral, yet this disturbs students who have been led to believe that all education within the university should be "neutral." On the first day of classes, I talk about my approach, about the ways the class may be different from other classes as we work to create strategies of learning to meet our needs—and of course we must discover together what those needs are. Even though I explain that the class will be different, students do not always take it seriously. One central difference is that all students are expected to contribute to class discussion, if not spontaneously, then through the reading of paragraphs and short papers. In this way, every student makes a contribution, every student's voice is heard. Despite the fact that this may be stated at the onset of class, written clearly on the syllabus, students will complain and whine about having to speak. It is only recently that I have begun to see much of the complaining as "change back" behavior. Students and teachers find it hard to shift their paradigms even though they have been longing for a different approach.

Struggling to educate for liberation in the corporate university is a process that I have found enormously stressful. Implementing new teaching strategies that aim to subvert the norm, to engage students fully, is really a difficult task. Unlike the oppressed or colonized, who may begin to feel as they engage in education for critical consciousness a newfound sense of power and identity that frees them from colonization of the mind, that liberates, privileged students are often downright unwilling to acknowledge that their minds have been colonized, that they have been learning how to be oppressors, how to dominate, or at least how to passively accept the domination of others. This past teaching year, a student confronted me (a black male student from a middle-class urban experience) in class with the question of what I expected from them (like his tone of voice was: did I have the right to expect anything). Seriously, he wanted to know what I wanted from them. I told him and the class that I thought the most important learning experience that could happen in our classroom was that students would learn to think critically and analytically, not just about the required books, but about the world they live in. Education for critical consciousness that encourages all students—privileged or non-privileged—who are seeking an entry into class privilege rather than providing a sense of freedom and release, invites critique of conventional expectations and desires. They may find such an experience terribly threatening. And even though they may approach the situation with great openness, it may still be difficult, and even painful.

This past semester, I taught a course on black women writers in which students were encouraged to think about the social context in which literature emerges, the impact of politics of domination—racism, sexism, class exploitation—on the writing. Students stated quite openly and honestly that reading the literature in the context of class discussion was making them feel pain. They complained that everything was changing for them, that they were seeing the world differently, and seeing things in that world that were painful to face. Never before had a group of students so openly talked about the way in which learning to see the world critically was causing pain. I did not belittle their pain or try to rationalize it. Initially, I was uncertain about how to respond and just asked us all to think about it. Later, we discussed the way in which all their comments implied that to experience pain is bad, an indication that something is wrong. We talked about changing how we perceive pain, about our society's approach to pain, considering the possibility that this pain could be a constructive sign of growth. I shared with them my sense that the experience should not be viewed as static, that at another point the knowledge and new perspectives they had might lead to clarity and a greater sense of well-being.

Education for liberation can work in the university setting but it does not lead students to feel they are enjoying class or necessarily feeling positive about me as a teacher. One aspect of radical pedagogy that has been difficult for me is learning to cope with not being seen positively by students. When one provides an experience of learning that is challenging, possibly threatening, it is not entertainment, or necessarily a fun experience, though it can be. If one primary function of such a pedagogy is to prepare students to live and act more fully in the world, then it is usually when they are in that context, outside the classroom, that they most feel and experience the value of what they have shared and learned. For me, this often means that most positive feedback I receive as a teacher comes after students have left the class and rarely during it.

Recently talking with a group of students and faculty at Duke University, we focussed on the issue of exposure and vulnerability. One white male professor, who felt his politics to be radical, his teaching to be an education for liberation, his teaching strategies subversive, felt it was important that no one in the university's bureaucratic structure know what was happening in the classroom. Fear of exposure may lead teachers with radical visions to suppress insight, to follow set norms. Until I came to teach at Yale, no one outside my classes had paid much attention to what was going on inside them. At Yale, students talked a lot outside about my classes, about what happens in them. This was very difficult for me as I felt both exposed and constantly scrutinized. I was certainly subjected to much critical feedback both from students in my classes and faculty and students who heard about them. Their responses forced recognition of the way in which teaching that is overtly political, especially if it radically challenges the status quo, requires acknowledgement that to choose education as the practice of freedom is to take a political stance that may have serious consequences.

Despite negative feedback or pressures, the most rewarding aspect of such teaching is to influence the way students mature and grow intellectually and spiritually. For those students who wish to try to learn in a new way but who have fears, I try to reassure them that their involvement in different types of learning experiences need not threaten their security in other classes; it will not destroy the backing system of education, so they need not panic. Of course, if all they can do is panic, then that is a sign that the course is not for them. My commitment to education as the practice of freedom is strengthened by the large number of students who take my courses and, by doing so, affirm their longing to learn in a new way. Their testimony confirms that education as the practice of liberation does take place in university settings, that our lives are transformed there, that there we do meaningful radical political work.

Textual Questions

1. When hooks describes her early schooling ("an oppressive drag") and the conflicting attitudes toward education of her community, she is establishing one of the two poles of the essay: education for domination. How does she define this kind of education?

2. How does she define the other pole: education for liberation?

3. Why were her years at Stanford "difficult"? Although her critical pedagogy as a teacher made students as well as her colleagues uncomfortable, and was for her "enormously stressful," she sees it as worth the pain. Why?

Rhetorical Questions

4. Does hooks's definition of most college work as "education for domination" make you uncomfortable? If so, why? If not, how has she failed in her goal?

5. What is the value of making students speak, write, and become uncomfortable in class, according to hooks? Why does hooks not value other professors who share her views but fail to practice them in class? Have you experienced such teaching?

6. Students pursuing "an entry into class privilege" rather than "a sense of freedom and release," hooks argues, have misunderstood the Promise of America. What does she mean by this distinction?

Intertextual Questions

7. What is different about hooks's view of education at selective universities from the views of Carus at Cal Tech and Douthat at Harvard (later in this chapter)?

8. Using hooks's language and concepts, evaluate Mike Rose's attitude toward his education, most particularly his view of the students in the "bonehead class." Which of the two writers has a clearer sense of education as fulfilling the promise of America?

Thinking Beyond the Text

9. If hooks is right, college teaching would have to undergo large changes, particularly in the "corporate university." For instance, large lectures classes would need to disappear. What changes would be required at your school?

10. Is hooks herself misconceiving the purpose of college, by failing to respect the desire of most students to get good jobs and salaries?

For Writing & Discussion

11. Why did you decide to go to college and how did you choose your present college? Is your goal "an entry into class privilege," "a sense of freedom and release," or some combination of the two? Or is it simply to get a better job and salary?

STANLEY FISH

Stanley Fish, born in 1938, earned degrees from the University of Pennsylvania and Yale University, and has worked as an English professor at the University of California, Berkeley, the University of Illinois, Chicago, and Johns Hopkins University. Early in his career, his writings about the interpretation of literature were— and still are—both controversial and influential. He later applied his literary theory to legal studies and in 1986 began working at Duke University as both the chair of the Department of English and a professor of law.

Fish has also written extensively about political and social issues in books such as *There's No Such Thing as Free Speech and It's a Good Thing, Too*; *Professional Correctness*; and *The Trouble with Principles*. "Reverse Racism, or How the Pot Got to Call the Kettle Black," in which Fish addresses the controversial issue of affirmative action, first appeared in 1993 in the *Atlantic Monthly*.

Reverse Racism, or How the Pot Got to Call the Kettle Black

∾ Prereading Question

Think about your own educational history. In terms of race, what was the makeup of one school that you attended—from elementary school through high school? Was there one racial group that comprised the bulk of the student body? Were most of the teachers of this same racial group? What other racial groups existed at the school you describe (among both teachers and students)? Do you feel that any racial group received special privileges or speical disadvantages at the school you describe?

I take my text from George Bush, who, in an address to the United Nations on September 23, 1991, said this of the UN resolution equating Zionism with racism: "Zionism . . . is the idea that led to the creation of a home for the Jewish people. . . . And to equate Zionism with the intolerable sin of racism is to twist history and forget the terrible plight of Jews in World War II and indeed throughout history." What happened in the Second World War was that 6 million Jews were exterminated by people who regarded them as racially inferior and a danger to Aryan purity. What happened after the Second World War was that the survivors of that Holocaust established a Jewish state—that is, a state centered on Jewish history, Jewish values, and Jewish traditions: in short, a Jewo-centric state. What President Bush objected to was the logical sleight of hand by which these two actions were declared equivalent because they were both expressions of racial exclusiveness. Ignored, as Bush said, was the *historical* difference between them—the difference between a program of genocide and the determination of those who escaped it to establish a community in which they would be the makers, not the victims, of the laws.

Only if racism is thought of as something that occurs principally in the mind, a falling-away from proper notions of universal equality, can the desire of a victimized and terrorized people to band together be declared morally identical to the actions of their would-be executioners. Only when the actions of the two groups are detached from the historical conditions of their emergence and given a purely abstract description can they be made interchangeable. Bush was saying to the United Nations, "Look, the Nazis' conviction of racial superiority generated a policy of systematic genocide; the Jews' experience of centuries of persecution in almost every country on earth generated a desire for a homeland of their own. If you manage somehow to convince yourself that these are the same, it is you, not the Zionists, who are morally confused, and the reason you are morally confused is that you have forgotten history."

Ↄↄ

A Key Distinction

What I want to say, following Bush's reasoning, is that a similar forgetting of history has in recent years allowed some people to argue, and argue persuasively, that affirmative action is reverse racism. The very phrase "reverse racism" contains the argument in exactly the form to which Bush objected: In this country whites once set themselves apart from blacks and claimed privileges for themselves while denying them to others. Now, on the basis of race, blacks are claiming special status and reserving for themselves privileges they deny to others. Isn't one as bad as the other? The answer is no. One can see why by imagining that it is not 1993 but 1955, and that we are in a town in the South with two more or less distinct communities, one white and one black. No doubt each community would have a ready store of dismissive epithets, ridiculing stories, self-serving folk myths, and expressions of plain hatred, all directed at the other community, and all based in racial hostility. Yet to regard their respective racisms—if that is the word—as equivalent would be bizarre, for the hostility of one group stems not from any wrong done to it but from its wish to protect its ability to deprive citizens of their voting rights, to limit access to educational institutions, to prevent entry into the economy except at the lowest and most menial levels, and to force members of the stigmatized group to ride in the back of the bus. The hostility of the other group is the result of these actions, and whereas hostility and racial anger are unhappy facts wherever they are found, a distinction must surely be made between the ideological hostility of the oppressors and the experience-based hostility of those who have been oppressed.

Not to make that distinction is, adapting George Bush's words, to twist history and forget the terrible plight of African Americans in the more than two hundred years of this country's existence. Moreover, to equate the efforts to remedy that plight with the actions that produced it is to twist history even further. Those efforts, designed to redress the imbalances caused by long-standing discrimination, are called affirmative action; to argue that affirmative action, which gives preferential treatment to disadvantaged minorities as part of a plan to achieve social equality, is no different from the policies that created the disadvantages in the first place is a travesty of reasoning. "Reverse racism" is a cogent description of affirmative action only if one considers the cancer of racism to be morally and medically indistinguishable from the therapy we apply to it. A cancer is an invasion of the body's equilibrium, and so is chemotherapy; but we do not decline to fight the disease because the medicine we employ is also disruptive of nominal functioning. Strong illness, strong remedy: The formula is as appropriate to the health of the body politic as it is to that of the body proper.

At this point someone will always say, "But two wrongs don't make a right; if it was wrong to treat blacks unfairly, it is wrong to give blacks preference and thereby treat whites unfairly." This objection is just another version of the forgetting and rewriting of history. The work is done by the adverb "unfairly," which suggests two more or less equal parties, one of whom has been unjustly penalized by an incompetent umpire. But blacks have not simply been treated unfairly; they have been subjected first to decades of slavery, and then to decades of second-class citizenship, widespread legalized discrimination, economic persecution, educational deprivation, and cultural stigmatization. They have been bought, sold, killed, beaten, raped, excluded, exploited, shamed, and scorned for a very long time. The word "unfair" is hardly an adequate description of their experience, and the belated gift of "fairness" in the form of a resolution no longer to discriminate against them legally is hardly an adequate remedy for the deep disadvantages that the prior discrimination has produced. When the deck is stacked against you in more ways than you can even count, it is small consolation to hear that you are now free to enter the game and take your chances.

⟢

A Tilted Field

The same insincerity and hollowness of promise infect another formula that is popular with the anti-affirmative-action crowd: the formula of the level playing field. Here the argument usually takes the form of saying "It is undemocratic to give one class of citizens advantages at the expense of other citizens; the truly democratic way is to have a level playing field to which everyone has access and where everyone has a fair and equal chance to succeed on the basis of his or her merit." Fine words—but they conceal the facts of the situation as it has been given to us by history: The playing field is already tilted in favor of those by whom and for whom it was constructed in the first place. If mastery of the requirements for entry depends upon immersion in the cultural experiences of the mainstream majority, if the skills that make for success are nurtured by institutions and cultural practices from which the disadvantaged minority has been systematically excluded, if the language and ways of comporting oneself that identify a player as "one of us" are alien to the lives minorities are forced to live, then words like "fair" and "equal" are cruel jokes, for what they promote and celebrate is an institutionalized unfairness and a perpetuated inequality. The playing field is already tilted, and the resistance to altering it by the mechanisms of affirmative action is in fact a determination to make sure that the present imbalances persist as long as possible.

One way of tilting the field is the Scholastic Aptitude Test. This test figures prominently in Dinesh D'Souza's book *Illiberal Education* (1991), in which one finds many examples of white or Asian students denied admission to colleges and universities even though their SAT scores were higher than the scores of some others—often African Americans—who were admitted to the same institution. This, D'Souza says, is evidence that as a result of affirmative-action policies colleges and universities tend "to depreciate the importance of merit criteria in admissions." D'Souza's assumption—and it is one that many would share—is that the test does in fact measure *merit*, with merit understood as a quality objectively determined in the same way that body temperature can be objectively determined.

In fact, however, the test is nothing of the kind. Statistical studies have suggested that test scores reflect income and socioeconomic status. It has been demonstrated again and again that scores vary in relation to cultural background; the test's questions assume a certain uniformity in educational experience and lifestyle and penalize those who, for whatever reason, have had a different experience and lived different kinds of lives. In short, what is being measured by the SAT is not absolutes like native ability and merit but accidents like birth, social position, access to libraries, and the opportunity to take vacations or to take SAT prepcourses.

Furthermore, as David Owen notes in *None of the Above: Behind the Myth of Scholastic Aptitude* (1985), the "correlation between SAT scores and college grades . . . is lower than the correlation between weight and height; in other words you would have a better chance of predicting a person's height by looking at his weight than you would of predicting his freshman grades by looking only at his SAT scores." Everywhere you look in the SAT story, the claims of fairness, objectivity, and neutrality fall away, to be replaced by suspicions of specialized measures and unfair advantages.

Against this background a point that in isolation might have a questionable force takes on a special and even explanatory resonance: The principal deviser of the test was an out-and-out racist. In 1923 Carl Campbell Brigham published a book called *A Study of American Intelligence*, in which, as Owen notes, he declared, among other things, that we faced in America "a possibility of racial admixture . . . infinitely worse than that faced by any European country today, for we are incorporating the Negro into our racial stock, while all of Europe is comparatively free of this taint." Brigham had earlier analyzed the Army Mental Tests using classifications drawn from another racist text, Madison Grant's *The Passing of the Great Race,* which divided American society into four distinct racial strains, with Nordic, blue-eyed, blond people at the pinnacle and the American Negro at the bottom. Nevertheless, in 1925 Brigham became a director of testing for the College Board, and developed the SAT. So here is the great SAT test, devised by a racist in order to confirm racist assumptions, measuring not native ability but cultural advantage, an uncertain indicator of performance, an indicator of very little except what money and social privilege can buy. And it is in the name of this mechanism that we are asked to reject affirmative action and reaffirm "the importance of merit criteria in admissions."

The Reality of Discrimination

Nevertheless, there is at least one more card to play against affirmative action, and it is a strong one. Granted that the playing field is not level and that access to it is reserved for an already advantaged elite, the disadvantages suffered by others are less racial—at least in 1993—than socioeconomic. Therefore shouldn't, as D'Souza urges, "universities . . . retain their policies of preferential treatment, but alter their criteria of application from race to socioeconomic disadvantage," and thus avoid the unfairness of current policies that reward middle-class or affluent blacks at the expense of poor whites? One answer to this question is given by D'Souza himself when he acknowledges that the overlap between minority groups and the poor is very large—a point underscored by the former Secretary of Education Lamar Alexander, who said, in response to a question about funds targeted for black students, "Ninety-eight percent of race-specific scholarships do not involve constitutional problems." He meant, I take it, that 98 percent of race-specific scholarships were also scholarships to the economically disadvantaged.

Still, the other 2 percent—nonpoor, middle-class, economically favored blacks—are receiving special attention on the basis of disadvantages they do not experience. What about them? The force of the question depends on the assumption that in this day and age race could not possibly be a serious disadvantage to those who are otherwise well positioned in the society. But the lie was given dramatically to this assumption in a 1991 broadcast of the ABC program "PrimeTime Live." In a stunning fifteen-minute segment reporters and a camera crew followed two young men of equal education, cultural sophistication, level of apparent affluence, and so forth around St. Louis, a city where neither was known. The two differed in only a single respect: one was white, the other black. But that small difference turned out to mean everything. In a series of encounters with shoe salesmen, record-store employees, rental agents, landlords, employment agencies, taxicab drivers, and ordinary citizens, the black member of the pair was either ignored or given a special and suspicious attention. He was asked to pay more for the same goods or come up with a larger down payment for the same car, was turned away as a prospective tenant, was rejected as a prospective taxicab fare, was treated with contempt and irritation by clerks and bureaucrats, and in every way possible was made to feel inferior and unwanted.

The inescapable conclusion was that alike though they may have been in almost all respects, one of these young men, because he was black, would lead a significantly lesser life than his white counterpart: He would be housed less well and at greater expense; he would pay more for services and products when and if he was given the opportunity to buy them; he would have difficulty establishing credit; the first emotions he would inspire on the part of many people he met would be distrust and fear; his abilities would be discounted even before he had a chance to display them; and, above all, the treatment he received from minute to minute would chip away at his self-esteem and self-confidence with consequences that most of us could not even imagine. As the young man in question said at the conclusion of the broadcast, "You walk down the street with a suit and tie and it doesn't matter. Someone will make determinations about you, determinations that affect the quality of your life."

Of course, the same determinations are being made quite early on by kindergarten teachers, grade school principals, high school guidance counselors, and the like, with results that cut across socioeconomic lines and place young black men and women in the ranks of the disadvantaged no matter what the bank accounts of their parents happen to show. Racism is a cultural fact, and although its effects may to some extent be diminished by socioeconomic variables, those effects will still be sufficiently great to warrant the nation's attention and thus the continuation of affirmative-action policies. This is true even of the field thought to be dominated by blacks and often cited as evidence of the equal opportunities society now affords them. I refer, of course, to professional athletics. But national self-congratulation on this score might pause in the face of a few facts: A minuscule number of African Americans ever receive a paycheck from a professional team. Even though nearly sixteen hundred daily newspapers report on the exploits of black athletes, they employ only seven full-time black sports columnists. Despite repeated pledges and resolutions, major-league teams have managed to put only a handful of blacks and Hispanics in executive positions.

∽

Why Me?

When all is said and done, however, one objection to affirmative action is unanswerable on its own terms, and that is the objection of the individual who says, "Why me? Sure, discrimination has persisted for many years, and I acknowledge that the damage done has not been removed by changes in the law. But why me? I didn't own slaves; I didn't vote to keep people on the back of the bus; I didn't turn water hoses on civil-rights marchers. Why, then, should I be the one who doesn't get the job or who doesn't get the scholarship or who gets bumped back to the waiting list?"

I sympathize with this feeling, if only because in a small way I have had the experience that produces it. I was recently nominated for an administrative post at a large university. Early signs were encouraging, but after an interval I received official notice that I would not be included at the next level of consideration, and subsequently I was told unofficially that at some point a decision had been made to look only in the direction of women and minorities. Although I was disappointed, I did not conclude that the situation was "unfair," because the policy was obviously not directed at me—at no point in the proceedings did someone say, "Let's find a way to rule out Stanley Fish." Nor was it directed even at persons of my race and sex—the policy was not intended to disenfranchise white males. Rather, the policy was driven by other considerations, and it was only as a by-product of those considerations—not as the main goal—that white males like me were rejected. Given that the institution in question has a high percentage of minority students, a very low percentage of minority faculty, and an even lower percentage of minority administrators, it made perfect sense to focus on women and minority candidates, and within that sense, not as the result of prejudice, my whiteness and maleness became disqualifications.

I can hear the objection in advance: "What's the difference? Unfair is unfair: you didn't get the job; you didn't even get on the short list." The difference is not in the outcome but in the ways of thinking that led up to the outcome. It is the difference between an unfairness that befalls one as the unintended effect of a policy rationally conceived and an unfairness that is pursued as an end in itself. It is the difference between the awful unfairness of Nazi extermination camps and the unfairness to Palestinian Arabs that arose from, but was not the chief purpose of, the founding of a Jewish state.

∽

The New Bigotry

The point is not a difficult one, but it is difficult to see when the unfairness scenarios are presented as simple contrasts between two decontextualized persons who emerge from nowhere to contend for a job or a place in a freshman class. Here is student A; he has a board score of 1,300. And here is student B; her board score is only 1,200, yet she is admitted and A is rejected. Is that fair? Given the minimal information provided, the answer is of course no. But if we expand our horizons and consider fairness in relation to the cultural and institutional histories that have brought the two students to this point, histories that weigh on them even if they are not the histories' authors, then both the question and the answer suddenly grow more complicated.

The sleight-of-hand logic that first abstracts events from history and then assesses them from behind a veil of willed ignorance gains some of its plausibility from another key word in the anti-affirmative-action lexicon. That word is "individual," as in "The American way is to focus on the rights of individuals rather than groups." Now, "individual" and "individualism" have been honorable words in the American political vocabulary, and they have often been well employed in the fight against various tyrannies. But like any other word or concept, individualism can be perverted to serve ends the opposite of those it originally served, and this is what has happened when in the name of individual rights, millions of individuals are enjoined from redressing historically documented wrongs. How is this managed? Largely in the same way that the invocation of fairness is used to legitimize an institutionalized inequality. First one says, in the most solemn of tones, that the protection of individual rights is the chief obligation of society. Then one defines individuals as souls sent into the world with equal entitlements as guaranteed either by their Creator or by the Constitution. Then one pretends that nothing has happened to them since they stepped onto the world's stage. And then one says of these carefully denatured souls that they will all be treated in the same way, irrespective of any of the differences that history has produced. Bizarre as it may seem, individualism in this argument turns out to mean that everyone is or should be the same. This dismissal of individual difference in the name of the individual would be funny were its consequences not so serious: It is the mechanism by which imbalances and inequities suffered by millions of people through no fault of their own can be sanitized and even celebrated as the natural workings of unfettered democracy.

"Individualism," "fairness," "merit"—these three words are continually misappropriated by bigots who have learned that they need not put on a white hood or bar access to the ballot box in order to secure their ends. Rather, they need only clothe themselves in a vocabulary plucked from its historical context and made into the justification for attitudes and policies they would not acknowledge if frankly named.

Textual Questions

1. At the beginning of the last paragraph of the essay, Fish lists three words "that are continually misappropriated by bigots." Define each of these words as Fish uses them and then as the "bigots" use them.

2. What is wrong, from Fish's perspective, with abstracting events and language from history? Summarize Fish's argument that it is wrong to call affirmative action "reverse racism." What are Fish's arguments against the use of the SAT for college admissions?

3. Describe how Fish uses a narrative to demonstrate the persistence of racism in American culture.

Rhetorical Questions

4. Much of the argument here focuses on the proper and improper use of analogies, for instance on whether Zionism can be called a form of racism. Select another analogy that Fish sees as improper and wrong. Explain why Fish sees it that way. How do you see this analogy?

5. Detail Fish's argument that his losing a position in part because he was a white male is not racial discrimination. Do you find this argument convincing? Why? Or why not?

6. Who do you think is the imagined audience for this essay? Do you include yourself in that audience? Who is Fish's ideal audience for this essay? That is, who would be most persuaded by this argument?

Intertextual Questions

7. Does Mike Rose's experience in school confirm or deny (or both) the position taken by Fish?

8. How do issues of racism affect the promise of America? Select two other essays in this chapter that deal with racism and use them, along with Fish's essay, to draw some conclusions on the topic.

Thinking Beyond the Text

9. Following the logic of Fish's attack on the SAT, should all colleges stop requiring it for admission? Assuming Fish is right, what other arguments can you bring to support that position?

10. If Fish were right, colleges ought by now to have abandoned the SAT. But many have not. Why?

For Writing & Discussion

11. More than ten years have passed since Fish wrote this essay. Have conditions changed? Are the issues he discusses settled? If they are settled, then how have they been put to rest? If they are not settled, then can they ever be?

MICHAEL J. SANDEL

Michael J. Sandel is a professor of government at Harvard University, where he teaches courses in political philosophy. His books include *Democracy's Discountent: America in the Search of a Public Philosophy* (1996), an influential book addressing politics, philosophy, and law.

Sandel's essays have appeared in the *Atlantic Monthly,* the *New Republic*, and the *New York Times*. Sandel's 1997 essay "Marketers Are Storming the Schoolhouse" first appeared in the "Hard Questions" column of the *New Republic.*

Marketers Are Storming the Schoolhouse

∽ Prereading Question

Think of your own education experiences from preschool to high school graduation. In what ways were you—during all those hours you were required to be in school—the target of someone's marketing (from soda companies to manufacturers of sporting equipment to advertisers on television programs that were viewed during class time)?

When the Boston Red Sox installed a display of giant Coke bottles above the left field wall this season, local sportswriters protested that such tacky commercialism tainted the sanctity of Fenway Park. But ballparks have long been littered with billboards and ads. Today, teams even sell corporations the right to name the stadium: the Colorado Rockies, for example, play in Coors Field. However distasteful, such commercialism does not seem to corrupt the game or diminish the play.

The same cannot be said of the newest commercial frontier—the public schools. The corporate invasion of the classroom threatens to turn schools into havens for hucksterism. Eager to cash in on a captive audience of consumers-in-training, companies have flooded teachers with free videos, posters and "learning kits" designed to sanitize corporate images and emblazon brand names in the minds of children. Students can now learn about nutrition from curricular materials supplied by Hershey's Chocolate or McDonald's, or study the effects of the Alaska oil spill in a video made by Exxon. According to *Giving Kids the Business*, by Alex Molnar, a Monsanto video teaches the merits of bovine growth hormone in milk production, while Proctor & Gamble's environmental curriculum teaches that disposable diapers are good for the earth.

Not all corporate-sponsored educational freebies promote ideological agendas; some simply plug the brand name. A few years ago, the Campbell Soup Company offered a science kit that showed students how to prove that Campbell's Prego spaghetti sauce is thicker than Ragu. General Mills distributed science kits containing free samples of its Gusher fruit snacks, with soft centers that "gush" when bitten. The teacher's guide suggested that students bite into the Gushers and compare the effect to geothermal eruptions. A Tootsie Roll kit on counting and writing recommends that, for homework, children interview family members about their memories of Tootsie Rolls.

While some marketers seek to insinuate brand names into the curriculum, others take a more direct approach: buying advertisements in schools. When the Seattle School Board faced a budget crisis last fall, it voted to solicit corporate advertising. School officials hoped to raise $1 million a year with sponsorships like "the cheerleaders, brought to you by Reebok" and "the McDonald's gym." Protests from parents and teachers forced the Seattle schools to suspend the policy this year, but such marketing is a growing presence in schools across the country.

Corporate logos now clamor for student attention from school buses to book covers. In Colorado Springs, advertisements for Mountain Dew adorn school hallways, and ads for Burger King decorate the sides of school buses. A Massachusetts firm distributes free book covers hawking Nike, Gatorade and Calvin Klein to almost 25 million students nationwide. A Minnesota broadcasting company pipes music into school corridors and cafeterias in fifteen states, with twelve minutes of commercials every hour. Forty percent of the ad revenue goes to the schools.

The most egregious example of the commercialization in schools is Channel One, a twelve-minute television news program seen by 8 million students in 12,000 schools. Introduced in 1990 by Whittle Communications, Channel One offers schools a television set for each classroom, two VCRs and a satellite link in exchange for an agreement to show the program every day, including the two minutes of commercials it contains. Since Channel One reaches over 40 percent of the nation's teenagers, it is able to charge advertisers a hefty $200,000 per thirty-second spot. In its pitch to advertisers, the company promises access to the largest teen audience in history in a setting free of "the usual distractions of telephones, stereos, remote controls, etc." The Whittle program shattered the taboo against outright advertising in the classroom. Despite controversy in many states, only New York has banned Channel One from its schools.

Unlike the case of baseball, the rampant commercialization of schools is corrupting in two ways. First, most corporate-sponsored learning supplements are ridden with bias, distortion and superficial fare. A recent study by Consumers Union found that nearly 80 percent of classroom freebies are slanted toward the sponsor's product. An independent study of Channel One released earlier this year found that its news programs contributed little to students' grasp of public affairs. Only 20 percent of its airtime covers current political, economic or cultural events. The rest is devoted to advertising, sports, weather and natural disasters.

But, even if corporate sponsors supplied objective teaching tools of impeccable quality, commercial advertising would still be a pernicious presence in the classroom because it undermines the purposes for which schools exist. Advertising encourages people to want things and to satisfy their desires: education encourages people to reflect on their desires, to restrain or to elevate them. The purpose of advertising is to recruit consumers; the purpose of public schools is to cultivate citizens.

It is not easy to teach students to be citizens, capable of thinking critically about the world around them, when so much of childhood consists of basic training for a commercial society. At a time when children come to school as walking billboards of logos and labels and licensed apparel, it is all the more difficult—and all the more important—for schools to create some distance from a popular culture drenched in consumerism.

But advertising abhors distance. It blurs the boundaries between places, and makes every setting a site for selling. "Discover your own river of revenue at the schoolhouse gates!" proclaims the brochure for the 4th Annual Kid Power Marketing Conference, held last May in New Orleans. "Whether it's first-graders learning to read or teenagers shopping for their first car, we can guarantee an introduction of your product and your company to these students in the traditional setting of the classroom!" Marketers are storming the schoolhouse gates for the same reason that Willie Sutton robbed banks—because that's where the money is. Counting the amount they spend and the amount they influence their parents to spend, 6-to 19-year-old consumers now account for $485 billion in spending per year.

The growing financial clout of kids is itself a lamentable symptom of parents abdicating their role as mediators between children and the market. Meanwhile, faced with property tax caps, budget cuts and rising enrollments, cash-strapped schools are more vulnerable to the siren song of corporate sponsors. Rather than raise the public funds we need to pay the full cost of educating our schoolchildren, we choose instead to sell their time and rent their minds to Burger King and Mountain Dew.

Textual Questions

1. What is "hucksterism" (paragraph 2) and why does Sandel dislike it?

2. Irony is a technique that says one thing on the surface but means something quite different. Describe the irony in "students can now learn about nutrition from curricular materials supplied by Hershey's Chocolate or McDonald's" (paragraph 2). Find other ironies in paragraph 2 and explain what Sandel really means by them.

3. What, in Sandel's view, makes Channel One "the most egregious example of the commercialism in schools"?

Rhetorical Questions

4. Sandel delays until paragraph 8 the clear statement of his argument. Locate that statement and consider the reasons for that delay. Is it more or less effective to build to the thesis statement in this way?

5. The last sentence of paragraph 8 speaks of the goals of education: "The purpose of public schools is to create citizens." What evidence does Sandel give for that assertion? How persuasive is that evidence? Or, in the light of Chapter 1 of this book, does he even need to give evidence for that assertion?

6. The last paragraph suggests a particular audience for this short essay. Who is that audience? What are its characteristics? Do you feel included in it?

Intertextual Questions

7. Sandel sees the movement of commercialism into schools as a form of corruption. But another way to see it might be as a business-oriented school reform and a means of enhanced financing. Compare the advantages and disadvantages of what Sandel describes with two other proposals for school reform in this chapter. Which seems best to you? Or is the present situation better still?

8. Compare Sandel's views to those of Carus (in this chapter). Since Carus comes from the business community, should we expect him to be in favor of the commercialism that Sandel deplores? Write a critique of Sandel's views from the perspective of Carus.

Thinking Beyond the Text

9. If Sandel is right, we need to protect children from the corrupting influences of commercialism. How might we do that, both in school and elsewhere? Is it even possible to protect children in this way? Why or why not?

10. Is Sandel exaggerating the evils of commercialism? Or is commercialism even more evil than Sandel realizes?

For Writing & Discussion

11. Has the climate of commercialism in present-day America corrupted or enhanced the promise of America? In modern America, does this aspect of the American dream—the attainment of an education—require corporate sponsorship?

KENYATTA MATTHEWS

Kenyatta Matthews has worked as a copy editor for *Ms.*, an influential magazine in the women's movement.

In "Black College in (White) America," she describes her experience in the 1990s attending Howard University, a traditionally predominantly black university in Washington, D.C.

Black College in (White) America

Prereading Question

What kinds of prejudice existed at your high school? Put another way, for what reasons were people discriminated against at your high school? Who were the people on the lower rungs of the social hierarchy and what put them there/kept them there? Race? Economics? Fashion?

Entering Howard in 1994, I had two beliefs: there were no black people in Denver or Delaware, and sisterhood was best achieved through a sorority.

My relatives, high school teachers, guidance counselors, and some friends had another belief: you won't be successful in the real (read: white) world with a degree from a historically black college or university (HBCU). I worried that they were right. Let's face it—if college prepares you for the real world, then time at an HBCU is like being schizophrenic. Spending four years or more isolated in a predominantly black environment while the rest of the world moves along to the drum of a powerful white majority seems to be a bit detached from reality—not to mention a waste of money. When you graduate, you're going to most likely deal with a white boss and work with white colleagues. And because you were off in a black world, you'll be out of the all-important networks essential for getting ahead in your field.

Well, Howard proved us wrong on all counts. I found that black people lived everywhere, from Bridgeport, Connecticut (another place that I was sketchy about) to Belize. I learned how to do headwraps from some New Jersey women, developed a taste for tart tamarind balls thanks to a Trini student, and learned firsthand how critical the situation is for women in Kenya when a student shared her story of how hard she had to fight to come to Howard instead of marry.

In an environment with people who looked just like me, I garnered the strength I needed to really accept who I was. Sisterhood became less about sororities and surface similarities and more about seeking diversity in the company I kept. My five girls and I were the Benetton of Howard; all different skin tones, hair textures, sizes. We overcame the anxieties of good versus bad hair, light versus dark skin. However, other insecurities surfaced. Class caused conflict when we searched for apartments that each of us could afford.

With the freedom to accept who I was came awareness. I became a feminist in my own way, although I never called it that in college. Wearing my hair natural, championing abortion and reproductive rights, and reading feminist literature amounted to anything but the "f" word in my mind. I had seen how feminists were received. A young woman who called herself one was booed during a class discussion and asked if she was a lesbian. Students, both men and women, complained because my favorite English professor added feminist works to the American Literature syllabus. There were no major marches to protest the two known rapes in my dorm freshman year. (They were finally acknowledged a few years later by candidates for the student association, to show that they were sensitive to safety issues.) My most enlightened girl called herself a womanist.

My feminist leanings came to the fore sophomore year when my friends and I decided to forgo the "official" female vigil on campus in support of the Million Man March and attend the real thing—despite warnings to stay away. Bounding down the Mall amid a sea of black men, some of whom told us to go home and called us disrespectful, is, to this day, one of the most vivid and explicit ways I have claimed space as a black woman. So, when it came to applying for internships my last years in college, I had no fear about my ability to compete. I had chosen to watch history in person instead of from the sidelines; I had competed with male colleagues in my classes (which were usually headed by a white professor—another myth debunked, that Howard professors were all people of color). I boldly walked into interviews, pouf of afro atop my head, and articulated my goals and why I was qualified with a clear strong voice, because I felt as if I belonged in this world—me with round hips and butt, chubby brown cheeks, nappy hair, and wealth of intelligence. I never worried that my natural hair would cost me my first editorial internship; that my African name would stop an employer from reading the rest of my resume; or that Howard University was a signpost for incompetence.

Being at an HBCU gave me a chance to make the rest of the world's problems with me secondary, and allowed me to make my problems with myself a priority. It was worth every minute.

Textual Questions

1. What are the two kinds of prejudice that Matthews was able to overcome?

2. In the second paragraph, Matthews speaks of her initial goal for college: "getting ahead in your field." What does this mean? How does her goal change, if it does, after getting to college?

3. What does "diversity" mean, in paragraph 4? What is the "f" word in paragraph 5? Why was it not respected in an HBCU?

Rhetorical Questions

4. Who is the audience for this essay? How can you tell? Racially/socially/economically, is there an ideal audience for this essay?

5. What is the purpose and effect of the author's downplaying racial issues in the essay? Does the author convince you that she learned how to accept herself as "I really was" at Howard? If so, how does that happen? If not, what should have been changed?

6. This is a brief essay about college, but it has nothing to say about academics. Why?

Intertextual Questions

7. Compare Matthews's experience at Howard with bell hooks's experience at her schools. How does this comparison illustrate the advantages and disadvantages of going to school with "people who looked just like me"?

8. What might Matthews think of laws such as No Child Left Behind? Considering her arguments about being educated among people physically similar to her, what might Matthews think of schools that are segregated by race (in practice but not by law)? Or schools where female students take classes such as math or physical education only with other female students? What do you think of such segregation?

Thinking Beyond the Text

9. Following Matthew's argument, construct a similar argument for the kind of education that would most reinforce your own self-acceptance.

10. Question Matthew's assertion that self-acceptance is the best route to realizing the Promise of America.

For Writing & Discussion

11. Is "the need to accept who I really was" an appropriate goal for college? Why or why not? What are the arguments for and against a college with students all of the same race, sex, or religion?

BLOUKE CARUS

Blouke Carus received a degree in electrical engineering from the California Institute of Technology in 1949 and went on to become chairman of an Illinois-based chemical company. He has also been active in education organizations, including the National Council on Education Research and Citizens' Committee to establish Illinois Valley Community College. He is chairman of Carus Publishing Company, which produces educational materials including magazines for children such as *Cricket* and *Cicada*.

Carus gave the speech "Education Reform: Teachers and Schools" to the Hegeler Carus Foundation Advisory Board, in LaSalle, Illinois, on September 18, 2004.

Education Reform: Teachers and Schools

∾ Prereading Question

American education is often compared to education in other countries, and the comparison is rarely favorable for the American system. Can one system of education be compared to another, legitimately? Or is any comparison between educational systems in different nations flawed because of cultural, political, and economic differences between those nations? Can educational systems in one part of the United States even be legitimately compared to systems in other parts of the United States? Can test scores from rural Montana be compared to those from New York City and Tucson, Arizona, for example?

Thank you for participating in this Hegeler Carus Foundation Advisory Board meeting. We appreciate your interest and hope you will find the time here enjoyable and rewarding.

As you know, education has been a lifelong interest of mine, ever since I studied in a humanistic Gymnasium in Freiburg, Germany in 1939, before World War II. Fortunately I never took any courses in education, so I was never influenced by the prevailing mindset of the schools of education. Instead, I developed my knowledge of education through what I learned from executive responsibilities with a dozen or so for-profit and not-for-profit organizations, through comparisons of the education of American students versus those from the industrial nations of the world, through reading most of Paul Carus' books (Paul Carus was very skeptical about John Dewey's philosophy), and through information provided by the Council for Basic Education and the books they reviewed (books by Bestor, Fadiman, Barzun, Rickover, Koerner, Trace, and others). As an autodidact, I was therefore much more fortunate than most students of education, and so I was free to pursue my passion and to devote my time and energy to what I found was missing, or what I thought was important.

After studying our son André's textbooks in first grade in Germany and comparing them to his first grade textbooks in America, Trace's book, *What Ivan Knows That Johnny Doesn't*, hit me over the head like a sledge-hammer. My wife Marianne and I were incredulous when we saw the stack of so-called textbooks we purchased for André's library. It was this comparison and Trace's book that precipitated our odyssey into the never-never land of our American educational malaise.

The textbook aspect of that story is well told by Harold Henderson in his forthcoming book, *Beyond Traditionalism and Progressivism*. From 1970 on, the International Baccalaureate (IB) fascinated me, so I started working with Alec Peterson, the Director General in Geneva, Switzerland, to cultivate that great institution. The story about the International Baccalaureate is well covered by Jay Mathews and Ian Hill in their forthcoming book, tentatively entitled *Supertest: The Development of the International Baccalaureate*, which Open Court will release next Spring, and the origins and rationale for *CRICKET* and our other magazines are well covered by *Celebrate CRICKET3*, which Marianne published last year. And our passion about laying the foundations for liberal education starting in the early grades is well discussed in a book called Liberal Education in a Knowledge Society, which includes some interesting proposals of Carl Bereiter, which we discussed here in the Mansion about six years ago. So, in the remaining 28 minutes of my introduction, I'll spare you the time of storytelling to one of conclusions about my views of the most important aspects of educational reform.

Let's start with the Greeks, who laid the foundation for the systematic education of young people. Socrates, Plato, and Aristotle were the great philosophers who laid the foundations for logic, critical thinking, and science. Starting in the latter half of the 5th century BC they were critical of the sophists; yet the father of education is now generally recognized to have been one of the greatest sophists, namely Isocrates, who lived for 98 years and died in 338 BC.

I like to quote his summary conclusion and the goals of education from his *Panathenaicus*, written when he was 94 years old:

Whom, then, do I call "educated?" Those who manage well the daily circumstances of their lives, who possess accurate judgment and rarely miss the expedient course of action; those who are decent and honorable, good-natured, slow to take offense, disciplined in their pleasures, brave under misfortune, unspoiled by success.

Isocrates concludes,

Those who have a character which is in accord, not with one of these things, but with all of them, these are the wise and complete men, possessed of all the virtues.

I like to point out that the Greeks had a great vision for education, which led to the artes liberales in the Middle Ages, which in turn paved the way for the establishment of the European universities in the 11th and 12th centuries in Italy and Paris. Each one of the major movements in Europe—the Renaissance, Humanism, and the Enlightenment—had an influence on the various faculties. However, until the beginning of the 19th century it was only a tiny fraction of the population, drawn from all classes, who could tolerate the intellectual discipline, the Spartan conditions in the monasteries, and the lack of incentives. The academic life was only a minuscule part of society, but it did maintain the classical literature and many of the basic concepts from ancient Greece and Rome and succeeding generations.

I would like to divide my comments into three areas: higher education, secondary education, and elementary education.

$\sim$

Higher Education

Today, it is obvious to all of us that the research university of the past two centuries has played a fundamental role in the development of the modern world. But I believe strongly that we don't yet fully appreciate the university's original and basic concepts, its development, and where it is headed. Of course, today a much larger proportion of the population attends universities. Unfortunately, however, there is evidence that the pursuit and dissemination of truth is no longer its unquestioned first principle as demonstrated by the student revolts of 1969–1970; the current attitudes towards so-called diversity, political correctness, and sports; and other distractions. I'm afraid that the "multiversity," as it has been called, is here to stay, with hundreds of different faculties, each with their own agendas.

We tell ourselves that our American higher education is the best in the world, and I agree that in several cases that belief is correct. My alma mater, Caltech, recently rated #1 among academic institutions in America, is a remarkable institution in many ways. The intellectual climate there is one of the most exhilarating on this planet. I have visited two of our regional universities. Bradley and Illinois Wesleyan, and I'm gratified to observe their aspirations for academic excellence, as well. However, when we see the demise of liberal education throughout higher education in America over the past 50 years, we note that 50% of our graduate students come from abroad, that over 50% of the undergraduates are taking remedial English or remedial Math, and we note the enormous dropout rates, then we must have second thoughts.

Our competitors, the other industrial nations of the world, have stronger, broader, much more rigorous K-12 systems, which educate ten times as many students per capita with much higher academic standards, as well as provide a much broader and more challenging education for occupational students. With more poorly prepared students entering higher education in our country, we'll have to recognize that higher education in America is in deep trouble. We still have a few Caltechs around, and the major research universities are maintaining their standards and striving for excellence, but these few won't provide enough future leaders in the professions, in statecraft, and in the private sector.

When I read *In Denial* by Klehr and Haynes and heard from the authors how the history professors in American universities are unwilling to accept historical documents and deliberately misconstrue what happened in the Cold War, I get the impression that the truth no longer seems to be a priority.

In contrast to the other industrial countries, humanities in American universities seem to take Derrida, Foucault, and deconstructivism seriously. The Hegeler Institute, under the leadership of Barry Smith and David Steele, organized a seminar a few years ago on this subject, and *The Monist* published the proceedings on this sad state of affairs. With the humanities not being well-taught in the first place and now being deconstructed, we are abandoning our cultural heritage and truncating our weltanschauung.

The natural science faculties are also not immune to irresponsibility. Although we hear a lot about the toxicity of chemicals and how the environment is at risk, universities are still not providing courses in toxicity, nor in "green chemistry" for B.S. or Ph.D. majors in chemistry.

Another failure of our institutions of higher learning is in our schools of education, which are basically ineffective. I know this to be the case because we have spent the last 40 years developing a reading and language arts program (which includes writing) based upon solid research of what works and what does not work in the classroom. At first I didn't think we could find any professors of education who could help us, but we were pleasantly surprised when our work put us in touch with a small group of brilliant educators and researchers who had the intelligence, the courage, and the independence to do what is needed to help us develop textbooks that make it possible to teach the 3Rs to literally all students in America.

Over the decades our Open Court textbooks have been attacked for dozens of reasons, mostly the wrong ones. It wasn't only for our strong (and very unusual) approach to teaching phonics, but we were highly criticized for our unique classroom organization, for various forms of student practices, for the integration of all of the language arts, for uncontrolled vocabulary, for classical literature, for teaching students to do research in the middle grades—almost everything, mostly because these assumptions and practices have not been taught in the schools of education.

Because of the diversity of reading programs, namely the basal series published by the major publishers, the universities failed to determine which are research-based, so they simply abdicated any responsibility for teaching elementary school teachers about reading and language arts pedagogy. They told their student teachers that they would have to learn reading methods when they got a job in teaching.

As a result, we faced an uphill struggle for the entire period from 1962 until 1996, when we sold our textbook division to SRA/McGraw-Hill. We had decades of experience to learn about the incompetence of the professors of education, which I am told by our friends to still be the case today in almost all teacher training institutions in America, despite the evidence that we know what methods and materials are effective and which are simply myths, and despite the survival issue to meet the needs of the new Federal legislation, No Child Left Behind.

And reading and writing instruction are not the only problems. For about 12 years we spent our lifeblood also on our elementary math program, which was just as innovative and effective as our reading program. We called it Real Math, and with it we faced similar if not even more difficult problems.

It's hard to teach students something you don't know yourself, yet that is the major problem we face in the middle schools, in grades four and above, when teachers should start teaching the foundations of algebra, geometry, probability and statistics, and problem solving. The fundamental difficulty is that over half of the elementary teachers in the middle schools have never studied math or science in colleges or universities—even the dumbed-down versions taught in colleges of education. And to top it off, the best teachers in math and science can make a much better living by leaving the classroom, so we're left with the incompetents. It's one of the toughest problems we face in education, and I have a proposal for you to consider, which I will discuss in a few minutes. You may disagree, but I'd like your opinion in any case.

Admiral H.G. Rickover, brilliant Russian Jewish émigré and father of the atomic submarine, pointed out something about higher education that I believe has been overlooked by philosophers and scholars of education. It can be summarized as follows:

It was the humanist and scholar Wilhelm von Humboldt in Berlin who established a broad and deep secondary education system for Prussia with a set of rigorous external examinations in the humanities, sciences, and social sciences. It took about 50 years for this to spread throughout all of Continental Europe, but this system of a rigorous pre-liberal arts curricula with external examinations never crossed the English Channel nor traveled to any of the Anglo-Saxon countries.

Rickover's main point is that by reducing the load of remediation of the basics in the European universities, it allowed the universities to take on research. This provided the opportunity for universities to become "research universities"—something new in the history of higher education, which contributed mightily to the development of the modern world.

That is why the university became the main institution to provide the systematic development of knowledge, as well as helping the talent and the leadership to continue this development. In other words, since 1815, the research universities have been the primary engine driving the world toward an ever-expanding base of scientific, medical, historical knowledge, and knowledge in general.

America didn't catch on until 1876, when Johns Hopkins adopted the model of the German research universities. Unfortunately, we never developed a system of preparing students for rigorous academic work in higher education. The Committee of Ten Report in 1893 was a valiant attempt, but the schools did not pay attention to it, so that was a tragic loss. So now we're paying for this oversight dearly because colleges and universities have to provide remedial education in the 3Rs, as European universities did before 1815, when the basics should have been mastered at the K-12 level. The college-level remediation is not only extremely costly (hundreds of billions), but it's too late for a large number of the students who enter higher education and drop out—also an enormous waste of time, resources, and human potential.

As Carl Bereiter points out in *Liberal Education in a Knowledge Society*, liberal education itself needs rethinking, starting in the early grades with "knowledge building." Subject matter knowledge is essential, but we need to move significantly beyond it so as to be able to encourage all students to develop a life of the mind and to cultivate lifelong learning in much more productive ways.

ॐ

Secondary Education

I don't think I need to document the lack of rigor in teaching secondary students about our cultural heritage in literature, the arts, foreign languages, and the humanities; about the missing knowledge and skills in history, geography, and economics needed to participate in a democracy; and in the deficiency of knowledge and skills students get in mathematics and in the sciences to be able to understand our role in the modern world and to be able to work productively.

We're almost two centuries behind the Continental European system and now rapidly falling behind the rising giants in Asia. That is why secondary reforms are not only urgent, but essential for the fulfillment of our own American higher education system, and for providing the future leadership of America in all fields.

It should be just as important to win these educational and cultural wars, as it was to win any war in the last century. Our future, if we are to have one, depends upon it! We may have the strongest economy now, but ultimately our economy, our system of government, and our very way of life depend upon the disciplined intelligence of our people. And we are falling behind in that. I shudder to think of the consequences if we continue what we are now doing—suffering for the vested interests of the educational establishment to maintain the status quo—leaving us with only incremental instead of fundamental reforms.

9/11 was a wake-up call to fight global terrorism, but we must not forget the Nation at Risk wake-up call in 1983 that there is an even more urgent call to wage the war against educational mediocrity.

The good news is that there are a number of interesting reforms now available for secondary schools, which are worth considering: The Advanced Placement Program of the College Board started from nothing in the 1950s, and now almost 25% of seniors in high school are taking one or more AP courses. This provides students with the opportunity to take college level courses in high school, and if they take the AP exams and do well, students will receive college credit. Approximately 1,000,000 students take AP exams every year, and that number is still growing. This has a profound effect upon each high school and on the students taking the exams; namely, the school leaders are recognizing the need for more rigor in the middle schools. It is already a major successful reform and worth expanding.

The International Baccalaureate Program offers a complete and balanced curriculum and a set of external exit examinations. The full IB Diploma Program has nine distinct components and requires the equivalent of taking about six AP examinations.

Because it is roughly the common ground of the European curricula and external examinations, the IB Diploma is recognized by almost all major universities around the world as an entrance qualifier, and therefore the IB Program is the only world-class curriculum available in America. Fortunately it is growing about as rapidly as can be tolerated by the IB Organization in Geneva, the UK, and the New York City offices, with about 500 IB secondary schools in the United States alone. I have personally been involved with the IB since 1970, and I can provide lots of background information for those interested. I recommend you take a careful look at the IB examinations.

The American Diploma Project (ADP) is extremely well conceived, and, as of this year, is available for implementation. Rather than arbitrarily developing standards by recognized scholars or leaders, the ADP staff interviewed university professors, admissions officers, as well as business leaders, human resources executives, etc., to determine what the students need to know and what they should be able to do in English and mathematics to benefit from higher education or to work productively in the real world. Over the next several years, the ADP will require all states to gradually upgrade their academic skill standards and content standards and in turn the accompanying state assessments. If the educators and state legislators accept this challenge for high stakes external examinations for graduation from secondary schools and entrance into universities, we will take a giant step towards developing a genuine restructuring of education in America to meet the needs of our students in today's world. But that's a big IF, and it will take a lot of effort and support from all of us if we are willing to do something about our educational malaise.

The Perkins Reauthorization is now being discussed in Congress and in my view has the potential to reorganize occupational education (as opposed to the former vocational education) and to take its place as a serious and well-conceived reform in secondary school and in community colleges. The proposal is for community colleges to offer curricula and assessments in areas of economic need in their own community and state, and to articulate these curricula with their feeder schools. The legislation in Congress is still in the process of development, but I am optimistic about it, and I look forward to working with the State of Illinois and our local Illinois Valley Community College to implement these reforms in our area.

There are many other reforms being discussed and experimented with, but these four are the major ones, as far as I know at the present time.

⁓

Elementary Education

This is the bottom third of our educational ladder, and this is where many of our problems in K-12 education and university education originate. We have therefore spent the past 40+ years in attempting to make changes, and we have made a bit of progress. After reading *What Ivan Knows that Johnny Doesn't* in January of 1962, I organized a meeting of Dr. Arther S. Trace, Priscilla McQueen, and a designer/printer from Donnelley's Press in 1962 to decide what to do.

The basic problem of course was that we had very few resources in the bank to do anything, and we did not know much about publishing. We did not have a clue how many millions the major publishers spent on a basal, K-12 reading program to develop a series—not to mention to publish it and sell it to schools.

But in a sense this was also our advantage: We had no investment in the then-current *Dick and Jane* basal readers, or their equivalents from other publishers, so we had to rethink everything from scratch. All we knew was that *Dick and Jane* were failing miserably, so we were hell-bent on burying *Dick and Jane*.

After 42 years, the end result is that McGraw-Hill is now taking full advantage of the research-based program we developed for over 30 years. The Open Court Reading Program is now becoming one of America's widely recognized programs because of its inclusion of research-based pedagogy, the high quality of literature, and the integration of all of the language arts, so that it has the potential to teach all children how to read and write, and offering good literature to introduce them into our culture.

David Packard, Jr. has given over $80,000,000 to train Open Court teachers in 28 districts in California, and the investment paid off handsomely in the sense that now about half of the children in California are using Open Court and learning to read and write more effectively than ever before.

The usage of Open Court finally reached Los Angeles schools, and after two years the average reading scores of all first graders went from the 36th (percentile exceeding the national average) to the 56th percentile. From my knowledge, no other large metropolitan district has ever made such gains, and I am pleased to say that now other major districts are also implementing Open Court: Baltimore, Detroit, Indianapolis, Houston, among others.

Despite our efforts to reform mathematics instruction starting in 1970, we were not so successful. We gathered a super team of authors and invested what we could afford over a 12-year period to develop what we called Real Math. We developed the most innovative, the broadest, and the most effective program on the market by 1992, but the market was not ready for it. By that I mean that the math supervisors were afraid their teachers could not handle the elements of algebra, geometry, number sense, probability, and statistics, etc., in the elementary grades.

It's only now, with the advent of No Child Left Behind in every school, and all children being tested in mathematics, that administrators are recognizing the need to do more than teach just arithmetic, as they have been doing for the past 200 years. So SRA/McGraw-Hill is responding very positively and aggressively and bringing Real Math up to date with a new revision, so we are optimistic that we can make a difference in mathematics education, as well.

Our major problem is, of course, the lack of teacher competency in the middle school level, which many have known for decades to be one of the major weaknesses. When almost all other First World countries are challenging their students in the middle school with rigorous instruction in reading, teaching children to write, beginning algebra and geometry, and serious study of history, geography, and foreign languages; our American students are falling behind.

I don't see the universities coming to the rescue here in any significant way, do you? Rather, I see the only way to make progress is to do what they practice in the Far East, namely, lifelong learning in each building. In the Far East, teachers get together with a master teacher daily to review what they did that day, to discuss how they can improve upon their activities, and to prepare for tomorrow's lessons. The main thing holding us back from this practice is the lack of master teachers (two hundred thousand).

My own recommendation is that we need to put the control of instruction into the hands of secondary teachers or other specialists who do have the appropriate subject matter expertise to be able to give the focus and direction, and to cultivate a master teacher in each elementary school building to fulfill this need of lifelong learning and the professionalization of our teachers.

Conclusion

In conclusion, the work we've done over the past 40+ years sounds as necessary and obvious as apple pie and motherhood, but it's important to keep in mind the continuing struggles against the all-pervasive hostile environment we faced daily, as well as the daily presence of the wolf at our door, always eager to blow our house down.

The main problems we faced—and we knew about our adversaries from Day One—were the Progressive Educators. This long-term struggle is well documented and well described in Harold Henderson's forthcoming book, but can only be appreciated if you study the above-cited references and read Diane Ravitch's book, *Left Behind: A Century of Battles Over School Reform*, and Harold Stevenson and James Stigler's book, *The Learning Gap*, Simon & Schuster. Although we have made some progress in reforming education in America over the last 40 years, I'm afraid that Alec Peterson was right. He said, "It is harder to reform education than it is to move a cemetery." In 1983, U.S. Secretary of Education Terence Bell, published a seminal commission report, "A Nation At Risk," and I'm afraid that our nation is still at risk. More at risk than ever. Education is far too important for our future to be left in the hands of the educators alone, and if our leaders and the public only knew how deeply we are at risk and why we are at risk and what to do about it, we would see more fundamental improvements. Just take a look at reading instruction, for example, and the lead article in last week's Education Week about Reid Lyon, who participated in our reading instruction seminar here in this Mansion in 1997, and who was one of the main architects of No Child Left Behind. In my view, America took a giant leap forward with this new Federal legislation and is now providing $6,000,000,000 to improve reading instruction alone, yet the vested interests of the old establishment are kicking and screaming to get rid of it. All this, despite the fact that inadequate reading instruction is increasing the learning gap between privileged and underprivileged children, ruining the lives of millions of our children, and costing the nation hundreds of billions per year! For the little progress we have made. I could never have done this work alone without the unwavering support of Marianne and our immediate family: my parents, our children André and Inga, and my older brother, Paul II, and dozens of others too numerous to mention. Thank you.

Textual Questions

1. What is Carus's background in education? What differences between education in Germany before World War I and in present American schools does he describe?

2. What, if any, connection does Carus draw between the Greek model of character education he describes in paragraph 4 and his ideals for American education?

3. When Carus speaks of "our competitors" around the world with "much higher academic standards," what does he mean by "higher academic standards"?

Rhetorical Questions

4. Look closely at the writing and list some of the ways you can tell that Carus is a CEO of a corporation and not a student or a teacher.

5. What evidence does Carus give for his statement that American education is doing a bad job, particularly compared to other nations? What other means of persuasion does Carus use, as he argues for particular programs he has developed?

6. Does the audience for this speech include the parents of people like Mike Rose or bell hooks? If not, why not?

Intertextual Questions

7. Prepare a short response to Carus's talk as if given by Mike Rose.

8. If bell hooks described the history of education, how might her history differ from that offered by Carus?

Thinking Beyond the Text

9. Assume that Carus's proposal for high schools of "rigor" and enrollments in college restricted to only the well-prepared were put in place. What would be the results?

10. What kinds of students would benefit from Carus's plans and what kinds of students would not?

For Writing & Discussion

11. Carus has his vision, as a CEO, of the Promise of America. What does it include and what does it leave out? How close is it to your vision of the Promise of America? To what degree did your own elementary and secondary education illustrate the problems that Carus attributes to American education?

DACIA CHARLESWORTH

Dacia Charlesworth, who earned a PhD from Southern Illinois University, is a professor of communications at Robert Morris University, where she is also director of the university's Honors Program. She has published several articles about education and women's issues.

"Which Number Will You Be?" is a speech she delivered at the National Society of Collegiate Scholars Induction Ceremony for Robert Morris University students in Moon Township, Pennsylvania, on September 19, 2004.

Which Number Will You Be?

A Challenge for National Society of Collegiate Scholars Inductees

∾ **Prereading Question**

Consider the reasons that brought you to where you are now—sitting in a college classroom and pursuing a degree. Why are you here and what do you hope to get from your degree? Money? Prestige? Knowledge?

2.4 million. This is the number of college degrees that the U.S. Census projects will be conferred this year. Since all of today's inductees are well on their way to being one of the 27% of our nation's adults 25 and over who have a least a bachelor's degree, I am wondering which of the following numbers you will choose to be: Will you be like one of the 106 million who voted in the 2000 Presidential election? Or will you be like one of the 100 million who did not? Will you be like one of the 83.9 million people who volunteered their time in 2003? Or will you be like one of the 106.8 million who did not? The reason I ask which number you will be is because the number you are shapes who you will become.

This year marks a significant anniversary for me as an educator. Ten years ago, in 1994, I first entered the college classroom as a teacher. As a graduate teaching assistant, I was young and naïve. So much so in fact, that I began every class the same way for five years: I began by asking students to tell me why they were pursuing a college degree. The answers I received varied and included: "To further my education," "To become more well-rounded," "Because I want to study more about my major," and "To get a job and make money." You probably noticed that I said I only asked this question for the first five years of my life as a teacher. The reason I quit beginning my classes this way is because although the question was the same, the answers, initially, were not. Then one semester, I began to notice that one answer began appearing more and more until it was heard above all others, and that answer was "To get a job and make money." Today, it is my hope that you, the members of the National Society of Collegiate Scholars, will once again offer different answers so that I might dare ask that question again.

As NSCS inductees, you have already demonstrated your ability to succeed in the classroom; through my remarks today, I hope that you come to recognize your obligation to succeed in ways that transcend a grade point average, both inside and outside the classroom. NSCS was founded on the principle that with scholarship comes a responsibility to obtain leadership and a duty to perform service. One primary way for you to fulfill these obligations is for you to become defenders of education. In order to do so, you must first understand the link between education and citizenry and the current state of higher education. Finally, I will offer you four tenets by which I hope you strive to live your lives, not only as scholars but also as citizens.

Education, while still relatively valued, was once prized above all else. Turning first to the bedrock of Western civilization, Ancient Greece, we encounter Isocrates, a some-time Sophist. While philosophers including Socrates, Plato and Aristotle have managed to be kindly remembered by history, Sophists have not been as fortunate. Though you may have never heard of the Sophists, I am sure that you are aware of the word that today still designates one as knowledgeable and worldly: Sophisticated. Isocrates was Athenian-born, a noble, and devoted his life to developing good citizens through education. Isocrates's students studied debate, speaking, writing, philosophy, prose and poetry, math, science and history. They studied these subjects so that they could fulfill their duties as citizens and be actively engaged in the political process. Does this Ancient Greek curriculum seem familiar? It should, for it is upon Isocrates's instruction that we have based our conceptualization of liberal education. Now, what exactly is a liberal education supposed to do? The answer to this is simple; look to the root of the word. A liberal education is intended to liberate the learner so that he or she may live a questioning, fulfilling life.

The Romans, as they were like to do, took the Greek notion of liberal education and amended it. In the Institutes of Oratory, Quintilian posits that citizens should be taught rhetoric from "the cradle to the grave." Here we see the ideals of a civilized culture, one in which its citizens desire to be life-long learners. In that same text, Quintilian, echoing the claims of Isocrates and many others, defines a rhetorician as "a good man speaking well." Here we see the inextricable link between education and citizenry. To be a good speaker and, in turn a good leader, one must also be a good person.

During the Renaissance, education was also viewed as a way to improve one's status as well as one's nation. Citizens were expected to live vita activa. In this "active life," citizens were expected to place the needs of their country first, then consider the needs of other citizens, then consider the needs of their family and friends, and then finally consider their own needs. Contemporary U.S. culture, being as individualistic as it is, does not easily lend itself to vita activa.

What the U.S. culture does lend itself to, however, is the belief that education has an intrinsic value. We only need to consider the social movements that have occurred during our nation's history to understand the relationship between education and civil rights. For example, this year marks the 50th anniversary of the Brown vs. Board of Education decision. Who can forget the images of the African-American students being escorted by armed men into the hallowed halls of various schools? Certainly, education is equivalent to civil rights.

Despite the historic link between education and citizenry, we have somehow lost sight of it and the current state of higher education worries me at times. When I am advising a student, listening to class discussion, or just talking informally to students, it breaks my heart when I hear students report that they do not understand why it is that they have to take an Arts and Humanities class, a History class, or an Intercultural communication class. These statements break my heart because they make me realize how we, educators within the humanities, have failed our students. For whatever reasons, those who have come before me and those of us who teach now have been content to allow student's discontent to rise. We have failed to inform students of their obligations once they leave our classrooms and our colleges. We have failed to persuade students that a myopic education is not the goal of a university degree. We have failed, quite simply, to teach students about the value of a degree—a value that transcends money, a job, and a career.

As evidence of our failure, consider the common distinction between the "real-world" and the college experience. Few things raise my ire more than hearing someone refer to their world as "real" as if what I am doing in the college classroom is not real. What I teach my students is not only real, but it matters. Consider this: Would members of our culture so readily distinguish between the "real-world" and the experiences within my classroom if they truly believed that we were developing good citizens? Would students be so quick to draw this distinction if they themselves believed that we were truly preparing them for life within a nation, within a state, within a community?

Perhaps most students do not consider their college experience as a "real-world" experience because of the student-as-consumer metaphor that some individuals in higher education are so fond of using. William Lowe Bryan once said, "Education is one of the few things a person is willing to pay for and not get." When individuals in higher education refer to students as consumers, we encourage students to enter the classroom with a sense of entitlement and watch them develop a sense of apathy. For if students are encouraged to view themselves as consumers, how can we be surprised when the only commodity they want is a final grade rather than the knowledge that accompanies it? The continual use of this metaphor detracts from the noble goals of education and categorizes education as nothing more than a commodity that can be bought and sold just as easily as one purchases fast food: The end result is expected immediately and the lasting effect is negligible. If we are to reclaim the link between education and citizenry, we must help others understand the value of a liberal education, that a college experience is a "real" experience, and that we only harm students when we encourage them to view themselves as consumers.

To reclaim this link between education and citizenry, I offer you the following four tenets for you to live by. In an attempt to convince you to consider these and actually remember them, I have developed these tenets in the form of a mnemonic device: NSCS.

My first goal for you: N. Never forget the power of education.

bell hooks, an English professor and extraordinary writer, explains how she viewed herself as a student: "I entered the classroom with the conviction that it was crucial for me and every other student to be an active participant, not a passive consumer. . . . Education connects the will to know with the will to become. Learning is a place where paradise can be created."

My second goal for you: S. Seek out knowledge; not because you have to, but because you want to.

Voltaire once said "Judge a man by his questions, rather than by his answers."

My third goal for you: C. Cultivate yourself as a person of good character, extreme intelligence, and as an excellent citizen.

On July 1, 1776, our beloved Robert Morris voted against the Declaration of Independence because he wished to hold out for reconciliation. On July 4, he declined to vote. On August 2, however, he signed the Declaration pronouncing "I am not one of those politicians that run testy when my own plans are not adopted. I think it is the duty of a good citizen to follow when he cannot lead."

My final goal for you: S. Support others in their desire to learn by teaching and modeling.

Gwendolyn Brooks, a noted poet, wrote, "We are each other's harvest; we are each other's business; we are each other's magnitude and bond."

Albert Einstein once said "People like us, who believe in physics, know that the distinction between past, present, and future is only a stubborn, persistent illusion." Break that illusion and let the past beliefs about the importance of education and citizenry intermingle with your present pursuit of scholarship and your future actions as a good citizen.

For those of you who know me, you know that my personal role model is the Rev. Dr. Anna Howard Shaw who, despite tremendous obstacles, was able to earn degrees in theology and medicine from Boston University during a time when women were not even expected to complete elementary school. Shaw went on to become an instrumental figure in our nation's temperance and suffrage movements. Later in her life, she was addressing a group of college students and she offered them the following advice: "There always have been and always will be eager runners who bear the torch of life's ideals ahead of the multitude, but that which inspires and leads them on comes from a great love of humanity, a love which nothing can quench. [This love] can endure all things and still trust with such an abiding faith that it saves, if not others, at least oneself." It is up to you to be the torchbearers at Robert Morris University: Lead the way in the classroom, lead the way in our community, and do so, if not for the respect of others, then for the love of yourselves.

I would like to thank the officers and the membership of NSCS for not only bestowing upon me this great honor, but for also allowing me the privilege to share my vision of my ideal world with you. Students, please remember, as is stated in Luke 12:48, "For unto whomsoever much is given, of him shall be much required." We are giving you much and are expecting more: we want you to never forget the power of education, to seek out knowledge, to cultivate your desire to be a good citizen, and to support others in their desire to learn. Fulfill these obligations as members of NSCS. Fulfill these obligations so that, as 27% of our nation's adults who have at least a bachelor's degree, you will be like one of the 106 million who voted in the 2000 Presidential election and will you be like one of the 83.9 million people who volunteered their time in 2003. When you consider which number you will be, be a number that matters and makes a positive difference.

Textual Questions

1. Charlesworth argues that a college degree has "value that transcends money, a job, and a career." Explain what she means by this.

2. What was the educational plan developed by Isocrates? What was its goal?

3. Charlesworth challenges you to think differently about two common terms: college as *not* the "real world" and the college student as consumer. Why does she disagree with these concepts and the assumptions behind them? Charlesworth summarizes her "ideal world" with the initials NSCS. What are the four tenets these letters stand for?

Rhetorical Questions

4. Notice who the audience is for this speech. Do you feel yourself part of that audience? If so, why? If not, why not?

5. How convincing is the argument that Charlesworth presents for her "ideal world"? Is there some other ideal that you would support?

6. Are Charlesworth's historical references still relevant? How does the quotation from Einstein argue for them? Is the argument persuasive?

Intertextual Questions

7. Carus also cites the Greek ideal of education and draws different conclusions about education from that ideal. Compare and contrast the arguments of Carus and Charlesworth, looking particularly at the way they use the Greek model in their essays.

8. To what degree does Mike Rose's description of education follow the ideals that Charlesworth presents, in his quest to realize the promise of America?

Thinking Beyond the Text

9. If you were to follow Charlesworth's advice, how would your college major and your plans for the future be different from what they now are?

10. Is Charlesworth so interested in her "ideal world" that she is out of touch with the world that we now must live in?

For Writing & Discussion

11. Many college students and college advisers will consider general education courses in English, philosophy, and history, for example, as work to be "gotten out of the way" so the serious work of the major can begin. What would Charlesworth say about this approach to education? Why? What do you think is the value of the courses you are required to take that are outside of your major?

V I C T O R I A   M U R P H Y

Victoria Murphy is a staff writer for *Forbes* magazine, where she covers business and technology.

"Where Everyone Can Overachieve," an article about an experimental high school called High Tech High, was first published on October 11, 2004.

Where Everyone Can Overachieve

◈ Prereading Question

Examining the generation born in the mid-1980s, a generation sometimes called the Echo Boomers, cultural critics often observe that the members of this group are all told, from the earliest age on, that they are exceptional. They all get trophies simply for participation in a competition. They are sheltered from games—such as dodgeball—in which losers are often left feeling humiliated. In your experience, are such observations in any way accurate? What consequences might this attitude that everyone is both equal and excellent have?

> *Larry Rosenstock is doing wonders with disaffected high schoolers in San Diego, the first step in a grand plan to reverse America's failure at mass education. The nation's richest philanthropists are lining up behind him.*

As an eighth-grader at Kroc Middle School in San Diego, Sasha Knox was trouble. She would throw punches at kids and hurl vitriol at teachers. Security guards once had to drag her out of history class while the teacher stood by, sobbing. Her great-grandfather was an alcoholic. Her grandmother, on drugs, slept in the streets. Her dad had left home, and her mother, a bipolar who smoked pot three times daily, was stumbling on and off welfare.

She was the kind of kid no one bothered to save. Four years ago a friend persuaded her to attend an experimental high school called High Tech High. It's a three-hour commute by bus and trolley each way from her shabby one-bedroom apartment in southeast San Diego to the school in Point Loma, a sun-bleached bayside community.

At High Tech, when Sasha rolled around the floor screaming, she got an arm around the shoulder and guidance. Her English teacher noticed that Sasha's troublemaking would always start because she finished her class assignments early. So her teachers boosted the workload. For a while she had only one minute to get from class to class, with a teacher escort. "They told me it was a privilege to be here and I had to stop acting like a brat," she says.

Sasha is a senior now. With a report card of straight As, she's applying to Clark Atlanta University and UC, San Diego. She writes poetry and is on the prom committee and student council. She goes in on weekends to help organize data for the school's state report card.

High Tech High has enrolled 650 kids since 2000 and produced two graduating classes, in 2003 and 2004, of 49 and 105 students, respectively. All students go to college, with 80% heading to four-year institutions (among them UC, Berkeley, Stanford, Northwestern, MIT and Johns Hopkins). Fifty-six percent were the first in their families to attend college; in some cases, the first to finish high school. Students at High Tech High test better than peers statewide. (In physics, for example, 42% reach proficiency versus 17% in California.) Everyone at High Tech graduates, too. At San Diego High only three out of four who start ever graduate.

This new school's philosophy, put into practice every day by its principal and chief executive, Larry G. Rosenstock, is that if you treat kids like adults, even the most bruised and battered will play up to the role. There are no bells to mark class times, yet most students show up before class begins. Doors are unlocked from 7 a.m. to 6 p.m. with no security guards. The only graffiti is an urban-inspired art project hanging in the school's sunlit hallway. Kids caught with drugs or alcohol are kicked out for a full semester, but this has happened just twice in the school's four-year existence.

Rosenstock, 56, is betting that schools like this one can work anywhere, as long as they're kept small. Size, he says, is one of the things that doom city high schools: "These are factories, not places you want to go to learn." Nationwide, 30% of ninth-graders drop out before graduating. One study of 2,000 big schools found a 40% dropout rate.

High schools are failing to do the two things they're supposed to do: help families move up the economic ladder and provide skilled labor for businesses. In a survey done by Public Agenda in 2001, employers and college professors rated the majority of high schoolers fair or poor in the basics—grammar and spelling, addition and subtraction, work habits. Without a diploma, jobs are tougher than ever to come by. In the next few years 70% of the fastest-growing job categories will require education beyond high school, according to the Department of Labor. Traditionally, elementary schools got the reform dollars. High schools receive only 5% of federal funds for low-performing schools.

The small-school movement has galvanized the foundations of the wealthiest Americans, including Bill Gates, Michael Dell, the Walton family, Qualcomm's Jacobs family and Gap's Donald and Doris Fisher. The Bill and Melinda Gates Foundation has pledged $647 million over the next four years to build 1,457 small high schools similar to High Tech High. Much of that money will go toward chopping up big, dysfunctional urban high schools into miniacademies. (San Diego High was split into six small schools this year.)

In four years Rosenstock has created a network of ten new urban charter schools, five in California, with others in Arizona and Illinois. Another five schools are opening in the fall of 2005, including ones in New Mexico and Massachusetts. Though these new schools will rely mostly on public funds, they're getting $10 million of Gates' money—$1,000 per student in each of their first three years—and will operate largely outside the rules and unions of the public system.

Like San Diego's High Tech High, each of these schools has fewer than 500 kids and a more narrowly focused curriculum of four classes instead of the usual seven per day. Students at High Tech High often teach each other. In one calculus class the students propose their own questions and answer them in front of everyone else. Internships and group projects replace a lot of textbook reading. Twice the physics class has built a working submarine. A biology class published a 120-page field guide on San Diego's harbor with a foreword by celebrity zoologist Jane Goodall. Rosenstock thinks this encourages a natural pull-up system, where high achievers inspire the less motivated to do better. "You can't do the same thing the same way and expect different results," says Rosenstock.

Each High Tech High pays Rosenstock's organization 8% of its operating budget for a slew of services, including building management, record-keeping, payroll accounting, audits, technical support, teacher credentials and compliance work (charter schools are required to report to ten different agencies). By some estimates, these same services in a public school system eat 21% of the budget.

But Rosenstock demands that the model not be tampered with. A prospective school in Philadelphia learned that the hard way. Its administrators wanted to track students, separating them by academic ability, a big no-no in Rosenstock's view. "You want to transform where kids are going, not replicate where they've come from," he says. The school lost its shot at a contract and now operates on its own.

San Diego's High Tech High broke even last year on $2.6 million in revenue, even though, as a charter school, it only gets 73% of the average $8,100 per pupil of taxpayer money that San Diego public high schools get. Rosenstock hires young teachers, most of them with less than five years' experience, and puts them on one-year contracts. There's no football or baseball or band. Rosenstock's salary is comparable to that of a headmaster at a private independent school.

The teachers at High Tech High have a hand in budget decisions, spurring them to look for ways to be stingy. At one Wednesday morning meeting they proposed handing out $20 Starbucks gift cards to teachers as incentives for perfect attendance, instead of spending $110 a day on substitutes.

This year High Tech High had three times as many applicants as spots available. Though it doesn't cherry-pick the best applicants—students are selected randomly by zip codes—its student body tends to be better off than those at the toughest schools. Families with the smarts to find out about the school and the willingness to fill out the form tend to be higher on the economic ladder. Only 15% qualify for federal free lunches, compared with 40% at San Diego High. Kids willing to put up with long bus rides are likely to be motivated.

Rosenstock is in a controversial line of business. There are 3,300 charter schools in the U.S., educating 800,000 students, or 1.6% of the total enrolled in the public system. Nationwide 9% of charter schools created in the last decade have closed down, often for financial reasons. This August 60 charter schools run by an organization in Victorville, Calif. shut down, leaving thousands of students suddenly school-less. The American Federation of Teachers argues many kids in charter schools are actually worse off than those in the public system.

But Rosenstock thinks he can prove his system works with even the toughest cases, so he's sending his students to go recruit others in churches and community centers in the city's poorest neighborhoods. He is negotiating with San Diego's transit chief to get more bus lines aimed at High Tech High. He delves into the school's funds to offer bus coupons, lunches and even SAT fee waivers.

His days are spent finagling for resources. For three years the San Diego school district forced High Tech High not only to forgo $190,000 in special education funding but also pay $130,000 to cover the district's overall deficit. On top of that it had to use some iffy specialists sent by the district. One speech therapist struggled with English. "I could not understand one word this woman said, and she was claiming kids had hearing deficits," says Rosenstock.

Rosenstock outsmarted the bureaucrats last year by joining a school district 150 miles away just for its special education funding. "The problems are never because of the kids, the problems are because of adults," he says.

Kids knock on Rosenstock's door all day long. He can't walk five feet without launching stories about each of the kids he walks by. "Great kid. Came from Mexico," he says passing a boy in the school's big, airy entrance hall. Rounding the corner, he spots a girl with her friends and he says, "You should've seen her dance performance. Man, she's got rhythm."

Each year Rosenstock, like all his teachers, spends two weeks of afternoons schlepping to advisees' homes. One of his was a Cambodian-Vietnamese girl who lived with eight family members in a two-bedroom apartment. The TV was constantly blaring. "That was their way of having privacy," says Rosenstock. "I couldn't hear myself think." He told her to stay late after school and do her homework there. (She's now at UC, San Diego).

Catharine Hart, an 18-year-old graduate of High Tech High (now a freshman at Cal State, Los Angeles), cruised through middle school. Her teachers didn't check her homework, so she often just regurgitated questions in spaces left for answers. "You knew how to just get by, not be noticed too much. Its all about working the system," she says. When she got to High Tech High, she found a system that was too intimate to disappear into. "We're the Jewish parents these kids don't have. We're constantly asking them, 'Did you do it? Did you hand in the work?'" says arts teacher Jeffrey Robin.

A skeptic would point at High Tech High and insist it cannot be repeated. When asked how many lookalikes it would take before the original magic wore off, its school director, Benjamin Daley, throws back a question: "How many Larry Rosenstocks are there?"

As a single dad in the late 1970s, Rosenstock went to law school at Boston University, but he would skip classes to teach carpentry to kids with psychiatric problems. He eventually got his degree but continued running woodworking classes. After a few years he started to sense that the practice of segregating vocational students was shortchanging any academic potential these kids had. While in residence at the Harvard Center for Law & Education in the late 1980s, he co-wrote legislation that would redirect funding for vocational education toward classic academics. George H.W. Bush signed it into law in 1990.

Soon after, Rosenstock took the job as principal at Rindge School of the Technical Arts. He was eventually picked to run both Rindge and its sister school, Cambridge Latin, making him responsible for 2,000 students. He lasted six years. Five teachers that he had fired for poor performance ended up at other local schools within months. It took him more than a year to get rid of one teacher, who handed out sex questionnaires to 15-year-old girls. When the school board rejected his plan to merge Latin's vocational training with traditional academics, he left.

He spent the next three years visiting 50 public high schools for a federally funded study of what makes a high school successful. "It was sobering. No one could give us nominations for great schools," he says.

He was soon to meet another frustrated soul on the West Coast, this one with resources. Irwin Jacobs, billionaire founder of San Diego wireless technology firm Qualcomm, was struggling to hire 800 engineers a year, and had to spend thousands of dollars apiece teaching them basic communication skills. Jacobs thought the root of the problem was poor math and science training. He wanted to back a school rich in a tech curriculum, and enlisted his oldest son, Gary.

In December 1998 the Jacobses called a meeting with Rosenstock, who had moved out to San Diego to run Price Club founder Sol Price's $75 million foundation. They talked of either opening a charter school with public money or funding one on their own. Either way it would be small and tech-focused. (This was back in the dot-com bubble of 1998.) Rosenstock couldn't get the idea out of his head. The next morning he phoned Gary with an offer. "I'll build it, start it, then run it." They hurriedly penciled out Rosenstock's contract on the back of recycled letterhead. Qualcomm pledged $100,000 a year for five years.

Rosenstock spent three months trying to find a location, eventually scoring a 105,000-square-foot former Navy training center being used as a book depot for a community college. He had to get permission from the Navy to begin construction. Gary and his wife, Jerri-Ann, donated $6 million. Irwin gave $1 million of his own money and Rosenstock got $1 million from the state.

Rosenstock set out to hire the best teachers he could find, a task he knew would be complicated. Any unionized teacher would lose precious tenure by going to High Tech High, a nonunion shop. Rosenstock tried to get around this by negotiating with the San Diego teacher's union to create a special three-year leave of absence with full tenure if they returned to the public system. The union's board unanimously voted down the deal. Four teachers switched camps anyway; the other eight spots went to recruits from other fields or right out of college.

For nine months the new staff labored out of two trailers in a dusty lot. It was often hot, and more often smelly—one of the portable toilets started leaking three months into the project. Good fortune brought an unexpected visitor in the spring of 2000: the Gates Foundation's education czar Thomas Vander Ark. "I knew after ten minutes we wanted to support this guy in any way we could," he says. A few months later the Gates Foundation pledged $1,000 per student enrolled. In July 2000 the school sent out 40,000 flyers with applications, filling the mailboxes of every eighth-grader in San Diego. The school got 1,000 applicants for 150 spots. (Competition for slots is easier now since Rosenstock no longer markets the school so widely.)

In the first year students were in class only three hours a day, with unstructured time for individual projects filling afternoons. Too many kids filled those hours socializing or playing Internet games instead of completing assignments. So the school ended the classless afternoons, filling them with project work closely attended by teachers. "We made mistakes," says Rosenstock. "We knew what we didn't want to be more than we knew what we wanted to be."

But the flexibility was paradise for kids like Billy Miller. Until High Tech High, he was bored in class and tried to teach himself after school. "I read five books a week," he says. Yearning for change (and eager to leave east San Diego's poverty-stricken City Heights neighborhood), Billy rearranged his bedroom furniture every two weeks. Though he could have done well at any school, here he learned at a gallop. By senior year Billy was taking college-level courses at San Diego City College. He is now a freshman at MIT on a full-tuition scholarship. His mother, from Mexico, is a cashier in a tortilla factory. She sports an MIT baseball cap instead of a hair net. "She'd heard of Harvard and Stanford. I had to convince her MIT was just as good," he says.

Textual Questions

1. In paragraph 8, Murphy details what she sees wrong with American high schools, which "are failing to do the two things they're supposed to do." What are these "two things"?

2. What examples of the "small school movement" does Murphy give? What is the purpose of these examples? What are the particular features of the small schools, like High Tech High, which seem so promising to the writer?

3. List some of the narratives, the little personal stories, that mark this essay. What is their purpose?

Rhetorical Questions

4. What is the evidence presented for the great success of the small school movement? Is it convincing? Why or why not? What other kinds of evidence might you look for in a description of a successful school?

5. Notice the business style of the essay, published originally in a business journal, *Forbes*, with its short, punchy paragraphs. What else makes this style different from some of the other essays you have read?

6. Who is the audience for this audience? How can you tell? Are you part of that audience?

Intertextual Questions

7. Do a computer search for John Dewey and "progressive education." Compare Dewey's ideas about reforming high schools with those described by Murphy in this essay.

8. Return to the "two things" that high school is supposed to do, as described by Murphy in paragraph 8. To what degree do these goals relate to the promise of america? Be sure to use as reference some of the other goals of schooling described by other essays in this chapter.

Thinking Beyond the Text

9. If Murphy can be believed, Larry Rosenstock has discovered the way to make every high school student successful. How would your high school have been different if it fit that model?

10. Why has the small school movement not made much of an impression on public schools in general, if it is such a sure success? Are there problems with that model that Murphy does not speak about?

For Writing & Discussion

11. What are some practical problems for public schools in following the charter school model described by Murphy? For instance, are there some valid reasons for teacher unions to resist the hiring of teachers without teaching credentials? What changes in the model might make some of its features possible for public schools?

GERALD W. BRACEY

Gerald W. Bracey, who earned a PhD in psychology from Stanford University, has been an independent researcher and writer on education issues since 1991. He has held positions at several universities, and has published several books, including *What You Need to Know About the War Against America's Public Schools* (2003), *The Death of Childhood and the Destruction of Public Schools* (2003), and *Put to the Test: An Educator's and Consumer's Guide to Standardized Testing* (2002),

"The Perfect Law: No Child Left Behind and the Assault on Public Schools" was published in *Dissent Magazine* in 2004. In the article, Bracey attacks the No Child Left Behind law, the President George W. Bush administration-sponsored initiative which passed in 2001.

The Perfect Law: No Child Left Behind and the Assault on Public Schools

⤳ Prereading Question

Consider your own education pre-college. What were the most positive aspects of the education you received in elementary school? Junior high school? High school? What were the most negative aspects of the education you received at each of these levels?

Imagine a law that would transfer hundreds of billions of dollars a year from the public sector to the private sector, reduce the size of government, and wound or kill a large Democratic power base. Impossible, you say. But the law exists. It is Title I of the Elementary and Secondary Education Act of 2001, better known as the No Child Left Behind law (NCLB).

The Bush administration has often been accused of Orwellian double-speak in naming its programs, and NCLB is a masterpiece of a law to accomplish the opposite of what it apparently intends. While claiming to be the law that—finally!—improves public education, NCLB sets up public schools to fail, setting the stage for private education companies to move in on the $400 billion spent annually on K-12 education ($500 billion according to recent statements by Secretary of Education Rod Paige). The consequent destruction or reduction of public education would shrink government and cripple or eliminate the teachers' unions, nearly five million mostly Democratic voters. It's a law to drool over if you're Karl Rove or Grover Norquist. The Perfect Law, in fact, as in The Perfect Storm.

It doesn't look that way at first glance. Indeed, NCLB appears to fly in the face of all that the Bush administration stands for. That administration has tried to deregulate and outsource virtually everything it touches. Yet from this most deregulatory of administrations comes NCLB laying 1,100 pages of law and reams of regulations on public schools. On closer inspection, those pages are just the law's shiny surface to blind and confuse onlookers.

The principal means to accomplish this amazing end is called Adequate Yearly Progress or AYP. All schools that accept Title I money from the federal government are compelled by the law to show AYP. If they don't, they are labeled "failing schools." The official tag is "in need of improvement" but no one outside of the U.S. Department of Education uses that term.

The concept of AYP in Title I is not new, but NCLB yokes it to sanctions that become increasingly punitive with each consecutive year of failure. These sanctions alone should have been a clue to Democrats that the law was not what it said it was, for punishment is not an effective means to achieve either individual or institutional change.

NCLB requires not only that each school make AYP, but that each of many subgroups make AYP. For many schools, once test scores are disaggregated by gender, ethnicity, socioeconomic status, special education, and English Language Learners, there are thirty-seven separate categories. All categories must make AYP. If one fails, the school fails. Not surprisingly, a study found that more diverse schools were more likely to fail—the odds that one group doesn't make it are against them. Even if all subgroups make AYP, it counts only if 95 percent of the kids in each group showed up on test day. If not, the school fails.

Here's how it works: all schools must test all students every year in grades three through eight in reading and math (and in a couple of years, science as well) and test one high school grade. For these tests, each state establishes a baseline of achievement. Its plan for AYP must be such that by the year 2014, 100 percent of the state's children achieve at the "proficient" level. At the moment, each state defines "proficient," but that will likely change. For some states, the progress from baseline to end state is a straight line. Other states have an accelerating curve with little required initially but a great deal of improvement required as the witching year of 2014 approaches.

How realistic is a goal of 100 percent proficiency? Well, at the 2004 convention of the American Educational Research Association (AERA), the California Department of Education presented projections indicating that by 2014, under AYP, 99 percent of its schools would be failing. In fact, this projection appears to be optimistic. It was predicated on assumptions about how fast test scores will improve. So far, these assumptions are not being met.

A reader might say, "Yes, but that is California. California is so educationally awful that it inspired a John Merrow PBS special, 'From First to Worst: The Rise and Fall of California's Public Schools.'" And it is true that in the National Assessment of Educational Progress's 2003 reading assessment California was at the bottom: forty-ninth at the fourth-grade level and tied with Hawaii for fiftieth at the eighth-grade level.

But consider a 2004 headline in the *St. Paul Pioneer Press*: "All Minnesota Left Behind?" The article beneath the headline described a report from the state's legislative auditor projecting that by 2014 some 80 percent of Minnesota's schools would be failing and that many of them would have failed for five consecutive years, a condition that unleashes the most draconian of NCLB's sanctions.

Academically, Minnesota is not California. In the Third International Mathematics and Science Study (TIMSS), twenty-five of forty-one participating nations outscored California in mathematics and only four (Iran, Kuwait, Colombia, and South Africa) scored lower (the remaining twelve scored about the same). In science, twenty scored higher and six scored lower. For Minnesota, the numbers are quite different. Only six of the forty-one nations outscored Minnesota in math, and only one outscored it in science.

This means that in a few years 80 percent of the schools in a state that outscores virtually the entire world will be labeled as failures.

Why would anyone foist such a no-win system on the public schools? To answer this question we must go back to the original legislation and note that it contained Bush-backed voucher amendments. If passed in this form, students would have been able to use these vouchers at any school that would accept them.

Congress struck the voucher provisions from the law. In the 2000 elections, voucher referenda in California and Michigan had suffered more than two-to-one defeats. The defeats were unusually decisive and not just because of the margins. Milton Friedman had argued that voucher efforts lose because, although the voucher proposals are "well thought out and initially warmly received, the educational establishment—administrators and teachers' unions—then launches an attack that is notable for its mendacity but is backed by much larger financial resources than the proponents can command and succeeds in killing the proposals."

In the 2000 refetenda, though, advocates outspent opponents—in California by two to one—and the outcome was still not close. The public at large decisively rejected the concept of vouchers in one liberal and one conservative state. After these referenda, even ardent voucher advocates such as Harvard's Paul Peterson opined that vouchers would be of interest only to a small proportion—perhaps 5 percent—of parents, mostly those with kids in inner-city schools. Congress decided that they had no place in NCLB.

If Bush succeeds in his reelection campaign, vouchers will be back. Actually, they already are. Bush proposed a $75 million voucher program for a half-dozen cities. Congress trimmed it to a $15 million program for only the District of Columbia. The proposal passed the House by a single vote but was repeatedly rejected by the Senate until it was attached to a $328 billion omnibus spending bill. Even Democrats who opposed vouchers thought that law too important to kill just to keep vouchers out of the District. The bill passed sixty-five to twenty-eight. A second-term Bush would no doubt broaden the scope of voucher proposals.

Vouchers, of course, send money to private schools and remove money from public schools. At present, the principal beneficiaries of vouchers are religious schools, especially Catholic schools. In Cleveland, one of two cities with ongoing, tax-funded voucher programs, 96 percent of voucher-using students attend church-affiliated schools and 67 percent attend Catholic schools.

The D.C. program will offer a child up to $7,500 per year, but the elite privates in the D.C. area charge more than $20,000 tuition per year. Independent private schools have also shown no interest in vouchers out of fear that government money will lead to government control.

Catholic schools, on the other hand, charge much less and have been hemorrhaging students. In 1960, Catholic schools accounted for 12.4 percent of all students. In 2000, 4.7 percent. The Catholic connection was made clear when Bush made his strongest pitch for the D.C. voucher proposal in the East Room of the White House to 250 members of the National Catholic Education Association, in town to mark their 100th anniversary. It could be seen as a cynical ploy to buy the Catholic vote in November. (Democratic presidential nominee John Kerry opposes vouchers. As a presidential candidate, John Edwards voiced similar opposition. Both expressed the position that vouchers help only the few, draw resources away from public schools, and inappropriately send taxpayer dollars to private institutions.)

Thus, after the 2000 elections, even voucher proponents concluded that the middle classes were pretty much satisfied with their schools. To make vouchers attractive to the middle classes, some way would have to be found to drive a wedge between the parents and their public schools and shatter that satisfaction. AYP's impossible standards provide the way. At the AERA convention mentioned earlier, representatives from the Boulder Valley School District, the district that surrounds the University of Colorado at Boulder, reported that parents were surprised when some of their "good" schools failed. It causes, the researchers said, "dissonance" in the parents. One can only wonder how much louder the dissonance will clang as the number of failing schools grows. Already the law appears to be taking its toll. A June 2004 survey by Educational Testing Service found that in 2001, 8 percent of parents gave public schools an "A" and 35 percent gave them a "B." In 2004, the figures had fallen to 2 percent and 20 percent, respectively.

Currently, there are few non-religious schools to receive vouchers, but if the vouchers are there, one can expect the for-profit Educational Management Organizations to expand (currently, there are 53 such companies managing 461 schools). Indeed, the first overbearingly ambitious plan from the largest such company, Edison Schools, Inc., depended on Bush's father and his father's secretary of education, Lamar Alexander. Alexander was once a paid consultant to and board member of Edison's then-parent company, Whittle Communications. Edison's founder, Chris Whittle, had planned to have one thousand private schools by 2000; and that plan hinged on Bush *père* and Alexander's pushing vouchers through Congress (though it was never mentioned in any Edison press releases). When Bush lost to Clinton, the plan came a cropper and left Whittle managing a few schools, not owning a thousand. But Chris Whittle is an ambitious man, and if the vouchers are there, he will come.

One can get some sense of where people think NCLB will lead by looking at what is being said about it by organizations that should, ideologically, oppose it. In 1996, for example, the Heritage Foundation, whose mission statement says it promotes free enterprise and limited government, condemned federal intrusion into education as a "liberal solution." Yet, this organization, once dubbed by *Slate* editor Michael Kinsley as "a right-wing propaganda machine," not only endorses NCLB but also brags that one of its policy analysts, Krista Kafer, "produced two papers that helped define the lines of debate" over NCLB.

The most ardent voucher proponent in academia is Harvard's Paul Peterson, also a senior fellow at the Hoover Institution. Hoover proudly announced that Peterson, along with Erik Hanushek, another senior fellow, had been named to a Bush-sponsored National Education Panel to evaluate NCLB.

The Eagle Forum's Phyllis Schlafly contended "the tests mandated by NCLB had ripped back the curtain and exposed a major national problem." But, she went on, NCLB wouldn't do much about that problem. We need "innovative solutions to introduce competition into the monopoly system." Vouchers, in other words.

With the voucher-touting right solidly lined up in favor of NCLB, shouldn't the center and the left be just a bit suspicious of it?

Even with each state having a unique definition of proficient, most schools fail. The situation will likely get worse. If each state has a unique definition, no two states can be compared. Lack of comparability alone would make some people uncomfortable, but some of the early results seemed, well, anomalous. In the first estimate of how many schools would fail, Michigan projected fifteen hundred, while Arkansas foresaw none. This finding did not produce, so far as is known, a stampede of Michigan parents seeking to educate their children in the Razorback state.

There will be pressure to seek a common yardstick that, in this most normative of nations, will let people compare the states. It exists. It is called the National Assessment of Educational Progress (NAEP). NAEP reports results two ways: in terms of scores on the tests and in terms of what percentage of the students attained its three "achievement levels": basic, proficient (the magic word), and advanced. Secretary Paige has already said that he will use the discrepancy between NAEP and state test results to shame the states into better performance (ironically, the biggest discrepancy turned up in Texas, where Paige had been superintendent of Houston public schools. Texas said 91 percent of its eighth-graders were proficient in math, NAEP said 24 percent).

The result from Texas gives some idea of the problem. The NAEP achievement levels are ridiculously high. In the 2003 math assessment, for instance, only 32 percent of the nation's fourth graders reached the proficient level. Even in high-scoring Minnesota, only 42 percent were designated proficient (for some minorities, nationally, the percentage proficient fell as low as 5 percent). American fourth-graders were well above average on the TIMSS math test and third in the world in science. But only about a third showed up as proficient on NAEP math and science tests administered the same year. Kids who are virtually on top of the world are not proficient? It makes no sense.

And it gets worse. The NAEP levels are not only ridiculously high, they are "fundamentally flawed," to use the words of the National Academy of Sciences. The NAEP achievement levels have been examined and found wanting by the National Center for Research on Evaluation, Standards, and Student Testing; the National Academy of Education; the National Academy of Sciences: the General Accounting Office; and individual psychometricians. The reports say that the process is confusing, internally inconsistent, and lacking in evidence for validity. These conclusions would condemn any proposed commercial test to the trash bin. But NAEP chugs along ignoring the flaws. Having many students score low has political uses.

If NAEP comes to be the common yardstick, the dissonance in people's minds will only increase because the NAEP standards ensure that no one will ever attain 100 percent proficiency for any group. Asian American students score considerably higher than other ethnic groups in math, but on the 2003 NAEP math assessment, their best performance was 48 percent proficient at the eighth grade. In his AERA presidential address in 2003, Robert Linn of the University of Colorado estimated that we could have all twelfth graders proficient in math in 166 years.

Many other problems with NCLB are smaller and of a more technical nature. For instance, the role of summer loss in poor students but not middle class or affluent students, meaning that some schools that do well during the school year will not make AYP because of what happens when they are closed. Then there is the impact of the "choice option." Students in schools that have failed for two consecutive years must be offered the option of choosing another school. This requirement leads to logistical nightmares—currently Chicago must offer the option to two hundred thousand students but has only five hundred spaces—and to peculiar alterations in the schools' test scores. Purportedly, the choice option must be offered first to the "neediest" students, namely those with the lowest test scores. But if these kids leave, the sending school's average score goes up through no merit of its own. At the other end, the receiving school will find it harder to maintain AYP with these incoming hard-core non-achievers.

And no one seems to have thought much about mobility. In some schools, the kids in the building in May are not the kids who were there in September. How, then, can the school be held accountable for their performance?

Although private companies are not yet taking over schools, they are already cashing in on the law. The law makes provisions for "secondary providers"—private firms—to tutor lowscoring students and provide other services. The *Wall Street Journal* estimated that there are some 24.3 billion dollars for companies to lust after in aid to high-poverty schools, reading programs, technology improvements, and building and running charter schools. Educational Testing Service vice president Sharon Robinson is said to have called NCLB a full employment act for test publishers.

The big problem with NCLB, though, remains that its intent is the opposite of what it claims. Former assistant secretary of education, Chester E. Finn, Jr., once said, "The public education system as we know it has proved that it cannot reform itself. It is an ossified government monopoly." As the preordained casualties from NCLB mount, the Chester Finns, George W. Bushes, and the think tanks on the right will intensify their attacks on the "government monopoly" while holding vouchers as the solution. If their attacks on public schools are successful, NCLB will indeed have proved to be The Perfect Law.

Textual Questions

1. Bracey defines "Orwellian doublespeak" in the sentence opening paragraph 2. How is the term "doublespeak" used in George Orwell's novel *1984* and what does it mean in this essay?

2. Why, in Bracey's ironic view, is NCLB the "perfect law" for a Republican administration?

3. What, in Bracey's view, is wrong with the system that designates schools as "failing"? What does Bracey find wrong with school vouchers as a means of reforming public schools?

Rhetorical Questions

4. Who is the audience for this essay? How can you tell? Do you feel yourself included in that audience? Why, or why not?

5. What does Bracey use for evidence that the assessments included in NCLB destine all schools for failure? Is that argument convincing?

6. How does Bracey make his case that the real purpose of NCLB is "the destruction or reduction of public education" for political purposes? In the next to last paragraph, Bracey foresees private companies "taking over the schools" as a result of NCLB. Why does he see this as a bad result?

Intertextual Questions

7. Review the essays by bell hooks and by Victoria Murphy in this chapter. In one paragraph, explain what hooks would think of Bracey's essay. In a second paragraph, explain what Murphy would think of Bracey's essay.

8. NCLB, in its title, suggests that the ideal is for nobody to be "left behind." What kind of race does that imply? How does it relate to the "overachievement" that Victoria Murphy celebrates in her praise of charter schools?

Thinking Beyond the Text

9. If Bracey is right, the public schools need to be defended against the assault on them in the new law. What arguments does Bracey make, and what arguments can you add, that might make up that defense? What actions have some states (such as Utah) taken in defense of their public schools? What's happening in your own state to undermine or defend public schools?

10. If Bracey is not right, American public schools would be reformed and improved by being replaced by charter schools and other private schools. In your experience, are the public schools failing, and, if so, how would privatization improve the situation?

For Writing & Discussion

11. Is the Promise of America better served by the present system of public schools or by a new system of charter and private schools? How effective is the present system of testing in the public schools, in your experience? Does the enhanced testing mandated by NCLB improve matters? Make them worse? In the end, what purpose does the competition for good scores on mandated tests serve?

ROSS DOUTHAT

Ross Douthat is a reporter and researcher at the *Atlantic Monthly*.
"The Truth About Harvard," which first appeared in the *Atlantic Monthly*, is an excerpt from his book *Privilege: Harvard and the Education of the Ruling Class* (2005). In the book, Douthat, a 2002 Harvard graduate, criticizes the university and tries to debunk the mythic reputation the school has as the paragon of academics.

The Truth About Harvard

∾ **Prereading Question**

In 1954 the US Supreme Court, in the case of Brown vs. Board of Education of Topeka, *ruled that every American had the right to an education equal to that of every other American. Despite this ruling, are some educations "more equal" than others (to use George Orwell's description of equality from* Animal Farm*)? Does—or should—the right to equal education apply to a university education?*

At the beginning of every term Harvard students enjoy a one-week "shopping period," during which they can sample as many courses as they like and thus—or so the theory goes—concoct the most appropriate schedule for their semesters. There is a boisterous quality to this stretch, a sense of intellectual possibility, as people pop in and out of lecture halls, grabbing syllabi and listening for twenty minutes or so before darting away to other classes.

The enthusiasm evaporates quickly once the shopping period ends. Empty seats in the various halls and auditoriums multiply as the semester rattles along, until rooms that were full for the opening lecture resemble the stadium of a losing baseball team during a meaningless late-August game. There are pockets of diehards in the front rows, avidly taking notes, and scattered observers elsewhere—students who overcame the urge to hit the snooze button and hauled themselves to class, only to realize that they've missed so many lectures and fallen so far behind that taking notes is a futile exercise. Better to wait for the semester's end, when they can take exhaustive notes at the review sessions that are always helpfully provided—or simply go to the course's Web site, where the professor has uploaded his lecture notes, understanding all too well the character and study habits of his seldom-glimpsed students.

But during the shopping period the campus bubbles with academic energy. And so Harvard Hall 101 was packed on the February day in 2001, midway through my junior year, when Harvey Mansfield gave the semester's first lecture in "The History of Modern Political Philosophy." Every seat was filled; the overflow jammed the aisles and windowsills and spilled out the door.

It was a good setting for an act of political theater.

Mansfield cuts a distinctive figure on campus, both physically and intellectually. Short and trim, tanned and handsome, with an angular face, bright eyes, and a wide, sharklike grin, he is dapper in an age of professorial slovenliness, favoring fedoras, pastel shirts, and unusual ties. He is famously conservative, well known for his opposition to affirmative action and gay rights and for his (sometimes cryptic) critiques of feminism and political correctness.

"Before I begin the lecture, I have a brief announcement concerning the class's grading policy," he said that day. "As many of you know, I have often been, ah, outspoken concerning the upward creep of Harvard grades over the last few decades. Some say that this climb—in which what were once Cs have become Bs, and those Bs are now fast becoming As—is a result of meritocracy, which has ensured that Harvard students today are, ah, *smarter* than their forebears. This may be true, but I must tell you that I see little evidence of it."

He paused, flashed his grin, and went on. "Nevertheless, I have recently decided that hewing to the older standard is fruitless when no one else does, because all I succeed in doing is punishing students for taking classes with me. Therefore I have decided that this semester I will issue two grades to each of you. The first will be the grade that you actually deserve—a C for mediocre work, a B for good work, and an A for excellence. This one will be issued to you alone, for every paper and exam that you complete. The second grade, computed only at semester's end, will be your, ah, ironic grade—'ironic' in this case being a word used to mean *lying*—and it will be computed on a scale that takes as its mean the average Harvard grade, the B-plus. This higher grade will be sent to the registrar's office, and will appear on your transcript. It will be your public grade, you might say, and it will ensure, as I have said, that you will not be penalized for taking a class with me." Another shark's grin. "And of course, only you will know whether you actually deserve it."

Mansfield had been fighting this battle for years, long enough to have earned the sobriquet "C-minus" from his students, and long enough that his frequent complaints about waning academic standards were routinely dismissed by Harvard's higher-ups as the out-of-touch crankiness of a conservative fogey. But the ironic-grade announcement changed all that. Soon afterward his photo appeared on the front page of *The Boston Globe,* alongside a story about the decline of academic standards. Suddenly Harvard found itself mocked as the academic equivalent of Garrison Keillor's Lake Wobegon, where all the children are above average.

This was somewhat unfair—if only because, as the article made clear, Harvard was hardly alone. Still, its numbers were particularly staggering. More than 90 percent of the class of 2001 had earned grade-point averages of B-minus or higher. Half of all the grades given the year before were As or A-minuses; only six percent were C-pluses or lower. By way of comparison, in 1940 C-minus was the most common GPA at Harvard, and in 1955 just 15 percent of undergraduates had a GPA of B-plus or higher.

What lay behind this trend? Writing in the college newspaper, the *Crimson,* Mansfield posited some historical factors. "Grade inflation got started . . . when professors raised the grades of students protesting the war in Vietnam," he argued. "At that time, too, white professors, imbibing the spirit of the new policies of affirmative action, stopped giving low grades to black students, and to justify or conceal this, also stopped giving low grades to white students." (As you might imagine, this theory was hotly contested.) But the main culprit now was simply this: "The prevalence in American education of the notion of self-esteem." Mansfield wrote, "According to that therapeutic notion, the purpose of education is to make students feel capable and 'empowered,' and professors should hesitate to pass judgment on what students have learned."

This may be partly true, but I think that the roots of grade inflation—and, by extension, the overall ease and lack of seriousness in Harvard's undergraduate academic culture—run deeper. Understanding grade inflation requires understanding the nature of modern Harvard and of elite education in general—particularly the ambitions of its students and professors.

The student's ambitions are those of a well-trained meritocratic elite. In the semi-aristocracy that Harvard once was, students could accept Cs, because they knew their prospects in life had more to do with family fortunes and connections than with GPAs. In today's meritocracy this situation no longer obtains. Even if you could live off your parents' wealth, the ethos of the meritocracy holds that you shouldn't, because your worth as a person is determined not by clan or class but by what you do and whether you succeed at it. What you do, in turn, hinges in no small part on what is on your résumé, including your GPA.

Thus the professor is not just a disinterested pedagogue. As a dispenser of grades he is a gatekeeper to worldly success. And in that capacity professors face upward pressure from students ("I can't afford a B if I want to get into law school"); horizontal pressure from their colleagues, to which even Mansfield gave way; downward pressure from the administration ("If you want to fail someone, you have to be prepared for a very long, painful battle with the higher echelons," one professor told the *Crimson*); and perhaps pressure from within, from the part of them that sympathizes with students' careerism. (Academics, after all, have ambitions of their own, and are well aware of the vicissitudes of the marketplace.)

It doesn't help that Harvard students are creatively lazy, gifted at working smarter rather than harder. Most of my classmates were studious primarily in our avoidance of academic work, and brilliant largely in our maneuverings to achieve a maximal GPA in return for minimal effort. It was easy to see the classroom as just another résumé-padding opportunity, a place to collect the grade (and recommendation) necessary to get to the next station in life. If that grade could be obtained while reading a tenth of the books on the syllabus, so much the better.

Sometimes you didn't have to do even that much. One of the last papers I wrote in college was assigned in "The American West, 1780–1930." The professor handed out two journal articles on the theory and practice of "material history"—essentially, historical research based on the careful analysis of objects. We were told to go to the Peabody, Harvard's museum of archaeology and ethnology, where the professor had set out three pairs of objects from the frontier era. One object in each pair had been made by Indians, one by Europeans, and we were to write a ten-page paper that compared the objects in a given pair. Aside from the articles on material history and a general text, *North American Indian Jewelry and Adornment*, we were to use no sources.

I picked a Sioux war club and an American revolver with its carrying case. As I stood in the museum taking notes, the assignment seemed impossible. How could I eke out ten pages when I knew nothing about the provenance of the weapons or the significance of their markings?

Sitting at my desk two weeks later, I realized I had been wrong. The paper was pathetically easy to write—not despite the dearth of information but *because* of it. Knowing nothing meant I could write anything. I didn't need to do any reading, absorb any history, or learn anything at all.

Some excerpts give the flavor of what I came up with.

> Chief Running Antelope's war club is less a weapon than a talisman of super-natural power . . . The club's red paint and eagle feather link the weapon and its holder to sacred, invisible worlds; the "H. A. Brigham" inscription, a 19th century version of the modern logo, reinforces the revolver's connection to a capitalist order in which weapons are mass-produced, rather than individu-ally crafted . . . The case is clearly an impractical method of *carrying* the gun . . . it is, rather, an eminently practical method of *displaying* a gun, with the para-doxical corollary that the gun is displayed by *not* being displayed . . . The book-like case, with its gold leaf and intricate images, transforms the gun by containing its potential for violence . . .

By the time I had finished, I almost believed it. My professor must have too: the paper got an A.

Not every class was so easy. Those that were tended to be in history and English, classics and foreign languages, art and philosophy—in other words, in those departments that provide what used to be considered the meat of a liberal arts education. Humanities students generally did the least work, got the highest grades, and cruised academically, letting their studies slide in favor of time-sucking extracurriculars, while their science- and math-minded classmates sometimes had to struggle to reach the B plus plateau.

The theory is often advanced that grade inflation is worst in the humanities because grading English essays and history papers is more sub-jective than marking problem sets and lab reports, and thus more vulnera-ble to student pressure and professorial weakness. There is a teaspoon of truth to that claim, I suppose. But I think the problem in the humani-ties, as with grade inflation in general, can be traced to the roots of elite America—and specifically to the influence of the free market.

Attempting to explain the left-wing biases of his Harvard colleagues, the libertarian philosopher Robert Nozick once hypothesized that most professors oppose capitalism because they consider themselves far smarter than boobish businessmen, and therefore resent the economic system that rewards practical intelligence over their own gifts. I'm inclined to think that such resentment—at least in money-drunk America—increasingly coexists with a deep inferiority complex regard-ing modern capitalism, and a need, however unconscious, to justify academic life in the face of the fantastic accumulation of wealth that takes place outside the ivory tower.

If I am right, some areas of academic life aren't vulnerable to this crisis of confidence in the importance of one's work. Scientists can rest secure in the knowledge that their labors will help shove along the modern project of advancing health—and wealth. Abstruse genomic work could one day yield *in utero* engineering; mucking around with chemicals could produce a cure for AIDS, or the next Viagra.

Then there is economics, the new queen of the sciences—a discipline perfectly tailored to the modern market-driven university, and not coincidentally the most popular concentration during my four years of college. It's also no coincidence that economics was the only department at Harvard in which the faculty tilted to the right, at least on issues of regulation and taxation. (Martin Feldstein, who taught Economics 10, Harvard's most popular class, was an economic adviser to President Ronald Reagan.) To tilt to the right is in some sense to assert a belief in absolute truth; and the only absolute truth that the upper class accepts these days is the truth of the market.

The humanities have no such reservoirs of confidence. And attempts by humanities professors to ape the rigor of their scientific colleagues have led to a decades-long wade in the marshes of postmodern academic theory, where canons are scorned, books exist only as texts to be deconstructed, and willfully obscure writing is championed over accessible prose. All this has merely reinforced capitalism's insistence that the sciences are the only important academic pursuits, because only they provide tangible, quantifiable (and potentially profitable) results. Far from making the humanities scientific, postmodernism has made them irrelevant.

The retreat into irrelevance is visible all across the humanities curriculum. Philosophy departments have largely purged themselves of metaphysicians and moralists; history departments emphasize exhaustive primary research and micro-history. In the field of English there is little pretense that literature is valuable in itself and should be part of every educated person's life, rather than serving as grist for endless academic debates in which every mention of truth is placed in sneering quotation marks.

Sure, historians believe in their primary sources, English scholars in their textual debates, philosophers in their logic games. But many of them seem to believe that they have nothing to offer students who don't plan to be historians, or literary theorists, or philosophers. They make no effort to apply their work to what should be the most pressing task of undergraduate education: to provide a general education, a liberal arts education, to future doctors and bankers and lawyers and diplomats.

In this environment who can blame professors if, when it comes time to grade their students, they sometimes take the path of least resistance—the path of the gentleman's B-plus?

One might expect Harvard's Core Curriculum to step into the breach. But the Core is a late-1970s version of a traditional liberal arts curriculum, and it's even worse than that description makes it sound. It has long been an object of derision among students (during my junior year the *Crimson* called it a "stifling and stagnant attempt" at a liberal arts education), and a curricular-review committee recently joined the chorus, observing dryly that the Core "may serve to constrain intellectual development" and recommending that it be replaced with "a new system of general education." (Harvard's faculty will begin voting on the committee's recommendations this spring.) At its inception, in 1978, the Core was seen as a less elitist alternative to the Great Books programs offered at Columbia and other universities. It has no universally required courses, mandating instead that students take, at some point before graduation, at least one class in seven of eleven areas—areas whose titles and subject matter *sound* suitably comprehensive. They include Literature and Arts, Historical Study, Science, Foreign Cultures, Quantitative Reasoning, Moral Reasoning, and Social Analysis.

But although these subject areas are theoretically general, the dozen or so classes offered annually in each of them (nearly all Core courses are designed for the Core) tend to be maddeningly specific and often defiantly obscure. The Core makes no attempt to distinguish between "Understanding Islam and Contemporary Muslim Societies" and "Tel Aviv: Urban Culture in Another Zion" in terms of importance; either will satisfy the Foreign Cultures requirement. For Science a student might choose "Human Evolution"—or he might choose "The Biology of Trees and Forests" or "Dinosaurs and Their Relatives." For his Social Analysis requirement he might decide to study basic economic principles in Martin Feldstein's Ec 10—or he might take "Food and Culture" or "Psychological Trauma" or "Urban Revolutions: Archaeology and the Investigation of Early States." And for Literature and Arts he might decide to take Helen Vendler's wide-ranging course "Poems, Poets, Poetry"—but then again, he might be drawn to "Women Writers in Imperial China: How to Escape From the Feminine Voice."

This is not to denigrate the more whimsical and esoteric choices that fill out a course catalogue. A computer-science major, his head spinning with lines of code, might be well served by dipping into "The Cuban Revolution: 1956–71: A Self-Debate." But under Harvard's system that might easily turn out to be the only history class he takes. It seems deeply disingenuous, at best, to suggest that in the development of a broadly educated student body the study of Castro's regime carries the same weight as, say, knowledge of the two world wars, or the French Revolution, or the founding of America. (During my four years at Harvard the history department didn't offer a single course focusing on the American Revolution.)

As if in reply to this complaint, the Core's mission statement asserts, with a touch of smugness, that "the Core differs from other programs of general education. It does not define intellectual breadth as the mastery of a set of Great Books, or the digestion of a specific quantum of information . . . rather, the Core seeks to introduce students to the major approaches to knowledge in areas that the faculty considers indispensable to undergraduate education."

These words, which appear in the course catalogue each year, are the closest that Harvard comes to articulating an undergraduate educational philosophy. They suggest that the difference in importance between, say, "Democracy, Development, and Equality in Mexico" and "Reason and Faith in the West" (both offerings in Historical Study) does not matter. As the introduction to the history courses puts it, both courses offer a "historical" approach to knowledge that is presumably more valuable than mere "facts" about the past. Comprehending history "as a form of inquiry and understanding" trumps learning about actual events. The catalogue contains similarly pat introductions to the other disciplines. In each case the emphasis is squarely on methodology, not material.

My experience of the Core was probably typical. I set out with the intention of picking a comprehensive roster of classes that would lead me in directions at once interesting and essential, providing perspectives that were unavailable in my concentration: American history and literature. The first Core course I wandered into—"Concepts of the Hero in Greek Civilization"—proved to be spectacular, notwithstanding its nickname, "Heroes for Zeroes." It was a survey course with a twist, in which an enthusiastic professor took an initially reluctant crowd of students on a whirlwind tour of the classics, with assists from contemporary films such as *Blade Runner* and *When We Were Kings*.

During the next three years I sought other courses that offered what this one had: Great Books and great teaching. What I found were unengaged professors and over-burdened teaching assistants who seemed to be marking time until they could return to the parochial safety of their departmental classes. Indeed, parochialism often overtook even the broadest-sounding Core classes. "Understanding Islam" involved only cursory analysis of the Koran, the history of Islamic civilization, and the rise of radical Islam, but devoted weeks to Muslim diaspora communities in London and Muslim-animistic syncretism in Africa. I chose another class, "The Portrait," because it seemed likely to offer something of a crash course in art history. And for the first few weeks it did, focusing on E. H. Gombrich's comprehensive *The Story of Art*. The rest of the time, however, was devoted to police photography in nineteenth-century France, sexual fetishism in Victorian daguerreotypes, aboriginal head-shrinking . . . The list goes on, but I didn't: by the middle of the semester I had stopped going to the lectures.

The few Core classes that are well taught are swamped each year, no matter how obscure the subject matter. The closest thing to a Harvard education—that is, to an intellectual corpus that most Harvard graduates have in common—is probably obtained in such oversubscribed courses as "The Warren Court and the Pursuit of Justice," "First Nights: Five Performance Premieres," and "Fairy Tales, Children's Literature, and the Construction of Childhood."

A Harvard graduate may have read no Shakespeare or Proust; he may be unable to distinguish Justinian the Great from Julian the Apostate, or to tell you the first ten elements in the periodic table (God knows I can't). But one need only mention "Mass Culture in Nazi Germany" or "Constructing the Samurai" and his eyes will light up with fond memories.

As in a great library ravaged by a hurricane, the essential elements of a liberal arts education lie scattered everywhere at Harvard, waiting to be picked up. But little guidance is given on how to proceed with that task.

I remember vividly the moment late in my high school senior year when Harvard's course catalogue arrived in the mail. It was a doorstop of a book, filled with descriptions of hundreds, maybe thousands, of classes. I pored over it, asking myself how I could choose just thirty-two classes, four years' worth, from the sea of fascinating choices.

Harvard never attempted to answer that question—perhaps the most important question facing any incoming freshman. I chose my classes as much by accident as by design. There were times when some of them mattered to me, and even moments when I was intoxicated. But achieving those moments required pulling myself away from Harvard's other demands, whether social, extracurricular, or pre-professional, which took far more discipline than I was usually able to exert.

Mostly I logged the necessary hours in the library and exam rooms, earned my solid (if inflated) GPA and my diploma, and used the rest of the time to keep up with my classmates in our ongoing race to the top of America (and the world). It was only afterward, when the perpetual motion of undergraduate life was behind me, that I looked back and felt cheated.

Afterward, too, I began chuckling inwardly when some older person, upon discovering my Harvard affiliation, would nod gravely and ask, But wasn't it such hard work?

It was—but not in the way the questioner meant. It was hard work to get into Harvard, and then it was hard work competing for offices and honors and extracurriculars with thousands of brilliant and driven young people; hard work keeping our heads in the swirling social world; hard work fighting for law-school slots and investment-banking jobs as college wound to a close . . . yes, all of that was heavy sledding. But the academics—the academics were another story.

Whatever nostalgists think, there was never a golden age when students did all their work and attended every lecture. When Aquinas held forth in Paris, and Heidegger in Freiburg, lazy undergraduates were doubtless squirreled away in their rooms, frantically skimming other people's notes to prep for the final exam. What makes our age different is the moment that happened over and over again at Harvard, when we said *This is going to be hard* and then realized *No, this is easy.* Maybe it came when we boiled down a three-page syllabus to a hundred pages of exam-time reading, or saw that a paper could be turned in late without the frazzled teaching fellow's docking us, or handed in C-quality work and got a gleaming B-plus. Whenever the moment came, we learned that it wasn't our sloth alone, or our constant pushing for higher grades, that made Harvard easy.

No, Harvard was easy because almost no one was pushing back.

Textual Questions

1. Describe what Douthat means by "the overall ease and lack of seriousness in Harvard's undergraduate academic culture."

2. Harvard, Douthat says, used to train a "semi-aristocracy" but now deals with "a meritocratic elite." Define these terms and clarify the difference between them.

3. Describe the pressures on faculty from students, colleagues, and the administration that, according to Douthat, lead to grade inflation. How do those pressures relate to "a deep inferiority complex regarding modern capitalism"?

Rhetorical Questions

4. What does Douthat assume about his audience and its attitudes toward education?

5. Look closely at the evidence Douthat gives for his repeated assertion that the academics at Harvard are "easy." Are you convinced? What does Douthat suggest about the Harvard faculty's ethics and politics? Does his evidence support his innuendos?

6. What does Douthat dislike most about Harvard's core curriculum and what does he imply it should require instead?

Intertextual Questions

7. Several of the essays in this chapter argue for a particular kind of education for the elite—those students with the background and resources to gain entry into the top American colleges. For instance, Carus is concerned with students at Cal Tech, another highly selective school. Referring to two of these other essays, compare and evaluate their assumptions about what future leaders of the country should know and be able to do.

8. Compare and contrast the educational problems that Douthat focuses on with those that Rose and hooks attend to. Why are their definitions of those problems so different?

Thinking Beyond the Text

9. Imagine that Douthat is an accurate observer of education at Harvard and propose the kind of general education courses and requirements he would approve. Then propose an argument for the increased value of your new core curriculum in comparison to the one he describes.

10. Imagine that Douthat is not an accurate observer of education at Harvard. Develop an essay that shows his evidence to be weak and his conclusions dubious.

For Writing & Discussion

11. Read the description of Harvard's core curriculum as it is posted at http://www.fas.harvard.edu. (A search at that site for "core curriculum" in June 2005 yielded 27 entries). Compare the information you have retrieved from the Web site with Douthat's description of the program based on his experience. In an essay, explain at least two points of similarity and two points of difference between Douthat's description and that available from Harvard's official Web site.

JAMES TRAUB

A lifelong New Yorker, James Traub is a contributing writer to *The New York Times Magazine*. He has published several books, including *City on a Hill* (1994), about changes at the City College of New York caused by open admissions, and *The Devil's Playground* (2004), about the transformation of Times Square over time.

"The Moral Imperative," an article about a growing chain of charter schools focusing on "character education," first appeared in the winter 2005 issue of *Education Next*.

The Moral Imperative

Prereading Question

The history of education in the West is filled with debates about the possibility of developing character in students—developing a solid sense of right and wrong, a strong sense of morality (although the definition of what is moral has, of course, changed over time). In your experience, is it possible for education in America to produce students who are not only smart but also moral? Possible or not, should schools even be involved in such a pursuit?

Earlier this year, at the Hyde School, a private high school in Bath, Maine, dedicated to "family-based character education," I witnessed a confrontation in an 11th-grade honors English class the likes of which, it is safe to say, few educators or scholars have ever seen. The teacher, Barbara Perry, asked if everyone had finished reading the assigned novel, Edwidge Danticat's *The Farming of Bones*. All but two of the dozen or so students had. It was a Monday, and Perry asked Brad, one of the two, if he had done any of the reading at all over the weekend.

"No," said Brad. "It was a really rough weekend for me. I've had a lot of trouble with believing in myself, and I've been trying to figure out where it comes from. Mr. Gauld [Malcolm Gauld, president and CEO of the Hyde Schools] thought it came from my father, and I should talk to him. I brought it up, and he got really upset."

One of the kids jumped on Brad. "You say you don't believe in yourself, but you don't give yourself an opportunity to believe in yourself. It's like how you didn't go to lacrosse practice on Saturday. I don't know how not doing your work, not going to lacrosse, is going to make you believe in yourself."

A chorus of "uh-huh"s rose around the room. Miss Perry said gently, "Do you know what you're doing?"

"Do I know what I'm doing?" Brad repeated, in a heart-breakingly toneless, defeated voice. "Hardly."

And now the other students tried to direct Brad to the deeper causes of his malaise. He was, they said, holding something back. "I'm really worried about you," said one of the girls.

A boy turned to Brad and said, "I was talking about you to my mom yesterday—how you have this reputation for being the kid who fluctuates the most. It's up to you whether you're going to be in charge or not."

Brad listened silently. Finally, he said, "So I guess I should leave now?"

"It's up to you," Miss Perry said. Brad pushed his chair back, gathered up his books, and left. And only then did the class begin to discuss *The Farming of Bones*.

Both students and teachers assured me that this exercise in tough love was nothing out of the ordinary at Hyde; several kids said that they had been on the receiving end of it themselves, to their lasting benefit. Radical truth telling, accompanied by an ethos of mutual responsibility known as "Brother's Keeper," lies at the core of Hyde's vision of character development. And these principles are meant to guide the conduct of not just the students but all the adults in what is very consciously referred to as "the Hyde community"—teachers, administrators, parents. Everyone is obliged to hold everyone else to the standards they themselves would wish to be held to. The Hyde experience is, if nothing else, exhausting.

❧

A Secular Morality

The Hyde School is scarcely typical of schools professedly dedicated to character education; it is, if anything, the extreme case, where principles that elsewhere have been applied halfheartedly have been most deeply considered and uncompromisingly followed. Hyde is, in fact, so peculiar, so supremely dedicated to its eccentric founding principles, that it's not easy to imagine the school's serving as a useful exemplar of anything. Nonetheless, Hyde schools are now flourishing in Woodstock, Connecticut, and in the inner-city systems of New Haven, Connecticut, and Washington, D.C. The school's founder, Joseph Gauld, Malcolm's father, says that he hopes to have charter schools operating in New York City and Oakland, California, by 2005. In the great, ongoing laboratory project known as whole-school reform, Hyde may turn out to be the leading entry under the heading "character education."

And a very large heading it is, too. (See sidebar, pages 200–203) Thomas Lickona, the head of the Center for the Fourth and Fifth Rs (the fourth and fifth being respect and responsibility) at the State University of New York at Cortland and a leading figure in the field, says that two-thirds of the states' schools are now required either by legislative mandate or by administrative regulation to implement programs in character education. The U.S. Department of Education has been awarding grants in the field since 1995; the No Child Left Behind Act of 2001 established the new Partnership in Character Education Program, which gives $25 million annually to schools. In part, perhaps, because the very term "character education" evokes such an all-American image of wholesomeness and high moral purpose, this is one bandwagon that educators are almost sure to be climbing aboard in growing numbers.

(Continues on page 203)

From McGuffey's Reader to Musical Chairs: A Brief History of "Character Education"

The expression "character education" would have seemed a redundancy until quite recently in history. Virtually all elite private education, whether at prep schools or colleges, was designed to ensure that young men of the better classes were prepared for the leadership positions in government and the professions to which they were destined. And the public schools were unabashed about their role in turning the children of immigrant families into Americans. Not until the age of John Dewey and the progressives was this inculcation of civic and personal virtue questioned; Dewey mocked the rigid pieties of

McGuffey's Reader and called for a pedagogy that would liberate the child's own questioning nature, that would replace inculcation itself with a more "child-centered" form of learning. And by midcentury, as a testdriven meritocracy made deep inroads into the old world of inherited privilege, character began to take a back seat to intellect at the elite institutions.

The modern character education movement began as a reaction to the aggressively value-neutral school culture that emerged thanks to this combination of progressivism and meritocracy. In *The Closing of the American Mind*, which appeared in 1987, Alan Bloom wrote that among young people "openness" had ascended to the status of supreme moral principle, just as "relativism" had become axiomatic in philosophy. Bloom's call for a return to the search for truth and meaning, in school as well as in intellectual life, struck a deep chord, or so the staggering sales of his rather dense tome implied. At the same time, neoconservative thinkers like Gertrude Himmelfarb were extolling the much-denigrated virtues of the Victorian age. The word "virtue" itself began to take on an almost talismanic power, especially in the wake of William Bennett's *Book of Virtues*, published in 1992. The very willingness to use the word meant that you accepted the principle that some things were true and some were not, as against the woolly relativism and permissiveness that pervaded the schools.

This philosophical and ideological assault on liberal, secular-minded culture put character education on the public agenda. But many parents and educators who had no interest in fighting the culture wars lamented the generalized loss of authority of traditional institutions. They felt angry that schools had succumbed to an anything-goes ethos that was harmful to both the schools and the young people passing through them. The killings at Columbine and elsewhere seemed to offer terrifying proof that the schools had somehow lost their way. Schools had left the development of values to parents at the very moment when parents were leaving it to . . . whomever. This widespread sense of unease lent an impetus to the intellectual critique and shifted the debate toward less ideological and more pragmatic objectives.

Character education really took wing, before Columbine, in 1992, at a conference sponsored by the Josephson Institute of Ethics, in Aspen, Colorado. There a group of educators and ethicists agreed on a list of values—not virtues—that they felt transcended sectarian, partisan, or class distinctions. These were codified as "The Six Pillars of Character" (trustworthiness, respect, responsibility, fairness, caring, citizenship). The following year, the institute established the Character Counts! program to help schools and communities incorporate the six pillars. At the same time, a group of civic and education organizations formed the Character Education Partnership, which now functions as the movement's clearinghouse and professional organization (and promotes its own "Eleven Principles" of character). President Clinton seized on the fledgling movement as one of the cost-free, nonpartisan

CONTINUED >

initiatives he was then touting. The White House began sponsoring annual conferences on "Character Building for a Civil and Democratic Society" in 1994. And in 1996 the president gave the movement the ultimate blessing when he said, in his State of the Union address, "I challenge all our schools to teach character education, to teach good values and good citizenship." By that time, according to a survey by the National School Boards Association, 45 percent of school districts said they had instituted character education programs, while another 38 percent said they planned to do so. Thus the character education bandwagon swiftly became a juggernaut.

Education publishers now offer kits and exercises designed to teach every virtue and every value known to man. The Character Counts! folks, for example, offer a 45-minute lesson plan designed to teach caring to teens. The class begins with a moralized version of musical chairs, in which the kids form groups of three the moment the music stops. Some kids inevitably get excluded in each round. "How did it feel to be left out?" the teacher asks. "What words describe the way you were treated? Do students at your school ever treat other students that way in real life?" The teacher delivers a potted lecture on caring. She then produces a golf ball, which she tosses to a student, who is asked to "name something that makes people hard to like." The teacher asks, "Does a person's neighborhood, size, or color give us the right to drop our standards?" The instruction sheet does not indicate whether there is more than one answer to this question.

The tens of thousands of schools now obliged to institute character education programs need materials, and a world of providers stands ready to help them. A company called Integrity Matters offers "entertaining, attention-capturing character education videos" on 35 "basic moral values" (including "Virtue"). Tolerance is a mini-industry all its own, with manuals offering "proven strategies" to stamp out hate. A curriculum program called "The Seven Cs of Thinking Clearly" (Criticism, Creativity, Curiosity, Concentration, Communication, Correction, and Control) helps children identify "faulty thinking practices" by way of "The Stink'n Think'n Gang," a gang of nogoodniks whose members include Iwannit Now, Judge B. Fore, and—well, you get the picture. The most hopeful thing one can say about most of these lessons-in-a-box is that they are so hokey and tone-deaf that it is hard to imagine a child, even one of tender years, taking them seriously. At the same time, they constitute a terrible waste of a precious commodity. Whatever time you spend revamping your faulty thinking practices or stamping out hate is time you are not spending studying history or chemistry.

If tossing a golf ball while delivering stilted homilies about caring can be considered character education, it is probably safe to say that the field has a serious quality-control problem. But what about schools like Hyde or others that have taken this reform seriously? Are they effective? And if so, at what are they effective? Some studies have found that character education programs do, in fact, build character, though none of these studies is rigorous enough to be remotely definitive. The largest of them is a study by researchers at South Dakota State University of 8,419 students in schools that have adopted Character Counts! The study concluded that between 1998 and 2000 the number of students who reported various acts of cheating, stealing, drinking, drug taking, class cutting, and the like decreased significantly.

Many an ulcerous principal would be delighted to adopt a program that promised greater student compliance; this very prospect probably impels many schools to go the character education route. But a central premise of the field is that character is a matter not only of social behavior but also of accomplishment. This is what Thomas Lickona means when he says, "Virtue is human excellence. To be a school of character, a community of virtue, is to be equally committed to two great goals: intellectual excellence and moral excellence."

If this is so, then character education programs should improve academic performance. In the maiden issue of the *Journal of Character Education,* a team of researchers reports on a study of the relative academic performance of schools in California that described themselves as having substantial character education components. They concluded that performance on standardized tests from 1999 to 2002 was "significantly positively correlated" with "a school's ability to ensure a clean and safe physical environment," "evidence that its parents and teachers modeled and promoted good character education" and opportunities "for students to contribute in meaningful ways to the school and its community." The findings were based on self-reporting, which is scarcely conclusive. The researchers struck a note of modest hopefulness, but cautioned that "no evidence exists for a broader relationship that spans a range of character education approaches in a large sample of schools."

Should one expect such evidence to surface? Not if character education means pious sermonettes on tolerance. But even if virtue is understood as human excellence, it's naive to expect instant results. "It's all about how you tap into and help them exercise their will," says Karen Bohlin, coauthor of *Building Character in Schools.* "That's where the real work is. And we don't see the results immediately. The really stable dispositions show up much later." That may well be true, especially where character education has been densely woven into the fabric of intellectual life. You have to wonder, however, if the same will be true at a school like Hyde, where character is understood as a kind of antidote to excessive academicism.

—*James Traub*

Indeed, although the character education movement began essentially as the educational wing of a campaign of conservative moral uplift, it long ago shed those dowdy Victorian garments. Whatever values schools wish to propagate nowadays, whether multicultural sensitivity or teamwork, now travel under this glorious banner. And character education has come increasingly to be seen as an educational rather than a social reform, with measurable inputs producing measurable consequences, for both student behavior and academic performance. Indeed, if the vast and various character education movement is unified by anything, it is the conviction that schools can, and must, consciously and explicitly develop a healthy peer culture because such a culture is the indispensable foundation for successful learning.

∽

Hyde Origins

Like so many of the programs of reform now competing for primacy, the Hyde idea emerged entirely from the mind of one extremely determined and deeply dissatisfied individual. This was Joe Gauld, a math teacher and administrator at the New Hampton prep school in New Hampshire in the late 1950s and early 1960s. It was the early days of the burgeoning postwar meritocracy, and Gauld felt increasingly repelled by the ethos of "giftedness" and the honors track and the rat race for college placement. The schools, he concluded—not just New Hampton but all schools—were failing children by rewarding innate ability rather than seeking to draw out each child's "unique potential." And so this lonely dissenter from the post-Sputnik fixation on academic achievement quit his job as assistant headmaster in order to pursue his flinty New England faith in self-improvement and transcendence. Gauld ultimately scraped together the funds to purchase the 145-acre Hyde family estate in Bath, in southern Maine, and the Hyde School opened its doors in 1966. "Instead of relying on intellect to produce good grades and high test scores," Gauld writes in *Character First: The Hyde School Difference*, "students at Hyde learn to follow the dictates of their conscience so they can develop the character necessary to bring out their unique potential."

The history of the school, as Gauld recounts it, was a sequence of moral dramas in which the founder insisted on clinging to the original vision in the face of threats to Hyde's very existence. The kids demanded the right to smoke; Gauld refused. A boy of admirable character but limited intellect couldn't pass math; Gauld eliminated academic requirements for graduation for the entire school. Gauld demanded that teachers subject themselves to the same searching self-scrutiny as the kids; a third of them left, and Hyde soldiered on. The board forced Gauld out of his own school in 1980; Malcolm stayed on and was able to engineer his father's return five years later. After all these years of choosing purity of doctrine and bloodlines over pragmatic calculation, the Hyde School today has an atmosphere charged with the dedication to first principles of a religious community as well as the air of immemorial ritual of an old Maine summer camp. Only about 220 students, almost all of them boarders, attend grades 9 through 12.

Hyde charges $32,000 a year in tuition, room, and board; nevertheless, the school has almost no endowment, and both its facilities and its faculty pay scale are very modest by the standards of New England prep schools. The school can afford no more than a dozen or so scholarships a year, which means that the student body is overwhelmingly white.

Joe Gauld wanted to work with the kids who hadn't been comfortable in the orthodox academic settings that he himself had spurned. From the outset Hyde attracted children who, for a variety of reasons, had failed in more conventional schools. Hyde very quickly gained a reputation, which it has never shaken, as a turnaround school. The Gaulds chafe under this unsought distinction, but recognize that they are powerless to change it. For many kids, Hyde is the last stop before some terrifying tough-love, boot-camp institution socked away deep in some western wilderness (as Malcolm, strikingly, says it was for himself). An appalling fraction of the kids I talked to had drug or alcohol problems and also had parents with drug or alcohol problems—all of which they talked about with stunning candor. Hyde has no electrified fences or muscle-bound counselors. But the rules forbid everything the kids were used to back home—smoking, drinking, sex, cheating, and mistreating your fellow adolescents. Most of the kids arrive kicking and screaming.

"We're not the school the kids want to go to," as Malcolm Gauld puts it. "We're the school the *parents* want the kids to go to." Several of the kids I spoke to singled out the school's rigid schedule for special loathing: up at 6:30; breakfast at 7:30; jobs at 8; then classes, lunch, more classes, performing arts, sports, "Discovery Group"; dinner; then study hall or "Mandatory Fun." The school sometimes feels to the kids like prison on the honor code. About 40 percent of each class drops out. One senior told me that she was one of 9 kids remaining from her freshman class of 25 or 30.

But the most demanding aspect of Hyde is the Brother's Keeper code, for it is conscience, rather than fear of punishment, that is meant to guide behavior at Hyde. And each individual must act as a guardian of the conscience of others, even—and especially—if that requires a painful confrontation. This is a principle that the Gaulds bluntly call "truth over harmony." It sounds like a dreadful weapon in the hands of 15-year-olds, and in fact a teacher in Hyde's school in Washington, D.C., the Hyde Leadership Public Charter School, said that they were "trying to get away from the Jerry Springer thing." But I never witnessed an abuse of this power. I don't know how Brad, the student in the honors English class at the Bath campus, felt about being on the receiving end of the Brother's Keeper ordeal, but it was plain that the message was, We're not going to stand by and watch you fail. Many of the kids described to me the painful process of seeing themselves for the first time as others saw them. Sarah Flint was one of the small number of Hyde students who had been perfectly successful in her previous school, in Charlotte, North Carolina. (Her brothers had preceded her as students at Hyde.) "I hated it here," she said, "because they were being honest with me." Students and faculty accused her of coasting and demanded that she work harder. And, she said, she did.

Joe Gauld writes that his wife, Blanche, was an alcoholic and that he himself had abused alcohol. This painful history may account for the cult of honesty that sometimes makes life at Hyde feel like a free-floating session of Alcoholics Anonymous. Students at Hyde must tell rule breakers to turn themselves in; if that doesn't work, they have to inform the administration themselves. In the outside world, this last practice goes by the name of snitching, and it violates the adolescent code of conduct as profoundly as does the practice of confronting one's friends. Many of the kids resist this most of all; but seniors, who are given a large hand in running the school, are expected to fully accept this responsibility. James is an obviously bright kid who had been through a wilderness program, a "lockdown facility," and an alcoholism treatment center—and was now, he said, clean and sober. He explained, "If you report several people for an infraction, they'll stop whatever we're doing and the whole community will go down to the Pit," the outdoor auditorium. "They'll say, 'We think there's an awful lot of dishonesty going on.'" James said that the ensuing outbreak of penitence often leads students to confess absurdly trivial transgressions.

The comfort zone is the great enemy of the Hyde ethos. As innate talent is denigrated, so pressing against your limits is celebrated. Every student is required to go on wilderness trips, to engage in demanding physical activities, to play team sports, and to perform on stage. For boys who have never sung or girls who have never run—or vice versa—this can be a terrifying prospect. But of course the whole idea is to force students to find in themselves the courage to face something they never thought they could face. The Gaulds are great believers in the character-building qualities of team sports. The Hyde school in D.C. has the nation's only all-black rugby team, and the coach, Tal Bayer, told me proudly not only how well the team had fared against far more experienced opponents, but also how extravagantly they had been praised by other coaches and parents. Good character is meant to lead to good performance, just as it is supposed to produce academic excellence.

◆

Parental Involvement

Hyde is by no means the only school that seeks to transform peer culture; that, after all, is the foundation of successful parochial schools, though the transformation they seek is of a slightly different nature. But Hyde's ambitions run deeper still. After years of meeting the parents of his students, many of them utterly blithe in the face of their own child's manifest unhappiness and apathy, Joe Gauld concluded that he could not work lasting changes in the child unless he could force the parents to undergo the same painful process of growth through self-scrutiny. Gauld is a social critic, but his sense of the world is guided less by the neo-Victorianism of today's conservatives than by a kind of New England transcendentalism— the exacting spirit of the old evangelicals. "The American family today," he writes, "is spiritually sick," obsessed with status and acquisition, deaf to the deeper registers. The lives of the children of such parents, he writes, "are empty, devoid of meaning." Gauld takes the view—and here he parts ways from much of the reform world—that even the most powerful school culture will eventually lose out to a larger, pernicious culture. As Laura Gauld, Malcolm's wife, a former Hyde student (along with her four siblings) and now the director of Hyde's Family Education Programs, puts it, "If you're not going to change the parents, you're not going to change the kids."

Hyde admits families as much as it does students. The interview process serves as an eye-opening introduction to the school's truth-seeking ethos. Lauren Franklin, an admissions officer (and a former Hyde student), says that she will ask the parents what "personal issues"—of theirs—they would like Hyde to address. This question flummoxes most parents, who typically take the position that while their children may have very serious problems, they don't. But since Hyde's premise is that the child's problems originate within the family, the school asks a great deal of parents, above and beyond the annual check. Parents are expected to gather for "regional meetings" at one another's homes every month, to attend family weekends at the Bath campus twice a year, and to spend three days each year at the school's Family Learning Center, also on campus. Parents spend a great many hours with one another and one another's children, even overcoming their mortification in theatrical and dance performances. The Hyde literature is full of stories of world-beating dads who finally abandon their defenses in these settings and admit to their anger, their insecurity, their alcoholism; and of families crying together in relief. Many of the kids told me that their relationship with their parents had for the first time moved beyond the superficially amicable or the ritualistically hostile.

All adults at Hyde, including the faculty, are expected to conduct themselves according to the school's dictates. Each teacher at Bath is paired with a student to talk about issues in their own life; in the D.C. school, teachers anonymously adopt a senior and correspond with him or her. The faculty in Bath has a monthly seminar in which they talk about their own progress as teachers and individuals. And at the end of the year, students gather to collectively evaluate their teachers. I attended one such session in Washington, where teachers advanced, one by one, to a folding chair set up in the front of the auditorium. Kids popped up from the audience to say "You always gave me good advice," or "I want to thank you for not giving up on me when I was in your class." The criticism tended to be mild: "You could be more patient." (It would certainly have been harsher in Bath, where the truth is usually delivered unvarnished.) One refrain I scarcely expected was, "You could be a little harder on us, especially if we're trying to take advantage of you." The kids' relationship to school authority had the character of a social contract rather than of submission to a higher power.

⟨∾⟩

The Hyde Truths

The Hyde experience culminates in an exercise that is, in a way, the ultimate test of character and of the virtues of the doctrine of radical truth telling. Seniors are expected to stand, one by one, before the entire class and the entire faculty and relate how they have grown at Hyde, how they have fallen short, and how they envision their future; then they propose the level of honors with which they deserve to graduate. When they are finished, everyone is invited to comment. As transparency is another incontestable virtue at Hyde, I was invited to sit in on one such session. A muscular Asian boy named Tim, a fine athlete and a sweet kid, took what is known as "the hot seat." His voice quaking, his head cast down, Tim commenced to lacerate himself for his shortcomings. "I was very afraid to look at myself," said Tim. "I would rely on my hard work and my personality." He deprecated his "people-pleasing attitude" and his "achievement-oriented attitude"— attributes that, one might think, would take him a long way in life. Tim seemed to have overdosed on the Hyde Kool-Aid. And the kids, strikingly buoyed him up. "You're so much greater than you think you are said one," and everyone sees it but you." "You have to deal with your father," said another. "You have to deal with being adopted. He had pegged himself at the middle of the three levels of attainment, but the kids and the teachers almost unanimously agreed that he deserved the top.

It was like watching psychoanalysis practiced by a community of loving amateurs: I didn't know whether to cover my eyes or join in a group hug. I said later to Paul Hurd, an administrator who first came to Hyde in 1966, that the truth does not, after all, always set one free. He replied, "It may feel that way at the time, but it's been our experience over the years that this is what works for the kids." And the kids themselves say much the same thing. It's true that the ones I met were the survivors. But this hardy remnant talked about the school in salvific terms. Two of the kids at the Hyde Leadership School in D.C. told me that they and their friends often came to school even when there were no classes. The school is open most weekends and holidays. "We love it here," said Dawnyetta Burke, a senior. "It's our second home."

Joe Gauld, a prophet and evangelizer in the great New England tradition, has always believed that the Hyde model is destined to replace what he sees as a dead-end academic-achievement model. So far, however, Hyde's efforts at self-replication, which Gauld has headed, have been rocky. In the early 1990s, the Hyde team tried and failed to open schools in nearby Gardiner; in Springfield, Massachusetts; and in Baltimore. In several cases, say the Gaulds, they were blocked by hostile teacher unions, since they demanded the right to hire their own faculty. Hyde now enrolls about 1,400 students at its four schools. The New Haven school is widely considered successful, but the Hyde content has drained out of it almost altogether. Only in D.C. can one test whether the Hyde model can be applied to a public school rather than to a private residential one and to a school that serves disadvantaged kids rather than financially privileged ones. Most of the seven hundred or so children who attend this K-12 institution located in a tough neighborhood in Northeast Washington enter scoring well below their grade level in reading and math; the school is overwhelmingly black and largely poor or working-class. Joanne Goubourn, the headmistress, said that she had had to scuttle certain aspects of Brother's Keeper for fear of ensuing "fights out in the street." She notes that parental involvement is much less than it is at Bath (though still significant by the standards of urban public schools). Goubourn feels that it may take another five years before the school is fully Hyde-ified.

It may be that the spiritual dedication at Bath depends on its monastic enclosure and the wounded souls there. Indeed, at times, Hyde feels almost like a cult, or at least a caste. Joe Gauld's son, Malcolm, married his former classmate Laura, whose sister Claire married Malcolm's classmate Ken, who founded Hyde's Woodstock school. Malcolm's sister Laurie married Paul Hurd; together they started Hyde's New Haven school. Another of Joe's daughters, Gigi, married another faculty member, and together *they* established the Washington, D.C., school, which Joe continues to visit at least monthly. It is as if the supreme level of engagement required to maintain the Hyde culture depends, in the end, on tribal bonds. If this is so, of course, the culture may begin to wane as soon as the institution becomes too large for the family to control. Indeed, Joanne Goubourn told me she can't quite imagine how the school would carry on without Joe Gauld.

∽

A Gradual Soul Turning

Many theoreticians of character education recognize that character cannot be taught as if it were an article of knowledge. Our characters are formed by slow accretion and by innumerable adaptations to the totality of our experience. If school is to consciously shape this process, it will have to do so pervasively, but indirectly. As Malcolm and Laura Gauld write, "Character is inspired; it is not imparted." In *Building Character in Schools,* one of the most thoughtful works in the field, Kevin Ryan and Karen Bohlin cite

Socrates' comment, recorded in Plato's *Republic:* "The instrument with which one learns is like an eye that cannot be turned around from darkness to light without turning the whole body." Education, Socrates goes on, is thus an act of "gradual soul turning." This, Ryan and Bohlin remark, is the perfect metaphor for character education.

The Hyde schools are a model of gradual soul turning. They do not, for example, teach courage; instead, daily life at the school, as well as the periodic baptism-under-fire experience, is designed to foster courage. Thomas Lickona, of the Center for the Fourth and Fifth Rs, says that he believes the Brother's Keeper code has effected profound changes in Hyde's peer culture, adding that he was "deeply impressed" by the school in Bath and "even more impressed" by the Washington charter school. But there are other models for an all-pervasive character culture.

Karen Bohlin is now the headmistress of the Montrose School, a Catholic girls school in Natick, Massachusetts. Bohlin is also an admirer of Hyde; but she is skeptical of "radical truth telling" and says that she has not been able to bring parents as deeply into the fold as Hyde does. Montrose, she explains, was founded "in reaction to the mushy sixties stuff" and is organized around the principle of seeking truth as the goal of intellectual endeavor and a commitment to service. Since the school does not need to pierce the self-delusion of deeply troubled adolescents, as Hyde does, character education is more directly linked to intellectual development. Issues of character and leadership suffuse the daily life of the school, but always, says Bohlin, with a sense of intellectual purpose. Students might, for example, discuss the difference between character and personality or between justice and fairness.

Gradual soul turning requires a deep commitment, a deep understanding, and a deep well of patience. And while character education is bound to attract pioneers who will embrace it in full, the ordinary mortals who come in their wake will not be so zealous. Laura Gauld told me that she is often asked to visit schools professing Hyde-like principles. "Character education," she says, "means you get a group together and they come up with a set of words they want to focus on. They all agree on 'tolerance,' because tolerance is the one thing everyone can agree on."

This blithe celebration of tolerance was, of course, the chief sign of the value-neutral culture that moral traditionalists vowed to upend; now it's the starting point of character education programs. This vapid, if benign, form of behavior modification can produce some immediate results. The actual goal of many of these programs, Laura Gauld says, is to reduce graffiti, bullying, and the various other outward signs of an aimless school culture. The implicit message, she says, is that character education "is going to help you clean up your act." Gauld says that so long as these obligations apply only to the kids and not to the whole adult community, and so long as "character" is understood in such narrow and utilitarian terms, the results are bound to be superficial.

༂

The American Character

Character education has legs. It is a reform so thoroughly in the American grain, not to mention so various and adaptable, that it cannot be dismissed as just another shiny and insubstantial bubble. Moreover, the wish for schools to somehow address the sense of drift and anomie in the larger culture is not likely to abate. And so the issue is not whether we will have character education, but instead, what kind we will have and what relationship it will bear to the ongoing campaign to improve children's academic skills.

Joe Gauld founded the Hyde School in opposition to what he considered the excessively academic focus of conventional schools. Gauld has not changed his view. In an exchange of e-mail, he wrote me: "The emphasis on academic achievement is basically elitist," since "roughly 10 percent naturally respond to classroom instruction," while the other 90 percent either give up or "seek recognition elsewhere." Most education reformers would reel at this sweeping dismissal; in any case they would argue that the problem lies in the means or the content of instruction. Gauld insists that the bottom 90 percent will not succeed academically until they are reached by some other means. And he puts very little faith in schools that aim to change those odds. While he concedes that kids who go to the new crop of academically rigorous inner-city schools, like the KIPP Academy, may do better on tests than his kids, he is confident that Hyde students will be likelier to stay in college and succeed in life. Were it not so, after all, he would be forced to reexamine his central premise.

At bottom, Gauld shares that deep American fear of the soul-killing effect of academic learning that long predates John Dewey. Ralph Waldo Emerson famously expressed it when he wrote, "I had better never see a book than be warped by its attraction clean out of my own orbit, and made a satellite inside of a system." Gauld is inclined to think of academic success not as the royal route out of a life of poverty and ignorance, but rather as a beguiling snare. In his e-mail he also declared that "every study done so far has found either no or an inverse relationship between grades and test scores with success and fulfillment in life." This is an astounding statement, backed up with some eccentric documentation, including a study by AT&T that apparently found that managers with high SAT scores "were reliably less happy and more psychologically mal-adjusted by their mid-adult years" than those with lower scores. Gauld also noted that Bill Gates had dropped out of college, and he observed that Thomas Edison, the Wright brothers, and Winston Churchill were "terrible students."

But I saw few signs that Hyde had discovered the key to intellectual growth. Adam, one of the seniors, said to me, "Academics kind of takes a back seat here." Classes were often adjourned in the name of some higher good—an emergency session at the Pit, for example. Both teachers and students talk about personal issues, not intellectual ones, among themselves. One reason why Hyde has trouble attracting conventionally able students is that it relegates academics to a secondary status. Only in the past few years has it introduced a series of honors classes to appeal to more academically ambitious students. And the honors English class I sat in on didn't seem terribly demanding: The students were reading four books that trimester, and they were expected to produce a standard five-paragraph essay on each as well as a final project "designed to capture your process through Hyde"—a characteristically self-referential assignment. Seniors are typically admitted to second- or third-tier colleges, though it is a point of pride that a high fraction of these students find the inner resources to graduate from college. (The same is true at Hyde's other prep school, in Woodstock, which serves a similar population.)

Rich kids with behavior problems are not, of course, the demographic for whom most school reforms are intended; poor and working-class black kids are. The success or failure of the Hyde school in Washington is thus a matter of real importance.

"We've got some high school kids who can't decode," Joanne Goubourn says. The Gaulds had no idea that children could suffer from such profound academic deficits when they opened the D.C. school in 1999, and they quickly discovered that a healthier peer culture wasn't going to improve anyone's reading comprehension. Only in the past few years has the school begun focusing intently on the teaching of basic skills, and there has been no startling progress on test scores. And yet Hyde must be doing something right: all 13 of last year's seniors graduated, enrolled in four-year colleges, and made it through the first year. And all 30 of this year's seniors are scheduled to attend four-year colleges. Hyde may have had very little effect on the kids' cognitive development, but it still had a great effect on the kind of behaviors—self-discipline, steady work habits, respect for others—that lead to success in school.

Joe Gauld says that he is now working with Craig Ramey, a founding director of the famed Abecedarian Project on early childhood development, on a school for children ages birth to five that would combine parental involvement, character formation, and cognitive development. He believes that he can infuse into little children the confidence and the drive he finds sadly lacking in so many of the older kids. One can only hope that he is right. It is, after all, widely understood that the academic gap between blacks and whites, and for that matter between whites and Asians, has a great deal to do with the expectations, habits, and values the children bring with them from home. Most schools view all that as a given; they are left, in effect, to work the margins. Hyde proposes to go to the heart of the matter.

Textual Questions

1. The "sidebar" insert in this essay gives a history and evaluation of character education in school. What are the principal characteristics of character education and where does the idea come from? Character education, Traub tells us, depends on a "healthy peer culture" which, in turn, is "the indispensable foundation for successful learning." What is a "healthy peer culture" and how can an observer tell if it exists in a school?

2. What is the connection, as Joe Gauld developed the idea, between character education and the attempt to "draw out each child's unique potential"?

3. What are the characteristics of the Hyde School (including its cost, its doctrines, and its limited student body) that keep it from being a model for other schools?

Rhetorical Questions

4. Traub gives several examples of "radical truth telling" at Hyde and of its effects on students, parents, and teachers. What is the purpose of these narratives for the essay?

5. What is the relation between character education and the academic success the school seeks? What does the school say about this relation? What does the author of the essay say?

6. How would you describe Traub's attitude toward the Hyde School? Give evidence from the text to support what you say.

Intertextual Questions

7. What would Mike Rose say about the Hyde school and its emphasis on character education?

8. A large part of the promise of America has to do with education leading to active citizenship, high income, and high social status. Give examples from this chapter of essays arguing that education has succeeded in promoting these goals, and contrary examples arguing that education has failed. In your own view, to what degree has education in America succeeded in furthering this promise? How might we as a society improve this important role for education?

Thinking Beyond the Text

9. Joe Gauld, Traub tells us, "is inclined to think of academic success not as the royal route out of a life of poverty and ignorance, but rather as a

beguiling snare." If Gauld is right, what changes would need to be made in American schooling in order to realize the promise of America?

10. Traub is skeptical about the effects of the Hyde emphasis on character and the fact that the school "relegates academics to a secondary status." What evidence does he give for this skepticism and does he convince you to share it?

For Writing & Discussion

11. If you were able to make school reforms, what would you change, if anything, from the present patterns of American schools? What principles would you follow and what examples would you draw from? How would your reforms help the schools help their students realize the promise of America? Which authors in this chapter would most/least support your reforms?

DAVID LEONHARDT

David Leonhardt is a writer for the *New York Times*.

"The College Dropout Boom" appeared in the *New York Times* on May 24, 2005 as part of a multi-authored series focusing on how social class in America affects all aspects of society, including health, education, and marriage. The 14-article series was reproduced later that year in a book titled *Class Matters*. Of the book, Barbara Ehrenreich, author of *Nickel and Dimed*, said, "*Class Matters* is a beautifully reported, deeply disturbing portrait of a society bent out of shape by harsh inequalities."

The College Dropout Boom

∾ Prereading Question

Consider your decision to pursue a college degree. What reasons pushed you to make this decision as you have? What reasons argued against it? What economic or social forces pushed you in this direction? What forces pushed you away?

One of the biggest decisions Andy Blevins has ever made, and one of the few he now regrets, never seemed like much of a decision at all. It just felt like the natural thing to do.

In the summer of 1995, he was moving boxes of soup cans, paper towels and dog food across the floor of a supermarket warehouse, one of the biggest buildings here in southwest Virginia. The heat was brutal. The job had sounded impossible when he arrived fresh off his first year of college, looking to make some summer money, still a skinny teenager with sandy blond hair and a narrow, freckled face.

But hard work done well was something he understood, even if he was the first college boy in his family. Soon he was making bonuses on top of his $6.75 an hour, more money than either of his parents made. His girlfriend was around, and so were his hometown buddies. Andy acted more outgoing with them, more relaxed. People in Chilhowie noticed that.

It was just about the perfect summer. So the thought crossed his mind: maybe it did not have to end. Maybe he would take a break from college and keep working. He had been getting C's and D's, and college never felt like home, anyway.

"I enjoyed working hard, getting the job done, getting a paycheck," Mr. Blevins recalled. "I just knew I didn't want to quit."

So he quit college instead, and with that, Andy Blevins joined one of the largest and fastest-growing groups of young adults in America. He became a college dropout, though nongraduate may be the more precise term.

Many people like him plan to return to get their degrees, even if few actually do. Almost one in three Americans in their mid-20's now fall into this group, up from one in five in the late 1960's, when the Census Bureau began keeping such data. Most come from poor and working-class families.

The phenomenon has been largely overlooked in the glare of positive news about the country's gains in education. Going to college has become the norm throughout most of the United States, even in many places where college was once considered an exotic destination—places like Chilhowie (pronounced chill-HOW-ee), an Appalachian hamlet with a simple brick downtown. At elite universities, classrooms are filled with women, blacks, Jews and Latinos, groups largely excluded two generations ago. The American system of higher learning seems to have become a great equalizer.

In fact, though, colleges have come to reinforce many of the advantages of birth. On campuses that enroll poorer students, graduation rates are often low. And at institutions where nearly everyone graduates—small colleges like Colgate, major state institutions like the University of Colorado and elite private universities like Stanford—more students today come from the top of the nation's income ladder than they did two decades ago.

Only 41 percent of low-income students entering a four-year college managed to graduate within five years, the Department of Education found in a study last year, but 66 percent of high-income students did. That gap had grown over recent years. "We need to recognize that the most serious domestic problem in the United States today is the widening gap between the children of the rich and the children of the poor," Lawrence H. Summers, the president of Harvard, said last year when announcing that Harvard would give full scholarships to all its lowest-income students. "And education is the most powerful weapon we have to address that problem."

There is certainly much to celebrate about higher education today. Many more students from all classes are getting four-year degrees and reaping their benefits. But those broad gains mask the fact that poor and working-class students have nevertheless been falling behind; for them, not having a degree remains the norm.

That loss of ground is all the more significant because a college education matters much more now than it once did. A bachelor's degree, not a year or two of courses, tends to determine a person's place in today's globalized, computerized economy. College graduates have received steady pay increases over the past two decades, while the pay of everyone else has risen little more than the rate of inflation.

As a result, despite one of the great education explosions in modern history, economic mobility—moving from one income group to another over the course of a lifetime—has stopped rising, researchers say. Some recent studies suggest that it has declined over the last generation.

Put another way, children seem to be following the paths of their parents more than they once did. Grades and test scores, rather than privilege, determine success today, but that success is largely being passed down from one generation to the next. A nation that believes that everyone should have a fair shake finds itself with a kind of inherited meritocracy.

In this system, the students at the best colleges may be diverse—male and female and of various colors, religions and hometowns—but they tend to share an upper-middle-class upbringing. An old joke that Harvard's idea of diversity is putting a rich kid from California in the same room as a rich kid from New York is truer today than ever; Harvard has more students from California than it did in years past and just as big a share of upper-income students.

Students like these remain in college because they can hardly imagine doing otherwise. Their parents, understanding the importance of a bachelor's degree, spent hours reading to them, researching school districts and making it clear to them that they simply must graduate from college.

Andy Blevins says that he too knows the importance of a degree, but that he did not while growing up, and not even in his year at Radford University, 66 miles up the Interstate from Chilhowie. Ten years after trading college for the warehouse, Mr. Blevins, 29, spends his days at the same supermarket company. He has worked his way up to produce buyer, earning $35,000 a year with health benefits and a 401(k) plan. He is on a path typical for someone who attended college without getting a four-year degree. Men in their early 40's in this category made an average of $42,000 in 2000. Those with a four-year degree made $65,000.

Still boyish-looking but no longer rail thin, Mr. Blevins says he has many reasons to be happy. He lives with his wife, Karla, and their year-old son, Lucas, in a small blue-and-yellow house at the end of a cul-de-sac in the middle of a stunningly picturesque Appalachian valley. He plays golf with some of the same friends who made him want to stay around Chilhowie.

But he does think about what might have been, about what he could be doing if he had the degree. As it is, he always feels as if he is on thin ice. Were he to lose his job, he says, everything could slip away with it. What kind of job could a guy without a college degree get? One night, while talking to his wife about his life, he used the word "trapped."

"Looking back, I wish I had gotten that degree," Mr. Blevins said in his soft-spoken lilt. "Four years seemed like a thousand years then. But I wish I would have just put in my four years."

❧

The Barriers

Why so many low-income students fall from the college ranks is a question without a simple answer. Many high schools do a poor job of preparing teenagers for college. Many of the colleges where lower-income students tend to enroll have limited resources and offer a narrow range of majors, leaving some students disenchanted and unwilling to continue.

Then there is the cost. Tuition bills scare some students from even applying and leave others with years of debt. To Mr. Blevins, like many other students of limited means, every week of going to classes seemed like another week of losing money—money that might have been made at a job.

"The system makes a false promise to students," said John T. Casteen III, the president of the University of Virginia, himself the son of a Virginia shipyard worker.

Colleges, Mr. Casteen said, present themselves as meritocracies in which academic ability and hard work are always rewarded. In fact, he said, many working-class students face obstacles they cannot overcome on their own.

For much of his 15 years as Virginia's president, Mr. Casteen has focused on raising money and expanding the university, the most prestigious in the state. In the meantime, students with backgrounds like his have become ever scarcer on campus. The university's genteel nickname, the Cavaliers, and its aristocratic sword-crossed coat of arms seem appropriate today. No flagship state university has a smaller proportion of low-income students than Virginia. Just 8 percent of undergraduates last year came from families in the bottom half of the income distribution, down from 11 percent a decade ago.

That change sneaked up on him, Mr. Casteen said, and he has spent a good part of the last year trying to prevent it from becoming part of his legacy. Starting with next fall's freshman class, the university will charge no tuition and require no loans for students whose parents make less than twice the poverty level, or about $37,700 a year for a family of four. The university has also increased financial aid to middle-income students.

To Mr. Casteen, these are steps to remove what he describes as "artificial barriers" to a college education placed in the way of otherwise deserving students. Doing so "is a fundamental obligation of a free culture," he said.

But the deterrents to a degree can also be homegrown. Many low-income teenagers know few people who have made it through college. A majority of the nongraduates are young men, and some come from towns where the factory work ethic, to get working as soon as possible, remains strong, even if the factories themselves are vanishing. Whatever the reasons, college just does not feel normal.

"You get there and you start to struggle," said Leanna Blevins, Andy's older sister, who did get a bachelor's degree and then went on to earn a Ph.D at Virginia studying the college experiences of poor students. "And at home your parents are trying to be supportive and say, 'Well, if you're not happy, if it's not right for you, come back home. It's O.K.' And they think they're doing the right thing. But they don't know that maybe what the student needs is to hear them say, 'Stick it out just one semester. You can do it. Just stay there. Come home on the weekend, but stick it out.'"

Today, Ms. Blevins, petite and high-energy, is helping to start a new college a few hours' drive from Chilhowie for low-income students. Her brother said he had daydreamed about attending it and had talked to her about how he might return to college.

For her part, Ms. Blevins says, she has daydreamed about having a life that would seem as natural as her brother's, a life in which she would not feel like an outsider in her hometown. Once, when a high-school teacher asked students to list their goals for the next decade, Ms. Blevins wrote, "having a college degree" and "not being married."

"I think my family probably thinks I'm liberal," Ms. Blevins, who is now married, said with a laugh, "that I've just been educated too much and I'm gettin' above my raisin'."

Her brother said that he just wanted more control over his life, not a new one. At a time when many people complain of scattered lives, Mr. Blevins can stand in one spot—his church parking lot, next to a graveyard—and take in much of his world. "That's my parents' house," he said one day, pointing to a sliver of roof visible over a hill. "That's my uncle's trailer. My grandfather is buried here. I'll probably be buried here."

Taking Class into Account

Opening up colleges to new kinds of students has generally meant one thing over the last generation: affirmative action. Intended to right the wrongs of years of exclusion, the programs have swelled the number of women, blacks and Latinos on campuses. But affirmative action was never supposed to address broad economic inequities, just the ones that stem from specific kinds of discrimination.

That is now beginning to change. Like Virginia, a handful of other colleges are not only increasing financial aid but also promising to give weight to economic class in granting admissions. They say they want to make an effort to admit more low-income students, just as they now do for minorities and children of alumni.

"The great colleges and universities were designed to provide for mobility, to seek out talent," said Anthony W. Marx, president of Amherst College. "If we are blind to the educational disadvantages associated with need, we will simply replicate these disadvantages while appearing to make decisions based on merit."

With several populous states having already banned race-based preferences and the United States Supreme Court suggesting that it may outlaw such programs in a couple of decades, the future of affirmative action may well revolve around economics. Polls consistently show that programs based on class backgrounds have wider support than those based on race.

The explosion in the number of nongraduates has also begun to get the attention of policy makers. This year, New York became one of a small group of states to tie college financing more closely to graduation rates, rewarding colleges more for moving students along than for simply admitting them. Nowhere is the stratification of education more vivid than here in Virginia, where Thomas Jefferson once tried, and failed, to set up the nation's first public high schools. At a modest high school in the Tidewater city of Portsmouth, not far from Mr. Casteen's boyhood home, a guidance office wall filled with college pennants does not include one from rarefied Virginia. The colleges whose pennants are up—Old Dominion University and others that seem in the realm of the possible—have far lower graduation rates.

Across the country, the upper middle class so dominates elite universities that high-income students, on average, actually get slightly more financial aid from colleges than low-income students do. These elite colleges are so expensive that even many high-income students receive large grants. In the early 1990's, by contrast, poorer students got 50 percent more aid on average than the wealthier ones, according to the College Board, the organization that runs the SAT entrance exams.

At the other end of the spectrum are community colleges, the two-year institutions that are intended to be feeders for four-year colleges. In nearly every one are tales of academic success against tremendous odds: a battered wife or a combat veteran or a laid-off worker on the way to a better life. But over all, community colleges tend to be places where dreams are put on hold.

Most people who enroll say they plan to get a four-year degree eventually; few actually do. Full-time jobs, commutes and children or parents who need care often get in the way. One recent national survey found that about 75 percent of students enrolling in community colleges said they hoped to transfer to a four-year institution. But only 17 percent of those who had entered in the mid-1990's made the switch within five years, according to a separate study. The rest were out working or still studying toward the two-year degree.

"We here in Virginia do a good job of getting them in," said Glenn Dubois, chancellor of the Virginia Community College System and himself a community college graduate. "We have to get better in getting them out."

◌ᴗ

"I Wear a Tie Every Day"

College degree or not, Mr. Blevins has the kind of life that many Americans say they aspire to. He fills it with family, friends, church and a five-handicap golf game. He does not sit in traffic commuting to an office park. He does not talk wistfully of a relocated brother or best friend he sees only twice a year. He does not worry about who will care for his son while he works and his wife attends community college to become a physical therapist. His grandparents down the street watch Lucas, just as they took care of Andy and his two sisters when they were children. When Mr. Blevins comes home from work, it is his turn to play with Lucas, tossing him into the air and rolling around on the floor with him and a stuffed elephant.

Mr. Blevins also sings in a quartet called the Gospel Gentlemen. One member is his brother-in-law; another lives on Mr. Blevins's street. In the long white van the group owns, they wend their way along mountain roads on their way to singing dates at local church functions, sometimes harmonizing, sometimes ribbing one another or talking about where to buy golf equipment.

Inside the churches, the other singers often talk to the audience between songs, about God or a grandmother or what a song means to them. Mr. Blevins rarely does, but his shyness fades once he is back in the van with his friends.

At the warehouse, he is usually the first to arrive, around 6:30 in the morning. The grandson of a coal miner, he takes pride, he says, in having moved up to become a supermarket buyer. He decides which bananas, grapes, onions and potatoes the company will sell and makes sure that there are always enough. Most people with his job have graduated from college.

"I'm pretty fortunate to not have a degree but have a job where I wear a tie every day," he said.

He worries about how long it will last, though, mindful of what happened to his father, Dwight, a decade ago. A high school graduate, Dwight Blevins was laid off from his own warehouse job and ended up with another one that paid less and offered a smaller pension.

"A lot of places, they're not looking that you're trained in something," Andy Blevins said one evening, sitting on his back porch. "They just want you to have a degree."

Figuring out how to get one is the core quandary facing the nation's college nongraduates. Many seem to want one. In a New York Times poll, 43 percent of them called it essential to success, while 42 percent of college graduates and 32 percent of high-school dropouts did. This in itself is a change from the days when "college boy" was an insult in many working-class neighborhoods. But once students take a break—the phrase that many use instead of drop out—the ideal can quickly give way to reality. Family and work can make a return to school seem even harder than finishing it in the first place.

After dropping out of Radford, Andy Blevins enrolled part-time in a community college, trying to juggle work and studies. He lasted a year. From time to time in the decade since, he has thought about giving it another try. But then he has wondered if that would be crazy. He works every third Saturday, and his phone rings on Sundays when there is a problem with the supply of potatoes or apples. "It never ends," he said. "There's a never a lull."

To spend more time with Lucas, Mr. Blevins has already cut back on his singing. If he took night classes, he said, when would he ever see his little boy? Anyway, he said, it would take years to get a degree part-time. To him, it is a tug of war between living in the present and sacrificing for the future.

༄

Few Breaks for the Needy

The college admissions system often seems ruthlessly meritocratic. Yes, children of alumni still have an advantage. But many other pillars of the old system—the polite rejections of women or blacks, the spots reserved for graduates of Choate and Exeter—have crumbled.

This was the meritocracy Mr. Casteen described when he greeted the parents of freshmen in a University of Virginia lecture hall late last summer. Hailing from all 50 states and 52 foreign countries, the students were more intelligent and better prepared than he and his classmates had been, he told the parents in his quiet, deep voice. The class included 17 students with a perfect SAT score.

If anything, children of privilege think that the system has moved so far from its old-boy history that they are now at a disadvantage when they apply, because colleges are trying to diversify their student rolls. To get into a good college, the sons and daughters of the upper middle class often talk of needing a higher SAT score than, say, an applicant who grew up on a farm, in a ghetto or in a factory town. Some state legislators from Northern Virginia's affluent suburbs have argued that this is a form of geographic discrimination and have quixotically proposed bills to outlaw it.

But the conventional wisdom is not quite right. The elite colleges have not been giving much of a break to the low-income students who apply. When William G. Bowen, a former president of Princeton, looked at admissions records recently, he found that if test scores were equal a low-income student had no better chance than a high-income one of getting into a group of 19 colleges, including Harvard, Yale, Princeton, Williams and Virginia. Athletes, legacy applicants and minority students all got in with lower scores on average. Poorer students did not.

The findings befuddled many administrators, who insist that admissions officers have tried to give poorer applicants a leg up. To emphasize the point, Virginia announced this spring that it was changing its admissions policy from "need blind"—a term long used to assure applicants that they would not be punished for seeking financial aid—to "need conscious." Administrators at Amherst and Harvard have also recently said that they would redouble their efforts to take into account the obstacles students have overcome.

"The same score reflects more ability when you come from a less fortunate background," Mr. Summers, the president of Harvard, said. "You haven't had a chance to take the test-prep course. You went to a school that didn't do as good a job coaching you for the test. You came from a home without the same opportunities for learning."

But it is probably not a coincidence that elite colleges have not yet turned this sentiment into action. Admitting large numbers of low-income students could bring clear complications. Too many in a freshman class would probably lower the college's average SAT score, thereby damaging its ranking by *U.S. News & World Report,* a leading arbiter of academic prestige. Some colleges, like Emory University in Atlanta, have climbed fast in the rankings over precisely the same period in which their percentage of low-income students has tumbled. The math is simple: when a college goes looking for applicants with high SAT scores, it is far more likely to find them among well-off teenagers.

More spots for low-income applicants might also mean fewer for the children of alumni, who make up the fund-raising base for universities. More generous financial aid policies will probably lead to higher tuition for those students who can afford the list price. Higher tuition, lower ranking, tougher admission requirements: they do not make for an easy marketing pitch to alumni clubs around the country. But Mr. Casteen and his colleagues are going ahead, saying the pendulum has swung too far in one direction.

That was the mission of John Blackburn, Virginia's easy-going admissions dean, when he rented a car and took to the road recently. Mr. Blackburn thought of the trip as a reprise of the drives Mr. Casteen took 25 years earlier, when he was the admissions dean, traveling to churches and community centers to persuade black parents that the university was finally interested in their children.

One Monday night, Mr. Blackburn came to Big Stone Gap, in a mostly poor corner of the state not far from Andy Blevins's town. A community college there was holding a college fair, and Mr. Blackburn set up a table in a hallway, draping it with the University of Virginia's blue and orange flag.

As students came by, Mr. Blackburn would explain Virginia's new admissions and financial aid policies. But he soon realized that the Virginia name might have been scaring off the very people his pitch was intended for. Most of the students who did approach the table showed little interest in the financial aid and expressed little need for it. One man walked up to Mr. Blackburn and introduced his son as an aspiring doctor. The father was an ophthalmologist. Other doctors came by, too. So did some lawyers.

"You can't just raise the UVa flag," Mr. Blackburn said, packing up his materials at the end of the night, "and expect a lot of low-income kids to come out."

When the applications started arriving in his office this spring, there seemed to be no increase in those from low-income students. So Mr. Blackburn extended the deadline two weeks for everybody, and his colleagues also helped some applicants with the maze of financial aid forms. Of 3,100 incoming freshmen, it now seems that about 180 will qualify for the new financial aid program, up from 130 who would have done so last year. It is not a huge number, but Virginia administrators call it a start.

◦◦◦

A Big Decision

On a still-dark February morning, with the winter's heaviest snowfall on the ground, Andy Blevins scraped off his Jeep and began his daily drive to the supermarket warehouse. As he passed the home of Mike Nash, his neighbor and fellow gospel singer, he noticed that the car was still in the driveway. For Mr. Nash, a school counselor and the only college graduate in the singing group, this was a snow day.

Mr. Blevins later sat down with his calendar and counted to 280: the number of days he had worked last year. Two hundred and eighty days—six days a week most of the time—without ever really knowing what the future would hold.

"I just realized I'm going to have to do something about this," he said, "because it's never going to end."

In the weeks afterward, his daydreaming about college and his conversations about it with his sister Leanna turned into serious research. He requested his transcripts from Radford and from Virginia Highlands Community College and figured out that he had about a year's worth of credits. He also talked to Leanna about how he could become an elementary school teacher. He always felt that he could relate to children, he said. The job would take up 180 days, not 280. Teachers do not usually get laid off or lose their pensions or have to take a big pay cut to find new work.

So the decision was made. On May 31, Andy Blevins says, he will return to Virginia Highlands, taking classes at night; the Gospel Gentlemen are no longer booking performances. After a year, he plans to take classes by video and on the Web that are offered at the community college but run by Old Dominion, a Norfolk, Va., university with a big group of working-class students.

"I don't like classes, but I've gotten so motivated to go back to school," Mr. Blevins said. "I don't want to, but, then again, I do."

He thinks he can get his bachelor's degree in three years. If he gets it at all, he will have defied the odds.

Textual Questions

1. Why, in paragraph 7, does Leonhardt include the information that dropouts are most likely to be from poor or working-class families? How does this make the story of Andy Blevins more than a simple story about one dropout's experience?

2. What does Leonhardt mean when he refers to educational privileges as an "inherited meritocracy"?

3. For what reasons do lower income students drop out of college, according to Leonhardt? Is his presentation of these reasons convincing? Are there other possible reasons that you can think of?

Rhetorical Questions

4. What argument—intentionally or unintentionally—does Leonhardt make about education, race, class, and gender in America?

5. How does Leonhardt use the story of Andy Blevins to organize his essay? Is this organization built around a narrative thread effective or ineffective? Why?

6. How does Leonhardt use traditional and nontraditional definitions of Affirmative Action to construct his argument?

Intertextual Questions

7. In what ways do Mike Rose and bell hooks (in this chapter) make arguments similar to Leonhardt? How do the arguments of these three writers compare/contrast?

8. Consider the essay by Barbara Ehrenreich at the end of Chapter 5. In what ways does the argument that Leonhardt makes here—about class, employment, and so on—echo the arguments that Ehrenreich makes in her essay?

Thinking Beyond the Text

9. Interview at least three people in one of your classes. What brought them to college? What keeps them there? What do they hope to do when they graduate? In your own estimation, does the information you gathered confirm or reject Leonhardt's arguments about class and education in America?

10. Consider your personal and family history. What social class would you label yourself as being a part of? Why? What jobs do the members of your immediate family hold? Aside from student, what job (or jobs) do you currently hold? How much security do any of these jobs afford? Is job security part of the reason you have chosen to pursue a given profession?

For Writing & Discussion

11. Searching online or in professional journals for your major field of study, find official statistics for education, pay, and employment for people in your chosen profession. In an essay, analyze the data you have found. Does the information make you feel hopeful for your professional future? Or is the future (possibly) more grim than you would have hoped? Did you find any of the information you located surprising? Does the information you found contradict what you know and/or have been told by others in your field?

FOCAL POINT

Exploring Images of The Promise of Education

FOCAL POINT

Exploring Images of The Promise of Education

Questions

1. How does the image on page 226 (top) show the reality of segregation and integration in American schools throughout much of the twentieth century? In this photograph, the African-American student sits apart from his classmates. Based on this student's placement, what mood does the photograph convey? What other elements in this photograph contribute to the mood? Do you think the African-American student faced the same, more, or fewer academic challenges than his white counterparts? Why?

2. In the photograph on page 226 (bottom), angry white students harass an African-American student on her first day of class. What could the African-American student have been thinking as she walked through the crowd to her new school? Do you think her thoughts were similar or different than the African-American student portrayed in the photograph on page 226 (top)? What message does this photograph send to viewers about the reaction of white students to school integration? How do you think the nation reacted to this photograph? How does this photograph make you feel about school integration? Why?

3. What aspects of the photograph on page 227 (top) suggest that it is a modern American classroom (rather than a classroom from the past or from another nation)? If the picture on page 226 (top) sends a message about school integration in its early years, then what message does this photograph send?

4. Although the student standing at the snack machine and digging for his wallet dominates the foreground of this photograph on page 227 (bottom), what image dominates the background? Put together, what point about modern American schools do the foreground and background images in this photograph suggest?

5. How do the two characters in this comic—Zipper and Cricket—compare and contrast with one another (page 228)? What setting are they in and why? What argument does this cartoon make about modern college students and the choices they may make? Does this argument only apply to today's students or would it apply to college students from past decades as well?

THE PROMISE OF A FREE PRESS

Few Americans ever meet the individuals who make the decisions affecting public and private life in this nation. In a nation of almost 300 million people, individual citizens have, realistically, a 0 percent chance of actually meeting and talking with the President of the United States and an only slightly better chance with a Senator or Representative (although we might get a quick handshake during a biannual election stop). Even at the lower levels of government, from the state governor to the local mayor, public access to publicly elected leaders is slim—yet the decisions these women and men make govern our lives, from laws about the legality or illegality of abortion to allocations of city budget expenditures to maintain the roads around our homes. This limited access to the representatives who wield power in our name is a feature of any republican democracy rather than being either a weakness or criticism.

What we know of these decision makers, we know secondhand at best. This is also true of our knowledge of most things beyond our own locality, family, and circle of friends. Our knowledge of national and international events, like our knowledge of the decisions of local and national leaders, comes to us through the news media. We read the local newspaper and watch the news on local television network affiliates. We listen to local and national radio broadcasts and consult Web sites—from the *New York Times* online to blogs by citizens in Iraq.

In short, we put together our picture of the world beyond our door via a patchwork of information provided in various media. And we make decisions about how to live based upon this information, from our choice of toothpaste to our vote for senator.

The Founding Fathers understood that a republican democracy is built not only on an educated citizenry but also on an informed citizenry, and thus they protected the freedom of the press in the First Amendment to the U.S. Constitution. This system breaks down, however, in two ways: (1) When the information provided by the news media is fundamentally flawed and (2) when the freedom of the press itself is denied. The readings in this chapter will lead you through a consideration of both of these breakdowns—in theory and in practice.

The information provided by the news media is flawed when it is incorrect, of course. When such flawed information is provided inadvertently, through simple human error, it is usually corrected and/or retracted, though often such retractions are published or broadcast only in obscure places. But incorrect information also comes from a source other than human error: bias. When information is presented in a biased way, favoring one political party over another, for example, the information may be incorrect by omission—incorrect because it is incomplete—or even by deliberate distortion. Bias can also be caused by less obvious means: The selection of images to accompany a story on poverty could, for example, focus on members of one racial group more than another, thus making the story "about" poverty among that racial group. Or a story about President George W. Bush could, by only including the commentary of politically liberal experts, be biased against the president.

Like incorrect information, infringing on the freedom of the press is not necessarily a deliberate act, although deliberate acts of censorship do occur. In 2004, for example, the ABC News program *Nightline* aired an episode titled "The Fallen," in which the newsanchor read the names and displayed the photographs of soldiers killed during the war in Iraq; the Sinclair Broadcast Group, believing that this program was an attack against President Bush and his policies toward Iraq, refused to allow this episode of *Nightline* to air on its eight ABC affiliates. While the program aired without incident at hundreds of ABC affiliates across America, the freedom of journalists at those eight affiliates was denied, and viewers in those broadcast areas were denied even the chance to choose or refuse to watch this program. While this decision by the Sinclair Broadcast Group was an example of a direct act of censorship—like a librarian taking a book out of circulation because he/she finds its political commentary offensive—it also suggests the much larger danger to the freedom of the press in America: the possible dangers of corporate ownership. In modern America, the "free press" is embodied in the "news business," and the "news business" is, obviously, a *business*. To continue to exist, businesses must be profitable, and the demands of the profit margin are not necessarily conducive to the demands of good journalism, which may occasionally outrage its customers with inconvenient truths. Thus the freedom of the press, in an ideal sense, is likely on occasion to call up what we might call corporate censorship, as the drive for larger and larger profits conflicts with the demands of good journalism.

As you read the selections in this chapter, consider these questions: Is a free press, guaranteed by the U.S. Constitution, even possible, or is it a promise that is bound to be broken? Is unbiased coverage of events possible, and if so, then how? Most importantly, consider how citizens can make decisions about their lives—about how to vote, about what to believe about their nation and the world—given that most information is mediated by a journalist who works for a corporation that is owned by a larger corporation that is, at the highest levels, likely to be tied to the political interests of the powerful elite. Or is the recent popularity of computer blogs an underground answer to such potential bias?

WALTER LIPPMANN

Walter Lippmann (1889–1974) was one of the twentieth century's most influential political journalists and critics of the press. Graduating from Harvard in 1910, Lippmann worked as a newspaper reporter, assistant to famous muckraking journalist Lincoln Steffens and a secretary to a mayor before publishing his first book, *A Preface to Politics*, in 1913 and becoming one of the founding editors of the *New Republic* in 1914. During World War I, he was an advisor to President Woodrow Wilson and helped draft Wilson's *Fourteen Points*. He wrote several important books about the press, politics, and public opinion, as well, and wrote a regular long-running and influential political column for the *New York Herald Tribune* and then the *Washington Post*.

"Censorship and Privacy" is from Lippmann's 1922 book *Public Opinion*. In the book, Lippmann analyzed public opinion and how it is influenced by politics and the media.

Censorship and Privacy

∾ Prereading Question

How much control should the military have over the ways in which journalists cover ongoing military conflicts? How could media coverage harm members of the military, directly and indirectly? Does the potential for harm mean the media should be tightly controlled?

1

The picture of a general presiding over an editorial conference at the most terrible hour of one of the great battles of history seems more like a scene from *The Chocolate Soldier* than a page from life. Yet we know at first hand

from the officer who edited the French communiqués that these conferences were a regular part of the business of war; that in the worst moment
of Verdun, General Joffre and his cabinet met and argued over the nouns,
adjectives, and verbs that were to be printed in the newspapers the
next morning.

"The evening communiqué of the twenty-third (February 1916)"
says M. de Pierrefeu,[1] "was edited in a dramatic atmosphere. M. Berthelot, of the Prime Minister's office, had just telephoned by order of
the minister asking General Pellé to strengthen the report and to
emphasize the proportions of the enemy's attack. It was necessary
to prepare the public for the worst outcome in case the affair turned into
a catastrophe. This anxiety showed clearly that neither at G. H. Q. nor at
the Ministry of War had the Government found reason for confidence.
As M. Berthelot spoke, General Pellé made notes. He handed me the
paper on which he had written the Government's wishes, together with
the order of the day issues by General von Deimling and found on some
prisoners, in which it was stated that this attack was the supreme offensive to secure peace. Skilfully used, all this was to demonstrate that
Germany was letting loose a gigantic effort, an effort without precedent,
and that from its success she hoped for the end of the war. The logic of
this was that nobody need be surprised at our withdrawal. When, a half
hour later, I went down with my manuscript, I found gathered together
in Colonel Claudel's office, he being away, the major-general, General
Janin, Colonel Dupont, and Lieutenant-Colonel Renouard. Fearing that
I would not succeed in giving the desired impression, General Pellé had
himself prepared a proposed communiqué. I read what I had just done.
It was found to be too moderate. General Pellé's, on the other hand,
seemed too alarming. I had purposely omitted von Deimling's order of
the day. To put it into the communiqué *would be to break with the
formula to which the public was accustomed,* would be to transform it
into a kind of pleading. It would seem to say: 'How do you suppose we
can resist?' There was reason to fear that the public would be distracted
by this change of tone and would believe that everything was lost.
I explained my reasons and suggested giving Deimling's text to the
newspapers in the form of a separate note.

"Opinion being divided, General Pellé went to ask General de Castel-
nau to come and decide finally. The General arrived smiling, quiet and
good humored, said a few pleasant words about this new kind of literary
council of war, and looked at the texts. He chose the simpler one, gave
more weight to the first phrase, inserted the words 'as had been anticipated,' which supply a reassuring quality, and was flatly against inserting
von Deimling's order, but was for transmitting it to the press in a special

[1]G. Q. G., pp. 126–129.

note. . . " General *Joffre* that evening read the communiqué carefully and approved it.

Within a few hours those two or three hundred words would be read all over the world. They would paint a picture in men's minds of what was happening on the slopes of Verdun, and in front of that picture people would take heart or despair. The shopkeeper in Brest, the peasant in Lorraine, the deputy in the Palais Bourbon, the editor in Amsterdam or Minneapolis had to be kept in hope, and yet prepared to accept possible defeat without yielding to panic. They are told, therefore, that the loss of ground is no surprise to the French Command. They are taught to regard the affair as serious, but not strange. Now, as a matter of fact, the French General Staff was not fully prepared for the German offensive. Supporting trenches had not been dug, alternative roads had not been built, barbed wire was lacking. But to confess that would have aroused images in the heads of civilians that might well have turned a reverse into a disaster. The High Command could be disappointed, and yet pull itself together; the people at home and abroad, full of uncertainties, and with none of the professional man's singleness of purpose, might on the basis of a complete story have lost sight of the war in a mêlée of faction and counter-faction about the competence of the officers. Instead, therefore, of letting the public act on all the facts which the generals knew, the authorities presented only certain facts, and these only in such a way as would be most likely to steady the people.

In this case the men who arranged the pseudo-environment knew what the real one was. But a few days later an incident occurred about which the French Staff did not know the truth. The Germans announced[2] that on the previous afternoon they had taken Fort Douaumont by assault. At French headquarters in Chantilly no one could understand this news. For on the morning of the twenty-fifth, after the engagement of the XXth corps, the battle had taken a turn for the better. Reports from the front said nothing about Douaumont. But inquiry showed that the German report was true, though no one as yet knew how the fort had been taken. In the meantime, the German communiqué was being flashed around the world, and the French had to say something. So headquarters explained. "In the midst of total ignorance at Chantilly about the way the attack had taken place, we imagined, in the evening communiqué of the 26th, a plan of the attack which certainly had a thousand to one chance of being true." The communiqué of this imaginary battle read:

A bitter struggle is taking place around Fort de Douaumont which is an advanced post of the old defensive organization of Verdun. The position taken this morning by the enemy, *after several unsuccessful assaults that cost him very*

[2]On February 26, 1916. Pierrefeu, G. Q. G., pp. 133 et seq.

heavy losses, has been reached again and passed by our troops whom the enemy has not been able to drive back.[3]

What had actually happened differed from both the French and German accounts. While changing troops in the line, the position had somehow been forgotten in a confusion of orders. Only a battery commander and a few men remained in the fort. Some German soldiers, seeing the door open, had crawled into the fort, and taken everyone inside prisoner. A little later the French who were on the slopes of the hill were horrified at being shot at from the fort. There had been no battle at Douaumont and no losses. Nor had the French troops advanced beyond it as the communiqués seemed to say. They were beyond it on either side, to be sure, but the fort was in enemy hands.

Yet from the communiqué everyone believed that the fort was half surrounded. The words did not explicitly say so, but "the press, as usual, forced the pace." Military writers concluded that the Germans would soon have to surrender. In a few days they began to ask themselves why the garrison, since it lacked food, had not yet surrendered. "It was necessary through the press bureau to request them to drop the encirclement theme."[4]

∾

2

The editor of the French communiqué tells us that as the battle dragged out, his colleagues and he set out to neutralize the pertinacity of the Germans by continual insistence on their terrible losses. It is necessary to remember that at this time, and in fact until late in 1917, the orthodox view of the war for all the Allied peoples was that it would be decided by "attrition." Nobody believed in a war of movement. It was insisted that strategy did not count, or diplomacy. It was simply a matter of killing Germans. The general public more or less believed the dogma, but it had constantly to be reminded of it in face of spectacular German successes.

[3]This is my own translation: the English translation from London published in the *New York Times* of Sunday, Feb. 27, is as follows:

> London, Feb 26 (1916). A furious struggle has been in progress around Fort de Douaumont which is an advance element of the old defensive organization of Verdun fortresses. The position captured this morning by the enemy after several fruitless assaults which cost him extremely heavy losses, (*) was reached again and gone beyond by our troops, which all the attempts of the enemy have not been able to push back."

(*) The French text says "pertes très élevées." Thus the English translation exaggerates the original text.

[4]Pierrefeu, *ap. cit.,* pp. 134–135.

"Almost no day passed but the communiqué. . . . ascribed to the Germans with some appearance of justice heavy losses, extremely heavy, spoke of bloody sacrifices, heaps of corpses, hecatombs. Likewise the wireless constantly used the statistics of the intelligence bureau at Verdun, whose chief, Major Cointet, had invented a method of calculating German losses which obviously produced marvelous results. Every fortnight the figures increased a hundred thousand or so. These 300,000, 400,000, 500,000 casualties put out, divided into daily, weekly, monthly losses, repeated in all sorts of ways, produced a striking effect. Our formulae varied little: 'according to prisoners the German losses in the course of the attack have been considerable '. . . 'it is proved that the losses' . . . 'the enemy exhausted by his losses has not renewed the attack' . . . Certain formulae, later abandoned because they had been overworked, were used each day: 'under our artillery and machine gun fire' . . . 'mowed down by our artillery and machine gun fire' . . . Constant repetition impressed the neutrals and Germany itself, and helped to create a bloody background in spite of the denials from Nauen (the German wireless) which tried vainly to destroy the bad effect of this perpetual repetition."[5]

The thesis of the French Command, which it wished to establish publicly by these reports, was formulated as follows for the guidance of the censors:

> This offensive engages the active forces of our opponent whose manpower is declining. We have learned that the class of 1916 is already at the front. There will remain the 1917 class already being called up, and the resources of the third category (men above forty-five, or convalescents). In a few weeks, the German forces exhausted by this effort, will find themselves confronted with all the forces of the coalition (ten millions against seven millions).[6]

According to M. de Pierrefeu, the French command had converted itself to this belief. "By an extraordinary aberration of mind, only the attrition of the enemy was seen; it appeared that our forces were not subject to attrition. General Nivelle shared these ideas. We saw the result in 1917."

We have learned to call this propaganda. A group of men, who can prevent independent access to the event, arrange the news of it to suit their purpose. That the purpose was in this case patriotic does not affect the argument at all. They used their power to make the Allied publics see affairs as they desired them to be seen. The casualty figures of Major Cointet which were spread about the world are of the same order. They were intended to provoke a particular kind of inference, namely that the war of attrition was going in favor of the French. But the inference is not

[5]*Op. cit.*, pp. 138–139.
[6]*Op. cit.*, p. 147.

drawn in the form of argument. It results almost automatically from the creation of a mental picture of endless Germans slaughtered on the hills about Verdun. By putting the dead Germans in the focus of the picture, and by omitting to mention the French dead, a very special view of the battle was built up. It was a view designed to neutralize the effects of German territorial advances and the impression of power which the persistence of the offensive was making. It was also a view that tended to make the public acquiesce in the demoralizing defensive strategy imposed upon the Allied armies. For the public, accustomed to the idea that war consists of great strategic movements, flank attacks, encirclements, and dramatic surrenders, had gradually to forget that picture in favor of the terrible idea that by matching lives the war would be won. Through its control over all news from the front, the General Staff substituted a view of the facts that comported with this strategy.

The General Staff of an army in the field is so placed that within wide limits it can control what the public will perceive. It controls the selection of correspondents who go to the front, controls their movements at the front, reads and censors their messages from the front, and operates the wires. The Government behind the army by its command of cables and passports, mails and custom houses and blockades increases the control. It emphasizes it by legal power over publishers, over public meetings, and by its secret service. But in the case of an army the control is far from perfect. There is always the enemy's communiqué, which in these days of wireless cannot be kept away from neutrals. Above all there is the talk of the soldiers, which blows back from the front, and is spread about when they are on leave.[7] An army is an unwieldy thing. And that is why the naval and diplomatic censorship is almost always much more complete. Fewer people know what is going on, and their acts are more easily supervised.

3

Without some form of censorship, propaganda in the strict sense of the word is impossible. In order to conduct a propaganda there must be some barrier between the public and the event. Access to the real environment must be limited, before anyone can create a pseudo-environment that he thinks wise or desirable. For while people who have direct access can misconceive what they see, no one else can decide how they shall misconceive it, unless he can decide where they shall look, and at what. The military censorship is the

---

[7]For weeks prior to the American attack at St. Mihiel and in the Argonne-Meuse, everybody in France told everybody else the deep secret.

simplest form of barrier, but by no means the most important, because it is known to exist, and is therefore in certain measure agreed to and discounted.

At different times and for different subjects some men impose and other men accept a particular standard of secrecy. The frontier between what is concealed because publication is not, as we say, "compatible with the public interest" fades gradually into what is concealed because it is believed to be none of the public's business. The notion of what constitutes a person's private affairs is elastic. Thus the amount of a man's fortune is considered a private affair, and careful provision is made in the income tax law to keep it as private as possible. The sale of a piece of land is not private, but the price may be. Salaries are generally treated as more private than wages, incomes as more private than inheritances. A person's credit rating is given only a limited circulation. The profits of big corporations are more public than those of small firms. Certain kinds of conversation, between man and wife, lawyer and client, doctor and patient, priest and communicant, are privileged. Directors' meetings are generally private. So are many political conferences. Most of what is said at a cabinet meeting, or by an ambassador to the Secretary of State, or at private interviews, or dinner tables, is private. Many people regard the contract between employer and employee as private. There was a time when the affairs of all corporations were held to be as private as a man's theology is to-day. There was a time before that when his theology was held to be as public a matter as the color of his eyes. But infectious diseases, on the other hand, were once as private as the processes of a man's digestion. The history of the notion of privacy would be an entertaining tale. Sometimes the notions violently conflict, as they did when the Bolsheviks published the secret treaties, or when Mr. Hughes investigated the life insurance companies, or when somebody's scandal exudes from the pages of Town Topics to the front pages of Mr. Hearst's newspapers.

Whether the reasons for privacy are good or bad, the barriers exist. Privacy is insisted upon at all kinds of places in the area of what is called public affairs. It is often very illuminating, therefore, to ask yourself how you got at the facts on which you base your opinion. Who actually saw, heard, felt, counted, named the thing, about which you have an opinion? Was it the man who told you, or the man who told him, or someone still further removed? And how much was he permitted to see? When he informs you that France thinks this and that, what part of France did he watch? How was he able to watch it? Where was he when he watched it? What Frenchmen was he permitted to talk to, what newspapers did he read, and where did they learn what they say? You can ask yourself these questions, but you can rarely answer them. They will remind you, however, of the distance which often separates your public opinion from the event with which it deals. And the reminder is itself a protection.

Textual Questions

1. Lippmann opens his essay with a story about control exerted by the French military over the way in which the ongoing battle for Verdun would be described in the newspaper. Why open with this story? What point does it make that summarizes Lippmann's overall point in the essay?

2. What does it mean that the description of the battle drafted by the military leaders created a "pseudo-environment"?

3. How does Lippmann define "propaganda"? What examples does he use to construct this definition?

Rhetorical Questions

4. Lippmann's argument is divided into three sections. How does section 1 logically build to section 2? How do both section 1 and 2 build logically to section 3? Would the essay be just as effective without the clear divisions into sections?

5. According to Lippmann, how is the making of inferences a part of the creation of propaganda? Would you agree with Lippmann's arguments about propaganda and patriotism in section 2 of his essay?

6. How is censorship a necessary component of propaganda, according to Lippmann? Are there other forms of propaganda that Lippmann's definition does not account for?

Intertextual Questions

7. How are Lippmann's arguments about the military and propaganda similar to Ben H. Bagdikian's arguments (later in this chapter) about business interests and media bias? Is media bias a form of propaganda? Whom does such bias serve?

8. How does Lippmann's definition of propaganda compare to the definition offered by Edward S. Herman and Noam Chomsky (the following reading)?

Thinking Beyond the Text

9. Searching in your school library, find at least two accounts on the siege of Verdun in World War I. How do the accounts you have found confirm/refute Lippmann's arguments about propaganda?

10. Is propaganda just another name for someone else's version of the truth? During a time of war, does every nation necessarily engage in propagandizing its efforts toward victory?

For Writing & Discussion

11. Consider the military conflicts that have taken place during your lifetime. Searching online, find video news coverage of one event from one of these conflicts. In an essay, summarize the news coverage and describe the ways in which it seems, to you, to be propaganda (or not to be propaganda).

EDWARD S. HERMAN AND NOAM CHOMSKY

Noam Chomsky, a professor at the Massachusetts Institute of Technology, is considered one of the most important intellectuals of the twentieth century. In the 1950s, he revolutionized the field of linguistics by proposing a theory of "universal grammar," which suggests that all people are born with language-learning capabilities and all languages have underlying similarities that people are born to acquire. Chomsky went on to become an important social critic and theorist, writing books about American foreign policy, politics, and the mass media. He has written more than 70 books. Edward S. Herman, professor emeritus at the University of Pennsylvania, is an economist and media analyst. He is the author of several books, including three co-authored with Chomsky.

"Propaganda Mill" was first published in 1988 in the journal *The Progressive.* That same year, Herman and Chomsky's *Manufacturing Consent: The Political Economy of the Mass Media* was published. The book, like "Propaganda Mill," claims that the media purposefully misinform the American public about the U.S. government, functioning more as propagandists rather than a free and informative press.

Propaganda Mill

◌ **Prereading Question**

Consider the relationship between a news reporter and his/her subject. In what ways are the reporter and the subject dependent upon one another? Can either be antagonistic to the other? (For example, can a reporter who covers Washington politics be a harsh critic of Washington politics?)

It is a primary function of the mass media in the United States to mobilize public support for the special interests that dominate the Government and the private sector.

This is our conclusion after years of studying the media. Perhaps it is an obvious point—but the common assumption seems to be that the media are independent and committed to discovering and reporting the truth. Leaders of the media claim that their news judgments rest on unbiased, objective criteria. We contend, on the other hand, that the powerful are able to fix the premises of discourse, decide what the general populace will be allowed to see, hear, and think about, and "manage" public opinion by mounting regular propaganda campaigns.

We do not claim this is all the mass media do, but we believe the propaganda function to be a very important aspect of their overall service.

In countries where the levers of power are in the hands of a state bureaucracy, monopolistic control of the media, often supplemented by official censorship, makes it clear that media serve the ends of the dominant elite. It is much more difficult to see a propaganda system at work where the media are private and formal censorship is absent.

This is especially true where the media actively compete, periodically attack and expose corporate and governmental malfeasance, and aggressively portray themselves as spokesmen for free speech and the general community interest. What is not evident (and remains undiscussed in the media) is the severely limited access to the private media system and the effect of money and power on the system's performance.

Critiques of this kind are often dismissed by Establishment commentators as "conspiracy theories," but this is merely an evasion. We don't rely on any kind of conspiracy hypothesis to explain the performance of the media; in fact, our treatment is much closer to a "free-market" analysis.

Most of the bias in the media arises from the selection of right-thinking people, the internalization of preconceptions until they are taken as self-evident truths, and the practical adaptation of employees to the constraints of ownership, organization, market, and political power.

The censorship practiced within the media is largely self-censorship, by reporters and commentators who adjust to the "realities" as they perceive them. But there are important actors who do take positive initiatives to define and shape the news and to keep the media in line. This kind of guidance is provided by the Government, the leaders of the corporate community, the top media owners and executives, and assorted individuals and groups who are allowed to take the initiative.

The media are not a solid monolith on all issues. Where the powerful are in disagreement, the media will reflect a certain diversity of tactical

From *The Progressive,* June 1988, 14–17.

judgments on how to attain generally shared aims. But views that challenge fundamental premises or suggest that systemic factors govern the exercise of State power will be excluded.

The pattern is pervasive. Consider the coverage from and about Nicaragua. The mass media rarely allow their news columns—or, for that matter, their opinion pages—to present materials suggesting that Nicaragua is more democratic than El Salvador and Guatemala; that its government does not murder ordinary citizens, as the governments of El Salvador and Guatemala do on a routine basis; that it has carried out socioeconomic reforms important to the majority that the other two governments somehow cannot attempt; that Nicaragua poses no military threat to its neighbors but has, in fact, been subjected to continuous attack by the United States and its clients and surrogates, and that the U.S. fear of the Nicaraguan government is based more on its virtues than on its alleged defects.

The mass media also steer clear of discussing the background and results of the closely analogous attempt of the United States to bring "democracy" to Guatemala in 1954 by means of a CIA-supported invasion, which terminated Guatemalan democracy for an indefinite period. Although the United States supported elite rule and organized terror in Guatemala (among many other countries) for decades, actually subverted or approved the subversion of democracy in Brazil, Chile, and the Philippines (again, among others), is now "constructively engaged" with terror regimes around the world, and had no concern about democracy in Nicaragua so long as the brutal Somoza regime was firmly in power, the media take U.S. Government claims of a concern for "democracy" in Nicaragua at face value.

In contrast, El Salvador and Guatemala, with far worse records, are presented as struggling toward democracy under "moderate" leaders, thus meriting sympathetic approval.

In criticizing media biases, we often draw on the media themselves for at least some of the "facts." That the media provide some information about an issue, however, proves absolutely nothing about the adequacy or accuracy of media coverage. The media do, in fact, suppress a great deal of information, but even more important is the way they present a particular fact—its placement, tone, and frequency of repetition—and the framework of analysis in which it is placed. That a careful reader looking for a fact can sometimes find it, with diligence and a skeptical eye, tells us nothing about whether that fact received the attention and context it deserved, whether it was intelligible to most readers, or whether it was effectively distorted or suppressed.

The standard media pattern of indignant campaigns and suppressions, of shading and emphasis, of carefully selected context, premises, and general agenda, is highly useful to those who wield power. If, for example, they are able to channel public concern and outrage to the abuses of enemy states, they can mobilize the population for an ideological crusade.

Thus, a constant focus on the victims of communism helps persuade the public that the enemy is evil, while setting the stage for intervention, subversion, support for terrorist regimes, an endless arms race, and constant military conflict—all in a noble cause. At the same time, the devotion of our leaders—and our media—to this narrow set of victims raises public patriotism and self-esteem, demonstrating the essential humanity of our nation and our people.

The public does not notice media silence about victims of America's client states, which is as important as the media's concentration on victims of America's enemies. It would have been difficult for the Guatemalan government to murder tens of thousands over the past decade if the U.S. press had provided the kind of coverage it gave to the difficulties of Andrei Sakharov in the Soviet Union or the murder of Jerzy Popieluszko in Poland. It would have been impossible to wage a brutal war against South Vietnam and the rest of Indochina, leaving a legacy of misery and destruction that may never be overcome, if the media had not rallied to the cause, portraying murderous aggression as a defense of freedom.

Propaganda campaigns may be instituted either by the Government or by one or more of the top media firms. The campaigns to discredit the government of Nicaragua, to support the Salvadoran elections as an exercise in legitimizing democracy, and to use the Soviet shooting down of the Korean airliner KAL 007 as a means of mobilizing support for the arms buildup were instituted and propelled by the Government. The campaigns to publicize the crimes of Pol Pot in Cambodia and the allegations of a KGB plot to assassinate the Pope were initiated by the *Reader's Digest,* with strong follow-up support from NBC television, *The New York Times,* and other major media companies.

Some propaganda campaigns are jointly initiated by the Government and the media; all of them require the media's cooperation.

The mass media are drawn into a symbiotic relationship with powerful sources of information by economic necessity and reciprocity of interest. The media need a steady, reliable flow of the raw material of news. They have daily news demands and imperative news schedules. They cannot afford to have reporters and cameras at all places where important stories may break, so they must concentrate their resources where significant news often occurs, where important rumors and leaks abound, and where regular press conferences are held.

The White House, the Pentagon, and the State Department are central nodes of such news activity at the national level. On a local basis, city hall and the police department are regular news beats for reporters. Corporations and trade groups are also regular and credible purveyors of stories deemed newsworthy. These bureaucracies turn out a large volume of material that meets the demands of news organizations for reliable, scheduled flows. They also have the great merit of being recognizable and credible because of their status and prestige.

Another reason for the heavy weight given to official sources is that the mass media claim to be "objective" dispensers of the news. Partly to maintain the image of objectivity, but also to protect themselves from criticism of bias and the threat of libel suits, they need material that can be portrayed as presumptively accurate. This also reduces cost: Taking information from sources that may be presumed credible reduces investigative expense, whereas material from sources that are not *prima facie* credible, or that will draw criticism and threats, requires careful checking and costly research.

The Government and corporate bureaucracies that constitute primary news sources maintain vast public-relations operations that ensure special access to the media. The Pentagon, for example, has a public-information service that involves many thousands of employees, spending hundreds of millions of dollars every year and dwarfing not only the public-information resources of any dissenting individual or group but the aggregate of *all* dissenters.

During a brief interlude of relative openness in 1979 and 1980, the U.S. Air Force revealed that its public-information outreach included 140 newspapers with a weekly total circulation of 690,000; *Airman* magazine with a monthly circulation of 125,000; thirty-four radio and seventeen television stations, primarily overseas; 45,000 headquarters and unit news releases; 615,000 hometown news releases; 6,600 news media interviews; 3,200 news conferences; 500 news media orientation flights; fifty meetings with editorial boards, and 11,000 speeches. Note that this is just the Air Force. In 1982, *Air Force Journal International* indicated that the Pentagon was publishing 1,203 periodicals.

To put this into perspective, consider the scope of public-information activities of the American Friends Service Committee and the National Council of the Churches of Christ, two of the largest nonprofit organizations that consistently challenge the views of the Pentagon. The Friends' main office had an information services budget of less than $500,000 and a staff of eleven in 1984–1985. It issued about 200 press releases a year, held thirty press conferences, and produced one film and two or three slide shows. The Council of Churches office of information has an annual budget of about $350,000, issues about 100 news releases, and holds four press conferences a year.

Only the corporate sector has the resources to produce public information and propaganda on the scale of the Pentagon and other Government bodies. These large actors provide the media with facilities and with advance copies of speeches and reports. They schedule news conferences at hours geared to news deadlines. They write press releases in usable language. They carefully organize "photo-opportunity" sessions.

In effect, the large bureaucracies of the powerful subsidize the mass media, and thereby gain special access. They become "routine" news sources, while nonroutine sources must struggle for access and may be ignored.

Because of the services they provide, the continuous contact they sustain, and the mutual dependency they foster, the powerful can use personal relationships, threats, and rewards to extend their influence over the news media. The media may feel obligated to carry extremely dubious stories, or to mute criticism, to avoid offending sources and disturbing a close relationship. When one depends on authorities for daily news, it is difficult to call them liars even if they tell whoppers.

Powerful sources may also use their prestige and importance as a lever to deny critics access to the media. The Defense Department, for example, refused to participate in discussions of military issues on National Public Radio if experts from the Center for Defense Information were invited to appear on the same program. Assistant Secretary of State Elliott Abrams would not appear on a Harvard University program dealing with human rights in Central America unless former Ambassador Robert White were excluded. Claire Sterling, a principal propagandist for the "Bulgarian connection" to the plot to assassinate the Pope, refused to take part in television programs on which her critics would appear.

The relation between power and sourcing extends beyond official and corporate provision of news to shaping the supply of "experts." The dominance of official sources is undermined when highly respectable unofficial sources give dissident views. This problem is alleviated by "coopting the experts"—that is, putting them on the payroll as consultants, funding their research, and organizing think tanks that will hire them directly and help disseminate their messages.

The process of creating a body of experts who will confirm and distribute the opinions favored by the Government and "the market" has been carried out on a deliberate basis and a massive scale. In 1972. Judge Lewis Powell, later elevated to the Supreme Court, wrote a memo to the U.S. Chamber of Commerce in which he urged business "to buy the top academic reputations in the country to add credibility to corporate studies and give business a stronger voice on the campuses."

During the 1970s and early 1980s, new institutions were established and old ones reactivated to help propagandize the corporate viewpoint. Hundreds of intellectuals were brought to these institutions, their work funded, and their output disseminated to the media by a sophisticated propaganda effort.

The media themselves also provide "experts" who regularly echo the official view. John Barron and Claire Sterling are household names as authorities on the KGB and terrorism because the *Reader's Digest* has funded, published, and publicized their work. The Soviet defector Arkady Shevchenko became an expert on Soviet arms and intelligence because *Time*, ABC television, and *The New York Times* chose to feature him, despite his badly tarnished credentials. By giving these vehicles of the preferred view much exposure, the media confer status and make them the obvious candidates for opinion and analysis.

Another class of experts whose prominence is largely a function of their serviceability to power consists of former radicals who have "come to see the light." The motives that induce these individuals to switch gods, from Stalin (or Mao) and communism to Reagan and free enterprise, may vary, but so far as the media are concerned, the ex-radicals have simply seen the error of their ways. The former sinners, whose previous work was ignored or ridiculed by the mass media, are suddenly elevated to prominence and anointed as experts.

Media propaganda campaigns have generally been useful to elite interests. The Red Scare of 1919–1920 helped abort the postwar union-organizing drive in steel and other major industries. The Truman-McCarthy Red Scare of the early 1950s helped inaugurate the Cold War and the permanent war economy, and also weakened the progressive coalition that had taken shape during the New Deal years.

The chronic focus on the plight of Soviet dissidents, on enemy killings in Cambodia, and on the Bulgarian Connection helped weaken the Vietnam Syndrome, justify a huge arms buildup and a more aggressive foreign policy, and divert attention from the upward distribution of income that was the heart of the Reagan Administration's domestic economic program. The recent propaganda attacks on Nicaragua have averted eyes from the savageries of the war in El Salvador and helped justify the escalating U.S. investment in counterrevolution in Central America.

Conversely, propaganda campaigns are *not* mobilized where coverage of victimization, though it may be massive, sustained, and dramatic, fails to serve the interests of the elite.

The focus on Cambodia in the Pol Povera was serviceable, for example, because Cambodia had fallen to the communists and useful lessons could be drawn from the experience of their victims. But the many Cambodian victims of U.S. bombing *before* the communists came to power were scrupulously ignored by the U.S. press. After Pol Pot was ousted by the Vietnamese, the United States quietly shifted its support to this "worse than Hitler" villain, with little or no notice in the press, which once again adjusted to the official political agenda.

Attention to the Indonesian massacres of 1965–1966, or to the victims of the Indonesian invasion of East Timor since 1975, would also be distinctly unhelpful as bases of media campaigns, because Indonesia is a U.S. ally and client that maintains an open door to Western investment. The same is true of the victims of state terror in Chile and Guatemala— U.S. clients whose basic institutional structures, including the state terror system, were put in place by, or with crucial assistance from, the United States.

No propaganda campaigns are mounted in the mass media on behalf of such victims. To publicize their plight would, after all, conflict with the interests of the wealthy and powerful.

Textual Questions

1. Why do Herman and Chomsky open with their thesis statement? What effect does this have on their argument?

2. What "propaganda service" do the media in America provide according to the authors of this essay? Who benefits and who is penalized by this service? Where, according to Herman and Chomsky, does media bias originate? How does it manifest itself?

3. Instead of being antagonistic to powerful institutions, the media are "drawn into a symbiotic relationship" with them according to the authors of this essay. Why? What are the consequences of this symbiosis?

Rhetorical Questions

4. Herman and Chomsky use Nicaragua as an example in their argument. How effective is this example? What makes it effective or ineffective?

5. What, according to Herman and Chomsky, is more important than the fact that the media "do, in fact, suppress a great deal of information"? How does the attempt to seem objective cripple the work of the news media?

6. Herman and Chomsky contrast the Air Force's ability to reach the news via various media with the abilities of both the American Friends Service Committee and the National Council of the Churches of Christ. How does this comparison fit into their argument? Is it a good, credible comparison—or is it a straw man, a construct built only to support their argument in a simplistic, yet satisfying, way?

Intertextual Questions

7. In what ways do Herman and Chomsky agree with such later writers in this chapter as Eric Alterman and Bernard Goldberg?

8. How does the argument of Herman and Chomsky echo the argument of Ben Bagdikian? How do the two arguments diverge?

Thinking Beyond the Text

9. Herman and Chomsky argue that they are not advocating a conspiracy theory about power and control, yet they clearly argue that the public is controlled by both the government and powerful media corporations. Despite their denial, do you believe their argument—or do you believe that this is only a one-sided conspiracy theory?

10. At the end of their argument, Herman and Chomsky argue that the propaganda service provided by the media serves specific bait-and-witch needs for the people in power, diverting public attention from "real" issues to phantom issues under the control of the powerful. Is this analysis credible and believable? How does it connect with your own experience of media coverage during events such as the War on Terror and the ongoing war in Iraq?

For Writing & Discussion

11. Herman and Chomsky refer to numerous examples of propaganda campaigns—in Nicaragua, Poland, the former Soviet Union, and others. Pick one of these examples and research the events/news coverage Herman and Chomsky describe. What makes these good/bad, effective/ineffective examples of propaganda? Are there times when propaganda is a necessary tool for mobilizing public support—after the terrorist attacks of 9/11, the tsunami disaster of December 2004, or such "dated" events as the Japanese attack on Pearl Harbor? Or is propaganda always a lie, whether it sells bleach, new Buicks, or the belief that one way of life is better than another?

NEIL POSTMAN
AND STEVE POWERS

Neil Postman (1931–2003) and Steve Powers (born in 1934) collaborated on the book *How to Watch TV News,* published in 1992. Postman was a scholar who published numerous books about education reform and criticism of television. Powers has extensive experience in radio and television broadcasting.

"The Bias of Language, the Bias of Pictures" is an excerpt from *How to Watch TV News*, which analyzes the medium of television news and its limitations in providing information to viewers.

The Bias of Language, the Bias of Pictures

∾ Prereading Question

It's often said that "a picture is worth a thousand words." Is this true—that a single image contains as much meaning/information as a four-page essay? Which can present a more accurate description of the meaning of an event, words or pictures?

When a television news show distorts the truth by altering or manufacturing facts (through re-creations), a television viewer is defenseless even if a re-creation is properly labeled. Viewers are still vulnerable to misinformation since they will not know (at least in the case of docudramas) what parts are fiction and what parts are not. But the problems of verisimilitude posed by re-creations pale to insignificance when compared to the problems viewers face when encountering a straight (no-monkey-business) show. All news shows, in a sense, are re-creations in that what we hear and see on them are attempts to represent actual events, and are not the events themselves. Perhaps, to avoid ambiguity, we might call all news shows "re-presentations" instead of "re-creations." These re-presentations come to us in two forms: language and pictures. The question then arises: what do viewers have to know about language and pictures in order to be properly armed to defend themselves against the seductions of eloquence (to use Bertrand Russell's apt phrase)?

Let us take language first. Below are three principles that, in our opinion, are an essential part of the analytical equipment a viewer must bring to any encounter with a news show.

∾

1. Whatever Anyone Says
Something Is, it Isn't

This sounds more complex—and maybe more pretentious—than it actually is. What it means is that there is a difference between the world of events and the world of words about events. The job of an honest reporter is to try to find words and the appropriate tone in presenting them that will come as close to evoking the event as possible. But since no two people will use exactly the same words to describe an event, we must acknowledge that for every verbal description of an event, there are multiple possible alternatives. You may demonstrate this to your own satisfaction by writing a two-paragraph description of a dinner you had with at least two other people, then asking the others who were present if each of them would also write, independently, a two-paragraph description of the "same" dinner. We should be very surprised if all of the descriptions include the same words, in the same order, emphasize the same things, and express the same feelings. In other words, "the dinner itself" is largely a nonverbal event. The words people use to describe this event are not the event itself and are only abstracted re-presentations of the event. What does this mean for a television viewer? It means that the viewer must never assume that the words spoken on a television news show are exactly what happened. Since there are so many alternative ways of describing what happened, the viewer must be on guard against assuming that he or she has heard "the absolute truth."

∿

2. Language Operates at Various Levels of Abstraction

This means that there is a level of language whose purpose is to *describe* an event. There is also a level of language whose purpose is to *evaluate* an event. Even more, there is a level of language whose purpose is to *infer* what is unknown on the basis of what is known. The usual way to make these distinctions clear is through sentences such as the following three:

Manny Freebus is 5′ 8″ and weighs 235 pounds.
Manny Freebus is grossly fat.
Manny Freebus eats too much.

The first sentence may be said to be language as pure description. It involves no judgments and no inferences. The second sentence is a description of sorts, but is mainly a judgment that the speaker makes of the "event" known as Manny Freebus. The third sentence is an inference based on observations the speaker has made. It is, in fact, a statement about the unknown based on the known. As it happens, we know Manny Freebus and can tell you that he eats no more than the average person but suffers from a glandular condition which keeps him overweight. Therefore, anyone who concluded from observing Manny's shape that he eats too much has made a false inference. A good guess, but false nonetheless.

You can watch television news programs from now until doomsday and never come across any statement about Manny Freebus. But you will constantly come across the three kinds of statements we have been discussing—descriptions, judgments, and inferences. And it is important for a viewer to distinguish among them. For example, you might hear an anchor introduce a story by saying: "Today Congress ordered an investigation of the explosive issue of whether Ronald Reagan's presidential campaign made a deal with Iran in 1980 to delay the release of American hostages until after the election." This statement is, of course, largely descriptive, but includes the judgmental word "explosive" as part of the report. We need hardly point out that what is explosive to one person may seem trivial to another. We do not say that the news writer has no business to include his or her judgment of this investigation. We do say that the viewer has to be aware that a judgment has been made. In fact, even the phrase "made a deal" (why not "arranged with Iran"?) has a somewhat sleazy connotation that implies a judgment of sorts. If, in the same news report, we are told that the evidence for such a secret deal is weak and that only an investigation with subpoena power can establish the truth, we must know that we have left the arena of factual language and have moved into the land of inference. An investigation with subpoena power may be a good idea but whether or not it can establish the truth is a guess on the journalist's part, and a viewer ought to know that.

∞

3. Almost All Words Have Connotative Meanings

This suggests that even when attempting to use purely descriptive language, a journalist cannot avoid expressing an attitude about what he or she is saying. For example, here is the opening sentence of an anchor's report about national examinations: "For the first time in the nation's history, high-level education policymakers have designed the elements for a national examination system similar to the one advocated by President Bush." This sentence certainly looks like it is pure description although it is filled with ambiguities. Is this the first time in our history that this has been done? Or only the first time that high-level education policymakers have done it? Or is it the first time something has been designed that is similar to what the President has advocated? But let us put those questions aside. (After all, there are limits to how analytical one ought to be.) Instead, we might concentrate on such words as "high-level," "policymakers," and "designed." Speaking for ourselves, we are by no means sure that we know what a "high-level policymaker" is, although it sounds awfully impressive. It is certainly better than a "low-level policymaker," although how one would distinguish between the two is a bit of a mystery. Come to think of it, a low-level "policymaker" must be pretty good, too, since anyone who makes policy must be important. It comes as no surprise, therefore, that what was done was "designed." To design something usually implies careful thought, preparation, organization, and coherence. People design buildings, bridges, and furniture. If your experience has been anything like ours, you will know that reports are almost never designed; they are usually "thrown together," and it is quite a compliment to say that a report was designed. The journalist who paid this compliment was certainly entitled to do it even though he may not have been aware of what he was doing. He probably thought he had made a simple description, avoiding any words that would imply favor or disfavor. But if so, he was defeated in his effort because language tends to be emotion-laden. Because it is people who do the talking, the talk almost always includes a feeling, an attitude, a judgment. In a sense, every language contains the history of a people's feelings about the world. Our words are baskets of emotion. Smart journalists, of course, know this. And so do smart audiences. Smart audiences don't blame anyone for this state of affairs. They are, however, prepared for it.

It is not our intention to provide here a mini-course in semantics. Even if we could, we are well aware that no viewer could apply analytic principles all the time or even much of the time. Anchors and reporters talk too fast and too continuously for any of us to monitor most of their sentences. Besides, who would want to do that for most of the stories on a news show? If you have a sense of what is important, you will probably judge most news stories to be fluff, or nonsense, or irrelevancies, not worthy of your analytic weaponry. But there are times when stories appear that are of major significance from your point of view. These are the times when your level of attention will reach a peak and you must call upon your best powers of interpretation. In those moments, you need to draw on whatever you know about the relationship between language and reality; about the distinctions among statements of fact, judgment, and inference; about the connotative meanings of words. When this is done properly, viewers are no longer passive consumers of news but active participants in a kind of dialogue between a news show and themselves. A viewer may even find that he or she is "talking back to the television set" (which is the title of a book by former FCC commissioner Nicholas Johnson). In our view, nothing could be healthier for the sanity and well-being of our nation than to have ninety million viewers talking back to their television news shows every night and twice on Sunday.

Now we must turn to the problem of pictures. It is often said that a picture is worth a thousand words. Maybe so. But it is probably equally true that one word is worth a thousand pictures, at least sometimes—for example, when it comes to understanding the world we live in. Indeed, the whole problem with news on television comes down to this: all the words uttered in an hour of news coverage could be printed on one page of a newspaper. And the world cannot be understood in one page. Of course, there is a compensation: television offers pictures, and the pictures move. Moving pictures are a kind of language in themselves, but the language of pictures differs radically from oral and written language, and the differences are crucial for understanding television news.

To begin with, pictures, especially single pictures, speak only in particularities. Their vocabulary is limited to concrete representation. Unlike words and sentences, a picture does not present to us an idea or concept about the world, except as we use language itself to convert the image to idea. By itself, a picture cannot deal with the unseen, the remote, the internal, the abstract. It does not speak of "man," only of *a* man; not of "tree," only of *a* tree. You cannot produce an image of "nature," any more than an image of "the sea." You can only show a particular fragment of the here-and-now— a cliff of a certain terrain, in a certain condition of light; a wave at a moment in time, from a particular point of view. And just as "nature" and "the sea" cannot be photographed, such larger abstractions as truth, honor, love, and falsehood cannot be talked about in the lexicon of individual pictures. For "showing of" and "talking about" are two very different kinds of processes: individual pictures give us the world as object; language, the world as idea. There is no such thing in nature as "man" or "tree." The universe offers no such categories or simplifications; only flux and infinite variety. The picture documents and celebrates the particularities of the universe's infinite variety. Language makes them comprehensible.

Of course, moving pictures, video with sound, may bridge the gap by juxtaposing images, symbols, sound, and music. Such images can present emotions and rudimentary ideas. They can suggest the panorama of nature and the joys and miseries of humankind.

Picture—smoke pouring from the window, cut to people coughing, an ambulance racing to a hospital, a tombstone in a cemetery.

Picture—jet planes firing rockets, explosions, lines of foreign soldiers surrendering, the American flag waving in the wind.

Nonetheless, keep in mind that when terrorists want to prove to the world that their kidnap victims are still alive, they photograph them holding a copy of a recent newspaper. The dateline on the newspaper provides the proof that the photograph was taken on or after that date. Without the help of the written word, film and videotape cannot portray temporal dimensions with any precision. Consider a film clip showing an aircraft carrier at sea. One might be able to identify the ship as Soviet or American, but there would be no way of telling where in the world the carrier was, where it was headed, or when the pictures were taken. It is only through language—words spoken over the pictures or reproduced in them—that the image of the aircraft carrier takes on specific meaning.

Still, it is possible to enjoy the image of the carrier for its own sake. One might find the hugeness of the vessel interesting; it signifies military power on the move. There is a certain drama in watching the planes come in at high speeds and skid to a stop on the deck. Suppose the ship were burning: that would be even more interesting. This leads to an important point about the language of pictures. Moving pictures favor images that change. That is why violence and dynamic destruction find their way onto television so often. When something is destroyed violently it is altered in a highly visible way; hence the entrancing power of fire. Fire gives visual form to the ideas of consumption, disappearance, death—the thing that burned is actually taken away by fire. It is at this very basic level that fires make a good subject for television news. Something was here, now it's gone, and the change is recorded on film.

Earthquakes and typhoons have the same power. Before the viewer's eyes the world is taken apart. If a television viewer has relatives in Mexico City and an earthquake occurs there, then he or she may take a special interest in the images of destruction as a report from a specific place and time; that is, one may look at television pictures for information about an important event. But film of an earthquake can be interesting even if the viewer cares nothing about the event itself. Which is only to say, as we noted earlier, that there is another way of participating in the news— as a spectator who desires to be entertained. Actually to see buildings topple is exciting, no matter where the buildings are. The world turns to dust before our eyes.

Those who produce television news in America know that their medium favors images that move. That is why they are wary of "talking heads," people who simply appear in front of a camera and speak. When talking heads appear on television, there is nothing to record or document, no change in process. In the cinema the situation is somewhat different. On a movie screen, close-ups of a good actor speaking dramatically can sometimes be interesting to watch. When Clint Eastwood narrows his eyes and challenges his rival to shoot first, the spectator sees the cool rage of the Eastwood character take visual form, and the narrowing of the eyes is dramatic. But much of the effect of this small movement depends on the size of the movie screen and the darkness of the theater, which make Eastwood and his every action "larger than life."

The television screen is smaller than life. It occupies about 15 percent of the viewer's visual field (compared to about 70 percent for the movie screen). It is not set in a darkened theater closed off from the world but in the viewer's ordinary living space. This means that visual changes must be more extreme and more dramatic to be interesting on television. A narrowing of the eyes will not do. A car crash, an earthquake, a burning factory are much better.

With these principles in mind, let us examine more closely the structure of a typical newscast, and here we will include in the discussion not only the pictures but all the nonlinguistic symbols that make up a television news show. For example, in America, almost all news shows begin with music, the tone of which suggests important events about to unfold. The music is very important, for it equates the news with various forms of drama and ritual—the opera, for example, or a wedding procession—in which musical themes underscore the meaning of the event. Music takes us immediately into the realm of the symbolic, a world that is not to be taken literally. After all, when events unfold in the real world, they do so without musical accompaniment. More symbolism follows. The sound of teletype machines can be heard in the studio, not because it is impossible to screen this noise out, but because the sound is a kind of music in itself. It tells us that data are pouring in from all corners of the globe, a sensation reinforced by the world map in the background (or clocks noting the time on different continents). The fact is that teletype machines are rarely used in TV news rooms, having been replaced by silent computer terminals. When seen, they have only a symbolic function.

Already, then, before a single news item is introduced, a great deal has been communicated. We know that we are in the presence of a symbolic event, a form of theater in which the day's events are to be dramatized. This theater takes the entire globe as its subject, although it may look at the world from the perspective of a single nation. A certain tension is present, like the atmosphere in a theater just before the curtain goes up. The tension is represented by the music, the staccato beat of the teletype machines, and often the sight of news workers scurrying around typing reports and answering phones. As a technical matter, it would be no problem to build a set in which the newsroom staff remained off camera, invisible to the viewer, but an important theatrical effect would be lost. By being busy on camera, the workers help communicate urgency about the events at hand, which suggests that situations are changing so rapidly that constant revision of the news is necessary.

The staff in the background also helps signal the importance of the person in the center, the anchor, "in command" of both the staff and the news. The anchor plays the role of host. He or she welcomes us to the newscast and welcomes us back from the different locations we visit during the filmed reports.

Many features of the newscast help the anchor to establish the impression of control. These are usually equated with production values in broadcasting. They include such things as graphics that tell the viewer what is being shown, or maps and charts that suddenly appear on the screen and disappear on cue, or the orderly progression from story to story. They also include the absence of gaps, or "dead time," during the broadcast, even the simple fact that the news starts and ends at a certain hour. These common features are thought of as purely technical matters, which a professional crew handles as a matter of course. But they are also symbols of a dominant theme of television news: the imposition of an orderly world—called "the news"—upon the disorderly flow of events.

While the form of a news broadcast emphasizes tidiness and control, its content can best be described as fragmented. Because time is so precious on television, because the nature of the medium favors dynamic visual images, and because the pressures of a commercial structure require the news to hold its audience above all else, there is rarely any attempt to explain issues in depth or place events in their proper context. The news moves nervously from a warehouse fire to a court decision, from a guerrilla war to a World Cup match, the quality of the film most often determining the length of the story. Certain stories show up only because they offer dramatic pictures. Bleachers collapse in South America: hundreds of people are crushed—a perfect television news story, for the cameras can record the face of disaster in all its anguish. Back in Washington, a new budget is approved by Congress. Here there is nothing to photograph because a budget is not a physical event; it is a document full of language and numbers. So the producers of the news will show a photo of the document itself, focusing on the cover where it says "Budget of the United States of America." Or sometimes they will send a camera crew to the government printing plant where copies of the budget are produced. That evening, while the contents of the budget are summarized by a voice-over, the viewer sees stacks of documents being loaded into boxes at the government printing plant. Then a few of the budget's more important provisions will be flashed on the screen in written form, but this is such a time-consuming process—using television as a printed page—that the producers keep it to a minimum. In short, the budget is not televisable, and for that reason its time on the news must be brief. The bleacher collapse will get more time that evening.

While appearing somewhat chaotic, these disparate stories are not just dropped in the news program helter-skelter. The appearance of a scattershot story order is really orchestrated to draw the audience from one story to the next—from one section to the next—through the commercial breaks to the end of the show. The story order is constructed to hold and build the viewership rather than place events in context or explain issues in depth.

Of course, it is a tendency of journalism in general to concentrate on the surface of events rather than underlying conditions; this is as true for the newspaper as it is for the newscast. But several features of television undermine whatever efforts journalists may make to give sense to the world. One is that a television broadcast is a series of events that occur in sequence, and the sequence is the same for all viewers. This is not true for a newspaper page, which displays many items simultaneously, allowing readers to choose the order in which they read them. If newspaper readers want only a summary of the latest tax bill, they can read the headline and the first paragraph of an article, and if they want more, they can keep reading. In a sense, then, everyone reads a different newspaper, for no two readers will read (or ignore) the same items.

But all television viewers see the same broadcast. They have no choices. A report is either in the broadcast or out, which means that anything which is of narrow interest is unlikely to be included. As NBC News executive Reuven Frank once explained:

> A newspaper, for example, can easily afford to print an item of conceivable interest to only a fraction of its readers. A television news program must be put together with the assumption that each item will be of some interest to everyone that watches. Every time a newspaper includes a feature which will attract a specialized group it can assume it is adding at least a little bit to its circulation. To the degree a television news program includes an item of this sort. . . it must assume that its audience will diminish.

The need to "include everyone," an identifying feature of commercial television in all its forms, prevents journalists from offering lengthy or complex explanations, or from tracing the sequence of events leading up to today's headlines. One of the ironies of political life in modern democracies is that many problems which concern the "general welfare" are of interest only to specialized groups. Arms control, for example, is an issue that literally concerns everyone in the world, and yet the language of arms control and the complexity of the subject are so daunting that only a minority of people can actually follow the issue from week to week and month to month. If it wants to act responsibly, a newspaper can at least make available more information about arms control than most people want. Commercial television cannot afford to do so.

But even if commercial television could afford to do so, it wouldn't. The fact that television news is principally made up of moving pictures prevents it from offering lengthy, coherent explanations of events. A television news show reveals the world as a series of unrelated, fragmentary moments. It does not—and cannot be expected to—offer a sense of coherence or meaning. What does this suggest to a TV viewer? That the viewer must come with a prepared mind—information, opinions, a sense of proportion, an articulate value system. To the TV viewer lacking such mental equipment, a news program is only a kind of rousing light show. Here a falling building, there a five-alarm fire, everywhere the world as an object, much without meaning, connections, or continuity.

Textual Questions

1. How is a "re-presentation" different from a "re-creation"? How does language, no matter how carefully chosen and crafted, distort the reality of an event?

2. Consider the organization of Powers and Postman's essay. The discussion of language is broken into three sections, yet pictures are discussed in a single section. Why might they have chosen this organizational pattern? How effective is it for you, as a reader?

3. How effective is Powers and Postman's analysis of "a typical newscast"? Based upon your own experience watching the television news, is their analysis fair and accurate?

Rhetorical Questions

4. What differences do Powers and Postman draw between connotative and denotative meanings of words? Are the differences as significant as they say?

5. What does it mean to say that the "television screen is smaller than life"? And why does it matter?

6. How is a "typical newscast" mostly "theatre"? Why do Powers and Postman argue that the content of a typical television news broadcast is best described as "fragmented"? Why is this a problem?

Intertextual Questions

7. Read (or reread) President George W. Bush's speech in the introduction to this book, "We Have Seen the State of Our Union." Find examples in this speech where President Bush describes something in a mostly neutral way, evaluates something positively or negatively, and makes inferences not directly supported by his words. Consider both the connotative and denotative definitions of the words he uses.

8. In Chapter 2, you read many essays about education in America, focusing on issues such as race, social class, and so on. You also wrote about schools in your region. Now, consider how those same local schools are discussed by the local news media. To do this, watch one episode of your local news (and tape it to allow many viewings) and take note of how local schools are described. What images are shown and what words are used? What is a viewer led to believe about local schools from viewing this report?

Thinking Beyond the Text

9. Postman and Powers argue that "most news stories [are] fluff, or nonsense, or irrelevancies." Do you believe this to be true? Why might Postman and Powers make this argument? And, if we allow that this is/might be true, how does this fluff and nonsense affect how TV news viewers think about their lives and about the wider world?

10. Postman and Powers argue that every word spoken in a one-hour news broadcast can fit onto a single page of a newspaper, "And the world cannot be understood in one page." Would you agree that the world is too complex to be summarized in such a space—or is this criticism, primarily, an example of knee-jerk cynicism about the limitations of television and backhanded praise for the virtues of newspapers?

For Writing & Discussion

11. Tape an episode of the local or national news broadcast on one of the major networks—ABC, CBS, FOX, or NBC. With the sound turned off, watch one story at least five times. As you watch, list the images that are shown and the order in which they are shown. In an essay, explain what impact the images alone have on a viewer.

FRANK RICH

Born on June 2, 1949, in Washington, D.C., Frank Rich is a graduate of its public schools. He earned a B.A. degree in American history and literature, graduating magna cum laude from Harvard College in 1971. At Harvard, he was editorial chairman of *The Harvard Crimson*, an honorary Harvard College scholar, and a member of Phi Beta Kappa. A writer for the *New York Times* since 1980, when he was named chief theater critic, he now writes a weekly 1500-word essay on the intersection of culture and news for its op-ed page.

In addition to his work at the *Times*, Mr. Rich has written about culture and politics for many other publications. His childhood memoir, *Ghost Light*, was published in 2000 by Random House and as a Random House trade paperback in 2001. The film rights to *Ghost Light* have been acquired by Story-line Entertainment. A collection of Mr. Rich's drama reviews, *Hot Seat: Theater Criticism for The New York Times, 1980–1993*, was published by Random House in October 1998. His newest book is *The Greatest Story Ever Sold: The Decline and Fall of Truth from 9/11 to Katrina*, published by Penguin in 2006. In the book, according to *Kirkus Reviews*, Rich "delivers a savaging sermon on the U.S. government's rampant cronyism, the empty sloganeer-ing of 'compassionate conservativism,' the reckless lack of plan-ning for all government operations except tax cuts—and so much more."

The following article was published July 9, 2006 in the *Times*, in response to the George W. Bush administration's attacks on the newspaper for publishing information it felt should be kept secret. When the president's press secretary, Tony Snow, was asked about the column in a press briefing the fol-lowing day, he declined to join that attack, saying, with some irony, "No, I see Frank Rich enjoying his First Amendment options, which he does in a way that many of us consider quite enjoyable." In an earlier confrontation, Fox News's Bill O'Reilly said: "The *New York Times* and others prove that we are now in an age where control of information flow has become a serious war of words."

All the News That's Fit to Bully

∾ **Prereading Question**

Consider the types of programs on television that purport to deliver "news" about the world—from programs that deliver entertainment news to the nighty news broadcast of the major networks to the "news magazine" programs (from "E!" to "ABC Nightly News" to "20/20" to "The Daily Show," [or also the monologues of Jay Leno and David Letterman], for example). Which of these programs seems to present the most "honest" view of the world, in your opinion?

July 9, 2006 Sunday

Late Edition – Final

Two weeks and counting, and the editor of *The New York Times* still has not been sentenced to the gas chamber. What a bummer for one California radio talk-show host, Melanie Morgan, who pronounced *The Times* guilty of treason and expressly endorsed that punishment. She and the rest of the get-the-press lynch mob are growing restless, wondering why newspapers haven't been prosecuted under the Espionage Act. "If Bush believes what he is saying," taunted Pat Buchanan, "why does he not do his duty as the chief law enforcement officer of the United States?"

Here's why. First, there is no evidence that *the Times* article on tracking terrorist finances either breached national security or revealed any "secrets" that had not already been publicized by either the administration or Swift, the Belgian financial clearinghouse enlisted in the effort. Second, the legal bar would be insurmountable: even Gabriel Schoenfeld, who first floated the idea of prosecuting *The Times* under the Espionage Act in an essay in *Commentary*, told *The Nation* this month that the chance of it happening was .05 percent.

But the third and most important explanation has nothing to do with the facts of the case or the law and everything to do with politics. For all the lynch mob's efforts to single out *The Times*—"It's the old trick, go after New York, go after big, ethnic New York," as Chris Matthews put it—three papers broke Swift stories on their front pages. Even in this bash-the-press environment, the last spectacle needed by a president with an approval rating in the 30s is the national firestorm that would greet a doomed Justice Department prosecution of *The Times*, *The Wall Street Journal* and *The Los Angeles Times*.

The administration has a more insidious game plan instead: it has manufactured and milked this controversy to reboot its intimidation of the press, hoping journalists will pull punches in an election year. There are momentous stories far more worrisome to the White House than the less-than-shocking Swift program, whether in the chaos of Anbar Province or the ruins of New Orleans. If the press muzzles itself, its under-the-radar self-censorship will be far more valuable than a Nixonesque frontal assault that ends up as a 24/7 hurricane veering toward the Supreme Court.

Will this plan work? It did after 9/11. The chilling words articulated at the get-go by Ari Fleischer (Americans must "watch what they say") carried over to the run-up to the Iraq war, when the administration's W.M.D. claims went unchallenged by most news organizations. That this strategy may work again can be seen in the fascinating escalation in tactics by the Bush White House's most powerful not-so-secret agent in the press itself, *The Wall Street Journal* editorial page. *The Journal* is not Fox News or an idle blogger or radio bloviator. It's the establishment voice of the party in power. The infamous editorial it ran on June 30 ("Fit and Unfit to Print"), an instant classic, doesn't just confer its imprimatur on the administration's latest crusade to conflate aggressive journalism with treason, but also ups the ante.

The editorial was ostensibly a frontal attack on *The Times*, accusing its editors of not believing America is "really at war" and of exercising bad faith in running its report on the Swift operation. But an attack on *The Times* by *The Journal*'s editorial page is a shrug-inducing dog-bites-man story; the paper's conservative editorialists have long dueled with a rival whose editorials usually argue the other side. (And sometimes *The Times* opinion writers gleefully return the fire.) What was groundbreaking and unsettling about *The Journal* editorial was that it besmirched the separately run news operation of *The Journal* itself.

By any standard, *The Journal* is one of the great newspapers in the world, whether you agree with its editorials or not. As befits a great newspaper, its journalists are fearless in pursuit of news, as tragically exemplified by Daniel Pearl. Like reporters at *The Times*, those at *The Journal* operate independently of the paper's opinion pages. Witness *The Journal*'s schism during the Enron scandal. Its editorial page belittled the scandal's significance most of the way, resisting even mild criticisms of Enron (it was "partly a victim of its own success") until it filed for bankruptcy. The dearly departed Ken Lay, after all, was the leading Bush financial patron; to *The Journal* editorialists, the "Clintonian moral climate" of the 1990s was a root cause of Enron's problems. Meanwhile, *The Journal*'s investigative reporters had gone their own way months earlier, helping unearth the scandal. So much so that Mr. Lay tried to argue his innocence in the spring by testifying that a "witch hunt" by the paper's reporters had more to do with his company's demise than he did.

It was a similarly top-flight *Journal* reporter, Glenn Simpson, who wrote his paper's Swift story. But *The Journal* editorial page couldn't ignore him if it was attacking *The Times* for publishing its Swift scoop on the same day. So instead it maligned him by echoing Tony Snow's official White House line: *The Journal* was merely following *The Times* once it knew that *The Times* would publish anyway. As if this weren't insulting enough, the editorial suggested that the Treasury Department leaked much of the story to *The Journal* and that a *Journal* reporter could be relied upon to write a "straighter" account more to the government's liking than that of a *Times* reporter.

This version of events does not jibe with an e-mail sent by *The Journal*'s own Washington bureau chief, Gerald Seib, on the day the Swift articles ran. "I was surprised to see your news story about *The New York Times* 'scoop' on the government program to monitor international bank transactions," Mr. Seib wrote to Joe Strupp of the trade publication *Editor & Publisher.* "As you could tell from the lead story on the front page of *The Wall Street Journal* today, we had the same story. Moreover, we posted it online early last evening, virtually at the same time *The Times* did. In sum, we and *The Times* were both chasing the story and crossed the finish line at the same time—and well ahead of *The Los Angeles Times*, which posted its story well after ours went up."

In other words, *The Journal*'s journalists were doing their job with their usual professionalism. But by twisting this history, *The Journal* editorial page was sending an unsubtle shot across the bow, warning those in the newsroom (and every other newsroom) that their patriotism would be impugned, as *The Times*'s had been, if they investigated administration conduct in wartime in ways that displeased the White House.

Any fan of *The Journal*'s news operation expects it to stand up to this bullying. But the nastiness of *The Journal* editorial is a preview of what we can expect from the administration and all of its surrogates this year. In *The One Percent Doctrine*, the revelatory book about wartime successes and failures now (happily) outpacing Ann Coulter at Amazon.com, the former *Wall Street Journal* reporter Ron Suskind explains just how tough it is for a reporter in this climate "to report about national affairs and, especially, national security in this contentious period demands at least a spoonful of disobedience—a countermeasure to strong assurances by those in power that the obedient will be rewarded or, at the very least, have nothing to worry about."

The trouble is we have plenty to worry about. For all the airy talk about the First Amendment, civil liberties and Thomas Jefferson in the debate over the Swift story and the National Security Agency surveillance story before it, there's an urgent practical matter at stake, too. Now more than ever, after years of false reports of missions accomplished, the voters need to do what Congress has failed to do and hold those who mismanage America's ever-expanding war accountable for their performance in real time.

As George Will wrote in March, all three members of the "axis of evil"—Iraq, Iran and North Korea—are "more dangerous than they were when that phrase was coined in 2002." So is Afghanistan, which is spiraling into Taliban-and-drug-lord anarchy, without nearly enough troops or other assistance to secure it. On the first anniversary of the London bombings, and on a surging wave of new bin Laden and al-Zawahiri videos, the two foremost Qaeda experts outside government, Peter Bergen and the former C.I.A. officer Michael Scheuer, both sounded alarms that contradict the insistent administration refrain that the terrorists are on the run.

We can believe instead, if we choose to, that all is well and that the press shouldn't question our government's account of how it is winning the war brilliantly at every turn. (The former C.I.A. analytical chief, Jami Miscik, decodes this game in *The One Percent Doctrine*: the administration tells "only half the story, the part that makes us look good," and keeps the other half classified.) We can believe that reporters, rather than terrorists, are the villains. We can debate whether traitorous editors should be sent to gas chambers or merely tarred and feathered.

Or we can hope that the press will rise to the occasion and bring Americans more news we can use, not less, at a perilous time when every piece of information counts.

Textual Questions

1. What are the three reasons Rich gives that make federal prosecution of the *New York Times* unlikely? Which one does he see as most important and why?

2. What is the difference between censorship and self-censorship? Which does Rich see as more damaging to freedom of the press?

3. What is the political motive that Rich attributes to the Bush administration?

Rhetorical Questions

4. Pick out some of the language Rich uses to describe those attacking the *New York Times*. What is the effect of such terms on you as a reader?

5. What does Rich mean by voters holding the government "accountable"? What is the traditional role of a free press in that process?

6. Why would it be wrong, according to Rich, for the voters to decide "that reporters, rather than terrorists, are the villains"?

Intertextual Questions

7. By referring to "all the airy talk about the First Amendment, civil liberties and Thomas Jefferson," Rich links his argument to other occasions in American history when the government tried to connect a free press to treason. Where else in this chapter has this issue been raised?

8. Research the progressive abolition of freedom of the press in recent years under President Putin in Russia. Why has it been so important for Putin to gain control over the press? Compare that situation to the control of the media in Italy under the magnate and politician Silvio Berlusconi. To what degree is freedom of the press in the United States comparable (or not) to freedom of the press in these countries?

Thinking Beyond the Text

9. What is the line between freedom of the press and treasonous divulging of secrets to the enemy?

10. Have the development of the Internet and the popularity of bloggers made the issue of freedom of the press irrelevant to the future?

For Writing & Discussion

11. Compare the way three wartime American presidents—Abraham Lincoln, Franklin D. Roosevelt, and George W. Bush—dealt with aggressive journalists and their newspapers. Which of them, in your view, was most successful in balancing the need to preserve important secrets with freedom of the press?

BERNARD GOLDBERG

Bernard Goldberg (born in 1945) has worked for several media organizations, including the Associated Press and Home Box Office (HBO). However, most of his career was spent working for the Columbia Broadcasting System (CBS) as a reporter and correspondent for such shows as *CBS Evening News with Dan Rather* and *48 Hours.* After leaving CBS, he wrote several books, including *Bias: A CBS Insider Exposes How the Media Distort the News* (2001) and *Arrogance: Rescuing America from the Media Elite* (2003).

"They Think You're a Traitor" is the introduction to *Bias.* In the book, Goldberg claims that the media twists facts, ignores conservative opinions, and fabricates stories to further its liberal agenda. Goldberg wrote *Bias* after retiring from CBS.

"They Think You're a Traitor"

∾ Prereading Question

Liberals often argue that television news is hostile to their views; conservatives often make the same argument. Journalists themselves argue that they are neutral observers who simply report the facts, leaving viewers to reach their own conclusions. With which group would you most agree—liberals, conservatives, or the journalists?

I have it on good authority that my liberal friends in the news media, who account for about 98 percent of *all* my friends in the news media, are planning a big party to congratulate me for writing this book. As I understand it, media stars like Dan Rather and Tom Brokaw and Peter Jennings will make speeches thanking me for actually saying what they either can't or won't. They'll thank me for saying that they really do slant the news in a leftward direction. They'll thank me for pointing out that, when criticized, they reflexively deny their bias while at the same time saying their critics are the ones who are really biased. They'll thank me for observing that in their opinion liberalism on a whole range of issues from abortion and affirmative action to the death penalty and gay rights is not really liberal at all, but merely reasonable and civilized. Finally, they'll thank me for agreeing with Roger Ailes of Fox News that the media divide Americans into two groups—moderates and right-wing nuts.

My sources also tell me that Rather, Brokaw, or Jennings—no one is sure which one yet—will publicly applaud me for alerting the networks that one reason they're all losing viewers by the truckload is that fewer and fewer Americans trust them anymore. He'll applaud, too, when I say that the media need to be more introspective, keep an open mind when critics point to specific examples of liberal bias, and systematically work to end slanted reporting.

According to the information I've been able to gather, this wonderful event will take place at a fancy New York City hotel, at eight o'clock in the evening, on a Thursday, exactly three days after Hell freezes over.

Okay, maybe that's too harsh. Maybe, in a cheap attempt to be funny, I'm maligning and stereotyping the media elites as a bunch of powerful, arrogant, thin-skinned celebrity journalists who can dish it out, which they routinely do on their newscasts, but can't take it. Except I don't think so, for reasons I will come to shortly.

First let me say that this was a very difficult book to write. Not because I had trouble uncovering the evidence that there is in fact a tendency to slant the news in a liberal way. That part was easy. Just turn on your TV set and it's there. Not every night and not in every story, but it's there too often in too many stories, mostly about the big social and cultural issues of our time.

What made doing this book so hard was that I was writing about people I have known for many years, people who are, or once were, my friends. It's not easy telling you that Dan Rather, whom I have worked with and genuinely liked for most of my adult life, really is two very different people; and while one Dan is funny and generous, the other is ruthless and unforgiving. I would have preferred to write about strangers. It would have been a lot easier.

Nor is it easy to write about other friends at CBS News, including an important executive who told me that of course the networks tilt left—but also warned that if I ever shared that view with the outside world he would deny the conversation ever took place.

I think this is what they call a delicious irony. A news executive who can tell the truth about liberal bias in network news—*but only if he thinks he can deny ever saying it!* And these are the people who keep insisting that all they want to do is share the truth with the American people!

It wasn't easy naming names, but I have. I kept thinking of how my colleagues treat cigarette, tire, oil, and other company executives in the media glare. The news business deserves the same hard look because it is even more important.

Fortunately, I was on the inside as a news correspondent for twenty-eight years, from 1972, when I joined CBS News as a twenty-six-year-old, until I left in the summer of 2000. So I know the business, and I know what they don't want the public to see.

Many of the people I spoke to, as sources, would not let me use their names, which is understandable. They simply have too much to lose. You can talk freely about many things when you work for the big network news operations, but liberal bias is not one of them. Take it from me, the liberals in the newsroom tend to frown on such things.

And there are a few things that are not in this book—information I picked up and confirmed but left out because writing about it would cause too much damage to people, some powerful, some not, even if I didn't use any names.

But much of what I heard didn't come from Deep Throat sources in parking garages at three o'clock in the morning, but from what the big network stars said on their own newscasts and in other big public arenas, for the world to hear.

When Peter Jennings, for example, was asked about liberal bias, on *Larry King Live* on May 15, 2001, he said, "I think bias is very largely in the eye of the beholder." This might offend the two or three conservative friends I have, but I think Peter is right, except that instead of saying "*very largely*" he should have left it as "*sometimes* in the eye of the beholder." Because it's true that some people who complain about liberal bias think Al Roker the weatherman is out to get conservatives just because he forecast rain on the Fourth of July. And some people who say they want the news without bias really mean they want it without *liberal* bias. *Conservative* bias would be just fine.

Some of Dan, Tom, and Peter's critics would think it fine if a story about affirmative action began, "Affirmative action, *the program that no right-thinking American could possibly support*, was taken up by the U.S. Supreme Court today." But I wouldn't. Bias is bias.

It's important to know, too, that there isn't a well-orchestrated, vast left-wing conspiracy in America's newsrooms. The bitter truth, as we'll see, is arguably worse.

Even though I attack liberal *bias*, not liberal *values*, I will be portrayed by some of my old friends as a right-wing ideologue. Indeed, I've already faced this accusation. When I wrote an op-ed for the *Wall Street Journal* in 1996 about liberal bias among the media elites, my professional life turned upside down. I became radioactive. People I had known and worked with for years stopped talking to me. When a *New York Post* reporter asked Rather about my op-ed, Rather replied that he would not be pressured by "political activists" with a "political agenda" "inside or outside" of CBS News. The "inside" part, I think, would be me.

Sadly, Dan doesn't think that any critic who utters the words "liberal bias" can be legitimate, even if that critic worked with Dan himself for two decades. Such a critic cannot possibly be well-meaning. To Dan, such a critic is Spiro Agnew reincarnated, spouting off about those nattering nabobs of negativism. Too bad. A little introspection could go a long way.

I know that no matter how many examples I give of liberal bias, no matter how carefully I try to explain how it happens, some will dismiss my book as the product of bad blood, of a "feud" between Dan Rather and me. How do I know this? Because that is exactly how Tom Brokaw characterized it when I wrote a second *Wall Street Journal* piece about liberal bias in May 2001.

In it I said that as hard as it may be to believe, I'm convinced that Dan and Tom and Peter "don't even know what liberal bias is." "The problem," I wrote, "is that Mr. Rather and the other evening stars think that liberal bias means just one thing: going hard on Republicans and easy on Democrats. But real media bias comes not so much from what party they attack. Liberal bias is the result of how they see the world."

The very same morning the op-ed came out, Tom Brokaw was on C-SPAN promoting his new book, when Brian Lamb, the host, asked about my op-ed. Tom smiled and said he was "bemused" by the column, adding, "I know that he's [Goldberg's] had an ongoing feud with Dan; I wish he would confine it to that, frankly."

Here's a bulletin: in my entire life I have mentioned Dan Rather's name only once in a column, be it about liberal media bias or anything else. Five years earlier, when I wrote my first and only other piece about liberal bias, I did in fact talk about the "media elites," of which Dan surely is one. So counting that (and before this book), I have written exactly two times about Dan Rather and liberal bias—or, for that matter, about Dan Rather and any subject, period!

Two times! And that, to Tom Brokaw, constitutes a "feud," which strikes me as a convenient way to avoid an inconvenient subject that Tom and many of the other media stars don't especially like to talk about or, for that matter, think too deeply about.

I also suspect that, thanks to this book, I will hear my named linked to the words "disgruntled former employee" and "vindictive." While it's true I did leave CBS News when it became clear that Dan would "never" (his word) forgive me for writing about liberal bias in the news, let me state the following without any fear whatsoever that I might be wrong: *Anyone who writes a book to be vindictive is almost certainly insane and at any moment could find himself standing before a judge who, acting well within the law, might sign official papers that could result in that "vindictive" person being committed to a secure facility for people with mental defects.*

I don't know this from firsthand experience, but my guess is it would be easier to give birth to triplets than write a book, especially if you've never written one before. Staring at a blank page on a computer screen for hours and hours and hours is not the most efficient way to be vindictive. It seems to me that staring at the TV set for a couple of seconds and blowing a raspberry at the anchorman would take care of any vindictive feelings one might have.

So, does all of this lead to the inevitable conclusion that all the big-time media stars bat from the left side of the plate? Does it mean that there are no places in the media where the bent is undeniably conservative? Of course not!

Talk radio in America is overwhelmingly right of center. And there are plenty of conservative syndicated newspaper columnists. There are "magazines of opinion" like the *Weekly Standard* and *National Review.* There's Fox News on cable TV, which isn't afraid to air intelligent conservative voices. And there's even John Stossel at ABC News, who routinely challenges the conventional liberal wisdom on all sorts of big issues. But, the best I can figure, John's just about the only one, which says a lot about the *lack* of diversity inside the network newsrooms.

On February 15, 1996, two days after my op-ed on liberal bias came out in the *Wall Street Journal*, Howard Kurtz of the *Washington Post* wrote about the firestorm it was creating. "The author was not some conservative media critic, but Bernard Goldberg, the veteran CBS News correspondent. His poison-pen missive has angered longtime colleagues, from news division president Andrew Heyward and anchor Dan Rather on down."

Kurtz quoted several dumbfounded CBS News people, one of whom suggested I resign, and ended his story with something I told him, more out of sadness than anything else. Journalists, I said, "admire people on the outside who come forward with unpopular views, who want to make something better. But if you're on the inside and you raise a serious question about the news, they don't embrace you. They don't admire you. They think you're a traitor."

I am not a traitor, nor am I the enemy. And neither are the millions of Americans who agree with me. The enemy is arrogance. And I'm afraid it's on the other side of the camera.

Textual Questions

1. Why does Goldberg open with the description of the thanks he'll receive from members of the news media "exactly three days after Hell freezes over"? How does this tongue-in-cheek opening establish the thesis of Goldberg's essay?

2. If there is no "vast left-wing conspiracy" slanting the news in a liberal direction, then how does Goldberg prove that the reality is "arguably worse"?

3. What examples does Goldberg use in his editorials to describe liberal media bias? How effective are these examples?

Rhetorical Questions

4. What image of himself does Goldberg create in this essay? How does he do this and how effective is it in making him credible?

5. How does Goldberg define *liberal bias*? And how is this different from *liberal values*?

6. Why is Goldberg defined by his critics as a "traitor"? How does he argue that the real "enemy [of the television news media] is arrogance" rather than a maligned "traitor"? Why would Goldberg be defined as a "whistle-blower"? How would he benefit from such a definition of himself and of his actions? Does this definition seem accurate to you?

Intertextual Questions

7. How does Goldberg's argument about liberal bias connect with Steve Powers and Neal Postman's arguments about bias in language and pictures? How do the two support one another?

8. After reading both Goldberg and Eric Alterman, which argument do you find most persuasive? Are the media biased liberally or conservatively? Or both? Or neither?

Thinking Beyond the Text

9. Watch the local news in your home town—or in the town where you attend school—for one week. Make a list of the stories that are covered and, beside each, indicate whether you think the bias in the story was liberal, conservative, or neutral. After a week of careful viewing, do you believe Goldberg's argument that the news media are liberally biased, overall? Or is Goldberg wrong?

10. Do you believe that the media are biased overwhelmingly in favor of liberal views, as Goldberg argues? If the media are biased in such a way, then why do you believe that conservative politicians during George W. Bush's presidency were able to control both houses of Congress and the White House itself?

For Writing & Discussion

11. Goldberg focuses his analysis on a simple binary: liberal and conservative. These are the biases he sees. Are there other biases in the news media? In an essay, explain what one of these biases may be. Be sure to define the bias you see and to analyze at least one story to support your conclusion.

ERIC ALTERMAN

Eric Alterman (born in 1960) is a journalist who has written for *Rolling Stone*, the *New York Times*, the *Washington Post, Vanity Fair*, and other publications. His writings often address what he sees as an assault on democracy by the government and corporations in manipulating public interests. Alterman's books include *Sound and Fury: The Washington Punditocracy and the Collapse of American Politics* (1992), *Who Speaks for America?: Why Democracy Matters in Foreign Policy* (1998), and *When Presidents Lie: A History of Official Deception and Its Consequences* (2004).

"You're Only As Liberal As the Man Who Owns You" is an excerpt from Alterman's 2003 book *What Liberal Media?: The Truth about Bias and the News,* where Alterman argues against the belief that the media is liberally biased.

You're Only As Liberal As the Man Who Owns You

∽ Prereading Question

If a journalist works for a given company, is it possible for him/her to report accurate and honest information about that company to the general public? Under what conditions is the journalist's integrity compromised? How can such compromising circumstances be avoided? Do they need to be? Why?

"Repeat something often enough and people will believe it" goes the adage, and this is nowhere truer than in American political journalism. As four scholars writing in the *Journal of Communication* observed in a study of the past three elections, "claiming the media are liberally biased perhaps has become a core rhetorical strategy by conservative elites in recent years." As a result, these unsupported claims have become a "necessary mechanism for moving (or keeping) analytical coverage in line with their interests." Another way of saying this is that conservatives have successfully cowed journalists into repeating their baseless accusations of liberal bias by virtue of their willingness to repeat them . . . endlessly.

The psychological effects of conservatives' persistent attacks on the SCLM (so-called liberal media) are significant. In seeking to explain why, well before 9/11, President Bush's life was "more pleasant than Clinton's ever was, even at the start of his presidency," *Washington Post* White House reporter John Harris pointed to "one big reason for Bush's easy ride; There is no well-coordinated corps of aggrieved and methodical people who start each day looking for ways to expose and undermine a new president." Harris expanded on the difference:

> There was just such a gang ready for Clinton in 1993. Conservative interest groups, commentators and congressional investigators waged a remorseless campaign that they hoped would make life miserable for Clinton and vault themselves to power. They succeeded in many ways. One of the most important was their ability to take all manner of presidential miscues, misjudgments or controversial decisions and exploit them for maximum effect. Stories like the travel office firings flamed for weeks instead of receding into yesterday's news. And they colored the prism through which many Americans, not just conservative ideologues, viewed Clinton. It is Bush's good fortune that the liberal equivalent of this conservative coterie does not exist.

It does not matter that the evidence for liberal bias often disintegrates upon careful scrutiny. It works anyway. To be fair, it is enormously difficult to design an intellectually respectable study that tells us much of significance about journalistic bias because no one can control for events. George W. Bush earned enormously more generous coverage in the aftermath of the 9/11 attacks than he had in nine previous months of his presidency. But the composition of the press corps was obviously unchanged. Did reporters turn less liberal overnight—in which case, the entire argument about the SCLM is now consigned to history's proverbial dustbin? Or did the composition of the relevant issues change? And in an atmosphere of constantly changing issues, how is it possible to measure, scientifically, the treatment the issues receive in the media?

Another problem with accusations of liberal bias in the media is definitional. Just what constitutes a "liberal" bias anyway? The folks at Fox News Channel stake the network's identity on the claim that its programs are "fair and balanced," rather than "conservative." Whenever a reporter inquires about this, Fox's chairman and CEO, Roger Ailes, dismisses the question as itself evidence of liberal bias and says something like: "Fox is not a conservative network! I absolutely, totally deny it." According to Ailes, Fox's mission is no more controversial than "to provide a little more balance to the news" and "to go cover some stories that the mainstream media won't cover." No one believes this; in fact, it's hard to believe that even Ailes does, which helps explain why he felt free to send memos to Karl Rove offering post–9/11 political advice to George W. Bush. But the tendency to insist that reality is whatever happens to comport with one's own ideological bias is not restricted to conservatives. The British reporter Robert Fisk is perhaps the most anti-American correspondent employed by a major English-language newspaper. His reports in the London-based *Independent* are no less biased than the average FNC broadcast, albeit in the opposite direction. But Fisk sees the problem with the other side as simply "the cowardly, idle, spineless way in which American journalists are lobotomizing their stories." Like his opposite numbers at Fox, Fisk seems to believe that the problem of truth is no more complex than the fact that he gets it and the other guys don't. "Why do we journalists try so hard to avoid the truth?" he asks. "All we have to do is tell the truth."

But no content study can measure truth. Philosophers cannot even define it. Most, therefore, do not even try. Content studies, therefore, are rarely "scientific" in the generally understood connotation of the term. Many are merely pseudoscience, ideology masquerading as objectivity. When, in the spring of 2002, an independent Web site ran some numbers and pronounced the *New York Times*'s Paul Krugman—also an economist at Stanford, Princeton, and MIT—to be the most partisan of newspaper pundits by virtue of the mathematical ratio of the number of remarks critical of the Bush Administration per word published, Krugman made the following argument in response:

> Suppose, just for the sake of argument, that the Bush administration was, in a fundamental way, being dishonest about its economic plans. Suppose that the numbers used to justify the tax cut were clearly bogus, and that the plan was in fact obviously a budget-buster. Suppose that the Social Security reform plan simply ignored the system's existing obligations, and thus purported to offer something for nothing. Suppose that the Cheney energy report deliberately misstated the nature of the country's actual energy problems, and used that misstatement to justify subsidies to the energy industry. Suppose also that I found myself writing an economics column as these plans were being sold— and that I was a highly competent economist, if I say so myself. Suppose that as an economist able to do my own analysis, not obliged to rely on conflicting quotes from the usual suspects, I was in a position to spot right away that some of the stuff being peddled made no sense—and clued in enough to get hold of experts who could tell me what was wrong with the other stuff. Suppose that I had been repeatedly proved right in my critiques of the Bush administration's assertions, even in cases where nobody else in the media was willing to take my criticisms seriously—for example, suppose that, because I understand microeconomics a lot better than your average columnist, I realized that economists who said that California's electricity crisis had a lot to do with market manipulation were probably right, more than a year before conventional wisdom was willing to contemplate the possibility. In this hypothetical situation, what sort of columns should I have been writing? Does the ideal of "nonpartisanship" mean that I should have mixed my critiques of Bush policies with praise, or with attacks on the hapless, ineffectual Democrats, just for the sake of perceived balance? Given what I knew to be the truth, would that even have been ethical?

Because these kinds of objections are well known, some researchers seeking to demonstrate the liberal bias of the elite press corps have turned to other means to try to prove that reporters are liberals who vote Democratic and look down their noses at people who don't. The right's Rosetta Stone in this regard is the now famous poll of "Washington bureau chiefs and congressional correspondents" released in 1996 by the Freedom Forum. "Ever since a now-legendary poll from the Media Studies Center showed that 89 percent of Washington journalists voted for Clinton in 1992, it has been hard to deny that the press is 'liberal,'" wrote Christopher Caldwell, a *Weekly Standard* writer, in the *Atlantic Monthly,* in one typical rendering. Caldwell's rendering could stand for thousands more such assertions.

The conservative pundit James Glassman employed these results to declare in the *Washington Post*: The people who report the stories are liberal Democrats. This is the shameful open secret of American journalism. That the press itself . . . chooses to gloss over it is conclusive evidence of how pernicious the bias is." Here Glassman makes a common tautological claim, insisting that the denial of crime is evidence of guilt. In addition he equates Clinton voters with "liberal Democrats," again positing no evidence. Such carelessness ought to be intellectually indefensible to anyone who takes a moment to consider it. Bill Clinton ran in 1992 quite self-consciously as a "New Democrat," heavily supported by the centrist Democratic Leadership Council. He hailed from a conservative Southern state. He supported the death penalty, "free trade," and "an end to welfare as we know it." In foreign policy, his hawkish views won him the support of right-wingers like William Safire and many hard-line neoconservatives. The only way to conclude that a Clinton voter is de facto a "liberal Democrat" is by refusing to make any distinctions between the words "liberal" and "Democrat"—a distinction that keeps the Democrats in office in much of the southern and western parts of the nation.

Taken outside of the singular context of U.S. politics, moreover, the insistence that "Democrat" equals "liberal" grows even more problematic. The entire context of American politics exists on a spectrum that is itself well to the right of that in most industrialized democracies. During the 1990s, Bill Clinton was probably further to the right than most ruling West European conservatives, such as Germany's Helmut Kohl and France's Jacques Chirac. Indeed, virtually the entire axis of political conversation in the United States takes place on ideological ground that would be considered conservative in just about every nation in democratic Western Europe.

In late October 2002, I took a trip to five cities in France, Spain, Italy, and Germany to meet with dozens of influential writers, editors, and cultural voices, both individually and in groups, in these four countries. Everywhere people voiced considerable admiration and affection for "America" in the abstract and a deep, if sometimes baffling, attraction to

American culture, both popular and literary. The once-reflexive anti-Americanism inspired by the Vietnam War and the Cold War romance with communism among these elites had been entirely dispelled. Almost all expressed solidarity with America vis-à-vis the 9/11 attacks. Alessandro Portelli, editor of an Italian literary magazine, voiced the hope that America's recognition of its own vulnerability might help the nation develop some empathy for the vulnerable elsewhere in the world, who lack the ability to act on the world stage with impunity. Yet the primary response, as Portelli saw it, as voiced in the media and among well-known American intellectuals, has "a rhetoric of the exceptionalism of American sorrow," with a ready-made accusation of "anti-Americanism" employed to silence anyone who questions the views of the current administration. Similarly, in Paris, Jacques Rupnik of the Centre d'Etudes et de Recherches Internationales—a close friend and adviser to both ex-Prime Minister Lionel Jospin as well as the powerfully pro-American Czech President Vaclav Havel—endorsed the U.S. military response in both Afghanistan and the Balkans, expressing sincere gratitude. But, as with virtually everyone to whom I spoke, he took profound offense at "the extraordinary, almost staggering moral self-righteousness of this administration" toward the good opinion of the rest of the democratic world.

Virtually no one in high European media and cultural circles appeared willing to support or even defend the manner in which the Bush administration chose, unilaterally and without any prior consultation, to withdrawal from the Kyoto Protocol on global warming. Nor was anyone to be found who thought it wise for the United States to refuse to accept the jurisdiction of the nascent International Criminal Court. Without questioning Israel's right to live freely and securely within internationally recognized boundaries, nobody at all in these nations had a good word for the administration's unstinting support for the campaign of Israel's Ariel Sharon to expand Israeli settlements beyond the "Green Line," isolate Yasir Arafat, destroy the Palestinian Authority, and re-occupy Palestinian lands. Nor could I find anyone among the many dozens of people I met who thought it wise or prudent for the United States to engage in a pre-emptive war in Iraq, though Saddam Hussein and his brutal regime inspired neither excuses nor illusions. The very idea of the administration's campaign to legitimate its declared right of "pre-emption" filled most of my fellow discussants with horror and dread. Europeans were also virtually unanimous in their disapproval of Bush's enthusiasm, while governor of Texas, for the death penalty, and shocked in particular at what they deemed to be the moral callousness of his comments regarding the frequency with which he was willing to employ it.

In the U.S. media, such views are routinely dismissed as the products of old-fashioned European anti-Americanism at best, anti-Semitism at worst, or frequently, both. But these views were repeated to me across the political spectrum by conservatives as well as liberals, by "pro-American" writers and thinkers as well as those who had traditionally been aligned with resistance to American power; they were spoken in nations whose leadership had agreed to support the administration in its efforts to organize the global community for war in Iraq as well as in those that opposed it, by Jews and gentiles alike. Whether one shares these views or not, the conclusion is inescapable: in autumn 2002, a consensus had formed across the Atlantic on virtually every significant issue facing the U.S.-Atlantic community that located itself well to the left of the mainstream views that dominated debate in America's SCLM. The neoconservative domination of the U.S. media's foreign policy debate is hardly atypical. Suffice to say that the domestic fault line within European media and intellectual circles is far enough to the left to be considered off the map in our own SCLM.

Fundamental European assumptions across the political spectrum regarding the value of social welfare programs, cultural Puritanism, labor rights, gun control, public financing of elections, public goods for all, and the need to invest in public education might place most editors closer to the center of gravity of a *Nation* magazine editorial board meeting than "responsible" opinion in respectable SCLM circles. Indeed, the right's ideological offensive of the past few decades has succeeded so thoroughly that the very idea of a genuinely philosophically "liberal" politics has come to mean something quite alien to Amerian politics.

Contemporary intellectual definitions of liberalism derive by common accord from the work of the political theorist John Rawls. The key concept upon which Rawls bases his definition is what he terms the "veil of ignorance"; the kind of social compact based on a structure that would be drawn up by a person who has no idea where he or she fits into it. In other words, such a structure would be equally fair if judged by the person at the bottom as well as the top; the CEO as well as the guy who cleans the toilets. In real-world American politics, this proposition would be considered so utopian as to be laughable. In 2001, the average CEO of a major company received $15.5 million in total compensation, or 245 times, on average, what they paid their employees. The steps that would need to be taken to reach a Rawlsian state in such a situation are politically unthinkable, beginning (and ending) with a steeply progressive income tax, to say nothing of making universally available, high-quality health care, education, housing, public parks, beaches, and last but not least, political power. The ethical philosopher Peter Singer notes, moreover, in his study of the morals of globalization that even Rawls' demanding standards do not take into account our responsibilities as citizens to those who live beyond our borders, in places where starvation, disease, and child mortality are rampant. These too are fundamental liberal causes, almost entirely unmentionable in a society that offers the world's poor barely one-tenth of one percent of its gross domestic product in development aid. Judged by this standard, even to begin to argue on behalf of a genuinely liberal political program is to invite amused condescension . . . at best.

But if we put the question of ideology aside for a moment, it is not hard to see that in 1992 journalists had strong self-interested reasons to prefer Bill Clinton to George Bush. A second Bush administration, peopled with many of the same figures who had served in the three administrations that preceded it, would have meant a full sixteen years without a break during which journalists would be forced to cover the same old guys saying the same old things about the same old issues. What could possibly be the fun in that? More than enough careers had already been made during the Reagan/Bush years, and it was time now to give a new bunch of people a chance to show their stuff.

I would not deny that I sensed a great deal of excitement among the press corps in Little Rock on Election Day 1992, but it had little to do with ideology. Part of the thrill was generational. Bush was part of Reagan's generation; Clinton was, like most reporters, a baby boomer. Part of the exhilaration was substantive. Clinton was king of the political policy wonks, armed and ready with blueprints for a decade's worth of ambitious programs. He and his advisers would make politics fun again in a way that Republican, button-down CEOs could not. Moreover, Democrats generally admit to liking journalists and enjoy both leaking to, and socializing with, them. They are also not terribly good about disciplining themselves when they disagree with one another—which is most of the time—and hence, prove to be talkative sources. In addition, lest we forget, Clinton's reputation as the world's biggest horndog was by this time well known to all of us. Careers could be made in scandal reporting—just look at David Brock. Paul Gigot, the fiercely conservative columnist, now editor of the *Wall Street Journal*'s editorial page, has quipped, "Clinton was a gold mine. I often joke that if I had known back in 1992 what he would do for my career, I probably would have voted for him."

Even with all of these caveats, the case is not closed on the Freedom Forum poll. The study itself turns out to be based on only 139 respondents out of 323 questionnaires mailed, a response rate so low that most social scientists would reject it as inadequately representative. What's more, the responders were not the right 139. Independent investigative journalist Robert Parry contacted the Roper Center in Connecticut, where the results were tabulated, and was given a list of the company affiliations of the original recipients. This too proved problematic. Fewer than 20 percent of the questionnaires were sent to the major elite media outlets such as the *New York Times, Washington Post,* CBS, NBC, ABC, *Time,* and *Newsweek.* The bulk went to middle-sized-market papers such as the *Modesto Bee,* the *Denver Post,* and the *Dallas Morning News.* Roughly a quarter went to small-circulation newspapers where the job "bureau chief" actually means "entire bureau." These included the 58,000-circulation

Green Bay (Wis.) Press-Gazette, the 27,000-circulation *Sheboygan (Wis.) Press*, the *Mississippi Press*, *Fort Collins Coloradoan*, *Grand Junction (Colo.) Daily Sentinel*, and the *Thibodaux (La.) Daily Comet*. The same was true, Parry found, regarding the magazines included. *Time* and *Newsweek* were statistically overshadowed by publications like *Indian Country Today*, *Hill Rag*, *El Pregonero*, *Senior Advocate*, *Small Newspaper Group*, *Washington Citizen*, *Washington Blade*, and *Government Standard*. Interestingly, Parry noted, "What was most dramatically missing from the list were many of the principal conservative journals." This is due, he reasoned, to the fact that many conservative journals are organized as nonprofit corporations in order to be able to solicit tax-deductible donations. While many writers for conservative journals are extremely influential in the national media, they often cannot secure credentials from the congressional press gallery. The net result was that this particular survey, with its tiny numbers and somewhat randomly created data base, could easily have underestimated the conservatives' presence. It certainly overemphasized the influence of people without much influence in the national debate.

Then again, let's not kid ourselves. The percentage of elite journalists who voted for Bill Clinton in 1992 was probably consistent with the percentage he received among all well-educated urban elites, which was pretty high, Most people who fit this profile do indeed hold socially "liberal" views on issues like gun control, abortion, and school prayer, and I have no doubts that most journalists do too. The journalists whose alleged biases concern conservatives, live, according to the current parlance, in "blue" states and, when it comes to social issues, carry with them typical "blue state" values. The vast majority are pro-choice, pro-gun control, pro-separation of church and state, pro-feminism, pro-affirmative action, and supportive of gay rights.

Most journalists, as the sociologist Herbert Gans explained, are also congenitally "reformist." They believe in the possibility of improving things or they would not have chosen the profession in the first place. But both reformist sympathy and the "elite" association can cut more than one way, in political terms. Beginning with the 1980 election of Ronald Reagan and accelerating with the "Gingrich Revolution" of 1994, conservatives began to capture the language of reformism, in opposition to what Gingrich termed "reactionary liberalism." Much of the media bought into this etymological transformation and hence, a bias toward "reform" gives little clue about a person's ideology anymore. Journalists were naturally in sympathy with liberal (and in the case of John McCain, conservative) efforts to reform our campaign finance laws, But they also appeared quite well-disposed to conservative efforts to "reform" the nation's Social Security system so as to introduce private stock market accounts—at least before the Nasdaq crashed.

Also, lest we forget, journalists are not entirely immune to the seductions of affluence. While they are not nearly as well paid as the nation's corporate, legal, or medical elite, high-level Washington and New York journalists do make considerably more money than most Americans. They have spouses who do too, and hence, live pretty well. According to a study conducted by the sociologist David Croteau, 95 percent of elite journalists' households earned more than $50,000 a year, and 31 percent earned more than $150,000. He points out, "High levels of income tend to be associated with conservative views on economic issues such as tax policy and federal spending." And journalists are no different. The journalists' views on economic matters are generally consistent with their privileged position on the socioeconomic ladder, and, hence, well to the right of most Americans. They are more sympathetic to corporations, less sympathetic to government-mandated social programs, and far more ideologically committed to free trade than to the protection of jobs than are their fellow citizens. Polls, of course, are always of limited value, and comparing ones taken at different moments in history, based on differently worded questions, invites rhetorical abuse, I would not take any of these individual statistics to the bank. Nevertheless the overall pattern is undeniably consistent, and it is not "liberal."

But if top Washington journalists are personally social liberals and economic conservatives, one must still ask what it means insofar as identifying a bias in coverage. The answer to that question has to be, "it is not entirely clear."

When it comes to news content, the journalists are often the low people on the totem poll. They are "labor," or if they are lucky, "talent." They are not "management." They do not get to decide by themselves how a story should be cast. As *Washington Post* columnist Gene Weingarten put it in a column he wrote about an editorial disagreement with his bosses:

> My company is a large, liberal-minded institution that thrives on convivial collegial consensus among persons who—as human people professionally partnered in common goal-oriented pursuits—are complete coequals right up to the time an actual disagreement occurs. At this point, the rules of the game change slightly. We go from Candy Land to rock-paper-scissors. Editors are rock. Writers are those gaily colored wussy plastic paper clips. In short, I was given a choice: I could see the lucent wisdom of my editors' point of view and alter the column as directed, or I could elect to write a different column altogether, or (in an organization this large and diverse, there are always a multitude of options) I could be escorted to the front door by Security.

Weingarten is a much-beloved columnist and so is given quite a bit of freedom. Moreover, he does not cover politics—this column was published in the Style section, which affords him even more latitude. But even so, print journalists have editors who have editors above them who have publishers above them and who, in most cases, have corporate executives above them. Television journalists have producers and executive producers and network executives who worry primarily about ratings, advertising profits, and the sensibilities of their audience, their advertisers, and their corporate owners. When it comes to content, it is these folks who matter, perhaps more than anyone.

Examine, for a moment, the corporate structure of the industry for which the average top-level journalist labors. Ben Bagdikian, former dean of the journalism school at the University of California at Berkeley, has been chronicling the concentration of media ownership in five separate editions of his book, *The Media Monopoly*, which was first published in 1983 when the number of companies that controlled the information flow to the rest of us—the potential employment pool for journalists—was fifty. Today we are down to six.

Consider the following: When AOL took over TimeWarner, it also took over: Warner Brothers Pictures, Morgan Creek, New Regency, Warner Brothers Animation, a partial stake in Savoy Pictures, Little Brown & Co., Bullfinch, Back Bay, Time-Life Books, Oxmoor House, Sunset Books, Warner Books, the Book-of-the-Month Club, Warner/Chappell Music, Atlantic Records, Warner Audio Books, Elektra, Warner Brothers Records, Time-Life Music, Columbia House, a 40 percent stake in Seattle's Sub-Pop records, *Time* magazine, *Fortune, Life, Sports Illustrated, Vibe, People, Entertainment Weekly, Money. In Style, Martha Stewart Living, Sunset, Asia Week, Parenting,* Weight Watchers, *Cooking Light,* DC Comics, 49 percent of the Six Flags theme parks, Movie World and Warner Brothers parks, HBO, Cinemax, Warner Brothers Television, partial ownership of Comedy Central, E!, Black Entertainment Television, Court TV, the Sega channel, the Home Shopping Network, Turner Broadcasting, the Atlanta Braves and Atlanta Hawks, World Championship Wrestling, Hanna-Barbera Cartoons, New Line Cinema, Fine Line Cinema, Turner Classic Movies, Turner Pictures, Castle Rock productions, CNN, CNN Headline News, CNN International, CNN/SI, CNN Airport Network, CNNfi, CNN radio, TNT, WTBS, and the Cartoon Network. The situation is not substantially different at Disney, Viacom, General Electric, the News Corporation, or Bertelsmann.

The point of the above is to illustrate the degree of potential conflict of interest for a journalist who seeks to tell the truth, according to the old *New York Times* slogan, "without fear or favor," about not only any one of the companies its parent corporation may own, but also those with whom one of the companies may compete, or perhaps a public official or regulatory body that one of them may lobby, or even an employee at one of them with whom one of his superiors may be sleeping, or divorcing, or remarrying, or one of *their* competitors, or competitors' lovers, ex-lovers, and so on. While the consumer is generally unaware of these conflicts, the possibilities are almost endless—unless one is going to restrict one's journalism to nothing but preachy pabulum and celebrity gossip. The natural fear for journalists in this context is direct censorship on behalf of the parent's corporate interests. The number of incidents of even remotely documented corporate censorship is actually pretty rare. But focusing on examples of direct censorship in the U.S. media misses the point. Rarely does some story that is likely to arouse concern ever go far enough to actually need to be censored at the corporate level. The reporter, the editor, the producer, and the executive producer all understand implicitly that their jobs depend in part on keeping their corporate parents happy.

Television viewers received a rare education on the corporate attitude toward even the slightest hint of criticism of the big cheese when, on the morning after Disney took over ABC, *Good Morning America* host Charles Gibson interviewed Thomas S. Murphy, chairman of Capital Cities/ABC, and Disney's Michael D. Eisner. "Where's the little guy in the business anymore?" Gibson asked. "Is this just a giant that forces everybody else out?" Murphy, now Gibson's boss, replied, "Charlie, let me ask you a question. Wouldn't you be proud to be associated with Disney? . . . I'm quite serious about this."

While some editors and producers profess to be able to offer the same scrutiny to properties associated with their own companies that they offer to the rest of the world, in most cases, it taxes one's credulity to believe them. Journalists, myself included, are usually inclined to give their friends a break. If you work for a company that owns a lot of other companies, then you automatically have many such friends in journalism, in business, and in government. Michael Kinsley, the founding editor of Slate.com, which is funded entirely by the Microsoft Corporation, did the world a favor when he admitted, "Slate will never give Microsoft the skeptical scrutiny it requires as a powerful institution in American society—any more than *Time* will sufficiently scrutinize Time Warner. No institution can reasonably be expected to audit itself. . . . The standard to insist on is that the sins be of omission, not distortion. There will be no major investigations of Microsoft in Slate." Eisner said much the same thing, perhaps inadvertently, when he admitted (or one might say, "instructed"), "I would prefer ABC not to cover Disney. . . . I think it's inappropriate."

Media magnates have always sought to reign in their reporters, albeit with mixed success. In 1905, Standard Oil baron John D. Rockefeller predicted of the New York *World*, in 1905, "The owner of the *World* is also a large owner of property, and I presume that, in common with other newspaper owners who are possessed of wealth, his eyes are beginning to be opened to the fact that he is like Samson, taking the initiative to pull the building down upon his head." Similarly, advertisers have always attempted to exert pressure on the news and occasionally succeeded. What has changed is the scale of these pressures, given the size and the scope of the new media conglomerates, and the willingness of news executives to interfere with the newsgathering process up and down the line. One-third of the local TV news directors surveyed by the

Pew Project for Excellence in Journalism in 2000 indicated that they had been pressured to avoid negative stories about advertisers, or to do positive ones. Again, by the time you get to actual pressure on an editor or writer, a great many steps have already been taken. A 2000 Pew Research Center study found that more than 40 percent of journalists felt a need to self-censor their work, either by avoiding certain stories or softening the ones they wrote, to benefit the interests of the organizations for which they work. As the editors of the *Columbia Journalism Review* put it: "The truth about self-censorship is that it is widespread, as common in newsrooms as deadline pressure, a virus that eats away at the journalistic mission." And it doesn't leave much room for liberalism.

Conservative critics of the SCLM often neglect not only the power of owners and advertisers, but also the profit motive to determine the content of the news. Any remotely attentive consumer of news has noticed, in recent years, a turn away from what journalists like to term "spinach," or the kind of news that citizens require to carry out their duties as intelligent, informed members of a political democracy, toward pudding—the sweet, nutritionally vacant fare that is the stock in trade of news outlets. The sense of a news division acting as a "public trust," the characterization of the major networks throughout the Cold War—has given way to one that views them strictly as profit centers, which must carry the weight of shareholder demands the same way a TV sitcom or children's theme park must.

The net result has been the viral growth of a form of "news" that owes more to sitcoms and theme parks than to old-fashioned ideas of public and civic life. Instead of John Kennedy and Nikita Khrushchev as the iconic images of the world of "news," we are presented the comings and goings of Madonna, O. J. Simpson, Princess Diana, Gary Condit, and Chandra Levy. Again, this tabloid contagion, which afflicts almost all commercial news programs and newspapers, has many unhappy implications, but one obvious one is that the less actual "news" one covers, the less opportunity alleged liberals have to slant it.

Moreover, the deeply intensified demand for profit places renewed pressure on almost all media outlets to appeal to the wealthiest possible consumer base, which pretty much rules out the poor and the oppressed as the topic of investigative entrepreneurship. As *New York*'s Michael Wolff observed of the creation of two new "leisure" sections in the *New York Times* and the *Wall Street Journal*, "They don't want to be old-fashioned newspapers at all, but information brands, sensibility vehicles, targeted upscale-consumer media outlets. . . . The battle that has been joined is for the hearts and minds of the 2 million or 3 million wealthiest and best-educated people in the nation." In the not-so-distant past, Wolff notes, this kind of market-driven, consumerist definition of news would have inspired journalistic purists into principled opposition. But, "There's very little of that now: Any journalist with any career prospects is also a marketer, and packager, and all-around design- and demographic-conscious media professional. Every journalist is also a worried journalist, united with the business side in concerns about 'being viable.'" Even in a tough year like 2001, media companies were demanding—and receiving—profit margins in the 20 percent range. There is not much room for an overriding liberal bias on the great issues of the day between that particular rock and hard place, I'm afraid, even with the best (or worst) of intentions. Reporters could be the most liberal people on earth. But for all the reasons discussed above, it would hardly matter. They simply do not "make" the news.

The intensified emphasis on profits of recent years has resulted in a few high-profile scandals in the business. The *Los Angeles Times* sold its soul to the Staples Center in exchange for a pittance in paid advertising, offering to share advertising revenue in a phony magazine supplement designed to look like a genuine news report. Meanwhile, ABC News almost gave Ted Koppel, its most distinguished journalist, his walking papers for a comedy program with lower ratings but higher advertising profits. *San Jose Mercury-News* publisher Jay Harris resigned in a loud and eloquent protest against Knight Ridder's adherence to the "tyranny of the markets" that he said was destroying his newspaper. But no less important than the scandals are the non-scandals, the ones that are perhaps even more egregious in terms of the news values but, for whatever reason, are never brought before the public.

These priorities were never more evident than in the winter of 2002 during the long, drawn-out debate over campaign finance reform. The dramatic events in question dominated domestic coverage for weeks, if not months—a fact that many conservatives attributed to liberal media bias, since Americans, while supportive of reform, did not appear to be passionately interested in the story. But even within this avalanche of coverage, virtually no one in the media thought it worthwhile to mention that media industry lobbyists had managed to murder a key provision of the bill that would have forced the networks to offer candidates their least expensive advertising rates. True, it was a hard story for which to create snappy visuals; "Dead behind the eyes" in Dan Rather's parlance. But why is that not viewed as a challenge rather than a cause for capitulation? Political campaigns have become a get-rich-quick scheme for local television station owners, whose profit margins reflect the high rates they charge for political advertisements. This is no small factor in the mad pursuit of money that characterizes virtually every U.S. political campaign and makes a mockery of our claims to be a "one-person, one-vote" democracy.

Estimates of the income derived from these advertisements are up to $750 million per election cycle and continue to rise. The provision in question, originally passed by the Senate by a 69 to 31 margin, died in the House of Representatives following a furious lobbying campaign by the National Association of Broadcasters and the cable television industry.

After the House vote, *Broadcasting & Cable* magazine reported, "Back in their headquarters, the National Association of Broadcasters popped the champagne, deeply appreciative of the strong bipartisan vote stripping the [advertising provision]." The broadcasters' victory left the United States alone among 146 countries, according to one study, in refusing to provide free television time to political candidates.

The silent treatment given the advertising amendment was, in many ways, a repeat of the non-coverage of an even more significant story: The 1996 Telecommunications Act. When the Republicans took over Congress in 1994, the party leadership invited telecommunications corporate heads to Washington, sat down with them, and asked, "What do you want" The result, after many millions of dollars worth of lobbying bills, was a milestone of deregulation that vastly increased the ability of the big media conglomerates to increase (and combine) their market share in almost every medium. This expansion came, virtually without exception, at the expense of the smaller voices in those markets. The net result turned out to be a significant diminution in the opportunities for citizens to experience, and participate in, democratic debate. Based on a quick perusal of TV listings for 1995, apparently not one of the major TV news magazines of Westinghouse/CBS (*48 Hours, 60 Minutes*), Disney/Cap Cities/ABC (*Primetime Live, 20/20*), or General Electric/NBC (*Dateline NBC*) devoted even a minute of their 300 or so hours of airtime to the bill or the issues that lay beneath it. Where, one might ask, were the SCLM when their corporate owners were rewriting the rules of democratic debate to increase their own profits?

Ultimately, as Tom Johnson, former publisher of the *LA Times* and later president of CNN, would observe,

> It is not reporters or editors, but the owners of the media who decide the quality of the news. . . produced by or televised by their news departments. It is they who most often select, hire, fire, and promote the editors and publishers, top general managers, news directors, and managing editors—the journalists—who run the newsrooms. . . . Owners determine newsroom budgets, and the tiny amount of time and space allotted to news versus advertising. They set the standard of quality by the quality of the people they choose and the news policy they embrace. Owners decide how much profit should be produced from their media properties. Owners decide what quality levels they are willing to support by how well or how poorly they pay their journalists.

To ignore the power of the money at stake to determine the content of news in the decisions of these executives—given the role money seems to play in every other aspect of our society—is indefensibly childish and naive. The two heads of AOL Time Warner, Gerald Levin and Steve Case, took home a combined $241 million in 2001. Michael Eisner of Disney pulled down nearly $73 million. Leave aside the fact that stocks of each of these companies performed miserably in the same years, something you will probably not find discussed much in the myriad media properties they control. Ask yourself if the men and women who earn numbers like these are really sending forth aggressive investigators of financial and political malfeasance, charged, as the saying goes, to "afflict the comfortable and comfort the afflicted"? As longtime editor Harold Evans pointed out, in a situation like the current one, "The problem that many media organizations face is not to stay in business, but to stay in journalism."

Textual Questions

1. Why, according to Alterman, is it difficult to scientifically "prove" bias in the news media? How is the denial of liberal bias in the media used by some to make a "tautological claim"?

2. Does "Democrat" equal "liberal"? "Republican" equal "conservative"? What other labels might be more accurate?

3. According to Alterman, how do Europeans feel about America, both as a specific nation and as an abstraction? Why do they feel this way, and what connection do these feelings have with the news media?

Rhetorical Questions

4. How and why does Alterman argue that "truth" is a big, slippery concept? According to Alterman, how did coverage of 9/11 slant— liberal or conservative or some other way? Why?

5. What image of himself does Alterman create in his argument? Based on the argument he makes and the examples he uses, what do you think his own political bias might be? Or is he strictly neutral?

6. Why does Alterman list the companies controlled by the AOL/Time-Warner merger, a list starting with Warner Brothers Pictures and ending with Cartoon Network? What effect does this list have on a reader? Why does he imply that this kind of massive control is (a) good for business and (b) bad for the public interest?

Intertextual Questions

7. In the Bill of Rights, how is the "free press" described? Why is it necessary that the press be free—and what must it be free from? Based on Alterman's analysis, is the press in America free? Or is it somehow enslaved—and by what/whom?

8. Consider the arguments of both Bernard Goldberg and Alterman. Regardless of your own feelings about how the television news media may be biased, which of these two writers makes the most credible and persuasive argument? How does he do this more effectively than his opponent? How would Ben H. Bagdikian (in the next reading) respond to both Goldberg and Alterman?

Thinking Beyond the Text

9. Explaining why Bill Clinton was covered so favorably in 1992, Alterman argues that "A second Bush administration . . . would have meant a full sixteen years without a break during which journalists would be forced to cover the same old guys saying the same old things about the same old issues." Do you believe that this boredom with conservatives and desire for a change explains positive, excitement-filled coverage of Bill Clinton's run for the presidency? Or is this radically oversimplified? Or simply wrong?

10. Do you believe, like Alterman, that the media have a heavy control over how America thinks about its leaders—a control so total that it can affect the outcome of presidential elections?

For Writing & Discussion

11. Visit "Who Owns What": http://www.cjr.org/tools/owners/. In an essay, describe one of the corporations covered on this site and explain the scope of this corporations media holdings—from TV to newspaper to online venues.

BEN H. BAGDIKIAN

Ben H. Bagdikian (born in 1920) has worked for several publications, including the *Saturday Evening Post* and the *Washington Post*. For 40 years, he has written, edited, and contributed to numerous books focusing on analyzing and criticizing the media.

In 1983, Bagdikian's book *The Media Monopoly* was published, criticizing the monopolization of media content. The book was so successful it went through six reprints through 2000. "Common Media for an Uncommon Nation" is the first chapter in 2004's *The New Media Monopoly*, a revised and updated version of the book.

Common Media for an Uncommon Nation

∾ Prereading Question

List the sources from which you regularly get your information about the world—local, regional, national, and international. Consider every possible source of information, from e-mail and blogs to the campus newspaper and the nightly television news. What do you know about each of these sources of information? Are they biased in any clear ways, arguing specific political agendas or ideological viewpoints? Who controls each? (For example, is your school newspaper under the control of a publications committee, faculty advisor, etc.?)

> Power corrupts; absolute
> power corrupts absolutely.
>
> Lord Acton, 1887

> New York Times, *February 20, 2003. . . Senator Byron Dorgan, Democrat of North Dakota, had a potential disaster in his district when a freight train carrying anhydrous ammonia derailed, releasing a deadly cloud over the city of Minot. When the emergency alert system failed, the police called the town radio stations, six of which are owned by the corporate giant, Clear Channel. According to news accounts, no one answered the phone at the stations for more than an hour and a half. Three hundred people were hospitalized, some partially blinded by the ammonia. Pets and livestock were killed.*
>
> *Anhydrous ammonia is a popular fertilizer that also creates a noxious gas, irritating the respiratory system and burning exposed skin. It fuses clothing to the body and sucks moisture from the eyes. To date, one person has died and 400 have been hospitalized.*
>
> —HTTP://WWW.UCC.ORG/UCNEWS/MAY02/TRAIN.HTM

Clear Channel is the largest radio chain in the United States. It owns 1,240 radio stations with only 200 employees. Most of its stations, including the six in Minot, N. Dak., are operated nationwide by remote control with the same prerecorded material.

The United States, as said so often at home with pride and abroad with envy or hostility, is the richest country in the world. A nation of nineteen thousand cities and towns is spread across an entire continent, with the globe's most diverse population in ethnicity, race, and country of origin. Its people live in regional cultures as different as Amherst is from Amarillo. In contrast to other major nations whose origins go back millennia, the United States is a new country, less than three hundred years old. Consequently, it has not inherited the baggage of centuries of monarchs, czars, and religious potentates who held other populations powerless with absolute authority. From its birth, the United States' most sacred principle has been government by consent of the governed.

But the United States has always been in a state of constant change. Today it is living through one of the most sweeping technological innovations in its history. The speed with which the digital revolution has penetrated an entire society has been breathtaking. The computer and Internet, added to one of the world's largest quantity of mass media outlets, have altered the way millions live their daily lives. The new technology has almost miraculous functions that at their best have led to the betterment of numberless aspects of life, like science, scholarship, and medicine.

The country is unique in yet another way. It has left to each community control of its own schools, its own land use, its own fire and police, and much else, functions that in other developed countries are left solely to nationwide agencies. Given the United States' unique dependence on local civic decision making and its extraordinary multiplicity of local self-governing units and hundreds of media outlets, a rational system for a nation with such a vast diversity of people and places would be hundreds of individual local media owners, each familiar with the particular needs of his or her own community. It would be a reasonable assumption that only then would an American community receive the media programming it needs.

It would be a reasonable assumption. But it would be wrong.

Five global-dimension firms, operating with many of the characteristics of a cartel, own most of the newspapers, magazines, book publishers, motion picture studios, and radio and television stations in the United States. Each medium they own, whether magazines or broadcast stations, covers the entire country, and the owners prefer stories and programs that can be used everywhere and anywhere. Their media products reflect this. The programs broadcast in the six empty stations in Minot, N. Dak., were simultaneously being broadcast in New York City.

These five conglomerates are Time Warner, by 2003 the largest media firm in the world; The Walt Disney Company; Murdoch's News Corporation, based in Australia; Viacom; and Bertelsmann, based in Germany. Today, none of the dominant media companies bother with dominance merely in a single medium. Their strategy has been to have major holdings in all the media, from newspapers to movie studios. This gives each of the five corporations and their leaders more communications power than was exercised by any despot or dictatorship in history.

(In the manic-depressive cycle of corporate mergers that has transpired throughout the various editions of this book, the names of the Time and

Warner media conglomerates have changed four times. *Time* magazine was created in 1923 by Henry Luce and his Yale classmate Briton Hadden. Luce bought out Hadden, created Time, Incorporated, and went on to issue additional magazines like *Life*. In the first edition of this book in 1983, the firm was simply Time, Incorporated. In 1990—the fourth edition—Time merged with Warner Communications to form Time Warner. In 2000—the sixth edition—America Online, the Internet server, bought it all for $182 billion in the largest merger in history and renamed the firm AOL Time Warner. In 2003, the Securities and Exchange Commission announced that it would investigate AOL's accounting methods in the prelude to AOL's purchase of Time Warner, an investigation with embarrassing implications. In October 2003, the Board of Directors voted to drop "AOL" from the firm's U.S. title. Nevertheless, "AOL Time Warner" continues to have a separate corporate life overseas, as does AOL as a separate entity. In this—the seventh edition—the company, as leader of the Big Five, returns to its former name, Time Warner, except where the business context and the date make sense to use AOL Time Warner. Whatever its title, it is still the largest media firm in the world.)

No imperial ruler in past history had multiple media channels that included television and satellite channels that can permeate entire societies with controlled sights and sounds. The leaders of the Big Five are not Hitlers and Stalins. They are American and foreign entrepreneurs whose corporate empires control every means by which the population learns of its society. And like any close-knit hierarchy, they find ways to cooperate so that all five can work together to expand their power, a power that has become a major force in shaping contemporary American life. The Big Five have similar boards of directors, they jointly invest in the same ventures, and they even go through motions that, in effect, lend each other money and swap properties when it is mutually advantageous.

It is not necessary for a single corporation to own everything in order to have monopoly power. Nor is it necessary to avoid certain kinds of competition. Technically, the dominant media firms are an oligopoly, the rule of a few in which any one of those few, acting alone, can alter market conditions. The most famous global cartel, the Organization of Petroleum Exporting Countries (OPEC), has had brutal shooting wars between some of its members, and there are mutual jealousies among others. But when it comes to the purpose of their cartel—oil—they speak with one voice.

Thus, Time Warner, the largest media firm in the group, competes against another member of the Big Five, Bertelsmann, the largest publisher of English-language books in the world. But in Europe, AOL Time Warner is a partner with both Bertelsmann and News Corporation in the European cable operation, Channel V. According to the Securities and Exchange Commission (SEC), in 2001 AOL Time Warner needed to inflate AOL ad sales figures quickly for stock market reasons. So, in a complex set of transactions, Bertelsmann agreed to buy $400 million worth of advertising in its "competitor," AOL Time Warner, in return for AOL Time Warner transferring to Bertelsmann additional shares in a European firm in which they were already partners. Thus, Bertelsmann, according to the SEC, helped its "competitor" look healthier than it really was.

The Big Five "competitors" engage in numerous such cartel-like relations. News Corporation, for example, has a joint venture with the European operations of Paramount Pictures, which belongs to Viacom, another of its "competitors" in the Big Five. According to French and American securities agencies, Vivendi, the disintegrating French media conglomerate, had agreed to place $25 million worth of advertising in AOL media in return for AOL giving the French firm a share of one of its operations in France.

Some competition is never totally absent among the Big Five media conglomerates. The desire to be the first among many is as true for linked corporations as it is for politicians and nations. It was true two decades ago when most big media companies aspired to command market control in only one medium, for example, Gannett in newspapers; Time, Incorporated in magazines; Simon & Schuster in books; the three TV networks in radio; CBS in television; Paramount in motion pictures. But completion of that process fed an appetite for expansion toward a new and more powerful goal, a small group of interlocked corporations that now have effective control over all the media on which the American public says it depends.

ᧁ

Free Markets or Free Lunches?

Corporate life and capitalist philosophy are almost synonymous, and at the heart of capitalism is competition, or the contemporary incantation, "the free market." If the dominant media corporations behaved in accordance with classical capitalist dogma, each would experiment to create its own unique product. In the media world, *product* means news, entertainment, and political programs. It would mean offering differing kinds of programs that reflect the widely different tastes, backgrounds, and activities of the American population. To compete outright would mean unique products and the goal of a winner-take-all victory. Instead, the Big Five indulge in mutual aid and share investments in the same media products. They jointly conform to the periodic ratings that presume to show what kinds of programs have fractionally larger audiences, after which "the competitors" then imitate the winners and take slightly varying shares of the total profits.

One result of this constricted competition is that the thousands of media outlets carry highly duplicative content. Another result is that an innovative newcomer can hope to become a significant participant in the industry only as one of the many subsidiaries of the billion-dollar established giants. It is only in legends that David beats Goliath. In the history of modern media, if two experimenters in a garage create an ingenious invention that could revolutionize their industry, ultimately they have limited choices: either sell their device for millions or billions to a dominant firm or risk a hostile takeover or being crushed by the vast promotion and financial resources of a threatened Goliath. In the end, Goliath wins.

Practitioners of current American capitalism do not reflect Adam Smith's eighteenth-century image of an all-out rivalry in which merchants compete by keeping prices lower and quality higher than their fellow merchants. That classical mythology would create a final battlefield with one victor and four companies reduced to leftovers or worse. No dominant media firm, given its size and wealth, wishes to risk such a loss. The Ford Motor Company and General Motors do not compete to the death because each has too much to lose in an all-or-nothing rivalry. Similarly, the major media maintain their cartel-like relationships with only marginal differences among them, a relationship that leaves all of them alive and well—but leaves the majority of Americans with artificially narrowed choices in their media. It is the small neighborhood stores and restaurants that truly compete in products, price, and quality and are willing to risk failure in the process.

The narrow choices the dominant firms offer the country are not the result of a conspiracy. Dominant media members do not sit around a table parceling out market shares, prices, and products, as is done literally by OPEC. The five dominant media firms don't need to. They share too many of the same methods and goals. But if a new firm will strengthen their ability to promote the companies they already own, they will compete with each other to add it to their collections.

The possibilities for mutual promotion among all their various media is the basic reason the Big Five have become major owners of all kinds of media. For example, actors and actresses in a conglomerate's wholly owned movie studio can appear on the same company's television and cable networks, photographs of the newly minted celebrities can dominate the covers of the firm's wholly owned magazines, and those celebrities can be interviewed on the firm's wholly owned radio and television talk shows. The conglomerate can commission an author from its wholly owned book publishing firm to write a biography or purported autobiography of the new stars, which in turn is promoted on the firms' other media.

In addition to jousting for fractional points in broadcast ratings, each of the Big Five wants its shares on the stock market higher than the others (which also increases the value of shares and stock options owned by top executives). Although, if one conglomerate is momentarily ahead, it is tolerable for the others because being a momentary "loser" still allows prodigious profits. Television stations, for example, regard 30 percent profit a year as "low" (being a "loser") because the more successful TV stations that may be Number One at the moment can make 60 percent profit a year. As one of the executives in their trade, Barry Diller, once said of TV stations, "This is a business where if you are a birdbrain you have a thirty-five percent margin. Many good broadcasters have a forty-to-sixty-percent margin."

Though not a literal cartel like OPEC, the Big Five, in addition to cooperation with each other when it serves a mutual purpose, have interlocking members on their boards of directors. An interlock exists when the same board member sits on the board of more than one corporation (this is illegal only if the interlocked firms would form a monopoly if they merged). According to a study by Aaron Moore in the March/April 2003 *Columbia Journalism Review,* News Corporation, Disney, Viacom, and Time Warner have forty-five interlocking directors.

It is a more significant cooperation that closely intertwines all five into a mutual aid combine. The dominant five media conglomerates have a total of 141 joint ventures, which makes them business partners with each other. To cite only one example, News Corporation shares a financial interest with its "competitors" in 63 cable systems, magazines, recording companies, and satellite channels in the United States and abroad. All five join forces in one of Washington's most powerful lobbies, the National Association of Broadcasters, to achieve the laws and regulations that increase their collective power over consumers. In 2000, for example, the National Association of Broadcasters spent $2.5 million lobbying on communications issues, using 24 of its own lobbyists plus four independent lobbying firms, and that year made 64 percent of its campaign contributions to Republicans and 36 percent to Democrats. This is in addition to the lobbying and campaign money spent by the major media corporations on their own.

The media conglomerates are not the only industry whose owners have become monopolistic in the American economy. But media products are unique in one vital respect. They do not manufacture nuts and bolts: they manufacture a social and political world.

New technology has expanded the commercial mass media's unprecedented power over the knowledge and values of the country. In less than a generation, the five intertwined media corporations have enlarged their influence in the home, school, and work lives of every citizen. Their concentrated influence exercises political and cultural forces reminiscent of the royal decrees of monarchs rejected by the revolutionists of 1776.

The Big Five have become major players in altering the politics of the country. They have been able to promote new laws that increase their corporate domination and that permit them to abolish regulations that inhibit their control. Their major accomplishment is the 1996 Telecommunications Act. In the process, power of media firms, along with all corporate power in general, has diminished the place of individual citizens. In the history of the United States and in its Constitution, citizens are presumed to have the sole right to determine the shape of their democracy. But concentrated media power in news and commentary, together with corporate political contributions in general, have diminished the influence of voters over which issues and candidates will be offered on Election Day.

Conservative policies have traditionally been preferred by all large corporations, including the large media conglomerates. The country's five dominant media corporations are now among the five hundred largest corporations in the world. These five corporations dominate one of the two worlds in which every modern person is destined to live.

It is still true, of course, that the face-to-face, flesh-and-blood environment continues to be the daily reality for human beings. It is part of human evolution and if it has any order and social principles it is the result of the millennia of insights, conventions, and experiences of the human race.

In contrast, the mass media world began in earnest only two hundred fifty years ago. Many of its most dramatic and influential elements have emerged within the lifetimes of the present generation. The media world—newspapers, magazines, books, radio, television, movies, and now the Internet—occupies a major role in the commerce and private life of the entire population.

∾

New Media in a New World

Media corporations have always possessed the power to affect politics. That is not new in history. But the five dominant corporations—Time Warner, Disney, News Corporation, Viacom, and Bertelsmann—have power that media in past history did not, power created by new technology and the near uniformity of their political goals. The political and social content projected by these media to the country's population has had real consequences: the United States has the most politically constricted voter choices among the world's developed democracies. That raises fundamental questions about how and by whom the nature of democracy shall be determined.

The magnitude of the change may be more readily understood by looking back from today's twenty-first century. In retrospect, the awesome power of the contemporary mass media has in one generation been a major factor in reversing the country's progressive political, social, and economic momentum of the twentieth century. As a result, in the United States, the twenty-first century inherited a new, more extreme brand of conservative policies.

Twentieth-century politics began with a Republican president, Theodore Roosevelt (1901–1909), at a time when every city of any size had five or more competing newspapers with a broad range of politics, right, center, and left. With the support of a number of influential periodicals and a portion of its newspapers, Theodore Roosevelt initiated historic conservation of natural resources and dismantled huge interlocked corporate conglomerates, then called *trusts*. The control of trusts in writing laws, bribing officials, and damaging the social welfare had been exposed month after month by some of the country's leading writers in its most influential periodicals—Lincoln Steffens, Owen Wister, Ida Tarbell, Louis Brandeis (sixteen years before he became a member of the U.S. Supreme Court), Upton Sinclair, and many others. Their investigative articles appeared in major media—newspapers published by Joseph Pulitzer, E.W. Scripps, and the early Hearst. Articles asking for reform were centerpieces of influential national magazines like *Harper's, Atlantic, Cosmopolitan, McClure's,* and *Century.*

That fundamental period of confronting the urgent new needs of industrial democracy ended when J. P. Morgan and John D. Rockefeller decided to buy *Harper's* and *Atlantic* and other angry financiers paid high salaries to the most skilled editors to take positions more compatible with the vision of Wall Street banking houses. That, along with World War I, ended the period of reform.

A similar period of reform repaired the chaos created by the wildly uninhibited free markets of the 1920s. Franklin Roosevelt's New Deal (1932–1945) established new social and regulatory agencies after the Great Depression's corporate breakdowns. The New Deal also established immediate jobs and agencies for housing and feeding the country's poor and middle-class families. While Franklin Roosevelt, unlike his cousin Theodore, had no overwhelming media support before his election, the newspapers, which were the only medium that really counted at the time, had lost much of their credibility. They had glorified the failed policies that produced the shambles of the Wall Street Crash of 1929 and the Great Depression that followed. By the time that Franklin Roosevelt ran for president in 1932, desperate unemployment and murmurings of popular revolt were ominous. Fear led many of the once-conservative or neutral newspapers and magazines to moderate their opposition to the election of Roosevelt.

Roosevelt created what were, for that period, radical reforms, like the Securities and Exchange Commission to monitor corporations that sold shares to the public; Social Security to create old age pensions for much of the population; and laws that prevented banks from speculating in the stock market with their depositors' money. The uninhibited free market had created the wild euphoria of every-man-a-millionaire in the 1920s, which then led to the chaos. This had a temporary chastening effect on the main media's normal philosophy of "leave business alone."

In contrast, the presidencies of Ronald Reagan (1981–1988) and of the Bushes—George H.W. Bush (1989–1993), the forty-first president, and his son, George W. Bush, the forty-third president, who took office in 2000—again created an abrupt reversal. After his ascendancy to the presidency in 2000, the younger Bush engaged in a systematic reversal or cancellation of earlier natural resource conservation plans, reduced welfare, and adopted economic policies that hastened the flow of wealth to the most wealthy. The theory espoused by President Reagan had been that the wealth at the top would trickle down to create jobs for middle-class and poor workers. It was a long-discredited theory characterized by John Kenneth Galbraith: "If you feed the horse with enough oats, sooner or later it will leave something behind for the sparrows."

Any dynamic democracy inevitably changes political direction as conditions and public desires evolve. The radical changes of the late twentieth century obviously reflected universal alterations in technology, world economics, and other underlying tides. But the contemporary power of mass media imagery controlled by a small number of like-minded giant corporations played a powerful role. The media of that period, particularly broadcasters, were compliant with requests of the Reagan White House, for example, to limit access of reporters to the president himself. The former actor's folksy personality distracted much of the public's attention from the disastrous consequences that followed an expanded national debt. What happened after the 1990s in the American economy was an eerie echo of the wild storms of the 1920s that brought the crash of 1929.

There are multiple reasons for the politics of any country to change, but with growing force the major media play a central role in the United States. In the years after 1980, conservatives began the chant of "get the government off our backs" that accelerated the steady elimination of a genuinely progressive income tax. They adopted the goal of uninhibited corporate power. Political slogans advocating a shrinking government and arguments involving that idea filled the reportorial and commentary agendas of most of the country's major news outlets. It was the beginning of the end of government-as-protector-of-the-consumer and the start of government-as-the-protector-of-big-business. And the news industry, now a part of the five dominant corporations, reflected this new direction.

By the time Bush the Younger had become president, the most influential media were no longer the powerful *Harper's, Century,* and other influential national organs of one hundred years earlier that had helped to expose abuses and campaigned to limit the power of massive corporations. In sharp contrast to the major media that led to Theodore Roosevelt's reforms, the most adversarial media in 2000, both in size of audience and political influence, were the right-wing talk shows and a major broadcast network, the Murdoch News Corporation's Fox network, with its overt conservatism. Murdoch went further and personally created the *Weekly Standard,* the intellectual Bible of contemporary American conservatism and of the administration of Bush the Younger. Murdoch's magazine is delivered each week to top-level White House figures. The office of Vice President Cheney alone receives a special delivery of thirty copies.

It is not simply a random artifact in media politics that three of the largest broadcast outlets insistently promote bombastic far-right political positions. Murdoch's Fox radio and television have almost unwavering right-wing commentators. The two largest radio groups, Clear Channel and Cumulus, whose holdings dwarf the rest of radio, are committed to a daily flood of far-right propagandistic programming along with their automated music. Twenty-two percent of Americans polled say their main source of news is radio talk shows. In a little more than a decade, American radio has become a powerful organ of right-wing propaganda. The most widely distributed afternoon talk show is Rush Limbaugh's, whose opinions are not only right-wing but frequently based on untruths.

Dominant media owners have highly conservative politics and choose their talk show hosts accordingly. Editor Ron Rodriques of the trade magazine *Radio & Records* said, "I can't think of a single card-carrying liberal talk show syndicated nationwide." The one clearly liberal talk show performer, Jim Hightower of ABC, was fired in 1995 by the head of Disney, Michael Eisner, the week after Eisner bought the Disney company, which owns ABC.

The political content of the remaining four of the Big Five is hardly a counter to Fox and the ultraconservatism and bad reporting of dominant talk shows. American television viewers have a choice of NBC (now owned by General Electric), CBS (now owned by one of the Big Five, Viacom), and ABC, now owned by another of the Big Five, Disney. Diversity among the tens of thousands of United States media outlets is no longer a government goal. In 2002, the chairman of the Federal Communications Commission, Michael Powell, expressed the opinion that it would not be so bad if one broadcast giant owned every station in an entire metropolitan area.

The machinery of contemporary media is not a minor mechanism. The 280 million Americans are served, along with assorted other small local and national media, by 1,468 daily newspapers, 6,000 different magazines, 10,000 radio stations, 2,700 television and cable stations, and 2,600 book publishers. The Internet gave birth to a new and still unpredictable force, as later portions of this book will describe. Though today's media reach more Americans than ever before, they are controlled by the smallest number of owners than ever before. In 1983 there were fifty dominant media corporations; today there are five. These five corporations decide what most citizens will—or will not—learn.

It may not be coincidental that during these years of consolidation of mass media ownership the country's political spectrum, as reflected in its news, shifted. As noted, what was once liberal is now depicted as radical and even unpatriotic. The shift does not reflect the political and social values of the American public as a whole. A recent Harris poll showed that 42 percent of Americans say they are politically moderate, middle-of-the-road, slightly liberal, liberal, or extremely liberal, compared to 33 percent for the same categories of conservatives, with 25 percent saying "Don't know or haven't thought about it."

Dollars versus Votes

One force creating the spectrum change has been, to put it simply, money—the quantities of cash used to gain office. Spontaneous national and world events and the accidents of new personalities inevitably play a part in determining a country's legislation and policies. But in American politics, beyond any other single force, money has determined which issues and candidates will dominate the national discourse that, in turn, selects the issues and choices available to voters on Election Day.

The largest source of political money has come from corporations eager to protect their expanded power and treasure. The country's massive media conglomerates are no different—with the crucial exception that they are directly related to voting patterns because their product happens to be a social-political one. It is, tragically, a self-feeding process: the larger the media corporation, the greater its political influence, which produces a still larger media corporation with still greater political power.

The cost of running for office has risen in parallel with the enlarged size of American industries and the size of their political contributions to preferred candidates and parties.

In 1952, the money spent by all candidates and parties for all federal election campaigns—House, Senate, and presidency—was $140 million (sic). In 2000, the races spent in excess of $5 billion. Spending in the 2000 presidential campaign alone was $1 billion.

The growth of money in politics is multiplied by what it pays for—the growth of consultants skilled in, among other things, the arts of guile and deception that have been enhanced by use of new technology in discovering the tastes and income of the public.

Television political ads are the most common and expensive campaign instrument and the largest single expenditure in American political campaigns. Typically, the commercials are brief, from a few seconds to five minutes, during which most of the content consists of slogans and symbols (waving Americans flags are almost obligatory), useless as sources of relevant information. Television stations and networks are, of course, the recipients of most of the money that buys air time. This is why the country's political spectrum is heavily influenced by which candidate has the most money.

Incumbents always have an advantage in attracting money from all sources because even conservative business leaders want influence with whoever happens to vote for legislation, even if it is a liberal. Nevertheless, if one eliminates incumbents, the big spenders have almost always been the winners. Beginning in 1976, candidates who spent more than $500,000 were increasingly Republicans. Conservatives perpetually accuse Democrats of bowing to *special interests.* In the conservative lexicon, these are code words for labor unions. And, indeed, labor unions in 2000, for example, gave Democrats $90 million and Republicans only $5 million. But in the 1990s, corporate and trade association political action committees gave Republicans twice as much money as they gave to Democrats and in quantities many multiples larger than labor union political contributions. In the crucial midterm 2002 elections, when control of the Senate depended on a few votes, Democrats spent $44 million and Republicans $80 million. Republicans gained control of Congress, undoubtedly helped by President Bush, who, two months before the election, suddenly declared that the country would go to war against Iraq and that opponents would be seen as supporters of Saddam Hussein's tyranny. That alone took domestic economic troubles off the front pages and out of TV news programs.

Increasingly, House and Senate candidates have spent their own money on campaigns, a choice available only to multimillionaires. Thus, the money both of the wealthy and of corporate interests has come to dominate American politics in the single generation during which the country's political spectrum has shifted far to the right.

◌◌

The View from the Top

The major news media overwhelmingly quote the men and women who lead hierarchies of power. Powerful officials are a legitimate element in news because the public needs to know what leaders in public and private life are saying and doing. But official pronouncements are only a fraction of the realities within the population. Complete news requires more. Leaders, whether in public or private life and whatever their personal ethical standards, like most human beings, seldom wish to publicize information that discloses their mistakes or issues they wish to keep in the background or with which they disagree. Officials do not always say the whole truth.

Citizen groups issuing serious contrary studies and proposals for mending gaps in the social fabric get only sporadic and minimal attention in the major media. Consequently, some of the country's most pressing problems remain muted. Unless powerful official voices press for attention and remedies for those missing issues, the pressing problems remain unresolved.

It is not rare for speakers and large organizations to complain publicly that it is shameful for the richest and most powerful country in the world to have increasing numbers of citizens homeless, that the United States is the only industrial country in the world without universal health care, or that its rhetorical support of education seems to believe that this requires no additional money from the federal government—even though it is the federal government that requires local schools to meet higher standards. Or that the country withdrew unilaterally from previous treaties to protect the planetary environment. Or that, despite agreement to restrict existing stocks of Russian and American nuclear weapons, President Bush the Younger announced that he would consider military action against countries initiating nuclear weapons research while simultaneously announcing that the United States would restart its own nuclear weapons research.

These issues are not absent from major news media. They are reported but then they are dropped, though national stories about a distant kidnapped child can continue on front pages and television news for weeks. There is nothing harmful and often some good in persistent stories about individual human tragedies. But in the national news agenda, there is no such media persistence with problems that afflict millions. It is an unrelenting tragedy that more than 41 million Americans remain without health care, that millions of young people are jammed into inadequate classrooms with inadequate teaching staffs, that deterioration threatens Planet Earth as a human habitat, or that a similar threat is growth of nuclear weaponry in the United States and the rest of the world. Or that preemptive war as a permanent policy is the law of the jungle.

News executives claim periodically that no one's really interested in unmet domestic needs, or people are tired of bad news, or we had a story on that. This is the same industry that is proud of its ability to be artful and ingenious in making any kind of story interesting, in which many of the same editors pursue the "lost child story" that, in fact, interests only part of the audience and is ignored by the rest. Every reader of a newspaper or viewer of television will pay close attention and absorb copious detail on an issue that affects that reader personally, whether it is a jobless bookkeeper or the national prospects for the unemployed or a family member desperate for possible treatments for Alzheimer's disease.

The major news media fail to deal systematically with the variety of compelling social needs of the entire population. Those needs remain hidden crises, obscured in the daily flood of other kinds of news. Yet the weight of most reputable surveys shows that, in the late twentieth and early twenty-first century, most Americans were deeply concerned with systematic lack of funds for their children's education, access to health care, the growing crises in unemployment, homelessness, and steady deterioration of city and state finances.

But these issues are not high priorities among the most lavish contributors to political candidates and parties. Corporations have other high-priority issues. There is a world of wealth, stratospheric in its imperial heights, which is so beyond the life of most Americans that it is barely imaginable.

∾

When There Are No Limits

Though not typical of the average profitable corporation, disclosures in recent years show excesses that can be achieved by "getting the government off our backs." It was only through divorce paper filings that shareholders of General Electric (GE) and the public learned about the lack of limits on compensation that some large corporate leaders quietly grant themselves while keeping their stockholders and the public unaware of their almost obscene money and perquisites.

The most striking disclosure was the compensation and pension benefits for Jack Welch, the much-celebrated leader of General Electric, learned only when his wife's divorce filings became public. Mr. Welch, while still CEO of GE, received $16.7 million a year; access to the corporate aircraft; use of an $80,000-a-month Manhattan apartment, with its expenses (including wine, food, laundry, toiletries, and newspapers) paid for by the company; along with floor-level seats to New York Knicks basketball games, VIP seating at Wimbledon tennis games, a box at Yankee Stadium and Boston Red Sox games, four country club fees, security and limousine service at all times, satellite TV in his four homes, and dining bills at a favorite restaurant.

In retirement, Welch's pension continues most of the perquisites for life, plus $86,535 for the first thirty days of each year's consultancy, plus $17,307 for each additional day. These otherworldly heights of excess not only were hidden from the average American but also were vague to shareholders, thanks to obscure or undecipherable footnotes in annual reports.

Tyco, one of the Enron-like fiascos, forgave a $19 million loan to executive Dennis Koslowski, who needed it to pay for an additional home in Florida. Kozlowski and his partners were later charged with looting $600 million from their company.

∾

Vain Ambition Produced No "Big Six"

When Vivendi, the house of cards concocted by French corporate adventurer Jean-Marie Messier, came apart, his dream of a media empire gave GE a chance to join the Big Five that now dominate American media. Under Messier, Vivendi's buying spree had included the United States' last major independent publishing house, Houghton Mifflin, based in Boston, which was then sold to an investment group that operated it with changes in the company's mix of printed and online services.

Messier's hard-headed successor, Jean-Renee Fourtou, salvaged Vivendi by GE's $3.8 billion purchase and assumption of $1.6 billion in debt, giving GE 80 percent ownership of Vivendi-Universal, which includes Universal studios. This purchase also gave GE's new chairman, Jeffrey Immelt, the foundation to convert GE from a large collection of older industrial assets (weaponry, jet engines, etc.) to the new hot industry, the media. Immelt has said that the old industries were paying one-digit profits while the media pay 25–60 percent.

Immelt foresees an enlarged GE as a vertically integrated media firm overshadowing its older products. GE already owned the NBC TV network and cable networks including the USA Network, Sci-Fi, CNBC, MSNBC, Bravo, and Trio. The deal added Universal Pictures, Universal Television (producer of the high-profit program *Law & Order*), shares in five theme parks, and Telemundo, the big Spanish-language network. Barry Diller owns 7 percent of Vivendi. Despite Immelt's vision of GE as a major media conglomerate, GE was also planning to acquire the London-based medical firm Amersham for $9.5 billion and still promotes sales of GE gas turbines and wind energy, high-tech ovens, and medical devices like magnetic resonance imaging (MRI).

Immelt still has to escape what Hollywood calls "the Curse of Universal," a threat based on a long line of business and other failures of former owners of the studio, from its founder Carl Laemmle in 1912 to the unfortunate Messier.

New names, systems, and services inevitably will, like GE, emerge; they add an increment to the media scene but do not approach the magnitude and power of the truly giant all-media conglomerates described in this book.

"Humble" Domination

The phrase "humble beginning" is almost obligatory in many corporate histories. Often it has been even more humble than displayed in the company's history. In the case of all parties to the $107 billion in Messier's deals, they were, indeed, if not humble at least not magisterial. Messier's former company name had been a water company and became a major builder of such systems worldwide. But it really began humbly as sewage. The original Vivendi firm inherited the bumbling Louis Napoleon's attempt to regain stature by constructing the Paris sewers. Vivendi's target, Seagram, for which Messier paid $34 million in stock, had the reputation of humbly shipping impressive quantities of liquor from Canada into the United States during Prohibition via groups the tabloids insisted on calling "gangs," using the word "smuggling," although neither word appeared in Seagram official company literature. Seagram was started as a humble Canadian saloon by the Bronfman family.

There has also been genuine public service by the senior Bronfman, who helped rescue European Jews from persecution or worse and was instrumental in exposing the Nazi collaboration of Kurt Waldheim, former secretary-general of the United Nations. He also helped track down Swiss bankers who profited from money once deposited by Jews murdered in the Holocaust.

A Built-in Imbalance

Most of the more conventionally wealthy families are able to buy private services that ordinary families cannot obtain in a publicly funded school or other community and national facilities that suffer from budget cuts made, among other reasons, to provide tax cuts for the wealthy.

The many decades of only passing consideration of the major needs of most people have produced hopelessness about the possibility for change. Consequently, masses of potential voters have become resigned to the assumption that what the major media tell them is the norm and now unchangeable. In the first edition of this book, twenty years ago, I observed "media power is political power." The five dominant media firms, now among the largest in the world, have that power and use it to enhance the values preferred by the corporate world of which they are a part.

The imbalance between issues important to corporate hierarchies and those most urgent to the population at large is obscured by the neutralist tone of modern news. The rightward impact of modern news is not in the celebrated inflamed language that once characterized nineteenth-century sensationalist headlines and language. Today the imbalance is in what is chosen—or not chosen—for print or broadcast. Media politics are reflected in the selection of commentators and talk show hosts. It is exercised powerfully in what their corporations privately lobby for in legislation and regulations, and in the contributions they and their leaders make to political parties and candidates. It is the inevitable desire of most large corporations to have a political environment that is friendly to weakening minimum standards for public service and safety in order to produce maximum corporate profit levels and lower the corporate share of city, state, and federal taxes. But these seldom provide comparable benefits for the common good, like health care, safe environments, and properly funded public education.

In the last twenty-five years, the media world has experienced accelerated inventions and with them conflicts and uncertainties about which media will survive and which will die off. Yet again, newspeople agonize whether a new method of communication that distracts the country's youths might condemn the daily newspaper to an early death. Similar questions have arisen about other traditional media, like magazines and books, to be dealt with later.

As Gutenberg's movable type was in his day, the new electronic media as a social force remain in a still-uncertain balance. Today, massive demonstrations protesting a government policy have been gathered solely marshaling sympathizers by Internet. At the same time, the digital revolution has made ambiguous the privacy within one's home because a government official, or anyone else with enough skill, can enter the citizen's computer from a remote location and thereby end the historic assumption that "my home is my castle."

That question hovers over the extraordinary but unpredictable innovations of the electronic media and the transformations that are continuing in our time.

Textual Questions

1. How does Bagdikian use the opening quotation from a news story to set readers up for his argument about Clear Channel?

2. According to Bagdikian, in what ways is the United States of America unique in the world? How does this "uniqueness" fit into Bagdikian's overall argument?

3. How does Bagdikian use history to build his argument about the present—and to raise alarm about the future? How does Bagdikian connect the Big Five to the history of America, the rise of political advertising, and the use and abuse of political power in the United States? How effectively are these links established?

Rhetorical Questions

4. Which corporations have monopoly power over media outlets in America? Legally, how are they able to amass and maintain this power? What are the costs and benefits to the public?

5. What effect does Bagdikian hope to achieve by referring to the Big Five as cartels? What connotative meanings does this specific term contain?

6. How does Bagdikian support his contention that media power and political power are inseparable? Do you believe this part of his argument to be accurate? Based on your close reading of his essay, what political views do you think Bagdikian holds? How do his political views cause you to react to his overall argument?

Intertextual Questions

7. In what ways does Bagdikian's argument echo that of Herman and Chomsky? How are their arguments alike? How are they different?

8. Although they are focused on very different issues and examples, how do Bagdikian and Frank Rich's arguments reinforce one another? Do both Bagdikian and Rich seem to hold the same view of the promise of a free press?

Thinking Beyond the Text

9. Bagdikian clearly believes that corporate interests are very different from the best interests of the American public. How does he support his belief, how convincing is his argument, and do you agree or disagree with him about this clear and present "danger" to freedom?

10. Is the issue of corporate ownership truly as dangerous to the public as Bagdikian believes it to be? Or is his argument simply alarmist rhetoric?

For Writing & Discussion

11. List all of the local media outlets in your region—from the local newspaper(s) to the local television network affiliates to the local soft-rock channel on the FM dial. Working in groups, research these media outlets to find the names of their parent companies. In an essay, explain who owns what in your region.

VIRGIL SCUDDER

Virgil Scudder works as a media trainer, preparing corporate executives, government leaders, and public relations representatives on how to effectively work with newspapers, television news channels, and other forms of media. After working for years in large public relations firms, he founded Virgil Scudder & Associates in 1977. The firm of "media trainers" has worked with clients throughout the United States as well as several countries overseas.

"The Importance of Communication in a Global World: Not 'Me to Me to Me'" is a speech Scudder delivered June 11, 2004, to the Canadian Public Relation Society in Quebec, Canada. In the speech, he addressed several recent examples of officials communicating with the public, criticizing both Presidents Bill Clinton and George W. Bush for misleading people and lauding former

New York Mayor Rudolph Giuliani for his accurate updates following the terrorist attacks of September 11, 2001.

The Importance of Communication in a Global World: Not "Me to Me to Me"

∽ Prereading Question

Depending on the critic, the Internet either brings people closer together or isolates people even more from the larger world. In your opinion, does the Internet enhance our sense of belonging to a community—from a local to national to international community—or does it isolate us (keeping us at home, alone, typing away at our keyboards)?

Merci, David. Bonjour, bon apres-midi. C'est un plaisir de m'addresser a quelques uns des plus grand communicateurs du monde. It's customary at this point to say, "for those of you who don't speak French, here's what I just said." But, since the quality of my French is poor, I'll instead say, "for those of you who do speak French, here's what I said.

I said, and I mean, "it's a pleasure to speak to some of the world's greatest communicators."

Over the years I've had the honor of addressing audiences in many countries. And, I'm always interested in the way I'm described in the program.

In Sydney, Australia, the line read: "Virgil is a very animated speaker." Now I'm not sure whether that's a compliment or an insult. But, since business audiences in Australia tend to be fairly restrained, I worry.

In one country in Asia I was described simply as "U.S. expert." That means they lost the bio.

The Columbia Journalism Review called me "avuncular." I had to look that one up. It means "uncle-like."

According to Forbes.com, I "harrumphed" an answer to a reporter's question. I guess I did.

I believe the original adjective that CPRS's materials applied to me was "provocative."

I'll try not to provoke too many of you today or be excessively animated. But, I might fall short on both counts since I intend to raise some serious questions and speak with my usual candor.

As I began to prepare these remarks I thought back to my first visit to this beautiful city last July during its renowned summer festival.

I was struck by how truly international Quebec City was and how the festival brought people together through music, dance, magic, and other forms of entertainment. The atmosphere was warm, friendly, and welcoming. Everybody had a good feeling. In words, music, and action, people communicated.

Fun and humor were everywhere. Asking for donations, one of the street performers said: "remember—the more you give . . . the more I will have." Another noted, "even a dollar will help; for you Americans that's three dollars in Canadian currency." Sounds like we had a lawyer moonlighting as an acrobat.

I attended a wonderful concert down the street at the Church of the Holy Trinity—music of Vivaldi, Bach, Mozart, Albinoni—superbly played by the Cologne Philharmonic Chamber Orchestra. While the group is based in Germany, its musicians came from wide and far—Australia, the U.S., Germany, of course, and even Uzbekistan.

When I stopped to congratulate the musicians afterward on their excellent performance, the Uzbeki gave me his e-mail address and said: "I need your help. I want to immigrate to Canada."

"I can't help you," I told him. "I'm not Canadian. I'm American."

He replied: "U.S. OK."

Those are words Americans haven't heard much lately—"U.S. OK." It sounds like my country needs a good PR firm.

Communication can be easy at play. It's harder at work, especially when there are significant differences in culture, goals, and perspectives. You are right to focus on perspectives in this conference called "Perspectives on Perspective."

We all live in Marshall MacLuhan's global village. I wonder what that great Canadian philosopher and futurist would think of it today.

Today's technology has made it easier for us to talk to each other. For example, I am in frequent e-mail contact with a business partner in Malaysia and China—unthinkable a short time ago.

Growing up in the farmlands of Indiana, I never dreamed that I would some day fly non-stop from Moscow to New York.

But, has technology resulted in better communication? Often it has not. The reason is that too much communication is one way—"me to me to me." Such an approach is a path to failure. In this area globalization has a long way to go.

Look at India. Few countries have seen more economic benefit from globalization. Yet, the government recently fell because it could not convey to people of lower incomes how the economic boom from globalization was helping them.

The government spoke but it hadn't listened to their concerns. Would their children have a chance for a good education? When would they get sanitary water and indoor plumbing? What about health care? Those concerns had not been adequately addressed.

I was troubled recently to read a quote from U.S. Defense Secretary Donald Rumsfeld saying, "I've stopped reading the newspapers." I do hope he was joking. That's me to me to me thinking.

Any successful communication starts with an analysis of the audience. What are their interests, concerns, and perspectives? What pleases them, excites them, offends them?

There is a time-honored way in which public relations professionals find out these things. It's called research. Too often business and government don't bother with this vital first step. Failures of communication are often failures of research.

A good example comes from a recent story from Kenya.

Women across Africa have always carried babies on their backs. But not long ago strollers and prams began to be introduced in major cities across the continent. Traditionalists were horrified.

There were several problems with this marketing effort.

- Most roads and pathways are not good enough to accommodate these little vehicles.
- They are too expensive for much of the population.
- And, most important, their use flies in the face of culture.

You see, many Africans view babies on backs as following their mothers in warmth and comfort—perfect bonding. Thus, to many, that is the only proper method for carrying children.

One Kenya psychiatrist noted that ". . . pushing babies and toddlers in prams and strollers is the utmost in pushing children away from you." Thus, a total product bomb.

Look at some of the mistakes the U.S. has made in Iraq. The administration believed that the coalition troops would be welcomed as liberators. Instead, we are regarded as heartless occupiers. What happened? The government didn't do good research. It listened to the wrong people and just heard what it wanted to hear. Thus, a communications—and diplomatic—failure. "Me to me to me communication."

Good communication begins with listening. Until you understand where others are coming from, you cannot set realistic communications objectives and design a program that will work.

There was no better example of this than when the White House hired an advertising whiz a couple of years ago to improve America's image in the Arab world. The result was production of a series of videos showing how great life could be for Muslims in America. The effort flopped.

Nobody in the Mideast doubted that Muslim Arabs could be successful in the U.S. People in those countries were upset about what was happening to them, not their cousins in Detroit or Los Angeles.

That U.S. image enhancement program should have been handled by public relations professionals. Sending an advertising expert to handle a public relations problem is about as smart as sending a tax lawyer to represent a murder defendant.

Very often the failure to listen and understand is unintentional. Former Prime Minister Trudeau expressed it well some years ago in describing concerns about the size and power of the U.S. Why, he was asked, should he have fears about a country that has always been a best friend to Canada? His answer was simple and effective.

He likened Canada's situation to sleeping next to an elephant. "The elephant may be friendly," Trudeau told us, "but you can never be sure it won't roll over in the middle of the night."

That's a thought that never crosses the elephant's mind . . . unless he's had a dialogue with his smaller buddy.

Far too often a failure to communicate is the result of indifference and arrogance—a lack of respect for local culture. Some years ago a U.S.-based company moved its international headquarters to Geneva, Switzerland. Years later a surprising number of the company's executives told me they still didn't speak a word of French even though they had lived and worked in Geneva for years. Yes, you can get by in Geneva speaking only English. But, can you really communicate?

The Columbia Journalism Review, a journalists' trade publication, recently pointed out that it's getting harder and harder to get straight answers from leaders of business and government in the U.S. I agree.

Two reasons were cited.

- A belief by newsmakers that evasion works.
- And the influence of media trainers.

I disagree on both counts.

My firm conducts media training around the world. And one of the first things we tell every client is this: "do not lie, mislead or deceive." You may win a short-term victory but you will pay for it in the long run. I doubt that you tell your clients or bosses anything different.

But President Bush has not followed such advice. Nor did President Clinton. And they both paid dearly for it in terms of credibility.

President Bush has been severely criticized for his performance at a recent news conference in which he gave a direct answer to less than half of reporters' questions. When asked about why weapons of mass destruction hadn't been found in Iraq, he basically told us that Saddam Hussein was a terrible man. Same answer when asked if he had made any mistakes: he couldn't think of any but Saddam Hussein was a terrible man.

PR professionals often preach about "staying on message." But, too often they overlook something equally important: staying credible and responsive.

Former President Clinton—caught in a compromising situation—quibbled about how one would define "sex." Most of us feel we can do that. But that feeble word game caused a loss of credibility that crippled his ability to get legislation passed in the final year of his term. And, I believe, it opened the door to his impeachment.

The perception of stonewalling hurt Martha Stewart in her trial for insider trading. Her lawyers had promised the jury that she would testify—she would tell her story to them. But, the lawyers later changed their minds and she never took the stand to defend herself.

That is her right. But, jurors said they felt cheated and they made her pay with a guilty verdict.

We all know that actions often speak louder than words. I recently joined the board of WiRED International, a nonprofit organization that is providing computers and computer access to medical information to doctors and medical students in Iraq. Let me read to you portions of a letter to Professor Gary Selnow, the organization's head. It comes from Dr. Khalid Mayah, director of the Basra Teaching Hospital.

Dr. Kahlid said that Iraqi doctors' access to medical information on line—quote—"may be the best thing done for Iraq. Your effort to help Iraqian doctors get instant access to the world of scientific research and information was the best thing done by all NGOs."

Professor Selnow's action; Dr. Kahlid's grateful words.

This is real communication. This is the kind of story we PR professionals need to promote and publicize. Even when we're not getting paid for it.

We need to encourage our corporate clients to do more—especially in the areas of disease, poverty, and ignorance; and to be aware of—and respond to—real needs. I might point out that one of your major sponsors, Pfizer, is a generous contributor to WiRED. This is good corporate citizenship.

A superb example of honest and effective communication came on 9/11 and the days that followed when we in New York suddenly came under aerial attack.

Mayor Rudolph Giuliani immediately took center stage and provided frequent updates on the situation. He was calm, clear, and reassuring. But nothing was exaggerated. And nothing was sugar-coated.

Most of all, he was honest. When asked what the final death toll would be, he told us it would be "too awful to contemplate."

I think of that each morning when I ride the train through that dreadful hole called "Ground Zero."

Giuliani understood our fears, our anger, and our frustration. And he especially understood our need for the truth.

Real communication in a society also requires a free press. But much of the world's press is still not free. And, the situation does not seem to be improving.

Last month I was working with a public relations professional in Singapore and he gave me some rather depressing figures about the media in Asia.

- A survey by the global media industry watchdog Freedom House concluded that only 17 of 39 Asia Pacific countries surveyed had a free press. Not very good.
- But, even that figure is misleading. Most of the 17 are tiny island nations like Palau, the Marshall Islands, Tuvalu and Samoa.
- Only seven percent of the region's population have access to a free press.
- And, of Asian countries experiencing free press changes, most are going backwards.
- Those losing ground include Thailand, the Philippines, Indonesia, Sri Lanka, Afghanistan, and Hong Kong—now, of course, a part of China.

In Russia, the news media are being muffled more every day. The public dialogue in Vladimir Putin's new Russia is getting closer to that of the old Soviet Union.

What can we—as public relations professionals—do about the problem of "me to me to me" communication? How can we influence leaders of business, governments and NGO's to engage more in dialogue and less in diatribe . . . speaking across instead of down?

How can we help promote peace through understanding?

For one thing we must fight for our seat at the table. Many of us have C-level knowledge, experience, and intelligence. Our role can be as critical as that of chief legal officer, chief financial officer, or chief operating officer in protecting a company's vital interests. We must continue to push for that place at the head table.

Once there, we must convince managements that oneway communication doesn't work.

We also need to go beyond our roles in business.

Public relations needs a seat in the councils of our governments—seats occupied by real PR people who will counsel truth and true dialogue, not deception and oneway communication.

We must be more aggressive in selling our profession and its value. PR needs better PR.

When I was working for a large public relations agency in New York some years ago a long-time client told me: "If your company handled our PR the way you handle your own, you wouldn't have had us for two weeks." I have never forgotten that remark.

Isn't this true of our industry today?

We need to establish ourselves as a leadership industry. After all, we have thinkers. Just look around this room. We have expertise in dealing with different cultures and attitudes. We work globally. Yet our voice is too seldom heard on major issues of the day.

We have to position ourselves as thought leaders and be influencers of global policy.

We have to get on television more, speaking out on critical issues. We need to make our voices heard through op-eds and bylined articles. And we need to increasingly speak through non-traditional media.

We need to publish surveys that draw on our expertise and perspectives. Journalists get surveyed all the time. The public hears about them and hears their reflections on society's convolutions today. People survey lawyers, accountants, and doctors.

In contrast, public relations associations primarily survey themselves—in order to improve member services. Surveys put weight behind the voices of our industry's leaders like Jean Valin, Lisa Homer, and Del Galloway.

The good news is that many in the profession—like yourselves—are stepping up to the plate and making some good things happen. There is no better example than this conference with its focus on ethics, corporate social responsibility, and international standards of practice.

There is tremendous promise in the work of the Global Alliance, bringing together public relations societies from many nations to share thoughts and policies and attempt to develop international standards of responsible behavior.

And, one of my PR colleagues in the U.S. has been asked by a friend of hers in Russia to help create and design strategies for what they are calling "Democracy Roundtables." This is exactly the kind of arena in which we can be effective.

Let me close by calling your attention to one further effort at better understanding of the world in which we live and the people with whom we share it.

Two years ago the International Section of the Public Relations Society of America created a series of international public affairs symposia. They bring together top journalists, scholars, U.N. officials, government leaders, and international experts to provide insights into our globalized world.

Here comes the commercial. I encourage you to join us for the next one which will be held on January 27 and 28, 2005, at U.N. headquarters in New York.

The title will be "Bridging Global Communications Divides—Political, Cultural, Economic, Religious, and Media." We invite not only your attendance but also your participation in this event.

In sum, we as public relations professionals can do a lot to change "me to me to me" communication. But it won't be easy.

I leave you with some words from an industrial giant, Lee Iacocca. When he was resurrecting Chrysler he loved to say, "lead, follow, or get out of the way." To public relations professionals I say, "delete the last two options."

Lead!

Merci, gracias, grazie, and thank you.

Textual Questions

1. Following age-old advice, Scudder opens his address with a joke. How effective is this opening as a setup for his argument?

2. According to Scudder, why, in June of 2004, does America need "a good PR firm"?

3. What is communication that is "me to me to me"? What example does Scudder use most effectively? How does Scudder connect his argument to the war in Iraq? How persuasive and effective are his arguments about this war?

Rhetorical Questions

4. One aspect of an effective speech is that it fits the occasion and the place of its delivery—that it is, in Attic Greek, *kairotic*. How does Scudder make his speech *kairotic*?

5. For Scudder, what is effective communication? What are the features of ineffective communication?

6. In some ways, Scudder's argument is built upon one example after another. How well does this construction make and develop his points about effective communication? How effectively does Scudder use the idea of "me to me to me" communication to pull the disparate parts of his argument together?

Intertextual Questions

7. How does Scudder's argument about the value of a free press compare/contrast with the arguments of Eric Alterman, Ben H. Bagdikian, and Bernard Goldberg?

8. How would journalists Daniel Drezner and Henry Farrell respond to Scudder's arguments?

Thinking Beyond the Text

9. Scudder argues about communication and failures of the United States in Iraq. How effective are these arguments in explaining the problems of the U.S. occupation of Iraq?

10. Scudder argues that both President Clinton and President Bush lost credibility. How did they lose it, according to him? Do you believe that this is true? What other examples would you cite?

For Writing & Discussion

11. Scudder argues that the vast majority of the world's population does not have access to a free press. Select one nation other than the United States and research the controls that do/do not exist on its news media. Focus your analysis of this nation's news media on either television, radio, the Internet, or print journalism—not on two or all three.

DANIEL W. DREZNER
AND HENRY FARRELL

Daniel W. Drezner is a professor of political science at the University of Chicago and previously taught at the University of Colorado at Boulder and Donetsk Technical University in the Republic of Ukraine. Henry Farrell is a political science professor at George Washington University and previously taught at the University of Toronto.

"Web of Influence," about the growing phenomenon of people getting news from web logs or "blogs," was first published in the November/December 2004 issue of *Foreign Policy*. Drezner and Farrell explore blogs further in the forthcoming book they edited entitled *The Political Promise of Blogging*.

Web of Influence

∾ Prereading Question

How much of your information about the world comes directly from an online source—email, blogs, and so on? How do you judge which information is most redible?

> *Every day, millions of online diarists, or "bloggers," share their opinions with a global audience. Drawing upon the content of the international media and the World Wide Web, they weave together an elaborate network with agenda-setting power on issues ranging from human rights in China to the U.S. occupation of Iraq. What began as a hobby is evolving into a new medium that is changing the landscape for journalists and policymakers alike.*

It was March 21, 2003—two days after the United States began its "shock and awe" campaign against Iraq—and the story dominating TV networks was the rumor (later proven false) that Saddam Hussein's infamous cousin, Ali Hassan al-Majid ("Chemical Ali"), had been killed in an airstrike. But, for thousands of other people around the world who switched on their computers rather than their television sets, the lead story was the sudden and worrisome disappearance of Salam Pax.

Otherwise known as the "Baghdad Blogger," Salam Pax was the pseudonym for a 29-year-old Iraqi architect whose online diary, featuring wry and candid observations about life in wartime, transformed him into a cult figure. It turned out that technical difficulties, not U.S. cruise missiles or Baathist Party thugs, were responsible for the three-day Salam Pax blackout. In the months that followed, his readership grew to millions, as his accounts were quoted in the *New York Times,* BBC, and Britain's *Guardian* newspaper. If the first Gulf War introduced the world to the "CNN effect," then the second Gulf War was blogging's coming out party. Salam Pax was the most famous blogger during that conflict (he later signed a book and movie deal), but myriad other online diarists, including U.S. military personnel, emerged to offer real-time analysis and commentary.

Blogs (short for "weblogs") are periodically updated journals, providing online commentary with minimal or no external editing. They are usually presented as a set of "posts," individual entries of news or commentary, in reverse chronological order. The posts often include hyperlinks to other sites, enabling commentators to draw upon the content of the entire World Wide Web. Blogs can function as personal diaries, political analysis, advice columns on romance, computers, money, or all of the above. Their number has grown at an astronomical rate. In 1999, the total number of blogs was estimated to be around 50; five years later, the estimates range from 2.4 million to 4.1 million. The Perseus Development Corporation, a consulting firm that studies Internet trends, estimates that by 2005 more than 10 million blogs will have been created. Media institutions have adopted the form as well, with many television networks, newspapers, and opinion journals now hosting blogs on their Web sites, sometimes featuring dispatches from their own correspondents, other times hiring full-time online columnists.

Blogs are already influencing U.S. politics. The top five political blogs together attract over half a million visitors per day. Jimmy Orr, the White House Internet director, recently characterized the "blogosphere" (the all-encompassing term to describe the universe of weblogs) as instrumental, important, and underestimated in its influence. Nobody knows that better than Trent Lott, who in December 2002 resigned as U.S. Senate majority leader in the wake of inflammatory comments he made at Sen. Strom Thurmond's 100th birthday party. Initially, Lott's remarks received little attention in the mainstream media. But the incident was the subject of intense online commentary, prodding renewed media attention that converted Lott's gaffe into a full-blown scandal.

Political scandals are one thing, but can the blogosphere influence global politics as well? Compared to other actors in world affairs—governments, international organizations, multinational corporations, and even non-governmental organizations (NGOs)—blogs do not appear to be very powerful or visible. Even the most popular blog garners only a fraction of the Web traffic that major media outlets attract. According to the 2003 Pew Research Center for the People and the Press Internet Survey, only 4 percent of online Americans refer to blogs for information and opinions. The blogosphere has no central organization, and its participants have little ideological consensus. Indeed, an October 2003 survey of the blogosphere conducted by Perseus concluded that "the typical blog is written by a teenage girl who uses it twice a month to update her friends and classmates on happenings in her life." Blogging is almost exclusively a part-time, voluntary activity. The median income generated by a weblog is zero dollars. How then can a collection of decentralized, contrarian, and nonprofit Web sites possibly influence world politics?

Blogs are becoming more influential because they affect the content of international media coverage. Journalism professor Todd Gitlin once noted that media frame reality through "principles of selection, emphasis, and presentation composed of little tacit theories about what exists, what happens, and what matters." Increasingly, journalists and pundits take their cues about "what matters" in the world from weblogs. For salient topics in global affairs, the blogosphere functions as a rare combination of distributed expertise, real-time collective response to breaking news, and public-opinion barometer. What's more, a hierarchical structure has taken shape within the primordial chaos of cyberspace. A few elite blogs have emerged as aggregators of information and analysis, enabling media commentators to extract meaningful analysis and rely on blogs to help them interpret and predict political developments.

Under specific circumstances—when key weblogs focus on a new or neglected issue—blogs can act as a focal point for the mainstream media and exert formidable agenda-setting power. Blogs have ignited national debates on such topics as racial profiling at airports and have kept the media focused on scandals as diverse as the exposure of CIA agent Valerie Plame's identity to bribery allegations at the United Nations. Although the blogosphere remains cluttered with the teenage angst of high school students, blogs increasingly serve as a conduit through which ordinary and not-so-ordinary citizens express their views on international relations and influence a policymaker's decision making.

The Ties that Bind

University of Michigan history Professor Juan Cole had a lot to say about the war on terror and the war in Iraq. Problem was, not many people were listening. Despite an impressive résumé (he's fluent in three Middle Eastern languages), Cole had little success publishing opinion pieces in the mainstream media, even after September 11, 2001. His writings on the Muslim world might have remained confined to academic journals had he not begun a weblog called "Informed Comment" as a hobby in 2002. Cole's language proficiency allowed him to monitor news reports and editorials throughout the region. "This was something I could not have been able to do in 1990, or even 1995," he told a Detroit newspaper, referring to the surge of Middle Eastern publications on the Internet. "I could get a level of texture and detail that you could never get from the Western press."

Fellow bloggers took an interest in his writings, especially because he expressed a skepticism about the U.S. invasion and occupation of Iraq that stood apart from the often optimistic mainstream media coverage following the successful overthrow of the Baathist regime. Writing in the summer of 2003, Cole noted: "The Sunni Arabs north, east and west of Baghdad from all accounts hate the U.S. and hate U.S. troops being there. This hatred is the key recruiting tool for the resistance, and it is not lessened by U.S. troops storming towns. I wish [the counterinsurgency operation] well; maybe it will work, militarily. Politically, I don't think it addresses the real problems, of winning hearts and minds."

As a prominent expert on the modern history of Shiite Islam, Cole became widely read among bloggers—and ultimately journalists—following the outbreak of Iraqi Shiite unrest in early 2004. With his blog attracting 250,000 readers per month, Cole began appearing on media outlets such as National Public Radio (NPR) and CNN to provide expert commentary. He also testified before the Senate Foreign Relations Committee. "As a result of my weblog, the *Middle East Journal* invited me to contribute for the Fall 2003 issue," he recalls. "When the Senate staff of the Foreign Relations Committee did a literature search on Moktada al-Sadr and his movement, mine was the only article that came up. Senate staff and some of the senators themselves read it and were eager to have my views on the situation."

Cole's transformation into a public intellectual embodies many of the dynamics that have heightened the impact of the blogosphere. He wanted to publicize his expertise, and he did so by attracting attention from elite members of the blogosphere. As Cole made waves within the virtual world, others in the real world began to take notice.

Most bloggers desire a wide readership, and conventional wisdom suggests that the most reliable way to gain Web traffic is through a link on another weblog. A blog that is linked to by multiple other sites will accumulate an ever increasing readership as more bloggers discover the site and create hyperlinks on their respective Web pages. Thus, in the blogosphere, the rich (measured in the number of links) get richer, while the poor remain poor. This dynamic creates a skewed distribution where there are a very few highly ranked blogs with many incoming links, followed by a steep falloff and a very long list of medium- to low-ranked bloggers with few or no incoming links. One study by Clay Shirky, an associate professor at New York University, found that the Internet's top dozen bloggers (less than 3 percent of the total examined) accounted for approximately 20 percent of the incoming links. Some link-deprived blogs may become rich over time as top bloggers link to them, which helps explain why new bloggers are not discouraged.

Consequently, even as the blogosphere continues to expand, only a few blogs are likely to emerge as focal points. These prominent blogs serve as a mechanism for filtering interesting blog posts from mundane ones. When less renowned bloggers write posts with new information or a new slant, they will contact one or more of the large focal point blogs to publicize their posts. In this manner, poor blogs function as fire alarms for rich blogs, alerting them to new information and links. This self-perpetuating, symbiotic relationship allows interesting arguments and information to make their way to the top of the blogosphere.

The skewed network of the blogosphere makes it less time-consuming for outside observers to acquire information. The media only need to look at elite blogs to obtain a summary of the distribution of opinions on a given political issue. The mainstream political media can therefore act as a conduit between the blogosphere and politically powerful actors. The comparative advantage of blogs in political discourse, as compared to traditional media, is their low cost of real-time publication. Bloggers can post their immediate reactions to important political events before other forms of media can respond. Speed also helps bloggers overcome their own inaccuracies. When confronted with a factual error, they can quickly correct or update their post. Through these interactions, the blogosphere distills complex issues into key themes, providing cues for how the media should frame and report a foreign-policy question.

Small surprise, then, that a growing number of media leaders—editors, publishers, reporters, and columnists—consume political blogs. *New York Times* Executive Editor Bill Keller said in a November 2003 interview, "Sometimes I read something on a blog that makes me feel we screwed up." Howard Kurtz, one of the most prominent media commentators in the United States, regularly quotes elite bloggers in his "Media Notes Extra" feature for the *Washington Post*'s Web site. Many influential foreign affairs columnists, including Paul Krugman and Fareed Zakaria, have said that blogs form a part of their information-gathering activities.

Around the World in Blogs

Plenty of bloggers discuss international affairs, but a few, in addition to those mentioned in this article, stand out from the crowd. Jeff Jarvis's "BuzzMachine" is the single best source for information on the global expansion of the blogosphere. University of California, Berkeley, economist Brad DeLong ("Brad DeLong's Semi-Daily Journal") is perhaps the most influential economics blogger, while Tyler Cowen and Alex Tabarrok comment on microeconomic theory and the globalization of culture at "Marginal Revolution." The group weblog "Oxblog" has won serious media attention for its campaign promoting an assertive U.S. foreign policy supporting human rights and democracy.

Blog coverage varies throughout the world. Although Salam Pax paved the way for Iraqi bloggers, he has stopped blogging himself, and only around 70 Iraqi blogs have picked up where he left off. Among the more prominent: "Iraq: The Model" and "Baghdad Burning," which respectively support and oppose the U.S. military intervention. Western Europe has a sizeable number of blogs, especially in Britain, with the right-wing "Edge of England's Sword" and the pro-war leftist. "Harry's Place." "Slugger O'Toole" covers the Northern Ireland beat, while "A Fistful of Euros" seeks to provide an overview of Western European politics. Elsewhere, "BlogAfrica" syndicates blogs from across that continent, while "Living in China" offers an expatriate perspective on Chinese politics and society. Last is the blog of Japanese tech entrepreneur and venture capitalist Joi Ito ("Joi Ito's Web"). He reportedly visits 190 blogs regularly and averages five hours a day reading and writing blogs.

—FP

For direct links to all of these blogs, visit www.foreignpolicy.com.

For the mainstream media—which almost by definition suffer a deficit of specialized, detailed knowledge—blogs can also serve as repositories of expertise. And for readers worldwide, blogs can act as the "man on the street," supplying unfiltered eyewitness accounts about foreign countries. This facet is an especially valuable service, given the decline in the number of foreign correspondents since the 1990s. Blogs may even provide expert analysis and summaries of foreign-language texts, such as newspaper articles and government studies, that reporters and pundits would not otherwise access or understand.

Even foreign-policy novices leave their mark on the debate. David Nishimura, an art historian and vintage pen dealer, emerged as an unlikely commentator on the Iraq war through his blog, "Cronaca," which he describes as a "compilation of news concerning art, archaeology, history, and whatever else catches the chronicler's eye, with the odd bit of opinion and commentary thrown in." In the month after the fall of Hussein's regime in April 2003, there was much public hand-wringing about reports that more than 170,000 priceless antiques and treasures had been looted from the Iraqi National Museum in Baghdad. In response to these newspaper accounts, a number of historians and archaeologists scorned the U.S. Defense Department for failing to protect the museum. Nishimura, however, scrutinized the various media reports and found several inconsistencies. He noted that the 170,000 number was flat-out wrong; that the actual losses, though serious, were much smaller than initial reports suggested; and that museum officials might have been complicit in the looting. "Smart money still seems to be on the involvement of Ba'athists and/or museum employees," he wrote. "The extent to which these categories overlap has been danced around so far, but until everything has been properly sorted out, it might be wise to remember how other totalitarian states have coopted cultural institutions, enlisting the past to remake the future." Prominent right-of-center bloggers, such as Glenn Reynolds, Andrew Sullivan, and Virginia Postrel, cited Nishimura's analysis to focus attention on the issue and correct the original narrative.

As the museum looting controversy reveals, blogs are now a "fifth estate" that keeps watch over the mainstream media. The speed of real-time blogger reactions often compels the media to correct errors in their own reporting before they mushroom. For example, in June 2003, the *Guardian* trumpeted a story in its online edition that misquoted Deputy U.S. Secretary of Defense Paul Wolfowitz as saying that the United States invaded Iraq in order to safeguard its oil supply. The quote began to wend its way through other media outlets worldwide, including Germany's *Die Welt*. In the ensuing hours, numerous bloggers led by Greg Djerijian's "Belgravia Dispatch" linked to the story and highlighted the error, prompting the *Guardian* to retract the story and apologize to its readers before publishing the story in its print version.

Bloggers have become so adept at fact-checking the media that they've spawned many other high-profile retractions and corrections. The most noteworthy was CBS News' acknowledgement that it could not authenticate documents it had used in a story about President George W. Bush's National Guard service that bloggers had identified as forgeries. When such corrections are made, bloggers create the impression at times that contemporary journalism has spun out of control. Glenn Reynolds of "Instapundit" explained to the *Online Journalism Review* that he sees parallels between the impact of the blogosphere and Russia's post-Soviet glasnost. "People are appalled, saying it's the decline of journalism . . . . But it's the same as when Russia started reporting about plane crashes and everyone thought they were just suddenly happening. It was really just the first time people could read about them." Media elites rightly retort that blogs have their own problems. Their often blatant partisanship discredits them in many newsrooms. However, as Yale University law Professor Jack Balkin says, the blogosphere has some built-in correction mechanisms for ideological bias, as "bloggers who write about political subjects cannot avoid addressing (and, more importantly, linking to) arguments made by people with different views. The reason is that much of the blogosphere is devoted to criticizing what other people have to say."

The blogosphere also acts as a barometer for whether a story would or should receive greater coverage by the mainstream media. The more blogs that discuss a particular issue, the more likely that the blogosphere will set the agenda for future news coverage. Consider one recent example with regard to U.S. homeland security. In July 2004, Annie Jacobsen, a writer for Womens WallStreet.com, posted online a first-person account of suspicious activity by Syrian passengers on a domestic U.S. flight: "After seeing 14 Middle Eastern men board separately (six together, eight individually) and then act as a group, watching their unusual glances, observing their bizarre bathroom activities, watching them congregate in small groups, knowing that the flight attendants and the pilots were seriously concerned and now knowing that federal air marshals were on board, I was officially terrified," she wrote. Her account was quickly picked up, linked to, and vigorously debated throughout the blogosphere. Was this the preparation for another September 11-style terrorist attack? Was Jacobsen overreacting, allowing her judgment to be clouded by racial stereotypes? Should the U.S. government end the practice of fining "discriminatory" airlines that disproportionately search Arab passengers? In just one weekend, 2 million people read her article. Reports soon followed in mainstream media outlets such as NPR, MSNBC, *Time,* and the *New York Times,* prompting a broader national debate about the racial profiling of possible terrorists.

Some bloggers purposefully harness the medium to promote wider awareness of their causes. With the assistance of experts including Kenneth Roth, the executive director of Human Rights Watch, and Samantha Power, the Pulitzer Prize-winning author of *"A Problem from Hell": America and the Age of Genocide,* cyberactivist Joanne Cipolla Moore set up a blog and Web site, "Passion of the Present," devoted to collecting news and information about genocide in Sudan. Moore sought out dozens of elite bloggers to link to her site and spread the word about Sudan. The blog of Ethan Zuckerman, a researcher at Harvard Law School's Berkman Center for Internet & Society, not only links to Moore's site but has issued a call to arms to the entire blogosphere: "Blogs let us tell offline media what we want. When blog readers made it clear we wanted to know more about Trent Lott's racist comments, mainstream media picked up the ball and dug deeper into the story . . . . What sort of effort would it take to choose an important issue—say the Sudanese government's involvement in Darfur—and get enough momentum in the blogosphere that CNN was forced to bring a camera crew to the region?"

In all of these instances, bloggers relied on established media outlets for much of their information. However, blogs also functioned as a feedback mechanism for the mainstream media. In this way, the blogosphere serves both as an amplifier and as a remixer of media coverage. For the traditional media—and ultimately, policymakers—this makes the blogosphere difficult to ignore as a filter through which the public considers foreign-policy questions.

❧

Rage Inside the Machine

Blogs are beginning to emerge in countries where there are few other outlets for political expression. But can blogs affect politics in regimes where there is no thriving independent media sector?

Under certain circumstances, they can. For starters, blogs can become an alternative source of news and commentary in countries where traditional media are under the thumb of the state. Blogs are more difficult to control than television or newspapers, especially under regimes that are tolerant of some degree of free expression. However, they are vulnerable to state censorship. A sufficiently determined government can stop blogs it doesn't like by restricting access to the Internet, or setting an example for others by punishing unauthorized political expression, as is currently the case in Saudi Arabia and China. The government may use filtering technologies to limit access to foreign blogs. And, if there isn't a reliable technological infrastructure, individuals will be shut out from the blogosphere. For instance, chronic power shortages and telecommunications problems make it difficult for Iraqis to write or read blogs.

Faced with various domestic obstacles, bloggers inside these countries (or expatriates) can try to influence foreign blogs and the media through indirect effects at home. Political scientists Margaret Keck of Johns Hopkins University and Kathryn Sikkink of the University of Minnesota note that activists who are unable to change conditions in their own countries can leverage their power by taking their case to transnational networks of advocates, who in turn publicize abuses and lobby their governments. Keck and Sikkink call this a "boomerang effect," because repression at home can lead to international pressure against the regime from abroad. Blogs can potentially play a role in the formation of such transnational networks.

Iran is a good example. The Iranian blogosphere has exploded. According to the National Institute for Technology and Liberal Education's Blog Census, Farsi is the fourth most widely used language among blogs worldwide. One service provider alone ("Persian Blog") hosts some 60,000 active blogs. The weblogs allow young secular and religious Iranians to interact, partially taking the place of reformist newspapers that have been censored or shut down. Government efforts to impose filters on the Internet have been sporadic and only partially successful. Some reformist politicians have embraced blogs, including the president, who celebrated the number of Iranian bloggers at the World Summit on the Information Society, and Vice President Muhammad Ali Abtahi, who is a blogger himself. Elite Iranian blogs such as "Editor: Myself" have established links with the English-speaking blogosphere. When Sina Motallebi, a prominent Iranian blogger, was imprisoned for "undermining national security through 'cultural activity,'" prominent Iranian bloggers were able to join forces with well-known English-language bloggers including Jeff Jarvis ("BuzzMachine"), Dan Gillmor ("Silicon Valley"), and Patrick Belton ("OxBlog") to create an online coalition that attracted media coverage, leading to Motallebi's release.

An international protest campaign also secured the freedom of Chinese blogger Liu Di, a 23-year-old psychology student who offended authorities with her satirical comments about the Communist Party. Yet, even as Di was released, two individuals who had circulated online petitions on her behalf were arrested. Such is life in China, where an estimated 300,000 bloggers (out of 80 million regular Internet users) uneasily coexist with the government. Bloggers in China have perfected the art of self-censorship, because a single offensive post can affect an entire online community—as when Internet censors temporarily shut down leading blog sites such as Blogcn. com in 2003. Frank Yu, a Program Manager at Microsoft Research Asia's Advanced Technology Center in Beijing, described this mind-set as he profiled a day in the life of a fictional Chinese blogger he dubbed "John X": "After reading over his new posting, he checks it for any politically sensitive terms which may cause the government to block his site . . . . Although he is not concerned as much about being shut down, he does not want all the writers that share the host server with him to get locked out as well. Living in China, we learn to pick the battles that we feel strongly about and let the host of other indignities pass through quiet compliance." Text messaging is a much safer medium for the online Chinese community. Some bloggers, however, do manage to push the envelope, as when Shanghai-based Microsoft employee Wang Jianshuo offered candid, firsthand accounts (including photos) of the SARS and Avian Flu outbreaks.

North Korea is perhaps the most blog-unfriendly nation. Only political the elites and foreigners are allowed access to the Internet. As might be expected, there are no blogs within North Korea, nor any easy way for ordinary North Koreans to access foreign blogs. However, even in that country, blogs may have an impact. A former CNN journalist, Rebecca MacKinnon, has set up "NKZone," a blog that has rapidly become a focal point for North Korea news and discussion. As MacKinnon notes, this blog can aggregate information in a way that ordinary journalism cannot. North Korea rarely allows journalists to enter the country, and when it does, it assigns government minders to watch them constantly. However, non-journalists can and do enter the country. "NKZone" gathers information from a wide variety of sources, including tourists, diplomats, NGOs, and academics with direct experience of life in North Korea, and the blog organizes it for easy consumption. It has already been cited in such prominent publications as the Asian *Wall Street Journal* and the *Sunday Times* of London as a source for information about North Korea.

ℳ

Blogo Ergo Sum

The growing clout of bloggers has transformed some into "blog triumphalists." To hear them tell it, blogging is the single most transformative media technology since the invention of the printing press. Rallying cries, such as "the revolution will be blogged," reflect the belief that blogs might even supplant traditional journalism. But, as the editor of the Washington, D.C.-based blog "Wonkette," Ana Marie Cox, has wryly observed, "A revolution requires that people leave their house."

There remain formidable obstacles to the influence of blogs. All bloggers, even those at the top of the hierarchy, have limited resources at their disposal. For the moment, they are largely dependent upon traditional media for sources of information. Furthermore, bloggers have become victims of their own success: As more mainstream media outlets hire bloggers to provide content, they become more integrated into as usual. Inevitably, blogs will lose some of their novelty and immediacy as they start being co-opted by the very institutions they purport to critique, as when both major U.S. political parties decided to credential some bloggers as journalists for their 2004 nominating conventions.

Bloggers, even those in free societies, must confront the same issues of censorship that plague traditional media. South Korea recently blocked access to many foreign blogs, apparently because they had linked to footage of Islamic militants in Iraq beheading a South Korean. In the United States, the Pentagon invoked national security to shut down blogs written by troops stationed in Iraq. Military officials claimed that such blogs might inadvertently reveal sensitive information. But Michael O'Hanlon, a defense specialist at the Brookings Institution, told NPR that he believes "it has much less to do with operational security and classified secrets, and more to do with American politics and how the war is seen by a public that is getting increasingly shaky about the overall venture."

One should also bear in mind that the blogosphere, mirroring global civil society as a whole, remains dominated by the developed world—a fact only heightened by claims of a digital divide. And though elite bloggers are ideologically diverse, they're demographically similar. Middle-class white males are overrepresented in the upper echelons of the blogosphere.

Reflecting those demographics, an analysis conducted by Harvard University's Ethan Zuckerman found that the blogosphere, like the mainstream media, tends to ignore large parts of the world.

Nevertheless, as more Web diarists come online, the blogosphere's influence will more likely grow than collapse. Ultimately, the greatest advantage of the blogosphere is its accessibility. A recent poll commissioned by the public relations firm Edelman revealed that Americans and Europeans trust the opinions of "average people" more than most authorities. Most bloggers are ordinary citizens, reading and reacting to those experts, and to the media. As Andrew Sullivan has observed in the online magazine *Slate*, "We're writing for free for anybody just because we love it. . . . That's a refreshing spur to write stuff that actually matters, because you can, and say things you believe in without too many worries."

Textual Questions

1. Who is Salam Pax? How do Drezner and Farrell describe him and his political "power"?

2. How is a blog different from a journal, diary, or other traditional print source?

3. What effects have blogs had on how business and political activities are performed?

Rhetorical Questions

4. What does it mean to call blogs a "fifth estate"?

5. Why might the U.S. government have "shut down blogs written by troops stationed in Iraq"? What tone do Drezner and Farrell take toward their subject? That is, how do they seem to feel about the power of blogs and how are their feelings apparent to readers?

6. Online, who can take on the role of expert? What if Salam Pax were, in fact, a teenage boy in Kansas pretending to be an Iraqi citizen? Would such a deception matter if, ultimately, the blog was accurate?

Intertextual Questions

7. Visit http://www.thebaghdadblog.com/home/ and read chapter one of *The Baghdad Blog*. What argument is made in this chapter, and how does it echo the argument of Drezner and Farrell?

8. Visit http://dear_raed.blogspot.com/ and read the blog of Salam Pax. How does reading this blog affect your feelings about the argument made by Drezner and Farrell?

Thinking Beyond the Text

9. Is the Internet a powerful tool for the spread of freedom? Why, or why not? What else is the Internet, aside from a global pornography warehouse?

10. Are blogs truly a grassroots effort to harness the power of the Internet to affect real change in the world? Are they more effective than other traditional means of affecting change? Why, or why not?

For Writing & Discussion

11. Using a free online site such as blogger.com, begin your own blog on a topic of personal/professional interest to you. Post to your blog at least three times per week for five weeks. After you have done this, write a short essay in which you consider your own blogging activities. How does capturing your thoughts on a blog help you clarify your thinking? Who, if anyone, has visited your blog? What responses have they given?

B O B   W R I G H T

Bob Wright is chairman and chief executive officer of NBC Universal, the company created with the 2004 merger of the National Broadcasting Company and Vivendi Universal Entertainment. Wright has been with NBC since 1986, giving him one of the longest tenures of any major media corporation chief. During his tenure, NBC went from a broadcast network to a global media powerhouse.

Wright delivered the speech "Technology and the Rule of Law in the Digital Age" on October 27, 2004, at the Media Institute and Benefactors Awards Banquet upon receiving the Freedom of Speech Award.

Technology and the Rule of Law in the Digital Age

Protection of Intellectual Property

⚭ Prereading Question

In what ways are copyrights routinely violated in the day-to-day world—from the illegal copying of DVDs or VCR tapes to peer-to-peer sharing of MP3 files to photocopying of entire books? Who "pays" for these violations, ultimately?

Thank you, Tim [Russert], for those kind words. Every Sunday morning, you do as much as any American to promote the values of the First Amendment, so it is certainly fitting for you to be here. I admit, however, I'm very glad you are introducing me, and not interviewing me, which would be a lot tougher.

By the way, I understand Tim's white board is enshrined behind bullet-proof glass over at the Newseum. He's negotiating with them to get it back for Tuesday night. It looks like he may be needing it—we are expecting a long night.

I also want to thank Patrick Maines and the Media Institute, not just for recognizing me and NBC Universal, which is indeed a great honor, but also for leading the way when it comes to freedom of speech.

Speaking personally, the Institute has been our ally on a number of issues over the years—usually involving the tension between the government's desire to control the news, and the obligation of NBC News to report the news. We all appreciate these efforts.

Nearly 170 years ago, in *Democracy in America*, the Frenchman Alexis de Tocqueville wrote: "The sovereignty of the people and the liberty of the press may be looked on as correlative institutions."

Put more simply: You can't have a free people without a free press.

And, as Thomas Jefferson pointed out, you can't have a free people without having an informed people.

Which is why I'm so proud of Tim and the work of all his colleagues in helping keep Americans informed, especially as we head into next week's election.

This is a critical time for our nation. That is why, as a news organization, we are alarmed at the flood of subpoenas that government at all levels is serving on journalists, including some of our own. These are courageous men and women, who are simply doing their jobs. If the current legal climate has a chilling effect on newsgathering, the consequences are serious—and could not come at a worse time.

NBC Universal with join with other major news organizations to highlight this issue. At no time in our history has the work of a free and unencumbered press been more important. We will be working together to make sure the appropriate shield laws are in place at both the state and federal levels, so that journalists can do their jobs without fear of government intrusion.

We are also concerned about the recent movement in Washington toward content regulation. We are facing an extraordinary set of pressures, easily the most alarming in my twenty-four years in this industry. The vast majority of broadcast licensees do an excellent job of knowing where to draw the line when it comes to content. We as a society certainly have much less to fear from obscene, indecent, or profane content than we do from an overzealous government willing to limit First Amendment protections and censor creative expression.

There is another part of the Constitution that applies to creative expression, along with the First Amendment: It is Article 1, Section 8—the Copyright Clause—which authorizes Congress to grant to "authors and inventors the exclusive right to their respective writings and discoveries." Congress has consistently enforced this for more than 200 years.

It has survived the high-speed printing press, the telegraph, the video recorder, and even the invention of xerography, which represents the ultimate test of Congress's will to apply the full measure of copyright laws. Think about it: It's a machine called . . . the copier. And copyright law survived.

This is what enables companies like NBC Universal to invest millions of dollars to transform a creative idea into a movie or television show.

Today, this constitutional protection is under enormous pressure and requires our vigilant attention. I know that the Media Institute will be our ally on this issue, too, which is a threat not only to media but to a broad cross-section of U.S. industries and export businesses.

Those in the media business are well aware that digital technology is poised to unleash an amazing world of possibility, in which the most compelling entertainment video content will be available to consumers around the globe anytime, anyplace, and on any one of numerous platforms or devices.

The potential of the digital age goes far beyond media, however. Virtually every industry stands on the cusp of a digital transformation, with untold benefits for consumers.

At NBC Universal, we are eager to roll out new digital, on-demand services. Working together with software developers and the consumer electronics industry, we would like nothing more than to make accessing video as easy as Apple's iPod has made accessing music. But the experience of the recording industry—decimated by illegal downloads—teaches an important lesson: If the technology isn't managed properly, it has the power to do a lot of damage, by facilitating theft, not commerce.

Despite countless man-hours devoted to this problem, we are far from having in place the necessary industry standards, filtering technologies, and legislative protection.

The costs of not getting this right are huge—and not just for media companies. More and more, our nation's economy is driven by high-value, service-based businesses, with intellectual property becoming an ever-larger part of the total picture. Copyright industries such as television, motion pictures, publishing, and software, whose capital is almost entirely composed of intellectual property, constitute the nation's largest source of exports, and 6% of our gross national product. If you include economic sectors that support these industries or are dependent on them, the figure doubles to 12% of GDP, or $1.25 trillion, with employment of more than 11 million Americans.

And if you added to this the intellectual property components of other commercial activity—in, say, pharmaceuticals, engineering, semiconductors, microtechnologies, and so on—it's entirely likely that more than 20% of our national economy could be traced to intellectual property of some sort. This is a very big piece of the national pie to have at risk.

Already, the economic costs of intellectual property theft are staggering. According to the Office of the U.S. Trade Representative, it amounts to $250 billion a year—more than the combined global revenues of the nation's top 25 media companies. This represents thousands of jobs, and millions in lost taxes.

The best solutions to IP theft will come from technology, not legislation. Given what is at stake, why so little progress?

For one thing, we hear repeatedly that intellectual property violations are a fair price to pay for the advent of a new digital age. And that technological progress demands a downgrading of the exclusive rights of creators, and a weakening of the legal status of copyrights and patents.

It is a mistake to think that entering this exciting world means embracing intellectual property theft. Time and again, we see that the inherent power of a technology drives its success, not the theft of protected content. Whether it be a digital camera, a new medical technology, or a novel piece of software, innovations ultimately succeed or fail depending on the capabilities and advantages they offer, not on whether or not they facilitate theft.

Second, the challenge of protecting intellectual property belongs to the core of U.S. industries and export businesses, not just the media. Today, all data and information is reducible to zeroes and ones, easily replicable, and able to be distributed at the speed of light around the world. Anyone who has information to transmit or an idea to share has a stake in this issue. Virtually anyone at work in the twenty-first century needs to be aligned with the cause of ensuring the safe management of electronic information and data, whether it be a movie, a military secret, or an e-mail.

Our collective challenge is to create new rules of the road for a digital world. Rules that encourage technological progress yet at the same time uphold the values that make commerce possible.

In the near term, there are three specific ways we can move closer to this goal:

- We need support for the House Judiciary Committee's package of antipiracy bills, which is currently in limbo.

- We need all interested parties to work in good faith with the Senate Judiciary Committee to develop appropriate legal safeguards against illegal peer-to-peer file-sharing.
- And we need to support the Attorney General's intellectual property enforcement recommendations, just announced two weeks ago, so that its strong rhetoric becomes reality.

But our long-term success depends on a greater degree of international cooperation, and cooperation among industries. In the recent past, a host of industry groups have collaborated to create interoperability standards, which enable a variety of different devices to work together.

Only the same degree of commitment will enable us to reach the point where consumers can enjoy the digital access they want, and rights holders have the protections they need.

Obviously, a great deal of time and effort has been spent on these issues. It is now time for the leadership of the industries involved to come together to find a collaborative solution, so that the long-awaited marriage of technology and content can finally take place. The solutions are there. What's needed is the will to develop and implement them.

Our founding fathers knew how important intellectual property rights were to the economic development of a new nation. That's why they granted exclusive rights to creators, to "promote the progress of science and the useful arts," in the words of the Constitution.

Congress has been upholding this commitment to progress for more than 200 years, with the judiciary committees in the House and Senate devoting a good deal of time trying to keep these protections up to date. U.S. business needs to do its part. Because now more than ever, the health of our economy depends on the effective protection of our intellectual property.

When he traveled through America in the 1830s, Alexis de Tocqueville was not only impressed by our tradition of freedom of speech.

"Everything is extraordinary in America," he wrote. Let's make sure this remains the case. Let's make sure we vigorously defend our First Amendment freedoms and protect our most important national assets in the digital age. Thank you.

Textual Questions

1. How does Wright support the argument that "You can't have a free people without a free press"?

2. Why, in October of 2004, does Wright argue that "At no time in our history has the work of a free and unencumbered press been more important"?

3. What threats to the Copyright Clause exist in the modern world? How is everyone invested in the protection of copyright, according to Wright?

Rhetorical Questions

4. How effectively does Wright connect the freedom of the press to the protection of copyright? How must technology and legislation work together to protect copyright?

5. How does Wright use history and appeals to the men who founded America to support his argument? How effective is this use of American history?

6. Wright makes his argument without using a single specific example. How effective is this? Why? What examples would you use to make his argument stronger? What examples would you use to refute his argument?

Intertextual Questions

7. How does Wright's argument about technology connect to Edward S. Herman and Noam Chomsky's argument about propaganda?

8. How would Edward S. Herman and Noam Chomsky respond to Wright's argument about technology and copyright?

Thinking Beyond the Text

9. Wright argues that the music industry has been "decimated by illegal downloads." Would you agree that this is true? Or is this an exaggeration?

10. What risk exists to the American economy if nothing is done to protect copyright in the digital age? Does Wright's argument seem reasonable, or is this alarmist, Chicken-Little-the-sky-is-falling rhetoric?

For Writing & Discussion

11. Consider the times you or someone you know has photocopied a book or article, burned a copy of a DVD, or downloaded music with peer-to-peer file sharing software. Did this activity violate any law? Is the ethical argument against such activity stronger or weaker than the legal prohibition? Research the effects of illegal downloading—normally via peer-to-peer file sharing software—of music on the recording industry. In an essay, explain the effect that peer-to-peer file sharing has had.

FOCAL POINT

Exploring Images of The Promise of a Free Press

FOCAL POINT

Exploring Images of The Promise of a Free Press

Questions

1. In this picture of the toppling of a statue of Saddam Hussein in Baghdad during Operation Iraqi Freedom (page 331), what messages are sent by the raised hands in the crowd? Why might the photographer have included the dome of a mosque in the background?

2. Like the picture on page 331, this photograph (page 332, top) shows the statue of Saddam Hussein being pulled down. What message does this picture send about the war that led to this moment? How does this message contrast with the message of the photograph on page 331? How would this image affect an American viewer? How might it affect an Iraqi viewer?

3. In the photograph on page 332 (bottom), Winston Churchill, Franklin D. Roosevelt, and Joseph Stalin—sometimes referred to as the "Big Three"—sit side-by-side. What does this photograph imply about the alliance of the three nations these men represent—Great Britain, the United States, and the Soviet Union—in opposition to Nazi Germany and Imperial Japan? Why might an image such as this be prominently displayed in newspapers in all three nations?

4. In this image from 1975 (page 333, top), American and South Vietnamese refugees crowd onto helicopters to escape the city of Saigon as it is overrun by the North Vietnamese Army. What do you think these refugees could have been thinking as they were taken away from their homeland? What message might this image have delivered to American viewers at the time?

5. What message does this cartoon (page 333, bottom) seem to send about President Bush and Vice President Cheney and their relationship with the *New York Times*? Whose political and/or economic interests are best served by a cartoon such as this? Historically speaking, are there times when any President of the United States and the press might have different definitions of "truth"? When? Why? Whose definition should matter most to the American people? Why?

4

THE PROMISE OF HEALTH

At no point in the Declaration of Independence, the U.S. Constitution, or the Bill of Rights is any citizen guaranteed the right to visit a doctor when ill, the right to affordable prescription medication, or the right to low-priced emergency room treatment in the event of a traumatic injury. Such rights are never discussed.

But the American promise of healthy living is implicit in a nation founded on every citizen's right to life, liberty, and the pursuit of happiness. *Life*, liberty, and the pursuit of happiness. Access to health care, never discussed directly in any detail in any foundational American documents, is listed first and foremost in the trinity of Truths the nation's founders held to be self-evident. Although the founders could hardly have imagined the kinds of health problems we now face—such as AIDS—or the kinds of advances in medicine we now enjoy, they knew well that a healthy life would always be crucial for human happiness.

Childhood is defined, culturally and legally, as a time of carefully managed safety. Day-care workers, like teachers, must be licensed. Advertising of dangerous products, such as cigarettes, is not allowed to use rhetorical strategies designed to appeal most to children, such as the infamous Joe Camel. The sale of such products to children is also restricted—and violators are punished. Age of Consent laws, which vary by state, combine with child pornography laws to protect children too young to defend themselves from sexual exploitation. Legally, the hours children can work and drive are restricted to protect them from exploitation and harm, respectively. Their health, in short, is as pro-tected as possible.

The health of adults in America is no less of a public concern. Seatbelt laws and safety standards protect them when they drive. The Food and Drug Administration and local health inspectors protect them while they eat and when they take medication. OSHA standards keep them safe in the workplace, and consumer safety groups (and the Better Business Bureau) keep them safe at home and elsewhere. Labels warn of harm and advise of benefits on every product from cigarettes to alcohol to corn chips. And the exercise and diet industries are both multibillion dollar components of the American economic machine.

But a borderline obsession with health has not led Americans to be healthy.

Current studies—both by governmental and private researchers—predict that as many as one in three Americans will be obese in his/her lifetime—obese enough to endanger health and to cost the larger economy billions of dollars in medical expenses and lost wages. Additionally, Americans over the age of eighteen—informed about the costs and benefits of every product they consume—are free to make poor choices in relation to their health, leaving emergency rooms packed with alcohol-related injuries and hospital rooms filled by patients with lung and heart conditions related directly to their use of tobacco. While all Americans have equal access to the freedom to make informed (and often poor) choices that leave them suffering from health problems, their equal access to treatment is denied.

Throughout the end of the twentieth century, the price of prescription drugs rose, sometimes precipitously. At the same time, more Americans found themselves without health care—or adequate health care—and more and more Americans became senior citizens (who, upon retirement, often lost health care benefits and, concurrently, found themselves living on much-reduced incomes). In 2006 the failing health-care system reached a crisis point, and a new Medicare Prescription Drug Plan was inaugurated with the intention of helping senior citizens live a better, healthier life. The program was not without faults, and, at the time of this writing, is still in the process of truly being implemented for all eligible seniors.

But the intent of such programs—and the laws and customs discussed earlier—is the same: Keep Americans healthy. The reasoning is, at its heart, syllogistic: Healthy Americans are productive Americans. Productive Americans are happy Americans. Therefore, healthy Americans are happy Americans. As you read the selections that follow, consider this syllogism about happiness and health—and the promise of Life in the promise of America.

TERRY TEMPEST WILLIAMS

Terry Tempest Williams (1955–) is a naturalist, environmental advocate, and author. Williams has written and edited more than a dozen books, including *An Unspoken Hunger: Stories from the Field* (1994), *Red: Patience and Passion in the Desert* (2001), *The Open Space of Democracy* (2004), and two children's books. In 2005, the Center for the American West gave Williams the Wallace Stegner Award, and she is in the Ecology Hall of Fame. An internationally known speaker, Williams currently teaches at the University of Utah as the Annie Clark Tanner Scholar in the Environmental Humanities Program.

"The Clan of One-Breasted Women" is the epilogue from Williams's most famous book, her award-winning 1991 memoir *Refuge: An Unnatural History of Family and Place*. Written while Williams was the naturalist-in-residence at the Utah Museum of Natural History, *Refuge* juxtaposes her mother's dying from ovarian cancer with the flooding of the Bear River Migratory Bird Refuge in 1983. Williams grew up in Utah, downwind of the Nevada Nuclear Test Site, and in this epilogue she draws connections between fallout from the above-ground nuclear tests of the 1950s and 1960s and the very high cancer rates among "downwinders," including most of the women in her family.

Williams's writing demonstrates how human actions can have profound effects on human health long after the actions take place.

The Clan of One-Breasted Women

∾ Prereading Question

Williams, in the following essay, says the 11 years of atomic weapons testing in Nevada is "a well-known story in the Desert West." Do you know of this story? If so, how did you find out about it? If not, why do you think you have not heard of it? What is the right balance between developing weapons for the military and protecting the health of those put at risk by that development?

I belong to a Clan of One-Breasted Women. My mother, my grandmothers, and six aunts have all had mastectomies. Seven are dead. The two who survive have just completed rounds of chemotherapy and radiation.

I've had my own problems: two biopsies for breast cancer and a small tumor between my ribs diagnosed as a "borderline malignancy."

This is my family history.

Most statistics tell us breast cancer is genetic, hereditary, with rising percentages attached to fatty diets, childlessness, or becoming pregnant after thirty. What they don't say is living in Utah may be the greatest hazard of all.

We are a Mormon family with roots in Utah since 1847. The "word of wisdom" in my family aligned us with good foods—no coffee, no tea, tobacco, or alcohol. For the most part, our women were finished having their babies by the time they were thirty. And only one faced breast cancer prior to 1960. Traditionally, as a group of people, Mormons have a low rate of cancer.

Is our family a cultural anomaly? The truth is, we didn't think about it. Those who did, usually the men, simply said, "bad genes." The women's attitude was stoic. Cancer was part of life. On February 16, 1971, the eve of my mother's surgery, I accidentally picked up the telephone and overheard her ask my grandmother what she could expect.

"Diane, it is one of the most spiritual experiences you will ever encounter."

I quietly put down the receiver.

Two days later, my father took my brothers and me to the hospital to visit her. She met us in the lobby in a wheelchair. No bandages were visible. I'll never forget her radiance, the way she held herself in a purple velvet robe, and how she gathered us around her.

"Children, I am fine. I want you to know I felt the arms of God around me."

We believed her. My father cried. Our mother, his wife, was thirty-eight years old.

A little over a year after Mother's death, Dad and I were having dinner together. He had just returned from St. George, where the Tempest Company was completing the gas lines that would service southern Utah. He spoke of his love for the country, the sandstoned landscape, bare-boned and beautiful. He had just finished hiking the Kolob trail in Zion National Park. We got caught up in reminiscing, recalling with fondness our walk up Angel's Landing on his fiftieth birthday and the years our family had vacationed there.

Over dessert, I shared a recurring dream of mine. I told my father that for years, as long as I could remember, I saw this flash of light in the night in the desert—that this image had so permeated my being that I could not venture south without seeing it again, on the horizon, illuminating buttes and mesas.

"You did see it," he said.

"Saw what?"

"The bomb. The cloud. We were driving home from Riverside, California. You were sitting on Diane's lap. She was pregnant. In fact, I remember the day, September 7, 1957. We had just gotten out of the Service. We were driving north, past Las Vegas. It was an hour or so before dawn, when this explosion went off. We not only heard it, but felt it. I thought the oil tanker in front of us had blown up. We pulled over and suddenly, rising from the desert floor, we saw it, clearly, this golden-stemmed cloud, the mushroom. The sky seemed to vibrate with an eerie pink glow. Within a few minutes, a light ash was raining on the car."

I stared at my father.

"I thought you knew that," he said. "It was a common occurrence in the fifties."

It was at this moment that I realized the deceit I had been living under. Children growing up in the American Southwest, drinking contaminated milk from contaminated cows, even from the contaminated breasts of their mothers, my mother—members, years later, of the Clan of One-Breasted Women.

It is a well-known story in the Desert West, "The Day We Bombed Utah," or more accurately, the years we bombed Utah: above ground atomic testing in Nevada took place from January 27, 1951 through July 11, 1962. Not only were the winds blowing north covering "low-use segments of the population" with fallout and leaving sheep dead in their tracks, but the climate was right. The United States of the 1950s was red, white, and blue. The Korean War was raging. McCarthyism was rampant. Ike was it, and the cold war was hot. If you were against nuclear testing, you were for a communist regime.

Much has been written about this "American nuclear tragedy." Public health was secondary to national security. The Atomic Energy Commissioner, Thomas Murray, said, "Gentlemen, we must not let anything interfere with this series of tests, nothing."

Again and again, the American public was told by its government, in spite of burns, blisters, and nausea, "It has been found that the tests may be conducted with adequate assurance of safety under conditions prevailing at the bombing reservations." Assuaging public fears was simply a matter of public relations. "Your best action," an Atomic Energy Commission booklet read, "is not to be worried about fallout." A news release typical of the times stated, "We find no basis for concluding that harm to any individual has resulted from radioactive fallout."

On August 30, 1979, during Jimmy Carter's presidency, a suit was filed, *Irene Allen v. The United States of America.* Mrs. Allen's case was the first on an alphabetical list of twenty-four test cases, representative of nearly twelve hundred plaintiffs seeking compensation from the United States government for cancers caused by nuclear testing in Nevada.

Irene Allen lived in Hurricane, Utah. She was the mother of five children and had been widowed twice. Her first husband, with their two oldest boys, had watched the tests from the roof of the local high school. He died of leukemia in 1956. Her second husband died of pancreatic cancer in 1978.

In a town meeting conducted by Utah Senator Orrin Hatch, shortly before the suit was filed, Mrs. Allen said, "I am not blaming the government, I want you to know that, Senator Hatch. But I thought if my testimony could help in any way so this wouldn't happen again to any of the generations coming up after us . . . I am happy to be here this day to bear testimony of this."

God-fearing people. This is just one story in an anthology of thousands.

On May 10, 1984, Judge Bruce S. Jenkins handed down his opinion. Ten of the plaintiffs were awarded damages. It was the first time a federal court had determined that nuclear tests had been the cause of cancers. For the remaining fourteen test cases, the proof of causation was not sufficient. In spite of the split decision, it was considered a landmark ruling. It was not to remain so for long.

In April 1987, the Tenth Circuit Court of Appeals overturned Judge Jenkins's ruling on the ground that the United States was protected from suit by the legal doctrine of sovereign immunity, a centuries-old idea from England in the days of absolute monarchs.

In January 1988, the Supreme Court refused to review the Appeals Court decision. To our court system it does not matter whether the United States government was irresponsible, whether it lied to its citizens, or even that citizens died from the fallout of nuclear testing. What matters is that our government is immune: "The King can do no wrong."

In Mormon culture, authority is respected, obedience is revered, and independent thinking is not. I was taught as a young girl not to "make waves" or "rock the boat."

"Just let it go," Mother would say. "You know how you feel, that's what counts."

For many years, I have done just that—listened, observed, and quietly formed my own opinions, in a culture that rarely asks questions because it has all the answers. But one by one, I have watched the women in my family die common, heroic deaths. We sat in waiting rooms hoping for good news, but always receiving the bad. I cared for them, bathed their scarred bodies, and kept their secrets. I watched beautiful women become bald as Cytoxan, cisplatin, and Adriamycin were injected into their veins. I held their foreheads as they vomited green-black bile, and I shot them with morphine when the pain became inhuman. In the end, I witnessed their last peaceful breaths, becoming a midwife to the rebirth of their souls.

The price of obedience has become too high.

The fear and inability to question authority that ultimately killed rural communities in Utah during atmospheric testing of atomic weapons is the same fear I saw in my mother's body. Sheep. Dead sheep. The evidence is buried.

I cannot prove that my mother, Diane Dixon Tempest, or my grandmothers, Lettie Romney Dixon and Kathryn Blackett Tempest, along with my aunts developed cancer from nuclear fallout in Utah. But I can't prove they didn't.

My father's memory was correct. The September blast we drove through in 1957 was part of Operation Plumbbob, one of the most intensive series of bomb tests to be initiated. The flash of light in the night in the desert, which I had always thought was a dream, developed into a family nightmare. It took fourteen years, from 1957 to 1971, for cancer to manifest in my mother—the same time, Howard L. Andrews, an authority in radioactive fallout at the National Institutes of Health, says radiation cancer requires to become evident. The more I learn about what it means to be a "downwinder," the more questions I drown in.

What I know, however, is that as a Mormon woman of the fifth generation of Latter-day Saints, I must question everything, even if it means losing my faith, even if it means becoming a member of a border tribe among my own people. Tolerating blind obedience in the name of patriotism or religion ultimately takes our lives.

When the Atomic Energy Commission described the country north of the Nevada Test Site as "virtually uninhabited desert terrain," my family and the birds at Great Salt Lake were some of the "virtual uninhabitants."

One night, I dreamed women from all over the world circled a blazing fire in the desert. They spoke of change, how they hold the moon in their bellies and wax and wane with its phases. They mocked the presumption of even-tempered beings and made promises that they would never fear the witch inside themselves. The women danced wildly as sparks broke away from the flames and entered the night sky as stars.

And they sang a song given to them by Shoshone grand-mothers:

Ah ne nah, nah	Consider the rabbits
nin nah nah—	How gently they walk on the earth—
ah ne nah, nah	Consider the rabbits
nin nah nah—	How gently they walk on the earth—
Nyaga mutzi	We remember them
oh ne nay—	We can walk gently also—
Nyaga mutzi	We remember them
oh ne nay—	We can walk gently also—

The women danced and drummed and sang for weeks, preparing themselves for what was to come. They would reclaim the desert for the sake of their children, for the sake of the land.

A few miles downwind from the fire circle, bombs were being tested. Rabbits felt the tremors. Their soft leather pads on paws and feet recognized the shaking sands, while the roots of mesquite and sage were smoldering. Rocks were hot from the inside out and dust devils hummed unnaturally. And each time there was another nuclear test, ravens watched the desert heave. Stretch marks appeared. The land was losing its muscle.

The women couldn't bear it any longer. They were mothers. They had suffered labor pains but always under the promise of birth. The red hot pains beneath the desert promised death only, as each bomb became a still-born. A contract had been made and broken between human beings and the land. A new contract was being drawn by the women, who understood the fate of the earth as their own.

Under the cover of darkness, ten women slipped under a barbed-wire fence and entered the contaminated country. They were trespassing. They walked toward the town of Mercury, in moonlight, taking their cues from coyote, kit fox, antelope squirrel, and quail. They moved quietly and deliberately through the maze of Joshua trees. When a hint of daylight appeared they rested, drinking tea and sharing their rations of food. The women closed their eyes. The time had come to protest with the heart, that to deny one's genealogy with the earth was to commit treason against one's soul.

At dawn, the women draped themselves in mylar, wrapping long streamers of silver plastic around their arms to blow in the breeze. They wore clear masks, that became the faces of humanity. And when they arrived at the edge of Mercury, they carried all the butterflies of a summer day in their wombs. They paused to allow their courage to settle.

The town that forbids pregnant women and children to enter because of radiation risks was asleep. The women moved through the streets as winged messengers, twirling around each other in slow motion, peeking inside homes and watching the easy sleep of men and women. They were astonished by such stillness and periodically would utter a shrill note or low cry just to verify life.

The residents finally awoke to these strange apparitions. Some simply stared. Others called authorities, and in time, the women were apprehended by wary soldiers dressed in desert fatigues. They were taken to a white, square building on the other edge of Mercury. When asked who they were and why they were there, the women replied, "We are mothers and we have come to reclaim the desert for our children."

The soldiers arrested them. As the ten women were blind-folded and handcuffed, they began singing:

You can't forbid us everything
You can't forbid us to think—
You can't forbid our tears to flow
And you can't stop the songs that we sing.

The women continued to sing louder and louder, until they heard the voices of their sisters moving across the mesa:

Ah ne nah, nah
nin nah nah—
Ah ne nah, nah
nin nah nah—

Nyaga mutzi
oh ne nay—
Nyaga mutzi
oh ne nay—

"Call for reinforcements," one soldier said.

"We have," interrupted one woman, "we have—and you have no idea of our numbers."

I crossed the line at the Nevada Test Site and was arrested with nine other Utahans for trespassing on military lands. They are still conducting nuclear tests in the desert. Ours was an act of civil disobedience. But as I walked toward the town of Mercury, it was more than a gesture of peace. It was a gesture on behalf of the Clan of One-Breasted Women.

As one officer cinched the handcuffs around my wrists, another frisked my body. She found a pen and a pad of paper tucked inside my left boot.

"And these?" she asked sternly.

"Weapons," I replied.

Our eyes met. I smiled. She pulled the leg of my trousers back over my boot.

"Step forward, please," she said as she took my arm.

We were booked under an afternoon sun and bused to Tonopah, Nevada. It was a two-hour ride. This was familiar country. The Joshua trees standing their ground had been named by my ancestors, who believed they looked like prophets pointing west to the Promised Land. These were the same trees that bloomed each spring, flowers appearing like white flames in the Mojave. And I recalled a full moon in May, when Mother and I had walked among them, flushing out mourning doves and owls.

The bus stopped short of town. We were released.

The officials thought it was a cruel joke to leave us stranded in the desert with no way to get home. What they didn't realize was that we were home, soul-centered and strong, women who recognized the sweet smell of sage as fuel for our spirits.

Textual Questions

1. In the opening paragraphs, Williams uses her own personal experience, and her family's, as a kind of story. How does that story relate to the actions that take place by the end of the essay?

2. What is the "deceit" that Williams mentions near the top of page 339?

3. Williams clearly values her family's long tradition in the Mormon church but raises a number of questions about that tradition. What are these questions?

Rhetorical Questions

4. This essay uses personal experience as part of its argument, a different approach to its topic than most of the pieces in this book. Do you find this approach more or less convincing than the usual argument, which makes claims and then supports the claims with data and other evidence?

5. Beginning on page 341 ("One night I dreamed . . . "), the writing changes tone radically. How would you describe this change? What effect does it have on you?

6. During the arrests of the protesting women at the end of the essay, Williams calls her pen and paper "weapons." What does she mean by this? How does it relate to the two definitions of "reinforcements" the women give the soldiers?

Intertextual Questions

7. Read or reread some of the documents in the long history of American protests against injustice, including the Declaration of Independence, or Martin Luther King's "Letter from Birmingham Jail" (in chapters one and six respectively). How does Williams's essay relate to this tradition?

8. Look ahead to Linda Peeno's essay later in this chapter. What do that essay and Williams's essay have in common? In what ways are they different?

Thinking Beyond the Text

9. Think of the Williams essay in relation to two different promises of America: the promise of equal and effective health care as part of the "general welfare" of all citizens, and the promise that protests against governmental injustice will be allowed or even encouraged. How does this essay connect those promises?

10. Is the promise of America different for public health issues (such as radiation danger, second-hand smoke, impure air or water, and so on) and for private health issues, such as individuals gaining access to affordable health care? If so, what is the difference and why is it different? Or if you see them as more similar than different, how would you frame that promise to include both?

For Writing & Discussion

11. What is the right balance between the rights of individuals and the perceived needs of society, when the two come into conflict? Assuming

that the government was correct when it claimed that nuclear testing was crucial to protect America, can those adversely affected by the tests still claim their rights were violated? In what other areas do these conflicts of rights occur? What is the best way to resolve such conflicts?

MARK H. TABAK

Mark H. Tabak (1950–) is the President and Chief Executive Officer of International Managed Care Advisors, a company he founded in 1996. The company's focus is on health care services in Latin America, Western and Central Europe, and Asia.[1] Tabak also serves as a managing partner in Healthcare Capital Partners, part of the investment fund Capital Z Partners. Before 1996, Tabak was the President and CEO of the companies Health America Development Corporation, Clinical Pharmaceuticals, Inc., Group Health Plan, and AIG Managed Care, Inc. Before his move to the private sector in the 1980s, Tabak worked for the United Auto Workers (UAW) as a "senior negotiator for health care benefits."

Tabak gave this talk on managed care in 1997 at the First International Ethics and Business Seminar in Buenos Aires, Argentina. Admitting that ethics is not his field, Tabak presents himself as a businessman who has spent 20 years implementing managed care plans such as Health Maintenance Organizations (HMOs) and Preferred Provider Organizations (PPOs). A strong advocate of such organizations, he describes the pre-managed care era as one of "unmanaged care." While Tabak admits to problems arising from managed care in the United States, he believes the benefits outweigh the disadvantages and he suggests ways that other countries might be more successful. Drawing on the work of Dr. Alain C. Enthoven, a professor in Stanford's Graduate School of Business, Tabak presents six "guiding principles" for making managed care work.

Tabak's focus on "cost, quality, and access" indicates the three-way balancing act involved in trying to control medical inflation while still making sure patients receive good health care.

---

[1]Info about IMCA's focus came from the biography that Tabak provided to ESC Medical Systems upon his being nominated to their Board of Directors in 1999.

Can Managed Care Make a Difference?

Chart a Sound Course with Ethically Guiding Principles

∞ Prereading Question

Tabak presents himself as a businessman not well qualified to speak of ethics in health care. Consider the role of business in relation to ethics. Are businessmen appropriate role models for ethical behavior? Why or why not? To what degree are the goals of business the same as the goals for health care? To what degree do they conflict? In what ways are businesses involved in the provision of health care for employees? Tabak also tells us he was a union negotiator for health care benefits. What do you know of the role of unions in relation to the provision of health care for their members?

Delivered to the First International Ethics and Business Seminar, Buenos Aires, Argentina, August 6–7, 1997

Thank you and good afternoon. I very much appreciate the opportunity to be a part of this landmark conference on ethics and business. It is indeed a great privilege for me to be in the company of so many outstanding leaders and thinkers on this most challenging of subjects. So let me say, and here I quote the beginning of Jose Hernandez' famous "Martin Fierro" poem: Aqui Me Pongo A Cantar. (Here, I start to sing).

Since the time Alberto Fernandez of Banco Provincia extended the invitation to me to participate in this conference, which was in June, I have given considerable thought as to how I might approach my remarks. This proved to be a very real challenge, in as much as my credentials hardly qualify me to speak as an authority on ethics in health care.

What I am is simply a businessman, and one who has had the good fortune of playing what has been, for me, a very exciting role in the managed care movement in the United States. It is a role I have enjoyed since the very beginning of that movement in the late 1970s.

Given this vantage point, and the fact that many of the practices of managed care in the U.S. are expected to become more widespread in many countries, including Argentina, in the coming years, I thought I should focus my remarks today on what I actually know something about. And that is managed care . . . more specifically, to share with you my vision for how managed care can make a difference in terms of creating a more equitable, more effective, and, I believe, more ethical health care system.

I, for one, am most optimistic that the coming years hold great promise for an exciting journey, a journey to play a pioneering role in helping shape the Argentine health care system into one of the most progressive in the world. And, I would like to emphasize, those are not just words.

My company, International Managed Care Advisors, together with Banco Provincia and the leadership of Alberto Fernandez, is making a substantial commitment to advance health care infrastructure and health care education here.

This commitment, first of all, is an investment which seeks to establish a platform for excellence in the organization and delivery of health care services. It also, I would like to point out, is an investment for the long term.

Frankly, we're not entirely sure that all that we have in mind will work as we envision it. But clearly, we are prepared to give it a try.

To be sure, this is a tall challenge. But I don't think most of us would be here today, contemplating ways to improve things, unless we were collectively committed to achieving large goals by attempting to do things differently . . . by attempting to experiment, and doing so even if we sometimes might fall short of our highest aspirations.

Career Experience as Pioneer

So that you can have a sense of my thinking, my frame of reference, I would like to start out by telling you a little about myself. I recognize that by doing that, I risk some criticism for being self-indulgent.

But, because my past experiences have significantly influenced my view of the future, at least with respect to health care, I thought at least a brief overview of my background would be appropriate.

One of the major themes of my career has been to be thrust into the position of pioneer . . . to be put in the fortunate position of being given an opportunity to break some new ground.

In the late 1970s and early Eighties I had the opportunity to be something of a pioneer within the ranks of organized labor in the United States. I was a senior negotiator for health care benefits for one of the largest union groups, the United Auto Workers.

In this capacity, I negotiated health benefit contracts covering millions of workers and their families, and, in so doing, played a role in transitioning large segments of America's workforce into managed care delivery systems, such as health maintenance organizations . . . HMOs, as they are popularly known.

This was very much a pioneering experience for me, and one which gave me a keen appreciation of the sensitivities associated with preserving and expanding workers' health benefit coverage.

The experience also gave me a keen appreciation of the health benefit costs borne by employers, and thus how expanding health coverage for workers needed to be balanced with health care management practices that contained costs while improving the quality of health care services and guaranteeing access.

Some years later, in the early 1980s, I left organized labor to join a for-profit company called HealthAmerica, whose goal was to become the largest operator of HMOs in the country.

HealthAmerica was very successful, and it did indeed achieve its goal.

It grew from a fragile start-up into a New York Stock Exchange company, a company with over one million members in HMOs spanning no fewer than 35 markets, and it did so in the short space of just four years.

What I learned from the HealthAmerica experience is that, while it can be a lot of fun to be a pioneer when you're on the company's side of the table, it was not necessarily "fun" for many of the members we brought into the HMO.

The health care freedoms our members had formerly enjoyed, freedoms under a health care system which permitted unlimited choice of physicians and unlimited freedom to pursue virtually any treatment regimen they wished, were far more restricted under HealthAmerica's managed care protocols.

This experience greatly sensitized me to the issues surrounding the doctor-patient relationship. It made me more aware of the needs and concerns of consumers and physicians with respect to health care. And, most broadly, it made me far more aware of the sensitivities that need to be borne in mind when a health care system moves along the managed care path.

In the early 1990s I had the good fortune of being named president of an HMO in St. Louis, an HMO which, at the time, had 120,000 members.

The membership included a commercial population, that is, employees whose health care coverage was linked to employer-sponsored benefit plans, and also Medicare members. As many of you are aware. Medicare is the government run program for the elderly in the United States, those 65 years of age and older.

In the early nineties, when I was at this St. Louis based HMO, the idea of transitioning a Medicare population from a fee-for-service environment to a managed care setting was considered not just a novel concept, but also a fairly radical one . . . mainly in view of the elderly's significant use of health care resources as well as their typically close and longstanding relationships with their doctors.

Once again, I found myself in a pioneering role which, in this case, sensitized me to the many issues associated with providing care to a segment of the population often described as "medically vulnerable."

In mid-1993 I had the privilege of being recruited by American International Group, AIG, to create an entirely new entity . . . an entity called AIG Managed Care.

The purpose was, again, of a pioneering nature: it was to help move this giant enterprise, an enterprise with 34,000 employees and nearly 25 billion dollars in revenues and operations in some 130 countries, into the managed care era.

In the U.S. market, this entailed introducing managed care techniques to the workers' compensation, that is, the occupational health care system. Internationally, it entailed applying the principles of managed care to AIG's large number of multinational clients . . . employers who were, and remain, quite concerned about securing access to high quality, cost-effective health care services for their expanding overseas work forces.

Thus, over the roughly 20 years since my union days with the United Auto Workers, I have been playing, to varying degrees, the role of pioneer, a role which, more often than not, enabled me to start with a fairly clean slate to attempt to do things differently . . . to try to shake up the status quo . . . and, above all, to try to make a difference.

I consider myself most fortunate, because all this has been very gratifying, and helps explain why I'm here in Argentina.

I'm here, as I suggested earlier, because I believe the opportunities to play a truly pioneering role with respect to the Argentine health care system have never been greater. And I say this mainly because I believe Argentina is not so far down any one path in health care that it has insurmountable barriers to creating a more effective system.

∾

U.S. Not a Managed Care Template

Now I know that some of you, perhaps many of you, may be thinking to yourselves, "Mr. Tabak, we've heard all about your health care system in the United States. Its got lots of problems. Why should we even consider the U.S. as a framework?"

Well, that is indeed a very good, a very reasonable, question to be asking. And I, for one, would not want to suggest, at least when it comes to managed care, that my experience, or what the United States as a whole has experienced, can or should serve as some kind of perfect model for the rest of the world. Hardly.

The U.S. has, and continues to have, many problems associated with its health care system, and many problems associated with managed care . . . problems, incidentally, which, in many respects, relate directly to ethics.

For those of you who might not be close followers of the U.S. health care system, let me tell you a little about what we're experiencing at the present time.

The U.S. managed care industry is currently facing a very real crisis in confidence, a very serious crisis in confidence.

The practices of managed care organizations are under intense scrutiny by the media, and a Presidential commission has even been established, within the last six months, to explore the idea of creating a "health care bill of rights" to protect consumers enrolled in managed care organizations.

With most Americans now obtaining their health care services through some type of managed care program, there is widespread concern that the accountability of managed care organizations is more to investors than to the well-being of their members.

It is this focus on profits, at the expense of members' health care needs, that has created a major credibility problem for U.S. managed care organizations.

In essence, many in the U.S. now perceive managed care organizations to be morally bankrupt . . . to be lacking any kind of "moral compass" . . . to be organizations that will do whatever it might take to save money on their members' health care needs, even if a member's life is placed in jeopardy.

Interestingly, what has caught the eye of regulators is a relatively few number of stories in the press about health care that was shortchanged . . . shortchanged because the rules of the system, that is, the policies or procedures of a given health plan, served either to delay care or to deny care . . . actions which had dire, and thus highly visible consequences.

And although U.S. managed care organizations have attempted to defend the legitimacy of their actions in these cases, many observers believe these organizations have already lost the battle in the court of public opinion. Hence the formation of the Presidential commission I just mentioned and, more generally, the creation of a climate of continuing intense scrutiny by the media.

Where all this will lead, no one can say with much certainty. But, despite several studies in the Eighties and Nineties which documented that the majority of members in managed care organizations were receiving care that was as good, if not better, than under the almost completely unfettered fee for service system and were also quite satisfied with the care they received, it seems, at least at this time, that the highly publicized ethical lapses of the managed care industry have sent the industry into a tailspin, and thus made ripe the conditions for more stringent government regulation.

Having said this, and recognizing your understandable skepticism about the U.S. health care system, the fact remains that the U.S. has accumulated a great deal of useful experience about organizing and managing the delivery of health care services more wisely than in the recent past.

We obviously have a long way to go before all of the short-comings of our system can be rectified. And it may well be that we never get to that point . . . that point where the familiar trilogy of health care issues, cost . . . quality . . . and access, are in perfect alignment.

Nevertheless, while managed care may be imperfect, managed care remains, at least at this point in time the only approach at our disposal to begin to more effectively address the ever present challenges of cost, quality and access. For this reason, I'd like to devote the balance of my remarks today to sharing some of the "lessons learned" in the United States with you, not so much with the idea that this information can serve as a "template" for health care in Argentina, but rather, so that it can serve, perhaps, as a helpful point of reference going forward.

We have a saying in our company, which is, "If you've seen one country . . . you've seen one country." We use that little phrase to remind ourselves that every country does indeed possess unique characteristics . . . hence the dangers of superimposing any one country's experience upon another's in a manner other than that which can be described as culturally sensitive.

General Comments on Managed Care

Before jumping to some of the more important lessons learned, or "guiding principles," that I have derived from my years in managed care, let me touch briefly on some of the more significant factors which created the backdrop to the managed care movement in the United States. Some of our problems may indeed ring familiar.

The opposite of managed care is what we had in the United States up until about the mid-1980s. It would not have been inaccurate to have labelled that period the era of unmanaged care.

Consider These Conditions

We had a health care system that was out of control. The costs of health care services were invariably described as a skyrocketing . . . climbing at double digit rates, year after year.

One of the major reasons why costs were skyrocketing was simply this: There was no link between providers of health care services and the payors of those services. Costs were out of control essentially because the system functioned on the basis of what was often lamented as "physician-induced demand."

In addition to cost problems, the quality of health care services was highly uneven . . . highly inconsistent. There were no broadly applied standards of care. There was no formally established provider accountability for quality.

And because most physicians were solo practitioners, health care "outcomes," meaning, the results of providers' medical services, were very uneven.

Additionally, the fragmented, cottage industry-like nature of the marketplace fostered wide variations in medical practice as well as widespread use of inappropriate services. Use of health care services was broadly described as indiscriminate.

- There were also few efforts to monitor the quality of health care services.
- Access to care was uneven and inconsistent.
- There was hardly any information available to the purchasers of health care services regarding quality. There were no rankings . . . no ratings . . . nothing that would enable you to know whether or not you, as an individual . . . as a small-company employer . . . or as a giant multinational corporation, were getting any value for your health care dollar.

Moreover, efforts to focus on important preventive health care services were more isolated than organized and systematic. Consequently, little attention was focused on some of the biggest contributors to the high consumption of health care resources contributors such as lack of exercise . . . smoking . . . alcohol, and the like.

Perhaps most fundamentally, only scant attention was paid to how to treat a patient most efficiently and effectively over the entire course of his or her illness. The focus was on putting, and keeping, patients in hospitals rather than in other, more effective and more patient friendly settings.

Lastly, in this era of unmanaged care, the notion of primary care took a distant back seat to specialist care. The result, of course, was ever-higher overall health care costs due to evermore expensive tests and procedures, a great many of which were found to be of negligible value.

Within this context, the managed care era was born, an era that, despite Federal legislation to stimulate the growth of HMOs dating back to the early Seventies, only began to take broad root some 15 years later, in the mid-1980s.

What managed care sought to do was to focus more intelligently on the entire health care environment in which a patient is handled.

Managed care was seen as a way to re-think how health care services should be organized . . . how such services might be reconfigured, not only so that health care resources could be consumed more wisely, but also, so that the quality of care could improve, as well.

This attempt to gain more intelligent control of the health care environment meant several things:

It meant intensely managing the individual not only as an inpatient, but also, as an outpatient.

It meant managing the entire process that brings the patient to recovery and back into the community as expeditiously as possible.

It meant identifying and contracting with a select group of primary care physicians, specialists and hospitals, providers who not only possessed the requisite credentials, but who also were committed to advancing shared goals with the health plan sponsor, the managed care organization.

And, by contracting with quality providers . . . by establishing standards of care . . . and by employing a variety of other tools and techniques, it came to mean that managed care was about striving to "do the right thing for the patient, by doing things right, the first time around."

So, for me, managed care did not come down to something about limiting the autonomy of doctors . . . or about delaying or denying care . . . or about undermining the doctor-patient relationship. No . . . for me, managed care became a way to organize the delivery of medical services and medical-support services in a manner that could be more efficient, less costly, of better quality . . . and thus more effective overall.

In short, managed care was not necessarily a cast-in-stone philosophy, but rather, an approach . . . an approach more about managing care wisely than about anything else.

❧

Some Guiding Principles

I want to be more specific about this idea of managing care and share with you some of my guiding principles, principles that, I believe, will serve to illustrate not only what not to do, but, above all, what to strive to achieve.

I would like to take a moment to point out that these principles rely largely on the intellectual guidance and writings of Alain C. Enthoven, the eminent health economist at Stanford University in California. Dr. Enthoven has provided what I would call truly pioneering thinking and, as such, has always been, for me, a highly influential intellectual beacon. As such, Dr. Enthoven's words and works have helped guide and shape my course as a health care executive over the years.

As I said earlier, I don't know if all that I'm about to discuss with you will work. I also don't know if we'll be able to win the support of all of the constituencies who are essential for an effective managed care delivery system. And I can't pretend to know all of the cultural issues that inevitably will have to be addressed.

But, if my career experience in health care is any guide, I do think we can, at the very least, begin to pioneer . . . which is to say, begin to move things forward in a constructive manner.

My guiding principles—Dr. Enthoven's guiding principles—constitute, for me, what it takes to establish and maintain a world-class managed care organization. These principles, and I want to emphasize this, are basic, and therefore sound deceptively simple . . . perhaps even simplistic.

But, make no mistake: Hardly any managed care organizations in the U.S. have been successful in executing all of these principles either consistently or particularly well, and, as a result, the managed care industry is very much under the gun, as I pointed out earlier.

Nevertheless. I thought these guiding principles would be most appropriate to share with you today, at this conference focused on ethics, because I believe that all of the principles are centered on doing the right thing, by doing things right, the first time around. As such, they are principles which can, I trust, provide, as I said earlier, a helpful reference point.

For the record, these principles are highlighted in an article by Dr. Enthoven and Carol Vorhaus, which appears in the May/ June 1997 issue of Health Affairs, one of the loading health policy journals in the United States.

∽

Guiding Principle Number One Is to Attract and Keep the Best Physicians

As one would suspect, the single most important determinant of a world-class managed care organization is embodied in the physicians associated with the organization, more specifically, their knowledge, their judgment, their overall skills-set.

A world-class managed care organization is therefore highly adept at the task of attracting the commitment and earning the loyalty of the best available physicians in the community . . . the best available primary care physicians and specialists.

By "best physicians in the community," I mean physicians who are committed to updating their knowledge and skills . . . physicians who can relate well to patients . . . who can work collaboratively with other physicians, that is, be the kind of doctors who can function well as part of a health care team . . . a team that is effective in coordinating a patient's total health care needs.

By "best physicians," I also mean primary care doctors who don't interpret the term "gatekeeper" to mean denying or delaying care, but rather who equate gatekeeper with functioning as the accountable steward, the accountable manager, of a patient's health care needs . . . that is, a doctor who knows what to do what actions to take . . . what services to perform, as well as what not to do.

By definition, then, a health plan which attracts these kinds of physicians is capable of identifying them and further, capable of creating the appropriate incentives to enable them to function as accountable stewards or managers of care.

And not only is a world-class managed care organization adept at the task of recruiting the best available physicians; it is also capable of monitoring their performance, meaning, monitoring their performance on the basis of data that is accurately collected on the outcomes of their services as well as on the level of satisfaction that their patients have with their services.

This ability to generate data on physician performance is important because it enables physicians to practice in a qualitatively better way with each passing year.

The data on physician performance is also important because it enables the managed care organization to be in an informed position to take corrective action if a physician's performance is found wanting.

All of this rigor associated with managing and monitoring physician performance is to suggest that a high-quality managed care organization invests heavily in information management systems, systems that track the use of resources . . . that track clinical outcomes . . . systems that facilitate the task of identifying and instituting a range of practices to improve overall performance.

It is also to suggest that, in a world-class managed care organization, the well-known, but not always vigorously practiced, concept of Continuous Quality Improvement is an essential goal of management.

As such, the leaders of a top-quality managed care organization make it a point to inculcate in their organization the importance of ongoing improvement of the various processes of care and of the ways in which services are delivered to patients.

Guiding Principle Number Two Is to Establish and Maintain a Strong Primary Care Orientation

Primary care easily accounts for the lion's share of medical interaction between patients and providers.

Attention to primary care needs is therefore fundamental to the avoidance of more serious and more costly health problems.

In a quality managed care organization, primary care must mean a strong sense of provider responsibility for each member's, each affiliate's, medical record.

Without this, there can be no real coordination of the total health care needs of the affiliate. This of course reflects what I mentioned earlier in describing managed care as the intelligent control of the entire health care environment.

Guiding Principle Number Three Is to Focus on Health Improvement

A world-class managed care organization needs to be focused on improving the health status of its affiliates. That means establishing and operating a managed care delivery system that is focused on health outcomes rather than on purely financial results.

To be effective in health improvement, the health plan must promote the use of disease management strategies for chronic illnesses, illnesses such as diabetes, asthma, arthritis, and the like. By definition, this means, as Dr. Enthoven has stated, embracing a broader epidemiological view of the entire affiliate population served by the health plan in order to effectively capture and analyze information on the health status, health risks and health problems of the population served by the managed care organization. Only in this way can effective interventions be identified and implemented.

☙

Guiding Principle Number Four, Which Is Closely Tied to Focusing on Health Improvement, Is to Focus on Patient Education and Involvement

As Dr. Enthoven has stated, "The fee-for-service system in the United States produced a culture of over-dependence on physicians selling their services and under-involvement of patients and families in their own health care."

In this context, a world-class managed care organization must appreciate that its role is not merely to sell patient services; rather, it is, as Enthoven suggests, to maintain and improve the health of each and every one of its affiliates.

And one of the most powerful ways to do this is, of course, to educate and involve patients and their families in the care processes and disease prevention activities.

It is now widely acknowledged in the United States that patient education and involvement can yield better care. To take but one example, prenatal childbirth education and parenting classes and patient involvement in treatments for chronic conditions often can prevent problems.

It is also important to note that a world-class managed care organization is careful to avoid instituting overly restrictive protocols which have the potential to produce undesirable events.

In one study of some 13,000 patients in six HMOs in the United States, overly restrictive lists of drugs that is, formularies that either limited pharmaceuticals within a certain medication class or excluded certain classes of drugs altogether, were associated with higher total costs of care. The study found that efforts to decrease drug utilization led to increased costs in emergency room visits or hospital admissions.

ᏬᏉ

Guiding Principle Number Five Is to Cooperate with Purchasers

A world-class health care organization also develops data about itself, not only for its own internal use, but also for external use. It views its data, in part, as something of a "community resource" to be used for continually improving the delivery of health care services.

In the U.S., coalitions of employers, large corporations, and others have in recent years demanded increasing amounts of quality performance information across the various health plans they offer to their respective employees. The response from managed care organizations has, by and large, been slow and often begrudging.

Employers want this information to assure themselves and their employees that their health plans are not cutting costs at the expense of quality of care, and that the choices that employers are offering their employees are indeed high quality choices.

In this context, a world-class managed care organization, as Dr. Enthoven puts it, needs to be able to report valid and reliable data so as to act as a real partner with purchasers to produce not just the best information, but the best knowledge for patients, providers and employers.

ᏬᏉ

Guiding Principle Number Six Is to Create Proper Financial Incentives to Improve the Health Status of Affiliates

A high quality health organization reduces the cost of, and need for, care by substituting better processes . . . not by restricting care.

Capitating physicians, that is, paying doctors a fixed amount of money on a prepaid basis to manage the total health care needs of their patients, can be a quality-enhancing incentive because it rewards prevention and tends to foster the physician's ability to get things right the first time around. Capitation also helps to overcome the fragmentation of care associated with the old fee-for-service system.

In no way is capitation designed to compromise any of the key elements of an effective doctor-patient relationship, elements that others have termed the six "Cs": choice . . . competence . . . communication . . . compassion . . . continuity . . . and the absence of any conflicts of interest.

As such, it is essential that whatever financial incentives are used, that they in no way undermine the trust of a patient in his or her physician.

I make a point of this because managed care, for a number of years, has put considerable strain on the doctor-patient relationship in the United States.

As a result, many advocacy groups are now lobbying to make certain that all patients enrolled in managed care organizations will not only have a right to know the criteria used by their health plan to select the doctors and hospitals they must use, but also, have a right to know how their doctors are paid.

The advocacy groups maintain that patients should be told of any potential conflicts of interest that may exist and any financial incentives or clinical rules that may cause doctors to provide less care than patients need.

Clearly, a world-class health plan establishes physician incentives which reward quality and patient satisfaction. By having clear financial incentives, the integrity of what might be termed the physician's fiduciary relationship with the patient can remain safely intact.

Concluding Comments

So, what have I said?

I said, it is essential to find and work with the best physicians.

I said, establish values that deliver top quality care, consistently.

I said, establish the incentives that foster desired provider and patient behavior.

I said, monitor performance.

I said, invest heavily in information management systems to capture data that drives continuous quality improvement and further, helps position your health plan as a partner of purchasers.

I said, establish a primary care ethic and use it as a foundation to focus on the total health care needs of both the individual and affiliate population as a whole.

To be sure, these guiding principles are familiar basic . . . fundamental. Yet, at the same time. I also see them as "ethically guiding" principles which can contribute importantly to the challenge of charting a sound course into the next millennium.

With that in mind, I thought I might close with the words of the great Argentine Jose Hernandez, who concluded his "Martin Fierro" with: No Es Para Mal De Ninguno, Pero Es Para Bien De Todos. "It isn't for anybody's harm, but for everybody's benefit."

I thank you, again. It has been a great privilege for me to be a participant at your conference. I very much look forward to working with our colleagues here in Argentina to advance this vision.

I also very much hope to have the privilege of spending considerably more time with many of you in the months and years ahead.

Textual Questions

1. What does Tabak mean by "managed care"? List its most important characteristics.

2. How do HMOs differ from the traditional doctor/patient pattern for Americans? List the problems Tabak sees in that "unmanaged care" system.

3. List the problems Tabak cites with managed care in the United States, most particularly the ethical ones. Why, in his view, should Argentina nonetheless learn from the American HMO model?

Rhetorical Questions

4. After an apology, Tabak presents his personal experience as evidence that he knows what he is talking about. Describe how he presents himself and consider if this procedure effectively supports his argument for managed care.

5. Tabak's argument for managed cared moves through a series of carefully titled sections. Describe the organization of the talk and its relation to the argument it makes.

6. Notice that the talk, despite its use of personal experience, is neither narrative nor particularly emotional. Select a typical sentence and examine its style. Why do you suppose that Tabak chose this style for his presentation?

Intertextual Questions

7. Linda Peeno takes a very different approach to managed care than does Tabak. Which writer is more convincing? Why?

8. How might Jessica Mitford respond to Tabak's arguments? Where would Tabak and Mitford most agree? Most disagree?

Thinking Beyond the Text

9. Since Tabak gave his talk, the managed care industry has come under increasing attack—even satire from comedians. To what degree have HMOs deserved this attack? How have they failed to deliver on the promise that Tabak sets out, if they have?

10. Describe your own experience with the health care system. Have you experienced care through an HMO? If you are enrolled in a college or university managed care program, how well does it work? To what degree is it like the program Tabak describes as ideal?

For Writing & Discussion

11. Did Argentina's leaders ultimately take Tabak's advice? Searching online, locate information about healthcare in Argentina's healthcare system. Does it deliver the promise of equal health care to its citizens any better-worse than the United States does?

JESSICA MITFORD

Jessica Mitford (1917–1996) combined political activism and journalism, a combination that caused *Time* magazine to dub her the "Queen of the Muckrakers" because of her penchant for digging up stories some people would prefer left untold. Her personal history shows the depth of her commitment to civil rights; in spite of the fact that her parents were British nobility and two of her older sisters were outspoken supporters of Hitler, Mitford joined the Communist Party (which she later left), moved to the United States in 1939, and became a civil rights activist and investigative journalist. Of her career, Mitford said, "You may not be able to change the world, but at least you can embarrass the guilty."

This excerpt, from Mitford's 1992 book *The American Way of Birth*, details causes of infant mortality in the United States and discusses what some health care workers, including those with Alabama's Gift of Life Foundation, are doing to reduce infant mortality rates among poor women.

Mitford wrote eight other books, including two autobiographies and a collection of magazine articles, *Poison Penmanship: The Art of Muckraking* (1979). Her most famous work, however, was her 1963 expose of the funeral industry, *The American Way of Death*, which led to an investigation by the Federal Trade Commission.

Although many of Mitford's books are out of print, The Mitford Project, Inc., continues her work by funding projects and organizations that address ongoing issues such as health care reform, prison reform, and other causes Mitford championed.

The Impoverished Way

∾ **Prereading Question**

Most middle class and wealthy Americans have little contact with the poor, who are often seen as lazy and irresponsible—they could move out of poverty if they really wanted to. Others see the persistent poverty in the richest country in the world as a sign that an important promise of America has not been fulfilled. Still others see the Biblical command to share what one has with the poor as an important obligation. What are your own attitudes toward those without enough money to live the American dream?

As the disgraceful statistics show year after year, the United States, with the highest per capita expenditure on health care of any country in the world, ranks twenty-fourth among Western industrial nations in infant mortality, due entirely to the not-so-benign political and bureaucratic neglect of the very poor, the uninsured (comprising an astonishing thirty-seven million Americans in 1990, up from 28.6 million in 1980), teenage mothers, and those who are alcoholic or drug-addicted. Estimates of the numbers of uninsured vary depending on the source, and how computed. Emily Friedman writing in JAMA, May 15, 1991, says that "most estimates" place the number between 31 and 36 million. In their April 1992 newsletter, the Public Citizen Health Research Group puts the figure at 40-plus million uninsured.

Focusing in for a close look at one example of the miserable experience confronting these women and their babies, a PBS crew directed by Robert Thurber produced a 1989 documentary called *Babies at Risk,* featuring Chicago's Cook County Hospital, where more than five thousand women were delivering babies each year. Some were on Medicaid, but a growing number had no insurance at all.

In this film, which as the producers have pointed out is merely illustrative of a situation that exists in every major U.S. city, we are shown agonizing pictures of skeletal newborns stuck full of tubes, struggling for life in their incubators. Thanks to modern technology, most could be expected to survive—but would likely require long periods of costly hospitalization throughout life. For starters, each day in the neonatal intensive care unit when the documentary was made cost $1,200. The average stay was about twenty days, or $24,000 a baby.

As for prenatal care—which the doctors believed could have prevented many of these disastrous outcomes for the baby—it was virtually nonexistent for their mothers. Since 1986, nine of Chicago's community hospitals serving poor communities had closed, due in large part to the growing number of uninsured patients and the low rate of reimbursement by Medicaid. Many of Chicago's better hospitals refused to accept poor women; instead, they transferred them to Cook County even if they were in advanced labor, a highly dangerous procedure known as "dumping."

According to the film, a pregnant woman seeking prenatal care in the clinics run by the Chicago Department of Health might have to wait as long as nine weeks before being given an appointment. Once this was accomplished, she might wait all day before she could see an obstetrician.

Gladly willing to fill this vacuum—and thereby bilk the tax-payer of a tidy sum—were private doctors who conduct a thriving business in store-front clinics in the poor Chicago neighborhoods, where they hold out the promise of prenatal care to Medicaid patients. Known by Cook County health professionals as "Medicaid mills," the clinics were charging Medicaid $28 per patient visit. They crammed in as many women as possible in any given day, doing virtually nothing for them—"The person loses, the tax-payer loses, and it's the worst kind of ripoff," said Jerry Stermer, president of Voices for Illinois Children. As Dr. Linda Powell of Cook County Hospital pointed out, "That's as bad, if not worse, than no prenatal care because the patients think they are having good care and they think everything's OK and in fact it's not, and they have very, very severe problems when they come to us."

So why haven't these bad actors been run out of the medical profession? Essentially, it would seem, because the Illinois State Medical Society, like its counterpart the California Medical Association (with its Board of Medical Quality Assurance), prefers to look the other way when fellow physicians might be "at risk"—never mind the risk to patients and their babies.[1]

Aside from segments showing the heroic efforts of dedicated public-health workers, swamped by the sheer volume of needy pregnant women, for this viewer the icing on the cake was provided by Governor of Illinois James Thompson, who explained on-camera:

> Illinois has really been, since I've been governor, at the forefront of infant mortality initiatives. Our infant mortality ranking is skewed by the statistics from Chicago.

Well done, Governor. Worthy of one of those *New Yorker* filler items headed "How's That Again?"

To get further specific details—the whys and wherefores, who is to blame, what if any solutions are in sight—I consulted Dr. Barbara Allen, a black pediatrician who since 1981 has been director of maternal and child health for Alameda County, California. In this vast, mainly urban area with a highly diversified population including

---

[1] A state-by-state list of licensing boards, furnished by BMQA in 1988, listed under the general heading "Illinois Department of Professional Regulation" the subheads "Medical Licensing Board" and "Medical Disciplinary Board," each with several locations in Illinois. None was mentioned by name in *Babies at Risk*.

blacks, Hispanics, plus Asian immigrants, Dr. Allen's job boggles the mind.

The great majority of her clientele are on Medi-Cal, the California medical assistance program for families on welfare. Maternity facilities for these clients are in East Oakland at Highland, the county hospital, supplemented by eight public-health clinics scattered throughout the county where a woman can go for prenatal care. However, said Dr. Allen, about 50 percent of the women who do come in to Highland have had no prenatal care. Why? I asked. "A variety of reasons. There's a hard-core group of women out there who are chemically dependent, whose addiction is so great that it's their primary reason for being, so prenatal care is not at all a priority in their minds. Some women out there are homeless and just walking from one place to another, and trying to get into prenatal care. Some try late in pregnancy to get care. And then a lot of clinics may not accept them late in pregnancy because by that time they are considered high-risk. Private doctors won't accept them late in pregnancy."

What happens then? "They either end up going to Highland emergency room or they just stay out of the system until it's time to deliver." An increasing number deliver at home, Dr. Allen told me—unattended, totally alone. "Again, a lot of these women are chemically dependent, and in particular on crack cocaine. And some of them are just so isolated, disconnected. A larger and larger percent of the mothers coming in are really destitute or chemically dependent or both."

As to physicians in private practice, a tiny handful will accept Medi-Cal patients—and at that, they limit these to only two or three a month.

Infant mortality? "The gap is widening," Dr. Allen said. "In the nonblack population the infant mortality rate and low-birth-weight rate continue to decline, but we see in the black population an increase in the rate.

"Anyway," she said, "infant mortality isn't really a medical issue. As long as our society has decided it's OK to have large numbers of people who have no place to live, just belong in the streets, who have insufficient food—no matter what the medical care, what we are finding is that they go right back into these dire living circumstances. So you may be telling her, 'I want you to take this medication X amount of times a day,' and if she's living on the streets somebody snatches her bag, her medication and so on.

"In order to correct the increase in infant mortality I think we're going to have to drastically modify how we see people in this society, especially the poor and the minorities in the community. It is always amazing to me when I hear what we're doing to fight drugs in other countries, the amount of money, and we're going to give them military technical assistance. Yet we have all these neighborhoods that are suffering from drug epidemics and things are out of control, and we can't care, or we don't consider war on drugs right in our backyards. It's like we've written off whole segments of our population."

In Dr. Allen's view, at least one answer would be a system "where everybody can be assured access to health care, a well-thought-out national health insurance program." In other countries, she added, "not only do they have that, but they have very good support programs for women and families—mandatory maternity leave for employed mothers, extended paternity leave where they get extra stipends."

Highland Hospital in East Oakland is a huge, forbidding, prison-like structure. Dr. James Jackson, black chairman of the Department of Maternal and Child Health and Chief of Obstetrics, has worked there since 1984, when he quit his private practice at Alta Bates Hospital to work for the county.

It has been a period of phenomenal growth, he told me. Births at Highland skyrocketed from fewer than 1,000 in 1981 to 2,800 in 1989. When Dr. Jackson first came, he had two physicians in the obstetrics department; in 1989, he had eleven. An indispensable component is the group of twelve certified nurse-midwives, who "do prenatal care on all of the normal patients and deliver more than half of the babies."

Another huge change in the general obstetrical scene is the decline—almost to the vanishing point—of private doctors willing to take Medi-Cal patients. "About 1983 and '84 we did a survey," said Dr. Jackson. "There were about eighty providers taking care of Medi-Cal patients. Today, if you did the same survey, I think you would find five on any one day. There are some closet providers who don't want it known that they take Medi-Cal cases."

Medi-Cal is, it seems, far from being the benign dispenser of health care for the poor; too often it's an almost insurmountable barrier to help of any kind.

"If the strategy was to drive out providers, they have done a marvelous job of driving out the providers throughout the state," said Dr. Jackson. "The worst thing a person can do is come into a doctor's office and wave a Medi-Cal card. You're like a pariah if you walk in with a Medi-Cal card. You can have a blue card, a green card, or any other card, but Medi-Cal has a bad reputation and connotation."

So, what to do? Like Dr. Allen, Dr. Jackson thinks that "medical intervention is to deal with illness, with poor outcomes. But we should be far more concerned with underlying causes. The social factors outweigh the medical factors." Like Dr. Allen, he supports a national, comprehensive health insurance law.

My introduction to the Alabama way of birth was a Pulitzer prize-winning series titled "A Death in the Family" in the *Alabama Journal* of September 14 to 18, 1987, which gave the state's infant mortality rate (babies who die before the age of one year) as 13.3 per thousand live births, at a time when the national figure was 10.4. For black babies, the rate was 19.9, for white, 9.7, a ratio that holds true for most of the country.

The five-part series, replete with human-interest stories—heartrending cases of grinding poverty and official dereliction—also afforded some glimpses into the politics of Alabama perinatal care for the indigent.

Governor Guy Hunt made rather good copy. Prodded by the reporters to explain his pocket veto of a legislative resolution calling for expansion of Medicaid coverage, he took the Reaganesque forgettability route: "I don't remember pocket-vetoing anything that dealt with it." His memory jogged by the persistent journalists, Hunt said he probably vetoed it "because it recommended that the amount obstetricians are paid for a Medicaid delivery be increased from $450 to $750."

Hunt disagreed with the opinion of some business experts that the high infant mortality rate discourages companies from relocating to Alabama because it indicates a poor quality of life. "We have not found this to be hindering our industrial development at the present time," he said, which has the ring of truth: corporations bent on finding a cheap source of labor in a largely nonunion state are hardly likely to worry about the infant mortality rate amongst those they seek to exploit.

The governor added, "I think it should be pointed out that the quality of care that we're receiving at a lot of our institutions in our state is the highest of anywhere in the world," a comment that enraged public-health workers toiling in the front lines of the battle to reduce infant mortality; for obvious reasons, they told the *Journal* reporters, the poor are not recipients of the kind of care that Governor Hunt was talking about.

Even more infuriating was the governor's proposal for a task force "to study the problem," that ever-handy device beloved by politicians wishing to deflect the slings and arrows of outraged constituents. "I want to examine the issue thoroughly before committing funds," he told the reporters, to which an exasperated health consultant replied, "We *know* about the problem. It shouldn't take long to study. You don't have to reinvent the wheel." And State Senator MacPherson: "That means 600 more babies are going to die in the next year without the attention they deserve. The problem has been studied long enough."

The cruelest blow of all was the *Journal's* revelation that Mississippi, which in 1985 had held the distinction of being at the very bottom of the fifty states in the infant death rate, had climbed to eighth worst, leaving Alabama in the Number 50 spot. To put this in context for readers unfamiliar with the particular sensitivities of the states involved: Alabama and Mississippi tend to run neck and neck in a perpetual race as to which is the worst in national statistics in just about anything to do with the public welfare: education, housing, mean annual income (and "mean" is the *mot juste*), health care, sanitation, etc.

The *Journal's* writing team donated its Pulitzer prize money to the Gift of Life Foundation, a newly organized Montgomery group "dedicated to lowering the state's infant mortality rate." In 1990, three years after the *Journal* series was published, I went to Montgomery to see Gift of Life in operation.

For starters, I met with Doris Barnette, acting director of the Alabama Department of Public Health's Family Health Service Bureau, whose functions include oversight of maternal and child care; the federal Special Supplemental Feeding Program for Women, Infants, and Children (WIC); and family planning, among several other subtasks. Mrs. Barnette is a large, expansive, charismatic woman who clearly inspires her staff and anyone else who comes into her orbit. As a staff member told me, "She keeps us going by her sheer enthusiasm; just being around her is like a shot of adrenaline." Mrs. Barnette is a Southerner born and bred, originally from Louisiana, a social worker by training who spent some years in Mississippi in health work before coming to Alabama in 1986.

The Gift of Life program, which functions under the aegis of her department, has accomplished a complete transformation in maternal care in Montgomery, she said: "It's an example of what can be done when a community comes together. Due to Gift of Life Montgomery went from terrible to almost tolerable."

As background, she described an audit done in 1987 by the General Accounting Office which "found Montgomery was the worst place anywhere in the United States to have a baby. There were three hospitals where indigents could give birth. People without resources came to the health department to get prenatal care. The director was an old doctor, not sensitive at all to the needs of the patients. The clinics were overrun; patients averaged less than three prenatal visits, whereas the American College of Obstetricians and Gynecologists recommends thirteen visits for a normal pregnancy—and a large number of these were high-risk."

Most nightmarish of all was the procedure for getting into a hospital once labor had started: "The three hospitals that accepted indigents rotated what they called 'Emergency Room of the Day.' If you were pregnant and about to get ready to deliver, you had to listen to the radio at six A.M. to find out which was the E.R. of the day."

Compounding the problems of women seeking prenatal care and admittance to a hospital for delivery was their wholesale abandonment by the medical profession. "Ten years ago, four hundred fifty obstetricians and family-practice doctors were delivering babies," said Mrs. Barnette. "Today it's less than two hundred, with practically no family physicians—less than twenty—delivering babies." The reason: malpractice insurance premiums in Alabama have risen to an average of $50,000, up to $65,000 in some rural areas. Those 450 family doctors each used to deliver from thirty to forty babies annually out of a total of sixty thousand births in Alabama.

When insurance companies forced them to pay premiums as high as those paid by obstetricians, they were forced to drop delivering babies from their practice. They couldn't even begin to pay the premiums with only thirty to forty deliveries per year.

"One of the fallouts from the malpractice situation is that doctors are refusing to take Medicaid patients because of their mistaken belief that poor people are more apt to sue for malpractice," said Mrs. Barnette. "I don't believe this. There are no statistics to back it up—furthermore, in my experience, poor people in the rural areas are on the whole suspicious of lawyers, and are not likely to seek one out. You'll hear such comments as 'When Uncle Joe was in trouble we got a lawyer and he charged plenty, but Joe went up to the penitentiary.' But it's the perception of physicians that counts, and what keeps a lot of them from accepting Medicaid cases."

In the four-county area surrounding Montgomery, Mrs. Barnette told me, there had been some twenty-five doctors delivering babies in the early 1980s, but by 1987 there were only thirteen, and others were planning to get out. "It was crisis. We were about to reach the point where every single obstetrician was about to stop delivering babies and you would not be able to have a baby in Montgomery or anywhere thereabouts, no matter what your income was."

Into this horrible mess stepped the Gift of Life Foundation, through which obstetricians and certified nurse-midwives provide comprehensive prenatal care and counseling at county health department clinics serving Montgomery and surrounding rural areas. About eighteen hundred babies a year are delivered in two Montgomery hospitals, also under the auspices of Gift of Life. The clientele is 75 percent black, 25 percent white—there is no appreciable Hispanic population in the Montgomery area, Mrs. Barnette said. In a typical year the program will have three to five FTE, or full-time equivalent, physicians; one FTE may actually be two part-time doctors. Gift of Life has about eight certified nurse-midwives and is constantly looking for more, but CNM's are very hard to get. "They're scarce as hens' teeth," said Mrs. Barnette. "We are recruiting all we can find . . . we hunt them, we hunt them."

Like health professionals everywhere, Mrs. Barnette is absolutely sold on the paramount importance of prenatal care in reducing the incidence of premature, low-weight births and ensuring a better outcome of the pregnancy. "It's pure magic," she said. "We don't quite know what it is about prenatal care that makes it magic. We only know that more and better prenatal care results in better babies."

Prenatal care as furnished by Gift of Life is a far cry from the crowded public-health clinic where a woman may wait for hours until she hears the words "Next, please." Ms. Next, whether she is a seasoned mother of six or a terrified fourteen-year-old expecting her first, will typically get a perfunctory examination by somebody she has never seen before—and likely will never see again, as personnel are constantly rotated—and be speedily ejected to make way for the next Ms. Next.

Not so in the Gift of Life setup. As explained by Mrs. Barnette and others in the program, the goal is to arrange for each patient to be followed throughout her pregnancy by the same individual: "This personal attention and concern may be the magic ingredient of prenatal care," she said, and recited a poignant line from a poem to illustrate the point: "*I had a nurse who knew my name . . .* "

A further step in the concept of maternity care as a one-on-one proposition is "case management," a program still in the initial stages as of 1990, designed to supplement the medical aspects of prenatal care. "The pregnant woman," said Mrs. Barnette, "is assigned *one* case manager, generally a social worker, to lead her by the hand through the highly confusing bureaucratic maze of services to which she is entitled. Where to get food stamps? How to apply for WIC benefits?

"What we have had are nurses who give the best prenatal care they can. But a nurse with a clinic and forty patients waiting to see her can't stop and, for example, help a single parent find housing. That's the sort of problem the case manager tries to cope with. An additional benefit is that the case manager is able to follow up the birth and see that the new mothers get into family-planning services for birth control. The object is to space the babies at least two years apart, but sometimes by the time a mother comes in for her postpartum checkup, she is pregnant again. That's because there was no one person working with them, before we started this program."

How much does all this cost and who pays for it? I asked. Needless to say, in a country whose proud and oft-repeated slogan is "the bottom line is the dollar sign," this is a crucial question.

The budget for three physicians and eight certified nurse-midwives is $1.2 million a year, said Mrs. Barnette. Seed money for the Gift of Life Foundation came from a variety of sources, both public and private: the state health department, cities and counties, churches, some grant money, and (surprisingly) even gifts from almost a dozen doctors, to the tune of $1,000 each.

For further elucidation, Doris Barnette steered me to two other movers and shakers in the Gift of Life setup: Dr. John Porter, chairman of the foundation, whose idea it was in the first place, and Martha Jinright, director of the program since its inception.

Before coming to Montgomery in 1981, Dr. Porter served for some years (1976 to 1981) as the only obstetrician in a small town in Mississippi—population ten thousand, plus another twenty thousand in the surrounding rural areas. He seemed driven, like many another who ventures into the quagmire of maternity facilities for the indigent, by twin and complementary passions: a fervent desire to accomplish at the very least a decent professional standard of care for the patients, and an abiding hatred of obstructionist politicians and bureaucratic foot-draggers.

"The working poor don't qualify for Medicaid," Dr. Porter told me. "Almost nobody in Alabama qualified. From 1981 to '87, I watched the horrendous time the poor had giving birth; there was not enough money from Medicaid and no private doctor would furnish prenatal care. The working poor and the indigent went to the health department for prenatal care but *not* for delivery. There was no continuity of care. Women just dropped into Emergency when they were already in labor. A bad system— Alabama was the worst state in the union."

At first, Dr. Porter encountered nothing but discouragement in his campaign to improve the situation: "We met with the county government, the county commissioners, the mayor, all the hospital administrators, and tried to get something accomplished. We got absolutely nowhere.

"The fact is the politicians are not interested in anything that won't get them votes; I really believe that's what it boils down to. It's just not an issue that's important to them, because it was a bunch of poor people who didn't matter anyway. So we got no help from the politicians.

"One day I got the idea, talking to my wife, that with more money from Medicaid plus private donations, we could hire CNM's and doctors." Having enlisted the support of the health department and assorted pediatricians, Dr. Porter and his colleagues raised enough money through private donations to employ four CNM's and two doctors. This proved to be an excellent goad with which to prod the politicians into action: "I think we shamed them because the initial start-up money was all volunteer donations, from individuals and from churches." Once the Gift of Life had proved to be outstandingly successful—and had across-the-board community support—the politicians soon swung behind it. "A politician would be committing suicide if he tried to end this program now," said Porter. "I think that you will find that the Gift of Life Foundation, how we did it and how we set it up, will be used as a prototype by many other communities."

When the search began for a director of the Gift of Life project, there were over a hundred applicants. Martha Jinright, who had worked for some years with the March of Dimes, which seeks to prevent birth defects, was one of eight to make it to the final stage, an interview by a committee of community leaders charged with the final selection. As the program was a brand-new proposition, the selection committee had little to go on, Ms. Jinright told me. "They called me back to tell me that I drew the short straw."

She began working at the inauguration of the project, in May 1988. "The Gift of Life started delivering in June of that year. We've delivered a little over three thousand in the twenty-two months that we've been in operation.[2]

Martha Jinright identified the three factors which, she believes, contributed most to the success of Gift of Life: "First, the nurse-midwives.

---

[2]My meeting with Martha Jinright was in March 1990. State health department statistics show that for the year 1990 there were 3,861 births in Montgomery County, of which Gift of Life delivered more than 1,600. In the first six months of 1991, Gift of Life delivered 738 babies. It would seem that Gift of Life is responsible for almost half of the births in Montgomery County.

I think we need our physicians—I don't want to shortchange them, but I think we could have hired twenty physicians and not had the success we've had with the nurse-midwifery component. The hands-on, woman-to-woman relationship, the personal relationship is a real, vital part of the project."

I was curious to know whether there was much opposition from Alabama physicians to the employment of nurse-midwives. "Not from those in our program," said Ms. Jinright. "But yes—from several in the medical profession in general. I think we have—I don't know any other term to describe them—the old coots. You can't tell them anything. They see the midwives as a threat, taking away their business. In my opinion, there's enough business out there to go around for everybody. It's interesting that they feel threatened. Is it because the midwives can do a better job? Is it because they do it for less money? I don't know."

The second key to success, she said, is the program of home visits by public-health nurses. "When our clients get back in their home setting, there are always issues that can't be addressed in a clinic or hospital, or in routine postpartum care. The home-visit nurses discuss things with the new mothers like how they're mixing their formula, the way they are taking care of their babies. The mothers suffer from information overload in the hospital and in the clinic; there are some things that need to be addressed personally in the home situation that can't be covered in the hospital."

The third ingredient in the Gift of Life's unique mix of services is what Doris Barnette described to me as "case management," via the social services. "This gives our clients a support mechanism, and someone they can call on for all kinds of help," Ms. Jinright said. "Not somebody who just measures their bellies and addresses their clinical needs in prenatal care, but someone who can assist them when they may have some emotional problems. Everything from stress, to coping, to 'I have a husband who's beating me on the weekends.'

"Then we have some ladies who are so poor, homeless, with basic needs: 'I have no food. I have nothing for my baby. It's thirty-two degrees outside and I have no blankets.' " Inspired by the Gift of Life organization, the community responded with "food, bibs, bottles,—what they call care packages. We've had a church use an old-fashioned pattern and make us some baby beds out of boxes. I know that some people think that's primeval, but some of these ladies have no place for their babies. The boxes are darling. They cover them with pretty wallpaper, donate pillows and handsewn pillowcases."

Doris Barnette had told me that the Gift of Life Foundation's board of directors range from ultraliberal—a black former aide to Martin Luther King, Jr.—to a white deep-dyed-conservative state senator. Martha Jinright elaborated: "We have fourteen board members, six of whom are black. Part of the fascination, I think, about the foundation and its origination is that these people were able to come together for a common goal. I think that in itself is a major accomplishment, particularly in the South." The black members include a member of the Board of Education, the dean of the black business college, and other community leaders. Do these work harmoniously with the white conservatives? I asked. "Yes. Although they may be adversaries on other issues, they work very harmoniously on our board."[3]

From these discussions, I gathered that the only way to reach into the hard hearts and shriveled souls of the Alabama old-line politicians is via the path suggested in the *Journal* series, viz., to play upon their embarrassment when Alabama is tagged as "the worst" place in the country to have a baby—even worse than Mississippi. Stalwarts in the Gift of Life program, well aware of this, have learned to fine-tune their approach to the powerful to jangle that particular sensitive nerve.

Brave little Dutch boys with fingers in the dyke, the Gift of Life workers have counterparts elsewhere, individuals who are dedicated to the well-being of mothers and their babies and who use great ingenuity—carrots and sticks, cajolery and threats—to get around the sloth, inefficiency, and miserliness of government and its officials in bureaucracies from Medicaid to local boards of health.

Those most closely involved with the day-to-day work of these programs have come to the inevitable conclusion that their efforts can only be a stopgap—a useful Band-Aid, but not a final solution to a huge and overriding problem.

Talking this over with Doris Barnette, I mentioned that the Netherlands, like most European countries, provides complete, free, comprehensive care for pregnant women, babies, and children, including everything from an adequate die to midwifery and medical and pediatric services. If a Dutch child age anywhere from three to ten is examined by health experts for such indicators as weight, height, and IQ, it is impossible to tell from these data whether the child comes from a rich, middle-class, or poor family, as he or she would have been entitled to all components of a healthy life regardless of financial status.

"That's a country that values its children regardless of their origin, because they are the future," Mrs. Barnette said, "and I think one could draw the conclusion based on the system we have here, although it sounds

---

[3]Listening to Doris Barnette, Martha Jinright, John Porter, and numerous coworkers, I might have been lulled into forgetting that I was in the Cradle of the Confederacy had it not been for a chance encounter with one of the pediatric nurses, who delivered a prototypically racist spiel about the patients she is supposed to serve. She assured me that her views are shared by all her friends, and by extension by a majority of whites in Alabama. I suspect she may be right about this. In essence, she thinks that black teenagers should be penalized for having babies, should be denied prenatal care and cut off from welfare or any other assistance. "Otherwise, two generations from now my grandchildren will be paying for the upkeep of *their* grandchildren, and on and on," the nurse said, casting her pretty blue eyes skyward at the exasperating thought.

like a real indictment, that perhaps we value only middle- and upper-income children. The data are there to tell us this is so."

I asked Martha Jinright what she would think of a program for the United States akin to those of England and Canada—a tax-supported national health service, providing free care to all. "I'm not so sure I agree with socialized medicine across the board," she said. "But I think, because of the maternity-care crisis we have in this nation, we could learn a lot from socialized medicine in addressing the obstetrical situation."

So it seems that from coast to coast those on the front line of maternity care—Drs. Allen and Jackson in California, Doris Barnette and Martha Jinright two thousand miles away in Alabama—are of like minds when it comes to the root cause of the ever-escalating crisis. If their energies, and those of health workers across the country, could be mobilized for a concerted push toward national legislation that would ensure free access to decent health care for all citizens, we might yet see some revolutionary changes.

Textual Questions

1. Several of the doctors interviewed in this essay say the problem with the high infant mortality rate among the poor is more a social issue than a medical issue. What do they mean by that?

2. How does Mitford apportion responsibility for Alabama's infant death rate among the mothers, the physicians, malpractice insurance, and the government? Where does she speak of the fathers' responsibilities?

3. Mitford gives one example of a way to solve the terrible problems she describes: the Gift of Life Foundation. List the reasons this institution is so effective. Why, despite all of these reasons, does she call it "a Band-Aid but not a final solution to a huge and overriding problem"? In what ways is the Netherlands proposed as offering a better promise of health care than does America?

Rhetorical Questions

4. This reading is taken from a popular book, rather than representing a scholar speaking to other scholars. How does the different audience affect the way Mitford writes?

5. Describe the organization of this reading and how it relates to the argument Mitford is making. Where does her controlling idea appear? Where does this controlling idea receive its strongest support

6. How does Mitford expect you to respond to this chapter and what kind of action does she seek to produce? Do you respond that way? If so, why? If not, why not?

Intertextual Questions

7. Mitford does not speak directly to the issues of morality and ethics, though she implies strongly that she thinks the situation she describes is wrong. Compare her approach to ethical health care to that used by Tabak in the preceding essay.

8. In the essay that follows, Sidney Taurel writes of aging and healthcare. While Mitford focuses much of her attention on race, is it possible that the age of parents is also a factor in Alabama's high infant mortality rate? How?

Thinking Beyond the Text

9. What kind of health care is available to the poor in your community? What about prenatal care for impoverished mothers? To what degree is it like or unlike the situation Mitford describes in Alabama?

10. What are the arguments for and against providing the same kind of health care for newborns of the poor that is available for those of the more well-to-do? What are the arguments against that view? Where do you stand on that issue?

For Writing & Discussion

11. Is there any way to reconcile the lack of health care for babies of the impoverished with the promise embodied in the statement that "all men are created equal"? If there is, how can that be done? If not, why has that promise been violated? What can be done?

SIDNEY TAUREL

Sidney Taurel (1949–) is the Chairman, President, and Chief Executive Officer of Eli Lilly and Company, a Fortune 500 pharmaceutical company that produces several well-known drugs, including Prozac. Taurel also is a member of the Board of Directors of Pharmaceutical Research and Manufacturers of America (PhRMA), of IBM's Audit Committee, and of the Board of Overseers of the Columbia Business School. He has been a member of the President's Export Council since 2003.

Taurel's talk on "The Future of Aging: Social Consequences of the Biomedical Revolution" was the 2001 Hatfield Lecture at The Johnson School, Cornell University's graduate school of management. Part boosterism, part analysis, the lecture examines the consequences of what Taurel calls "the age wave": the U.S. population as a whole is getting older as more of the population lives to ages well over 65. While Taurel acknowledges potential problems caused by an aging population, especially potential economic problems, he presents a more optimistic perspective. An aging population, he says, instead of causing a drain on the nation's resources, can create economic as well as social benefits as the baby boomers pass retirement age. In particular, he talks about ways that biomedical companies benefit other sectors of the industry, and argues that the health care industry may become the new driving force in the American economy.

Whether or not Taurel is correct about economics, his demographics are accurate; the 1990 census counted 31.2 million Americans ages 65 and over, and by 2000 that figure had increased to 35 million.[1] As the post-World War II baby boom (born 1945–1964) continues to age, this number is expected to increase.

The Future of Aging
Social Consequences of the Biomedical Revolution

✎ Prereading Question

You know, of course, that you will grow old and die some day. But it's sometimes hard for those who are relatively young to imagine what that will be like. It seems so far away, rather boring to think about. In fact, few young people have any real contact with the elderly, and few start saving money for their retirement voluntarily. But the economic and health issues now looming before the "baby boomers" born in the late 1940s have become more and more important in recent years. And it is not clear just how future generations will live as they age. Before reading this essay, imagine yourself at age 65 and on the point of retirement. What will your health be like? Where will your retirement income come from? What can you tell us about the life you have lived and how it prepared you for that later stage of life you will be starting?

Delivered to The 2001 Hatfield Lecture, Cornell University, Ithaca, New York, September 20, 2001

Thank you, President Rawlings. It is a very great honor to be invited to deliver the address as the Hatfield Fellow for 2001.

---

[1]Figures from "The 65 Years and Over Population: 2000," which is a "Census 2000 Brief" publisher by the U.S. Census Bureau.

Let me first say that this is still a very difficult time for the residents of New York and for people anywhere on the planet who value human life. I want to offer my deepest sympathy to anyone here who may have lost relatives or friends in this horrible attack.

But I am glad that the University has convened this event as scheduled. And I am proud to be a part of it.

I firmly believe that—beyond helping the victims and their families in any way we can—one of the positive things each one of us can do to respond to the terrorists is to deny them the spectacle of disorder and despondency they most want. And instead, to pick ourselves up and get on about our lives as quickly and vigorously as we can.

Also I am eager to speak to you because the message that I bring today is, ultimately, a hopeful and optimistic one about a subject that more commonly inspires anxiety and even fear.

My topic today is "the future of aging." The issue is by no means obscure. And yet it never seems to receive sustained focus in our national dialogue. Instead it seems to always be off on the periphery, claiming our attention only in occasional headlines about recent census data or future Social Security obligations.

Such occasional reports are the proverbial "tip of the iceberg." They only hint at the extraordinary mass lying just out of view. In fact, what they are is advance notice of a demographic event unprecedented in human history—a rapid and large-scale shift in the age distribution of our population.

In the United States a hundred years ago, about 4 percent of the population was over 65. By 1950, it was 8 percent. Today it is a little under 13 percent. By 2030, it will likely exceed 20 percent.

Nor is this something unique to the United States. By 2030, one of every three people in Germany and Japan, two of five in France will be over 65.

This is a change that will change everything else. Dealing with it, in one form or another, will very likely be the dominant public issue for the first half of this century.

Today, I want to outline the dynamics of this demographic event. In part, I think it's important just to fully acknowledge the reality, to look beneath the surface and try to understand the true dimensions of the phenomenon bearing down on us.

At the same time, I want to talk about some of the major societal and economic changes it will bring and suggest the choices we will have to make to accommodate an older society.

I think it's fair to say that the prevailing attitudes are pretty negative. To the extent that people think about the coming age shift at all, they see it as increasing the burden of social welfare costs.

I have a more positive view. I'll argue that this trend will also bring great benefits, which, I believe, will more than offset the costs.

Most of my case is based on well-known data. If I have any special angle of insight, it comes mainly from the fact that pharmaceutical companies play a big role in this story and we are keenly interested in how it will unfold.

Let's start with the factors driving this population shift. Demographers point to three great forces combining to create this "age wave." And I would add a fourth.

The first factor is obviously longevity—people are simply living longer. Americans have added 28 years to the average life expectancy over the last century.

That's an incredible accomplishment, but it's sometimes misunderstood. There is no evidence that we have managed to override our genetic programming and extend the lifespan of our species, although that may someday be possible. Rather, with enormous improvements in our standard of living, our public health infrastructure, and our medical technology, we have managed to sharply reduce the high incidence of premature death that human beings have suffered throughout history. A great many more of us are now able to enjoy a much greater share of our biological allotment.

Thus, as "Age Wave" expert Ken Dychtwald puts it, "throughout most of recorded history only 1 person in 10 could expect to live past 65. Today, nearly 80 percent of Americans will live to be that age."

That age and well beyond. More than two-fifths of the over-65 cohort is already over 75. The 2000 census shows that the population segment known as the "oldest old"—those over 85—is the fastest growing of all.

The second force is the approaching retirement of the baby boomers. The oldest of this generation of 76 million will reach 65 in 10 years. By sheer mass, the boomers have defined the center of gravity in American life from childhood on. As their numbers are added to the long-lived seniors ahead of them, markets, media, and politics will focus on the elderly.

The third force is the countertrend—the "baby bust" that followed the boomers. If the boomers create a peak to the age wave, the next generation accentuates the trough. Beginning in the 1970s, fertility rates in America have declined to historic lows. For three decades, they have been less than two-point-one children per woman of childbearing age—which means that, as a nation, we are not replacing ourselves. This statistic is of particular concern to policy makers, as we shall see.

And I would add a fourth component to the dynamic of the aging trend: namely the impact of biomedical innovation.

Better health care has been a multiplier in each of the three demographic trends I've just listed. Obviously, improvements in medicine have played a central role in extending life expectancy, especially with the powerful gains made in recent decades. But it is also worth observing that the baby boom generation was the first to benefit fully from vaccines and antibiotics, protecting those babies against the infectious diseases that had killed so many children in earlier times. Finally, among the causes of the "baby bust," surely one major one was "the pill," which gave American women, for the first time, full control over their fertility.

So these are the components of the evolving demographic shift, but what are the implications? What does the age wave really mean for America? Is it to be feared or welcomed?

Public attitudes seem to be mixed. The emerging story on longevity inspires a certain degree of awe, and that translates into a new sense of entitlement at the individual level. People clearly want to live longer, and now they expect to.

But in media accounts and political speeches, the message seems to be that this age wave represents, in the refrain of a popular song, "the end of the world as we know it."

The focus seems to be on the most worrisome entailments of the age shift, with an emphasis on economic concerns. The conventional perception is that a big increase in the number of elderly means a big increase in costs to society. Older people, we all know, have a greater burden of illness and disability. So health care costs are bound to shoot up. And extended lives require extended incomes, which surely means greater Social Security expenditures. The only question is "who is going to pay for this . . . and how?"

The answer that has worked for so long—taxing current workers to support current retirees—won't work much longer. That's the significance of the baby bust.

When Social Security began in 1935, there were 40 people of working age to support each retiree. By 1950, the ratio was 17 to 1. Today it is about 4 to 1. By 2020, it will be 3 to 1. By 2030, there will be roughly two workers to cover the benefits of each retiree.

If it's any consolation, Europe and Japan are moving along the same demographic track, but roughly 10 years ahead of the United States.

It's safe to conclude that the intergenerational "chain letter" is about to be, if not broken, then drastically revised.

In the meantime, the only course of action that public officials seem to have embraced is an effort to contain the costs of the benefits provided.

Health care and especially the pharmaceutical industry are right in the cross hairs of this effort. From this vantage point, new medical technology is seen as more of a problem than a solution. The argument is that high-tech therapies come with higher price tags and, because they work better, expand utilization. Some health economists have insisted that, given that we cannot slow down the increase in the number of elderly, our only option is to slow down the flow of expensive new technology to assist them.

No one acknowledges that, in fact, this is a way to slow down the increase in the number of elderly.

In any case, health care is merely the "target of opportunity" for the general mindset. The main assumption in policy circles is that the age shift is going to bring massive economic challenges, and rigorous cost control is going to be the only path to solutions.

I wouldn't say this conclusion is incorrect so much as it is incomplete. When several key details are added to the picture, I think the future looks much brighter than the conventional view. There is no question that a demographic shift of this magnitude will bring extraordinary challenges. But it will also bring some extraordinary benefits.

What the conventional view misses, I think, is an adequate understanding of the role of biomedical innovation in the future and, for that matter, in the present day. The pessimists don't see how technology is changing the aging process.

The key fact missing from the conventional view is the dramatic decline of disability among those over 65.

During the 1970s, disability rates among older Americans held fairly constant, averaging about 45 percent. By the late '80s, those rates had fallen significantly, to under 39 percent. The most recent study indicates that the disability rate today among people over 65 is less than 20 percent.

Some gerontologists summarize such findings by saying that we've added 10 years to what we might call our "health span," that is, years of life without a disabling condition.

By the way, this effect can't be explained by pointing to water treatment plants or any other part of our basic public health infrastructure. Healthier lifestyle choices are part of the story, but primarily this is medicine at work.

Moreover, it's clear that seniors are using this windfall of vitality in ways that would have amazed their own parents.

Retirees today are not buying rocking chairs. They are buying sea kayaks and tandem bikes. They are taking up distance running in their 60s, learning to tap dance in their 70s, signing up for walking tours at 80.

Their improved vitality is mental as well as physical. Far from shunning the new information technologies, seniors have rapidly learned to use the new tools of connectivity to fight isolation and loneliness.

Across the nation, colleges report steadily rising enrollments of the elderly in a broad range of courses. Learning for learning's sake seems to be a rapidly-growing pastime among retirees.

What we're witnessing is the emergence of a new life stage growing between what we have always called "middle age"—say age 50—and what we think of as truly "old age"—a boundary which has now moved out to 75 or 80. It's as if we've opened the circle of life and inserted a new wedge in it. Ken Dychtwald suggests that the people entering this new age will not turn into their grandfathers. Instead, they are turning out to be simply more experienced versions of themselves in middle age.

The conventional view of our future society misses this entirely. It still expects the majority of the elderly to fit the traditional stereotype of older people—failing physically, fading mentally, stuck in the past, and fearful of the future. In short, living lives ruled by entropy.

In fact, all evidence suggests that the new senior citizen will be a person characterized by energy.

And why does this matter so much?

Because that energy, that larger health span created by decades of medical innovation, may well turn out to be the most precious natural resource we have. The contributions of these "super seniors" may indeed make the difference between a future of economic stagnation and decline and one of continued vitality and economic growth.

Consider this: there are many components to economic growth, but one that is absolutely essential is a growing workforce.

Now, the demographic facts of life we've just reviewed suggest that the labor pool in the U.S. is not going to grow. It's going to shrink. That in turn suggests that at some point within the next two decades, our economy will bump up against a ceiling on workforce expansion, cutting off further growth.

This would be a far more serious matter than any other challenges created by the age shift. Everything that we have in this country—our rising standard of living, our capacity for building wealth in the private sector, our ability to meet the ever-expanding needs in the public sector, all of this depends on sustaining growth.

Some people think that immigration will make up the difference. And certainly, the U.S. economy will continue to benefit from a steady flow of new immigrant workers. But to replace a loss of 76 million boomers from the workforce, current levels of annual immigration would have to be increased something like 400 percent. The logistical difficulties, not to mention the political issues, of very large-scale immigration make this seem a highly unlikely solution.

So where will the needed workers come from?

Clearly, a significant fraction will have to come from the workforce of today and yesterday. Thanks to the new "health span," the lengthening of middle age, this is possible.

Thus, potentially, our future economy will have available the services of a large number of talented highly experienced workers—people who are at least able to work well beyond the current retirement age.

Whether they'll be willing to stay in or return to the workforce is another issue. After all, for a decade, at least, the trend has been toward earlier and earlier retirement. Reversing that trend is not going to be an easy sell.

Many will feel a strong financial pressure to stay longer. Clearly, the current compact for social security and health care can't be continued indefinitely without some major modifications—higher taxes, lower benefits, later eligibility dates, means testing, perhaps some combination of these measures.

And the boomers in general have been even worse than other generations at saving enough to carry their own retirement, especially in view of their added life expectancy. Many people now hoping to retire early are going to eventually do the math and realize they will, in fact, have to retire late.

The real issue is whether, in addition to this push from reality, we employers can't find some more appealing way to pull—to invite and induce—these skilled and experienced people back into the national workforce.

I can envision a broad range of experiments, essentially reengineering how we work. Indeed, employers might have to rethink the whole paradigm of a career path. In the modern era, for most people, a career is a 40-year climb up a steep mountain. The higher you go, the harder it gets and the more you are asked to carry. And then at about 65, wherever you are on the mountain, all at once you trade in your pack for a parachute and launch yourself off into retirement. Many people are eager to jump—they're simply tired of climbing that mountain.

I wonder if it absolutely has to be that way. I wonder if, instead of a sudden plunge, there could not also be an option of a gradual descent back down the mountain—a phased-in retirement, if you will. Arranging hours and adjusting financial incentives would be the easy part. The hard part would be creating psychological incentives so that workers would look forward to those extra years in the way that they now look forward to quitting work for good.

Changing the composition and culture of the workforce is only one aspect of how the senior boom might transform our economy.

In fact, the rising of the age wave is going to be the social equivalent of a "phase shift." Almost every part of our social and economic order will be forced to adjust.

But far from being a catastrophe, I believe this shift will act as an incredible driver of "creative destruction," making many familiar products and services obsolete and others—some not yet imagined—needed and desired. It will thus provide a tremendous stimulus to innovation, renewal, and economic growth.

Consider financial services. All of the traditional assumptions underpinning our pensions systems—public and private—need reworking. We'll need new instruments and incentives for retirement savings as well. And all forms of insurance, but especially health insurance, will need creative adjustments to reflect the new demographics.

Think of real estate: Will the building trends continue to favor two-story houses and increasing square footage? Or will the new seniors be looking for something very different? How important will connectivity be in future homes? Will new technologies to support independent living be developed and deployed in housing of the future? What locations will be the destinations of choice for new retirees? Will large cities be reenergized or avoided? Whatever the answers, this sector is likely to undergo massive change.

Businesses involved in travel and tourism should experience a windfall. Leisure time and disposable income are the key drivers of that sector, and even today, senior households have more of both than younger ones.

What about industries related to recreation and entertainment? When one in every five Americans is over 65, will movie producers still be targeting eighth graders? Will the music industry take notice? Will advertisers? At the very least, it seems likely that our cultural outlook may broaden beyond its current close focus on youth.

In fact, it's hard to see what economic sector will not feel this irresistible stimulus to change and thereby to grow. But it's easy to see which sector will emerge as the strongest driver of growth in our economy. It has to be those industries near the center of the biomedical revolution.

The discovery and decoding of DNA that began only 50 years ago has spawned the new science of genomics and related new disciplines, through which have come increasingly solid descriptions of biological processes at the level of the system, the cell, and the single molecule.

As we learn more about the fundamental processes underlying various diseases, we are beginning to develop a new wave of medicines that will make most of the things we're doing today look low-tech.

Other health technologies—diagnostics, imaging, medical devices, surgical practices—are undergoing revolutionary change as well.

In effect what is occurring is a rapid rise in our collective "medical IQ," increasing the odds that in the near future we will be able not only to more effectively treat and cure many diseases but even to predict and prevent them altogether.

As this technological cluster continues to grow, it pumps ever-larger volumes of money into other sectors as well, building demand for chemicals, machine tools, lab equipment, construction services. In particular, biomedical companies are huge consumers of information technology. Indeed, none of this could have happened without the augmentation of computing power from the earliest stages of drug discovery through the last stages of clinical trials.

Conversely, the fundamental advances occurring in biomedicine are finding new applications, and working parallel transformations, in other vital industries—agriculture and food production, environmental management, materials sciences, and more.

Already, the positive economic effect on the U.S. economy is profound. Hundreds of billions of dollars of wealth have been created for pension funds and individual retirement accounts. Billions of dollars in income taxes flow into government coffers every year. Ten million people now work in the health care industry.

And of course, with each passing year, the ultimate result is longer, healthier lives for millions of people.

As we move forward, this dynamic cycle of expanding solutions to expanding needs may indeed form a new paradigm so pervasive as to reshape the key industries of the U.S. into what one writer has called "the health care economy."

New reports suggest that health care is currently the strongest sector carrying our economy through this current downturn, accounting for as much as 30 percent of our nation's GDP growth over the past year and about 45 percent of new jobs created over the past year.

Those who hold the conventional view actually see this data as a cause for alarm. But this is because they see it only as a cost. They do not equate the creation of better health with the production of an economic good.

Charles Morris, the writer I alluded to, mocks this bias in an *Atlantic Monthly* article titled "The Health Care Economy is Nothing to Fear."

"Gouging coal out of mountains to run power plants so that we can waft cool air over the brows of investment bankers is totted up as industrial production—an unambiguous increase in national wealth, like jet skis and video games. But new hips that allow people to walk, intra-ocular implants that restore their vision, stents that put them back to work, are classified as non-productive services that somehow make us poorer."

I think he has it about right.

Except that, unlike jet skis and video games, money spent for medical improvements is something more than mere "production." It very often qualifies as "investment" because it usually produces a return far greater than its cost.

The current issue of the policy journal *Health Affairs* is entirely devoted to documenting this creation of value. In paper after paper, leading health economists show that new medical technologies more than pay for themselves by replacing less effective and more costly treatments, by preserving millions of days of worker productivity that otherwise would be lost to illness and, ultimately, by restoring many years of precious life for millions of individuals.

It would seem that, far from being something to fear, a health care economy may be something to cultivate.

Indeed, last week's issue of *Business Week* ran an article by Michael Mandel that made precisely that claim and reinforced many of the points I have been making today.

The article draws an interesting parallel between current health care spending and a similar rise in IT expenditures 15 years ago. Those investments, too, were originally dismissed as frivolous and not important for economic growth. Subsequently, it became clear that those investments, in fact, were the key drivers of growth through the '90s.

Mandel argues that those who see health care primarily as a drain on the economy are making the same mistake, for all the reasons I have presented today. He concludes by saying:

> "If the Information Revolution propelled the first decade of the New Economy, its second decade may be marked by the Health Care Revolution. And there's nothing wrong with that."

He's absolutely right. The goods and services associated with the life sciences are as viable an economic locomotive as any. The message from the age wave is that these goods and services are what our society will need and want most as we go forward.

When we consider all these effects in perspective, it seems to me there is every reason to view the future with hope, even with optimism. This is not to say that the coming age shift will not bring challenges. Clearly it will. Giving people longer lives, even with lower disability, does mean that as a society we will have to find ways to help a growing number of the very old, and that will consume resources.

But it is also clear that the net gain—the positive contribution of this new wave of elders—should more than offset the costs. Indeed, as I've suggested, they may be the key to our continuing prosperity as a nation.

Somehow, this potential—indeed, this whole subject—needs to receive more attention in policy circles.

When our legislators try to grapple with huge issues like Medicare reform and Social Security funding, the long-term needs of the population always seem to be overwhelmed by the short-term needs of the next election cycle. And the potential benefits of such programs always seem to be overshadowed by considerations of their costs. Our leaders need a broader outlook and a longer timeline.

Above all, they need to take great care not to enact any policy which may have the unintended consequence of shutting down investments in new medical technologies. Such a course would chain us to the past and forfeit a brighter future.

With a more balanced perspective, I believe many would conclude with me that, yes, the age wave may represent the end of the world as we know it.

But at the same time, it may just be the beginning of a better world than we have ever known. Thank you.

Textual Questions

1. List the negative economic and health problems that most people now associate with old age.

2. What are the arguments that Taurel sets out to combat the beliefs you just listed?

3. What evidence allows Taurel to conclude that "there is every reason to view the future with hope, even optimism"?

Rhetorical Questions

4. When Taurel says, "Most of my case is based on well-known data," what data is he referring to. What is the "key fact missing from the conventional view"?

5. How does Taurel present his interpretation of the data to lead to positive instead of negative conclusions?

6. Do you find Taurel's argument convincing? If so, why? If not, why not?

Intertextual Questions

7. To what degree does Taurel's vision of the future take into account the people that Mitford describes?

8. Compare Taurel's optimistic vision of what lies ahead with Peeno's pessimistic one. Which writer makes the better case for his or her prediction? What makes that case better?

Thinking Beyond the Text

9. What is the right balance of responsibilities for health care for the elderly? Among those to consider are the government, HMOs, insurance, pharmaceutical companies, the individual, and the family. As your parents age, who should cover their health care costs? Are you prepared to step in if needed?

10. Since Taurel gave his talk, the abandonment of standard pension plans (including medical benefits for retirees) by many companies has made the future of health care for the elderly even more problematic. United Airlines and IBM are two examples of this major shift. Research the effects of this shift on the workers of these two companies and consider whether you would consider working for either of them. If   you would, how might you prepare for your own retirement?

For Writing & Discussion

11. Has the American promise of access to health care for all been broken, as some writers claim? If so, where does the fault lie and how can that promise be restored? Or is Taurel right, that the promise remains and can be carried out, in the light of the biomedical revolution?

MICHAEL   J.   SCOTTI

Michael Scotti is an MD and retired two-star Major General in the Army. A former Senior Vice President of Professional Standards for the American Medical Association (AMA), he also has served as the AMA's Vice President of Medical Education and as President of the National Medical Veterans Society (NMVS). While in the Army, Scotti was a Family Practice Consultant, Chief of Graduate Medical Education, Director of Quality Assurance, and Director of Professional Services. He served as the Commanding General of Army Medicine in Europe during the Gulf War. He is currently president (through 2006) and council member (through 2007) of The Society of Medical Consultants to the Armed Forces (SMCAF).

Scotti gave this speech at the MCP Hahnemann University School of Medicine (now part of Drexel University) on September 12, 2001. In it he describes the magnitude of the AIDS epidemic in Africa and explains some of the complications of epidemiology in Africa, an understanding of which is necessary if the spread of AIDS is to be controlled. When Scotti gave this talk there were 15 million AIDS orphans in Africa, with predictions of 40 million by 2010.

Africa Is Different from a Poor American Neighborhood

AIDS as a World-Wide Socioeconomic Issue

∾ Prereading Question

This essay asks us to think about the importance of world health issues. Why should we do so? What difference does it make to us if people elsewhere are experiencing serious and large scale disease and death? What obligations do we have to deal with such matters? Is it a matter of charity toward others or do we have some self-interest here? What possible benefits can we gain if we spend much money and effort on problems on other continents?

Yesterday, all of us were witnesses to history—in the most literal and terrible sense of that word. Even as I speak, physicians in New York and Washington D.C. have rallied to help those who have survived.

Yet thousands are already presumed dead. No one has claimed responsibility.

It is difficult at such a time in our history to turn away—from the television reports and the newspapers.

But today, we are called to do so, because we have come together to talk about another killer—not of thousands, but of millions. It is a silent enemy that we as physicians know all too well.

That enemy is AIDS, and in the twenty years it has been with us, it has killed 21.8 million people throughout the world.

That year IBM put out its first personal computer. And physicians in San Francisco first identified the strange cluster of symptoms that later became known as the telltale signs of AIDS.

Since that time both PCs and AIDS have proliferated throughout the world, affecting all levels of society.

And while PCs have helped millions, AIDS has killed millions—particularly in the developing world.

Not long after AIDS was identified in the U.S., a few doctors and village healers in Africa began to notice an incurable illness that slowly wasted its victims.

On the border of Tanzania and Uganda, they called it "Slim."

It wasn't until 1983, a physician in Zambia connected the patients she was seeing in her clinic to the disease that was devastating the homosexual community in the United States and Europe.

AIDS had made its first public entry onto the stage of African history.

Today, HIV has traveled the world and the citizens of the globe share in the devastation.

However, we do not share it in equal parts.

In the developed world, the past twenty years have brought an explosion of information about AIDS.

Scientific advances have allowed us to transform it from an acute and inevitably fatal disease to one where those infected can lead outwardly normal lives.

And social changes—such as frank discussion about how HIV is transmitted through sex and needles—have helped to slow its spread.

Though the rate of new infections in the United States, at 40,000 cases per year, is nothing to brag about our numbers pale before the tragedy that is unfolding in Africa and other developing nations.

Consider these facts:

Today, 36.1 million people in the world have already contracted HIV.

Over two thirds of them reside in sub-Saharan Africa.

In the past minute, approximately 11 individuals were infected with AIDS. Ten of those 11 individuals live in southern Africa.

The figures are mind numbing and heart breaking.

And though AIDS kills only half as many people as another worldwide epidemic—tobacco—it is, in many ways, a far worse scourge.

Tobacco, as deadly as it is, doesn't create villages where there is no one—literally no one—over the age of fourteen.

It doesn't transform prosperous farming communities into subsistence farming communities.

And it doesn't wipe out those individuals who have preserved oral histories and tribal traditions through generations of colonization, civil war, and famine.

But AIDS does all this—because it kills men and women in the prime of life—and decimates family and community structures in the process.

And AIDS will only continue its path of destruction unless we—in conjunction with the nations of Africa—do something about it.

But we can't even begin to address the African pandemic until we understand that Africa is not like a poor neighborhood in Philadelphia or Los Angeles.

AIDS is devastating the developing world in ways that are alien to our experience—largely because developing nations often lack two basic weapons in their arsenal:

First, many of these countries do not have the medical infrastructure to deliver a complex regimen of care, nor do they have the resources to treat the multiple secondary infections associated with AIDS.

Second, these nations have too often lacked the political will to educate citizens about AIDS—even as widespread poverty has created conditions that facilitate the disease's spread.

Only when we acknowledge these lacks and gaps and differences, will we begin to see how AIDS could be treated, and prevented, in the developing world, especially sub-Saharan Africa.

Because the experience of AIDS in different countries and cultures is as variable as the different strains of HIV itself.

Let's begin with treatment.

Recently, there has been a great deal of discussion about the prohibitive cost of anti-retroviral drugs—and how that cost is preventing AIDS victims in Africa from receiving the care they need.

However it's not simply a matter of bringing down the price of AIDS medications and getting them on the ground.

On the television show *West Wing*, one of the White House characters put it this way: "You can't give pills that have to be taken every eight hours to a population that doesn't wear watches."

But the problem goes far beyond this. Much of Africa lacks basic public health infrastructure and basic medical infrastructure.

Such infrastructure is fundamental to the successful delivery of a complex regimen of care and to ensuring that those being treated stick to that regimen.

Indeed, problems with long-term compliance have already led to new, resistant forms of HIV.

Then there is the cost issue.

Even with the Indian pharmaceutical company, Cipla, promising to offer generic drugs at the cost of $1 per day—the price of anti-retroviral treatments is still out of reach for many poor African nations. Nations that don't have the funds to provide citizens with even the most basic medications and care.

As one physician on the ground recently said in an interview: "The people I deal with on a daily basis are asking for clean water, for food, for pain relief, for simple skin preparations for itchy skin."

And according to UNAIDS Executive Director, Peter Piot, hunger was the leading concern among rural Africans with HIV.

It has been estimated that simply addressing basic human needs could lengthen the lives of African AIDS victims by as much as eight years.

And though there is clearly a role for anti-retroviral medication in Africa—the suffering of many, many AIDS victims will not abate until the most basic material conditions of their lives improve.

That includes the creation of a public health and medical infrastructure where, in too many places, little or none exists.

But what about prevention?

Most of us know that the Prime Minister of one of the most seriously affected African countries, South Africa, has publicly expressed doubt that there is a connection between being HIV positive and having AIDS.

This is just the most egregious example of what has been an all too common unwillingness to face AIDS head on.

We in the U.S. are fortunate that the homosexual community rallied around the AIDS issue early, and loudly.

Our leaders could not not listen, and education and prevention became the first keys to slowing the epidemic.

In Africa, paternalistic governments with their heads in the sand combined with the crushing stigma surrounding AIDS in much of Africa has too often prevented aggressive education and prevention programs from being put into place.

And so today, in some parts of Africa, including South Africa and Kenya, some citizens are still so uninformed about HIV and how it is spread, that they believe that sex with a virgin will cure AIDS.

And in Sierra Leone, where the government is too preoccupied with war to focus on AIDS, some joke that AIDS stands for "American Intentions to Discourage Sex."

Though the political environment in Africa is changing, much of the damage has already been done.

Because in an atmosphere of complacency, the multiple burdens of poverty, ignorance and inequality have already fueled the spread of HIV.

Consider, if you will, this pattern.

In Africa, poverty often compels rural men to migrate to cities in search of work.

Separated from their wives and families for months at a time, they seek sexual release with prostitutes, often without the protection of a condom.

These women have resorted to prostitution because of their own poverty, lack of education and property rights.

Many of them are HIV positive. And those who are not infected are often more concerned with getting food for today, than with the prospect of AIDS in the distant future.

Eventually, the men return home, carrying the HIV virus.

But if wives ask their husbands to wear condoms, they risk being accused of adultery.

And so, they too, become infected. And unknowingly pass the virus on to their children.

After their husbands succumb to AIDS, the wives and children are often left impoverished.

In many cases these women do not even have the right to inherit what little property is left.

More often than not, AIDS strikes again—killing the remaining parent.

And so poverty, ignorance about HIV, and inequality between the sexes have helped create 15 million AIDS orphans in Africa.

These orphans are themselves at high risk for contracting HIV.

Children who have lost both parents to AIDS are more likely to be poor, more likely to be uneducated, and more likely to be abused or neglected or stigmatized.

In short, they are more likely to exhibit the economic and emotional needs—that make it more likely they will have unsafe sex.

By 2010, there will be 40 million such children living Africa.

But when these orphans get HIV and die, there will be nobody left to care for their children.

For just as HIV devastates the human body—so too does it decimate the social body.

What's more, as HIV prevalence increases, economic production drops.

A 10 percent HIV rate causes an annual loss of around one per cent of GDP growth. And the damage is cumulative.

And so the cycle of poverty and AIDS continues its terrible spiral downwards.

These are the reasons why AIDS is likely to eclipse every catastrophe in Africa's recorded history—including the famines and wars that have ravaged the continent for much of this century.

This is also why we must make sure we understand specific local cultures and needs—and have the courage to insist on change when custom gets in the way of care.

Finally, this is why we must dedicate resources in ways appropriate to each country's level of infrastructure.

Focusing first on basic sanitary and public health systems—before putting more sophisticated treatment protocols into place.

Some developments in Africa give cause for hope.

In countries such as Uganda and Senegal, government-funded and locally supported educational programs have already been proven effective in curtailing the spread of HIV.

In Senegal, an aggressive fourteen-year campaign has kept the infection rate hovering at about 2 percent.

In Uganda, prevalence has gone down from a shocking 14 percent in 1990—to approximately 8 percent ten years later.

Other countries are increasingly beginning to follow their lead.

And they should have a good road map, thanks to a study that will help determine which preventive measures have been most effective in curbing HIV in Uganda—so that these measures can be replicated throughout Africa.

The study, which is being funded by the Pfizer Foundation, will be implemented by the Uganda AIDS Commission, UNICEF and UNAIDS.

And there are other coalitions at work in Uganda—which are beginning to focus not just on prevention, but on infrastructure—and treatment.

One of these coalitions, a group called the Academic Alliance for AIDS Care and Prevention, will soon break ground in [site not chosen at time of first printing] for the first large-scale HIV clinic in Africa.

The clinic will have programs aimed at patients who lack access to even the most rudimentary care.

And it will provide training on the latest AIDS treatment options to medical personnel from across Africa.

As members of the Alliance, Uganda's Makere University, the Infections Disease Society of America, and various international and local non-governmental organizations will operate the clinic.

The Pfizer Foundation is providing funds.

This is what country-led initiatives can achieve—when they have committed international partners—and real money.

And not just in Uganda.

One of the African countries most devastated by AIDS—Botswana—is working to provide anti-retroviral drugs to expectant mothers—and prevent the vertical transmission of AIDS.

This care will someday be possible because the Gates Foundation has committed 50 million dollars to strengthening Botswana's primary health care system.

Because the pharmaceutical industry is supplying free drugs.

And, perhaps most importantly, because there is strong support from the Republic of Botswana itself.

Other partnership-based initiatives in Botswana—and elsewhere in Africa—are also making a difference.

Unfortunately, such partnerships are not yet the norm in Africa.

But with AIDS increasingly at the forefront of the international agenda, there is hope for more.

Hope for initiatives that are led by citizens and by democratically elected leaders. Leaders who know the culture and conditions best, and who are committed to meeting the challenge with whatever resources they have.

Hope also for initiatives—that are backed by committed international organizations—both for-profit and non-profit, by national governments, and, of course, by real funds.

Because these developing countries cannot help themselves without partnership from wealthier nations.

And all of our funding will come to nothing, unless these countries show a willingness to face up to the problem—and commit whatever resources they can to help themselves.

We, as physicians and as citizens, need to use our individual and collective authority—to encourage such partnerships, in Africa and elsewhere.

And also—though this has not been my focus—to support the research that may one day lead to a vaccine.

We must become involved in the debate at all levels and urge our country, its leaders, and leaders from the private sector—to provide the resources and create the policies that will help us make advances against this terrible disease.

We must do this for humanitarian reasons. And for reasons of enlightened self-interest.

As citizens of developed nations, we have a moral obligation to help bring the same level of prevention and care that we have in our countries—to developing nations, to the maximum extent possible.

We also have a responsibility to help create a stable world.

According to the National Intelligence Estimate, over the next 20 years, global infectious diseases like AIDS—and here I quote: "will endanger U.S. citizens at home and abroad, threaten armed forces deployed overseas, and exacerbate social and political instability in key countries and regions where the U.S has significant interests."

Clearly there is much at stake—for all of us.

Today, I have focused on Africa—on the heterosexual and vertical transmission of AIDS there—and on the conditions of poverty, inequality, and lack of education that have helped fuel that particular pandemic.

I have also described some reasons for hope.

But AIDS is spreading in Asia, South East Asia, and in the former Soviet Union.

In each of these areas, the cultural conditions of HIV transmission are different.

In one country, the primary means of transmission may be IV drug use. In another, infected sex workers. Still another may not have sufficiently addressed problems with its blood supply. And levels of infrastructure will vary greatly from nation to nation—from sophisticated to stressed to simply nonexistent.

Whatever the case, we can only hope to stop AIDS if we understand the local conditions that are facilitating its spread or hindering its treatment. And then act on that knowledge if we—and the other nations of the world—fail to do this, we will see 150 million people infected worldwide—in twenty years.

No person or nation or organization will be immune to the medical, social, economic, and political consequences of the AIDS pandemic.

The response of all of us must be maximal—and sustained.

As individual physicians, caring for AIDS patients.

And as citizens of an increasingly vulnerable world.

Textual Questions

1. What is the connection Scotti makes between AIDS and the terrorist attacks on New York and Washington on September 11, 2001?

2. List the facts on AIDS compiled by Scotti (as of 2001). Why is it "a far worse scourge" than tobacco?

3. What makes AIDS particularly disastrous for Africa? Why is prevention so difficult there?

Rhetorical Questions

4. Examine the structure of Scotti's argument. What is the connection between his compilation of facts at the beginning of the talk and his argument toward the end? How does his evidence relate to his argument?

5. What does Scotti want his listeners and readers to do?

6. List Scotti's arguments for why we should take action. Which are most effective and why?

Intertextual Questions

7. Search for any mention of AIDS in the essays you have read so far in this chapter. What do you find? Why do you suppose this is so?

8. Jessica Mitford discusses infant mortality in America, especially in Alabama. How, based on your reading of her essay, might she respond to Scotti's argument about AIDS in Africa?

Thinking Beyond the Text

9. What other world plagues besides AIDS have devastated world populations in the past? Choose one of these diseases and compare it to the effects of AIDS.

10. As this book goes to press, the international health care community is deeply concerned about a possible pandemic derived from avian flu, a disease of poultry that might jump to the human population and than be communicable from person to person. Many millions of people are likely to die from this flu. Review the expressions of concern in 2006 and report on the actual consequences. Was enough done to prepare for this terrible disease?

For Writing & Discussion

11. What happens to the Promise of America for affordable and accessible health care in the face of worldwide epidemics such as AIDS? Should some elements of the population, such as political leaders or the elderly, receive special protections? Should some kind of triage, or priorities, advantage some groups or some people over others for treatment or for medications not available to all? Or can we hope to keep epidemics away from the American shores by rigorous control over all who enter the country, so that we won't have to deal with such troubling issues?

LINDA PEENO

Linda Peeno is an MD and medical ethicist who writes and speaks about health care reform, especially the need for changes in the managed care industry. While working as a medical reviewer for Humana Inc. and a medical director for Blue Cross/Blue Shield, Peeno realized the harm done to patients when a Health Management Organization (HMO) puts profits ahead of patient care. Peeno is now an expert witness who has testified on behalf of patients in more than 50 trials as well as before the U.S. House of Representatives Subcommittee on Health and Environment.

In addition to serving as an expert witness, Peeno also works for health-care reform through involvement with various organizations. She founded the CARE Foundation, a nonprofit education and advocacy group, and she is a former chair of the ethics committee at the University of Louisville Hospital.

"Burden of Oath" was first published in the literary journal *Creative Nonfiction* and the special issue in which it appeared, "Rage and Reconciliation: Inspiring a Health-care Revolution," was re-released early in 2006 with more essays and an audio CD that includes a panel discussion about medical ethics. In 1998 Peeno also published a testimonial, "What Is the Value of a Voice?", in *U.S. News & World Report*, and a related story, "A Voice for Elizabeth," in *Reader's Digest*. The 2002 Showtime television movie *Damaged Care* portrays Peeno's life and her move from working for HMOs to helping prosecute their failures in patient care.

Burden of Oath

∾ Prereading Question

Sometimes as we pursue arguments about the abstraction "health care," with all of its economic and social dimensions, we forget about the sick person and his or her doctor. Imagine, for instance, a very old person in need of expensive health care. To be even more precise, imagine your parents in that position, or even yourself, for you will also, if you are lucky, be very old some day. How much money should be spent on that sick person? How much is that life "worth"? And who gets to make the decision about worth?

> *. . . And I will use regimens for the benefit of the ill, in accordance with my ability and my judgment, but from what is to their harm or injustice I will keep them . . .*
>
> *. . . And in a pure and holy way I will guard my life and my techne . . .*
>
> *. . . Into as many houses as I may enter, I will go for the benefit of the ill . . .*
> —Hippocrates, "Hippocratic Oath"
> Translated by Heinrich von Staden

A ninety-year-old man died, an event that wouldn't prompt many of us to take a second glance at the obituaries. Yet I spent eight hours today trying to explain a grim chain of events leading to this death. The harder I struggled to weave meaning, the more a lawyer, representing a large health insurance company, attempted to unravel it. In many ways, we simply played a chess game of words. Except I was under oath.

I attempted to reconstruct the events of the man's last days through a deposition, a legal procedure theoretically designed to reveal and challenge an expert's opinions in a lawsuit. As a physician with special knowledge about the inner workings of the health industry, I practice a kind of medicine Hippocrates never could have imagined. Instead of potions and procedures, my care of patients requires language and analysis.

I sit now at my kitchen table, a place of refuge. I should do something—eat, read mail, return calls, work—but the late afternoon sun presses across my chair, and the heat of the day immobilizes me. I can see tips of trees through the kitchen window. An early spring breeze ruffles them, causing speckles of light and shadow to flicker on the floor. I should open some windows and doors for air. But the slant of the late sun saddens me. With the day's end, I feel overwhelmed by all that's left undone.

I spent three days preparing for the deposition, reading and analyzing thousands of pages of documents. Last night I had only a few hours of sleep, waking early to work more. I always fear I will forget something critical from a contract, policy or testimony. But all that preparation seems futile now. The lawyer just spent hours dissecting my personal and professional life. The process was less about the facts of the patient's death, and more about intimidating me. The lawyer adeptly upended so much of what I had done, turned work about which I was pleased into something that appeared to be a failure, turned writings over which I had agonized into something for which I should be apologetic.

Why do this, I wonder.

It takes special knowledge to articulate long threads of casual connections between inappropriate cost-cutting and harmful patient care. My job demands painstaking exploration of whole systems most others ignore, discount or just don't understand. I see first-hand the ways we have created a health system unprecedented in its ill effects. Patients now suffer not only from their diseases, but also from the *management* of their diseases.

Although I can do little now for the man who died, I can help identify patterns of practice that risk harming other patients. Patients such as this man are evidence of processes gone tragically awry, but their stories are all too often dismissed as "mere anecdotes"—the health industry's means of explaining away responsibility, Yet when we understand the ways corporations affect patient care, we can potentially provide corrections—a nice, simple ideal that caused me to change my work as a physician several years ago. Now I work full-time assisting attorneys, policy makers and the public who try to gain correctives and recompense for people who have been or who are at risk of being abused by a system that puts profits over patient care.

When I first testified in a case against an HMO, I believed naively that public knowledge and legal accountability would change the actions of health care companies. Now, more than five years and fifty cases later, the only difference I see is in the increased subtlety of harm, in the ever more inventive elusion of responsibility. My house is a vault of suppressed information, an inaccessible archive of documents protected by sealed confidentiality orders and settlement agreements.

Today the lawyer referred repeatedly to the patient as just a "ninety-year-old man, wheelchair bound, with dementia"—suggesting, it seemed, that his age and condition justified the poor care he had received. I finally asked her directly if her characterization meant that the patient was too old and sick to deserve either the expense—or hope—of care. She feigned outrage at my accusation, but I was haunted through the entire deposition by the thought that this man had become *disposable.*

There are, of course, other persons, including some physicians, who would argue that such a man—that anyone sufficiently old and sufficiently sick—should receive a different kind of care, though they would never of course admit to using those criteria. Some would justify their position with claims of kindness: Why should we subject someone like this to prolonged life? Others would claim that it is necessary rationing: We can re-direct dollars spent on potentially futile care to those who need it more—children for example. These arguments sound rational in the abstract. But with particular patients, their fallacies multiply: Acts of so-called kindness can become ruses for cost-cutting, and savings from denials go not to needier patients, but more often to hungrier bottom-lines.

Medicine is inherently *particular,* as Dr. Francis Peabody once told Harvard medical students. One essential quality of the clinician, according to Dr. Peabody, is interest in humanity, for the secret of the care of patients is in caring for the patient. If we do not keep specific patients—particular human beings—in mind in our systems of care, we can become the causes, however remote, of cost accounting masked as beneficence, and harm masked as utility. We then perpetuate our peculiarly American brand of health delivery, the only health system that rations care for the financial benefit of those who are supposed to provide that care.

Today the lawyer avoided all my attempts to individualize the patient. The man, although ninety, had been living at home alone. His son described him as clear thinking and independent. After a fall, he went to his doctor with a complaint of pain in his leg. Even though an X-ray confirmed a fractured hip, and a note by the radiologist indicated the patient would be transported to the hospital for surgery, another document showed that some unidentifiable person cancelled the admission. The doctor sent the patient home instead, and ordered an evaluation by Hospice, the one treatment in this case that cost the doctor and health plan nothing—a benefit of their astute cost-shifting.

A Hospice nurse promptly told the doctor that the patient's non-terminal condition made him ineligible for Hospice care. So the patient suffered for several days at home, without assistance, pain medications or treatment for the fracture. As the pain worsened, the family pleaded with the doctor to admit the man to the hospital. Mysteriously, the patient acquired another diagnosis at the time of his admission: The doctor said he suffered from "dementia," something unsupported by other medical records, previous living conditions or history provided by the son.

Two days after the doctor finally performed surgery on the hip fracture, he sent the patient to a nursing home for rehabilitation and physical therapy. When the patient arrived there, he already had bed-sores from his hospitalization. Despite his medical needs, no doctor saw him during his week in the nursing home. A physical therapist told the doctor and the insurance company that the patient could not do therapy or rehabilitation without a special medical device to relieve pressure from the sores on his heels. A document in the records showed that someone first approved the device, but then deleted that approval before sending the request to the equipment company. A note found in the documents explained that the doctor objected to the cost, although it was less than $300. One is left to wonder if the doctor and insurance company thought that even a few hundred dollars was too much to spend on a man they believed moved closer every day to death.

The doctor, who had not seen the patient in the several days since his discharge from the hospital, sent the patient home after giving an order by telephone. At first, the doctor did not arrange home health care, but when family members pleaded again for help, home health nurses were allowed to visit. When the nurses complained about the increasingly infected, deepening wounds, the doctor responded, not with hospitalization, but with a discontinuation of home health care.

After receiving reports about worsening of the bedsores, the doctor made a house call, something that would, under other circumstances, signify an unusually caring physician. But this doctor didn't go because he cared so much; he went because he cared so little—he simply hoped to save the cost of a hospitalization. There at the patient's house, with the patient in his own bed, the doctor performed surgery—without proper instruments, and without anesthesia. With the patient writhing and screaming in bed, the doctor scraped rotting flesh down to the muscle and bone—living tissue that bled and registered pain.

After more pleading from the family, the doctor finally sent the patient back to the hospital. Later the man died from a massive infection caused by progressive, untreated pressure wounds.

I know there are persons who would argue that, at most, this was a case of physician negligence, or that the physician couldn't have prevented what happened, since the man was going to die anyway. The claim for inevitable death is a favorite among insurance companies. However, some particulars cannot be ignored.

Unbeknownst to the patient or his family, the primary care physician and the insurance company had a financial arrangement by which they each received bonuses when allotted money wasn't spent on medical care. This operated according to simple arithmetic: Spend less, make more. Furthermore, when doctors spent too much, they not only lost money, they risked deficits that would require them to pay penalties to the insurance company.

Maybe this arrangement had no effect on the decisions and outcome, as the insurance company argues. Or if it did, the insurance company is not responsible for how a doctor practices—another favorite argument. Some court of law or public opinion should consider if these financial arrangements resulted in a chain of deadly decisions for this man, a chain in which every point marked a cost-cutting choice without regard for the patient. The people of this country—every one a potential patient in such a system—should be allowed to determine if this is an isolated case, or if it is the logical result of a health care system in urgent need of correction.

My funk increases as the room darkens. The last light is a smudge of red just behind the lacy branches of the trees I can see. A faint rose glow now lights the room just beyond the kitchen. From my chair, I can see four boxes on the dining room floor—a new case. I groan, feeling oppressed as much by the burden of work that they represent as by the heat. As the boxes melt away into the darkening room, I realize how sick I am of this health care mess. I am sick of the fight, sick of the increasing sophistication of the health industry's dereliction of duty, sick of witnessing needless suffering, and most of all, sick of feeling impotent to make any real change.

My house overflows with paper—evidence of a monstrous change in medicine, something we now call "managed care." When I graduated from medical school in 1978, the term didn't exist in my vocabulary. Now I have more than 200 books about the subject. Piles of "managed care" documents—benefit books, policy and procedure manuals, contracts, financial reports, marketing materials, corporate communications, utilization and quality profiles—litter rooms once filled only with books on philosophy, literature, science and theology. I have read more of these documents than any person I know in this country. I tire of the health care industry's failed promises and the damage it does to patients. I shudder when I think that Hippocrates binds me to a 3,000-year-old oath outlining a way of life, not just the treatment of patients. These are words that take root, ground me.

Thirty years ago, almost to this day, a young family doctor begged me to apply to medical school. I had seen him a few times for simple ailments, typical colds and sore throats. One day, as I sat on his exam table, trying to describe a new, but vague illness, he stood back and asked directly: What is really wrong?

I burst into tears. I had just received a letter denying me admission to nursing school, a path I believed would always assure work so I could support my daughter and still pursue graduate work in philosophy. The head of the nursing school told me that the program was too demanding for a single mother with a small baby. Fortunately, upon hearing my story, my doctor spent time asking questions rather than doing tests, and what he prescribed was far more powerful than any drug.

A few days later, when I returned for a second visit, he told me he had been thinking about our conversation. Forget nursing school, he said. You should go to medical school. I have this vision, he went on, of you walking in a crisp white coat down the sunlit hall of a hospital.

Years later, long, fluorescent tubes, not the sun, lit the halls I walked. My white coat turned dingy with wear, and often hung limp after long hours of work. No day in my life as a doctor ever manifested the scene the way my doctor imagined it, but I carried that image—his ideal—through the hard years of training, my balm for fear, fatigue, doubt and despair.

At one point, the perfect image of that clean, bright hall blurred with a vision of a darker place. It came one hot afternoon. I had walked off a ward and turned down a long corridor, on my way to tell a mother about the death of her son. The oppressive heat had driven everyone to cooler places, and my steps echoed through the emptiness of the long hall. I walked as slowly as possible, at first to delay my encounter with the mother, and then to soften the sounds of the steps that magnified my loneliness. I longed for the hall to have no end and to make no sound.

As I walked, an image came to me. I was in another large hall, dimly lit and packed with people. All around me, people stood, sat or moved in and out of groups. Some laughed. Some whined or cried. Some were quiet, and others moved about frenetically. Some begged for help. Others tended to their needs. Periodically a door would open, and a name would be called. One by one, individuals exited the room and did not return.

The young boy who had just died had become a favorite patient. His disease and eventual death seemed inexplicable. I could think of nothing to tell his mother. Maybe this is just what life is like, I thought, as I imagined that hall filled with people. We pass through this room briefly, marking time until our name is called. Then we leave. Maybe that is all there is.

The sky is now so dark the trees are no longer visible. I have a fleeting urge to leave the house and walk to those imperceptible masses just to touch their trunks.

Today the lawyer spent nearly an hour asking questions about a patient whose death I caused. While working for an insurance company in 1987, I denied a man a life-saving procedure. It took years for me to understand what I had done, because an act of honest confession is unacceptable to the business of health care. The lawyer circled the issue round and round, attempting to break apart my words and feelings until they were meaningless and empty.

A young man caught what seemed to be a simple cold. Instead, he had a virus that attacked his heart, leaving him no hope of recovery without a heart transplant. After critical weeks had passed, a hospital in another state had a donor. While teams of surgical personnel prepared for the surgery, a clerk in the hospital's admissions department placed a call to our insurance company for authorization. A nurse at the company took the call, but could not give medical approval for the case. She referred it to the doctor in charge of "medical review."

I was that doctor, part of a new breed of medical professionals far removed from the bedside. I made decisions about the "medical necessity" of procedures that other physicians requested for their patients. Though new to me, this sort of work was generously reimbursed and quite easy compared to the physically exhausting work in an emergency room, the usual place for a moonlighting physician. No one questioned how it was possible for a physician distant from a patient and without the requesting physician's clinical knowledge and experience to make appropriate medical decisions, especially when those decisions altered a patient's course of care.

Although I had been working for only a few months, I was already familiar with the unspoken prime requirement of the job; Save the company as much money as possible. Most of the cases referred to physicians like me were more "economic" than "medical." More than once, my superior, also a physician, paid me visits to discuss the nature of my job and the decisions I made. I was told frequently that my medical degree helped give medical justification to economic decisions. He never failed to remind me that, in contrast to other work I might do as a physician, I was now an *employee* of a company, which, in case I should forget, issued my paycheck.

When the request for the heart transplant came to me, I thought my task was simple. Since we made determinations about medical necessity, I didn't understand why I had the case. Surely no physician would perform a medically *unnecessary* heart transplant. Believing it was a mistake, I simply called the transplant surgeon, documented the medical history and authorized the procedure.

Just as I started to stamp "APPROVE" on the request, a nurse burst into the office to tell me that I must call the surgeon back. We have a way to deny the case, she said. The benefits department discovered an exclusion for heart transplants in this man's contract.

With clear grounds for a technical denial, I called the surgeon to tell him we would not pay for the transplant. At first he couldn't believe it. He spat questions through the phone: How could we sell contracts like that? How did this man get on a transplant list and get to the hospital if his contract was so clear? Even if the contract was right, how could we deny him at this point? *Don't you realize, Dr. Peeno, that you have issued this man a death sentence?*

In the fury of the moment, these questions didn't register. I had just saved my company a $0.5 million dollars. Later that day, the Vice President for Medical Affairs complimented me on my good work, and assured me that I had finally grasped the nature of my professional responsibilities as a physician with the company. My fellow physician reviewers envied my moment of success.

Initially I felt a kind of confidence about my actions. I fulfilled the expectations of my job. We had a contract and could legitimately enforce it. Our country suffered from escalating health care costs that required us to limit expenditures. But a few days later, as I walked through the company's marble rotunda, I saw a new sculpture—a piece that I eventually discovered cost $3.8 million dollars, eight times the price of a heart transplant.

What had I done? I began to feel something deep but ill-defined, a sense of unnamable dread. I finally couldn't ignore reality: I participated in a young man's death by performing well a job I never questioned. Although everything about the new organization of health care conspired to diminish my sense of connection to the man, and though his initial facelessness diminished my sense of responsibility, I couldn't shake his presence.

Now, the world through the kitchen window is solid black, everything folded together. The heat from the day's sun, still trapped in my closed house, makes me miserable, yet I still cannot find the energy to move. Leaving my chair means a return to work, a return to the burden of an oath and a profession I continue to question.

Several weeks ago, I began reading a new philosophy book, essays by a French philosopher named Emmanuel Levinas. He writes about the primacy of the *other*, embodied, he believes, in the face-to-face experience. Responsibility, for Levinas, is not just our answer for that which we have originated, but commands that we answer even for situations we did not bring about. We are responsible, he claims, not only for our own deeds, but also for the deeds of others. It's a heavy burden, I think, but one that I realize has underpinned my evolving view of life and work as both a physician and a human being.

Some are guilty, says Jewish theologian Abraham Joshua Heschel, but all are responsible. Yet we live in a culture that makes us masters at eluding responsibility, even when the cause-effect chain of actions and responses seems direct and obvious. How easy it is to claim ignorance, impotence, indecision, incompetence, or any number of other mitigating conditions. And, of course, the easiest plea in a culture of legislation, administrative rules and professional codes is simply to say, I am not *required* to do this.

Levinas says to know a fellow person is not to thematize him or her as an object, but to greet the person. This requires an encounter, a kind of welcoming that binds us inextricably to all the individuals about us. Our fellow persons are not mere objects of perception, but persons who make appeals and require responses. An encounter, according to Levinas, can never be complete or total. There is always a surplus of available action: I can always do more. I create continuous conditions of possibility, and every decision I make is not only about what action to take, but also about what kind of person I want to be.

As a physician—even a physician who now only uses words as my tools for healing—my work is inherently linked to patients, real human beings who command something of me. These persons, with whom I have an unbreakable relationship, make demands of me, for they always have, as Levinas argues, a *face*—even if I do not physically see it. Because of the work I do now as a physician, I must struggle harder to give presence to patients, especially those made distant and abstract by the medical and legal systems. I must bring them close enough to disturb me and to disturb others too. To hear their cries, as Levinas writes.

To claim that kind of responsibility is to seek more, not less, as Hippocrates no doubt meant when he wrote the Hippocratic Oath. For all the frustration, the hours spent reading documents, the meetings with lawyers, the exhausting cross-country flights to depositions and trials, my life and work are intertwined in ways that ultimately make both richer. My oaths—medical and legal—require a way of being as well as doing, a way of acting as well as speaking. Yes, I risk and experience futility. But maybe the antidote lies in seeking out increasingly longer, more complex chains of interrelationships and responsibility, and understanding that what sometimes appears futile may just be the result of views which are still too narrow, and on which too little light has been shed.

I get up from my chair and get on with things. I must eat, read mail, return calls, work. I have four new boxes to open. First though, the house needs fresh air. When I open the kitchen window, a cool breeze blows through, and I see that the trees are now backlit by a clear, bright moon.

Textual Questions

1. Exactly what is Peeno's job and to whom is she accountable?

2. Detail the events that led to the death of the 90-year-old man in this story. Who was responsible for his death?

3. There are two different oaths—"medical and legal"—that are significant in this essay. What are they and how do they conflict?

Rhetorical Questions

4. This essay combines the narrative of the old man's death with the story of the writer's afternoon. How does Peeno link the two narratives?

5. The audience for this essay is not as obvious as it was for the speeches we have been reading in this chapter. Who is the audience here and how can you tell?

6. To what degree does this essay convince you that America has "a health care system in urgent need of correction"? Describe the argument and evidence that leads to your answer.

Intertextual Questions

7. Compare this essay with the argument in favor of managed care by Tabak, earlier in this chapter. Describe the conflicting views of the two writers. Do they have anything at all in common?

8. The essay by Mitford in this chapter focuses on the place of money in the health-care system; the essay by Taurel looks closely at the problems posed by an aging population. Choose one of these essays to compare and contrast its perspective with that of Peeno.

Thinking Beyond the Text

9. Some other countries have developed a national health-care system that removes money from decisions about patient care. Research one of those systems, such as in Canada or most countries in Europe, and consider the problems as well as the advantages such a system poses.

10. How might America remove or diminish the role of money in health care decisions and then redirect the money now spent on bureaucracy and litigation to the care of patients?

For Writing & Discussion

11. Will America now or in the future be able to afford to carry out the promise of health care accessible to all? If not, how would you redefine that promise? If so, where will the resources come from?

ROBBIE E. DAVIS-FLOYD

Robbie E. Davis-Floyd (1951–) is a Senior Research Fellow in Anthropology at the University of Texas, Austin and an Adjunct Associate Professor in Anthropology at Case Western Reserve University, Cleveland. Her ethnographic research on reproduction began in 1979 with the birth of her first child, Peyton, a traumatic experience that prompted her to interview 100 other women about their childbirth experiences. The interviews became the basis of her PhD dissertation and her first book, *Birth as An American Rite of Passage* (1992), from which "Gender and Ritual: Giving Birth the American Way" is excerpted.

Davis-Floyd has followed her initial 100 interviews with research on many topics, including midwifery, holistic medicine, and medical anthropology, in the United States, Mexico, and Brazil. She has published over 80 articles, co-edited eight books, and co-authored (with Gloria St. John) *From Doctor to Healer: The Transformative Journey*. Her analysis in "Gender and Ritual" shows how the typical American birthing experience—the woman supine in a hospital bed—ritualistically embodies the role of women in society. She compares American birthing practices with those in other cultures and countries, and explores how the American medical approach actually makes labor and delivery more difficult for both mothers and babies.

Like other authors in this chapter, Davis-Floyd looks closely at the balance of power in the American health-care system, and in particular at how it sometimes devalues or dehumanizes patients.

Gender and Ritual: Giving Birth the American Way

∽ **Prereading Question**

Think of some rituals we engage in that seem so natural that only a person from another culture or another planet would question them: the way we bathe and shampoo our hair, for instance, or the way we go on dates, or the ways we pursue our religions or our sports. Few of us question the meanings behind these rituals and the many others we engage in without thinking of how they contain cultural assumptions. It is always surprising, even shocking, when someone questions these assumptions, particularly if the questions challenge our belief that our rituals are simply natural. The following essay asks us to think about "major life transitions" in such a way; the writer sees the conduct of childbirth in modern America as such a ritual, with negative results for women's health. What other behaviors can you describe in a similar way?

Although the array of new technologies that radically alter the nature of human reproduction is exponentially increasing, childbirth is still an entirely gendered phenomenon. Because only women have babies, the way a society treats pregnancy and childbirth reveals a great deal about the way that society treats women. The experience of childbirth is unique for every woman, and yet in the United States childbirth is treated in a highly standardized way. No matter how long or short, how easy or hard their labors, the vast majority of American women are hooked up to an electronic fetal monitor and an

IV (intravenously administered fluids and/or medication), are encouraged to use pain-relieving drugs, receive an episiotomy (a surgical incision in the vagina to widen the birth outlet in order to prevent tearing) at the moment of birth, and are separated from their babies shortly after birth. Most women also receive doses of the synthetic hormone pitocin to speed their labors, and they give birth flat on their backs. Nearly one-quarter of babies are delivered by Cesarean section.

Many Americans, including most of the doctors and nurses who attend birth, view these procedures as medical necessities. Yet anthropologists regularly describe other, less technological ways to give birth. For example, the Mayan Indians of Highland Chiapas hold onto a rope while squatting for birth, a position that is far more beneficial than the flat-on-your-back-with-your-feet-in-stirrups (lithotomy) position. Mothers in many low-technology cultures give birth sitting, squatting, semi-reclining in their hammocks, or on their hands and knees, and are nurtured through the pain of labor by experienced midwives and supportive female relatives. What then might explain the standardization and technical elaboration of the American birthing process?

One answer emerges from the field of symbolic anthropology. Early in this century, Arnold van Gennep noticed that in many societies around the world, major life transitions are ritualized. These cultural *rites of passage* make it appear that society itself effects the transformation of the individual. Could this explain the standardization of American birth? I believe the answer is yes.

I came to this conclusion as a result of a study I conducted of American birth between 1983 and 1991. I interviewed over 100 mothers, as well as many of the obstetricians, nurses, childbirth educators, and midwives who attended them. While poring over my interviews, I began to understand that the forces shaping American hospital birth are invisible to us because they stem from the conceptual foundations of our society. I realized that American society's deepest beliefs center on science, technology, patriarchy, and the institutions that control and disseminate them, and that there could be no better transmitter of these core values and beliefs than the hospital procedures so salient in American birth. Through these procedures, American women are repeatedly told, in dozens of visible and invisible ways, that their bodies are defective machines incapable of giving birth without the assistance of these other, male-created, more perfect machines. . . .

&

Preservation of the Status Quo

A major function of ritual is cultural preservation. Through explicit enactment of a culture's belief system, ritual works both to preserve and to transmit the culture. Preserving the culture includes perpetuating its power structure, so it is usually the case that those in positions of power will have unique control over ritual performance. They will utilize the effectiveness of ritual to reinforce both their own importance and the importance of the belief and value system that legitimizes their positions.

In spite of tremendous advances in equality for women, the United States is still a patriarchy. It is no cultural accident that 99 percent of American women give birth in hospitals, where only physicians, most of whom are male, have final authority over the performance of birth rituals—an authority that reinforces the cultural privileging of patriarchy for both mothers and their medical attendants.

Nowhere is this reality more visible than in the lithotomy position. Despite years of effort on the part of childbirth activists, including many obstetricians, the majority of American women still give birth lying flat on their backs. This position is physiologically dysfunctional. It compresses major blood vessels, lowering the mother's circulation and thus the baby's oxygen supply. It increases the need for forceps because it both narrows the pelvic outlet and ensures that the baby, who must follow the curve of the birth canal, quite literally will be born heading upward, against gravity. This lithotomy position completes the process of symbolic inversion that has been in motion ever since the woman was put into that "upside-down" hospital gown. Her normal bodily patterns are turned, quite literally, upside-down—her legs are in the air, her vagina totally exposed. As the ultimate symbolic inversion, it is ritually appropriate that this position be reserved for the peak tranformational moments of the initiation experience—the birth itself. The doctor—society's official representative—stands in control not at the mother's head nor at her side, but at her bottom, where the baby's head is beginning to emerge.

Structurally speaking, this puts the woman's vagina where her head should be. Such total inversion is perfectly appropriate from a social perspective, as the technocratic model promises us that eventually we will be able to grow babies in machines—that is, have them with our cultural heads instead of our natural bottoms. In our culture, "up" is good and "down" is bad, so the babies born of science and technology must be delivered "up" toward the positively valued cultural world, instead of down toward the negatively valued natural world. Interactionally, the obstetrician is "up" and the birthing woman is "down," an inversion that speaks eloquently to her of her powerlessness and of the power of society at the supreme moment of her own individual transformation.

The episiotomy performed by the obstetrician just before birth also powerfully enacts the status quo in American society. This procedure, performed on over 90 percent of first-time mothers as they give birth, expresses the value and importance of one of our technocratic society's most fundamental markers—the straight line. Through episiotomies, physicians can deconstruct the vagina (stretchy, flexible, part-circular and part-formless, feminine, creative, sexual, non-linear), then reconstruct it in accordance with our cultural belief and value system. Doctors are taught (incorrectly) that straight cuts heal faster than the small jagged tears that sometimes occur during birth. They learn that straight cuts will prevent such tears, but in fact, episiotomies often cause severe tearing that would not otherwise occur (Klein 1992; Shiono et al. 1990; Thorp and Bowes 1989; Wilcox et al. 1989). These teachings dramatize our Western belief in the superiority of culture over nature. Because it virtually does not exist in nature, the line is most useful in aiding us in our constant conceptual efforts to separate ourselves from nature.

Moreover, since surgery constitutes the ultimate form of manipulation of the human body-machine, it is the most highly valued form of medicine. Routinizing the episiotomy, and increasingly, the Cesarean section, has served both to legitimize and to raise the status of obstetrics as a profession, by ensuring that childbirth will be not a natural but a surgical procedure.

Effecting Social Change

Paradoxically, ritual, with all of its insistence on continuity and order, can be an important factor not only in individual transformation but also in social change. New belief and value systems are most effectively spread through new rituals designed to enact and transmit them; entrenched belief and value systems are most effectively altered through alterations in the rituals that enact them.

Nine percent of my interviewees entered the hospital determined to avoid technocratic rituals in order to have "completely natural childbirth," yet ended up with highly technocratic births. These nine women experienced extreme cognitive dissonance between their previously held self-images and those internalized in the hospital. Most of them suffered severe emotional wounding and short-term post-partum depression as a result. But 15 percent did achieve their goal of natural childbirth, thereby avoiding conceptual fusion with the technocratic model. These women were personally empowered by their birth experiences. They tended to view technology as a resource that they could choose to utilize or ignore, and often consciously subverted their socialization process by replacing technocratic symbols with self-empowering alternatives. For example, they wore their own clothes and ate their own food, rejecting the hospital gown and the IV. They walked the halls instead of going to bed. They chose perineal massage instead of episiotomy, and gave birth like "primitives," sitting up, squatting, or on their hands and knees. One of them, confronted with the wheelchair, said "I don't need this," and used it as a luggage cart. This rejection of customary ritual elements is an exceptionally powerful way to induce change, as it takes advantage of an already charged and dramatic situation.

During the 1970s and early 1980s, the conceptual hegemony of the technocratic model in the hospital was severely challenged by the natural childbirth movement which these 24 women represent. Birth activists succeeded in getting hospitals to allow fathers into labor and delivery rooms, mothers to birth consciously (without being put to sleep), and mothers and babies to room together after birth. They fought for women to have the right to birth without drugs or interventions, to walk around or even be in water during labor (in some hospitals, Jacuzzis were installed). Prospects for change away from the technocratic model of birth by the 1990s seemed bright.

Changing a society's belief and value system by changing the rituals that enact it is possible, but not easy. To counter attempts at change, individuals in positions of authority often intensify the rituals that support the status quo. Thus a response to the threat posed by the natural childbirth movement was to intensify the use of high technology in hospital birth. During the 1980s, periodic electronic monitoring of nearly all women became standard procedure, the epidural rate shot up to 80 percent, and the Cesarean rate rose to nearly 25 percent. Part of the impetus for this technocratic intensification is the increase in malpractice suits against physicians. The threat of lawsuit forces doctors to practice conservatively—that is, in strict accordance with technocratic standards. As one of them explained:

> Certainly I've changed the way I practice since malpractice became an issue. I do more C-sections . . . and more and more tests to cover myself. More expensive stuff. We don't do risky things that women ask for—we're very conservative in our approach to everything. . . . In 1970 before all this came up, my C-section rate was around 4 percent. It has gradually climbed every year since then. In 1985 it was 16 percent, then in 1986 it was 23 percent.

The money goes where the values lie. From this macro-cultural perspective, the increase in malpractice suits emerges as society's effort to make sure that its representatives, the obstetricians, perpetuate our technocratic core value system by continuing through birth rituals to transmit that system. Its perpetuation seems imperative, for in our technology we see the promise of our eventual transcendence of bodily and earthly limitations—already we replace body parts with computerized devices, grow babies in test tubes, build space stations, and continue to pollute the environment in the expectation that someone will develop the technologies to clean it up!

We are all complicitors in our technocratic system, as we have so very much invested in it. Just as that system has given us increasing control over the natural environment, so it has also given not only doctors but also women increasing control over biology and birth. Contemporary middle-class women *do* have much greater say over what will be done to them during birth than their mothers, most of whom gave birth during the 1950s and 1960s under general anesthesia. When what they demand is in accord with technocratic values, they have a much greater chance of getting it than their sisters have of achieving natural childbirth. Even as hospital birth still perpetuates partriarchy by treating women's bodies as defective machines, it now also reflects women's greater autonomy by allowing them conceptual separation from those defective machines.

Epidural anesthesia is administered in about 80 percent of American hospital births. So common is its use that many childbirth educators are calling the 1990s the age of the "epidural epidemic." As the epidural numbs the birthing woman, eliminating the pain of childbirth, it also graphically demonstrates to her through lived experience the truth of the Cartesian maxim that mind and body are separate, that the biological realm can be completely cut off from the realm of the intellect and the emotions. The epidural is thus the perfect technocratic tool, serving the interests of the technocratic model by transmitting it, and of women choosing to give birth under that model, by enabling them to use it to divorce themselves from their biology:

> Ultimately the decision to have the epidural and the Cesarean while I was in labor was mine. I told my doctor I'd had enough of this labor business and I'd like to . . . get it over with. So he whisked me off to the delivery room and we did it. (Elaine)

For many women, the epidural provides a means by which they can actively witness birth while avoiding "dropping into biology." Explained Joanne, "I'm not real fond of things that remind me I'm a biological creature—I prefer to think and be an intellectual emotional person." Such women tended to define their bodies as tools, vehicles for their minds. They did not enjoy "giving in to biology" to be pregnant, and were happy to be liberated from biology during birth. And they welcomed advances in birth technologies as extensions of their own ability to control nature.

In dramatic contrast, six of my interviewees (6 percent), insisting that "I am my body," rejected the technocratic model altogether. They chose to give birth at home under an alternative paradigm, the *holistic model*. This model stresses the organicity and trustworthiness of the female body, the natural rhythmicity of labor, the integrity of the family, and self-responsibility. These homebirthers see the safety of the baby and the emotional needs of the mother as one. The safest birth for the baby will be the one that provides the most nurturing environment for the mother. Said Ryla,

> I got criticized for choosing a home birth, for not considering the safety of the baby. But that's exactly what I was considering! How could it possibly serve my baby for me to give birth in a place that causes my whole body to tense up in anxiety as soon as I walk in the door?

Although homebirthers constitute only about 2 percent of the American birthing population, their conceptual importance is tremendous, as through the alternative rituals of giving birth at home, they enact—and thus guarantee the existence of—a paradigm of pregnancy and birth based on the value of connection, just as the technocratic model is based on the principle of separation.

The technocratic and holistic models represent opposite ends of a spectrum of beliefs about birth and about cultural life. Their differences are mirrored on a wider scale by the ideological conflicts between biomedicine and holistic healing, and between industrialists and ecological activists. These groups are engaged in a core value struggle over the future—a struggle clearly visible in the profound differences in the rituals they daily enact.

Textual Questions

1. How does Davis-Floyd connect the physical positioning of women in childbirth to the symbolic position of women in society?

2. How does Davis-Floyd argue that the hospital procedure for childbirth is a matter of cultural choices rather than the best medical practice?

3. What does Davis-Floyd claim to be the reason for and the symbolic meaning of the increased use of Caesarian deliveries?

Rhetorical Questions

4. What audience is this essay written for? How can you tell?

5. What kind of evidence does Davis-Floyd use to support the claim that American childbirth procedures are a ritual rather than a medical advance?

6. Are you convinced by Davis-Floyd's argument? If so, what convinced you? If not, why not?

Intertextual Questions

7. Find in this chapter two other essays that speak about inequalities in the health-care system. Describe the causes of those inequalities as set out by the two authors and compare them to the causes detailed by Davis-Floyd. Which of the two essays you have chosen is the most convincing, and why?

8. Reread Terry Tempest Williams, "The Clan of the One-Breasted Women." Compare the way Williams argues a serious women's health issue with the way Davis-Floyd does. Note that both writers are making public an issue that some people think it impolite to discuss.

Thinking Beyond the Text

9. Research the heated debate over the use of anesthesia in childbirth in ninteenth-century England. What were the arguments against easing the pain of childbirth by using medication? How did Queen Victoria settle the issue?

10. Find out the relative amount of money now being spent on diseases of men, such as prostate cancer, and those of women, such as breast cancer. When you have dependable and comparative figures, use them as evidence for an argument on whether or not current medical research embodies sex bias.

For Writing & Discussion

11. Select a foreign country, such as India, which has made major advances recently in improving its health care. Then learn all you can about its predominant method of childbirth. To what degree is the "ritual" you discover (to use Davis-Floyd's term) an expression of the underlying cultural attitudes toward women in that country?

America's Promises

◌ Prereading Question

Here is a good point in this book to reconsider the meaning of the word "Promise." What meanings have you so far encountered in your reading and how do they relate to the common meaning of the word? For instance, to what degree does the word refer to good intentions rather than to something to be counted on? Under what conditions is it ethical to disregard one's promises? Are there different kinds of promises for different circumstances? Or is a promise, well, a promise to be fulfilled?

The New York Times *Editorial Friday, January 28, 2005*

Three years ago, President Bush created the Millennium Challenge Account to give more money to poor countries that are committed to policies promoting development. Mr. Bush said his government would donate billions in incremental stages until the program got to a high of $5 billion a year starting in 2006. While $5 billion is just 0.04 percent of America's national income, President Bush touted the proposal as proof that he cares about poverty in Africa and elsewhere. "I carry this commitment in my soul," the president said.

For the third straight year, Mr. Bush has committed a lot less than he promised. Michael Phillips of the *Wall Street Journal* reports that the White House has quietly informed the managers of the Millennium Challenge Account to expect about $3 billion in the next budget. This follows a sad pattern. Mr. Bush said he would ask Congress for $1.7 billion in 2004; he asked for $1.3 billion and got $1 billion. He said he would ask for $3.3 billion in 2005; he asked for $2.5 billion and got $1.5 billion.

So if past is prologue, the Republican Congress will cut the diluted 2006 pledge even further.

None of that appears to bother the Bush administration, which continues to send high-ranking officials into the world to promote the anemic Millennium Challenge Account to poor nations. The program—not the money, since the account has yet to pay out a single dollar—is high on the list of talking points for cabinet officials like the United States trade representative, Robert Zoellick, who visited Africa in December and cited the program every chance he got. Speaking to Latin American ambassadors in Washington this month, a Treasury under secretary, John Taylor, hailed it as a "major way in which we are working with countries to meet the challenge of increasing productivity growth."

Officials at the Millennium Challenge Account are quick to list the countries that, through good governance, have qualified for the aid program. They are not as quick to list the countries that have received a dime: there aren't any. Still, Paul Applegarth, chief executive of the Millennium Challenge Corporation, assured us last week that President Bush's program is "really moving at an extraordinarily quick pace."

Maybe the administration should tell that to the 300 million Africans who lack safe drinking water, or the 3,000 African children under the age of 5 who die every day from malaria, or the 1 in 16 African women who die in childbirth, or the 6,000 Africans who die each day of AIDS. But wait: Maybe the president is planning to deal with the African AIDS catastrophe through his 2003 proposal to increase AIDS funds by $10 billion over the following five years.

Not unless he is planning to finish with a bang, because the White House is expected to ask Congress for only $1.6 billion more next year. When added to the amount that AIDS funds increased in 2004 and 2005, that would leave a whopping more than $6 billion to get out of Congress in the next two years to meet Mr. Bush's pledge. Congress and Mr. Bush will point to the ballooning deficit and say they don't have the money. But that was a matter of choice. They chose to spend billions on tax cuts for the wealthy and the war in Iraq. They can choose to spend it instead to keep America's promises.

Textual Questions

1. List the specific promises cited in this editorial.

2. List the degree to which each of these promises have been fulfilled.

3. What conclusions does the editorial ask you to draw from the evidence it presents?

Rhetorical Questions

4. What is the audience for an editorial in *The New York Times*?

5. What kind of evidence does this editorial use to make its case, and do you find it convincing?

6. What is the relation between the evidence used and the expectations of the audience?

Intertextual Questions

7. Contrast the kind of evidence this editorial uses to the kind of evidence that Tabak uses in his speech. Why do the two pieces use evidence in such different ways? How does the kind of evidence used suggest different kinds of promises for health?

8. How would Linda Peeno respond to this editorial and why?

Thinking Beyond the Text

9. To what degree has America been defined (to Americans and to others) by its promise? What is the result if America's promises cannot be trusted?

10. To what degree does the Promise of America relate to problems in other countries? Do promises at home have a different meaning than those made to non-Americans? Is the Promise of America a local issue or does it imply an overall moral commitment?

For Writing & Discussion

11. Look up the circumstances of some of America's promises that have been broken to the rest of the world. For instance, President Wilson said the United States entered the first world war to "make the world safe for democracy," something that has not happened in the almost one hundred years since that promise was made. Why was that promise broken? Was the problem in the nature of the promise itself, in the way the promise was attempted to be carried out, or in some other factor or combination of factors? What was the result?

MALCOLM GLADWELL

Malcolm Gladwell (1963–) is a staff writer for *The New Yorker*. He also has written for *The Washington Post* and *The New Republic*. In 2001 his profile of inventor Ron Popeil received a National Magazine Award for Profiles, and the 2000 television movie *Runaway Virus* was based on an article he wrote in 1997. In 2005, *Time* listed him as one of their 100 Most Influential People. His writing also has earned him the honor of being profiled himself in a 2006 *New York Times* article titled "The Gladwell Effect."

In "The Moral-Hazard Myth," published in *The New Yorker* in August 2005, Gladwell discusses the need for universal health care in America, and possible reasons that six attempts at establishing it, starting in World War I, have failed.

Gladwell's other articles cover a wide range of subjects such as basketball, homelessness, elite college admissions, cookies, plagiarism, personality tests, diapers, caffeine, and many other topics. He also has two bestselling books, *The Tipping Point: How Little Things Can Make a Big Difference* (2000) and *Blink: The Power of Thinking Without Thinking* (2005). A movie adaptation of *Blink*, starring and produced by Leonardo DiCaprio, is in production and expected in 2007.

Born in the United Kingdom and raised in rural Ontario, Gladwell now lives in New York City. According to Gladwell, his family claims to be distantly related to Colin Powell.

The Moral-Hazard Myth
The Bad Idea Behind Our Failed Health-Care System

Prereading Question

On the left side of a piece of paper, running down the side, write numerals from one to your current age. Next to each number, list every medical procedure that was performed on you at that age—from ear surgery during your infancy to regular dentist visits during your teens to emergency room visits in your early twenties, and so on. Next to each number, also list any medications you took/are taking and anything else that seems applicable, including flu vaccinations and emergency shots for rabies or tetanus. Include anything and everything you can remember, even if that means you'll share this list with no one.

When your list is complete, consider the cumulative costs of all this health care. What did you—or someone else—pay directly for this care? Did you have insurance/lose insurance during any portion of your lifetime? How much do you—or someone else—pay for your health-care insurance?

Tooth decay begins, typically, when debris becomes trapped between the teeth and along the ridges and in the grooves of the molars. The food rots. It becomes colonized with bacteria. The bacteria feeds off sugars in the mouth and forms an acid that begins to eat away at the enamel of the teeth. Slowly, the bacteria works its way through to the dentin, the inner structure, and from there the cavity begins to blossom three-dimensionally, spreading inward and sideways. When the decay reaches the pulp tissue, the blood vessels, and the nerves that serve the tooth, the pain starts—an insistent throbbing. The tooth turns brown. It begins to lose its hard structure, to the point where a dentist can reach into a cavity with a hand instrument and scoop out the decay. At the base of the tooth, the bacteria mineralizes into tartar, which begins to irritate the gums. They become puffy and bright red and start to recede, leaving more and more of the tooth's root exposed. When the infection works its way down to the bone, the structure holding the tooth in begins to collapse altogether.

Several years ago, two Harvard researchers, Susan Starr Sered and Rushika Fernandopulle, set out to interview people without health-care coverage for a book they were writing, "Uninsured in America." They talked to as many kinds of people as they could find, collecting stories of untreated depression and struggling single mothers and chronically injured laborers—and the most common complaint they heard was about teeth. Gina, a hairdresser in Idaho, whose husband worked as a freight manager at a chain store, had "a peculiar mannerism of keeping her mouth closed even when speaking." It turned out that she hadn't been able to afford dental care for three years, and one of her front teeth was rotting. Daniel, a construction worker, pulled out his bad teeth with pliers. Then, there was Loretta, who worked nights at a university research center in Mississippi, and was missing most of her teeth. "They'll break off after a while, and then you just grab a hold of them, and they work their way out," she explained to Sered and Fernandopulle. "It hurts so bad, because the tooth aches. Then it's a relief just to get it out of there. The hole closes up itself anyway. So it's so much better."

People without health insurance have bad teeth because, if you're paying for everything out of your own pocket, going to the dentist for a checkup seems like a luxury. It isn't, of course. The loss of teeth makes eating fresh fruits and vegetables difficult, and a diet heavy in soft, processed foods exacerbates more serious health problems, like diabetes. The pain of tooth decay leads many people to use alcohol as a salve. And those struggling to get ahead in the job market quickly find that the unsightliness of bad teeth, and the self-consciousness that results, can become a major bar-rier. If your teeth are bad, you're not going to get a job as a receptionist, say, or a cashier. You're going to be put in the back somewhere, far from the public eye. What Loretta, Gina, and Daniel understand, the two authors tell us, is that bad teeth have come to be seen as a marker of "poor parenting, low educational achievement and slow or faulty intellectual development." They are an outward marker of caste. "Almost every time we asked inter-viewees what their first priority would be if the president established uni-versal health coverage tomorrow," Sered and Fernandopulle write, "the immediate answer was 'my teeth.' "

The U.S. health-care system, according to "Uninsured in America," has created a group of people who increasingly look different from others and suffer in ways that others do not. The leading cause of personal bank-ruptcy in the United States is unpaid medical bills. Half of the uninsured owe money to hospitals, and a third are being pursued by collection agen-cies. Children without health insurance are less likely to receive medical attention for serious injuries, for recurrent ear infections, or for asthma. Lung-cancer patients without insurance are less likely to receive surgery, chemotherapy, or radiation treatment. Heart-attack victims without health insurance are less likely to receive angioplasty. People with pneumonia who don't have health insurance are less likely to receive X rays or consul-tations. The death rate in any given year for someone without health insur-ance is twenty-five per cent higher than for someone with insurance. Because the uninsured are sicker than the rest of us, they can't get better jobs, and because they can't get better jobs they can't afford health insur-ance, and because they can't afford health insurance they get even sicker. John, the manager of a bar in Idaho, tells Sered and Fernandopulle that as a result of various workplace injuries over the years he takes eight ibupro-fen, waits two hours, then takes eight more—and tries to cadge as much prescription pain medication as he can from friends. "There are times when I should've gone to the doctor, but I couldn't afford to go because I don't have insurance," he says. "Like when my back messed up, I should've gone. If I had insurance, I would've went, because I know I could get treat-ment, but when you can't afford it you don't go. Because the harder the hole you get into in terms of bills, then you'll never get out. So you just say, 'I can deal with the pain.' "

One of the great mysteries of political life in the United States is why Americans are so devoted to their health-care system. Six times in the past century—during the First World War, during the Depression, during the Truman and Johnson Administrations, in the Senate in the nineteen-seventies, and during the Clinton years—efforts have been made to intro-duce some kind of universal health insurance, and each time the efforts have been rejected. Instead, the United States has opted for a makeshift system of increasing complexity and dysfunction. Americans spend $5,267 per capita on health care every year, almost two and half times the industrialized world's median of $2,193; the extra spending comes to hundreds of billions of dollars a year. What does that extra spending buy us? Americans have fewer doctors per capita than most Western countries. We go to the doctor less than people in other Western countries. We get admitted to the hospital less frequently than people in other Western countries. We are less satisfied with our health care than our counterparts in other countries. American life expectancy is lower than the Western average. Childhood-immunization rates in the United States are lower than average. Infant-mortality rates are in the nineteenth percentile of industrialized nations. Doctors here perform more high-end medical procedures, such as coronary angioplasties, than in other countries, but most of the wealthier Western countries have more CT scanners than the United States does, and Switzerland, Japan, Austria, and Finland all have more MRI machines per capita. Nor is our system more efficient. The United States spends more than a thousand dollars per capita per year—or close to four hundred billion dollars—on health-care-related paperwork and administration, whereas Canada, for example, spends only about three hundred dollars per capita. And, of course, every other country in the industrialized world insures all its citizens; despite those extra hundreds of billions of dollars we spend each year, we leave forty-five million people without any insurance. A country that displays an almost ruthless commitment to efficiency and performance in every aspect of its economy—a country that switched to Japanese cars the moment they were more reliable, and to Chinese T-shirts the moment they were five cents cheaper—has loyally stuck with a health-care system that leaves its citizenry pulling out their teeth with pliers.

America's health-care mess is, in part, simply an accident of history. The fact that there have been six attempts at universal health coverage in the last century suggests that there has long been support for the idea. But politics has always got in the way. In both Europe and the United States, for example, the push for health insurance was led, in large part, by organized labor. But in Europe the unions worked through the political system, fighting for coverage for all citizens. From the start, health insurance in Europe was public and universal, and that created powerful political support for any attempt to expand benefits. In the United States, by contrast, the unions worked through the collective-bargaining system and, as a result, could win health benefits only for their own members. Health insurance here has always been private and selective, and every attempt to expand benefits has resulted in a paralyzing political battle over who would be added to insurance rolls and who ought to pay for those additions.

Policy is driven by more than politics, however. It is equally driven by ideas, and in the past few decades a particular idea has taken hold among prominent American economists which has also been a powerful impediment to the expansion of health insurance. The idea is known as "moral hazard." Health economists in other Western nations do not share this obsession. Nor do most Americans. But moral hazard has profoundly shaped the way think tanks formulate policy and the way experts argue and the way health insurers structure their plans and the way legislation and regulations have been written. The health-care mess isn't merely the unintentional result of political dysfunction, in other words. It is also the deliberate consequence of the way in which American policymakers have come to think about insurance.

"Moral hazard" is the term economists use to describe the fact that insurance can change the behavior of the person being insured. If your office gives you and your co-workers all the free Pepsi you want—if your employer, in effect, offers universal Pepsi insurance—you'll drink more Pepsi than you would have otherwise. If you have a no-deductible fire-insurance policy, you may be a little less diligent in clearing the brush away from your house. The savings-and-loan crisis of the nineteen-eighties was created, in large part, by the fact that the federal government insured savings deposits of up to a hundred thousand dollars, and so the newly deregulated S. & L.s made far riskier investments than they would have otherwise. Insurance can have the paradoxical effect of producing risky and wasteful behavior. Economists spend a great deal of time thinking about such moral hazard for good reason. Insurance is an attempt to make human life safer and more secure. But, if those efforts can backfire and produce riskier behavior, providing insurance becomes a much more complicated and problematic endeavor.

In 1968, the economist Mark Pauly argued that moral hazard played an enormous role in medicine, and, as John Nyman writes in his book "The Theory of the Demand for Health Insurance," Pauly's paper has become the "single most influential article in the health economics literature." Nyman, an economist at the University of Minnesota, says that the fear of moral hazard lies behind the thicket of co-payments and deductibles and utilization reviews which characterizes the American health-insurance system. Fear of moral hazard, Nyman writes, also explains "the general lack of enthusiasm by U.S. health economists for the expansion of health insurance coverage (for example, national health insurance or expanded Medicare benefits) in the U.S."

What Nyman is saying is that when your insurance company requires that you make a twenty-dollar co-payment for a visit to the doctor, or when your plan includes an annual five-hundred-dollar or thousand-dollar deductible, it's not simply an attempt to get you to pick up a larger share of your health costs. It is an attempt to make your use of the health-care system more efficient. Making you responsible for a share of the costs, the argument runs, will reduce moral hazard: you'll no longer grab one of those free Pepsis when you aren't really thirsty. That's also why Nyman says that the notion of moral hazard is behind the "lack of enthusiasm" for expansion of health insurance. If you think of insurance as producing wasteful consumption of medical services, then the fact that there are forty-five million Americans without health insurance is no longer an immediate cause for alarm. After all, it's not as if the uninsured *never* go to the doctor. They spend, on average, $934 a year on medical care. A moral-hazard theorist would say that they go to the doctor when they really have to. Those of us with private insurance, by contrast, consume $2,347 worth of health care a year. If a lot of that extra $1,413 is waste, then maybe the uninsured person is the truly efficient consumer of health care.

The moral-hazard argument makes sense, however, only if we consume health care in the same way that we consume other consumer goods, and to economists like Nyman this assumption is plainly absurd. We go to the doctor grudgingly, only because we're sick. "Moral hazard is overblown," the Princeton economist Uwe Reinhardt says. "You always hear that the demand for health care is unlimited. This is just not true. People who are very well insured, who are very rich, do you see them check into the hospital because it's free? Do people really like to go to the doctor? Do they check into the hospital instead of playing golf?"

For that matter, when you have to pay for your own health care, does your consumption really become more efficient? In the late nineteen-seventies, the RAND Corporation did an extensive study on the question, randomly assigning families to health plans with co-payment levels at zero per cent, twenty-five per cent, fifty per cent, or ninety-five per cent, up to six thousand dollars. As you might expect, the more that people were asked to chip in for their health care the less care they used. The problem was that they cut back equally on both frivolous care and useful care. Poor people in the high-deductible group with hypertension, for instance, didn't do nearly as good a job of controlling their blood pressure as those in other groups, resulting in a ten-per-cent increase in the likelihood of death. As a recent Commonwealth Fund study concluded, cost sharing is "a blunt instrument." Of course it is: how should the average consumer be expected to know before-hand what care is frivolous and what care is useful? I just went to the dermatologist to get moles checked for skin cancer. If I had had to pay a hundred per cent, or even fifty per cent, of the cost of the visit, I might not have gone. Would that have been a wise decision? I have no idea. But if one of those moles really is cancerous, that simple, inexpensive visit could save the health-care system tens of thousands of dollars (not to mention saving me a great deal of heartbreak). The focus on moral hazard suggests that the changes we make in our behavior when we have insurance are nearly always wasteful. Yet, when it comes to health care, many of the things we do only because we have insurance—like getting our moles checked, or getting our teeth cleaned regularly, or getting a mammogram or engaging in other routine preventive care—are anything but wasteful and inefficient. In fact, they are behaviors that could end up saving the health-care system a good deal of money.

Sered and Fernandopulle tell the story of Steve, a factory worker from northern Idaho, with a "grotesque-looking left hand—what looks like a bone sticks out the side." When he was younger, he broke his hand. "The doctor wanted to operate on it," he recalls. "And because I didn't have insurance, well, I was like 'I ain't gonna have it operated on.' The doctor said, 'Well, I can wrap it for you with an Ace bandage.' I said, 'Ahh, let's do that, then.'" Steve uses less health care than he would if he had insurance, but that's not because he has defeated the scourge of moral hazard. It's because instead of getting a broken bone fixed he put a bandage on it.

At the center of the Bush Administration's plan to address the health-insurance mess are Health Savings Accounts, and Health Savings Accounts are exactly what you would come up with if you were concerned, above all else, with minimizing moral hazard. The logic behind them was laid out in the 2004 Economic Report of the President. Americans, the report argues, have too much health insurance: typical plans cover things that they shouldn't, creating the problem of overconsumption. Several paragraphs are then devoted to explaining the theory of moral hazard. The report turns to the subject of the uninsured, concluding that they fall into several groups. Some are foreigners who may be covered by their countries of origin. Some are people who could be covered by Medicaid but aren't or aren't admitting that they are. Finally, a large number "remain uninsured as a matter of choice." The report continues, "Researchers believe that as many as one-quarter of those without health insurance had coverage available through an employer but declined the coverage. . . . Still others may remain uninsured because they are young and healthy and do not see the need for insurance." In other words, those with health insurance are overinsured and their behavior is distorted by moral hazard. Those without health insurance use their own money to make decisions about insurance based on an assessment of their needs. The insured are wasteful. The uninsured are prudent. So what's the solution? Make the insured a little bit more like the uninsured.

Under the Health Savings Accounts system, consumers are asked to pay for routine health care with their own money—several thousand dollars of which can be put into a tax-free account. To handle their catastrophic expenses, they then purchase a basic health-insurance package with, say, a thousand-dollar annual deductible. As President Bush explained recently, "Health Savings Accounts all aim at empowering people to make decisions for themselves, owning their own healthcare plan, and at the same time bringing some demand control into the cost of health care."

The country described in the President's report is a very different place from the country described in "Uninsured in America." Sered and Fernandopulle look at the billions we spend on medical care and wonder why

Americans have so little insurance. The President's report considers the same situation and worries that we have too much. Sered and Fernandopulle see the lack of insurance as a problem of poverty; a third of the uninsured, after all, have incomes below the federal poverty line. In the section on the uninsured in the President's report, the word "poverty" is never used. In the Administration's view, people are offered insurance but "decline the coverage" as "a matter of choice." The uninsured in Sered and Fernandopulle's book decline coverage, but only because they can't afford it. Gina, for instance, works for a beauty salon that offers her a bare-bones health-insurance plan with a thousand-dollar deductible for two hundred dollars a month. What's her total income? Nine hundred dollars a month. She could "choose" to accept health insurance, but only if she chose to stop buying food or paying the rent.

The biggest difference between the two accounts, though, has to do with how each views the function of insurance. Gina, Steve, and Loretta are ill, and need insurance to cover the costs of getting better. In their eyes, insurance is meant to help equalize financial risk between the healthy and the sick. In the insurance business, this model of coverage is known as "social insurance," and historically it was the way health coverage was conceived. If you were sixty and had heart disease and diabetes, you didn't pay substantially more for coverage than a perfectly healthy twenty-five-year-old. Under social insurance, the twenty-five-year-old agrees to pay thousands of dollars in premiums even though he didn't go to the doctor at all in the previous year, because he wants to make sure that someone else will subsidize his health care if he ever comes down with heart disease or diabetes. Canada and Germany and Japan and all the other industrialized nations with universal health care follow the social-insurance model. Medicare, too, is based on the social-insurance model, and, when Americans with medicare report themselves to be happier with virtually every aspect of their insurance coverage than people with private insurance (as they do, repeatedly and overwhelmingly), they are referring to the social aspect of their insurance. They aren't getting better care. But they are getting something just as valuable: the security of being insulated against the financial shock of serious illness.

There is another way to organize insurance, however, and that is to make it actuarial. Car insurance, for instance, is actuarial. How much you pay is in large part a function of your individual situation and history: someone who drives a sports car and has received twenty speeding tickets in the past two years pays a much higher annual premium than a soccer mom with a minivan. In recent years, the private insurance industry in the United States has been moving toward the actuarial model, with profound consequences. The triumph of the actuarial model over the social-insurance model is the reason that companies unlucky enough to employ older, high-cost employees—like United Airlines—have run into such financial difficulty. It's the reason that automakers are increasingly moving their operations to Canada. It's the reason that small businesses that have one or two employees with serious illnesses suddenly face unmanageably high health-insurance premiums, and it's the reason that, in many states, people suffering from a potentially high-cost medical condition can't get anyone to insure them at all.

Health Savings Accounts represent the final, irrevocable step in the actuarial direction. If you are preoccupied with moral hazard, then you want people to pay for care with their own money, and, when you do that, the sick inevitably end up paying more than the healthy. And when you make people choose an insurance plan that fits their individual needs, those with significant medical problems will choose expensive health plans that cover lots of things, while those with few health problems will choose cheaper, bare-bones plans. The more expensive the comprehensive plans become, and the less expensive the bare-bones plans become, the more the very sick will cluster together at one end of the insurance spectrum, and the more the well will cluster together at the low-cost end. The days when the healthy twenty-five-year-old subsidizes the sixty-year-old with heart disease or diabetes are coming to an end. "The main effect of putting more of it on the consumer is to reduce the social redistributive element of insurance," the Stanford economist Victor Fuchs says. Health Savings Accounts are not a variant of universal health care. In their governing assumptions, they are the antithesis of universal health care.

The issue about what to do with the health-care system is sometimes presented as a technical argument about the merits of one kind of coverage over another or as an ideological argument about socialized versus private medicine. It is, instead, about a few very simple questions. Do you think that this kind of redistribution of risk is a good idea? Do you think that people whose genes predispose them to depression or cancer, or whose poverty complicates asthma or diabetes, or who get hit by a drunk driver, or who have to keep their mouths closed because their teeth are rotting ought to bear a greater share of the costs of their health care than those of us who are lucky enough to escape such misfortunes? In the rest of the industrialized world, it is assumed that the more equally and widely the burdens of illness are shared, the better off the population as a whole is likely to be. The reason the United States has forty-five million people without coverage is that its health-care policy is in the hands of people who disagree, and who regard health insurance not as the solution but as the problem.

Textual Questions

1. What example does Gladwell open his essay with and why?

2. How does Gladwell describe the costs—directly and indirectly—of going without health-care insurance?

3. In each section of his essay, what primary example does Gladwell focus upon or what primary example/kind of example does he use to develop his argument?

Rhetorical Questions

4. What do "bad teeth" mean in America, literally and figuratively? How do "bad teeth" serve as a significant example in Gladwell's argument?

5. How and where does Gladwell compare and contrast America to other nations of the world? What effect do these comparisons and contrast have on his argument?

6. How does Gladwell build his argument logically to the focus of the final section? How does the argument that comes before it make the argument within the final section more/less credible?

Intertextual Questions

7. In what ways do Gladwell's criticisms of America's health-care system compare and contrast to the criticisms of this same system made in *The New York Times* editorial "America's Promises"?

8. Which argument do you find more effective and why, Gladwell's argument in this essay or that made by Linda Peeno?

Thinking Beyond the Text

9. View a copy of the 1991 film *The Doctor* or read an excerpt from the 1988 memoir *A Taste of My Own Medicine*, upon which the film is based. In your estimation is the criticism of American health care made in this movie/book still accurate in modern America? Or have things improved/worsened since the publication of this book/release of this film?

10. Consider your own health insurance—or the reasons you do not have any. What is the financial cost of this insurance monthly/annually? What percentage of your monthly/annual income does this insurance take? What basic needs—such as annual dental checkups—are and are not covered by your insurance?

For Writing & Discussion

11. Interview someone you know well, someone who trusts you, who is at least two decades older than you are now. Ask him/her to describe his/her healthcare history just as you did before reading Gladwell's essay (see Prereading Question). Is he/she currently covered by healthcare insurance? If so, then how much does it cost and what percentage of this person's annual/monthly income does that amount to? If not, then why not? In an essay, describe this person's healthcare history and ongoing healthcare costs. How is the need for health care—affordable health care—a factor in decisions this person makes?

FOCAL POINT

Exploring Images of The Promise of Health

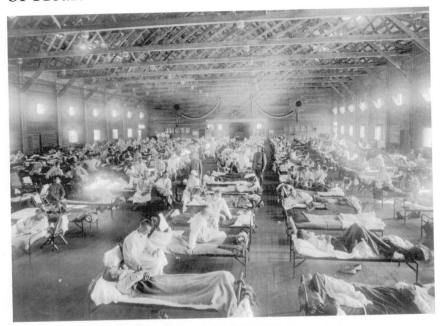

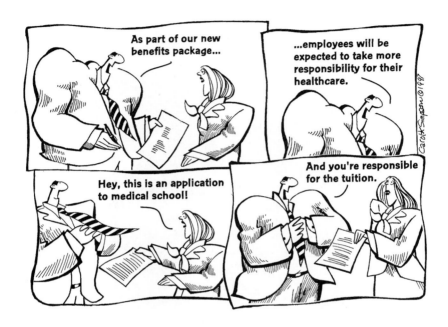

FOCAL POINT
Exploring Images of The Promise of Health

Questions

1. What message does the image on page 424 (top) depicting the flu epidemic that swept the world in 1918 send? What details support this message? Given the concerns today of a possible global pandemic, what reactions do you have to this photograph? Explain.

2. What does the image of the modern hospital waiting room on page 424 (bottom) say about the state of healthcare in America? Explain in detail.

3. The photograph on page 425 (top) shows the AIDS Quilt laid out in front of the United States Capitol. What is the significance of the quilt's placement in relation to the United States Capitol? What emotions does this image of the quilt invoke in you? Explain.

4. Does your reaction to the image of the AIDS Quilt on page 425 (bottom) differ from your reaction to the picture of the Quilt from afar? Which is more effective, the close-up or wide-shot? Why? Do the two photographs make the same argument? Similar arguments? Different arguments entirely?

5. There are three potential subjects being mocked in this cartoon (page 426)—the cost of insurance, the unavailability of healthcare for the employed, and the high cost of either tuition or (perhaps) medical care itself. Which of these possible topics seems dominant to you? Why? How does this cartoon support the argument made by the photograph of the crowded hospital waiting room on page 424 (bottom)?

5

THE PROMISE OF WORK AND SUCCESS

In the first reading in this book, former president Jimmy Carter touched on one of the foundational beliefs within the promise of America, commonly expressed as "Every generation does a little bit better." This is a belief in progress, in the progression of America—and all its citizens—into an ever-more-rosy future of personal happiness and financial security. Fundamental to this promise is belief in the value of hard work—the marker along the road to success. Like education, discussed in Chapter 2, dedication to work is a key to fulfilling the promise of America.

The rhetoric of work and success surrounds modern Americans. Consider two radically different examples:

1. When Hurricane Katrina devastated the Gulf Coast in 2005 and critics argued that the response of federal aid agencies was retarded by ignorance and inefficiency, officials from the president down did everything in their power to prove that, during the disaster, they worked hard to avert the cataclysmic events bearing down. Hundreds of e-mails were released to reporters, showing the constant flow of questions and answers that demonstrated men and women hard at work. Early in 2006 the White House released videotapes of teleconferences between the president and various advisors to show the extent of President Bush's work to save the Gulf Coast's citizens. But in some circles critics argued that the tapes showed a bored, disengaged president making little effort to lead. In short, they argued that the tapes showed a president who wasn't working hard enough.

2. Weekend and late-night cable television programming has, since the mid-1980s, been dominated by a growing number of infomercials, 30- or 60-minute long "paid advertisements" for everything from psychics and phone sex to fitness products and juice makers. By far the most common, however, are the infomercials that offer financial and educational opportunities. In both instances, the arguments are remarkably similar: Viewers who are working hard but not living the life they "deserve" should consider working even harder—by adding either online classes to their busy schedules or buying and selling real estate/makeup/diet products/and so on. The secret to success, these infomercials argue, is working harder—which eventually (but presumably quickly) leads to working less and living better. Hard work now—along with three easy payments—means success and security further down the line.

428

Both of these arguments—the former of life-and-death importance to thousands, the latter of little importance to most anyone—build upon the simple, pure, generally unstated belief that in America hard work and success are longtime partners, and one always leads to the other. Knowledge of this partnership is implicit in every aspect of American life, from the church to the school. Americans, historically, know the value of hard work.

Many Americans in the modern era know better.

At the end of the twentieth and beginning of the twenty-first centuries, many corporations began "dumping" their pension responsibilities to their employees—with corporations such as Enron leading the way. Workers who had paid into retirement funds—in some cases for decades—lost everything that was promised to them; their hard work led not to financial security but to financial ruin. Other corporations, such as Northwest Airlines, required workers to take massive cuts in pay and benefits—in some cases lowering annual income for employees by as much as 30 percent. Concurrently, many businesses began to employ multitiered systems in their employment practices—leaving "old" employees with reduced benefits and newly hired employees with few (or no) benefits at all.

As you read the selections that follow, consider the value of hard work in modern America. For some workers, the promise has been kept, and their hard work has paid off handsomely. But other workers now find themselves trapped in a terrible cycle. Unable to make a livable wage at a single job, they work two or more jobs simultaneously; working so many hours, they are unable to pursue educational or career opportunities that might, ultimately, allow them to receive a higher wage. Working many hours at one or more jobs, they may have no retirement fund through their employer(s) and no disposable income to invest for their own retirement. Working many hours at one or more jobs, they may have limited (or no) health insurance—and thus may be one accident or illness away from complete financial ruin.

Within such an economic reality, what can we say about the promise of work and the chance of success in America at the opening of the twenty-first century? What was it a generation ago? What will it be for you and your children?

JOHN STEINBECK

John Steinbeck (1902–1968), an American writer, is most remembered as a novelist who wrote classics such as *Cannery Row* (1945), *Of Mice and Men* (1937), and *The Grapes of Wrath* (1939). The latter, which describes the lives of migrant workers during the Great Depression, won a Pulitzer in 1939, and Steinbeck won the Nobel Prize for Literature in 1962. Seventeen of his books have been made into Hollywood films, and several have also been made into films in other countries, including Iran, Turkey, and Mexico. Steinbeck worked on films himself, including the adaptations of some of his books, and he wrote the screenplay for Alfred Hitchcock's 1944 movie, *Lifeboat*.

In addition to his impressive list of novels and novellas, Steinbeck also wrote nonfiction. During World War II he was a correspondent for the *New York Herald Tribune*, and he wrote a memoir about driving around America with his poodle, *Travels with Charley: In Search of America*, which was published in 1962.

"Harvest Gypsies" was originally published as a series of articles in the *San Francisco News* in 1936, then collected in 1938 into a pamphlet called *Their Blood is Strong*. In these articles, Steinbeck discusses the lives of migrant workers, the fact that the California agricultural economy could not function without them, and the shift happening at that time as fewer of the migrants were immigrants and more were landless citizens, with citizens' rights, forced west out of the Dust Bowl.

Harvest Gypsies

∾ Prereading Question

For the American economy to continue to function, is it necessary that there always be a group of people willing to do the work that no one else will do? Or that there be groups of people willing to do this work (or unable to do any other work)? For example, are there jobs done only by teenagers? By immigrants, legal or illegal? What would happen if the members of one of these groups simply stopped doing the work that only they do?

The squatters' camps are located all over California. Let us see what a typical one is like. It is located on the banks of a river, near an irrigation ditch or on a side road where a spring of water is available. From a distance it looks like a city dump, and well it may, for the city dumps are the sources for the material of which it is built. You can see a litter of dirty rags and scrap iron, of houses built of weeds, of flattened cans or of paper. It is only on close approach that it can be seen that these are homes.

Here is a house built by a family who have tried to maintain a neatness. The house is about 10 feet by 10 feet, and it is built completely of corrugated paper. The roof is peaked, the walls are tacked to a wooden frame. The dirt floor is swept clean, and along the irrigation ditch or in the muddy river the wife of the family scrubs clothes without soap and tries to rinse out the mud in muddy water. The spirit of this family is not quite broken, for the children, three of them, still have clothes, and the family possesses three old quilts and a soggy, lumpy mattress. But the money so needed for food cannot be used for soap nor for clothes.

With the first rain the carefully built house will slop down into a brown, pulpy mush; in a few months the clothes will fray off the children's bodies while the lack of nourishing food will subject the whole family to pneumonia when the first cold comes.

Five years ago this family had fifty acres of land and a thousand dollars in the bank. The wife belonged to a sewing circle and the man was a member of the grange. They raised chickens, pigs, pigeons and vegetables and fruit for their own use; and their land produced the tall corn of the middle west. Now they have nothing.

If the husband hits every harvest without delay and works the maximum time, he may make four hundred dollars this year. But if anythings happen, if his old car breaks down, if he is late and misses a harvest or two, he will have to feed his whole family on as little as one hundred and fifty.

But there is still pride in this family. Wherever they stop they try to put the children in school. It may be that the children will be in a school for as much as a month before they are moved to another locality.

Here, in the faces of the husband and his wife, you begin to see an expression you will notice on every face; not worry, but absolute terror of the starvation that crowds in against the borders of the camp. This man has tried to make a toilet by digging a hole in the ground near his paper house and surrounding it with an old piece of burlap. But he will only do things like that this year. He is a newcomer and his spirit and decency and his sense of his own dignity have not been quite wiped out. Next year he will be like his next door neighbor.

This is a family of six; a man, his wife and four children. They live in a tent the color of the ground. Rot has set in on the canvas so that the flaps and the sides hang in tatters and are held together with bits of rusty baling wire. There is one bed in the family and that is a big tick lying on the ground inside the tent.

They have one quilt and a piece of canvas for bedding. The sleeping arrangement is clever. Mother and father lie down together and two children lie between them. Then, heading the other way, the other two children lie, the littler ones. If the mother and father sleep with their legs spread wide, there is room for the legs of the children.

There is more filth here. The tent is full of flies clinging to the apple box that is the dinner table, buzzing about the foul clothes of the children, particularly the baby, who has not been bathed nor cleaned for several days. This family has been on the road longer than the builder of the paper house. There is no toilet here, but there is a clump of willows nearby where human feces lie exposed to the flies—the same flies that are in the tent.

Two weeks ago there was another child, a four year old boy. For a few weeks they had noticed that he was kind of lackadaisical, that his eyes had been feverish. They had given him the best place in the bed, between father and mother. But one night he went into convulsions and died, and the next morning the coroner's wagon took him away. It was one step down.

They know pretty well that it was a diet of fresh fruit, beans and little else that caused his death. He had no milk for months. With this death there came a change of mind in his family. The father and mother now feel that paralyzed dullness with which the mind protects itself against too much sorrow and too much pain.

And this father will not be able to make a maximum of four hundred dollars a year any more because he is no longer alert; he isn't quick at piece-work, and he is not able to fight clear of the dullness that has settled on him. His spirit is losing caste rapidly.

The dullness shows in the faces of this family, and in addition there is a sullenness that makes them taciturn. Sometimes they still start the older children off to school, but the ragged little things will not go; they hide in ditches or wander off by themselves until it is time to go back to the tent, because they are scorned in the school.

The better-dressed children shout and jeer, the teachers are quite often impatient with these additions to their duties, and the parents of the "nice" children do not want to have disease carriers in the schools.

The father of this family once had a little grocery store and his family lived in back of it so that even the children could wait on the counter. When the drought set in there was no trade for the store any more.

This is the middle class of the squatters' camp. In a few months this family will slip down to the lower class. Dignity is all gone, and spirit has turned to sullen anger before it dies.

The next door neighbor family of man, wife and three children of from three to nine years of age, have built a house by driving willow branches into the ground and wattling weeds, tin, old paper and strips of carpet against them. A few branches are placed over the top to keep out the noonday sun. It would not turn water at all. There is no bed. Somewhere the family has found a big piece of old carpet. It is on the ground. To go to bed the members of the family lie on the ground and fold the carpet up over them.

The three year old child has a gunny sack tied about his middle for clothing. He has the swollen belly caused by malnutrition.

He sits on the ground in the sun in front of the house, and the little black fruit flies buzz in circles and land on his closed eyes and crawl up his nose until he weakly brushes them away.

They try to get at the mucous in the eye-corners. This child seems to have the reactions of a baby much younger. The first year he had a little milk, but he has had none since.

He will die in a very short time. The older children may survive. Four nights ago the mother had a baby in the tent, on the dirty carpet. It was born dead, which was just as well because she could not have fed it at the breast; her own diet will not produce milk.

After it was born and she had seen that it was dead, the mother rolled over and lay still for two days. She is up today, tottering around. The last baby, born less than a year ago, lived a week. This woman's eyes have the glazed, far-away look of a sleep walker's eyes. She does not wash clothes any more. The drive that makes for cleanliness has been drained out of her and she hasn't the energy. The husband was a share-cropper once, but he couldn't make it go. Now he has lost even the desire to talk. He will not look directly at you for that requires will, and will needs strength. He is a bad field worker for the same reason. It takes him a long time to make up his mind, so he is always late in moving and late in arriving in the fields. His top wage, when he can find work now, which isn't often, is a dollar a day.

The children do not even go to the willow clump any more. They squat where they are and kick a little dirt. The father is vaguely aware that there is a culture of hookworm in the mud along the river bank. He knows the children will get it on their bare feet. But he hasn't the will nor the energy to resist. Too many things have happened to him. This is the lower class of the camp.

This is what the man in the tent will be in six months; what the man in the paper house with its peaked roof will be in a year, after his house has washed down and his children have sickened or died, after the loss of dignity and spirit have cut him down to a kind of subhumanity.

Helpful strangers are not well-received in this camp. The local sheriff makes a raid now and then for a wanted man, and if there is labor trouble the vigilantes may burn the poor houses. Social workers, survey workers have taken case histories. They are filed and open for inspection. These families have been questioned over and over about their origins, number of children living and dead. The information is taken down and filed. That is that. It has been done so often and so little has come of it.

And there is another way for them to get attention. Let an epidemic break out, say typhoid or scarlet fever, and the country doctor will come to the camp and hurry the infected cases to the pest house. But malnutrition is not infectious, nor is dysentery, which is almost the rule among the children.

The county hospital has no room for measles, mumps, whooping cough; and yet these are often deadly to hunger-weakened children. And although we hear much about the free clinics for the poor, these people do not know how to get the aid and they do not get it. Also, since most of their dealings with authority are painful to them, they prefer not to take the chance.

This is the squatters' camp. Some are a little better, some much worse. I have described three typical families. In some of the camps there are as many as three hundred families like these. Some are so far from water that it must be bought at five cents a bucket.

And if these men steal, if there is developing among them a suspicion and hatred of well-dressed, satisfied people, the reason is not to be sought in their origin nor in any tendency to weakness in their character.

The federal government, realizing that the miserable condition of the California migrant agricultural worker constitutes an immediate and vital problem, has set up two camps for the moving workers and contemplates eight more in the immediate future. The development of the camps at Arvin and at Marysville makes a social and economic study of vast interest.

The present camps are set up on leased ground. Future camps are to be constructed on land purchased by the Government. The Government provides places for tents. Permanent structures are simple, including washrooms, toilets and showers, an administration building and a place where the people can entertain themselves. The equipment at the Arvin camp, exclusive of rent of the land, costs approximately $18,000.

At this camp, water, toilet paper and some medical supplies are provided. A resident manager is on the ground. Campers are received on the following simple conditions: (1) That the men are bona fide farm people and intend to work, (2) that they will help to maintain the cleanliness of the camp and (3) that in lieu of rent they will devote two hours a week towards the maintenance and improvement of the camp.

The result has been more than could be expected. From the first, the intent of the management has been to restore the dignity and decency that had been kicked out of the migrants by their intolerable mode of life.

In this series the word "dignity" has been used several times. It has been used not as some attitude of self-importance, but simply as a register of a man's responsibility to the community. A man herded about, surrounded by armed guards, starved and forced to live in filth loses his dignity; that is, he loses his valid position in regard to society, and consequently his whole ethics toward society. Nothing is a better example of this than the prison, where the men are reduced to no dignity and where crimes and infractions of the rule are constant.

We regard this destruction of dignity, then, as one of the most regrettable results of the migrant's life, since it does reduce his responsibility and does make him a sullen outcast who will strike at our Government in any way that occurs to him.

The example at Arvin adds weight to such a conviction. The people in the camp are encouraged to govern themselves, and they have responded with simple and workable democracy. The camp is divided into four units. Each unit, by direct election, is represented in a central governing committee, an entertainment committee, a maintenance committee and a Good Neighbors committee. Each of these members is elected by the vote of his unit, and is recallable by the same vote. The manager, of course, has the right of veto, but he practically never finds it necessary to act contrary to the recommendations of the committee.

The result of this responsible self-government has been remarkable. The inhabitants of the camp came there beaten, sullen and destitute. But as their social sense was revived they have settled down. The camp takes care of its own destitute, feeding and sheltering those who have nothing with their own poor stores. The central committee makes the laws that govern the conduct of the inhabitants.

In the year that the Arvin camp has been in operation there has not been any need for outside police. Punishments are the restrictions of certain privileges such as admission to the community dances, or for continued anti-social conduct, a recommendation to the manager that the culprit be ejected from the camp.

A works committee assigns the labor to be done in the camp, improvements, garbage disposal, maintenance and repairs. The entertainment committee arranges for the weekly dances, the music for which is furnished by an orchestra made up of the inhabitants. So well do they play that one orchestra has been lost to the radio already. This committee also takes care of the many self-made games and courts that have been built.

The Good Neighbors, a woman's organization, takes part in quilting and sewing projects, sees that destitution does not exist, governs and watches the nursery, where children can be left while the mothers are working in the fields and in the packing sheds. And all of this is done with the outside aid of one manager and one part-time nurse. As experiments in natural and democratic self-government, these camps are unique in the United States.

In visiting these camps one is impressed with several things in particular. The sullen and frightened expression that is the rule among the migrants has disappeared from the faces of the Federal camp inhabitants. Instead there is a steadiness of gaze and a self-confidence that can only come of restored dignity.

The difference seems to lie in the new position of the migrant in the community. Before he came to the camp he had been policed, hated and moved about. It had been made clear that he was not wanted.

In the Federal camps every effort of the management is expended to give him his place in society. There are no persons on relief in these camps.

In the Arvin camp the central committee recommended the expulsion of a family which applied for relief. Employment is more common than in any similar group for, having something of their own, these men are better workers. The farmers in the vicinity seem to prefer the camp men to others.

The inhabitants of the Federal camps are no picked group. They are typical of the new migrants. They come from Oklahoma, Arkansas and Texas and the other drought states. Eighty-five per cent of them are former farm owners, farm renters or farm laborers. The remaining 15 per cent includes painters, mechanics, electricians and even professional men.

When a new family enters one of these camps it is usually dirty, tired and broken. A group from the Good Neighbors meets it, tells it the rules, helps it to get settled, instructs it in the use of the sanitary facilities; and if there are insufficient blankets or shelters, furnishes them from its own stores.

The children are bathed and cleanly dressed and the needs of the future canvassed. If the children have not enough clothes the community sewing circle will get busy immediately. In case any of the family are sick the camp manager or the part-time nurse is called and treatment is carried out.

These Good Neighbors are not trained social workers, but they have what is perhaps more important, an understanding which grows from a likeness of experience. Nothing has happened to the newcomer that has not happened to the committee.

A typical manager's report is as follows: "New arrivals. Low in food-stuffs. Most of the personal belongings were tied up in sacks and were in a filthy condition. The Good Neighbors at once took the family in hand, and by 10 o'clock they were fed, washed, camped, settled and asleep."

These two camps each accommodate about 200 families. They were started as experiments, and the experiments have proven successful. Between the rows of tents the families have started little gardens for the raising of vegetables, and the plots, which must be cared for after a 10 or 12-hours' day of work, produce beets, cabbages, corn, carrots, onions and turnips. The passion to produce is very great. One man, who has not yet been assigned his little garden plot, is hopefully watering a jimson weed simply to have something of his own growing.

The Federal Government, through the Resettlement Administration, plans to extend these camps and to include with them small maintenance farms. These are intended to solve several problems.

They will allow the women and children to stay in one place, permitting the children to go to school and the women to maintain the farms during the work times of the men. They will reduce the degenerating effect of the migrants' life, they will reinstil the sense of government and possession that have been lost by the migrants. Located near to the areas which demand seasonal labor, these communities will permit these subsistence farmers to work in the harvests, while at the same time they stop the wanderings over the whole state. The success of these Federal camps in making potential criminals into citizens makes the usual practice of expending money on tear gas seem a little silly.

The greater part of the new migrants from the dust bowl will become permanent California citizens. They have shown in these camps an ability to produce and to cooperate. They are passionately determined to make their living on the land. One of them said, "If it's work you got to do, mister, we'll do it. Our folks never did take charity and this family ain't takin' it now."

The plan of the Resettlement Administration to extend these Federal camps is being fought by certain interests in California. The arguments against the camps are as follows:

That they will increase the need for locally paid police. But the two camps already carried on for over a year have proved to need no locally paid police whatever, while the squatters' camps are a constant charge on the sheriff's offices.

The second argument is that the cost of schools to the district will be increased. School allotments are from the state and governed by the number of pupils. And even if it did cost more, the communities need the work of these families and must assume some responsibility for them. The alternative is a generation of illiterates.

The third is that they will lower the land values because of the type of people inhabiting the camps. Those camps already established have in no way affected the value of the land and the people are of good American stock who have proved that they can maintain an American standard of living. The cleanliness and lack of disease in the two experimental camps are proof of this.

The fourth argument, as made by the editor of The Yuba City *Herald*, a self-admitted sadist who wrote a series of incendiary and subversive editorials concerning the Marysville camp, is that these are the breeding places for strikes. Under pressure of evidence the Yuba City patriot withdrew his contention that the camp was full of radicals. This will be the argument used by the speculative growers' associations. These associations have said in so many words that they require a peon class to succeed. Any action to better the condition of the migrants will be considered radical to them.

Migrant families in california find that unemployment relief, which is available to settled unemployed, has little to offer them. In the first place there has grown up a regular technique for getting relief; one who knows the ropes can find aid from the various state and Federal disbursement agencies, while a man ignorant of the methods will be turned away.

The migrant is always partially unemployed. The nature of his occupation makes his work seasonal. At the same time the nature of his work makes him ineligible for relief. The basis for receiving most of the relief is residence.

But it is impossible for the migrant to accomplish the residence. He must move about the country. He could not stop long enough to establish residence or he would starve to death. He finds, then, on application, that he cannot be put on the relief rolls. And being ignorant, he gives up at that point.

For the same reason he finds that he cannot receive any of the local benefits reserved for residents of a county. The county hospital was built not for the transient, but for residents of the county.

It will be interesting to trace the history of one family in relation to medicine, work relief and direct relief. The family consisted of five persons, a man of 50, his wife of 45, two boys, 15 and 12, and a girl of 6. They came from Oklahoma, where the father operated a little ranch of 50 acres of prairie.

When the ranch dried up and blew away the family put its moveable possession in an old Dodge truck and came to California. They arrived in time for the orange picking in Southern California and put in a good average season.

The older boy and the father together made $60. At that time the automobile broke out some teeth of the differential and the repairs, together with three second-hand tires, took $22. The family moved into Kern County to chop grapes and camped in the squatters' camp on the edge of Bakersfield.

At this time the father sprained his ankle and the little girl developed measles. Doctors' bills amounted to $10 of the remaining store, and food and transportation took most of the rest.

The 15-year-old boy was now the only earner for the family. The 12-year-old boy picked up a brass gear in a yard and took it to sell. He was arrested and taken before the juvenile court, but was released to his father's custody. The father walked in to Bakersfield from the squatters' camp on a sprained ankle because the gasoline was gone from the automobile and he didn't dare invest any of the remaining money in more gasoline.

This walk caused complications in the sprain which laid him up again. The little girl had recovered from measles by this time, but her eyes had not been protected and she had lost part of her eyesight.

The father now applied for relief and found that he was ineligible because he had not established the necessary residence. All resources were gone. A little food was given to the family by neighbors in the squatters' camp. A neighbor who had a goat brought in a cup of milk every day for the little girl.

At this time the 15-year-old boy came home from the fields with a pain in his side. He was feverish and in great pain. The mother put hot cloths on his stomach while a neighbor took the crippled father to the county hospital to apply for aid. The hospital was full, all its time taken by bona fide local residents. The trouble described as a pain in the stomach by the father was not taken seriously.

The father was given a big dose of salts to take home to the boy. That night the pain grew so great that the boy became unconscious. The father telephoned the hospital and found that there was no one on duty who could attend to his case. The boy died of a burst appendix the next day.

There was no money. The county buried him free. The father sold the Dodge for $30 and bought a $2 wreath for the funeral. With the remaining money he laid in a store of cheap, filling food—beans, oatmeal, lard. He tried to go back to work in the fields. Some of the neighbors gave him rides to work and charged him a small amount for transportation.

He was on the weak ankle too soon and could not make over 75¢ a day at piece-work, chopping. Again he applied for relief and was refused because he was not a resident and because he was employed. The little girl, because of insufficient food and weakness from measles, relapsed into influenza.

The father did not try the county hospital again. He went to a private doctor who refused to come to the squatters' camp unless he were paid in advance. The father took two days' pay and gave it to the doctor who came to the family shelter, took the girl's temperature, gave the mother seven pills, told the mother to keep the child warm and went away. The father lost his job because he was too slow.

He applied again for help and was given one week's supply of groceries.

This can go on indefinitely. The case histories like it can be found in their thousands. It may be argued that there were ways for this man to get aid, but how did he know where to get it? There was no way for him to find out.

California communities have used the old, old methods of dealing with such problems. The first method is to disbelieve it and vigorously to deny that there is a problem. The second is to deny local responsibility since the people are not permanent residents. And the third and silliest of all is to run the trouble over the county borders into another county. The floater method of swapping what the counties consider undesirables from hand to hand is like a game of medicine ball.

A fine example of this insular stupidity concerns the hookworm situation in Stanislaus County. The mud along water courses where there are squatters living is infected. Several business men of Modesto and Ceres offered as a solution that the squatters be cleared out. There was no thought of isolating the victims and stopping the hookworm.

The affected people were, according to these men, to be run out of the county to spread the disease in other fields. It is this refusal of the counties to consider anything but the immediate economy and profit of the locality that is the cause of a great deal of the unsolvable quality of the migrants' problem. The counties seem terrified that they may be required to give some aid to the labor they require for their harvests.

According to several Government and state surveys and studies of large numbers of migrants, the maximum a worker can make is $400 a year, while the average is around $300, and the large minimum is $150 a year. This amount must feed, clothe and transport whole families.

Sometimes whole families are able to work in the fields, thus making an additional wage. In other observed cases a whole family, weakened by sickness and malnutrition, has worked in the fields, making less than the wage of one healthy man. It does not take long at the migrants' work to reduce the health of any family. Food is scarce always, and luxuries of any kind are unknown.

Observed diets run something like this when the family is making money:

Family of eight—Boiled cabbage, baked sweet potatoes, creamed carrots, beans, fried dough, jelly, tea.
Family of seven—Beans, baking-powder biscuits, jam, coffee.
Family of six—Canned salmon, cornbread, raw onions.
Family of five—Biscuits, fried potatoes, dandelion greens, pears.

These are dinners. It is to be noticed that even in these flush times there is no milk, no butter. The major part of the diet is starch. In slack times the diet becomes all starch, this being the cheapest way to fill up. Dinners during lay-offs are as follows:

Family of seven—Beans, fried dough.
Family of six—Fried cornmeal.
Family of five—Oatmeal mush.
Family of eight (there were six children)—Dandelion greens and boiled potatoes.

It will be seen that even in flush times the possibility of remaining healthy is very slight. The complete absence of milk for the children is responsible for many of the diseases of malnutrition. Even pellagra is far from unknown.

The preparation of food is the most primitive. Cooking equipment usually consists of a hole dug in the ground or a kerosene can with a smoke vent and open front. If the adults have been working 10 hours in the fields or in the packing sheds they do not want to cook. They will buy canned goods as long as they have money, and when they are low in funds they will subsist on half-cooked starches.

The problem of childbirth among the migrants is among the most terrible. There is no prenatal care of the mothers whatever, and no possibility of such care. They must work in the fields until they are physically unable or, if they do not work, the care of the other children and of the camp will not allow the prospective mothers any rest.

In actual birth the presence of a doctor is a rare exception. Sometimes in the squatters' camps a neighbor woman will help at the birth. There will be no sanitary precautions nor hygienic arrangements. The child will be born on newspapers in the dirty bed. In case of a bad presentation requiring surgery or forceps, the mother is practically condemned to death. Once born, the eyes of the baby are not treated, the endless medical attention lavished on middle-class babies is completely absent.

The mother, usually suffering from malnutrition, is not able to produce breast milk. Sometimes the baby is nourished on canned milk until it can eat fried dough and cornmeal. This being the case, the infant mortality is very great.

The following is an example: Wife of family with three children. She is 38; her face is lined and thin and there is a hard glaze on her eyes. The three children who survive were born prior to 1929, when the family rented a farm in Utah. In 1930 this woman bore a child which lived four months and died of "colic."

In 1931 her child was born dead because "a han' truck fulla boxes run inta me two days before the baby come." In 1932 there was a miscarriage. "I couldn't carry the baby 'cause I was sick." She is ashamed of this. In 1933 her baby lived a week. "Jus' died. I don't know what of." In 1934 she had no pregnancy. She is also a little ashamed of this. In 1935 her baby lived a long time, nine months.

"Seemed for a long time like he was gonna live. Big strong fella it seemed like." She is pregnant again now. "If we could get milk for um I guess it'd be better." This is an extreme case, but by no means an unusual one.

Textual Questions

1. What tone does Steinbeck take as he opens his essay, describing a family, its possessions, and its home? Why? What effect does this tone have on how readers respond to the essay?

2. What steps is the government taking, according to Steinbeck, to help the migrant workers? Which of these steps are most/least effective?

3. How does Steinbeck describe the Arvin camp and its inhabitants? To what purpose does he put this example? How effective is it, compared to the description of the families with which Steinbeck opens his essay?

Rhetorical Questions

4. Steinbeck's description of life in the squatters' camps is a description of disease, despair, and death. What is the effect of these descriptions on a reader? Do the details come together to have a cumulative effect, or are the details so overwhelming that a reader is unable to respond?

5. Why in a descriptive essay with such a sorrowful subject, does Steinbeck write of both pride and dignity among the workers? What does the inclusion of these two topics do to a reader's image of the migrant workers?

6. If the federal camps are vastly better than other camps for migrant workers, then what are the arguments against founding more of them? What interests are best served by *not* creating federal camps? How would anyone benefit from keeping migrant workers in the conditions described by Steinbeck early in his essay?

Intertextual Questions

7. How does Steinbeck's description of the lives of migrant workers compare to the description of the lives of Wal-Mart Associates in "Everyday Low Wages"?

8. How does Steinbeck's description of the three families in the squatters' camps compare to Charles Young's description of losers (later in this chapter)? Does Steinbeck's description and analysis of the plight of the migrant workers refute or support Young's definition of losing in America?

Thinking Beyond the Text

9. In America, is the worth of an individual defined by the value of the work he or she does? Should it be? If worth is dependent upon employment, then what happens to the unemployed?

10. Steinbeck's description of the lives of migrant workers is more than seven decades old, but are there groups in America which could be described in similar ways even now? Who?

For Writing & Discussion

11. Searching online (and analyzing the results of your searching), find answers to these questions: What is the unemployment rate in the state you live in? Who is most likely to be unemployed? Of those who are unemployed, how many receive some form of state assistance—welfare, subsidized daycare, and so forth? Aside from state assistance, what help is available to the unemployed, such as job training? What help seems most or least effective? In an essay, present the results of your research and analysis. How large is the unemployment problem in your state? What is being done—effectively or ineffectively—to reduce this problem?

S C O T T   R U S S E L L   S A N D E R S

Scott Russell Sanders (1945–) is a Distinguished Professor of English at Indiana University, where he has taught since 1971. Sanders writes both nonfiction and fiction and has won many awards, including the Associated Writing Programs Award in Creative Nonfiction, the Kenyon Review Award for Literary Excellence, the Great Lakes Book Award, the Ohioana Book Award, the Lannan Literary Award, the PEN Syndicated Fiction Award, and the Gamma Award. He has written 20 books, including six children's books, and his writing appears regularly in national publications such as *Audubon*, *Harper's*, *Orion*, and *Utne Reader*. His work is in more than 50 anthologies.

"The Men We Carry in Our Minds" was published in Sanders's essay collection *The Paradise of Bombs* in 1987, but it tells about his experiences as a scholarship student at Brown University in the 1960s. Sanders, who came from a poor rural community, first began considering the intersection of class and gender roles upon talking to affluent feminist classmates about the rights of white collar men—rights the women's movement claims for women as well—and the rights of blue collar men, "toilers and warriors," around whom he had lived all his life.

The Men We Carry in Our Minds

∾ Prereading Question

Think about the men in your life when you were a child. What did they do for a living? How did their work affect the rest of their lives? What did the women around you in your childhood do for a living? How were they affected by their work?

The first men, besides my father, I remember seeing were black convicts and white guards, in the cottonfield across the road from our farm on the outskirts of Memphis. I must have been three or four. The prisoners wore dingy gray-and-black zebra suits, heavy as canvas, sodden with sweat. Hatless, stooped, they chopped weeds in the fierce heat, row after row, breathing the acrid dust of boll-weevil poison. The overseers wore dazzling white shirts and broad shadowy hats. The oiled barrels of their shotguns flashed in the sunlight. Their faces in memory are utterly blank. Of course those men, white and black, have become for me an emblem of racial hatred. But they have also come to stand for the twin poles of my early vision of manhood—the brute toiling animal and the boss.

When I was a boy, the men I knew labored with their bodies. They were marginal farmers, just scraping by, or welders, steel workers, carpenters; they swept floors, dug ditches, mined coal, or drove trucks, their forearms ropy with muscle; they trained horses, stoked furnaces, built tires, stood on assembly lines wrestling parts onto cars and refrigerators. They got up before light, worked all day long whatever the weather, and when they came home at night they looked as though somebody had been whipping them. In the evenings and on weekends they worked on their own places, tilling gardens that were lumpy with clay, fixing broken-down cars, hammering on houses that were always too drafty, too leaky, too small.

The bodies of the men I knew were twisted and maimed in ways visible and invisible. The nails of their hands were black and split, the hands tattooed with scars. Some had lost fingers. Heavy lifting had given many of them finicky backs and guts weak from hernias. Racing against conveyor belts had given them ulcers. Their ankles and knees ached from years of standing on concrete. Anyone who had worked for long around machines was hard of hearing. They squinted, and the skin of their faces was creased like the leather of old work gloves. There were times, studying them, when I dreaded growing up. Most of them coughed, from dust or cigarettes, and most of them drank cheap wine or whiskey, so their eyes looked bloodshot and bruised. The fathers of my friends always seemed older than the mothers. Men wore out sooner. Only women lived into old age.

As a boy I also knew another sort of men, who did not sweat and break down like mules. They were soldiers, and so far as I could tell they scarcely worked at all. During my early school years we lived on a military base, an arsenal in Ohio, and every day I saw GIs in the guardshacks, on the stoops of barracks, at the wheels of olive drab Chevrolets. The chief fact of their lives was boredom. Long after I left the Arsenal I came to recognize the sour smell the soldiers gave off as that of souls in limbo. They were all waiting— for wars, for transfers, for leaves, for promotions, for the end of their hitch—like so many braves waiting for the hunt to begin. Unlike the warriors of older tribes, however, they would have no say about when the battle would start or how it would be waged. Their waiting was broken only when they practiced for war. They fired guns at targets, drove tanks across the churned-up fields of the military reservation, set off bombs in the wrecks of old fighter planes. I knew this was all play. But I also felt certain that when the hour for killing arrived, they would kill. When the real shooting started, many of them would die. This was what soldiers were *for,* just as a hammer was for driving nails.

Warriors and toilers: those seemed, in my boyhood vision, to be the chief destinies for men. They weren't the only destinies, as I learned from having a few male teachers, from reading books, and from watching television. But the men on television—the politicians, the astronauts, the generals, the savvy lawyers, the philosophical doctors, the bosses who gave orders to both soldiers and laborers—seemed as remote and unreal to me as the figures in tapestries. I could no more imagine growing up to become one of these cool, potent creatures than I could imagine becoming a prince.

A nearer and more hopeful example was that of my father, who had escaped from a red-dirt farm to a tire factory, and from the assembly line to the front office. Eventually he dressed in a white shirt and tie. He carried himself as if he had been born to work with his mind. But his body, remembering the earlier years of slogging work, began to give out on him in his fifties, and it quit on him entirely before he turned sixty-five. Even such a partial escape from man's fate as he had accomplished did not seem possible for most of the boys I knew. They joined the Army, stood in line for jobs in the smoky plants, helped build highways. They were bound to work as their fathers had worked, killing themselves or preparing to kill others.

A scholarship enabled me not only to attend college, a rare enough feat in my circle, but even to study in a university meant for the children of the rich. Here I met for the first time young men who had assumed from birth that they would lead lives of comfort and power. And for the first time I met women who told me that men were guilty of having kept all the joys and privileges of the earth for themselves. I was baffled. What privileges? What joys? I thought about the maimed, dismal lives of most of the men back home. What had they stolen from their wives and daughters? The right to go five days a week, twelve months a year, for thirty or forty years to a steel mill or a coal mine? The right to drop bombs and die in war? The right to feel every leak in the roof, every gap in the fence, every cough in the engine, as a wound they must mend? The right to feel, when the layoff comes or the plant shuts down, not only afraid but ashamed?

I was slow to understand the deep grievances of women. This was because, as a boy, I had envied them. Before college, the only people I had ever known who were interested in art or music or literature, the only ones who read books, the only ones who ever seemed to enjoy a sense of ease and grace were the mothers and daughters. Like the menfolk, they fretted about money, they scrimped and made-do. But, when the pay stopped coming in, they were not the ones who had failed. Nor did they have to go to war, and that seemed to me a blessed fact. By comparison with the narrow, ironclad days of fathers, there was an expansiveness, I thought, in the days of mothers. They went to see neighbors, to shop in town, to run errands at school, at the library, at church. No doubt, had I looked harder at their lives, I would have envied them less. It was not my fate to become a woman, so it was easier for me to see the graces. Few of them held jobs outside the home, and those who did filled thankless roles as clerks and waitresses. I didn't see, then, what a prison a house could be, since houses seemed to me brighter, handsomer places than any factory. I didn't realize—because such things were never spoken of—how often women suffered from men's bullying. I did learn about the wretchedness of abandoned wives, single mothers, widows; but I also learned about the wretchedness of lone men. Even then I could see how exhausting it was for a mother to cater all day to the needs of young children. But if I had been asked, as a boy, to choose between tending a baby and tending a machine, I think I would have chosen the baby. (Having now tended both, I know I would choose the baby.)

So I was baffled when the women at college accused me and my sex of having cornered the world's pleasures. I think something like my bafflement has been felt by other boys (and by girls as well) who grew up in dirt-poor farm country, in mining country, in black ghettos, in Hispanic barrios, in the shadows of factories, in Third World nations—any place where the fate of men is as grim and bleak as the fate of women. Toilers and warriors. I realize now how ancient these identities are, how deep the tug they exert on men, the undertow of a thousand generations. The miseries I saw, as a boy, in the lives of nearly all men I continue to see in the lives of many—the body-breaking toil, the tedium, the call to be tough, the humiliating powerlessness, the battle for a living and for territory.

When the women I met at college thought about the joys and privileges of men, they did not carry in their minds the sort of men I had known in my childhood. They thought of their fathers, who were bankers, physicians, architects, stockbrokers, the big wheels of the big cities. These fathers rode the train to work or drove cars that cost more than any of my childhood houses. They were attended from morning to night by female helpers, wives and nurses and secretaries. They were never laid off, never short of cash at month's end, never lined up for welfare. These fathers made decisions that mattered. They ran the world.

The daughters of such men wanted to share in this power, this glory. So did I. They yearned for a say over their future, for jobs worthy of their abilities, for the right to live at peace, unmolested, whole. Yes, I thought, yes yes. The difference between me and these daughters was that they saw me, because of my sex, as destined from birth to become like their fathers, and therefore as an enemy to their desires. But I knew better. I wasn't an enemy, in fact or in feeling. I was an ally. If I had known, then, how to tell them so, would they have believed me? Would they now?

Textual Questions

1. Why does Sanders open with the story of white guards and black prisoners? How does that story serve to set up the rest of his essay?

2. In paragraph 2, Sanders uses a long list of jobs to describe the hard work of the men who surrounded him in his childhood. What effect

does this list have on a reader? Where else does Sanders use this same basic stylistic strategy? To what effect?

3. How does Sanders use his father to pull the various parts of his essay together? How does he use his mother to do this, too?

Rhetorical Questions

4. Where in his essay does Sander address these topics: race, social class, and gender? How does he connect these three disparate topics into a single, focused essay?

5. How does Sanders align his own interests with those of the women he meets in college—women who dislike and distrust him because they have a different understanding of what he represents than he does?

6. At the top of page 446, Sanders makes a parenthetical point about tending babies versus tending to machinery. What point is he making here, and how effectively does he make this point? Would the essay be strengthened or weakened if this point were removed?

Intertextual Questions

7. How do Sanders's arguments about socio-economic status and power compare to the arguments made by Barbara Ehrenreich in "In Which I am Offered a 'Job'"?

8. In what ways are the lives of the men and women Sanders describes from his childhood similar to the lives of the men and women described by John Steinbeck?

Thinking Beyond the Text

9. At your school, what percentage of the student body is men? Women? In your chosen major, what is the percentage breakdown of men and women? What would account for the numbers breaking down as they do?

10. Consider the adult men and women who were around you during your childhood. What socioeconomic status were they, and what work did they do? Did they see themselves as people with power, people who controlled their lives, or did they see themselves as victims of some larger forces? Or did they see themselves some other way entirely?

For Writing & Discussion

11. As a child, what did you know about the working world? What did the adults you knew do for a living? How did you think about them and

what they did when they went to work? Pick one of the adults you knew as a child, preferably someone with whom you spent a great deal of time over several years—and describe your understanding of that person's work. What did you know about him/her and how did you know it?

CHARLES M. YOUNG

Charles M. Young (1951–) is a freelance journalist and former associate editor of *Rolling Stone* where he was referred to as the "Reverend Charles M. Young" and known for his irreverent prose. (In one early article, Young tells readers, whom he has accused of ignoring his musical recommendations, that the Ramones' use of "nigh-pure power chords and satire [. . .]—though enormously satisfying to smart people like myself—was too threatening to dumb people like you.") Since leaving *Rolling Stone* in the 1980s, Young has expanded his topics beyond music and, at least in some pieces, adopted a more serious tone.

Young's other accomplishments include a master's degree in journalism from Columbia University, nine months as executive editor at the now-defunct *Musician* magazine, and a stint as the bass player in the 1990s rock band Iron Prostate. He writes regularly for *Atlantic Monthly*, *Playboy*, *Guitar World*, and *Men's Journal*, where "Losing: An American Tradition" was first published in 2000. It was later anthologized in *Best American Sports Writing 2000*. Young has interviewed many notable public figures including Noam Chomsky, Howard Zinn, Ralph Nader, and Beavis and Butt-Head.

He is currently working on a book about the punk band the Butthole Surfers and has taken up Zen meditation.

Losing: An American Tradition

∾ Prereading Question

In what ways is competition a part of your life—from sports to online gaming to getting good grades? Is competition a healthy force that drives you to do better than you would do on your own? Or is competition a damaging element in your life, something that causes you more worry and anxiety than anything else?

Somebody's got to lose. Don't we all know the feeling?
—B.C.

Just North of the north end zone of Blackshear Stadium at Prairie View A&M University in Texas is an unmarked grave.

"We buried last season," said Greg Johnson, the Prairie View Panthers' coach, during a break in football practice. "In March, just before the start of spring practice, we had them write down everything they didn't like about the past—being 0–9 last season, the record losing streak. We used the example of Superman, this guy that nobody could stop unless you got him near some green kryptonite. We asked them, 'Well, what's your green kryptonite? What is it that keeps you from doing what you need to do in the classroom and on the football field? Is it a female? Is it your friends? Is it a drug? Is it alcohol? Lack of dedication? Not enough time in the weight room? You got a nagging injury that you didn't rehab?' Whatever they wanted to bury, they wrote it down on a piece of paper. And the last thing we did, we looked at the HBO tape. The segment that Bryant Gumbel did on us for *Real Sports,* where they laughed at us and ridiculed us as the worst team in the country—'How does it feel to be 0–75 since 1989?' or whatever it was at that point. I said, 'That's the last we'll ever see of that tape,' and I put it in a big plastic trash bag with the paper. We took it to a hole I had dug near the gate, and we threw it in. All the players and all the coaches walked by. Some of them kicked dirt on it, some of them spit on it. Some of them probably thought I was crazy. I said, 'This is the last time we're going to talk about last year. This is the last time we're going to talk about the losing streak. The past is dead, and anything that's dead ought to be buried. It's history. It's gone.' "

That took place in September 1998, when Prairie View's NCAA-record losing streak stood at 0–77. Now skip ahead to the postgame interviews of the January 9, 1999, AFC playoff game, in which the Denver Broncos beat the Miami Dolphins 38–3. Shannon Sharpe, the Broncos' tight end, called Miami's Dan Marino a "loser." Universally, this was viewed as a mortal insult, far beyond the bounds of acceptable trash talk.

"I cringed when I read that," said Mike Shanahan, the Broncos' coach. "I was really disappointed. Dan Marino's no loser."

So Sharpe, much humbled (and probably at Shanahan's insistence), groveled after the next Denver practice: "In no way, shape, or form is Dan Marino a loser. Dan, if I offended you or your family, your wife, your kids, your mother or father, your brothers or sisters, I apologize. I stand before you and sincerely apologize. I would never disrespect you as a person."

Which is odd. Football, along with every other major sport, is constructed to create losers. On any given game day, half the teams win, and half the teams lose. By the end of the playoffs, exactly one team can be called a winner, while thirty other teams are, literally, losers. So given that 96.7 percent of the players in the NFL can't help but be losers, why should calling somebody a loser be considered such an egregious violation of propriety that the guy who won must debase himself in public for pointing out that the guy who lost, lost?

Consider *Patton,* winner of the 1971 Academy Award for Best Picture and a favorite of coaches, team owners, and politicians ever since. It opens with George C. Scott standing in front of a screen-size American flag in the role of General George S. Patton, giving a pep talk to his troops. Using sports imagery to describe war (mirroring the sportswriters who use war imagery to describe sports), Patton delivers a succinct sociology lesson: "Americans love a winner, and will not tolerate a loser. Americans play to win all the time. I wouldn't give a hoot in hell for a man who lost and laughed. That's why Americans have never lost, and will never lose a war— because the very thought of losing is hateful to Americans."

Which is a view of most Americans that's shared by most Americans. Certain women of my acquaintance refer to men who score low on the Multiphasic Boyfriend Potentiality Scale as losers. *Cosmopolitan* has run articles on how to identify and dump losers before they have a chance to inseminate the unwary.

In *Jerry Maguire,* Tom Cruise suffers his worst humiliation when he spots his former girlfriend dating a rival agent at a *Monday Night Football* game. She makes an L with her fingers and mouths, "Loser."

In *American Beauty,* Kevin Spacey announces during his midlife crisis: "Both my wife and daughter think I'm this gigantic loser."

In *Gods and Monsters,* Lolita Davidovich, playing a bartender, dismisses the possibility of sex with her sometime lover, played by Brendan Fraser: "From now on, you're just another loser on the other side of the bar."

In *200 Cigarettes,* set in the ostensibly alternative subculture of Manhattan's Lower East Side, Martha Plimpton works herself into a state of despair considering the idea that no one will come to her New Year's Eve party. Then, considering an even worse possibility, she weeps: "All the losers will be here!"

At the real-life sentencing last February of Austin Offen for bashing a man over the head with a metal bar outside a Long Island night club, Assistant District Attorney Stephen O'Brien said that Offen was "vicious and brutal. He's a coward and a loser." Offen, displaying no shame over having crippled a man for life, screamed back: "I am not a loser!"

In his book *Turbo Capitalism: Winners and Losers in the Global Economy,* Edward Luttwak equates losing with poverty and observes that Americans believe that "failure is the result not of misfortune or injustice, but of divine disfavor."

I could list a hundred more examples, but you get the point.

Shannon Sharpe, in using the word *loser,* implied that Dan Marino was: unworthy of sex or love or friendship or progeny, socially clueless, stupid, parasitical, pathetic, poverty-stricken, cowardly, violent, felonious, bereft of all forms of status, beneath all consideration, hated by himself, hated by all good Americans, hated by God. And Dan Marino is one of the best quarterbacks ever to play football. [. . .]

The literal truth is, I may not be the worst college football player of all time. I've claimed that occasionally in the course of conversation, but I may be only the worst college football player of 1972. I was definitely the worst player on the Macalester College Scots of St. Paul, Minnesota, and we lost all of our games that season by an aggregate score of 312–46. The team went on to win one game in each of the following two seasons (after I graduated), then set the NCAA record with fifty straight losses. So, strictly speaking, the losing streak wasn't my fault. I do think I made a huge contribution to the atmosphere of despair and futility that led to the losing streak. I think that as Prairie View was to the '90s, Macalester was to the '70s. But in the final analysis, I think that over two decades at both schools, some athlete may have failed more than I did.

I may therefore merely be one of the worst, a weaker distinction that makes me even more pathetic than whoever it is who can make the case for sole possession of the superlative—if someone wants to make that case. [. . .]

A couple of weeks after I left PVU, the Panthers won a football game, 14–12, against Langston University, ending the losing streak at eighty. The campus erupted in a victory celebration that was typical of the orgiastic outpourings that people all over the world feel entitled to after an important win. I was happy for them. I felt bad for Langston, having to carry the stigma of losing to the losers of all time.

There being virtually no literature of losing, I became obsessed with reading books about winning, some by coaches and some by self-help gurus. All of them advised me to forget about losing. If you want to join the winners, they said, don't dwell on your past humiliations. Then I thought of George Santayana's dictum: "Those who forget the past are condemned to repeat it." So if I remembered losing, I'd be a loser. And if I forgot losing, I'd be a loser. Finally, I remembered a dictum of my own: "Anybody who quotes George Santayana about repeating the past will soon be repeating even worse clichés."

That Christmas, my local Barnes & Noble installed a new section called "Lessons from the Winners." Publishers put out staggering numbers of books with "win" in the title (as they do with *Zen and Any Stupid Thing*), and they make money because there's a bottomless market of losers who want to be winners. Almost all of these books are incoherent lists of aphorisms and advice on how to behave like a CEO ("Memorize the keypad on your cell phone so you dial and drive without taking your eyes off the road"). Most of these books are written by men who have made vast fortunes polluting the groundwater and screwing people who work for a living, and these men want to air out their opinions, chiefly that they aren't admired enough for polluting the groundwater and screwing people who work for a living. I thought of the ultimate winner,

Howard Hughes, who was once the richest man in the world, who had several presidents catering to his every whim, who stored his feces in jars. I got more and more depressed.

Maybe I was just hypnotized by my own history of failure, character defects, and left-wing politics. Maybe what I needed was a pep talk. Maybe what I needed was Ray Pelletier, a motivational speaker who has made a lot of money raising morale for large corporations and athletic teams. Pelletier, a member of the National Speakers Association Hall of Fame, wrote a book, *Permission to Win,* that Coach Johnson had recommended to me. Basically an exhortation to feel like a winner no matter how disastrous your circumstances happen to be, the book deals with losing as a problem of individual psychology. I asked Pelletier if he thought that the emphasis American culture places on competition was creating vast numbers of people who, on the basis of having lost, quite logically think of themselves as losers.

"I don't think you have to think of yourself as a loser," he said. "I think competition causes you to reach down inside and challenges you to be at your very best. The key is not to beat yourself. If you're better than I am and you're more prepared to play that day, you deserve to win. I have no problem with that. Every time I give a presentation, I want it to be better than the last one. I want to be sure I'm winning in everything that I do."

Yeah, but wasn't there a difference between excellence and winning?

"No, that's why I say that if I get beat by a team that's more talented, I don't have a problem with that."

When one guy won, was he not inflicting defeat on the other guy?

"No. I'll give you an example. The first time I worked with a female team before a big game, I was getting them all riled up and playing on their emotions, telling them how they deserved this win and how they worked really hard. A rah-rah, goose-pimple kind of speech. Just before we went on the court, the point guard said, 'Can I ask a question? Haven't the girls in the other locker room worked really hard, too? Don't they deserve to win, too?' "

Pelletier then veered off into a discussion of how the game teaches you about life, of how his talks are really for fifteen years down the line when your wife leaves you, or the IRS calls for an audit, or you can't pay your mortgage. I asked him how he replied to the point guard in the locker room.

"I said, 'Absolutely the other team deserves to win, too. What we have to do is find out if we can play together tonight as a team.' See, that's the biggest challenge facing corporate America today. We talk about teamwork but we don't understand the concept of team. Most of us have never been coached in anything. We've been taught, but not coached. There's a big difference. Great coaches challenge you to play at your best. The key is, you're in the game, trying to better yourself."

But Bill Parcells, the former coach of the Jets, is famous for saying that you are what the standings say you are . . .

"Winning is playing at your best. Do you know the number-one reason why an athlete plays his sport? Recognition. Once you understand that, everything else becomes easy. Lou Holtz says that win means 'What's Important Now.' "

That's just standard practice in books about winning, I told him. They redefine the word to include all human behavior with a good connotation. In *The Psychology of Winning*, Dr. Denis Waitley writes that winning is "unconditional love." Winning could hardly be a more conditional form of love. You are loved if you win, and scorned if you lose.

"I don't believe that."

If athletes play for recognition, don't they want to be recognized as winners? And if you've lost, won't you be recognized as a loser?

"I don't think they're labeled that way."

By the press? By the fans?

"To me, unconditional love is an aspect of winning. The problem is that you and I have not been trained to think positively. In one of my corporate seminars, I ask people to write down all the advantages there are to being negative. I want them to think about it seriously. It's an exercise that can take fifteen or twenty minutes, and then they have the 'Aha!' There is no advantage to negative thinking. None. And yet the biggest problem we face in America is low self-esteem."

Low self-esteem has its uses, though. Whenever you see a couple of male animals on a PBS nature special duking it out for the privilege of having sex with some female of the species, one of the males is going to dominate and the other male is either going to die or get low self-esteem and crawl off making obsequious gestures to the winner. The evolutionary value is obvious: Fight to the death and your genes die with you; admit you're a loser and you may recover to fight again or find another strategy for passing on your genes through some less selective female. Species in which one alpha male gets to have sex with most of the females—elephant seals are a good example—need a lot of low self-esteem among the beta males for social stability.

With 1 percent of the population possessing more wealth than the bottom 95 percent, the American economy operates a lot like a bunch of elephant seals on a rock in the ocean. And it simply must mass-produce low self-esteem in order to maintain social stability amidst such colossal unfairness.

According to the World Health Organization, mood disorders are the number-one cause worldwide of people's normal activities being impaired. In the United States alone, the WHO estimates, depression costs $53 billion a year in worker absenteeism and lost productivity. While that's a hell of a market for Ray Pelletier and the National Speakers Association, which has more than three thousand people giving pep talks to demoralized companies and sports teams, doledout enthusiasm is a palliative, not a curative. In fact, demoralization is a familiar management tool; the trick is creating just enough. Too much and you have work paralysis, mass depression, and suicide. Too little and you have a revolution. Ever hear a boss brag that he doesn't *have* ulcers, he *gives* them? He's making sure his employees are demoralized enough to stay in their place.

Consider the book *Shame and Pride,* by Dr. Donald L. Nathanson, a psychiatrist and the executive director of the Silvan S. Tomkins Institute in Philadelphia. Starting in the mid-1940s, Dr. Tomkins watched babies for thousands of hours and made a convincing case that humans are born preprogrammed with nine "affects"—potential states of emotion that can be triggered by a stimulus or memory. These affects are: interest-excitement, enjoyment-joy, surprise-startle, fear-terror, distress-anguish, anger-rage, dissmell (*dissmell* is similar to *distaste,* but related to the sense of smell), disgust, and shame-humiliation. These affects "amplify" an outside stimulus or memory to give you an increase in brain activity that eventually becomes full-blown emotion.

Until recent years, shame was the "ignored emotion" in psychology. But a few people, Nathanson most prominently, built on Tomkins and discovered the key to . . . well, not quite everything, but an awful lot. According to Tomkins and Nathanson, shame erupts whenever "desire outruns fulfillment." An impediment arises to the two positive affects (interest-excitement and enjoyment-joy), and suddenly your eyes drop, your head and body slump, your face turns red, and your brain is confused to the point of paralysis. [. . .]

So I called up Nathanson and asked if he had any thoughts about athletes and [*Shame. . . .*]

Sports events are often described as a morality play, I said, but there's nothing moral about it. Sports decide who will participate in power and who will be humiliated.

"That's understandable when you recognize that our sense of place in society is maintained by shame. Keeping people in their place is maintaining them at certain levels of shaming interaction at which they can be controlled. This issue of winning and losing, it throws us. It defines our identity, doesn't it?"

Calling someone a loser is probably the worst insult in the United States today.

"If you're calling someone that, the person must live in a perpetual state of shame. The only way he can live with himself is to have massive denial, disavowal of his real identity. He has to make his way in the world somehow, and he can't walk around constantly thinking of himself as a loser. Yet if someone in our eyes is a loser and he refuses to admit it, this is narcissism. He has an identity that can't be sustained by consensual validation."

Is there some value in competition, in creating all these losers?

"When you're young and you're learning and it's just a bunch of guys playing a game, that's not shame. That's just figuring out that Billy is faster than Johnny. When parents and schools and bureaucracies start getting involved and demanding wins, then it gets pathological."

Playing for the Chicago Bears, the Philadelphia Eagles, and the Dallas Cowboys from 1961 to 1972, Mike Ditka was All-Pro five times as a tight end, won an NFL championship with the Bears in 1963, won Super Bowl VI with the Cowboys, and was elected to the Hall of Fame. As the coach of the Bears from 1982 to 1992, he won Super Bowl XX with an 18–1 team generally acknowledged as one of the greatest ever and was named Coach of the Year twice. As the coach of the New Orleans Saints for the past three seasons, he had a 15–33 record and is now most vividly remembered for flipping off the fans and grabbing his crotch during and after an especially inept defeat. (He was fined $20,000.) I asked him if he thinks that football fans are inherently interested in the game, or in the hallucination of power they get when their team wins?

"They relate to the winning. Well, you can't say they aren't interested in the game. They watch the game. But the excitement comes from winning."

When football players snap at journalists in the locker room after a loss . . .

"That's only human nature. They probably snap at their wives when they get home, too. Are you saying, Does losing bother people? Sure it does. It's no different from a guy at IBM who loses a sale to a competitor. You just don't like to lose. Most people want to be associated with winning. When you work your butt off and don't get the results you want, you might be a little short-tempered as a coach. That's only life. But that's no different than any other segment of life. Football parallels society, period."

I've noticed that the worst thing you can call somebody in the United States is a loser.

"No. The word *quitter* is the worst thing you can call somebody. Lemme ask you something: If two teams play all year, and they reach the Super Bowl, the one that loses is a loser? Come on."

"I don't like the term. . . . It's not fair. I think as long as you compete and you do your best, if the other team is better, I don't think you really lose. I think you lose when you quit trying."

The problem with declaring a quitter to be a lower form of dirt than a loser is that you're still stigmatizing almost everybody. Studies indicate that up to 90 percent of children drop out of organized competitive sports by the age of fifteen. Extrapolating from my own experience, I would guess that they don't enjoy feeling like losers so that the jocks can feel like winners. Since they associate intense physical activity with feeling rotten, they grow up having problems with obesity and depression, both of which have become epidemic in the United States.

As Mike Ditka would say, it's not fair. But I think there's a way out. And I think that Alfie Kohn has seen it. Kohn, an educational philosopher, has helped inspire the opposition to standardized tests, an especially pernicious form of competition. His first book, *No Contest: The Case Against Competition*, cites study after study demonstrating that competition hinders work, play, learning, and creativity in people of all ages. (In fact, there is almost no evidence to the contrary in the social sciences.) The book is wonderfully validating for anyone who ever had doubts about the ostensible fun of gym class and spelling bees. I told Kohn that in my experience, people get unhinged when you question the value of making other people fail.

"Absolutely. It calls into question America's state religion, which is practiced not only on the playing field but in the classroom and the workplace, and even in the family. The considerable body of evidence demonstrating that this is self-defeating makes very little impression on people who are psychologically invested in a desperate way in the idea of winning. The real alternative to being number one is not being number two, but being able to dispense with these pathological ratings altogether. If people accepted the research on the destructiveness of competition, you wouldn't see all these books teaching how to compete more effectively. I hear from a lot of teachers and parents whose kids fall apart after losing in spelling bees and awards assemblies, and they feel dreadful about it. The adults start to think, *Hmm, maybe competition isn't such a good thing, at least for those kids.* It took me years to see that the same harms were being visited upon the winners. The kids who win are being taught that they are good only to the extent that they continue to beat other people. They're being taught that other people are obstacles to their own success, which destroys a sense of community as effectively as when we teach losers that lesson. And finally, the winners are being taught that the point of what they are doing is to win, which leads to diminished achievement and interest in what they are doing. What's true for kids is also true for adults. It's not a problem peculiar to those who lose. We're all losers in the race to win."

I'm very blessed that way. I didn't have the perspective to spell it out like Alfie Kohn, but I've known I was a total loser since my first college football practice. I've admitted it here publicly, and I am free. You, you're probably holding on to some putrefying little shred of self-esteem, denying that you're a loser in a country inhabited by Bill Gates and 260 million losers. You're still hoping to beat your friend at racquetball and make him feel as bad as you do when you lose, still looking to flatten some rival with just the right factoid in an argument, still craving the sports car in the commercial that accurately announces, "There's no such thing as a gracious winner." Give up, I say. Join me. Losers of the world, unite! You have nothing to lose but your shame.

Textual Questions

1. Why does Young open his essay with the story of an "unmarked grave"? How does this story set up the main points he makes about winning and losing/being a winner/loser?

2. What examples does Young use to show that hatred of losers is very common in American culture? How effectively does he use these examples?

3. What definitions of "winner" and "loser" does Young offer (directly or through quoting other sources)? With which definitions do you most agree and why? Which definitions of "winning" and "losing" seem most foolish to you?

Rhetorical Questions

4. How and where in the essay does Young use his personal experience with losing to help develop his points? How effective is his use of personal experience? How well does it connect with the other sections of this essay (such as the list of films and the discussion of books on winning)?

5. On page 450, Young gives readers a long, long list of what it means to call someone a "loser." How much of this list seems reasonable to you, and how much of it seems unreasonable? Do Americans actually attach this much meaning to the term "loser," or does Young go too far (maybe way, way too far)?

6. According to Young, what are the costs of losing—physically, emotionally, and financially? Which of these costs is best explained in the essay? Why? Which is least effectively explained? Why?

Intertextual Questions

7. Would Eric Schlosser agree with Young's argument about what it means to be a loser in America? Why/why not?

8. Assume that Young is correct when he asserts that Americans hate losers and hate to define themselves as losers. In President Bush's speech "We Have Seen the State of Our Union" and President Carter's speech "Energy Crisis," how does each President implicitly define Americans as good, strong, capable people who can overcome any challenge—as winners?

Thinking Beyond the Text

9. List the sports that are most popular among Americans. In how many of these sports do teams regularly end their games/matches in tied

scores? In how many of these sports is it even *possible* to end a game/match in a tied score? How do these results of your analysis of the sports on your list confirm/refute Young's arguments about winning and losing in America?

10. Think about the social divisions in your high school, middle school, or elementary school. Were even these social groupings somehow built on winning and losing? That is, were the people at the "top" of the social ladder the winners in some way while the people at the "bottom" of the social ladder were losers?

For Writing & Discussion

11. In an essay, describe some time when you took part in a competition— of any kind, from informal gaming with your friends to actual, formal competition. Describe what it was like either to win or to lose. As the winner/loser, what did you think and feel? How did your winning/losing make your competition feel? Are your feelings different now than they were then?

ERIC SCHLOSSER

Eric Schlosser (1959–) is the author of *Fast Food Nation: The Dark Side of the All-American Meal,* a 2001 exposé of the American fast food industry that was on the *New York Times* bestseller list for over two years. Schlosser has been nominated for several journalism awards and has won a National Magazine Award and Sidney Hillman Foundation Award for Reporting.

"Success," an excerpt from *Fast Food Nation,* reveals how franchises are owned and run. Focusing on Little Caesar's, McDonald's, and Subway, it looks at the effect of franchising on small businesses and small-business owners. As this chapter shows, *Fast Food Nation* looks beyond the culinary aspects of the fast food industry to the constellation of social, economic, and historical factors that surround it.

Schlosser's other work includes articles in *Rolling Stone,* the *Atlantic Monthly,* and *Mother Jones,* and the 2003 book *Reefer Madness: Sex, Drugs, and Cheap Labor in the American Black Market.* He is currently working on a book about the American prison system. The book will expand on his 1998 article in the *Atlantic Monthly,* "The Prison Industrial Complex" which, like his other writing, examines how a range of interests—legal, political, economic, and social—interact to feed an increase in the prison population despite a decrease in violent crime.

Schlosser and co-author Charles Wilson wrote a preteen adaptation of *Fast Food Nation* called *Chew on This: Everything You Don't Want to Know About Fast Food* (2006).

Success

∾ Prereading Question

What does it mean to "succeed" in America? Is being a success the same as being a winner? Are there general qualities that signal success—socially, economically, physically, spiritually, psychologically, and so on? Does success mean different things for members of different social groups? For different groups of workers?

Matthew Kabong glides his '83 Buick LeSabre through the streets of Pueblo, Colorado, at night, looking for a trailer park called Meadowbrook. Two Little Caesars pizzas and a bag of Crazy Bread sit in the back seat. "Welcome to my office," he says, reaching down, turning up the radio, playing some mellow rhythm and blues. Kabong was born in Nigeria and raised in Atlanta, Georgia. He studies electrical engineering at a local college, hopes to own a Radio Shack some day, and delivers pizzas for Little Caesars four or five nights a week. He earns the minimum wage, plus a dollar for each delivery, plus tips. On a good night he makes about fifty bucks. We cruise past block after block of humble little houses, white-washed and stucco, built decades ago, with pickup trucks in the driveways and children's toys on the lawns. Pueblo is the southern-most city along the Front Range, forty miles from Colorado Springs, but for generations a world apart, largely working class and Latino, a town with steel mills that was never hip like Boulder, bustling like Denver, or aristocratic like Colorado Springs. Nobody ever built a polo field in Pueblo, and snobs up north still call it "the asshole of Colorado."

We turn a corner and find Meadowbrook. All the trailers look the same, slightly ragged around the edges, lined up in neat rows. Kabong parks the car, and when the radio and the headlights shut off, the street suddenly feels empty and dark. Then somewhere a dog barks, the door of a nearby trailer opens, and light spills onto the gravel driveway. A little white girl with blonde hair, about seven years old, smiles at this big Nigerian bringing pizza, hands him fifteen dollars, takes the food, and tells him to keep the change. Behind her there's movement in the trailer, a brief glimpse of someone else's life, a tidy kitchen, the flickering shadows of a TV. The door closes, and Kabong heads back to the Buick, his office, beneath a huge sky full of stars. He has a $1.76 tip in his pocket, the biggest tip so far tonight.

The wide gulf between Colorado Springs and Pueblo—a long-standing social, cultural, political, and economic division—is starting to narrow. As you drive through the streets of Pueblo, you can feel the change coming, something palpable in the air. During the 1980s, the city's unemployment rate hovered at about 12 percent, and not much was built. New things now seem to appear every month, new roads around the Pueblo Mall, new movie theaters, a new Applebee's, an Olive Garden, a Home Depot, a great big Marriott. Subdivisions are creeping south from Colorado Springs along I-25, turning cattle ranches into street after street of ranch-style homes. Pueblo has not boomed yet; it seems ready, right on the verge, about to become more like the rest.

The Little Caesars where Kabong works is in the Belmont section of town, across the street from a Dunkin' Donuts, not far from the University of Southern Colorado campus. The small square building the Little Caesars occupies used to house a Godfather's Pizza and before that, a Dairy Bar. The restaurant has half a dozen brown Formica tables, red brick walls, a gumball machine near the counter, white-and-brown flecked linoleum floors. The place is clean but has not been redecorated for a while. The customers who drop by or call for pizza are college students, ordinary working people, people with large families, and the poor. Little Caesars pizzas are big and inexpensive, often providing enough food for more than one meal.

Five crew members work in the kitchen, putting toppings on pizzas, putting the pizzas in the oven, getting drinks, taking orders over the phone. Julio, a nineteen-year-old kid with two kids of his own, slides a pizza off the old Blodgett oven's conveyor belt. He makes $6.50 an hour. He enjoys making pizza. The ovens have been automated at Little Caesars and at the other pizza chains, but the pizzas are still handmade. They're not just pulled out of a freezer. Scott, another driver, waits for his next delivery. He wears a yellow Little Caesars shirt that says, "Think Big!" He's working here to pay off student loans and the $4,000 debt on his 1988 Jeep. He goes to the University of Southern Colorado and wants to attend law school, then join the FBI. Dave Feamster, the owner of the restaurant, is completely at ease behind the counter, hanging out with his Latino employees and customers— but at the same time seems completely out of place.

Feamster was born and raised in a working-class neighborhood of Detroit. He grew up playing in youth hockey leagues and later attended college in Colorado Springs on an athletic scholarship. He was an All-American during his senior year, a defenseman picked by the Chicago Black Hawks in the college draft. After graduating from Colorado College with a degree in business, Feamster played in the National Hockey League, a childhood dream come true. The Black Hawks reached the playoffs during his first three years on the team, and Feamster got to compete against some of his idols, against Wayne Gretzky and Mark Messier. Feamster was not a big star, but he loved the game, earned a good income, and traveled all over the country; not bad for a blue-collar kid from Detroit.

On March 14, 1984, Feamster was struck from behind by Paul Holmgren during a game with the Minnesota North Stars. Feamster never saw the hit coming and slammed into the boards head first. He felt dazed, but played out the rest of the game. Later, in the shower, his back started to hurt. An x-ray revealed a stress fracture of a bone near the base of his spine. For the next three months Feamster wore a brace that extended from his chest to his waist. The cracked bone didn't heal. At practice sessions the following autumn, he didn't feel right. The Black Hawks wanted him to play, but a physician at the Mayo Clinic examined him and said, "If you were my son, I'd say, find another job; move on." Feamster worked out for hours at the gym every day, trying to strengthen his back. He lived with two other Black Hawk players. Every morning the three of them would eat breakfast together, then his friends would leave for practice, and Feamster would find himself just sitting there at the table.

The Black Hawks never gave him a good-bye handshake or wished him good luck. He wasn't even invited to the team Christmas party. They paid off the remainder of his contract, and that was it. He floundered for a year, feeling lost. He had a business degree, but had spent most of his time in college playing hockey. He didn't know anything about business. He enrolled in a course to become a travel agent. He was the only man in a classroom full of eighteen- and nineteen-year-old women. After three weeks, the teacher asked to see him after class. He went to her office, and she said, "What are you doing here? You seem like a sharp guy. This isn't for you." He dropped out of travel agent school that day, then drove around aimlessly for hours, listening to Bruce Springsteen and wondering what the hell to do.

At a college reunion in Colorado Springs, an old friend suggested that Feamster become a Little Caesars franchisee. Feamster had played on youth hockey teams in Detroit with the sons of the company's founder, Mike Ilitch. He was too embarrassed to call the Ilitch family and ask for help. His friend dialed the phone. Within weeks, Feamster was washing dishes and making pizzas at Little Caesars restaurants in Chicago and Denver. It felt a long, long way from the NHL. Before gaining the chance to own a franchise, he had to spend months learning every aspect of the business. He was trained like any other assistant manager and earned $300 a week. At first he wondered if this was a good idea. The Little Caesars franchise fee was $15,000, almost all the money he had left in the bank.

∽

Devotion to a New Faith

Becoming a franchisee is an odd combination of starting your own business and going to work for someone else. At the heart of a franchise agreement is the desire by two parties to make money while avoiding risk. The franchisor wants to expand an existing company without spending its own funds. The franchisee wants to start his or her own business without going it alone and risking everything on a new idea. One provides a brand name, a business plan, expertise, access to equipment and supplies. The other puts up the money and does the work. The relationship has its built-in tensions. The franchisor gives up some control by not wholly owning each operation; the franchisee sacrifices a great deal of independence by having to obey the company's rules. Everyone's happy when the profits are rolling in, but when things go wrong the arrangement often degenerates into a mismatched battle for power. The franchisor almost always wins.

Franchising schemes have been around in one form or another since the nineteenth century. In 1898 General Motors lacked the capital to hire salesmen for its new automobiles, so it sold franchises to prospective car dealers, giving them exclusive rights to certain territories. Franchising was an ingenious way to grow a new company in a new industry. "Instead of the company paying the salesmen," Stan Luxenberg, a franchise historian, explained, "the salesmen would pay the company." The automobile, soft drink, oil, and motel industries later relied upon franchising for much of their initial growth. But it was the fast food industry that turned franchising into a business model soon emulated by retail chains throughout the United States.

Franchising enabled the new fast food chains to expand rapidly by raising the hopes and using the money of small investors. Traditional methods of raising capital were not readily available to the founders of these chains, the high school dropouts and drive-in owners who lacked "proper" business credentials. Banks were not eager to invest in this new industry; nor was Wall Street. Dunkin' Donuts and Kentucky Fried Chicken were among the first chains to start selling franchises. But it was McDonald's that perfected new franchising techniques, increasing the chain's size while maintaining strict control of its products.

Ray Kroc's willingness to be patient, among other things, contributed to McDonald's success. Other chains demanded a large fee up front, sold off the rights to entire territories, and earned money by selling supplies directly to their franchises. Kroc wasn't driven by greed; the initial McDonald's franchising fee was only $950. He seemed much more interested in making a sale than in working out financial details, more eager to expand McDonald's than to make a quick buck. Indeed, during the late 1950s, McDonald's franchisees often earned more money than the company's founder.

After selling many of the first franchises to members of his country club, Kroc decided to recruit people who would operate their own restaurants, instead of wealthy businessmen who viewed McDonald's as just another investment. Like other charismatic leaders of new faiths, Kroc asked people to give up their former lives and devote themselves fully to McDonald's. To test the commitment of prospective franchisees, he frequently offered them a restaurant far from their homes and forbade them from engaging in other businesses. New franchisees had to start their lives anew with just one McDonald's restaurant. Those who contradicted or ignored Kroc's directives would never get the chance to obtain a second McDonald's. Although Kroc could be dictatorial, he also listened carefully to his franchisees' ideas and complaints. Ronald McDonald, the Big Mac, the Egg McMuffin, and the Filet-O-Fish sandwich were all developed by local franchisees. Kroc was an inspiring, paternalistic figure who looked for people with "common sense," "guts and staying power," and "a love of hard work." Becoming a successful McDonald's franchisee, he noted, didn't require "any unusual aptitude or intellect." Most of all, Kroc wanted loyalty and utter devotion from his franchisees—and in return, he promised to make them rich.

While Kroc traveled the country, spreading the word about McDonald's, selling new franchises, his business partner, Harry J. Sonneborn, devised an ingenious strategy to ensure the chain's financial success and provide even more control of its franchisees. Instead of earning money by demanding large royalties or selling supplies, the McDonald's Corporation became the landlord for nearly all of its American franchisees. It obtained properties and leased them to franchisees with at least a 40 percent markup. Disobeying the McDonald's Corporation became tantamount to violating the terms of the lease, behavior that could lead to a franchisee's eviction. Additional rental fees were based on a restaurant's annual revenues. The new franchising strategy proved enormously profitable for the McDonald's Corporation. "We are not basically in the food business," Sonneborn once told a group of Wall Street investors, expressing an unsentimental view of McDonald's that Kroc never endorsed. "We are in the real estate business. The only reason we sell fifteen cent hamburgers is because they are the greatest producer of revenue from which our tenants can pay us our rent."

In the 1960s and 1970s McDonald's was much like the Microsoft of the 1990s, creating scores of new millionaires. During a rough period for the McDonald's Corporation, when money was still tight, Kroc paid his secretary with stock. June Martino's 10 percent stake in McDonald's later allowed her to retire and live comfortably at an oceanfront Palm Beach estate. The wealth attained by Kroc's secretary vastly exceeded that of the McDonald brothers, who relinquished their claim to 0.5 percent of the chain's annual revenues in 1961. After taxes, the sale brought Richard and Mac McDonald about $1 million each. Had the brothers held on to their share of the company's revenues, instead of selling it to Ray Kroc, the income from it would have reached more than $180 million a year.

Kroc's relationship with the McDonalds had been stormy from the outset. He deeply resented the pair, claiming that while he was doing the hard work—"grinding it out, grunting and sweating like a galley slave"— they were at home, reaping the rewards. His original agreement with the McDonalds gave them a legal right to block any changes in the chain's operating system. Until 1961 the brothers retained ultimate authority over the restaurants which bore their name, a fact that galled Kroc. He had to borrow $2.7 million to buy out the McDonalds; Sonneborn secured financing for the deal from a small group of institutional investors headed by Princeton University. As part of the buyout, the McDonald brothers insisted upon keeping their San Bernardino restaurant, birthplace of the chain. "Eventually I opened a McDonald's across the street from that store, which they had renamed The Big M," Kroc proudly noted in his memoir, "and it ran them out of business."

The enormous success of McDonald's spawned imitators not only in the fast food industry, but throughout America's retail economy. Franchising proved to be a profitable means of establishing new companies in everything from the auto parts business (Meineke Discount Mufflers) to the weight control business (Jenny Craig International). Some chains grew through franchised outlets; others through company-owned stores; and McDonald's eventually expanded through both. In the long run, the type of financing used to grow a company proved less crucial than other aspects of the McDonald's business model: the emphasis on simplicity and uniformity, the ability to replicate the same retail environment at many locations. In 1969, Donald and Doris Fisher decided to open a store in San Francisco that would sell blue jeans the way McDonald's, Burger King, and KFC sold food. They aimed at the youth market, choosing a name that would appeal to counterculture teens alienated by the "generation gap." Thirty years later, there were more than seventeen hundred company-owned Gap, GapKids, and babyGap stores in the United States. Among other innovations, Gap Inc. changed how children's clothing is marketed, adapting its adult fashions to fit toddlers and even infants.

As franchises and chain stores opened across the United States, driving along a retail strip became a shopping experience much like strolling down the aisle of a supermarket. Instead of pulling something off the shelf, you pulled into a driveway. The distinctive architecture of each chain became its packaging, as strictly protected by copyright law as the designs on a box of soap. The McDonald's Corporation led the way in the standardization of America's retail environments, rigorously controlling the appearance of its restaurants inside and out. During the late 1960s, McDonald's began to tear down the restaurants originally designed by Richard McDonald, the buildings with golden arches atop their slanted roofs. The new restaurants had brick walls and mansard roofs. Worried about how customers might react to the switch, the McDonald's Corporation hired Louis Cheskin—a prominent design consultant and psychologist—to help ease the transition. He argued against completely eliminating the golden arches, claiming they had great Freudian importance in the subconscious mind of consumers. According to Cheskin, the golden arches resembled a pair of large breasts: "mother McDonald's breasts." It made little sense to lose the appeal of that universal, and yet somehow all-American, symbolism. The company followed Cheskin's advice and retained the golden arches, using them to form the *M* in McDonald's.

Free Enterprise with Federal Loans

Today it costs about $1.5 million to become a franchisee at Burger King or Carl's Jr.; a McDonald's franchisee pays roughly one-third that amount to open a restaurant (since the company owns or holds the lease on the property). Gaining a franchise from a less famous chain—such as Augie's, Buddy's Bar-B-Q, Happy Joe's Pizza & Ice Cream Parlor, the Chicken Shack, Gumby Pizza, Hot Dog on a Stick, or Tippy's Taco House—can cost as little as $50,000. Franchisees often choose a large chain in order to feel secure; others prefer to invest in a smaller, newer outfit, hoping that chains like Buck's Pizza or K-Bob's Steakhouses will become the next McDonald's.

Advocates of franchising have long billed it as the safest way of going into business for yourself. The International Franchise Association (IFA), a trade group backed by the large chains, has for years released studies "proving" that franchisees fare better than independent businessmen. In 1998 an IFA survey claimed that 92 percent of all franchisees said they were "successful." The survey was based on a somewhat limited sample: franchisees who were still in business. Franchisees who'd gone bankrupt were never asked if they felt successful. Timothy Bates, a professor of economics at Wayne State University, believes that the IFA has vastly overstated the benefits of franchising. A study that Bates conducted for a federal loan agency found that within four to five years of opening, 38.1 percent of new franchised businesses had failed. The failure rate of new independent businesses during the same period was 6.2 percent lower. According to another study, three-quarters of the American companies that started selling franchises in 1983 had gone out of business by 1993. "In short," Bates argues, "the franchise route to self-employment is associated with higher business failure rates and lower profits than independent business ownership."

In recent years conflicts between franchisees and franchisors have become much more common. As the American market for fast food grows more saturated, restaurants belonging to the same chain are frequently being put closer to one another. Franchisees call the practice "encroachment" and angrily oppose it. Their sales go down when another outlet of the same chain opens nearby, drawing away customers. Most franchisors, on the other hand, earn the bulk of their profits from royalties based on total sales—and more restaurants usually means more sales. In 1978 Congress passed the first federal legislation to regulate franchising. At the time, a few chains were operated much like pyramid schemes. They misrepresented potential risks, accepted large fees up front, and bilked millions of dollars from small investors. The FTC now requires chains to provide lengthy disclosure statements that spell out their rules for prospective franchisees. The statements are often a hundred pages long, with a lot of small print.

Federal law demands full disclosure prior to a sale, but does not regulate how franchises are run thereafter. Once a contract is signed, franchisees are largely on their own. Although franchisees must obey corporate directives, they are not covered by federal laws that protect employees. Although they must provide the investment capital for their businesses, they are not covered by the laws that protect independent businessmen. And although they must purchase all their own supplies, they are not covered by consumer protection laws. It is perfectly legal under federal law for a fast food chain to take kickbacks (known as "rebates") from its suppliers, to open a new restaurant next door to an existing franchisee, and to evict a franchisee without giving cause or paying any compensation.

According to Susan Kezios, president of the American Franchise Association, the contracts offered by fast food chains often require a franchisee to waive his or her legal right to file complaints under state law; to buy only from approved suppliers, regardless of the price; to sell the restaurant only to a buyer approved by the chain; and to accept termination of the contract, for any cause, at the discretion of the chain. When a contract is terminated, the franchisee can lose his or her entire investment. Franchisees are sometimes afraid to criticize their chains in public, fearing reprisals such as the denial of additional restaurants, the refusal to renew a franchise contract at the end of its twenty-year term, or the immediate termination of an existing contract. Ralston-Purina once terminated the contracts of 642 Jack in the Box franchisees, giving them just thirty days to move out. A group of McDonald's franchisees, unhappy with the chain's encroachment on their territories, has formed an organization called Consortium Members, Inc. The group issues statements through Richard Adams, a former McDonald's franchisee, because its members are reluctant to disclose their names.

The fast food chains are periodically sued by franchisees who are upset about encroachment, about inflated prices charged by suppliers, about bankruptcies and terminations that seemed unfair. During the 1990s, Subway was involved in more legal disputes with franchisees than any other chain—more than Burger King, KFC, McDonald's, Pizza Hut, Taco Bell, and Wendy's combined. Dean Sager, a former staff economist for the U.S. House of Representatives' Small Business Committee, has called Subway the "worst" franchise in America. "Subway is the biggest problem in franchising," Sager told *Fortune* magazine in 1998, "and emerges as one of the key examples of every [franchise] abuse you can think of."

Subway was founded in 1965 by Frederick DeLuca, who borrowed $1,000 from a family friend to open a sandwich shop in Bridgeport, Connecticut. DeLuca was seventeen at the time. Today Subway has about fifteen thousand restaurants, second only to McDonald's, and opens about a thousand new ones every year. DeLuca is determined to build the world's largest fast food chain. Many of the complaints about Subway arise from its unusual system for recruiting new franchisees. The chain relies on "development agents" to sell new Subway franchises. The development agents are not paid a salary by Subway; they are technically independent contractors, salesmen whose income is largely dependent on the number of Subways that open in their territory. They receive half of the franchise fee paid by new recruits, plus one-third of the annual royalties, plus one-third of the "transfer fee" paid whenever a restaurant is resold. Agents who fail to meet their monthly sales quotas are sometimes forced to pay the company for their shortfall. They are under constant pressure to keep opening new Subways, regardless of how that affects the sales of Subways that are already operating nearby. According to a 1995 investigation by Canada's *Financial Post*, Subway's whole system seems "almost as geared to selling franchises as it is to selling sandwiches."

It costs about $100,000 to open a Subway restaurant, the lowest investment required by any of the major fast food chains. The annual royalty Subway takes from its franchisees—8 percent of total revenues—is among the highest. A top Subway executive has acknowledged that perhaps 90 percent of the chain's new franchisees sign their contracts without reading them and without looking at the FTC filings. Roughly 30 to 50 percent of Subway's new franchisees are immigrants, many of whom are not fluent in English. In order to earn a decent living, they must often work sixty to seventy hours a week and buy more than one Subway.

In November of 1999, Congressman Howard Coble, a conservative Republican from North Carolina, introduced legislation that would make franchisors obey the same fundamental business principles as other American companies. Coble's bill would for the first time obligate franchise chains to act in "good faith," a basic tenet of the nation's Uniform Commercial Code. The bill would also place limits on encroachment, require "good cause" before a contract can be terminated, permit franchisees to form their own associations, allow them to purchase from a variety of suppliers, and give them the right to sue franchisors in federal court. "We are not seeking to penalize anyone," Coble said, before introducing his plan for franchise reform. "We only seek to bring some order and sanity to a segment of our economy which is growing and may be growing out of control." Iowa adopted similar franchise rules in 1992, without driving Burger King or McDonald's out of the state. Nevertheless, the IFA and the fast food chains strongly oppose Coble's bill. The IFA has hired Allen Coffey, Jr., the former general counsel of the House Judiciary Committee, and Andy Ireland, a former Republican congressman who was the ranking member of the House Small Business Committee, to help thwart greater federal regulation of franchising. While in Congress, Ireland had criticized franchisees who sought legal reforms, calling them "whiny butts" who came running to the government instead of taking responsibility for their own business mistakes.

After congressional hearings were held on Coble's bill in 1999, the IFA claimed in a press release that federal regulation of franchising would interfere with "free enterprise contract negotiations" and seriously harm one of the most vital and dynamic sectors of the American economy. "Small businesses and franchising succeed by relying on marketplace solutions," said Don DeBolt, the president of the IFA. Despite its public opposition to any government interference with the workings of the free market, the IFA has long supported programs that enable fast food chains to expand using government-backed loans.

For more than three decades the fast food industry has used the Small Business Administration (SBA) to finance new restaurants—thereby turning a federal agency that was created to help independent, small businesses into one that eliminates them. A 1981 study by the General Accounting Office found that the SBA had guaranteed 18,000 franchise loans between 1967 and 1979, subsidizing the launch of new Burger Kings and McDonald's, among others. Ten percent of these franchise loans ended in default. During the same period, only 4 percent of the independent businesses receiving SBA loans defaulted. In New York City, the SBA backed thirteen loans to Burger King franchisees; eleven of them defaulted. The chain was "experimenting," according to a congressional investigation, using government-backed loans to open restaurants in marginal locations. Burger King did not lose money when these restaurants closed. American taxpayers had covered the franchise fees, paid for the buildings, real estate, equipment, and supplies.

According to a recent study by the Heritage Foundation, the SBA is still providing free investment capital to some of the nation's largest corporations. In 1996, the SBA guaranteed almost $1 billion in loans to new franchisees. More of those loans went to the fast food industry than to any other industry. Almost six hundred new fast food restaurants, representing fifty-two different national chains, were launched in 1996 thanks to government-backed loans. The chain that benefited the most from SBA loans was Subway. Of the 755 new Subways opened that year, 109 relied upon the U.S. government for financing.

The World Beyond Pueblo

The franchise agreement that Dave Feamster signed in 1984 gave him the exclusive right to open Little Caesars restaurants in the Pueblo area. In addition to the franchise fee, he had to promise the company 5 percent of his annual revenues and contribute an additional 4 percent to an advertising pool. Most Little Caesars franchisees have to supply the capital for the purchase or construction of their own restaurants. Since Feamster did not have the money, the company gave him a loan. Before selling a single pizza, he was $200,000 in debt.

Although Feamster had spent four years in college at Colorado Springs, less than an hour away, he'd never visited Pueblo. He rented a small house near his new restaurant, on a block full of steelworkers. It was the sort of neighborhood where he'd grown up. Feamster expected to stay there for just a few months, but wound up living there alone for six years, pouring all his energy into his business. He opened the restaurant every morning and closed it at night, made pizzas, delivered pizzas, swept the floors, did whatever needed to be done. His lack of experience in the restaurant business was offset by his skill at getting along with all sorts of different people. When an elderly customer phoned him and complained about the quality of a pizza, Feamster listened patiently and then hired her to handle future customer complaints.

It took Feamster three years to pay off his initial debt. Today he owns five Little Caesars restaurants: four in Pueblo and one in the nearby town of Lamar. His annual revenues are about $2.5 million. He earns a good income, but lives modestly. When I visited a Colorado Springs restaurant operated by a rival pizza chain, the company flew in a publicist from New York City to accompany me at all times. Feamster gave me free rein to interview his employees in private and to poke around his business for as long as I liked. He says there's nothing to hide. His small office behind the Belmont store, however, is in an advanced state of disarray, crammed with stacks of sagging banker's boxes. While his competitors use highly computerized operating systems that instantaneously display a customer's order on TV monitors in the kitchen, Feamster's restaurants remain firmly planted in the era of ballpoint pens and yellow paper receipts.

Feamster has established strong roots in Pueblo. His wife is a schoolteacher, a fifth-generation native of the city. His community work occupies much of his time and doesn't seem driven by publicity needs. He donates money to local charities and gives speeches at local schools. He pays some of the college tuition of his regular employees, so long as they maintain a 3.0 grade average or higher. And he recently helped organize the city's first high school hockey team, which draws players from throughout the district. Feamster paid for uniforms and equipment, and he serves as an assistant coach. The majority of the players are Latino, from the sorts of backgrounds that do not have a long and illustrious tradition on the ice. The team regularly plays against high schools from Colorado Springs, which have well-established hockey programs. The Pueblo hockey team has made it to the playoffs in two of its first three seasons.

Despite all the hard work, the future success of Feamster's business is by no means guaranteed. Little Caesars is the nation's fourth-largest pizza chain, but has been losing market share since 1992. Hundreds of Little Caesars restaurants have closed. Many of the chain's franchisees, unhappy with the company's management, have formed an independent association. Some franchisees have withheld their contributions to the chain's advertising pool. Feamster feels loyal to the Ilitch family and to the company that gave him a break, but worries about the reduced spending on ads. Even more worrying is the recent arrival of Papa John's in Pueblo. Papa John's is the fastest-growing pizza chain in the United States, adding about thirty new restaurants every month. In the fall of 1998, Papa John's opened its first unit in Pueblo, and the following year, it opened three more.

The fate of Dave Feamster's restaurants now depends on how his employees serve his customers at every meal. Rachel Vasquez, the manager of the Belmont Little Caesars, takes her job seriously and does her best to motivate crew members. She's worked for Feamster since 1988. She was sixteen at the time, and no one else would hire her. The following year she bought a car with her earnings. She now makes about $22,000 a year for a fifty-hour workweek. She also receives health insurance. And Feamster annually contributes a few thousand dollars to her pension fund. Rachel met her husband at this Little Caesars in 1991, when she was a co-manager and he was a trainee. "We made more than pizza," she says, laughing. Her husband's now employed as a clerk for an industrial supply company. They have two small children. A grandmother looks after the kids while Rachel is at work. At the back of the kitchen, inside a small storage closet, Rachel has a makeshift office. There's a black table, a chair, a battered filing cabinet, a list of employee phone numbers taped to a box, and a sign that says "Smile."

Fourteen of Feamster's employees meet at the Belmont store around seven o'clock on a Tuesday morning. Feamster has tickets to an event called "Success" at the McNichols Sports Arena in Denver. It starts at eight-fifteen in the morning, runs until six in the evening, and features a dozen guest speakers, including Henry Kissinger, Barbara Bush, and former British Prime Minister John Major. The event is being sponsored by a group called "Peter Lowe International, the Success Authority." The tickets cost Feamster $90 each. He's rented a van and given these employees the day off. He doesn't know exactly what to expect, but hopes to provide a day to remember. It seems like an opportunity not to be missed. Feamster wants his young workers to see "there's a world out there, a whole world beyond the south side of Pueblo."

The parking lot at the McNichols Arena is jammed. The event has been sold out for days. Men and women leave their cars and walk briskly toward the arena. There's a buzz of anticipation. Public figures of this stature don't appear in Denver every week. The arena is filled with eighteen thousand people, and almost every single one of them is white, clean-cut, and prosperous—though not as prosperous as they'd like. These people want more. They are salespeople, middle managers, franchisees. In the hallways and corridors where you'd normally buy hot dogs and Denver Nuggets hats, *Peter Lowe's Success Yearbook* is being sold for $19.95, "American Sales Leads on CD-Rom" is available for $375, and Zig Ziglar is offering "Secrets of Closing the Sale" (a twelve-tape collection) for $120 and "Everything of Zig's" (fifty-seven tapes, four books, and eleven videos) for the discount price of $995, thanks to "Special Day of Seminar Pricing."

Peter Lowe has been staging these large-scale events since 1991. He's a forty-two-year-old "success authority" based in Tampa, Florida. His parents were Anglican missionaries who gave up the material comforts of their middle-class life in Vancouver to work among the poor. Lowe was born in Pakistan and educated at the Woodstock School in Mussoorie, India, but he chose a different path. In 1984 he quit his job as a computer salesman and organized his first "success seminar." The appearance of Ronald Reagan at one of these events soon encouraged other celebrities to endorse Peter Lowe's work. In return, he pays them between $30,000 and $60,000 for a speech—for about half an hour of work. Among those who've recently joined Peter Lowe onstage are: George Bush, Oliver North, Barbara Walters, William Bennett, Colin Powell, Charlton Heston, Dr. Joyce Brothers, and Mario Cuomo.

Rachel Vasquez can hardly believe that she's sitting among so many people who own their own businesses, among so many executives in suits and ties. The Little Caesars employees have seats just a few yards from the stage. They've never seen anything like this. Though the arena's huge, it seems like these fourteen fast food workers from Pueblo can almost reach out and touch the famous people who appear at the podium.

"You are the elite of America," Brian Tracy, author of *The Psychology of Selling,* tells the crowd. "Say to yourself: I like me! I like me! I like me!" He is followed by Henry Kissinger, who tells some foreign policy anecdotes. And then Peter Lowe's attractive wife, Tamara, leads the audience in a dance contest; the winner gets a free trip to Disneyland. Four contestants climb onstage, dozens of beach balls are tossed into the crowd, the sound system blasts the Beach Boys' "Surfin' USA," and eighteen thousand people start to dance. Barbara Bush is next, arriving to "Fanfare for the Common Man," her smile projected onto two gigantic television screens. She tells a story that begins, "We had the whole gang at Kennebunkport . . ."

When Peter Lowe arrives, fireworks go off and multicolored confetti drops from the ceiling. He is a slender, red-haired man in a gray, double-breasted suit. He advises the audience to be cheerful, to train themselves for courage, to feed themselves with optimism, and never quit. He recommends his tape series, "Success Talk," on sale at the arena, which promises a monthly interview with "one of the most successful people of our time." After a short break, he reveals what is ultimately necessary to achieve success. "Lord Jesus, I need You," Peter Lowe asks the crowd to pray. "I want you to come into my life and forgive me for the things I've done."

Lowe has broken from the Christianity of his parents, a faith that now seems hopelessly out of date. The meek shall no longer inherit the earth; the go-getters will get it and everything that goes with it. The Christ who went among the poor, the sick, the downtrodden, among lepers and prostitutes, clearly had no marketing savvy. He has been transfigured into a latter-day entrepreneur, the greatest superstar salesperson of all time, who built a multi-national outfit from scratch. Lowe speaks to the crowd about mercy. But the worship of selling and of celebrity infuses his literature, his guest lists, his radio shows and seminars. "Don't network haphazardly," Peter Lowe preaches in his $19.95 *Peter Lowe's Success Yearbook*. "Set goals to meet key people. Imagine yourself talking to them. Plan in advance what questions to ask them . . . When there is an important individual you want to network with, be prepared to say something insightful to them that shows you're aware of their achievements . . . Everyone loves to receive a present. It's hard to be resistant or standoffish to someone who has just given you a nice gift . . . Adopt the attitude of a superstar . . . Smile. A smile tells people you like them, are interested in them. What an appealing message to send!" These are the teachings of his gospel, the good news that fills arenas and sells cassettes.

As the loudspeakers play the theme song from *Chariots of Fire*, Lowe wheels Christopher Reeve onstage. The crowd wildly applauds. Reeve's handsome face is framed by longish gray hair. A respirator tube extends from the back of his blue sweatshirt to a square box on his wheelchair. Reeve describes how it once felt to lie in a hospital bed at two o'clock in the morning, alone and unable to move and thinking that daylight would never come. His voice is clear and strong, but he needs to pause for breath after every few words. He thanks the crowd for its support and confesses that their warm response is one reason he appears at these events; it helps to keep his spirits up. He donates the speaking fees to groups that conduct spinal cord research.

"I've had to leave the physical world," Reeve says. A stillness falls upon the arena; the place is silent during every pause. "By the time I was twenty-four, I was making millions," he continues. "I was pretty pleased with myself . . . I was selfish and neglected my family . . . Since my accident, I've been real-izing . . . that success means something quite different." Members of the audience start to weep. "I see people who achieve these conventional goals," he says in a mild, even tone. "*None of it matters.*"

His words cut through all the snake oil of the last few hours, calmly and with great precision. Everybody in the arena, no matter how greedy or eager for promotion, all eighteen thousand of them, know deep in their hearts that what Reeve has just said is true—too true. Their latest schemes, their plans to market and subdivide and franchise their way up, whatever the cost, the whole spirit now gripping Colorado, vanish in an instant. Men and women up and down the aisles wipe away tears, touched not only by what this famous man has been through but also by a sudden awareness of something hollow about their own lives, something gnawing and unfulfilled.

Moments after Reeve is wheeled off the stage, Jack Groppel, the next speaker, walks up to the microphone and starts his pitch, "Tell me friends, in your lifetime, have you ever been on a diet?"

Textual Questions

1. What topic does Schlosser cover in each section of his essay? How do these sections (a) connect to one another directly and indirectly and (b) build upon one another to make Schlosser's point about success in America?

2. How does Schlosser describe Pueblo, Colorado? Why? What purpose does this description serve in his overall essay?

3. How does Schlosser describe the process of becoming a franchisee? What tone does his description seem to take? How does his description of this process connect with his profiles of Matthew Kabong and Dave Feamster? And what do any of these descriptions have to do with Pueblo, Colorado, and the meaning of "success" in America?

Rhetorical Questions

4. How does Schlosser use the profiles of various people to make his argument more than a simple hard-luck story of individual success and failure?

5. What details make the profile/history of Ray Kroc most effective? How does the description/history of Kroc and McDonald's connect to Schlosser's larger point in the essay?

6. What point is Schlosser making in his essay when he describes Christopher Reeve speaking to the crowd? How does this point connect to the argument made before Reeve's appearance? How does this point connect with the final paragraph of Schlosser's essay?

Intertextual Questions

7. Schlosser's description of the franchise business is less than flattering. How does his description compare to George Miller's description of Wal-Mart's business practices in "Everyday Low Wages"?

8. Compare Schlosser's use of profiles of individual people to the profiles used by Scott Russell Sanders in "The Men We Carry in Our

Minds" and John Steinbeck's profiles of individuals/families in "Harvest Gypsies." Are the uses of profiles similar or different in these three disparate texts? Which of them uses profiles most/least effectively and why?

Thinking Beyond the Text

9. Make a list of the businesses you pass on your route to and from school (or along some other route you regularly travel). Of the businesses on your list, how many are regional, national, or international franchises? How many of them are locally owned? Which do you tend to frequent most and why?

10. Consider all of the positives and negatives Schlosser describes about franchising—from the independence of being one's own boss to the borderline financial exploitation, the long hours and hard work (with only slim chances of success), and so on. Interview either a local franchise manager or teacher of business, and ask her/him about these positives and negatives. Are there other positives and negatives to franchising that Schlosser doesn't mention?

For Writing & Discussion

11. Visit the home page of the International Franchise Association (http://www.franchise.org). In an essay compare and contrast the ways in which Schlosser describes this group to the ways in which it describes itself on its home page. Which description seems more credible to you and why?

BENJAMIN CHEEVER

Benjamin Cheever is a writer and a former senior editor at *Reader's Digest.* He left the magazine in 1988 to publish a book of letters by his father, the famous novelist John Cheever, then began writing novels himself. He also has written for the *New York Times, The New Yorker, The Nation,* and *National Review.*

Cheever's first two novels, *The Plagiarist* (1994) and *The Partisan* (1994), were well received, but then he experienced a career slump and wrote a nonfiction book, *Selling Ben Cheever: Back to Square One in a Service Economy* (2001), from which "Nobody Beats the Wiz" is excerpted.

Written during the low spot in his fiction-writing career—his second novel had been published but his third had been repeatedly rejected—*Selling Ben Cheever* chronicles his attempts to get and keep a minimum-wage job. Nobody Beats the Wiz, referred to in this chapter, is an electronics store. Also mentioned is Cheever's wife, Janet Maslin, whose salary as a film critic supported their family during Cheever's foray into the working-for-low-wages class.

Since writing *Selling Ben Cheever* he has published two more novels, *Famous After Death* (2000) and *The Good Nanny* (2004), and he is currently working on a second nonfiction book, *Strides*, which is about running.

Nobody Beats the Wiz: "What Do People Fear More Than Death?"

Prereading Question

List the jobs you've had in your lifetime—from babysitting to clerking to being an intern or teaching assistant for one of your professors. What training was involved before you could "officially" perform the duties of each job? What training, skills, and experience did each job give you that led to another (hopefully better) job? Does every job necessarily (a) involve training of some kind and (b) prepare you to move on and do something else?

When I was training for a job at Nobody Beats the Wiz, I went one evening to see my wife participate in a panel discussion at the 92nd Street Y. Leonard Lopate moderated, and the panel's topic was "The Critics and the Criticized". The director Arthur Penn (*Bonnie and Clyde, Little Big Man*) was also on the panel and seemed notable for having missed the part in his artistic development where one learns arrogance and bad manners. From the audience, I could see Penn cheerfully deprecating himself and pouring everybody's water. The screenwriter Lorenzo Semple Jr. brought up a quotation from one of Janet's reviews, which he recited as an example of what he didn't like in critics. He was witty, but his voice was distorted by anger. He wouldn't sit up straight, nor would he pull his chair into the table.

After the last question from the audience, there was a rush for the stage. One of the people who came up had seen Janet on another panel. "That was a great night for film," he said. Then he pumped his arm in the air. He was wearing a wash-and-wear shirt buttoned to the throat. No necktie. "I love *Taxi Driver*," he said. "What a great movie! What a greeeaat movie!"

After most of the crowd and some of the panelists had departed, Lopate suggested that the rest of us go out for a drink. By this time a stranger had attached himself to Janet. He was wearing a leather jacket, scarf, and black jeans. Everything torn. He had his face about two and a half inches away from hers. I heard him say that he was an actor. I believe he had a screenplay with him. "I'm just trying to talk to Mizz Maselin," he said when somebody suggested that he might not join us for a drink.

Lopate was accompanied by a female producer who remembered me from the time I was on his radio show for one of my novels. "I was the person who read the book," she said. She was strikingly attractive, with hair just streaking gray. Remember when gray hair meant a woman was old? Now gray hair is apt to be a sign of vitality. The producer had a pleasant boyfriend; he had cigarettes. As a backsliding former smoker I was enjoying myself immensely, walking along the sidewalk, talking and smoking, but I was worried about Janet. The actor didn't seem to be quieting down at all. I expressed my concern. The producer said that if I wanted, she could help Janet. "Could you?" I asked. "That's my job," she said. So she sailed up to the actor, and words were exchanged. The next thing I knew, the actor had backed away and was violently giving both women the finger. "You don't need to diss me," he said, "I only wanted to talk to Mizz Maselin." Lopate interjected himself. Then I introduced myself to the actor as Janet's husband. We shook hands. I seem to have said something about how we were all human beings.

At this point it was decided that maybe a drink wasn't such a grand idea, and we all headed off in different directions.

I mention this only because the next day, when I showed up for class at the Nobody Beats the Wiz building at Thirty-first Street and Sixth Avenue, I saw the same actor. I looked away immediately and afterwards never allowed eye contact. I heard him ask if they were accepting applications. He and I got in the elevator together. I kept my face to the wall. Since I was already in class, and he was just applying for a job, we would head off in different directions when we got out of the elevator. I was terrified he'd recognize me before we reached our floors. He didn't. Nor did I ever see him again.

Status changes the way we see. And yet status changes quickly, and can be willfully disguised. When I first started the process of applying for the Wiz job at a different store in Scarsdale, New York, the entrance through which I walked was being swept furiously with a push broom by a man with black hair to his shoulders. I later learned that he was the manager of the entire store and presumably took down a fabulous salary, since Scarsdale was always among the top three for volume in a chain which then had fifty retail units.

I was beginning to get some idea of how little I was actually worth on the open market. New to me still, though, was the promise of riches.

I remember one evening when a man in his late fifties came and stopped at the stairs leading down into Home Office, the Wiz department where I ended up. He stood there like a bull elephant on a ridge, apparently expecting to be admired. A colleague grabbed my arm, pointed up at the stranger. "He earned a hundred and fifty thousand dollars last year," I was told in a hushed whisper.

"Selling what?" I whispered back.

"Home theatres."

But I'm getting ahead of myself. The sensation I remember most vividly the day I moved past the manager with the push broom and into the bowels of the Scarsdale branch was of having my pupils dilate violently. The surfaces in the building were covered with black velvet, or something designed to look like black velvet. The lighting was markedly subdued, as if this were a cave, or the lair of a college student and follower of the Grateful Dead.

I found a woman in a dark business suit with a cell phone in one hand and a sheaf of papers in the other. When she got off the phone, I gave her my résumé.

"You wrote two novels?" she asked.

"Yes."

"What were they?"

"You won't have heard of them. I'm not John Grisham."

"No," she said. "What were they about? I might have heard."

"'Bout life," I said, and shrugged.

"All right, then," she said, losing interest. "What's the difference between SVGA and VGS?"

"I don't know."

"If you're talking about a computer," she asked, without giving me a chance to recover, "what's a high-speed bus?"

"Some computers have them, and some don't," I said. "I think the better ones have them."

"What can we can do with a person who doesn't even know the fundamentals?" she said, and sighed.

I bristled. I told her I'd already sold computers for Comp USA. "I can answer the questions asked by nine out of ten customers," I said.

She backed away into the shadows. Moments later a young man appeared, also in a dark business suit, also with a cell phone. I was given twenty minutes in which to take a multiple-choice test. Then I was presented with a series of forms to fill out, including a schedule. On a sheet titled "Days and Hours You Can Work" I filled in a twenty-hour week with both Saturday and Sunday left blank.

The man in the suit took my papers away, then returned and said that my projected schedule wasn't going to work.

"But these are the hours I want," I said.

He went away into the darkness. When he returned, he said that in order to qualify for the special eight-day training program, I needed to put down that I planned to be available for a forty-hour week. Once I was out of training, he said, I could cut the job down to twenty hours a week. I'd need to work the precise schedule out with my manager.

I nodded dumbly. Then he filled out a fresh sheet, writing, "Open" for the schedule. And in the section titled "Days and Hours When You Are Unable to Work (Please provide reasons)" he wrote, "None".

I signed this along with several other forms. In one I promised to show up fifteen minutes early for each shift and not to sign out until the shift was over. I also vowed not to wear jeans or sneakers.

As the man who had interviewed and tested me gathered up my papers, he was given a form filled out by another applicant. "Souflé!" he exclaimed loudly. "I'm not talking with anybody named Souflé. What kind of name is that?"

Walking out of the building, I could hear the woman with the cell phone catechizing a new prospect: "What's the difference between SVGA and VGS?" Then from the darkness, I heard a faint, uncertain voice intensely reminiscent of my own. "I don't know," it said.

Which must not have mattered frightfully, because I at least was given an appointment for a urine test, and enrolled in the coveted eight-day training program.

My reluctance to work weekends and holidays was related to the fact that this book had not yet been sold. The proposal, which I had expected to have publishers fighting over like dogs over a steak sandwich, had been turned down repeatedly. I'd transformed myself from an author who couldn't get his third novel published into a hack who also couldn't sell nonfiction, and was spoiling his family life by holding a variety of humiliating and low-paying jobs that took him away from home on weekends and holidays. I figured I'd soldier on, but if possible, I'd contain the time I spent working so that I could still be of some use to my wife and children, the only people who seemed truly interested in my services.

So a couple of weeks after my interview, I showed up for classes, which were held on the fourth floor of the Wiz store at Thirty-first Street and Sixth Avenue in Manhattan. "Gentlemen must wear a suit, or sport jacket with tie, and dress slacks at all times," my form had said.

In place of a sport jacket, many of the other students had worn leather jackets. I, of course, was bibbed and tuckered, wearing a blue blazer and button-down shirt. The room in which we met had a man at a desk in front. The job candidates collected in chairs facing him. The man at the front of the room had me down as "Ben Cheves". I was given a time card and taught how to swipe in. There were about twenty of us; more than half of the men wore pagers. A third of the students were women. I was in my mid-forties at the time, and a good fifteen years older than everybody else in the class.

The room was freshly painted, with posters on the wall of Bruce Springsteen, Darth Vader, and a Sports Sony Walkman. There was a Poland

Springs water dispenser. Shortly after I arrived, another employee showed up for whom they didn't have a time card. "You're fucked," he was told cheerfully, but he sat with us and waited.

When the instructor appeared, we followed him into another, larger room, with chairs, tables, and a green blackboard. There were windows all along one wall. I learned that most of the women would be in the group briefly and then go on to specialized schooling as cashiers. Some of the men would also drop out early, since they were preparing to work in the stockroom. Only the sales counselors, the RAF of the Wiz, would be together for the full eight days.

Our instructor was a slender man of indeterminate age with bright eyes and a weak chin. He seemed keen on the program, but he also carried an aura of sorrow. He was enthusiastic about the Wiz, but I thought I could tell that he'd been enthusiastic about other employers in the past. Other, different employers. Ultimately it was this sorrow, and an irony I suspected but couldn't exactly locate, that made his positive attitude so difficult to resist.

"Welcome to Nobody Beats the Wiz, new-hire training," he told us after everybody found a seat. Benefits start after three months. After two months you're entitled to ten per cent off on Wiz merchandise.

"Two things we ask you to do," he said, and turned to write on the board:

1. Take responsibility

2. Have fun

"You need to get seventy per cent to pass," he said. "I haven't lost anybody yet. The thought of firing anybody makes me break out."

Ask questions, he told us. "The only question that's stupid," he said, is the one that doesn't get asked.

"Your training is important, because *you* are important. Because you're going to come in contact with the most valuable people at the Wiz: our customers."

He then passed around a sheet which had the words *Icebreaker* at the top followed by some statements. We were to sign our names next to the statements that applied to us. These included:

Has visited Niagara Falls
Owns an exotic pet
Views Rush Limbaugh
Knows what the acronym "SNAFU" stands for
Worked as a commissioned salesperson

We all scribbled away dutifully and then handed the form up to the front of the room.

Reading from it, the teacher told us that one man had a fruit bat, one woman owned a boa constrictor, and another man had a snake.

"What sort of snake?" he was asked.

"Just a regular snake," he said.

I got my name mentioned for having known what *SNAFU* stood for: "Situation Normal. All Fucked Up."

The instructor wanted to know if I'd been in the military.

I said that no, I had not.

I was sitting immediately to the right of a black kid in his late teens or early twenties. After I'd admitted missing military service, he tapped me on the shoulder. "But you do watch Rush Limbaugh?" he asked.

"No."

"You look like you'd watch him for sure," he said then, but without any edge to it.

"Thanks," I said, but without any edge to it.

Then the teacher, I'll call him Paul, asked which of us spoke a second language. Some hands went up. "English counts," he said, which got a laugh. "But, seriously, you all speak a second language," he said. "We all speak the language of the body."

The first thing we had to learn was the Wiz credo. The mnemonic acronym for it was ICER. The credo: Integrity, Customer, Excellence, and Respect.

> Integrity: To be totally honest with our customer, fellow workers, company, and yourself. Customer: To do whatever it takes to satisfy our customer. Excellence: To strive for excellence in everything we do. Respect: To respect our customer, fellow workers, company, and yourself. Give respect, and you will receive it in return.

Paul told us the Wiz was spending three thousand dollars on each of us for schooling. He said that philosophy was always important. When he'd worked at Neiman-Marcus, everybody had had to read *Minding the Store* by Stanley Marcus.

I asked if there was a book Wiz employees needed to read. Not really, he said. There would be texts handed out at the end of the day. And a training film called *The Wizard of Oz,* he said. I took this to be a joke.

He showed us how the initials *ICER* had been worked into the logo which was etched or painted at several places on the fourth floor.

We learned that the company had started in 1976 with a single store on Fulton Street in Brooklyn. Nobody Beats the Wiz was founded by Norman Jemal. Apparently, Norman Jemal's favorite Broadway show had been *The Wiz.* Norman had owned a construction company called Namron. *Namron* was Norman spelled backwards. Norman had since died, but the CEO of the Wiz was a man named Lawrence Jemal. The executive vice president was named Marvin Jemal. Stephen Jemal was head of Namron, which did all Wiz construction.

Paul handed out a sheet titled "Company Hierarchy". He told us the Jemals were "good people". He said we should remember how to spell their names. When this got a titter, he said, "It will be on the final."

This was in the early spring of 1996, and we were told that the Wiz was the largest regional home-electronics chain in the United States of America. "The goal of the company is to become a nationwide retailer," Paul told us.

Paul wrote "*FUD*" on the board. Then he wrote, "Fears, Uncertainties, Doubts". He told us that we must learn how to deal with our customers' FUDs.

The reason nobody beats the Wiz, we were told, is that we don't let them. If a customer has proof that a recognized competitor has a lower price, the salesperson should take the Wiz price, subtract the competitor's price from it, and multiply the difference by 25 per cent, or divide it by four. Then add a dollar. Subtract that total from the competitor's price, and that's the price you sell at.

So if the Wiz was selling something for one hundred dollars and a customer produced proof that a recognized competitor was selling it for ninety, then the customer could buy the product from the Wiz for $86.50.

We were told that there was a thirty-three-day price guarantee, and for that time customers were entitled to a refund, except for camcorders, which must be returned within five days. "Why?" Paul asked us.

Nobody knew.

"Vacations ordinarily last seven days," he told us. People would film their vacation, then return the camera. TVs with a screen larger than thirty inches also could not be returned. Why? Because customers were regularly buying huge projection-screen TVs and returning them on Super Bowl Monday with the rings from beer cans still on the housing, potato-chip crumbs in the speaker fabric.

"Not that we should criticize customers, ever," Paul said. Nor should we disparage the competition. "I refer to them as 'the enemy'", Paul said, and smiled, "but we shouldn't ever bad-mouth them to a customer." Another appliance chain called Tops had put up Wiz and P. C. Richards logos in their toilets, and the Wiz and P. C. Richards sued them. The case was settled out of court for twenty-five thousand dollars, Paul told us, which was given to charity.

Our role as employees could not be overestimated, Paul said. Word of mouth was a vital element in the business. Studies had shown that a satisfied customer tells three other people about his experience. A dissatisfied customer tells ten to twenty people.

"Forget the Golden Rule," Paul told us. "Learn instead the Platinum Rule: 'Do unto others as they would have you do unto them'".

A store loses 15 per cent of customers over a year. One per cent die. We couldn't do anything about them, but 58 per cent of those lost attribute their change to poor customer service.

We would be tested on the Five Cs of customer service. These were:

1. Caring
2. Considerate
3. Creative
4. Committed
5. Courteous

For those of us who spoke Spanish, the second letter of words two, three, and four provided a useful mnemonic: *oro,* the Spanish word for "gold". We could remember it by using the phrase "The customer is gold to me".

We had fifteen-minute break, and I went out of the building with the young black man who had taken me for a Limbaugh fan, a dittohead. He had his hair laid flat against his head in cornrows. I thought that this might be an expression of hostility, or at least of an unwillingness to mingle with white folk, but he seemed happy to speak with me. He had a bright, open face. He was trying for a job in the stockroom, he told me, and I automatically felt a little smarter than he was. Employees in the stockroom earned a flat salary, while sale counselors were entitled to commissions.

Paul was out in the street smoking, too. He had his sleeves rolled up and one arm displayed the tattoo "Jumpmaster".

He did not boast, but when questioned, he admitted that he had been an army paratrooper. He talked a little about night drops. He told about how he had been specifically warned never to jump a certain way when leaving the helicopter—and so of course he tried it.

"When you're young . . . " he said, and wagged his head.

Going back into the building, I asked him why none of the women were training to be sales counselors. He said that was an interesting question. He said that for some reason, they preferred to be cashiers. When they did become sales counselors, he told me, they often performed well.

I asked him how they selected people for the program. He said they kept out people who didn't speak English, or if "a guy comes up to me and says, 'I sell more drugs than anybody else on the block.' "

Back in the classroom, Paul told us that *The Wizard of Oz* could count as a training film because Dorothy could never have made it to Oz without the lion, the tin man, and the scarecrow. Teamwork was essential to Dorothy, he said, and would be essential to us.

He asked us what we thought teamwork was. Nobody seemed certain. "A team," he told us, "is a group of people working together for a common goal." He said we'd be tested on this.

The requirements for teamwork, he told us, were:

1. Communication
2. Cooperation

3. Consideration

4. Responsibility

To remember, he said, we should think of *co* and *tion* three times, and then *responsibility*.

We were each given stapled textbooks from which to study. These texts should be used for review, we were told. Anything on which we were going to be tested would be covered in class.

Right before we left that evening, Paul played *The Wizard of Oz* for us on a VCR. He made a point of showing us the part in the film where a stage-hand kills himself. I saw only shadows, which I was told represented a man climbing a stepladder, putting a noose around his neck, and jumping off.

The next day I showed up early and there was a lot of complaining about all the homework. One of the white students said that when somebody else in his family saw him doing all the paperwork, they figured he must be applying for welfare.

It developed that the one thing we all had in common was a devotion to electronics. Many of us had worked in computer stores before, and we all had systems and gadgets that exceeded any practical need. One of the other "cadets" had taken the one-thousand-dollar course whose classified I'd been ogling. The course promised to teach students to "build a computer from scratch". He'd gone to work at CompUSA afterwards as a techie, installing memory upgrades and the like.

He told me that people would buy computers, remove the innards, and then try to return them. There was another cadet from the Manhattan CompUSA. He spoke of a customer who used to come in every day and buy a different computer.

When I asked why anybody would do that, my new friend smiled. "I guess he just likes computers a lot."

"So if you have technical know-how, what are you doing here?" I asked the one who had taken the course, and he shrugged.

There was some discussion of the pay plan. As I understood it, we were being paid a lesser wage during training, but when we hit the stores we'd be entitled to a draw of seven dollars an hour. This was against unearned commissions. Our commissions were 1 per cent of sales. If we consistently failed to meet the draw, we'd be fired.

There were rumors of salespeople who had done very well at the Wiz. One of the other cadets had been working at a different computer store where there was no draw. "So, in other words, you could get dressed up, go to work—and earn nothing?" I asked.

"Yup," I was told.

Then there was talk of commissions at other establishments. Barney's, I was told, gave the salesperson 40 per cent. "So if you sell a guy a shirt for one hundred dollars, you make forty dollars?" I asked.

"A job at Barney's," I was told, "is like winning the lottery."

When Paul arrived, the chatter stopped. He told us that Lawrence Jemal was in the building. Paul suggested that we might want to straighten our neckties. I noticed that nobody straightened his necktie.

That morning we were given our first test. I was sitting next to the black guy who thought I must watch Rush Limbaugh, the one who wanted to work in the stockroom. The exam was multiple choice. Almost immediately my new friend began to make noises of distress. He rolled his eyes, smacked his forehead with the back of his hand. I thought, *He's going to fail. He doesn't even have the ambition to try to be a sales counselor, but he's still going to wash out.*

I was tempted to lean over and give hints on some of the harder questions. I was afraid that I'd get caught, though, and I had no doubt that Paul would throw me out for cheating. I kept my mouth shut.

These black kids may be nice, I thought, *but they haven't had my advantages.*

After the morning break, the tests were handed back, but folded, so that we couldn't see each other's marks, which were written at the top of the first page. I peeked and saw that I had gotten 98 points out of 100. After my friend had looked at his test, and screwed up his face with dismay, I reached over with my left hand and gave him a conciliatory pat on the shoulder. I wanted him to know that whatever grade he'd gotten on the test, I still considered him a splendid human being.

First Paul asked the class if anybody had a perfect score, and sure enough, a beautiful young cashier-in-training had gotten 100. Nobody had 99. I had raised my hand when he asked about 98s. Had anyone gotten 97? Several hands shot up, including that of my young stockroom friend, the one I had been so sure would fail.

Ask me today if I'm a racist, and I'll deny it still, but since that morning, I've been a little less passionate in my refutations.

There was a certain amount of product knowledge stirred into the second day of training, but there was also a good deal about body language. When dealing with customers, we were not to put our hands in our pockets. "If you put your hand in your pocket, you look as if you're concealing something," we were told.

I remembered reading of a young doctor who had studied at a Boston hospital early in the last century under an administration that insisted that all doctors-in-training sew their pockets closed.

We must listen, Paul told us. Most people don't listen, he said. Studies showed that adults spend 70 per cent of each day in verbal communication. Forty-five per cent of the time, they're listening, he said. "You do the math."

People speak at a rate of two hundred words a minutes, think at the rate of two thousand, we were told. So the listeners go on ahead and lose interest. Words account for less than 10 per cent of the message we get across, Paul told us. Not a cheering statistic if you mean to be a writer.

Paul wrote the word *yo* on the chalkboard and showed us with various inflections how that single word could be made to mean:

1. Yes.
2. No.
3. Hello.
4. Hello!
5. Stop that!
6. That's a pretty girl.
7. That's a bad idea.

While we must be acutely aware of the messages our posture, clothing, and tone of voice gave off, we should also be careful never to dismiss customers because of their posture or an unpromising wardrobe, Paul said. He told of a man who had come into the Neiman-Marcus at closing one day, looking like he'd been sleeping in the streets. Just to glance at him, you'd practically expect the guy to ask for a dollar, Paul told us, but instead this individual had gone over to the jewelry display, pulled out twenty-nine one-thousand-dollar bills, and made a purchase.

"Richard Gere shops in our NoHo store all the time. He looks like a hobo."

Which didn't mean, Paul told us again, that we could be sloppy ourselves. We should be neatly dressed and always equipped with pens, worksheets, measuring tapes, and a generous supply of mints. Bad breath was bad for business, he told us. "If you stink, you can't sell."

That afternoon we watched again the section of *The Wizard of Oz* in which the stagehand is supposed to hang himself in the background. I still couldn't see it.

By the end of the second day I was enthusiastic about the job. I liked Paul enormously. He was a gifted teacher. When a friend referred to the Wiz jokingly as "Everybody Beats the Wiz", I got quite sore. I was pleased to remember having gotten this email from another friend, when I was working at CompUSA and concerned with the morality of pushing the insurance:

Well, I can say that our Wiz purchase of a big screen (in Nov. 1989) with an insurance policy, which raised the total outlay to about $3,500, was a bargain. Now, 6+ years later, the set works fine, but we did have one catastrophic failure, just before the policy ran out. And the innards were repaired at no cost.

The keystone of faith in an electronics store is the insurance. The Wiz policy at the time was called Performance Plus and administered by Independent Dealer Services, Inc. If you believe the insurance offered by your store is good, you can believe in your job. I believed in my job.

In order to get to the classroom, you had to walk into the store downstairs. You could take the elevator from the first floor or climb the stairs up through the store. I was truly shocked one afternoon in the second week, when I saw the Casio watch I wore then on display and selling for a hundred dollars. It was the first G shock that lit up—"electroluminescence," they called it. I'd bought the watch at Caldor. This was two years beforehand, and it cost seventy-six dollars at the time. Electronics are supposed to go down in price, not up.

Back in the classroom, we were briefed about the electronic-product industry. There was an amazingly high level of technical knowledge among the students. The computer, we were told, stores everything in terms of a zero or a one. *Zero* represents "off"/"false"/"no". *One* represents "on"/"true"/"yes".

I don't quite know what the great fascination for gadgets is, but apparently the passion is basic to the species. I was cheered during my reading to discover that Samuel Pepys, that famous seventeenth-century diarist, was enraptured with his first pocket watch, a costly instrument that rarely kept the correct time.

The appetite has grown feverish as the gadgets have gotten better and also cheaper. The Wiz cadets seemed to share a belief that these infinitely clever creations would not only make us more efficient, but also improve the very essence of our lives.

During the 1990s, Paul told us, computer speed will double, storage requirements triple, and memory quadruple every eighteen months.

Each class had a name, Paul told us, and we would be the ice men, because, he said, "When I'm done with you, you'll be able to sell ice to Eskimos." He broke us into groups, had us interact, with one student as salesperson, one as prospect.

Never ask a customer what he or she wants to spend. "You've painted yourself into a corner." If possible, give a demonstration. "Demo the demo" was a slogan we learned to repeat.

Never, ever ask a customer, "Can I help you?" He's always going to say, "No." Be less threatening and more specific. "What features are you interested in?"

We were told how to focus on a "tie-down", a particular feature of a product, and then encourage the customer to imagine enjoying that feature. The new TVs with the picture-in-picture capacity were the favored example. Learn from the customer when he might want to know what was going on on two stations simultaneously and then let him inhabit that scene. Maybe he's interested in two different football games. Let Mr. Customer visualize himself sitting in a chair, with the control in his hand. Draw him into a reverie, then shut up.

We also learned about the "TO", or "takeover". If you've got a customer to the point where he or she seems almost ready to buy, but it has become a war of wills, a stalemate, then you signal another salesman to come in. If this can be done smoothly, the intervention of a second, enthusiastic witness is enough to ensure a sale.

"Hey, John, would you come over here for a second? Show Mr. Customer how the picture-in-picture works. Don't you have one of these sets at home?"

Paul also told us about spiffs. *The New Shorter Oxford English Dictionary* defines a spiff as "a money bonus given to an employee for selling old or unwanted stock". I knew from working at CompUSA that there were spiffs on some products. For instance, we'd had a particularly slow-moving computer: It was a desktop that had the Mac operating system, but it wasn't manufactured by Apple. If you sold one of these computers, the manufacturer gave the salesperson a direct bonus of two hundred dollars. Outside of this particular item, I had not been aware of spiffs while at CompUSA. At Nobody Beats the Wiz most items had spiffs. There were too many to recall, but this didn't matter, because at the Wiz the spiffs were written right into the product number, which was displayed near the item on sale. The spiff began after the first seven digits of the number and and ended before the last five. So the salesperson, looking at a long number with a trained eye, might see 25000 in the middle of it and know he was entitled to a cash bonus of $250 if he moved this particular turkey.

Paul asked if anybody had ever gone into a TV showroom and seen a Sony and a Panasonic and a brand you'd never heard of, and the Sony and Panasonic had horrible pictures, while Brand X had a picture that was crystal clear. That's because Brand X has a high spiff, he told us. So the salespeople in those stores have carefully adjusted the color and reception on the other TVs so that they look horrible.

He certainly didn't want us to do anything of the sort at the Wiz. We were nevertheless encouraged to know our spiffs. During an informal conversation I had with Paul after one of our breaks, he told me that a Sony representative had come into one of the stores and tried to buy a Sony. Sony, because of its excellent reputation, has low spiffs, or no spiffs at all, and so the salesman was determined not to sell a Sony to the man from Sony. In fact, he went on at considerable length and in detail about how weak the Sony line was. As a result, Sony was so angry at the Wiz that they threatened to withdraw their brand, Paul said.

One evening, our assignment was to shop the competition and take notes. The prize for best quote retrieved was given to the cadet who had asked a salesman a second question about a product at a competing store and was asked angrily, "Who do you think you are? John Gotti?"

Back in the classroom, we were given our numerical targets. Three out of ten customers should buy an insurance policy. Accessories should constitute 8 per cent of the total spent.

"This guy is going to do well," Paul said, pointing at me, after we'd been playacting. "He has charisma." I was genuinely pleased. I also thought, *Maybe I will do well.*

"Will you be using your Wiz card today?" is a question we were supposed to ask every customer. Wiz cards, which were obtainable at the moment of purchase, should be used in 35 per cent of transactions. When selling a Wiz card, we should also sell Wiz Guard. Wiz Guard was an insurance policy that cost seventy-five cents for every hundred dollars the customer spent and guaranteed that if the customer was killed or incapacitated or lost his job while he still owed on his purchase, the minimum payment would be made. The specter to be raised here, Paul explained, was that of unemployment.

"What do people fear more than death?" Paul asked us.

"Public speaking," I said.

Nope. "Recent studies show that the greatest fear felt by American voters today is that they will lose their job."

Textual Questions

1. How does Cheever describe his training for employment at Nobody Beats the Wiz? What tone does his description take? What is the intent of the training? What unintentional effects does it seem to have?

2. Why, in his description of his training program, does Cheever include acronyms such as SNAFU, FUD, and ICER—and details such as "the Five Cs of customer service" and the existence of "spiffs"? What do such details of the training do for his description?

3. When Cheever mentions seeing his own Casio watch on display, selling for $100, what point is he making about Nobody Beats the Wiz? How does this point foreshadow things that come later in the essay?

Rhetorical Questions

4. How does Cheever describe Paul, the man who leads the orientation program? Why? How does Cheever describe the other participants in the orientation program (both groups of people and individuals)? Why?

5. What part do race and social class play in Cheever's essay?

6. How effectively does Cheever build his essay to the point made in the final paragraph? What is most/least effective about the buildup to this concluding point?

Intertextual Questions

7. Compare Cheever's description of his training to work at Nobody Beats the Wiz with Barbara Ehrenreich's description of her training (in "In Which I am Offered a 'Job'"). How are the two descriptions similar? What are the goals of the two training programs and how are they similar/different?

8. How does Cheever's description of how people feel about unemployment compare to the description of unemployment offered by Scott Russell

Sanders in "The Men We Carry in Our Minds"? In both essays, is being unemployed the same as being a "loser" (as defined by Charles Young in "Losing: An American Tradition")?

Thinking Beyond the Text

9. Why would the training for a job such as the one Cheever seeks at Nobody Beats the Wiz involve anything but discussion of sales techniques and product specifications? Why discuss such topics as proper dress, bad breath, spiffs, integrity, responsibility, and so forth? Put another way, why does training such of this seem, at least in part, to involve cult-like indoctrination into a philosophy of life?

10. Cheever ends his essay by making the point that people fear unemployment more than they fear death or public speaking. Do you believe this to be true? Can you confirm this point of Cheevers, either through online or traditional research?

For Writing & Discussion

11. The next time you shop at an electronics store such as Nobody Beats the Wiz, BestBuy, or CompUSA, observe the behaviors of the salespeople. What do they do and/or say that seems to echo the training Cheever received?

ROBERT HINKLEY

Robert Hinkley was a corporate securities attorney for 23 years. He left his partnership at a successful law firm in 2000 after realizing how many problems are not only allowed but encouraged by corporate law. In 2002 he published this oft-cited article, "How Corporate Law Inhibits Social Responsibility" in the journal *Business Ethics: Corporate Social Responsibility Report* (January/ February 2002).

   In this article Hinkley challenges the nature of state-level corporate laws, which place companies' profits ahead of environmental, human, community, and employee rights, and argues for a simple legislative change that would reverse these priorities. He is currently working on a book about his Model Code for Corporate Citizenship, *The 28 Word Solution*.

Hinkley received the 1999 Economic Social Innovations Award and in a poll by *Business Week/Harris*, 95 percent of Americans agreed that corporations "should sometimes sacrifice some profit for the sake of making things better for their workers and communities."

In 2003, Hinkley co-founded a new tobacco company, Licensed to Kill, Inc., that mocks corporate irresponsibility with its motto, "We're Rich, You're Dead," and cigarette brand names like Global Massacre ("Guns kill a lot of people, but LtoK kills more!").

How Corporate Law Inhibits Social Responsibility

A Corporate Lawyer Proposes a "Code for Corporate Citizenship" in State Laws

∾ Prereading Question

A corporation must be responsible to its shareholders—must make them a profit to justify their investment. To whom should the corporation also be responsible? What does a corporation such as Wal-Mart owe to its full time employees, part time employees, customers, citizens of communities in which its stores are located, and so on?

Published in the January/February 2002 issue of Business Ethics: Corporate Social Responsibility Report

After 23 years as a corporate securities attorney—advising large corporations on securities offerings and mergers and acquisitions—I left my position as partner at Skadden, Arps, Slate, Meagher & Flom because I was disturbed by the game. I realized that the many social ills created by corporations *stem directly from corporate law*. It dawned on me that the law, in its current form, actually inhibits executives and corporations from being socially responsible. So in June 2000 I quit my job and decided to devote the next phase of my life to making people aware of this problem. My goal is to build consensus to change the law so it encourages good corporate citizenship, rather than inhibiting it.

The provision in the law I am talking about is the one that says the purpose of the corporation is simply to make money for shareholders. Every jurisdiction where corporations operate has its own law of corporate governance. But remarkably, the corporate design contained in hundreds of corporate laws throughout the world is nearly identical. That design creates a governing body to manage the corporation—usually a board of directors—and dictates the duties of those directors. In short, the law creates corporate purpose. That purpose is to operate in the interests of shareholders. In Maine, where I live, this duty of directors is in Section 716 of the business corporation act, which reads:

> . . . the directors and officers of a corporation shall exercise their powers and discharge their duties with a view to the interests of the corporation and of the shareholders. . . .

Although the wording of this provision differs from jurisdiction to jurisdiction, its legal effect does not. This provision is the motive behind all corporate actions everywhere in the world. Distilled to its essence, it says that the people who run corporations have a legal duty to shareholders, and that duty is to make money. Failing this duty can leave directors and officers open to being sued by shareholders.

Section 716 dedicates the corporation to the pursuit of its own self-interest (and equates corporate self-interest with shareholder self-interest). No mention is made of responsibility to the public interest. Section 716 and its counterparts explain two things. First, they explain why corporations find social issues like human rights irrelevant—because they fall outside the corporation's legal mandate. Second, these provisions explain why executives behave differently than they might as individual citizens, because the law says their only obligation in business is to make money.

This design has the unfortunate side effect of largely eliminating personal responsibility. Because corporate law generally regulates corporations but not executives, it leads executives to become inattentive to justice. They demand their subordinates "make the numbers," and pay little attention to how they do so. Directors and officers know their jobs, salaries, bonuses, and stock options depend on delivering profits for shareholders.

Companies believe their duty to the public interest consists of complying with the law. Obeying the law is simply a cost. Since it interferes with making money, it must be minimized—using devices like lobbying, legal hairsplitting, and jurisdiction shopping. Directors and officers give little thought to the fact that these activities may damage the public interest.

Lower-level employees know their livelihoods depend upon satisfying superiors' demands to make money. They have no incentive to offer ideas that would advance the public interest unless they increase profits. Projects that would serve the public interest—but at a financial cost to the corporation—are considered naive.

Corporate law thus casts ethical and social concerns as irrelevant, or as stumbling blocks to the corporation's fundamental mandate. That's the effect the law has inside the corporation. Outside the corporation the effect is more devastating. It is the law that leads corporations to actively disregard harm to all interests other than those of shareholders. When toxic chemicals are spilled, forests destroyed, employees left in poverty, or communities devastated through plant shutdowns, corporations view these as unimportant side effects outside their area of concern. But when the company's stock price dips, that's a disaster. The reason is that, in our legal framework, a low stock price leaves a company vulnerable to takeover or means the CEO's job could be at risk.

In the end, the natural result is that corporate bottom line goes up, and the state of the public good goes down. This is called privatizing the gain and externalizing the cost.

This system design helps explain why the war against corporate abuse is being lost, despite decades of effort by thousands of organizations. Until now, tactics used to confront corporations have focused on where and how much companies should be allowed to damage the public interest, rather than eliminating the reason they do it. When public interest groups protest a new power plant, mercury poisoning, or a new big box store, the groups don't examine the corporations' motives. They only seek to limit where damage is created (not in our back yard) and how much damage is created (a little less, please).

But the where-and-how-much approach is reactive, not proactive. Even when corporations are defeated in particular battles, they go on the next day, in other ways and other places, to pursue their own private interests at the expense of the public.

I believe the battle against corporate abuse should be conducted in a more holistic way. We must inquire why corporations behave as they do, and look for a way to change these underlying motives. Once we have arrived at a viable systemic solution, we should then dictate the terms of engagement to corporations, not let them dictate terms to us.

We must remember that corporations were invented to serve mankind. Mankind was not invented to serve corporations. Corporations in many ways have the rights of citizens, and those rights should be balanced by obligations to the public.

Many activists cast the fundamental issue as one of "corporate greed," but that's off the mark. Corporations are incapable of a human emotion like greed. They are artificial beings created by law. The real question is why corporations behave as if they are greedy. The answer is the design of corporate law.

We can change that design. We can make corporations more responsible to the public good by amending the law that says the pursuit of profit takes precedence over the public interest. I believe this can best be achieved by changing corporate law to make directors personally responsible for harms done.

Let me give you a sense of how director responsibility works in the current system. Under federal securities laws, directors are held personally liable for false and misleading statements made in prospectuses used to sell securities. If a corporate prospectus contains a material falsehood and investors suffer damage as a result, investors can sue each director personally to recover the damage. Believe me, this provision grabs the attention of company directors. They spend hours reviewing drafts of a prospectus to ensure it complies with the law. Similarly, everyone who works on the prospectus knows that directors' personal wealth is at stake, so they too take great care with accuracy.

That's an example of how corporate behavior changes when directors are held personally responsible. Everyone in the corporation improves their game to meet the challenge. The law has what we call an in terrorem effect. Since the potential penalties are so severe, directors err on the side of caution. While this has not eliminated securities fraud, it has over the years reduced it to an infinitesimal percentage of the total capital raised.

I propose that corporate law be changed in a similar manner—to make individuals responsible for seeing that the pursuit of profit does not damage the public interest.

To pave the way for such a change, we must challenge the myth that making profits and protecting the public interest are mutually exclusive goals. The same was once said about profits and product quality, before Japanese manufacturers taught us otherwise. If we force companies to respect the public interest while they make money, business people will figure out how to do both.

The specific change I suggest is simple: add 26 words to corporate law and thus create what I call the "Code for Corporate Citizenship." In Maine, this would mean amending section 716 to add the following clause. Directors and officers would still have a duty to make money for shareholders,

> . . . but not at the expense of the environment, human rights, the public safety, the communities in which the corporation operates or the dignity of its employees.

This simple amendment would effect a dramatic change in the underlying mechanism that drives corporate malfeasance. It would make individuals responsible for the damage companies cause to the public interest, and would be enforced much the same way as securities laws are now. Negligent failure to abide by the code would result in the corporation, its directors, and its officers being liable for the full amount of the damage they cause. In addition to civil liability, the attorney general would have the right to criminally prosecute intentional acts. Injunctive relief—which stops specific behaviors while the legal process proceeds—would also be available.

Compliance would be in the self-interest of both individuals and the company. No one wants to see personal assets subject to a lawsuit. Such a prospect would surely temper corporate managers' willingness to make money at the expense of the public interest. Similarly, investors tend to shy away from companies with contingent liabilities, so companies that severely or repeatedly violate the Code for Corporate Citizenship might see their stock price fall or their access to capital dry up.

Many would say such a code could never be enacted. But they're mistaken. I take heart from a 2000 *Business Week/Harris* Poll that asked Americans which of the following two propositions they support more strongly:

- *Corporations should have only one purpose—to make the most profit for their shareholders—and pursuit of that goal will be best for America in the long run.*
  or
- *Corporations should have more than one purpose. They also owe something to their workers and the communities in which they operate, and they should sometimes sacrifice some profit for the sake of making things better for their workers and communities.*

An overwhelming 95 percent of Americans chose the second proposition. Clearly, this finding tells us that our fate is not sealed. When 95 percent of the public supports a proposition, enacting that proposition into law should not be impossible.

If business people resist the notion of legal change, we can remind them that corporations exist only because laws allow them to exist. Without these laws, owners would be fully responsible for debts incurred and damages caused by their businesses. Because the public creates the law, corporations owe their existence as much to the public as they do to shareholders. They should have obligations to both. It simply makes no sense that society's most powerful citizens have no concern for the public good.

It also makes no sense to endlessly chase after individual instances of corporate wrongdoing, when that wrongdoing is a natural result of the system design. Corporations abuse the public interest because the law tells them their only legal duty is to maximize profits for shareholders. Until we change the law of corporate governance, the problem of corporate abuse can never fully be solved.

Textual Questions

1. How does Hinkley establish his own authority and credibility to write on this subject?

2. How does Hinkley describe "Section 716" and the effects it has on how businesses operate in America? What are the negative and positive effects—and for whom are they either positive or negative?

3. What changes does Hinkley advocate? How and where does he describe them in his essay?

Rhetorical Questions

4. Consider the direct quotations from "Section 716" that Hinkley uses in his essay. How does he build his argument to set up each quotation? How does he follow each quotation in a way that uses the quotation to advance his main argument?

5. In this essay Hinkley uses both "I" and "we." How does he construct himself—the "I" in this essay—in a way that is crafted to make readers respond positively to his argument? How does he construct the "we" in this essay to help support his argument? That is, who are "we" in Hinkley's argument?

6. How does Hinkley build his argument to his final points about businesses and needed changes? Which support does he use in his argument that seems most effective? Which support seems least effective?

Intertextual Questions

7. In what ways does Hinkley's argument here compare and contrast with the arguments made about Wal-Mart in "Everyday Low Wages" (later in this chapter)?

8. How does Hinkley construct his argument in similar/dissimilar ways to the argument made by Eric Schlosser in "Success"?

Thinking Beyond the Text

9. Searching online, locate at least one article about the Enron corporation and the disastrous effects its bankruptcy had on its employees. In the article you read, how is the topic of ethical/unethical business practices discussed? Are specific individuals at Enron—or specific actions—criticized as being unethical?

10. Consider one item that you use on a daily—or almost daily—basis, from your automobile to your iPod. What ethical business practices went into the manufacture and/or sale of that item? For example, did the maker of your automobile go beyond legal requirements when designing safety features? Did the maker of your iPod specifically design its controls with both able-bodied and physically handicapped individuals in mind?

For Writing & Discussion

11. Beginning at one of the major online search engines, type in "business ethics." After weeding out advertisements for books and seminars on this topic, and any random pornography that may appear, consider one of the online sources that you find. How does it define—explicitly

or implicitly—the idea of ethical business practices? Does it argue for any specific changes in business practices? Print this page and bring it to class for discussion.

A L A I N   D E   B O T T O N

Alain de Botton (1969–) is the author of eight books, four of which have been made into television series in the United Kingdom. He has received some of Europe's most prestigious literary awards; he is a Chevalier de l'Ordre des Arts et Lettres in France, won the Prix Européen de l'Essai Charles Veillon, and received the "Economics Book of the Year" prize from the *Financial Times* of Germany for his 2004 book *Status Anxiety.* His writing has been translated into 20 languages.

De Botton's nonfiction books blend essayist and novelist techniques to look at abstract concepts—romantic love, the psychology of travel, social status, and most recently architecture and concepts of beauty—and how they affect ordinary people's lives. "Workers of the World, Relax: The Pursuit of Happiness" was first published in the *International Herald Tribune* on September 7, 2004. It begins with a quick overview of the history of work in the Western world, then articulates how the increasing expectation that work will be satisfying inevitably has caused greater dissatisfaction. De Botton ends with an argument for demanding less of our jobs and of ourselves as workers.

Born in Switzerland and currently living in London, de Botton uses America as the focus of this article because, as he says, work is more central to society in America than in other parts of the Western world.

Workers of the World, Relax
The Pursuit of Happiness

∽ Prereading Question

List three people you know and, after each name, list the job he/she currently holds. Does this work make him/her "happy"—assuming, for the sake of simplicity, that "happiness" has a definition upon which you and they agree? How large a part in your own career choice and future career plans does the pursuit of happiness play? Does work need to make you happy—or is it the benefits of work, especially the paycheck, that lead to happiness rather than the work itself?

Tuesday, September 07, 2004

The most remarkable feature of the modern workplace has nothing to do with computers, automation or globalization. Rather, it lies in the Western world's widely held belief that our work should make us happy.

All societies throughout history have had work right at their center; but ours—particularly America's—is the first to suggest that it could be something other than a punishment or penance. Ours is the first to imply that a sane human being would want to work even if he wasn't under financial pressure to do so. We are unique, too, in allowing our choice of work to define who we are, so that the central question we ask of new acquaintances is not where they come from or who their parents are, but rather what it is they do—as though only this could effectively reveal what gives a human life its distinctive timbre.

It wasn't always like this, Greco-Roman civilization tended to view work as a chore best left to slaves. For both Plato and Aristotle, fulfillment could be reached only when one had the command of a private income and could escape day-to-day obligations and freely devote oneself to the contemplation of ethical and moral questions. The entrepreneur and the merchant may have had a nice villa and a heaping larder, but they played no role in the antique vision of the good life.

Early Christianity took a similarly bleak view of labor, adding the even darker thought that man was condemned to toil in order to make up for the sin of Adam. Working conditions, however abusive, could not be improved. Work wasn't accidentally miserable—it was one of the planks upon which earthly suffering was irrevocably founded. St. Augustine reminded slaves to obey their masters and accept their pain as part of what he termed, in "The City of God," the "wretchedness of man's condition."

The first signs of the modern, more cheerful attitude toward work can be detected in the city-states of Italy during the Renaissance and, in particular, in the biographies of the artists of the time. In descriptions of the lives of men like Michelangelo and Leonardo, we find some now familiar-sounding ideas about what our labors could ideally mean for us: a path to authenticity and glory. Rather than a burden and punishment, artistic work could allow us to rise above our ordinary limitations. We could express our talents on a page or on a canvas in a way we never could in our everyday lives. Of course, this new vision applied only to a creative elite (no one yet thought to tell a servant that work could develop his true self; that was a claim waiting for modern management theory), but it proved to be the model for all successive definitions of happiness earned through work.

It was not until the late 18th century that the model was extended beyond the artistic realm. In the writings of bourgeois thinkers like Benjamin Franklin, Diderot and Rousseau, we see work recategorized not only as a means to earn money, but also as a way to become more fully ourselves. It is worth noting that this reconciliation of necessity and happiness exactly mirrored the contemporary re-evaluation of marriage. Just as marriage was rethought as an institution that could deliver both practical benefits and sexual and emotional fulfillment (a handy conjunction once thought impossible by aristocrats, who saw a need for a mistress and a wife), so too work was now alleged to be capable of delivering both the money necessary for survival and the stimulation and self-expression that had once been seen as the exclusive preserve of the leisured.

Simultaneously, people began to experience a new kind of pride in their work, in large part because the way that jobs were handed out took on a semblance of justice. In his autobiography, Thomas Jefferson explained that his proudest achievement had been to create a meritocratic United States, where "a new aristocracy of virtue and talent" replaced the old aristocracy of unfair privilege and, in many cases, brute stupidity. Meritocracy endowed jobs with a new, quasi-moral quality. Now that prestigious and well-paid posts seemed to be available on the basis of actual intelligence and ability, your job title could perhaps say something directly meaningful about you.

During the 19th century, many Christian thinkers, especially in the United States, changed their views of money accordingly. American Protestant denominations suggested that God required his followers to lead a life that was successful both temporally and spiritually. Fortunes in this world were evidence that one deserved a good place in the next.

As meritocracy came of age, demeaning jobs came to seem not merely regrettable but, just like their more exciting counterparts, also deserved. No wonder people started asking each other what they did—and listening very carefully to the answers.

Though all this may seem like progress, in truth, modern attitudes toward work have unwittingly caused us problems. Today, claims are made on behalf of almost all kinds of work that are patently out of sync with what reality can provide. Yes, a few jobs are certainly fulfilling, but the majority are not and never can be. We would therefore be wise to listen to some of the pessimistic voices of the premodern period, if only to stop torturing ourselves for not being as happy in our work as we were told we could be. The American philosopher William James once made an acute point about the relationship between happiness and expectation. He argued that satisfaction with ourselves does not require us to succeed in every endeavor. We are not always humiliated by failing; we are humiliated only if we first invest our pride and sense of worth in a given achievement, and then do not reach it. Our goals determine what we will interpret as a triumph and what must count as a failure: "With no attempt there can be no failure; with no failure no humiliation." So our self-esteem in this world is determined by the ratio of our actualities to our supposed potentialities.

If happiness at work is now so hard to earn, perhaps it is because our pretensions have so substantially outstripped reality. We expect every job to deliver some of the satisfaction available to Sigmund Freud or Franklin Roosevelt. Perhaps we should be reading Marx instead. Marx was a poor historian and wrong in his prescriptions for a better world, but he was rather acute at diagnosing why work is so often miserable. In this respect, he drew on Immanuel Kant, who wrote in his "Groundwork of the Metaphysics of Morals" that behaving morally toward other people required that one respect them "for themselves" instead of using them as a "means" for one's enrichment or glory.

Thus Marx famously accused the bourgeoisie and its new science, economics, of practicing "immorality" on a grand scale: "Political economy knows the worker only as a working animal—as a beast reduced to strictest bodily needs." The wages paid to employees were, said Marx, just "like the oil which is applied to wheels to keep them turning," adding, "The true purpose of work is no longer man, but money."

Marx may have been erratically idealizing the preindustrial past and unduly castigating the bourgeoisie, but he ably captured the inescapable degree of conflict between employer and employee. Every commercial organization will try to gather raw materials, labor and machinery at the lowest possible price to combine them into a product that can be sold at the highest possible price.

And yet, troublingly, there is one difference between "labor" and other elements that conventional economics does not have a means to represent, or give weight to, but which is nevertheless unavoidably present: Labor feels pain and pleasure. When production lines grow prohibitively expensive, they may be switched off and will not cry at the seeming injustice of their fate. A business can move from using coal to natural gas without the neglected energy source walking off a cliff.

But labor has a habit of meeting attempts to reduce its price or presence with emotion. It sobs in toilet stalls, it gets drunk to ease its fears of underachievement, and it may choose death over redundancy.

These emotional responses point us to two, perhaps conflicting, imperatives coexisting in the workplace: an economic imperative that dictates that the primary task of business is to realize a profit, and a human imperative that leads employees to hunger for financial security, respect, tenure and even, on a good day, fun. Though the two imperatives may for long periods coexist without apparent friction, all wage-dependent workers live under an awareness that should there ever have to be a serious choice between the two, it is the economic one that must always prevail.

Struggles between labor and capital may no longer, in the developed world at least, be as bare-knuckled as in Marx's day. Yet, despite advances in working conditions and employee protections, workers remain tools in a process in which their own happiness or economic well-being is necessarily incidental. Whatever camaraderie may build up between employer and employed, whatever good will workers may display and however many years they may have devoted to a task, they must live with the knowledge and attendant anxiety that their status is not guaranteed—that it remains dependent on their own performance and the economic well-being of their organizations; that they are hence a means to profit, and never ends in themselves.

This is all sad, but not half as sad as it can be if we blind ourselves to the reality and raise our expectations of our work to extreme levels. A firm belief in the necessary misery of life was for centuries one of mankind's most important assets, a bulwark against bitterness, a defense against dashed hopes. Now it has been cruelly undermined by the expectations incubated by the modern worldview.

Now perhaps, as many of us return from summer vacations, we can temper their sadness by remembering that work is often more bearable when we don't, in addition to money, expect it always to deliver happiness.

Textual Questions

1. Why, according to de Botton, do Americans believe that work should be anything other than "punishment or penance"?

2. How does de Botton use history to develop his argument? How effective is this selective use of historical examples? Would personal or more modern examples be more effective support for the argument?

3. According to de Botton, what problems are caused by the modern idea that work should lead, at least on some level, to personal happiness?

Rhetorical Questions

4. How effectively can historical comparisons be drawn between men such as Michelangelo and large groups, such as slaves? And can either legitimately be used to make a comparison/contrast with modern American workers?

5. How is religion, directly or indirectly, a part of de Botton's argument? Does his use of religion seem effective or ineffective to you? Why?

6. How is personal happiness tied to our self image and internal expectations? How does this allow, at least in theory, for people to "fail" in the eyes of the larger American culture but to "succeed" in their own view?

Intertextual Questions

7. How do both Scott Russell Sanders (in "The Men We Carry in Our Minds") and Charles Young (in "Losing: An American Tradition") make the same argument as de Botton in regard to success, failure, and personal happiness in America?

8. Based upon de Botton's analysis of what it means to be happy at work, why might the workers described by John Steinbeck (in "Harvest Gypsies") feel personally responsible for their own unhappiness, even though their situation is largely beyond their control? Why might Barbara Ehrenreich (in "In Which I Am Offered a 'Job,'" later in this chapter) also feel unhappy in her potential work, based upon de Botton's analysis?

Thinking Beyond the Text

9. In modern America, are people defined by the work they do? What effects do such definitions have? Are there people who are paid little, in a financial sense, but who are respected greatly? Are people who make a great deal of money from their work given inordinate respect? What three examples of each group can you list?

10. According to de Botton, how are the drive for profit and the drive for personal financial security perhaps mutually exclusive? From a purely corporate standpoint, should worker happiness play any part in decisions? Why?

For Writing & Discussion

11. In modern America, workers are less and less likely to remain with a given employer for any significant amount of time—either because they choose to move on or because they are moved on by the corporation's decisions. Fewer and fewer employees who remain with a single corporation for a long stretch of time are paid any form of retirement benefit when they do leave their employer. This is a radical shift from the American workplace of a generation ago, when individual loyalty to a corporation was generally rewarded by financial stability and a steadily increasing (or at least not decreasing) standard of living. What, in your estimation, accounts for this change

in the American workplace? Is the change necessary, even if it is unfair to individuals? Does fairness have any place in the question or its answer? Loyalty?

GEORGE MILLER

George Miller (1945–) is a congressional representative from California. He is the ranking member of the Committee on Education and the Workforce, a member of the Committee on Resources, and chairman of the Democratic Policy Committee.

"Everyday Low Wages" discusses Wal-Mart's labor practices and details how much taxpayers spend supporting Wal-Mart employees who cannot afford housing, medical care, child care, and other necessities. It also addresses Wal-Mart's response to allegations of unfair labor practices. Miller also wrote a 2006 article for *The Nation*, "Employee Free Choice," which argues that all employees should have the right to form labor unions.

Miller's work on labor issues began long before his investigation of Wal-Mart. For example, he has advocated for labor reform in the Northern Marianas Islands, a U.S. territory that is exempt from most American labor laws. In 1999 he urged President Clinton to honor student involvement in a push to ban the use of sweatshop-made garments in university logo wear. Miller also has been closely involved in legislation about education and the environment. He was a co-signer of the No Child Left Behind Act, has resisted cuts to student financial aid, and supported the 1994 California Desert Protection Act.

Everday Low Wages

The Hidden Price We All Pay for Wal-Mart

∾ **Prereading Question**

Consider the area in which you live, work, and attend school. How many "big-box" stores do you have easy access to—from Target and K-Mart to Home Depot and Sam's Club? What items do you regularly purchase in such stores? What items do you purchase—regularly or occasionally—at smaller stores (that are either local chain stores or locally owned small businesses)?

February 16, 2004, A Report by the Democratic Staff of the Committee on Education and the Workforce, U.S. House of Representatives

Introduction

The retail giant Wal-Mart has become the nation's largest private sector employer with an estimated 1.2 million employees. The company's annual revenues now amount to 2 percent of the U.S. Gross Domestic Product. Wal-Mart's success is attributed to its ability to charge low prices in mega-stores offering everything from toys and furniture to groceries. While charging low prices obviously has some consumer benefits, mounting evidence from across the country indicates that these benefits come at a steep price for American workers, U.S. labor laws, and community living standards.

Wal-Mart is undercutting labor standards at home and abroad, while those federal officials charged with protecting labor standards have been largely indifferent. Public outcry against Wal-Mart's labor practices has been answered by the company with a cosmetic response. Wal-Mart has attempted to offset its labor record with advertising campaigns utilizing employees (who are euphemistically called "associates") to attest to Wal-Mart's employment benefits and support of local communities. Nevertheless—whether the issue is basic organizing rights of workers, or wages, or health benefits, or working conditions, or trade policy—Wal-Mart has come to represent the lowest common denominator in the treatment of working people.

This report reviews Wal-Mart's labor practices across the country and around the world and provides an overview of how working Americans and their allies in Congress are seeking to address the gamut of issues raised by this new standard-bearer of American retail.

Wal-Mart's Labor Practices

Workers' Organizing Rights

The United States recognizes workers' right to organize unions. Government employers generally may not interfere with public sector employees' freedom of association. In the private sector, workers' right to organize is protected by the National Labor Relations Act. Internationally, this right is recognized as a core labor standard and a basic human right.

Wal-Mart's record on the right to organize recently achieved international notoriety. On January 14, 2004, the International Confederation of Free Trade Unions (ICFTU), an organization representing 151 million workers in 233 affiliated unions around the world, issued a report on U.S. labor standards. Wal-Mart's rampant violations of workers' rights figured prominently. In the last few years, well over 100 unfair labor practice charges have been lodged against Wal-Mart throughout the country, with 43 charges filed in 2002 alone. Since 1995, the U.S. government has been forced to issue at least 60 complaints against Wal-Mart at the National Labor Relations Board. Wal-Mart's labor law violations range from illegally firing workers who attempt to organize a union to unlawful surveillance, threats, and intimidation of employees who dare to speak out.

With not a single Wal-Mart store in the United States represented by a union, the company takes a pro-active role in maintaining its union-free status. Wal-Mart has issued "A Manager's Toolbox to Remaining Union Free," which provides managers with lists of warning signs that workers might be organizing, including "frequent meetings at associates' homes" and "associates who are never seen together start talking or associating with each other." The "Toolbox" gives managers a hotline to call so that company specialists can respond rapidly and head off any attempt by employees to organize.

When employees have managed to obtain a union election and vote for a union, Wal-Mart has taken sweeping action in response. In 2000, when a small meatcutting department successfully organized a union at a Wal-Mart store in Texas, Wal-Mart responded a week later by announcing the phase-out of its meatcutting departments entirely. Because of deficient labor laws, it took the meatcutters in Texas three years to win their jobs back with an order that Wal-Mart bargain with their union. Rather than comply, Wal-Mart is appealing this decision.

Wal-Mart's aggressive anti-union activity, along with the nation's weak labor laws, have kept the largest private sector employer in the U.S. union-free. Breaking the law that guarantees workers' right to organize has material consequences for both the workers and the company. According to data released by the Bureau of Labor Statistics in January 2004, union workers earn median weekly salaries of $760, compared to non-union workers' median weekly salaries of $599—a difference of over 26 percent. In the supermarket industry, the union difference is even more pronounced, with union members making 30 percent more than non-union workers. Union representation also correlates with higher benefits. For instance, 72 percent of union workers have guaranteed pensions with defined benefits, while only 15 percent of non-union workers enjoy such retirement security. On the health care front, which will be explored in more detail later, 60 percent of union workers have medical care benefits on the job, compared to only 44 percent of non-union workers. For companies like Wal-Mart seeking to maintain low labor costs, these statistics obviously provide an incentive to remain union-free. Unfortunately, U.S. labor laws fail to provide a sufficient disincentive against violating workers' rights.

Low Wages

By keeping unions at bay, Wal-Mart keeps its wages low—even by general industry standards. The average supermarket employee makes $10.35 per hour. Sales clerks at Wal-Mart, on the other hand, made only

$8.23 per hour on average, or $13,861 per year, in 2001. Some estimate that average "associate" salaries range from $7.50 to $8.50 per hour. With an average on-the-clock workweek of 32 hours, many workers take home less than $1,000 per month. Even the higher estimate of a $13,861 annual salary fell below the 2001 federal poverty line of $14,630 for a family of three. About one-third of Wal-Mart's employees are part-time, restricting their access to benefits. These low wages, to say the least, complicate employees' ability to obtain essential benefits, such as health care coverage, which will be explored in a later section.

The low pay stands in stark contrast to Wal-Mart's slogan, "Our people make the difference." Now-retired Senior Vice President Don Soderquist has explained: "'Our people make the difference' is not a meaningless slogan— it's a reality at Wal-Mart. We are a group of dedicated, hardworking, ordinary people who have teamed together to accomplish extraordinary things." With 2002 company profits hitting $6.6 billion, Wal-Mart employees do indeed "accomplish extraordinary things." But at poverty level wages, these workers are not sharing in the company's success.

Unequal Pay and Treatment

Title VII of the Civil Rights Act prohibits discrimination in employment based on employees' race, color, religion, sex, or national origin. Additionally, the Equal Pay Act, an amendment to the Fair Labor Standards Act, prohibits unequal pay for equal work on the basis of sex. These basic labor and civil rights laws have become an issue at Wal-Mart.

In 2001, six women sued Wal-Mart in California claiming the company discriminated against women by systematically denying them promotions and paying them less than men. The lawsuit has expanded to potentially the largest class action in U.S. history—on behalf of more than 1 million current and former female employees. While two-thirds of the company's hourly workers are female, women hold only one-third of managerial positions and constitute less than 15 percent of store managers. The suit also claims that women are pushed into "female" departments and are demoted if they complain about unequal treatment. One plaintiff, a single mother of four, started at Wal-Mart in 1990 at a mere $3.85 an hour. Even with her persistent requests for training and promotions, it took her eight years to reach $7.32 an hour and seven years to reach management, while her male counterparts were given raises and promotions much more quickly. For this plaintiff, annual pay increases were as little as 10 cents and never more than 35 cents per hour.

Off-The-Clock Work

While wages are low at Wal-Mart, too often employees are not paid at all. The Fair Labor Standards Act (FLSA), along with state wage and hour laws, requires hourly employees to be paid for all time actually worked at no less than a minimum wage and at time-and-a-half for all hours worked over 40 in a week. These labor laws have posed a particular obstacle for Wal-Mart. As of December 2002, there were thirty-nine class-action lawsuits against the company in thirty states, claiming tens of millions of dollars in back pay for hundreds of thousands of Wal-Mart employees.

In 2001, Wal-Mart forked over $50 million in unpaid wages to 69,000 workers in Colorado. These wages were paid only after the workers filed a class action lawsuit. Wal-Mart had been working the employees off-the-clock. The company also paid $500,000 to 120 workers in Gallup, New Mexico, who filed a lawsuit over unpaid work.

In a Texas class-action certified in 2002 on behalf of 200,000 former and current Wal-Mart employees, statisticians estimated that the company shortchanged its workers $150 million over four years—just based on the frequency of employees working through their daily 15 minute breaks.

In Oregon, 400 employees in 27 stores sued the company for unpaid, off-the-clock overtime. In their suit, the workers explained that managers would delete hours from their time records and tell employees to clean the store after they clocked out. In December 2002, a jury found in favor of the workers. One personnel manager claimed that, for six years, she was forced to delete hours from employee time sheets.

In the latest class-action, filed in November 2003, noting evidence of systematic violations of the wage-and-hour law, a judge certified a lawsuit for 65,000 Wal-Mart employees in Minnesota. Reacting to the certification, a Wal-Mart spokesperson told the Minneapolis *Star Tribune:* "We have no reason to believe these isolated situations . . . represent a widespread problem with off-the-clock work."

Many observers blame the wage-and-hour problems at Wal-Mart on pressure placed on managers to keep labor costs down. In 2002, operating costs for Wal-Mart were just 16.6 percent of total sales, compared to a 20.7 percent average for the retail industry as a whole. Wal-Mart reportedly awards bonuses to its employees based on earnings. With other operating and inventory costs set by higher level management, store managers must turn to wages to increase profits. While Wal-Mart expects those managers to increase sales each year, it expects the labor costs to be cut by two-tenths of a percentage point each year as well.

Reports from former Wal-Mart managers seem to corroborate this dynamic. Joyce Moody, a former manager in Alabama and Mississippi, told the *New York Times* that Wal-Mart "threatened to write up managers if they didn't bring the payroll in low enough." Depositions in wage and hour lawsuits reveal that company headquarters leaned on management to keep their labor costs at 8 percent of sales or less, and managers in turn leaned on assistant managers to work their employees off-the-clock or simply delete time from employee time sheets.

Child Labor and Work Breaks Violations

The Fair Labor Standards Act and state wage and hour laws also govern child labor and work breaks. These work time regulations have likewise posed a problem at Wal-Mart stores.

In January 2004, the *New York Times* reported on an internal Wal-Mart audit which found "extensive violations of child-labor laws and state regulations requiring time for breaks and meals." One week of time records from 25,000 employees in July 2000 found 1,371 instances of minors working too late, during school hours, or for too many hours in a day. There were 60,767 missed breaks and 15,705 lost meal times.

According to the *New York Times* report: "Verette Richardson, a former Wal-Mart cashier in Kansas City, Mo., said it was sometimes so hard to get a break that some cashiers urinated on themselves. Bella Blaubergs, a diabetic who worked at a Wal-Mart in Washington State, said she sometimes nearly fainted from low blood sugar because managers often would not give breaks."

A store manager in Kentucky told the *New York Times* that, after the audit was issued, he received no word from company executives to try harder to cut down on violations: "There was no follow-up to that audit, there was nothing sent out I was aware of saying, 'We're bad. We screwed up. This is the remedy we're going to follow to correct the situation.'"

Unaffordable or Unavailable Health Care

In 2002, 43 million non-elderly Americans lacked health insurance coverage—an increase of almost 2.5 million from the previous year. Most Americans receive their health insurance coverage through their employers. At the same time, most of the uninsured are working Americans and their families, with low to moderate incomes. Their employers, however, either do not offer health insurance at all or the health insurance offered is simply unaffordable.

Among these uninsured working families are a significant number of Wal-Mart employees, many of whom instead secure their health care from publicly subsidized programs. Fewer than half—between 41 and 46 percent—of Wal-Mart's employees are insured by the company's health care plan, compared nationally to 66 percent of employees at large firms like Wal-Mart who receive health benefits from their employer. In recent years, the company increased obstacles for its workers to access its health care plan.

In 2002, Wal-Mart increased the waiting period for enrollment eligibility from 90 days to 6 months for full-time employees. Part-time employees must wait 2 years before they may enroll in the plan, and they may not purchase coverage for their spouses or children. The definition of part-time was changed from 28 hours or less per week to less than

34 hours per week. At the time, approximately one-third of Wal-Mart's workforce was part-time. By comparison, nationally, the average waiting period for health coverage for employees at large firms like Wal-Mart was 1.3 months.

The Wal-Mart plan itself shifts much of the health care costs onto employees. In 1999, employees paid 36 percent of the costs. In 2001, the employee burden rose to 42 percent. Nationally, large-firm employees pay on average 16 percent of the premium for health insurance. Unionized grocery workers typically pay nothing. Studies show that much of the decline in employer-based health coverage is due to shifts of premium costs from employers to employees.

Moreover, Wal-Mart employees who utilize their health care confront high deductibles and co-payments. A single worker could end up spending around $6,400 out-of-pocket—about 45 percent of her annual full-time salary—before seeing a single benefit from the health plan.

According to an AFL-CIO report issued in October 2003, the employees' low wages and Wal-Mart's cost-shifting render health insurance unaffordable, particularly for those employees with families. Even under the Wal-Mart plan with the highest deductible ($1,000)—and therefore with the lowest employee premium contribution—it would take an $8 per hour employee, working 34 hours per week, almost one-and-a-half months of pre-tax earnings to pay for one year of family coverage.

Wal-Mart's spending on health care for its employees falls well below industry and national employer-spending averages. A Harvard Business School case study on Wal-Mart found that, in 2002, Wal-Mart spent an average of $3,500 per employee. By comparison, the average spending per employee in the wholesale/retailing sector was $4,800. For U.S. employers in general, the average was $5,600 per employee.

In the end, because they cannot afford the company health plan, many Wal-Mart workers must turn to public assistance for health care or forego their health care needs altogether. Effectively, Wal-Mart forces taxpayers to subsidize what should be a company-funded health plan. According to a study by the Institute for Labor and Employment at the University of California–Berkeley, California taxpayers subsidized $20.5 million worth of medical care for Wal-Mart in that state alone. In fact, Wal-Mart personnel offices, knowing employees cannot afford the company health plan, actually encourage employees to apply for charitable and public assistance, according to a recent report by the PBS news program *Now With Bill Moyers.*

When a giant like Wal-Mart shifts health insurance costs to employees, its competitors invariably come under pressure to do the same. Currently engaged in the largest ongoing labor dispute in the nation, unionized grocery workers in southern California have refused to accept higher health care costs resulting from cost-shifting on health insurance premiums by their grocery chain employers—cost-shifting, the grocers say, inspired by the threat of Wal-Mart competition. Beginning on October 11, 2003, 70,000 grocery employees of Vons, Pavilions, Ralphs, and Albertsons have either been on strike or locked out. The companies want to dramatically increase workers' share of health costs, claiming that the change is necessary in order to compete with Wal-Mart's incursion in the southern California market. E. Richard Brown, the director of the Center for Health Policy at the University of California, Los Angeles, told the *Sacramento Bee* that, if the grocery chains drastically reduce health benefits, the trends toward cost shifting and elimination of health coverage will accelerate. Following the grocers' lead, more employers would offer fewer benefits, would require their workers to pay more, and may even drop health benefits altogether. Whether the current pressure from Wal-Mart is real or imagined or merely a convenient excuse for the grocers' cost-cutting bargaining position, Wal-Mart has sparked a new race to the bottom among American retail employers. Undeniably, such a race threatens to undermine the employer-based health insurance system.

Low Wages Mean High Costs to Taxpayers

Because Wal-Mart wages are generally not living wages, the company uses taxpayers to subsidize its labor costs. While the California study showed how much taxpayers were subsidizing Wal-Mart on health care alone, the total costs to taxpayers for Wal-Mart's labor policies are much greater.

The Democratic Staff of the Committee on Education and the Workforce estimates that one 200-person Wal-Mart store may result in a cost to federal taxpayers of $420,750 per year—about $2,103 per employee. Specifically, the low wages result in the following additional public costs being passed along to taxpayers:

- $36,000 a year for free and reduced lunches for just 50 qualifying Wal-Mart families.
- $42,000 a year for Section 8 housing assistance, assuming 3 percent of the store employees qualify for such assistance, at $6,700 per family.
- $125,000 a year for federal tax credits and deductions for low-income families, assuming 50 employees are heads of household with a child and 50 are married with two children.
- $100,000 a year for the additional Title I expenses, assuming 50 Wal-Mart families qualify with an average of Two children.
- $108,000 a year for the additional federal health care costs of moving into state children's health insurance programs (S-CHIP), assuming 30 employees with an average of two children qualify.
- $9,750 a year for the additional costs for low income energy assistance.

Among Wal-Mart employees, some single workers may be able to make ends meet. Others may be forced to take on two or three jobs. Others may have a spouse with a better job. And others simply cannot make ends meet. Because Wal-Mart fails to pay sufficient wages, U.S. taxpayers are forced to pick up the tab. In this sense, Wal-Mart's profits are not made only on the backs of its employees—but on the backs of every U.S. taxpayer.

The ultimate costs are not limited to subsidies for underpaid Wal-Mart workers. When a Wal-Mart comes to town, the new competition has a ripple effect throughout the community. Other stores are forced out of business or forced to cut employees' wages and benefits in order to compete with Wal-Mart. The Los Angeles City Council commissioned a report in 2003 on the effects of allowing Wal-Mart Supercenters into their communities. The report, prepared by consulting firm Rodino and Associates, found that Supercenters drive down wages in the local retail industry, place a strain on public services, and damage small businesses. It recommended that the City Council refuse to allow any Supercenters to be built in Los Angeles without a promise from Wal-Mart to increase wages and benefits for its employees.

The findings of the Rodino report are alarming. The labor impacts of a Wal-Mart Supercenter on low-income communities include:

- "Big box retailers and superstores may negatively impact the labor market in an area by the conversion of higher paying retail jobs to a fewer number of lower paying retail jobs. The difference in overall compensation (wages and benefits) may be as much as $8.00."
- "Lack of health care benefits of many big box and superstore employees can result in a greater public financial burden as workers utilize emergency rooms as a major component of their health care."
- "A study conducted by the San Diego Taxpayers Association (SDCTA), a nonprofit, nonpartisan organization, found that an influx of big-box stores into San Diego would result in an annual decline in wages and benefits between $105 million and $221 million, and an increase of $9 million in public health costs. SDCTA also estimated that the region would lose pensions and retirement benefits valued between $89 million and $170 million per year and that even increased sales and property tax revenues would not cover the extra costs of necessary public services."
- "[The threat of Wal-Mart's incursion into the southern California grocery market] is already triggering a dynamic in which the grocery stores are negotiating with workers for lowered compensation, in an attempt to re-level the 'playing field.'"
- "One study of superstores and their potential impact on grocery industry employees found that the entry of such stores into the

Southern California regional grocery business was expected to depress industry wages and benefits at an estimated range from a low of $500 million to a high of almost $1.4 billion annually, potentially affecting 250,000 grocery industry employees . . . [T]he full impact of lost wages and benefits throughout Southern California could approach $2.8 billion per year."

Reports such as these have provided supporting evidence to localities which seek to pass ordinances restricting "big box" or supercenter stores. Such ordinances were recently passed in Alameda and Contra Costa counties in California. Wal-Mart, however, has moved to overturn those ordinances. In Contra Costa, Wal-Mart launched a petition drive to challenge that county's ordinance in a referendum in March 2004. In Alameda, the company has filed a lawsuit to void an ordinance passed by the Board of Supervisors in January 2004.

One of the most cited studies on Wal-Mart's impact on local communities was performed by economist Kenneth Stone at Iowa State University in 1993. Stone looked at the impact of Wal-Mart on small towns in Iowa. He found a 3 percent spike in total retail sales in communities immediately after a Wal-Mart opened. But the longer term effects of Wal-Mart were disastrous for nearby independent businesses. Over the course of the next several years, retailers' sales of mens' and boys' apparel dropped 44 percent on average, hardware sales fell by 31 percent, and lawn and garden sales fell by 26 percent. Likewise, a Congressional Research Service report in 1994 explained that Wal-Mart uses a saturation strategy with store development. In other words, it builds stores in nearby connected markets in order to stifle any competition in the targeted area by the size of its presence.

By all accounts, Wal-Mart's development strategy has been working. Currently, Wal-Mart operates around 3,000 total stores and close to 1,400 Supercenters. It is the largest grocer in the U.S., with a 19 percent market share, and the third-largest pharmacy, with a 16 percent market share. According to Retail Forward, a global management consulting and research firm, for every one Supercenter that will open, two supermarkets will close. Since 1992, the supermarket industry has experienced a net loss of 13,500 stores. Over the next five years, Wal-Mart plans to open 1,000 more Supercenters in the U.S. By 2007, Wal-Mart is expected to control 35 percent of food and drug sales in the U.S.

Illegal Use of Undocumented Workers

Among the lowest paid workers in the U.S. economy are undocumented immigrants. As was reported in the fall of 2003, these workers are not foreign to the floors of Wal-Mart stores. On October 23, 2003, federal agents raided 61 Wal-Mart stores in 21 states. When they left, the agents had arrested 250 nightshift janitors who were undocumented workers.

Following the arrests, a grand jury convened to consider charging Wal-Mart executives with labor racketeering crimes for knowingly allowing undocumented workers to work at their stores. The workers themselves were employed by agencies Wal-Mart contracted with for cheap cleaning services. While Wal-Mart executives have tried to lay the blame squarely with the contractors, federal investigators point to wiretapped conversations showing that executives knew the workers were undocumented.

Additionally, some of the janitors have filed a class-action lawsuit against Wal-Mart alleging both racketeering and wage-and-hour violations. According to the janitors, Wal-Mart and its contractors failed to pay them overtime totaling, along with other damages, $200,000. One of the plaintiffs told the *New York Times* that he worked seven days per week for eight months, earning $325 for 60-hour weeks, and he never received overtime. A legal question now being raised is whether these undocumented workers even have the right to sue their employers.

Not surprisingly, this recent raid was not the first time Wal-Mart was caught using undocumented workers. In 1998 and 2001, federal agents arrested 102 undocumented workers at Wal-Marts around the country.

President Bush's newly proposed temporary foreign worker plan would legalize such undocumented workers without granting them an opportunity for citizenship, creating a new class of indentured servants and a safer source of cheap labor for companies like Wal-Mart.

Trading Away Jobs

Since the recession began in March 2001, the United States has lost 2.4 million jobs. In every recession, since the Great Depression, jobs were recovered within the first 31 months after the recession began—until now. The latest recession began 34 months ago and officially ended in November 2001, but the jobs have not been recovered. For American working families, by all accounts, the "jobless recovery" has been of little benefit to them. While GDP growth was strong or solid in the third and fourth quarters of 2003, real wages for workers remained stagnant and even declined.

Indeed, of the jobs that remain, the pay is low. The country has seen a dramatic shift from high-paying jobs to low-paying jobs. For instance, in New Hampshire, which still has not recovered the number of jobs it lost in the recession, new jobs pay 35 percent lower wages than lost jobs. In Delaware, those wages are 43 percent lower; in Colorado, 35 percent lower; in West Virginia, 33 percent lower. In fact, the low-pay shift has hit all but two of the fifty states.

Moreover, these changes in the labor market reveal themselves in a marked decline in living standards for low- and middle-income workers. The real weekly earnings for full-time workers age 25 and older fell for the bottom half of the workforce between the fourth quarters of 2002 and 2003. In particular, workers in the 10th percentile saw their weekly earnings fall 1.2 percent; in the 20th percentile, by 0.5 percent, in the 50th percentile, by 0.1 percent. Conversely, earners in the top percentiles of income experienced growth. The 90th percentile, for instance, saw a 1.1 percent increase in weekly earnings. As the Economic Policy Institute points out: "This pattern of earnings growth suggests that while the economy is expanding, the benefits of growth are flowing to those at the top of the wage scale."

These lower-paying jobs are largely service sector jobs, like retail, replacing traditionally higher-paying and unionized manufacturing jobs. Between January 1998 and August 2003, the nation experienced a net loss of 3 million manufacturing jobs. During the "recovery," 1.3 million manufacturing jobs disappeared. American manufacturers find it increasingly difficult to keep jobs in the U.S., given the availability of cheap labor abroad. In 2003, the U.S. trade deficit hit a record high of $551 billion, increasing 15 percent from 2002 and exceeding 5 percent of GDP.

Wal-Mart plays a curiously illustrative role in this jobs phenomenon— not just in the creation of low-paying jobs and the downward pressure on wages and benefits, but also in the export of existing manufacturing jobs to foreign countries offering cheap labor. Wal-Mart markets itself with a patriotic, small-town, red-white-and-blue advertising motif. But Wal-Mart's trade practices are anything but small-town. Indeed, Wal-Mart conducts international trade in manufactured goods on a scale that can bring down entire nations' economies.

While the red-white-and-blue banners remain, long-gone are the days when Wal-Mart abided by the mottos of "Buy American" and "Bring It Home to the USA." In 1995, Wal-Mart claimed only 6 percent of its merchandise was imported. Today an estimated 50–60 percent of its products come from overseas. In the past five years, Wal-Mart has doubled its imports from China. In 2002, the company bought 14 percent of the $1.9 billion of clothes exported by Bangladesh to the United States. Also in 2002, the company purchased $12 billion in merchandise from China, or 10 percent of China's total U.S.-bound exports, a 20 percent increase from the previous year. In 2003, these Chinese purchases jumped to $15 billion, or almost one-eighth of all Chinese exports to the United States. Today, more than 3,000 supplier factories in China produce for Wal-Mart.

Wal-Mart maintains an extensive global network of 10,000 suppliers. Whether American, Bangladeshi, Chinese, or Honduran, Wal-Mart plays these producers against one another in search of lower and lower prices.

American suppliers have been forced to relocate their businesses overseas to maintain Wal-Mart contracts. Overseas manufacturers are forced to engage in cutthroat competition that further erodes wages and working conditions of what often already are sweatshops. To keep up with the pressure to produce ever cheaper goods, factories force employees to work overtime or work for weeks without a day off. A Bangladeshi factory worker told the *Los Angeles Times* that employees at her factory worked from 8 a.m. to 3 a.m. for 10 and 15 day stretches just to meet Wal-Mart price demands. And still, Wal-Mart's general manager for Bangladesh complained of his country's factories, telling the *Los Angeles Times*, "I think they need to improve. When I entered a factory in China, it seemed they are very fast."

While low-wage jobs displace higher-paid manufacturing jobs in the United States, undercutting living standards at home, living standards abroad are not reaping the benefits one might expect. Reports indicate that Wal-Mart's bargaining power is able to maintain low wages and poor working conditions among its foreign suppliers. The *Washington Post* has explained: "As capital scours the globe for cheaper and more malleable workers, and as poor countries seek multinational companies to provide jobs, lift production, and open export markets, Wal-Mart and China have forged themselves into the ultimate joint venture, their symbiosis influencing the terms of labor and consumption the world over." Thanks to a ban on independent trade unions and a lack of other basic human rights, China offers Wal-Mart a highly-disciplined and cheap workforce. A Chinese labor official who asked to remain anonymous for fear of punishment told the *Washington Post* that "Wal-Mart pressures the factory to cut its price, and the factory responds with longer hours or lower pay. And the workers have no options."

One employee of a Chinese supplier described the difficulties of surviving on $75 per month. She could rarely afford to buy meat, and her family largely subsisted on vegetables. Over four years, she had not received a single salary increase.

Wal-Mart has countered that it insists that its suppliers enforce labor standards and comply with Chinese law. One-hundred Wal-Mart auditors inspect Chinese plants, and the company has suspended contracts with about 400 suppliers, mainly for violating overtime limits. An additional 72 factories were permanently blacklisted in 2003 for violating child labor standards. Still, critics point out that the Wal-Mart does not regularly inspect smaller factories that use middlemen to sell to the company. Nor does it inspect the factories of subcontractors. A Chinese labor organizer explained that the inspections are "ineffective," since Wal-Mart usually notifies the factories in advance. The factories "often prepare by cleaning up, creating fake time sheets and briefing workers on what to say."

The factories themselves complain that, because Wal-Mart demands such low prices, they have slim profit margins—if any. A manager of one Chinese supplier told the *Washington Post,* "In the beginning, we made money . . . But when Wal-Mart started to launch nationwide distribution, they pressured us for a special price below our cost. Now, we're losing money on every box, while Wal-Mart is making more money." Obviously, one way to regain a profit for such suppliers would be to begin cutting back on labor costs.

Finally, as testament to Wal-Mart's stalwart anti-union policy, none of its 31 stores in China are unionized, despite the fact that the Communist Party-controlled official union has told the company that it would not help workers fight for higher pay. Oddly enough, Article 10 of China's Trade Union Law requires that any establishment with 25 or more workers must have a union. Wal-Mart, however, claims that it has received assurances from the central government that it need not allow unions in any of its stores. As one reporter has explained, "The explanation for the apparent contradiction may be that the government's desire for foreign investment and jobs trumps any concern for workers' rights. That wouldn't be surprising in the Chinese environment, where strikes are forbidden and the official labor grouping actively supports the government's efforts to block the rise of independent unions." With China, any company in search of pliant and cheap labor has found a perfect mix of cooperative government officials and workers made submissive through fear.

Disability Discrimination

The Americans with Disabilities Act (ADA) prohibits discrimination against persons with disabilities in employment matters. In particular, an employer may not discriminate against an employee or prospective employee who is otherwise qualified to perform the job if given reasonable accommodations.

In addition to lawsuits over lost wages or unequal pay, Wal-Mart has faced a barrage of lawsuits alleging that the company discriminates against workers with disabilities. In 2001, Wal-Mart paid over $6 million to settle 13 such lawsuits. These cases were brought by the U.S. Equal Employment Opportunity Commission (EEOC) on behalf of disabled persons whom Wal-Mart failed to hire. The settlement also required Wal-Mart to change its procedures in dealing with disabled job applicants and provide more training for its employees on anti-discrimination laws.

Yet, on January 20, 2004, the EEOC filed another lawsuit against the retail giant on behalf of a job applicant who claims he was not hired because he needed a wheelchair. The lawsuit was filed in Kansas City after the EEOC failed to obtain a settlement with Wal-Mart.

Worker Safety

The Occupational Safety and Health Act (OSHA) is designed to protect workers from workplace injuries and illnesses. OSHA is enforced by the Department of Labor's Occupational Safety and Health Administration. Regulations issued by that agency lay out clear rules for such safety matters as the provision of exits for employees.

The latest Wal-Mart scandal to hit the news is its reported lockdown of its nighttime shift various stores around the country. According to a January 18, 2004, *New York Times* report, the company institutes a "lock-in" policy at some of its Wal-Mart and Sam's Club stores. The stores lock their doors at night so that no one can enter or leave the building, leaving workers inside trapped. Some workers are then threatened that, if they ever use the fire exit to leave the building, they will be fired. Instead, a manager is supposed to have a key that will unlock doors to allow employees to escape. Many workers have found themselves locked in without a manager who has a key, as the *New York Times* story detailed.

The company has claimed that the policy is designed to protect stores and employees from crime. Former store managers, however, have claimed the real reason behind the lockdown is to prevent "shrinkage"—i.e., theft by either employees or outsiders. It is also designed to eliminate unauthorized cigarette breaks or quick trips home.

Locked-in workers have had to wait for hours off-the-clock for a manager to show up to let them go home after they completed their shift. One worker claims to have broken his foot on the job and had to wait four hours for someone to open the door. Another worker alleges she cut her hand with box cutters one night and was forced to wait until morning to go to the hospital, where she received thirteen stitches.

In the history of American worker safety, some of the worst tragedies have involved employees locked in their workplaces in an emergency, including the Triangle Waist Company fire of 1911 in which 146 women died in a fire because the garment factory's doors were locked. As recently as 1991, 25 workers perished in a fire at a chicken processing plant in North Carolina. The plant's owner had locked the doors for fear of employee theft and unauthorized breaks. According to recent reports, ten percent of Wal-Mart's stores are subjected to the nighttime lockdown.

In 2002, in a telling junction of alleged labor law violations, the National Labor Relations Board (NLRB) issued a complaint against a Wal-Mart in Texas regarding health and safety threats made by management against employees. According to the complaint, a company official told workers that, after a worker filed complaints regarding unsafe conditions with the Occupational Safety and Health Administration (OSHA), any fines imposed upon the company would come out of employee bonuses.

∽

Wal-Mart's Response

Wal-Mart's response to this extensive list of labor problems has been to treat the charges as a public-relations matter and not a substantive issue of workplace fairness. Seemingly, Wal-Mart believes only its image—not its behavior—needs to be adjusted. In that regard, Wal-Mart has undertaken aggressive advertising campaigns, has financed its own economic-impact studies to counter those that show the costs of Wal-Mart to local communities, and has become a major political campaign contributor.

On the advertising front, Wal-Mart launched a television ad series called "Good Jobs" in early 2004. The ads feature Wal-Mart employees talking about how great it is to work at Wal-Mart. Spots also show Wal-Mart's community involvement. One ad features a Wal-Mart employee who attests that Wal-Mart health insurance made it possible to treat his 7-year-old son for liver disease. It is not known what the total cost of the ad series will be in the end.

Wal-Mart has also financed its own studies, to counter publicly commissioned reports which detail the burden that Wal-Mart imposes on communities. After the Rodino report was commissioned by Los Angeles City Council members, the Los Angeles Economic Development Corporation (LAEDC), a private non-profit corporation, released its own study. The LAEDC study was commissioned and financed by Wal-Mart Stores, Inc. Unsurprisingly, it claimed that Wal-Mart Supercenters would provide extraordinary benefits for the Los Angeles economy.

Because Wal-Mart would be charging lower prices, according to the report, households would experience greater savings. If Wal-Mart penetrates 20 percent of the market in the seven Southland counties, the savings, an estimated $3.6 billion, would then translate into the creation of an incredible 36,400 jobs annually. That is, while the study estimates that 3,000 to 5,000 jobs would be lost in the grocery business, consumer savings on food prices would turn into more consumer spending on non-grocery goods, creating more jobs in those sectors. Of course, it is not at all clear why job loss would be limited to the grocery business, since Supercenters, by their very nature, sell virtually any consumer good, except for durables like automobiles. According to the study, California consumers "may opt to spend their savings on sports equipment, continuing education classes, or restaurant meals." The study failed to mention that Wal-Mart already offers an extensive line of "sports equipment." The "continuing education classes" were presumably listed because they may constitute job training for better jobs. And where would those better jobs be? It can only be assumed, as more people spend their grocery savings for "restaurant meals," much of the claimed job creation would be in restaurants and similar low-paying service sector businesses, for which continuing education classes offer little advantage.

The ultimate household savings projections by the LAEDC study should also be questioned. First, downward pressure on wages and benefits, spurred by the giant employer, would cause people to have less money to spend. Thus, while they may spend less on groceries, they also make less or may be spending more on former benefits like health care. Indeed, the study appears to not take into account the loss of such benefits as health care and pensions that workers are likely to experience. Second, when Wal-Mart has successfully reduced the number of surrounding competitors, there is less pressure on the company to keep its prices low. Third, the claim that Wal-Mart does in fact charge consumers less is open to question. Economist Kenneth Stone has found that Wal-Mart lowers the prices of "price sensitive" items such as milk and bread. Consumers pay attention to the prices of these items—the kind of everyday items consumers buy most often—and less attention to the prices of other items such as light bulbs—which are not reduced and may be more expensive at Wal-Mart than at other retailers. The lower-priced items are displayed prominently, grabbing customers' attention and leading them to mistakenly believe that they are getting similarly low prices on other items throughout the store.

The LAEDC study also disputed the extent of wage and benefit differences between Wal-Mart employees and other retail or grocery workers. According to the LAEDC, wage comparisons are often skewed for two reasons. First, most Wal-Mart Supercenters have not been open long enough to allow employees to accumulate seniority and, therefore, higher rates of pay. Second, because Wal-Mart promotes to management from within its own ranks, those employees with the greatest longevity are usually no longer counted as hourly employees.

The first reason does not appear to square with prolific reports about the intense pressure on stores to keep labor costs down. This story first appeared in the *Wall Street Journal*:

> At Wal-Mart Stores Inc., managers are judged in part on their ability to keep payroll costs at a strict percentage of sales, according to former managers. Some say that puts extra pressure on higher-paid workers to be more productive.
>
> "You keep people making $ 10 an hour to a high standard," putting more pressure on them for small mistakes, said Lyndol Jackson, a Wal-Mart manager until he left for another job in 1998.
>
> Often, those workers quit and can be replaced less expensively, added Jackson, who lives in Memphis, Tenn.
>
> Former Wal-Mart cashier Dana Mailloux, 33, worked for eight years at a store in Fort Myers, Fla., moving up to $ 9.15 an hour. Last fall, her manager

called her and more than a dozen other longtime employees into his office and told them he had to lay them off because of lack of work.

That same day, Mailloux said, she passed a room with six new hires, red vests in hand, filling out paperwork.

Returning to the store that weekend, she said, she saw newly advertised positions listed on a bulletin board.

"Basically, I was thrown out like a piece of trash," said Mailloux.

Wal-Mart spokeswoman Sarah Clark said the company continually lays off and hires workers as sales rise and fall. She said that if "labor adjustments are necessary," the company before making cuts asks for volunteers to take time off and carefully controls hours.

"It is ludicrous and contrary to our business model to think the company would benefit from replacing experienced associates with new, lower-paid ones," Clark said in a statement. "It's clear that experienced associates are golden with us."

Clark declined to discuss Mailloux's dismissal, citing employee privacy.

In other words, there may be other reasons for the wage difference than just the frequency of store openings. Nor does the lack-of-longevity reason for the wage differences square with previously-mentioned accounts of actual pay raises of just a few cents per year.

The second reason claimed for wage differences—that Wal-Mart promotes its best employees to management—would appear to be exaggerated. To the extent that such promotions do happen, their effect on the average Wal-Mart wage must be minimal. Wal-Mart is not promoting half of its workforce. The average Wal-Mart store has one manager, one-to-three assistant managers, and 15 department heads (who may or may not be counted as hourly), compared to 300 to 350 "associates."

Moreover, according to the study, Wal-Mart's health care benefits are better than often portrayed. The authors acknowledge that the Wal-Mart health insurance plan is not as comprehensive as the unionized grocery store plans in Southern California and that Wal-Mart employees must pay part of the premium while union workers pay nothing. However, the authors note, the Wal-Mart plan does not include a cap on medical expenses, thereby protecting participating employees from the bankrupting costs of catastrophic illnesses. The unionized store plans do have a cap, according to the LAEDC study.

The relative worth of a catastrophic plan versus a more comprehensive health plan comes into focus when considering the frequency with which workers utilize various services. While childrens' vaccinations are covered by the union plans, such routine medical needs are excluded from Wal-Mart's coverge. Such out-of-pocket costs for these low-wage employees might be $75 per shot at a private clinic. On the other hand, Wal-Mart touts the 60 transplants it covers per year at a cost of $1 million each. As one commentator has noted, 60 transplants amounts to slightly over one-hundredth of one percent of Wal-Mart's 500,000 insured workers.

On the issue of health care coverage, the LAEDC study explained:

> Since they must pay some of the upfront costs of medical care, many Wal-Mart employees who are eligible for the coverage choose not to participate. This leads to much lower participation rates among Wal-Mart employees than among union workers, virtually all of whom participate since their up front costs are paid by their employer. It is worth noting that more than 90 percent of all Wal-Mart employees have health coverage from some source, including the company itself, a covered spouse, parents, through retirement benefits (from another job), etc.

According to the LAEDC, low participation rates in Wal-Mart's health plan are a matter of mere "choice," not affordability. Nevertheless, most Wal-Mart employees, according to the study, have health care from "some source," including "a covered spouse"—that is, a spouse at another company with better health care benefits, now subsidizing what should be Wal-Mart's labor cost. The study did not go into any further detail on what these unnamed other sources of coverage might be, but did not rule out public assistance programs. In July 2003, California Assemblywoman Sandy Lieber (D-San Jose) released copies of employee handouts from Wal-Mart which explained how to use an employment verification service when applying for Medicaid, food stamps, and other public services.

The LAEDC study continued on the topic of health care coverage: "The issue of participation rates may become moot in California, however. In October, Governor Davis signed SB2—Health Care for Working Families that mandates large employers to provide health coverage to all of their employees." While Wal-Mart currently covers about two-thirds of the costs of employee health care, SB2 would require Wal-Mart to cover 80 percent. The long waiting periods for Wal-Mart coverage would also have to be cut by 3 months for full-time workers and one-year and nine months for part-time workers. While the study claimed SB2 might render the debate over participation rates moot, it failed to mention that Wal-Mart has helped finance an employer-backed campaign for a referendum to repeal SB2.

Textual Questions

1. What tone is set by the opening three paragraphs? How is this tone set? How does this tone affect a reader's examination of the information that follows?

2. The body of this report describes eleven different aspects of Wal-Mart's business practices, from its active discouraging of unionization to its

record on worker safety. Which of these practices is described most effectively? Why? Which is least effectively described? Why?

3. After many pages of accusations of wrongdoing, the Wal-Mart response is comparatively short. As a reader, how effective is this response, in your opinion? Given the differing sizes between the charges and the rebuttal, how are the authors hoping to shape your response? Are you actually responding as they would want? Why/why not?

Rhetorical Questions

4. Like the introduction, the conclusion is only three paragraphs long. What points do both the introduction and the conclusion make, and how effectively do they make them? In a report of this length, is brevity more or less effective?

5. In the body of this report, serious allegations of illegal business practices are mixed with allegations of unfair business practices and unethical business practices. Why mix the charges against Wal-Mart together in this way rather than listing them in a least-to-most serious structure? Why not separate the illegal and the unethical into separate organizational categories entirely?

6. In your own estimation, which of the eleven charges leveled against Wal-Mart is the most serious? Why? Which is the least serious, in comparison? Why?

Intertextual Questions

7. How are the allegations made in this report similar to or different from the personal anecdotes related in Benjamin Cheever's essay "Nobody Beats the Whiz"?

8. Consider Alain de Botton's argument that only Americans (and only modern Americans, actually) believe that work should lead to personal happiness. Which of the charges against Wal-Mart made in this report have more to do with personal happiness than with questionable business practices?

Thinking Beyond the Text

9. Visit a local Wal-Mart or similar "big-box" store. While you are in the store, look for evidence that the store is a positive force in the community. For example, is a portion of the store's profit donated to local schools or charitable groups? At Christmas time does the store donate food or toys to local groups? How effective are such local actions at combating charges such as those made in this report?

10. Think about the unspoken rules of capitalism, a system in which better business models always put less effective business models out of business. Before the rise of the fast-food industry, many local "burger joints" existed. Now there are relatively few. Before the rise of multinational oil and gas corporations, there were many small, locally owned gas stations along America's highways and interstates. Now there are almost none. In a capitalist system such as that in modern America, then, is the rise of a business such as Wal-Mart not only logical but necessary?

For Writing & Discussion

11. Research the effects of Wal-Mart and/or similar "big box" stores on the economy of the town in which you now live—or the town in which you spent the longest time growing up. In an essay, describe how the "big box" store was a positive, negative, and neutral force acting on the community—from the loss/creation of jobs to the increase in traffic flow.

BARBARA EHRENREICH

Barbara Ehrenreich (1941–) is a journalist and activist who has published 18 books and had her work translated into several languages. Ehrenreich earned a PhD in biology from the Rockefeller University before deciding to work as a writer and political activist instead of as a research scientist. Her articles have appeared in many publications, including the *Atlantic Monthly*, *Mother Jones*, *Ms*, *The New Republic*, and the *New York Times*. Ehrenreich also is vice-president of the Democratic Socialists of America.

"In Which I Am Offered a 'Job'" comes from Ehrenreich's 2005 book, *Bait and Switch: The (Futile) Pursuit of the American Dream*. In this book, Ehrenreich follows up on the success of her 2001 book on low-wage jobs, *Nickel and Dimed: On (Not) Getting By In America*, by looking at unemployment among middle-class, white-collar Americans. Just as *Nickled and Dimed* exposed harsh realities for the working poor, *Bait and Switch* shows an alarming side of middle-class life by revealing that even getting a college degree and having a robust résumé may not be enough to land a job.

In Which I Am Offered a "Job"

◌ **Prereading Question**

Think of the jobs that you and the people in your circle of friends have had. How many of these jobs involved working for little or no pay (being a teacher's assistant or office intern, for example)? In a culture that values money, are such "jobs" completely without value in the eyes of most people? If not, then why not? If so, then why does anyone actually agree to spend time doing them?

In late May, six months into my search, I get an e-mail request for an actual interview. AFLAC, the insurance company, is looking for sales reps in the central Virginia area with opportunities for management positions and my resume—which they must have come across on one of the job boards—suggests that I may be just the woman for the job. This is not, of course, the first job offer that has found its way to my in-box. There was the one from a verbally disabled firm looking for female models, for example, stating:

> Whats good fam its your . . . bol JR . . . Check us out you wont be sorry. Plenty of pics and video, and guess what? We need new talent so you ladies in Washington DC, Baltimore, Virginia, Atlanta, Ga. and Houston, Texas that are interested in joining our team and ready to make some real money send me a short email along with a photo or two.

I have also been solicited to sell insurance against identity theft, and spent twenty-five minutes on the phone listening to a recorded "conference call" in which two male voices concurred happily that the problem is "growing exponentially." I got a bite from Melaleuca, a United Kingdom–based firm specializing in eco-friendly cleaning products and cosmetics and now seeking sales reps in the United States. In a phone conversation, Melaleuca's Steve assured me that "it's not one of those multilayer marketing-type jobs where you have to put a lot of money up front, It's really a matter of spreading the word in your social life."

"I get paid just to spread the word?" I asked.

"That's right; there's no pressure to perform. It's a word-of-mouth-type business."

I briefly try to envision a social life in which the subject of cleaning fluids would naturally arise on a regular basis, but the money aspect is less than appealing. Steve says he puts twenty hours a week into selling Melaleuca products and grosses about $300 in U.S. dollars, but he has to spend $75 to

$80 a month for the products he sells—for a net wage, I calculate, of around $11 an hour.

AFLAC, however, is a highly reputable and successful organization, as far as I know. Everyone has seen its irritating commercials, in which two people are complaining about their insurance problems while, completely unnoticed by them, a duck keeps proclaiming the solution: *AFLAC*. In preparation for my interview, I visit the AFLAC web site, where I learn that the product is "supplemental insurance" to round out the no-doubt inadequate health insurance your employer provides. Then I turn to Google and Nexis, where I hit pay dirt after less than thirty minutes: AFLAC has had problems with the training and management of its sales force. I will stun my interviewer with this information, followed by the unique management contribution I am prepared to make. Furthermore, there are suggestions that AFLAC has overplayed the duck. It's fine for attracting initial attention, but you need a more mature and serious approach if you're selling insurance. That's me—serious and mature—the antiduck.

It's a gorgeous drive over the Blue Ridge Mountains to Staunton, where the AFLAC office is located, but my perilous speed of fifteen miles per hour over the speed limit allows for no scenic appreciation. At the last minute before leaving home, I discovered a dim, archipelago-shaped stain on one sleeve of the tan suit, which required a quickie home dry-cleaning session, but I manage to arrive only five minutes late. The office occupies a far more humble rural site than I expected: half of a one-story building across from a rundown shopping center. Only one car is parked outside, and its vanity plate reads "AFLAC."

Despite my tardiness, Larry greets me enthusiastically and ushers me into a windowless room containing a table and a half-dozen chairs. To enhance the entombment effect, he shuts the door behind us, although, oddly enough, there is not a soul around to disturb us. Where is the bustling, high-energy team promised by the AFLAC web site, the "fun" atmosphere and instant camaraderie? Larry is about fifty, with pale blond hair, wearing a white shirt embossed with the word *AFLAC* and a yellow tie featuring many small ducks. Maybe it would be unwise to bring up the company's alleged overreliance on its barnyard spokesperson, since the only decoration the office contains, in addition to a large photo of the post-9/11 Manhattan skyline, is a rubber ducky on what appears to be a receptionist's desk.

What ensues is not what I would call an interview. Larry offers me a blue folder containing colored sheets of paper starting with one titled "A Career Opportunity with AFLAC" and starts reading aloud from his own folder while I attempt to follow along in mine. This seems to be the preferred method of corporate communication: reading aloud, either from paper or a PowerPoint, while the person being read to reads along too.

Is there some fear that no one will pay attention unless at least two senses—auditory and visual—are engaged simultaneously? Occasionally, Larry departs from the script, to tell me for example, that although AFLAC is "huge," that is not something they dwell on anymore: "You know, after Enron and WorldCom, we don't emphasize the bigness. We're a family run operation."

Now to the serious part, beginning with a sheet titled "Immediate Income/Paid for Past Efforts/Lifestyle." On the matter of lifestyle, "I don't try to turn people into perfect AFLAC robots," he assures me, though the tie, the shirt, and the vanity plate would seem to suggest that the botlike approach can't hurt. There is a reason for this unusual level of tolerance he explains: "If we were all the same, how could we open up new markets?" Also, I can work as hard or as little as I want; it's up to me how much I want to "produce." Low production, however, could lead to his flooding my market area with fresh competing salespeople, and with this he gives me a narrow look. I will want to hit the ground running, he warns, because the first few months' sales count for a lot.

I remind him that, as I wrote in an e-mail, I am not interested in a sales job; I want to *manage* salespeople—motivate them, mentor them, and work with them to devise a strategic approach to our allotted terrain. This, I decide, is the moment for my bombshell: the articles in the business literature arguing that AFLAC has had problems managing its sales force. But if Larry is impressed by my knowledge, he does a good job of concealing it, continuing on unfazed like a tour guide who's been through this museum a few too many times. Yes, yes, I can be a manager, though this seems to require recruiting my own salespeople to manage, just as he is apparently doing right now. There are in fact about ten blue folders spread out neatly on the table, attesting to a strenuous series of "interviews," of which mine could be, for all I know, the eleventh of the day.

On to the money part and a blinding sheet of numbers titled "Income Illustration" and showing that even a complete slacker can make $32,000 in her first year through a combination of commissions, bonuses, and policy renewals. Also, Larry ad-libs, "we have fun"—at company-sponsored trips to destinations like Las Vegas, Honolulu, and San Diego. As he returns to the numbers, highlighting here and there in brilliant yellow-green, I ponder my role in this "interview." Looking interested would seem to be the main thing, and I try on various faces meant to convey agreement, concern, fascination. I must look as freakish as Lisa—the volunteer with the ever-changing expressions at the McLean Bible Church—just sitting here trying on masks.

Business can only get better, he's telling me. Why? Because health insurance deductibles and co-pays are rising steadily, and because "people have less disposable income than at any other time," meaning they can't handle those deductibles and co-pays themselves. I nod cheerily at the good news. Here we are, in a weird corporate niche created by the total failure of the American health-care system, and I am grinning with delight at the deepening misery.

There occurs now the kind of physiological breakdown that could sink a genuine interview. A headache starts pinching in from my right temple; my throat begins to itch. When I break into an uncontrollable fit of alternating coughing and sneezing, he eventually notices and allows me to get some water from the cooler just outside the room. Either I'm allergic to something in the conference room, or carbon monoxide is being pumped in through the vents. Fortunately, we have reached the end of the sheets in the folder, and he asks whether I have any questions.

Yes, I do, like what are we doing in this windowless room while the Blue Ridge Mountains undulate beckoningly outside? But instead I ask him something guaranteed to please: Has he made any inroads into the University of Virginia, which is Churlottesville's largest employer? No, he says, and looks at me for the first time with something approaching interest Good, I tell him. I have lots of contacts there.

The next step? Some of the people he is interviewing this week will be invited back for a second interview—"that's where we get to know each other." He will let me know next week if I've made the cut. I tell him I'll be away next week but will try to check my e-mail, at which point he says, "Well, why don't we just make an appointment for the second interview right now?" So, just like that, I've made the cut.

Despite the promise that this second interview, which occurs two weeks later, will be our chance to "get to know each other," it proceeds exactly like the first one. Larry, again wearing an AFLAC shirt and duck tie, leads me through the still entirely unoccupied outer rooms to the windowless conference room, where the table is again stacked with blue folders. "I have a present for you," I tell him—a new hardcover book about the advertising agency that created the spokes-duck, sent to me by a friend in the publishing industry whom I had told about my possible AFLAC job. I have read the crucial duck section, in which a young ad man wanders the streets of Manhattan, muttering "AFLAC, AFLAC" over and over to himself, until, in a stunning epiphany, he realizes he sounds like a . . . But Larry is too baffled by this departure from the script to thank me. He glances at the cover, then pushes the book aside with one finger, as if rejecting a bribe.

Out of one of the blue folders (and this is a more advanced set than last time), he takes a bunch of stapled pages titled "Fast Track to Management" and begins highlighting phrases as he speaks them. I can become a CIT (Coordinator in Training) if I produce "a minimum of $50,000 AP" in six months, open a minimum of six new accounts, and recruit at least one other salesperson. Continuing with the "six" theme, I will have six responsibilities as a CIT, including "attending quarterly CDIs with the DSC, RSC, and SSC." I must in addition acquire an insurance broker's license and become "Flex and SmartApp Certified." Any questions?

Now he produces a Xeroxed calendar for July and begins highlighting the days I will spend in training classes, some of which will be conducted in another Virginia city, where AFLAC will pay for my motel room, assuming I am willing to share a room. A laptop will be required.

"Will the company give me one?" I inquire.

"No, but you'll make the money to pay for it in no time at all."

So, not counting the laptop, that's an initial investment of about $1,900 for the broker's license and courses leading up to it. We move on through the content of the courses AFLAC will be offering me, including "L.E.A.S.E. Secretary and Approach Memorization (DSC 1-on-1 Reinforcement)," and "Account Servicing, Billing Reconciliation, and NOI Networking." There will also be training in cold-calling, Larry adds, though this is not written down anywhere, perhaps because a cold call is the salesperson's equivalent of a cold douche, most people would do almost anything to avoid having to make one. I note that the calendar, in which almost every weekday is now high-lighted, indicates both full and new moons, and cannot help but wonder what use an AFLAC associate might make of this information.

He has taken on an increasingly bosslike tone, which I struggle to interpret positively. In the first interview, he was selling the job; now he's directing it. There is the need to clear my calendar immediately, the need to get cracking on the broker's exam, which will require mastery of a huge book. (Larry shows the book to me, though I will have to buy my own, and even he admits it's "boring.") "I hope you realize you've got the job if you want it," he says out of the blue, with nothing more than a quick upward glance from the folder in front of him.

He should smile at this point. He should shake my hand and offer a hearty "welcome to the team." But Larry seems to be too emotionally defended to pause for celebration. In fact, he follows up with an implied put-down. Waving dismissively at a printout of my résumé, he says, "It's not about this. I don't even understand what this is about"—as if my career had been in astrophysics. "I make my judgment based on how a person communicates. Whether they have people skills. Whether they're a good listener." Then he gives me a little nod, for indeed I have been a good listener, though this would seem to be a pretty minimal requirement for an interviewee. He returns seamlessly to the need to "hit the ground running" and "make a total commitment," Any questions?

"What about health insurance?"

"We're independent contractors; we get our own."

So he has people selling health insurance who have none of their own? More tactfully, I ask whether I will have an office to work out of.

"Umm, our associates use their home offices."

We shake hands and I set out to drive home, but some kind of monsoon strikes the mountains, forcing me off the road to sit and stare through the windshield wipers at the whiteout beyond. I have a job. I have been found fit to represent a major corporation to the general public, apparently on no other basis than my ability to sit still and listen meekly for two long and dreary hours. Or maybe I should give myself more credit for appearance and simulated enthusiasm; it's hard to say. That, anyway, is the bright side. On the dimmer side, this "job" offers no salary, no benefits, not even an office with fax machine and phones. I might as well have applied at Wal-Mart and been given a pushcart full of housewares to hawk on the streets. I never call back, nor does Larry call me.

There are thousands—tens of thousands—of "jobs" like this available to corporate rejects and malcontents. In 1995, 31 percent of the American workforce found themselves in some sort of "nonstandard" employment, characterized by a lack of benefits and weak bonds to their ostensible employers, and the number continues to grow.[1] Many of these people are pink-collar temp workers and blue-collar day laborers—lawn workers and housecleaners, for example.

But a growing number of the nonstandardly employed are former corporate employees, professionals and managers who have burned out or been expelled from their jobs. For the white-collar job seeker, the lures—or, as the case may be, snares—are everywhere. My in box always contains one or two exhortations to. "Be Your Own Boss!" and "Make as Much Money as You Want!" often accompanied by an eye-catching question like: "Sick of the Corporate Rat Race?" "Got a Case of the MONDAYS?" "Head Hurt From Hitting a Glass Ceiling?" "Lost That Loving Feeling for Your Job?" Recruiters to these quasi employments lurk at networking events, like the fellow I met at Fuddruckers who offered to match me to an appropriate franchising opportunity. I could have my own Merry Maids business, he assured me, and run it by remote control from the location of my choice.

Selling real estate is one of the more respectable and traditional alternatives to the corporate world and offers no more of an initial hurdle than selling insurance: all you have to do is pay for a course and pass a state-licensing exam. My brother does it in Missouri, my brother-in-law

---

[1]Arne L. Kallenberg, Barbara F. Reskin, and Ken Hudson, "Bad Jobs in America, Standard and Nonstandard Employment Relations and Job Quality in the United States," *American Sociological Review,* 65: 1 (2000), pp. 256–78. In personal communications, Kallenberg and Hudson assured me that the trend is continuing.

in Colorado, as do a number of geographically scattered friends and acquaintances. My brother is a corporate dropout and former owner of a motel in Arkansas; my brother-in-law came to real estate after a move to escape the high living costs in Hawaii derailed his career as a schoolteacher. When his teaching credentials proved nontransferable to Colorado without a several-thousand-dollar investment in further courses, he managed a Burger King for five years and spent a brief inter- lude as a paralegal before settling on real estate. One of my Atlanta contacts, a woman with a background in web-site design, has taken the real estate course and is considering taking the state exam. Clark Nickerson, whom I also met at Fuddruckers, had been an industrial sales manager for twenty-seven years and decided to enter the field after an "early retirement" proved financially nonfeasible and a yearlong job search bottomed out.

> By mid April [2003] I was doing everything you should do—going to net- working meetings, using the job boards—but I was really having a hard time staying motivated. My wife and I sat down—she struggles when I do—and she said, "This is just not working." What I realized then was I didn't want to get back into the industrial sales world. She said, "What about real estate?"

But as a default career for the white-collar unemployed, real estate is far from reliable. According to the respected industry magazine *Realty Times,* first-year realtors suffer an 86 percent failure rate, and of those who survive, 70 percent earn less than $30,000 a year. In my brother-in-law's opinion, real estate "is too easy to get into. A lot of people don't really see it as a profession, just an interim thing." For an "interim thing," though, he says the payoffs are slow to come.

> You need at least enough money to carry you for a year. I started with four hundred cold calls a week—door-to-door and phone calls—and didn't really make anything for six to eight months. Then, when you get a commission check, you don't realize at first that forty to fifty percent has to come out of it for expenses—everything from taxes to the desk fee a lot of agencies charge. After my first year, I had to get a bank loan just to pay our taxes.

Both my brother-in-law and his wife, my sister, toil away at his real estate business, grossing about $75,000 in 2004, of which half went for taxes and expenses.

In his midfifties and still in the early, nonremunerative phase of his real estate career, Clark Nickerson is hopeful: "It's going good, going great . . . It's a lot of training and learning and basic grunt work, but I'm fully confident that I'll have some clients and listings soon." All I could think of, when Clark told me this, was Cynthia, the woman who burst into tears, at

Patrick's boot camp, and Richard, who appeared to be on the verge of doing so himself—two realtors who had been unable to stay afloat and were restarting their job searches from scratch.

Another nonstandard form of employment held out to the unemployed is franchising, known to cynics as "buying your self a job" because the initial fee for the right to use the corporate franchisor's name is in the $15,000 to $40,000 range.[2] In an earlier era, people were more likely to start their own small businesses; today you can buy a sort of prefab business, in which operating procedures, as well as any products used or sold, are supplied, for a monthly "royalty," by the franchisor. About 400,000 Americans are franchisees, managing eight million employees and generating one-third of U.S. gross domestic product—everything from doughnuts and burgers to fitness centers. But as in real estate, the rewards are uncertain and the prospects of failure dauntingly high. In his study of franchisees in a variety of industries sociologist Peter M. Birkeland found a survival rate of only about 25 percent and average franchisee incomes of about $30,000.[3]

Finally, as an option for the white-collar unemployed, there are thousands of commission-only sales jobs such as the one AFLAC offered me. According to the Direct Selling Association, 13.3 million Americans worked in such sales jobs in 2003, selling $25 billion worth of goods. In many cases, like AFLAC, these jobs offer rewards not only for selling the product but for recruiting new people to do so as well. On its dark side, the direct-selling world is filled with costly traps for the unwary—pyramid schemes in which the ultimate product is vague or nonexistent. An outfit called JDO Media, for example, enticed people to make money by enlisting others to sell a sketchily defined "marketing program"—for which privilege each recruit had to put up as much as $3,500.[4]

Even the legitimate firms; offer only scant remuneration, with only 8 percent of commission-only salespeople earning more than $50,000 a year and over half earning less than $10,000.[5] Four years ago, an unemployed friend of mine got drawn into a vitamin-marketing scheme, in which the real rewards, again, came from recruiting others to the sales force. I went with him to a meeting led by a local doctor, and was impressed by the relative inattention to the vitamins' metits compared to the emphasis on enlisting others to sell them. For his efforts, my friend lost $400 but gained a vitamin supply that will hopefully help compensate for his lack of health insurance.

[2]According to www.francorp.com. Francorp bills itself as "The Leader, in Franchise Development and Consulting."

[3]Peter M. Birkeland, *Franchising Dreams: The Lure of Entrepreneurship in America* (Chicago: University of Chicago Press, 2002), pp. 1–2, 31, 115.

[4]Kris Hundely, "Get-Fleeced-Quick," *St. Petersburg Times*, April 12, 2004.

[5]Susan B. Garland, "So Glad You Could Come. Can I Sell You Anything?" *New York Times*, December 19, 2004.

I get a second "job" offer of the commission-only variety at a job fair, not long after my success with AFLAC. Mary Kay cosmetics was not one of the companies that attracted me to the fair,[6] and, when I get there, my impulse is to avoid the Mary Kay table, which from a distance seems to be loaded with candy—actually pink cosmetics. But since no potential recruits are lining up, Linda, the table's minder, is standing in front of it, and button-holes me as I loiter in a moment of indecision as to where to make my next pitch. If I fill out a form, she tells me, I could win $25 and a free makeover: "Just what you need when you're looking for a new job!"

She is a large woman in a mauve suit with a white lace top underneath, mauve eye shadow matching her suit, and a pink rhinestone pin in the shape of a high heel attached to her shoulder. Again, I have to wonder why my tasteful silver brooch was rejected by Prescott, especially if Linda can get away with this whimsical display. I fill out the form, which wants only contact information, and reveal that I am looking for a PR job. "I had a high-up corporate job for thirty-one years, and one day I realized I was sick of it," she says, her gaze drifting across the room: "The downsizing. Achieving so much and they can never afford a raise. You're up against everyone for promotions. You can't trust anyone. I never got the encouragement from management or the support from other women."

The "support from other women" part holds me rooted in place, trying to imagine this great valentine of a woman in the cutthroat corporate world she's described. Now Linda's problems are solved. "I work only twenty hours a week, and—you know what?—I make as much as I did before." In addition, she works two days a week in a needlepoint shop, "and you know who that is—*women*," in other words, potential Mary Kay customers. "Have you ever used Mary Kay cosmetics?" she asks me.

"No," I admit. "I guess I've been more into L'Oréal."

"That's OK," she says consolingly. "You can say it. You just haven't tried Mary Kay yet."

We set a phone appointment for the following week, and she wishes me "an awesome day." As instructed, I go to the Mary Kay web site and study the wisdom of Mary Kay herself, an elderly woman made up to resemble Dustin Hoffman in *Tootsie*, I learn that high earners can win a pink Cadillac and that the corporate philosophy is "God first, family second, career third." I also talk to Leah Gray, my unemployed acquaintance in Atlanta, because she had put in a stint with Mary Kay.

> When you join, there is a miniceremony in a dimly lit room in which the director lights each new consultant's handheld candle and says some encouraging words. I have to admit I thought it was cheesy and overdramatic for my taste. She was saying things like "You've all made the most important

---

[6]Internet announcements of job fairs generally offer a list of the "exhibiting" companies.

life-changing decision; to join Mary Kay." The ironic thing is that I am a very hard sell and fell into this trap.

When we finally connect, Linda is ebullient. "It's a very supportive business. It's awesome. It's hard for me to describe it without sounding like a nutcase."

"What do I need to spend up front?" I ask.

"Just one hundred dollars for the start-up kit, plus thirteen dollars for sales tax and shipping. You can't start any business in this world for just a hundred dollars! Barbara, I am going to get real, I'm sure you've thrown away a hundred dollars for something that's hanging in your closet."

She goes on about how easy it is to learn to do the "skin care classes" at customers' homes. "I teach you everything and provide you the words to say in the class. They don't care if you read it or memorize it."

It's hard to get a word in edgewise as Linda prattles on, but Leah warned me that she ended up spending over $700 on cosmetics before realizing that this was not for her. So I ask Linda how much I will need to spend on inventory in order to have enough to sell.

"Inventory," she responds meditatively. "I don't usually get that question. Of course, you don't have to buy one ounce. I don't recommend it, though. I suggest eighteen hundred dollars to start. Do you have to? No, but personally this is how I feel. Women don't want to wait for their lipstick and mascara."

So, $1,900 just to get started. "What do you do for health insurance?" I throw in, recklessly.

"You're totally on your own. I have coverage of my own which I've had for years. It's a big problem for the country, so it's not just us."

I have gotten the drift now and attempt to cut the call short by claiming an impending appointment. "Look," Linda says in summation, "don't overanalyze this. It's just a fun business and a great opportunity. I can't explain it to you more than that."

So, after almost seven months of job searching, an image makeover, an expensively refined and later upgraded résumé, and networking in four cities, I have gotten exactly two offers: from AFLAC and Mary Kay. But these are not jobs, not in the way I defined a job when I started this project, in that no salary, benefits, or workplace is provided. Surely there are plenty of actual sales jobs offering a salary and benefits in addition to commissions, but a real job involves some risk taking on the part of the employer, who must make an investment in order to acquire your labor. In real estate, franchising, and commission-only sales, the only risk undertaken is by the job seeker, who has to put out money up front and commit days or weeks to unpaid training. Then she is on her own, ever fearful that the market will soften or that the quasi employer will flood the area with competing sales reps or franchisees.

No one, apparently, is willing to take a risk on me. Is the fear that, if given health insurance for even a month, I will go on an orgy of body scans and elective surgery? The most any corporation seems willing to give me is the right to wear its logo on my chest and go about pushing its products.

I had pictured the corporate world that I seek to enter as a castle on a hill, outside of which the starving vagrants wander, set upon by wolves and barbarian hordes, begging for entry into the safety of the fortified towers. But now I see there is another zone out here: a somewhat settled encampment, where people toll for uncertain rewards at minor tasks invented by the castle dwellers. There is an advantage to occupying this zone: you are free of the rigid conformity required of those who dwell inside; you can actually "Be Your Own Boss!" A few do very well, acquiring pink Cadillacs or fortunes from real estate deals. Many more are ruined or pour themselves into efforts that generate near-poverty-level earnings year after year. There is no safety out here; the wolves keep circling.

Textual Questions

1. How does Ehrenreich describe her job interview (and the details of the job itself) at AFLAC? What details in the text make her attitude toward this "opportunity" clear to a reader?

2. What are the positive aspects of working for AFLAC, according to the details Ehrenreich includes from her two interviews. Why and how does she present these positive details as negatives? How do the positive aspects of working for AFLAC compare to the positive aspects of working for Mary Kay cosmetics?

3. Consider the sections into which Ehrenreich's essay is divided. What topic does she cover/story does she tell in each section? How does she link these sections together? How do they build upon one another's points to reach her concluding section?

Rhetorical Questions

4. For Ehrenreich, a job is only a real job if it involves direct pay for work done. Is this a useful and accurate definition of the term "job"? What other definitions of "job" might be more inclusive, might encompass work such as that which Ehrenreich refuses to do?

5. Of all the possible topics to include in this essay on "non-standard" employment, why might Ehrenreich have chosen AFLAC and Mary Kay? If she has been flooded with similar offers, as she claims, then why choose these two companies to target for her criticism of this labor practice?

6. At the end, Ehrenreich uses a metaphor in her last sentence, describing the world of the unemployed in America: "There is no safety out here; the wolves keep circling." Does the essay build logically, naturally, and effectively to this colorful image? Or is the drama of this image more than the essay truly can support?

Intertextual Questions

7. Although "In Which I Am Offered a 'Job'" and "Nobody Beats the Whiz" cover very different topics, in what ways are they similar? If you read both texts and did not know the authors' names, then might you believe that both were written by the same person? Why?

8. How does Ehrenreich's description of franchising compare to/contrast with the description of franchising offered by Eric Schlosser in "Success"?

Thinking Beyond the Text

9. Both Ehrenreich and Benjamin Cheever (in "Nobody Beats the Wiz") describe the work of salespeople in negative terms. Yet thousands of people do, in fact, make their living as salespeople. How can both of these "points" be true, that selling is a terrible job that pays badly and that selling is a way in which many people do in fact earn a living wage?

10. In *Death of a Salesman*, Arthur Miller describes the plight of Willy Loman, a befuddled Everyman whose life has spun far beyond his control; for Willy, the American Dream has turned nightmare, and the play ends with the dissolution of his family and his own suicide. In both the play and Ehrenreich's essay, the act of selling is described as (a) a perfect opportunity for a self-starter unafraid of working hard and (b) a nightmarish trap where hard work promises no reward—only more hard work. Why might the job of being a salesperson be presented in such a paradoxical way—as it is in both *Death of a Salesman* and "In Which I Am Offered a 'Job'"?

For Writing & Discussion

11. Examine AFLAC's official home page: http://www.aflac.com. In what ways does the description of a "career" with AFLAC support Ehrenreich's description of her experience with this company? Compare AFLAC's home page to that of another insurance company, such as State Farm or Farmer's Insurance. Do the descriptions of careers with these companies seem to match the description of a career with AFLAC? Does it all seem as rosy and promising—on the surface, at least—as Ehrenreich says?

FOCAL POINT
Exploring Images of The Promise of Work and Success

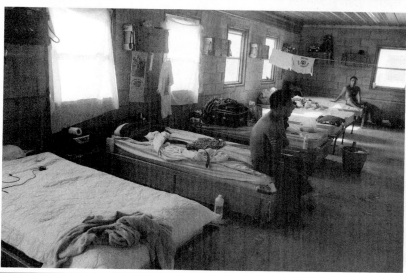

"We've done a computer simulation of your projected performance in five years. You're fired."

FOCAL POINT
Exploring Images of The Promise of Work and Success

Questions

1. What does the photograph of a California migrant labor camp in 1940 on page 535 (top) say about the people who lived there? How does this image support the argument made by John Steinbeck in "Harvest Gypsies"?

2. While the image on page 535 (top) shows a migrant camp from California in 1940, the photograph below it depicts a migrant labor camp in North Carolina in 2005. Despite the 65 years that separate them, do these photographs make similar arguments about the lives of migrant workers? Could this photograph serve to illustrate John Steinbeck's argument in "Harvest Gypsies," regardless of the difference in time?

3. This depiction of Wal-Mart on page 536 (top) looks like a cartoon that might be seen in a children's book or on a restaurant placemat. Viewed positively, what does this say about the success of Wal-Mart's business model? What's the negative interpretation of this cartoon? Which do you think the artist intended? If it were published side-by-side with the selection "Everyday Low Wages: The Hidden Price We All Pay for Wal-Mart," how would this cartoon likely be interpreted?

4. When workers at United Parcel Service (UPS) went on strike in 1997 for higher wages and better working conditions, it marked the first major strike called by the Teamsters Union in decades. Consider the photograph on page 536 (bottom). What argument about equality and fairness in employment do the striking workers seem to be making? To whom is their protest directed? Would your interpretation of the image be different if the striking workers were of a different age, race, or gender? What if the protesters were highly-paid "workers" such as baseball players? Why?

5. What message about technology and white-collar work in America does the cartoon on page 537 seem to send? In what ways has computer technology changed working conditions for American laborers? Which jobs have been most affected by technology? Which jobs have been least affected? Are the changes in working conditions caused by computer technology greater or lesser than changes caused by other technologies (such as the typewriter or mechanized assembly lines)? Explain.

6

THE PROMISE OF EQUALITY
AND CIVIL LIBERTY

The debate in America over civil liberties sometimes seems very recent, to have only really begun since the terrorist attacks on 9/11 and, shortly thereafter, the codification of the Patriot Act, viewed by some as one of the most effective tools in the War on Terror, viewed by others as the greatest assault on individual freedom since America's founding. The fire of this debate has been further fueled by the ongoing—but undeclared—wars in Afghanistan and Iraq, the continuing imprisonment of both American citizens and foreign nationals at Guantanamo Bay, and the revelations of "domestic spying" on individual Americans authorized by President George W. Bush (including collection of telephone records of Americans not suspected of committing any specific crime). But this perception that civil liberties are suddenly under assault for the first time is, ultimately, a misperception. Whenever civil rights, such as freedom of the press, or to privacy, or to petition the government, have appeared to come in conflict with national security or domestic tranquility—and in times of crisis they always do—these rights seem to many to carry too much risk. Throughout American history, the defense of these rights has come under attack from those whose primary concern is public order and defense of the country.

As the selections in Chapter 1 of this text demonstrate, America has from its very beginning been in the process of defining what freedom and equality mean, what legally protected civil liberties actually are, and to whom all of this legitimately applies. In that chapter, the primary focus was on the right to vote, one of the foundational rights granted in a republican democracy such as America and in flux from 1776 to the present day. Initially restricted to free white men, the right to vote was extended to African American men in 1868 (in the Fourteenth Amendment), to women in 1920 (in the Nineteenth Amendment), to all Native Americans in 1940 (when they were first recognized by Congress as American citizens, although their right to vote was not recognized by every state until 1947), and to all Americans 18 years old or older in 1971. Since the 2000 and 2004 elections, however, debate has become particularly heated over how the right to vote is abridged by advances in technology, changes in voting districts, dishonest campaigning, and legally questionable tactics of intimidation. The fight for the right to vote continues, with its implications for all other rights.

In this chapter, these debates return to some of this same territory and then branch into entirely new areas of civil liberty and the meaning of equality in America.

How does the ideal of democracy, first expressed in ancient Athens, work in modern America—how does the ideal become the actual? Whatever political perspective one may bring to that question, it is clear that America has made immense progress toward that ideal in its relatively brief history. It is also clear that we remain at some distance from the goal.

MARTIN LUTHER KING, JR.

Martin Luther King, Jr. (1929–1968) was a Baptist minister, Doctor of Theology, and civil rights activist. Among King's many notable actions as a civil rights leader were his involvement in the 1955–1956 Montgomery bus boycott, a protest against segregated buses; his leadership of the Southern Christian Leadership Conference, which was famous for its adherence to principles of nonviolence; and his helping organize the 1963 March on Washington for Jobs and Freedom.

King wrote his famous "Letter from Birmingham Jail" in 1963 after being arrested for joining an anti-segregation march for which a permit had not been granted. King wrote the letter during his 11 days in jail as a response to one written by eight local white clergymen that called for local African Americans to work with the local white citizens instead of with outsiders such as King. King's letter, which argues that nonviolent actions were necessary if social justice was to be obtained, was originally published in a June 1963 issue of *The New Leader* with the title "Letter from Birmingham City Jail."

Many of King's aims were accomplished with the passage of the Civil Rights Act of 1964 and the Voting Rights Act of 1965. He was awarded the Nobel Peace Prize in 1964, the youngest person ever to receive the award.

Letter from Birmingham Jail

∾ Prereading Question

Based upon your knowledge of American history—gleaned from courses you've taken, books you've read, movies you've seen, the television news, and so on—what did Martin Luther King, Jr. believe. That is, what did he stand for? What did he want for himself and for all blacks? And how did he want to achieve those goals?

∾

A Call for Unity
[By eight local clergymen]

April 12, 1963

We the undersigned clergymen are among those who, in January, issued "An Appeal for Law and Order and Common Sense," in dealing with racial problems in Alabama. We expressed understanding that honest convictions in racial matters could properly be pursued in the courts, but urged that decisions of those courts should in the meantime be peacefully obeyed.

Since that time there had been some evidence of increased forebearance and a willingness to face facts. Responsible citizens have undertaken to work on various problems which cause racial friction and unrest. In Birmingham, recent public events have given indication that we all have opportunity for a new constructive and realistic approach to racial problems.

However, we are now confronted by a series of demonstrations by some of our Negro citizens, directed and led in part by outsiders. We recognize the natural impatience of people who feel that their hopes are slow in being realized. But we are convinced that these demonstrations are unwise and untimely.

We agree rather with certain local Negro leadership which has called for honest and open negotiation of racial issues in our area. And we believe this kind of facing of issues can best be accomplished by citizens of our own metropolitan area, white and Negro, meeting with their knowledge and experience of the local situation. All of us need to face that responsibility and find proper channels for its accomplishment.

Just as we formerly pointed out that "hatred and violence have no sanction in our religious and political traditions," we also point out that such actions as incite to hatred and violence, however technically peaceful those actions may be, have not contributed to the resolution of our local problems. We do not believe that these days of new hope are days when extreme measures are justified in Birmingham.

We commend the community as a whole, and the local news media and law enforcement officials in particular, on the calm manner in which these demonstrations have been handled. We urge the public to continue to show restraint should the demonstrations continue, and the law enforcement officials to remain calm and continue to protect our city from violence.

We further strongly urge our own Negro community to withdraw support from these demonstrations, and to unite locally in working peacefully for a better Birmingham. When rights are consistently denied, a cause should be pressed in the courts and in negotiations among local leaders, and not in the streets. We appeal to both our white and Negro citizenry to observe the principles of law and order and common sense.

C.C.J. Carpenter, D. D., L.L.D., Bishop of Alabama; Joseph A. Durick, D. D., Auxiliary Bishop, Diocese of Mobile-Birmingham; Rabbi Milton L. Grafman, Temple Emanu-El, Birmingham, Alabama; Bishop Paul Hardin, Bishop of the Alabama-West Florida Conference of the Methodist Church; Bishop Nolan B. Harmon; Bishop of the North Alabama Conference of the Methodist Church; George M. Murray, D. D., L.L.D., Bishop Coadjutor, Episcopal Diocese of Alabama; Edward V. Ramage, Moderator, Synod of the Alabama Presbyterian Church in the United States; Earl Stallings, Pastor, First Baptist Church, Birmingham, Alabama.

℘

Letter From Birmingham Jail

April 16, 1963

My Dear Fellow Clergymen:

While confined here in the Birmingham city jail, I came across your recent statement calling my present activities "unwise and untimely."[1] Seldom do I pause to answer criticism of my work and ideas. If I sought to answer all the criticisms that cross my desk, my secretaries would have little time for anything other than such correspondence in the course of the day, and I would have no time for constructive work. But since I feel that you are men of genuine good will and that your criticisms are sincerely set forth, I want to try to answer your statement in what I hope will be patient and reasonable terms.

I think I should indicate why I am here in Birmingham, since you have been influenced by the view which argues against "outsiders coming in." I have the honor of serving as president of the Southern Christian Leadership Conference, an organization operating in every southern state, with headquarters in Atlanta, Georgia. We have some eighty-five affiliated organizations across the South, and one of them is the Alabama Christian

---

[1]This response to a published statement by eight fellow clergymen from Alabama (Bishop C.C.J. Carpenter, Bishop Joseph A. Durick, Rabbi Milton L. Grafman, Bishop Paul Hardin, Bishop Nolan B. Harmon, the Reverend George M. Murray, the Reverend Edward V. Ramage, and the Reverend Earl Stallings) was composed under somewhat constricting circumstances. Begun on the margins of the newspaper in which the statement appeared while I was in jail, the letter was continued on scraps of writing paper supplied by a friendly Negro trusty, and concluded on a pad my attorneys were eventually permitted to leave me. Although the text remains in substance unaltered, I have indulged in the author's prerogative of polishing it for publication. [King's note.]

Movement for Human Rights. Frequently we share staff, educational, and financial resources with our affiliates. Several months ago the affiliate here in Birmingham asked us to be on call to engage in a nonviolent direct-action program if such were deemed necessary. We readily consented, and when the hour came we lived up to our promise. So I, along with several members of my staff, am here because I was invited here. I am here because I have organizational ties here.

But more basically, I am in Birmingham because injustice is here. Just as the prophets of the eighth century B.C. left their villages and carried their "thus saith the Lord" far beyond the boundaries of their home towns, and just as the Apostle Paul left his village of Tarsus and carried the gospel of Jesus Christ to the far corners of the Greco-Roman world, so am I compelled to carry the gospel of freedom beyond my own home town. Like Paul, I must constantly respond to the Macedonian call for aid.

Moreover, I am cognizant of the interrelatedness of all communities and states. I cannot sit idly by in Atlanta and not be concerned about what happens in Birmingham. Injustice anywhere is a threat to justice everywhere. We are caught in an inescapable network of mutuality; tied in a single garment of destiny. Whatever affects one directly, affects all indirectly. Never again can we afford to live with the narrow, provincial "outside agitator" idea. Anyone who lives inside the United States can never be considered an outsider anywhere within its bounds.

You deplore the demonstrations taking place in Birmingham. But your statement, I am sorry to say, fails to express a similar concern for the conditions that brought about the demonstrations. I am sure that none of you would want to rest content with the superficial kind of social analysis that deals merely with effects and does not grapple with underlying causes. It is unfortunate that demonstrations are taking place in Birmingham, but it is even more unfortunate that the city's white power structure left the Negro community with no alternative.

In any nonviolent campaign there are four basic steps: collection of the facts to determine whether injustices exist; negotiation; self-purification; and direct action. We have gone through all these steps in Birmingham. There can be no gainsaying the fact that racial injustice engulfs this community. Birmingham is probably the most thoroughly segregated city in the United States. Its ugly record of brutality is widely known. Negroes have experienced grossly unjust treatment in the courts. There have been more unsolved bombings of Negro homes and churches in Birmingham than in any other city in the nation. These are the hard, brutal facts of the case. On the basis of these conditions, Negro leaders sought to negotiate with the city fathers. But the latter consistently refused to engage in good-faith negotiation.

Then, last September, came the opportunity to talk with leaders of Birmingham's economic community. In the course of the negotiations, certain promises were made by the merchants—for example, to remove the stores' humiliating racial signs. On the basis of these promises, the Reverend Fred Shuttleworth and the leaders of the Alabama Christian Movement for Human Rights agreed to a moratorium on all demonstrations. As the weeks and months went by, we realized that we were the victims of a broken promise. A few signs, briefly removed, returned; the others remained.

As in so many past experiences, our hopes had been blasted, and the shadow of deep disappointment settled upon us. We had no alternative except to prepare for direct action, whereby we would present our very bodies as a means of laying our case before the conscience of the local and the national community. Mindful of the difficulties involved, we decided to undertake a process of self-purification. We began a series of workshops on nonviolence, and we repeatedly asked ourselves: "Are you able to accept blows without retaliating?" "Are you able to endure the ordeal of jail?" We decided to schedule our direct-action program for the Easter season, realizing that except for Christmas, this is the main shopping period of the year. Knowing that a strong economic-withdrawal program would be the by-product of direct action, we felt that this would be the best time to bring pressure to bear on the merchants for the needed change.

Then it occurred to us that Birmingham's mayoralty election was coming up in March, and we speedily decided to postpone action until after election day. When we discovered that the Commissioner of Public Safety. Eugene "Bull" Connor, had piled up enough votes to be in the run-off, we decided again to postpone action until the day after the run-off so that the demonstrations could not be used to cloud the issues. Like many others, we waited to see Mr. Connor defeated, and to this end we endured postponement after postponement. Having aided in this community need, we felt that our direct-action program could be delayed no longer.

You may well ask: "Why direct action? Why sit-ins, marches, and so forth? Isn't negotiation a better path?" You are quite right in calling for negotiation. Indeed, this is the very purpose of direct action. Nonviolent direct action seeks to create such a crisis and foster such a tension that a community which has constantly refused to negotiate is forced to confront the issue. It seeks so to dramatize the issue that it can no longer be ignored. My citing the creation of tension as part of the work of the nonviolent-resister may sound rather shocking. But I must confess that I am not afraid of the word "tension." I have earnestly opposed violent tension, but there is a type of constructive, nonviolent tension which is necessary for growth. Just as Socrates felt that it was necessary to create a tension in the mind so that individuals could rise from the bondage of myths and half-truths to the unfettered realm of creative analysis and objective appraisal, so must we see the need for nonviolent gadflies to create the kind of tension in society that will help men rise from the dark depths of prejudice and racism to the majestic heights of understanding and brotherhood.

The purpose of our direct-action program is to create a situation so crisis-packed that it will inevitably open the door to negotiation. I therefore concur with you in your call for negotiation. Too long has our beloved Southland been bogged down in a tragic effort to live in monologue rather than dialogue.

One of the basic points in your statement is that the action that I and my associates have taken in Birmingham is untimely. Some have asked: "Why didn't you give the new city administration time to act?" The only answer that I can give to this query is that the new Birmingham administration must be prodded about as much as the outgoing one, before it will act. We are sadly mistaken if we feel that the election of Albert Boutwell as mayor will bring the millennium to Birmingham. While Mr. Boutwell is a much more gentle person than Mr. Connor, they are both segregationists, dedicated to maintenance of the status quo. I have hope that Mr. Boutwell will be reasonable enough to see the futility of massive resistance to desegregation. But he will not see this without pressure from devotees of civil rights. My friends, I must say to you that we have not made a single gain in civil rights without determined legal and nonviolent pressure. Lamentably, it is an historical fact that privileged groups seldom give up their privileges voluntarily. Individuals may see the moral light and voluntarily give up their unjust posture; but as Reinhold Niebuhr has reminded us, groups tend to be more immoral than individuals.

We know through painful experience that freedom is never voluntarily given by the oppressor; it must be demanded by the oppressed. Frankly, I have yet to engage in a direct-action campaign that was "well timed" in the view of those who have not suffered unduly from the disease of segregation. For years now I have heard the word "Wait!" It rings in the ear of every Negro with piercing familiarity. This "Wait" has almost always meant "Never." We must come to see, with one of our distinguished jurists, that "justice too long delayed is justice denied."

We have waited for more than 340 years for our constitutional and God-given rights. The nations of Asia and Africa are moving with jetlike speed toward gaining political independence, but we still creep at horse-and-buggy pace toward gaining a cup of coffee at a lunch counter. Perhaps it is easy for those who have never felt the stinging darts of segregation to say, "Wait." But when you have seen vicious mobs lynch your mothers and fathers at will and drown your sisters and brothers at whim; when you have seen hate-filled policemen curse, kick, and even kill your black brothers and sisters; when you see the vast majority of your twenty million Negro brothers smothering in an airtight cage of poverty in the midst of an affluent society; when you suddenly find your tongue twisted and your speech stammering as you seek to explain to your six-year-old daughter why she can't go to the public amusement park that has just been advertised on television, and see tears welling up in her eyes when she is told that Funtown is closed to colored children, and see ominous clouds of inferiority beginning to form in her little mental sky, and see her beginning to distort her personality by developing an unconscious bitterness toward white people; when you have to concoct an answer for a five-year-old son who is asking: "Daddy, why do white people treat colored people so mean?"; when you take a cross-country drive and find it necessary to sleep night after night in the uncomfortable corners of your automobile because no motel will accept you; when you are humiliated day in and day out by nagging signs reading "white" and "colored"; when your first name becomes "nigger," your middle name becomes "boy" (however old you are) and your last name becomes "John," and your wife and mother are never given the respected title "Mrs."; when you are harried by day and haunted by night by the fact that you are a Negro, living constantly at tiptoe stance, never quite knowing what to expect next, and are plagued with inner fears and outer resentments; when you are forever fighting a degenerating sense of "nobodiness"—then you will understand why we find it difficult to wait. There comes a time when the cup of endurance runs over, and men are no longer willing to be plunged into the abyss of despair. I hope, sirs, you can understand our legitimate and unavoidable impatience.

You express a great deal of anxiety over our willingness to break laws. This is certainly a legitimate concern. Since we so diligently urge people to obey the Supreme Court's decision of 1954 outlawing segregation in the public schools, at first glance it may seem rather paradoxical for us consciously to break laws. One may well ask: "How can you advocate breaking some laws and obeying others?" The answer lies in the fact that there are two types of laws: just and unjust. I would be the first to advocate obeying just laws. One has not only a legal but a moral responsibility to obey just laws. Conversely, one has a moral responsibility to disobey unjust laws. I would agree with St. Augustine that "an unjust law is no law at all."

Now, what is the difference between the two? How does one determine whether a law is just or unjust? A just law is a man-made code that squares with the moral law or the law of God. An unjust law is a code that is out of harmony with the moral law. To put it in the terms of St. Thomas Aquinas: An unjust law is a human law that is not rooted in eternal law and natural law. Any law that uplifts human personality is just. Any law that degrades human personality is unjust. All segregation statutes are unjust because segregation distorts the soul and damages the personality. It gives the segregator a false sense of superiority and the segregated a false sense of inferiority. Segregation, to use the terminology of the Jewish philosopher Martin Buber, substitutes an "I-it" relationship for an "I-thou" relationship and ends up relegating persons to the status of things. Hence segregation is not only politically, economically, and sociologically unsound, it is morally wrong and sinful. Paul Tillich has said that sin is separation. Is not segregation an existential expression of man's tragic separation, his awful estrangement, his terrible sinfulness? Thus it is that I can urge men to obey the 1954 decision of the Supreme Court, for it is morally right; and I can urge them to disobey segregation ordinances, for they are morally wrong.

Let us consider a more concrete example of just and unjust laws. An unjust law is a code that a numerical or power majority group compels a minority group to obey but does not make binding on itself. This is *difference* made legal. By the same token, a just law is a code that a majority compels a minority to follow and that it is willing to follow itself. This is *sameness* made legal.

Let me give another explanation. A law is unjust if it is inflicted on a minority that, as a result of being denied the right to vote, had no part in enacting or devising the law. Who can say that the legislature of Alabama which set up that state's segregation laws was democratically elected? Throughout Alabama all sorts of devious methods are used to prevent Negroes from becoming registered voters, and there are some counties in which, even though Negroes constitute a majority of the population, not a single Negro is registered. Can any law enacted under such circumstances be considered democratically structured?

Sometimes a law is just on its face and unjust in its application. For instance, I have been arrested on a charge of parading without a permit. Now, there is nothing wrong in having an ordinance which requires a permit for a parade. But such an ordinance becomes unjust when it is used to maintain segregation and to deny citizens the First Amendment privilege of peaceful assembly and protest.

I hope you are able to see the distinction I am trying to point out. In no sense do I advocate evading or defying the law, as would the rabid segregationist. That would lead to anarchy. One who breaks an unjust law must do so openly, lovingly, and with a willingness to accept the penalty. I submit that an individual who breaks a law that conscience tells him is unjust, and who willingly accepts the penalty of imprisonment in order to arouse the conscience of the community over its injustice, is in reality expressing the highest respect for law.

Of course, there is nothing new about this kind of civil disobedience. It was evidenced sublimely in the refusal of Shadrach, Meshach, and Abednego to obey the laws of Nebuchadnezzar, on the ground that a higher moral law was at stake. It was practiced superbly by the early Christians, who were willing to face hungry lions and the excruciating pain of chopping blocks rather than submit to certain unjust laws of the Roman Empire. To a degree, academic freedom is a reality today because Socrates practiced civil disobedience. In our own nation, the Boston Tea Party represented a massive act of civil disobedience.

We should never forget that everything Adolf Hitler did in Germany was "legal" and everything the Hungarian freedom fighters did in Hungary was "illegal." It was "illegal" to aid and comfort a Jew in Hitler's Germany. Even so, I am sure that, had I lived in Germany at the time, I would have aided and comforted my Jewish brothers. If today I lived in a Communist country where certain principles dear to the Christian faith are suppressed, I would openly advocate disobeying that country's anti-religious laws.

I must make two honest confessions to you, my Christian and Jewish brothers. First, I must confess that over the past few years I have been gravely disappointed with the white moderate. I have almost reached the regrettable conclusion that the Negro's great stumbling block in his stride toward freedom is not the White Citizen's Counciler or the Ku Klux Klanner, but the white moderate, who is more devoted to "order" than to justice; who prefers a negative peace which is the absence of tension to a positive peace which is the presence of justice; who constantly says: "I agree with you in the goal you seek, but I cannot agree with your methods or direct action"; who paternalistically believes he can set the timetable for another man's freedom; who lives by a mythical concept of time and who constantly advises the Negro to wait for a "more convenient season." Shallow understanding from people of good will is more frustrating than absolute misunderstanding from people of ill will. Lukewarm acceptance is much more bewildering than outright rejection.

I had hoped that the white moderate would understand that law and order exist for the purpose of establishing justice and that when they fail in this purpose they become the dangerously structured dams that block the flow of social progress. I had hoped that the white moderate would understand that the present tension in the South is a necessary phase of the transition from an obnoxious negative peace, in which the Negro passively accepted his unjust plight, to a substantive and positive peace, in which all men will respect the dignity and worth of human personality. Actually, we who engage in nonviolent direct action are not the creators of tension. We merely bring to the surface the hidden tension that is already alive. We bring it out in the open, where it can be seen and dealt with. Like a boil that can never be cured so long as it is covered up but must be opened with all its ugliness to the natural medicines of air and light, injustice must be exposed, with all the tension its exposure creates, to the light of human conscience and the air of national opinion before it can be cured.

In your statement you assert that our actions, even though peaceful, must be condemned because they precipitate violence. But is this a logical assertion? Isn't this like condemning a robbed man because his possession of money precipitated the evil act of robbery? Isn't this like condemning Socrates because his unswerving commitment to truth and his philosophical inquiries precipitated the act by the misguided populace in which they made him drink hemlock? Isn't this like condemning Jesus because his unique God-consciousness and never-ceasing devotion to God's will precipitated the evil act of crucifixion? We must come to see that, as the federal courts have consistently affirmed, it is wrong to urge an individual to cease his efforts to gain his basic constitutional rights because the quest may precipitate violence. Society must protect the robbed and punish the robber.

I had also hoped that the white moderate would reject the myth concerning time in relation to the struggle for freedom. I have just received a letter from a white brother in Texas. He writes: "All Christians know that the colored people will receive equal rights eventually, but it is possible that you are in too great a religious hurry. It has taken Christianity almost two thousand years to accomplish what it has. The teachings of Christ take time to come to earth." Such an attitude stems from a tragic misconception of time, from the strangely irrational notion that there is something in the very flow of time that will inevitably cure all ills. Actually, time itself is neutral; it can be used either destructively or constructively. More and more I feel that the people of ill will have used time much more effectively than have the people of good will. We will have to repent in this generation not merely for the hateful words and actions of the bad people but for the appalling silence of the good people. Human progress never rolls in on wheels of inevitability; it comes through the tireless efforts of men willing to be co-workers with God, and without this hard work, time itself becomes an ally of the forces of social stagnation. We must use time creatively, in the knowledge that the time is always ripe to do right. Now is the time to make real the promise of democracy and transform our pending national elegy into a creative psalm of brotherhood. Now is the time to lift our national policy from the quicksand of racial injustice to the solid rock of human dignity.

You speak of our activity in Birmingham as extreme. At first I was rather disappointed that fellow clergymen would see my nonviolent efforts as those of an extremist. I began thinking about the fact that I stand in the middle of two opposing forces in the Negro community. One is a force of complacency, made up in part of Negroes who, as a result of long years of oppression, are so drained of self-respect and a sense of "somebodiness" that they have adjusted to segregation; and in part of a few middle-class Negroes who, because of a degree of academic and economic security and because in some ways they profit by segregation, have become insensitive to the problems of the masses. The other force is one of bitterness and hatred, and it comes perilously close to advocating violence. It is expressed in the various black nationalist groups that are springing up across the nation, the largest and best-known being Elijah Muhammad's Muslim movement. Nourished by the Negro's frustration over the continued existence of racial discrimination, this movement is made up of people who have lost faith in America, who have absolutely repudiated Christianity, and who have concluded that the white man is an incorrigible "devil."

I have tried to stand between these two forces, saying that we need emulate neither the "do-nothingism" of the complacent nor the hatred and despair of the black nationalist. For there is the more excellent way of love and nonviolent protest. I am grateful to God that, through the influence of the Negro church, the way of nonviolence became an integral part of our struggle.

If this philosophy had not emerged, by now many streets of the South should, I am convinced, be flowing with blood. And I am further convinced that if our white brothers dismiss as "rabble-rousers" and "outside agitators" those of us who employ nonviolent direct action, and if they refuse to support our nonviolent efforts, millions of Negroes will, out of frustration and despair, seek solace and security in black-nationalist ideologies—a development that would inevitably lead to a frightening racial nightmare.

Oppressed people cannot remain oppressed forever. The yearning for freedom eventually manifests itself, and that is what has happened to the American Negro. Something within has reminded him of his birthright of freedom, and something without has reminded him that it can be gained. Consciously or unconsciously, he has been caught up by the *Zeitgeist*,[2] and with his black brothers of Africa and his brown and yellow brothers of Asia, South America, and the Caribbean, the United States Negro is moving with a sense of great urgency toward the promised land of racial justice. If one recognizes this vital urge that has engulfed the Negro community, one should readily understand why public demonstrations are taking place. The Negro has many pent-up resentments and latent frustrations, and he must release them. So let him march; let him make prayer pilgrimages to the city hall; let him go on freedom rides—and try to understand why he must do so. If his repressed emotions are not released in nonviolent ways, they will seek expression through violence; this is not a threat but a fact of history. So I have not said to my people: "Get rid of your discontent." Rather, I have tried to say that this normal and healthy discontent can be channeled into the creative outlet of nonviolent direct action. And now this approach is being termed extremist.

But though I was initially disappointed at being categorized as an extremist, as I continued to think about the matter I gradually gained a measure of satisfaction from the label. Was not Jesus an extremist for love: "Love your enemies, bless them that curse you, do good to them that hate you, and pray for them which despitefully use you, and persecute you." Was

<hr>

[2]*Zeitgeist* German for "spirit of the age."

not Amos an extremist for justice: "Let justice roll down like waters and righteousness like an ever-flowing stream." Was not Paul an extremist for the Christian gospel: "I bear in my body the marks of the Lord Jesus." Was not Martin Luther an extremist; "Here I stand; I cannot do otherwise, so help me God." And John Bunyan: "I will stay in jail to the end of my days before I make a butchery of my conscience." And Abraham Lincoln: "This nation cannot survive half slave and half free." And Thomas Jefferson: "We hold these truths to be self-evident, that all men are created equal. . . ." So the question is not whether we will be extremists, but what kind of extremists we will be. Will we be extremists for hate or for love? Will we be extremists for the preservation of injustice or for the extension of justice? In that dramatic scene on Calvary's hill three men were crucified. We must never forget that all three were crucified for the same crime—the crime of extremism. Two were extremists for immorality, and thus fell below their environment. The other, Jesus Christ, was an extremist for love, truth, and goodness, and thereby rose above his environment. Perhaps the South, the nation, and the world are in dire need of creative extremists.

I had hoped that the white moderate would see this need. Perhaps I was too optimistic; perhaps I expected too much. I suppose I should have realized that few members of the oppressor race can understand the deep groans and passionate yearnings of the oppressed race, and still fewer have the vision to see that injustice must be rooted out by strong, persistent, and determined action. I am thankful, however, that some of our white brothers in the South have grasped the meaning of this social revolution and committed themselves to it. They are still all too few in quantity, but they are big in quality. Some—such as Ralph McGill, Lillian Smith, Harry Golden, James McBride Dabbs, Ann Braden, and Sarah Patton Boyle—have written about our struggle in eloquent and prophetic terms. Others have marched with us down nameless streets of the South. They have languished in filthy, roach-infested jails, suffering the abuse and brutality of policemen who view them as "dirty nigger-lovers." Unlike so many of their moderate brothers and sisters, they have recognized the urgency of the moment and sensed the need for powerful "action" antidotes to combat the disease of segregation.

Let me take note of my other major disappointment. I have been so greatly disappointed with the white church and its leadership. Of course, there are some notable exceptions. I am not unmindful of the fact that each of you has taken some significant stands on this issue. I commend you, Reverend Stallings, for your Christian stand on this past Sunday, in welcoming Negroes to your worship service on a nonsegregated basis. I commend the Catholic leaders of this state for integrating Spring Hill College several years ago.

But despite these notable exceptions, I must honestly reiterate that I have been disappointed with the church. I do not say this as one of those negative critics who can always find something wrong with the church. I say this as a minister of the gospel, who loves the church; who was nurtured in its bosom; who has been sustained by its spiritual blessings and who will remain true to it as long as the cord of life shall lengthen.

When I was suddenly catapulted into the leadership of the bus protest in Montgomery, Alabama, a few years ago, I felt we would be supported by the white church. I felt that the white ministers, priests, and rabbis of the South would be among our strongest allies. Instead, some have been outright opponents, refusing to understand the freedom movement and misrepresenting its leaders; all too many others have been more cautious than courageous and have remained silent behind the anesthetizing security of stained-glass windows.

In spite of my shattered dreams, I came to Birmingham with the hope that the white religious leadership of this community would see the justice of our cause and, with deep moral concern, would serve as the channel through which our just grievances could reach the power structure. I had hoped that each of you would understand. But again I have been disappointed.

I have heard numerous southern religious leaders admonish their worshipers to comply with a desegregation decision because it is the law, but I have longed to hear white ministers declare: "Follow this decree because integration is morally right and because the Negro is your brother." In the midst of blatant injustices inflicted upon the Negro, I have watched white churchmen stand on the sideline and mouth pious irrelevancies and sanctimonious trivialities. In the midst of a mighty struggle to rid our nation of racial and economic injustice, I have heard many ministers say: "Those are social issues, with which the gospel has no real concern." And I have watched many churches commit themselves to a completely otherworldly religion which makes a strange, unbiblical distinction between body and soul, between the sacred and the secular.

I have traveled the length and breadth of Alabama, Mississippi, and all the other southern states. On sweltering summer days and crisp autumn mornings I have looked at the South's beautiful churches with their lofty spires pointing heavenward. I have beheld the impressive outlines of her massive religious-education buildings. Over and over I have found myself saying: "What kind of people worship here? Who is their God? Where were their voices when the lips of Governor Barnett dripped with words of interposition and nullification? Where were they when Governor Wallace gave a clarion call for defiance and hatred? Where were their voices of support when bruised and weary Negro men and women decided to rise from the dark dungeons of complacency to the bright hills of creative protest?"

Yes, these questions are still in my mind. In deep disappointment I have wept over the laxity of the church. But be assured that my tears have been tears of love. There can be no deep disappointment where there is not deep love. Yes, I love the church. How could I do otherwise? I am in the rather unique position of being the son, the grandson, and the great-grandson of preachers. Yes, I see the church as the body of Christ. But, Oh! How we have blemished and scarred that body through social neglect and through fear of being nonconformists.

There was a time when the church was very powerful—in the time when the early Christians rejoiced at being deemed worthy to suffer for what they believed. In those days the church was not merely a thermometer that recorded the ideas and principles of popular opinion; it was a thermostat that transformed the mores of society. Whenever the early Christians entered a town, the people in power became disturbed and immediately sought to convict the Christians for being "disturbers of the peace" and "outside agitators." But the Christians pressed on, in the conviction that they were "a colony of heaven," called to obey God rather than man. Small in number, they were big in commitment. They were too God-intoxicated to be "astronomically intimidated." By their effort and example they brought an end to such ancient evils as infanticide and gladiatorial contests.

Things are different now. So often the contemporary church is a weak, ineffectual voice with an uncertain sound. So often it is an archdefender of the status quo. Far from being disturbed by the presence of the church, the power structure of the average community is consoled by the church's silent—and often even vocal—sanction of things as they are.

But the judgment of God is upon the church as never before. If today's church does not recapture the sacrificial spirit of the early church, it will lose its authenticity, forfeit the loyalty of millions, and be dismissed as an irrelevant social club with no meaning for the twentieth century. Every day I meet young people whose disappointment with the church has turned into outright disgust.

Perhaps I have once again been too optimistic. Is organized religion too inextricably bound to the status quo to save our nation and the world? Perhaps I must turn my faith to the inner spiritual church, the church within the church, as the true *ekklesia* and the hope of the world. But again I am thankful to God that some noble souls from the ranks of organized religion have broken loose from the paralyzing chains of conformity and joined us as active partners in the struggle for freedom. They have left their secure congregations and walked the streets of Albany, Georgia, with us. They have gone down the highways of the South on tortuous rides for freedom. Yes, they have gone to jail with us. Some have been dismissed from their churches, have lost the support of their bishops and fellow ministers. But they have acted in the faith that right defeated is stronger than evil triumphant. Their witness has been the spiritual salt that has preserved the true meaning of the gospel in these troubled times. They have carved a tunnel of hope through the dark mountain of disappointment.

I hope the church as a whole will meet the challenge of this decisive hour. But even if the church does not come to the aid of justice, I have no despair about the future. I have no fear about the outcome of our struggle in Birmingham, even if our motives are at present misunderstood. We will reach the goal of freedom in Birmingham and all over the nation, because the goal of America is freedom. Abused and scorned though we may be, our destiny is tied up with America's destiny. Before the pilgrims landed at Plymouth, we were here. Before the pen of Jefferson etched the majestic words of the Declaration of Independence across the pages of history, we were here. For more than two centuries our forebears labored in this country without wages; they made cotton king; they built the homes of their masters while suffering gross injustice and shameful humiliation—and yet out of a bottomless vitality they continue to thrive and develop. If the inexpressible cruelties of slavery could not stop us, the opposition we now face will surely fail. We will win our freedom because the sacred heritage of our nation and the eternal will of God are embodied in our echoing demands.

Before closing I feel impelled to mention one other point in your statement that has troubled me profoundly. You warmly commended the Birmingham police force for keeping "order" and "preventing violence." I doubt that you would have so warmly commended the police force if you had seen its dogs sinking their teeth into unarmed, nonviolent Negroes. I doubt that you would so quickly commend the policemen if you were to observe their ugly and inhumane treatment of Negroes here in the city jail; if you were to watch them push and curse old Negro women and young Negro girls; if you were to see them slap and kick old Negro men and young boys; if you were to observe them, as they did on two occasions, refuse to give us food because we wanted to sing our grace together. I cannot join you in your praise of the Birmingham police department.

It is true that the police have exercised a degree of discipline in handling the demonstrators. In this sense they have conducted themselves rather "nonviolently" in public. But for what purpose? To preserve the evil system of segregation. Over the past few years I have consistently preached that nonviolence demands that the means we use must be as pure as the ends we seek. I have tried to make clear that it is wrong to use immoral means to attain moral ends. But now I must affirm that it is just as wrong, or perhaps even more so, to use moral means to preserve immoral ends. Perhaps Mr. Connor and his policemen have been rather nonviolent in public, as was Chief Pritchett in Albany, Georgia, but they used the moral means of nonviolence to maintain the immoral end of racial injustice. As T. S. Eliot has said: "The last temptation is the greatest treason: To do the right deed for the wrong reason."

I wish you had commended the Negro sit-inners and demonstrators of Birmingham for their sublime courage, their willingness to suffer, and their amazing discipline in the midst of great provocation. One day the South will recognize its real heroes. They will be the James Merediths, with the noble sense of purpose that enables them to face jeering and hostile mobs, and with the agonizing loneliness that characterizes the life of the pioneer. They will be old, oppressed, battered Negro women, symbolized in a seventy-two-year-old woman in Montgomery, Alabama, who rose up with a sense of dignity and with her people decided not to ride segregated buses, and who responded with ungrammatical profundity to one who inquired about her weariness: "My feets is tired, but my soul is at rest." They will be the young high school and college students, the young ministers of the gospel and a host of their elders, courageously and nonviolently sitting in at lunch counters and willingly going to jail for conscience' sake. One day the South will know that when these disinherited children of God sat down at lunch counters, they were in reality standing up for what is best in the American dream and for the most sacred values in our Judaeo-Christian heritage, thereby bringing our nation back to those great wells of democracy which were dug deep by the founding fathers in their formulation of the Constitution and the Declaration of Independence.

Never before have I written so long a letter. I'm afraid it is much too long to take your precious time. I can assure you that it would have been much shorter if I had been writing from a comfortable desk, but what else can one do when he is alone in a narrow jail cell, other than write long letters, think long thoughts, and pray long prayers?

If I have said anything in this letter that overstates the truth and indicates an unreasonable impatience, I beg you to forgive me. If I have said anything that understates the truth and indicates my having a patience that allows me to settle for anything less than brotherhood, I beg God to forgive me.

I hope this letter finds you strong in the faith. I also hope that circumstances will soon make it possible for me to meet each of you, not as an integrationist or a civil-rights leader but as a fellow clergyman and a Christian brother. Let us all hope that the dark clouds of racial prejudice will soon pass away and the deep fog of misunderstanding will be lifted from our fear-drenched communities, and in some not too distant tomorrow the radiant stars of love and brotherhood will shine over our great nation with all their scintillating beauty.

Yours for the cause of Peace and Brotherhood,
Martin Luther King, Jr.

Textual Questions

1. Consider the letter "A Call for Unity" to which King's own letter is a response. What points are made in "A Call for Unity"? How does King address each of these points in his own letter, directly and/or indirectly?

2. Where does King use "I" in his letter? Where does he use "we" and "us"? Where does he use "you"? Why, when he uses each of these pronouns, does he choose to do so?

3. Where and how does King define himself in his letter—and his goals and reasons for participating in the march that led to his confinement?

Rhetorical Questions

4. As a response, directly, to "A Call for Unity," how persuasive is "Letter from Birmingham Jail"? As an indirect call to the nation's people as a whole, how effective are both letters? What makes one weaker/stronger than the other?

5. Are both of these letters—"A Call for Unity" and "Letter from Birmingham Jail"—written to the same audience? If so, then how can you tell? If not, then to whom is each letter written, and how is this clear to you?

6. What references to religion does King make, where, and why? In what way are these references a response to "A Call for Unity"? In what way are these something else entirely?

Intertextual Questions

7. Compare "Letter from Birmingham Jail" with "I Have a Dream" (chapter one). How are these two texts alike? How are they different?

8. In what ways is President Lyndon B. Johnson's speech "The Great Society" (chapter one) similar to or different from King's "Letter from Birmingham Jail"?

Thinking Beyond the Text

9. Would King's "Letter from Birmingham Jail," with its many references to religion, be as persuasive if penned today as it was in the 1960s? Why? What has/has not changed in America that would affect the ways in which the religious rhetoric of this letter is perceived?

10. Given the massive inequities between white and black America in 1963, and the violence with which many civil rights marches were being met, how does King establish and maintain a reasonable, rational, moderate tone in his argument? Ultimately, do you believe that change occurred because of this moderation or in spite of it?

For Writing & Discussion

11. King's "Letter from Birmingham Jail" is a response to "A Call for Unity," but what were the immediate responses to King's letter itself? Searching online and/or in your school's library, locate at least one response to King's letter and bring it to class to read aloud.

R O B E R T   F .   K E N N E D Y

The younger brother of President John Fitzgerald Kennedy, Robert "Bobby" Kennedy (1925–1968) was Attorney General in his brother's administration and under Lyndon B. Johnson after JFK's assassination in 1963. From 1964–1968 Kennedy represented New York in the U.S. Senate, and he ran for the Democratic presidential nomination in 1968. A powerful civil rights advocate, Kennedy supported the integration of universities, busing in public schools, anti-poverty programs, and the Voting Rights Act of 1965. Kennedy was assassinated in June 1968, two months after the assassination of Martin Luther King, Jr.

Kennedy gave this unplanned, unscripted speech, "On the Death of Martin Luther King, Jr.," when he learned of King's death while on a campaign stop in Indianapolis, Indiana. Audience members, many of whom were African American, had not yet heard about the assassination. Considering the rioting in other cities following the announcement, some of his advisors suggested he cancel the speech. Instead Kennedy chose not only to appear but also to speak directly about the racism that King had dedicated his life to overcoming and to plead with his listeners, black and white, to continue King's work.

On the Death of Martin Luther King, Jr.

∿ Prereading Question

Assassinations of major political figures in America are, ultimately, quite rare, overall. Yet the 1960s saw many such assassinations—President John F. Kennedy, Medgar Evars, Martin Luther King, Jr., Robert Kennedy. Why?

April 4, 1968
Indianapolis, Indiana

I have bad news for you, for all of our fellow citizens, and people who love peace all over the world, and that is that Martin Luther King was shot and killed tonight.

Martin Luther King dedicated his life to love and to justice for his fellow human beings, and he died because of that effort.

In this difficult day, in this difficult time for the United States, it is perhaps well to ask what kind of a nation we are and what direction we want to move in. For those of you who are black—considering the evidence there evidently is that there were white people who were responsible—you can be filled with bitterness, with hatred, and a desire for revenge. We can move in that direction as a country, in great polarization—black people amongst black, white people amongst white, filled with hatred toward one another.

Or we can make an effort, as Martin Luther King did, to understand and to comprehend, and to replace that violence, that stain of bloodshed that has spread across our land, with an effort to understand with compassion and love.

For those of you who are black and are tempted to be filled with hatred and distrust at the injustice of such an act, against all white people, I can only say that I feel in my own heart the same kind of feeling. I had a member of my family killed, but he was killed by a white man. But we have to make an effort in the United States, we have to make an effort to understand, to go beyond these rather difficult times.

My favorite poet was Aesehylus. He wrote: "In our sleep, pain which cannot forget falls drop by drop upon the heart until, in our own despair, against our will, comes wisdom through the awful grace of God."

What we need in the United States is not division; what we need in the United States is not hatred; what we need in the United States is not violence or lawlessness; but love and wisdom, and compassion toward one another, and a feeling of justice toward those who still suffer within our country, whether they be white or they be black.

So I shall ask you tonight to return home, to say a prayer for the family of Martin Luther King, that's true, but more importantly to say a prayer for our own country, which all of us love—a prayer for understanding and that compassion of which I spoke.

We can do well in this country. We will have difficult times; we've had difficult times in the past; we will have difficult times in the future. It is not the end of violence; it is not the end of lawlessness; it is not the end of disorder.

But the vast majority of white people and the vast majority of black people in this country want to live together, want to improve the quality of our life, and want justice for all human beings who abide in our land.

Let us dedicate ourselves to what the Greeks wrote so many years ago: to tame the savageness of man and make gentle the life of this world.

Let us dedicate ourselves to that, and say a prayer for our country and for our people.

Textual Questions

1. Where does Kennedy use "I" and where does he use "we" in his speech? Why? What effect does each have, in its place?

2. How and where does Kennedy use the death of Martin Luther King, Jr. to make a larger point about America's present and future?

3. How is Kennedy's speech organized so that it builds logically and emotionally to its climax in the last two paragraphs?

Rhetorical Questions

4. Kennedy, on the campaign trail for President of the United States at the time, was advised not to mention the death of Martin Luther King, Jr., in his speech—even though it had just happened, and the members of his audience did not yet know. Why does he, instead, choose not only to mention the death of MLK but to use this tragedy to make a point about America? Why might his advisers have been against any mention of MLK?

5. Consider paragraphs 3 and 4. How effective is Kennedy's explanation of what could happen—paragraph 3—and what should happen (paragraph 4)? Is the effect of the latter heightened by its placement after the former? Why?

6. What call to action does Kennedy make in his speech, and how effectively does he make it?

Intertextual Questions

7. How does Kennedy's description of the possible legacies of the assassination of Martin Luther King, Jr. compare with the description of this same tragedy offered by Cesar Chavez (later in this chapter)?

8. If the dates of their assassinations were reversed, then how might Martin Luther King, Jr. have responded to the death of Robert F. Kennedy? Why?

Thinking Beyond the Text

9. Why would Robert Kennedy be in a position to speak with great authority on issues of racism, violence, and hatred in America?

10. Based upon the modern American definition, would you consider the assassination of Martin Luther King, Jr. a terrorist act? Would the assassinations of President John F. Kennedy and presidential candidate Robert Kennedy also be terrorist acts? Why/why not?

For Writing & Discussion

11. Searching online or in your library, examine how other prominent Americans responded to the death of Martin Luther King, Jr. In what ways were their responses similar to that of Robert Kennedy? How were their responses different?

MICHAEL LEVIN

Michael Levin (1944? –) is a professor of philosophy in the Honors College of the City College of New York (CCNY). He has published widely in scholarly journals and also in nonacademic publications including *Newsweek* and the *National Review*.

"The Case for Torture" was first published in *Newsweek* in 1982. It poses a range of hypothetical situations in which, Levin suggests, torture is in fact an acceptable option. Levin also has written on affirmative action, feminism, race, and other topics. His books include *Feminism and Freedom* (1987), *Why Race Matters: Race Differences and What They Mean* (1997), and *Sexual Orientation and Human Rights* (1999, with Laurence M. Thomas).

Levin, who has called for the repeal of the 1964 Civil Rights Act and other anti-discrimination legislation, has sparked considerable controversy. In the 1980s he was picketed at CCNY by student members of the International Committee Against Racism for an anti-affirmative action letter he wrote to the *New York Times*, and in 1988 was formally censured by the faculty senate at CCNY for another article, although the senate also supported his right to freedom of expression.

The Case for Torture

∾ Prereading Question

How do you define "torture"? What, physically, can be considered torturous? Mentally? Is there a "spiritual torture"?

It is generally assumed that torture is impermissible, a throwback to a more brutal age. Enlightened societies reject it outright, and regimes suspected of using it risk the wrath of the United States.

I believe this attitude is unwise. There are situations in which torture is not merely permissible but morally mandatory. Moreover, these situations are moving from the realm of imagination to fact.

Suppose a terrorist has hidden an atomic bomb on Manhattan Island which will detonate at noon on July 4 unless . . . (here follow the usual demands for money and release of his friends from jail). Suppose, further, that he is caught at 10 A.M. of the fateful day, but—preferring death to failure—won't disclose where the bomb is. What do we do? If we follow due process—wait for his lawyer, arraign him—millions of people will die. If the only way to save those lives is to subject the terrorist to the most excruciating possible pain, what grounds can there be for not doing so? I suggest there are none. In any case, I ask you to face the question with an open mind.

Torturing the terrorist is unconstitutional? Probably. But millions of lives surely outweigh constitutionality. Torture is barbaric? Mass murder is far more barbaric. Indeed, letting millions of innocents die in deference to one who flaunts his guilt is moral cowardice, an unwillingness to dirty one's hands. If *you* caught the terrorist, could you sleep nights knowing that millions died because you couldn't bring yourself to apply the electrodes?

Once you concede that torture is justified in extreme cases, you have admitted that the decision to use torture is a matter of balancing innocent lives against the means needed to save them. You must now face more realistic cases involving more modest numbers. Someone plants a bomb on a jumbo jet. He alone can disarm it, and his demands cannot be met (or if they can, we refuse to set a precedent by yielding to his threats). Surely we can, we must, do anything to the extortionist to save the passengers. How can we tell 300, or 100, or 10 people who never asked to be put in danger, "I'm sorry, you'll have to die in agony, we just couldn't bring ourselves to . . ."

Here are the results of an informal poll about a third, hypothetical, case. Suppose a terrorist group kidnapped a newborn baby from a hospital. I asked four mothers if they would approve of torturing kidnappers if that were necessary to get their own newborns back. All said yes, the most "liberal" adding that she would administer it herself.

I am not advocating torture as punishment. Punishment is addressed to deeds irrevocably past. Rather, I am advocating torture as an acceptable measure for preventing future evils. So understood, it is far less objectionable than many extant punishments. Opponents of the death penalty, for example, are forever insisting that executing a murderer will not bring back his victim (as if the purpose of capital punishment were supposed to be resurrection, not deterrence or retribution). But torture, in the cases described, is intended not to bring anyone back but to keep innocents from being dispatched. The most powerful argument against using torture as a punishment or to secure confessions is that such practices disregard the rights of the individual. Well, if the individual is all that important—and he is—it is correspondingly important to protect the rights of individuals threatened by terrorists. If life is so valuable that it must never be taken, the lives of the innocents must be saved even at the price of hurting the one who endangers them.

Better precedents for torture are assassination and preemptive attack. No Allied leader would have flinched at assassinating Hitler, had that been possible. (The Allies did assassinate Heydrich.) Americans would be angered to learn that Roosevelt could have had Hitler killed in 1943— thereby shortening the war and saving millions of lives—but refused on moral grounds. Similarly, if nation A learns that nation B is about to launch an unprovoked attack, A has a right to save itself by destroying B's military capability first. In the same way, if the police can by torture save those who would otherwise die at the hands of kidnappers or terrorists, they must.

There is an important difference between terrorists and their victims that should mute talk of the terrorists' "rights." The terrorist's victims are at risk unintentionally, not having asked to be endangered. But the terrorist knowingly initiated his actions. Unlike his victims, he volunteered for the risks of his deed. By threatening to kill for profit or idealism, he renounces civilized standards, and he can have no complaint if civilization tries to thwart him by whatever means necessary.

Just as torture is justified only to save lives (not extort confessions or recantations), it is justifiably administered only to those *known* to hold innocent lives in their hands. Ah, but how can the authorities ever be sure they have the right malefactor? Isn't there a danger of error and abuse? Won't We turn into Them?

Questions like these are disingenuous in a world in which terrorists proclaim themselves and perform for television. The name of their game is public recognition. After all, you can't very well intimidate a government into releasing your freedom fighters unless you announce that it is your group that has seized its embassy. "Clear guilt" is difficult to define, but when 40 million people see a group of masked gunmen seize an airplane on the evening news, there is not much question about who the perpetrators are. There will be hard cases where the situation is murkier. Nonetheless, a line demarcating the legitimate use of torture can be drawn. Torture only the obviously guilty, and only for the sake of saving innocents, and the line between Us and Them will remain clear.

There is little danger that the Western democracies will lose their way if they choose to inflict pain as one way of preserving order. Paralysis in the face of evil is the greater danger. Some day soon a terrorist will threaten tens of thousands of lives, and torture will be the only way to save them. We had better start thinking about this.

Textual Questions

1. How does Levin's opening paragraph make a point about torture that is completely reversed in paragraph 2? Why?

2. In paragraph 4, Levin asks and answers a short set of questions. How well does this Q&A structure work for you as a reader? Does it develop his points enough to allow them to be persuasive?

3. What examples does Levin use to construct his argument? What comparisons does he make? What ultimate point does he make about the use of torture by a nation such as the United States?

Rhetorical Questions

4. Levin's essay was published in 1982, nearly 20 years before the terrorist attacks of 9/11 and the long War on Terror. How would his essay need to be revised if it were to be published today? What changes would you make and why?

5. Levin writes that "Torturing the terrorist is unconstitutional? Probably. But millions of lives surely outweigh constitutionality." There are two assertions here, separated by "Probably." Do you agree with either/both? Why or why not?

6. Where does Levin appeal to reason in his essay? Where does he appeal to emotion? Which is most effective, in your opinion, and why? How does Levin, in his argument built around reason and emotion, build to his final paragraph? And do you agree or disagree with his final points? Why?

Intertextual Questions

7. How does Levin's discussion of torture compare with that of Andrew C. McCarthy in "Torture: Thinking about the Unthinkable" (Chapter 7)?

8. Based upon your reading of "Just War—or a Just War?" (Chapter 7) how would former President Jimmy Carter respond to Levin's argument—as a politician, a statesman, and a man of faith?

Thinking Beyond the Text

9. Levin's argument is built on a foundation of emotional logic: Of course it's better to hurt one person if the lives of millions can be saved. But is emotional logic enough? If a terrorist plans to attack a free nation of laws by killing millions of its citizens, what does it mean for the nation if its legal representative breaks its laws in order to save the lives of those millions? Lives are saved, but is the nation saved?

10. There are nations that allow what the United States considers torture of suspected criminals such as terrorists. Yet the information gained through torture is frequently flawed or fabricated, according to experts. If the information itself may prove useless, and the terrorist's attack may or may not be foiled because the terrorist is tortured, then is the use of torture justified? Logical? Ethical?

For Writing & Discussion

11. What nations allow the torture of prisoners—and under what circumstances? Where does the United States stand, legally, on the issue of torture? What treatment does the United States legally allow of its prisoners—either enemy combatants or criminals—that is/can be considered torture?

RONALD REAGAN

Ronald Reagan (1911–2004) served as governor of California from 1967–1975, and as president of the United States from 1981–1989. Before entering politics, he worked as a radio sports announcer, movie and television actor, and head of the Screen Actors Guild. As a politician, Reagan was a social and fiscal conservative and a strong promoter of supply-side economics and of a military buildup that was based on the concept of "peace through strength." Opponents liked to call Reagan "The Teflon President" because no criticism seemed to stick to him, while supporters dubbed him "The Great Communicator" because of his personable delivery.

In the speech "America's Best Days are Yet to Come," delivered at the 1992 Republican Convention in Houston, Reagan supported President George H. W. Bush and Vice-President Dan Quayle's bid for a second term. This and other speeches are available in *Speaking My Mind: Selected Speeches* (2004).

Reagan's 1992 speech shows his characteristic optimism and humor while also stressing the values that characterized his presidency. For example, Reagan is remembered for ending an American policy of détente and shifting the United States toward a more interventionist foreign policy. In keeping with that, his speech illustrates his belief that America's focus on civil rights should extend beyond its own citizens to people in other countries.

America's Best Days are Yet to Come

◌ **Prereading Question**

One aspect of the American dream is the belief that America is always getting better—safer, stronger, more prosperous. The implications of this for the present are two: (1) The future will be better than the present and (2) the past was, by definition, worse than the present. Would you agree that either of these assertions is true? Or are both simply easy ways of talking about the past/future that don't require any critical thought?

Delivered at the Republican National Convention, Houston, Texas, August 17, 1992

Thank you. Thank you very much. Thank you, Paul for that kind introduction. And Mr. Chairman, delegates, friends, fellow Americans, thank you so very much for that welcome.

You've given Nancy and me so many wonderful memories, so much of your warmth and affection, we cannot thank you enough for the honor of your friendship.

Over the years, I've addressed this convention as a private citizen, as a governor, as a presidential candidate, as a president. And now, once again tonight, as private citizen Ronald Reagan.

Tonight is a very special night for me. Of course, at my age, every night's a special night. After all—after all, I was born in 1911. Indeed, according to the experts, I have exceeded my life expectancy by quite a few years. Now, this is a source of great annoyance to some, especially those in the Democratic party.

But, here's the remarkable thing about being born in 1911. In my life's journey over these past eight decades, I have seen the human race through a period of unparalleled tumult and triumph. I have seen the birth of communism and the death of communism. I have witnessed the bloody futility of two World Wars, and Korea, Vietnam and the Persian Gulf. I have seen Germany united, divided and united again. I have seen television grow from a parlor novelty to become the most powerful vehicle of communication in history. As a boy, I saw streets filled with model-T's. As a man, I have met men who walked on the moon.

I have not only seen, but lived the marvels of what historians have called the "American Century." Yet, tonight is not a time to look backward. For while I take inspiration from the past, like most Americans, I live for the future.

So this evening, for just a few minutes, I hope you will let me talk about a country that is forever young.

There was a time when empires were defined by land mass, subjugated peoples, and military might. But the United States is unique because we are an empire of ideals. For two hundred years we have been set apart by our faith in the ideals of democracy, of free men and free markets, and of the extraordinary possibilities that lie within seemingly ordinary men and women. We believe that no power of government is as formidable a force for good as the creativity and entrepreneurial drive of the American people.

Those are the ideals that invented revolutionary technologies and a culture envied by people everywhere. This powerful sense of energy has made America synonymous for opportunity the world over. And after generations of struggle, America is the moral force that defeated communism—and all those who would put the human soul itself into bondage.

But in a few short years, we Americans have experienced the most sweeping changes of this century—the fall of the Soviet Union and the rise of the global economy. No transition is without its problems, but as uncomfortable as it may feel at the moment, the changes of the 1990s will leave America more dynamic and less in danger than at any time in my life.

A fellow named James Allen once wrote in his diary, "many thinking people believe America has seen its best days." He wrote that July 26, 1775. There are still those who believe America is weakening, that our glory was the brief flash of time called the 20th Century, that ours was a burst of greatness too bright and brilliant to sustain, that America's purpose is past. My friends, I utterly reject those views. That's not the America we know.

We were meant to be masters of destiny, not victims of fate. Who among us would trade America's future for that of any other country in the world? And who could possibly have so little faith in our American people that they would trade our tomorrow for our yesterday? I'll give you a hint. They put on quite a production in New York a few weeks ago.

You might even call it "slick."

A stone's throw from Broadway, it was. And how appropriate. Over and over they told us they were not the party they were. They kept telling us with straight faces that they're for family values, they're for a strong America, they're for less intrusive government. And they call me an actor!

To hear them—to hear them talk, you'd never know that the nightmare of nuclear annihilation has been lifted from our sleep. You'd never know that our standard of living remains the highest in the world. You'd never know that our air is cleaner than it was 20 years ago. You'd never know that we remain the one nation the rest of the world looks to for leadership.

All right. All right, thank you.

It always—or wasn't always this way. We mustn't forget, even if they would like to, the very different America that existed just twelve years ago—an America with 21 percent interest rates and back-to-back years of double-digit inflation; an America where mortgage payments doubled, pay-checks plunged, and motorists sat in gas lines; an America whose leaders told us it was our own fault, that ours was a future of scarcity and sacrifice, and that what we really needed was another good dose of government control and higher taxes.

It wasn't so long ago that the world was a far more dangerous place as well. It was a world where aggressive Soviet communism was on the rise and America's strength was in decline. It was a world where our children came of age under the threat of nuclear holocaust. It was a world where our leaders told us that standing up to aggressors was dangerous, that American might and determination were somehow obstacles to peace.

But we stood tall and proclaimed that communism was destined for the ash-heap of history. We never heard so much ridicule from our liberal friends. The only thing that got them more upset was two simple words: "Evil Empire."

But we knew then what the liberal Democrat leaders just couldn't figure out—the sky would not fall if America restored her strength and resolve, the sky would not fall if an American president spoke the truth. The only thing that would fall was the Berlin Wall.

I heard those speakers at that other convention saying "we won the Cold War." And I couldn't help wondering, just who exactly do they mean by "we"? All right. And to top it off—to top it off, they even tried to portray themselves as sharing the same fundamental values of our party. But, they truly don't understand the principle so eloquently stated by Abraham Lincoln:

> You cannot strengthen the weak by weakening the strong. You cannot help the wage-earner by pulling down the wage-payer. You cannot help the poor by destroying the rich. You cannot help men permanently by doing for them what they could and should do for themselves.

If we ever hear the Democrats quoting that passage by Lincoln and acting like they mean it, then my friends, we will know that the opposition has really changed. Until then, when we see all that rhetorical smoke blowing out from the Democrats, well Ladies and Gentlemen, I'd follow the example of their nominee—don't inhale.

All right. But listen to me. This fellow they've nominated claims he's the new Thomas Jefferson. Well, let me tell you something—I knew Thomas Jefferson. He was a friend of mine. And, governor, you're no Thomas Jefferson.

But now, let's not dismiss our current troubles. But where they see only problems, I see possibilities as vast and diverse as the American family itself. Even as we meet, the rest of the world is astounded by the pundits and fingerpointers who are so down on us as a nation.

Well I've said it before and I'll say it again: America's best days are yet to come.

Our proudest moments are yet to be. Our most glorious achievements are just ahead. America remains what Emerson called her 150 years ago, "the country of tomorrow." What a wonderful description and how true. And yet tomorrow might never have happened had we lacked the courage in the 1980s to chart a course of strength and honor.

All the more reason—all the more reason no one should underestimate the importance of this campaign and what the outcome will mean. The stakes are high. The presidency is serious business. We cannot afford to take a chance. We need a man of serious purpose, unmatched experience, knowledge and ability—a man who understands government, who understands our country and who understands the world—a man who has been at the table with Gorbachev and Yeltsin—a man whose performance as commander-in-chief of the bravest and most effective fighting force in history left the world in awe and the people of Kuwait free of foreign tyranny—yes, yes, yes, four more years, a man who has devoted more than half of his life to serving his country—a man of decency, integrity and honor.

And tonight I come to tell you that I warmly, genuinely, wholeheartedly support the reelection of George Bush as President of the United States.

All right. Okay. All right.

We know President Bush. By his own admission, he is a quiet man, not a showman. He is a trustworthy and level-headed leader who is respected around the world. His is a steady hand on the tiller through the choppy waters of the '90s, which is exactly what we need. We need George Bush!

Yes—yes—yes—we need Bush. We also need another real fighter, a man who happens to be with us this evening, someone—someone who has repeatedly stood up for his deepest convictions. We need our vice president, Dan Quayle.

Now—now—now, it's true. A lot of liberal Democrats are saying it's time for a change. And they're right. The only trouble is they're pointing to the wrong end of Pennsylvania Avenue.

What we should change is a Democratic Congress that wastes precious time on partisan matters of absolutely no relevance to the needs of the average American. So to all the entrenched interests along the Potomac—the gavel-wielding chairmen, the bloated staffs, the taxers and takers and congressional rulemakers—we have a simple slogan for November 1992: Clean House!

Yes, yes—

For you see, my fellow Republicans, we are the change! For 50 of the last 60 years, the Democrats have controlled the Senate. And they've had the House of Representatives for 56 of the last 60 years. It is time to clean house, to clean out the privileges and perks, clean out the arrogance and the big egos, clean out the scandals, the corner-cutting and the foot-dragging. What kind of job do you think they've done during all those years they've been running the Congress?

You're absolutely right.

You know, I used to say to some of those Democrats who chair every committee in the House: "You need to balance the Government's check-book the same way you balance your own." Then I learned how they ran the House bank—and I realized that was exactly what they had been doing!

Now just change what they would do if they controlled the Executive Branch, too!

This is the 21st presidential election in my lifetime, the 16th in which I will cast a ballot. Each of those elections had its shifting moods of the moment, its headlines of one day that were forgotten the next. There have been a few more twists and turns this year than in others, a little more shouting about who was up or down, in or out, as we went about selecting our candidates. But now we have arrived, as we always do, at the moment of truth—the serious business of selecting a president.

Now is the time for choosing.

As it did twelve years ago, and as we have seen many times in history, our country stands at a crossroads. There is widespread doubt about our public institutions and profound concern, not merely about the economy but about the overall direction of this great country. And as they did then, the American people are clamoring for change and sweeping reform. The kind of question we had to ask twelve years ago is the question we ask today, what kind of change can we Republicans offer the American people?

Some might believe that the things we've talked about tonight are irrelevant to the choice. These new isolationists claim that the American people don't care about how or why we prevailed in the great defining struggle of our age, the victory of liberty over our adversaries. They insist that our triumph is yesterday's news, part of a past that holds no lessons for the future.

Well nothing could be more tragic, after having come all this way on the journey of renewal we began 12 years ago, then if America herself forgot the lessons of individual liberty that she has taught to a grateful world.

Emerson was right. We are the country of tomorrow. Our revolution did not end at Yorktown. More than two centuries later, America remains on a voyage of discovery, a land that has never become, but is always in the act of becoming.

But just as we have led the crusade for democracy beyond our shores, we have a great task to do together in our own home. Now, I would appeal to you to invigorate democracy in your own neighborhoods.

Whether we come from poverty or wealth; whether we are Afro-American or Irish-American; Christian or Jewish, from the big cities or small towns, we are all equal in the eyes of God. But as Americans, that is not enough. We must be equal in the eyes of each other. We can no longer judge each other on the basis of what we are, but must, instead, start finding out who we are. In America, our origins matter less than our destinations and that is what democracy is all about.

A decade after we summoned America to a new beginning, we are beginning still. Every day brings fresh challenges and opportunities to match. With each sunrise we are reminded that millions of our citizens have yet to share in the abundance of American prosperity. Many languish in neighborhoods riddled with drugs and bereft of hope. Still others hesitate to venture out on the streets for fear of criminal violence. Let us pledge ourselves to a new beginning for them.

Let us apply our ingenuity and remarkable spirit to revolutionize education in America so that everyone among us will have the mental tools to build a better life. And while we do so, let's remember that the most profound education begins in the home.

And let us harness the competitive energy that built America into rebuilding our inner cities so that real jobs can be created for those who live there and real hope can rise out of despair.

Let us strengthen our health care system so that Americans of all ages can be secure in their futures without the fear of financial ruin.

And my friends, once and for all, let us get control of the federal deficit through a Balanced Budget Amendment—yes—yes—yes—, a budget amendment and a line item veto for the president.

And let us all renew our commitment, renew our pledge to day by day, person by person, make our country and the world a better place to live. Then when the nations of the world turn to us and say, "America, you are the model of freedom and prosperity," we can turn to them and say, "you ain't seen nothing, yet!"

For me, tonight is the latest chapter in a story that began a quarter of a century ago, when the people of California entrusted me with the stewardship of their dreams.

My fellow citizens—those of you here in this hall and those of you at home—I want you to know that I have always had the highest respect for you, for your common sense and intelligence and for your decency. I have always believed in you and in what you could accomplish for yourselves and for others.

And whatever else history may say about me when I'm gone, I hope it will record that I appealed to your best hopes, not your worst fears, to your confidence rather than your doubts. My dream is that you will travel the road ahead with liberty's lamp guiding your steps and opportunity's arm steadying your way.

My fondest hope for each one of you, and especially for the young people here—Friends, what this is, is my hope that you will love your country, not for her power or wealth, but for her selflessness and her idealism. May each of you have the heart to conceive, the understanding to direct, and the hand to execute works that will make the world a little better for your having been here.

May all of you as Americans never forget your heroic origins, never fail to seek divine guidance, and never lose your natural, God-given optimism.

And finally, my fellow Americans, may every dawn be a great new beginning for America and every evening bring us closer to that shining city upon a hill.

Before I go, I would like to ask the person who has made my life's journey so meaningful, someone I have been so very proud of over the years, to join me. Nancy—

My fellow Americans—my fellow Americans, on behalf of both of us, goodbye and God bless each and every one of you. And God bless this country we love.

Textual Questions

1. How does Ronald Reagan describe "the America that [he] know[s]"? How does his view of America contrast with the view of those who would argue against him?

2. Where and how does Ronald Reagan make references to American history, both recent and distant?

3. What major points does Ronald Reagan make in his concluding section, beginning with the single-sentence paragraph "Now is the time for choosing"? Which of these points are most persuasive and why? Which are least persuasive and why?

Rhetorical Questions

4. Ronald Reagan's text is addressed to two primary audiences—the immediate delegates at the 1992 Republican National Convention and the millions of television viewers. How does he tailor the speech simultaneously to both audiences—one obviously and entirely sympathetic to him and to his views of America and one that may agree, disagree, or not care at all?

5. How does Reagan use his own experiences, his first-person perspective, to organize his entire essay? How effective is this organization? Why? What makes this organization especially effective or ineffective for a speech made by this man at this time in this place?

6. Reread "America's Best Days are Yet to Come" and mark all/each of the words that has totally positive connotations and denotations—words such as "hope" and "faith," for example. How many of these kinds of words does Reagan use? Where? Why are there so many of them in so many places?

Intertextual Questions

7. How do former President Ronald Reagan's assertions in this speech directly contradict the assertions made by President Jimmy Carter in "Energy Problems: The Erosion of Confidence" (in the introduction to this textbook)?

8. How does Ronald Reagan's optimism about America and its future compare and contrast with the view of America offered by Michael Ignatieff in "Who Are Americans to Think That Freedom Is Theirs to Spread?" (Chapter 7)?

Thinking Beyond the Text

9. If the American generation that fought the Second World War is called "The Greatest Generation," as it often is, then doesn't that, by default, mean that America has been in a steady arc of descent since 1945? Could you, whether you believe it or not, construct a version of America's history that completely refutes that offered by former President Reagan? What events would you include?

10. Considering that the Republican candidate for President in 1992, George H. W. Bush, lost the election, why did American voters favor William Jefferson Clinton (in both the 1992 and 1996 elections)? What did Reagan perhaps leave out of his description of America, the Republican Party, and the Democratic Party that could account for the Republican loss?

For Writing & Discussion

11. Searching online or in your school's library, locate an archive of television campaign advertisements from 1980 and 1984, the two years in which Ronald Reagan was elected president of the United States. Select one ad and, in a short essay, explain how the ad expresses the same view of America that Reagan expresses in his speech.

CESAR CHAVEZ

Cesar Chavez (1927–1993) was a farm worker's rights advocate and founder of the National Farm Workers Association (NFWA) which later became the United Farm Workers (UFW).

Born and raised in a family of migrant farm workers, Chavez began working in the fields at the age of 10 when his family lost their Arizona farm during the Great Depression. He served in the U.S. Navy during World War II, then settled in California where he worked on farms and began his civil rights career by speaking out in favor of worker's rights. During the 1950s he worked for the Community Services Organization, a Latino civil rights group, and in 1962 he and Dolores Huerta founded the

NFWA/UFW. The UFW's first major campaign, a boycott of table grapes in support of California's migrant grape-pickers, was supported by then-Senator Robert Kennedy and was ultimately successful. The UFW has continued supporting farm workers in many states.

"Lessons of Dr. Martin Luther King, Jr." is a speech Chavez gave on King's birthday, January 12, in 1990. In it he describes King's life as one of actions as well as words, and calls for listeners to honor King by acting for social justice.

Chavez is now celebrated in many parts of the country. State workers in California have a paid holiday on his birthday, and Arizona, Colorado, and Texas also recognize the day. President Clinton awarded him a posthumous Presidential Medal of Freedom in 1994.

Lessons of Dr. Martin Luther King, Jr.

✎ Prereading Question

Early in his address, made in 1990, Chavez argues that America is at war both with its neighbors and with itself. Why, at that time, would he make this statement—in what ways was America at war with its neighbors and with itself?

My friends, today we honor a giant among men; today we honor the reverend Martin Luther King, Jr. Dr. King was a powerful figure of destiny, of courage, of sacrifice, and of vision. Few people in the long history of this nation can rival his accomplishment, his reason, or his selfless dedication to the cause of peace and social justice. Today we honor a wise teacher, an inspiring leader, and a true visionary, but to truly honor Dr. King we must do more than say words of praise. We must learn his lessons and put his views into practice, so that we may truly be free at last.

Who was Dr. King?

Many people will tell you of his wonderful qualities and his many accomplishments, but what makes him special to me, the truth many people don't want you to remember, is that Dr. King was a great activist, fighting for radical social change with radical methods. While other people talked about change, Dr. King used direct action to challenge the system. He welcomed it, and used it wisely. In his famous "Letter from the Birmingham Jail," Dr. King wrote that "The purpose of direct action is to create a situation so crisis-packed that it will inevitably open the door to negotiation."

Dr. King was also radical in his beliefs about violence. He learned how to successfully fight hatred and violence with the unstoppable power of nonviolence. He once stopped an armed mob, saying: "We are not advocating violence. We want to love our enemies. I want you to love our enemies. Be good to them. This is what we live by. We must meet hate with love." Dr. King knew that he very probably wouldn't survive the struggle that he led so well. But he said "If I am stopped, the movement will not stop. If I am stopped, our work will not stop. For what we are doing is right. What we are doing is just, and God is with us."

My friends, as we enter a new decade, it should be clear to all of us that there is an unfinished agenda, that we have miles to go before we reach the promised land. The men who rule this country today never learned the lessons of Dr. King, they never learned that non-violence is the only way to peace and justice. Our nation continues to wage war upon its neighbors, and upon itself. The powers that be rule over a racist society, filled with hatred and ignorance. Our nation continues to be segregated along racial and economic lines. The powers that be make themselves richer by exploiting the poor. Our nation continues to allow children to go hungry, and will not even house its own people.

The time is now for people, of all races and backgrounds, to sound the trumpets of change. As Dr. King proclaimed "There comes a time when people get tired of being trampled over by the iron feet of oppression." My friends, the time for action is upon us. The enemies of justice want you to think of Dr. King as only a civil rights leader, but he had a much broader agenda. He was a tireless crusader for the rights of the poor, for an end to the war in Vietnam long before it was popular to take that stand, and for the rights of workers everywhere.

Many people find it convenient to forget that Martin was murdered while supporting a desperate strike on that tragic day in Memphis, Tennessee. He died while fighting for the rights of sanitation workers. Dr. King's dedication to the rights of the workers who are so often exploited by the forces of greed has profoundly touched my life and guided my struggle. During my first fast in 1968, Dr. King reminded me that our struggle was his struggle too. He sent me a telegram which said "Our separate struggles are really one. A struggle for freedom, dignity, and for humanity." I was profoundly moved that someone facing such a tremendous struggle himself would take the time to worry about a struggle taking place on the other side of the continent.

Just as Dr. King was a disciple of Gandhi and Christ, we must now be Dr. King's disciples. Dr. King challenged us to work for a greater humanity. I only hope that we are worthy of his challenge. The United Farm Workers are dedicated to carrying on the dream of Reverend Martin Luther King, Jr. My friends, I would like to tell you about the struggle of the farmworkers who are waging a desperate struggle for our rights, for our children's rights, and for our very lives.

Many decades ago the chemical industry promised the growers that pesticides would bring great wealth and bountiful harvests to the fields. Just recently, the experts are learning what farmworkers, and the truly organized farmers have known for years. The prestigious National Academy of Sciences recently concluded an exhaustive five-year study which determined that pesticides do not improve profits and do not produce more crops. What, then, is the effect of pesticides? Pesticides have created a legacy of pain, and misery, and death for farmworkers and consumers alike.

The crop which poses the greatest danger, and the focus of our struggle, is the table grape crop. These pesticides soak the fields. They drift with the wind, pollute the water, and are eaten by unwitting consumers. These poisons are designed to kill, and pose a very real threat to consumers and farmworkers alike. The fields are sprayed with pesticides like Captan, Parathion, Phosdrin, and Methyl Bromide. These poisons cause cancer, DNA mutation, and horrible birth defects.

The Central Valley of California is one of the wealthiest agricultural regions in the world. In its midst are clusters of children dying from cancer. The children live in communities surrounded by the grape fields that employ their parents. The children come into contact with the poisons when they play outside, when they drink the water, and when they hug their parents returning from the fields. And the children are dying.

They are dying slow, painful, cruel deaths in towns called cancer clusters, in cancer clusters like McFarland, where the children's cancer rate is 800 percent above normal. A few months ago, the parents of a brave little girl in the agricultural community of Earlimart came to the United Farm Workers to ask for help. The Ramirez family knew about our protests in nearby McFarland and thought there might be a similar problem in Earlimart. Our union members went door to door in Earlimart, and found that the Ramirez family's worst fears were true.

There are at least four other children suffering from cancer in the little town of Earlimart, a rate 1200 percent above normal. In Earlimart, little Jimmy Candillo died recently from leukemia at the age of three. Three other young children in Earlimart, in addition to Jimmy and Natalie, are suffering from similar fatal diseases that the experts believe are caused by pesticides. These same pesticides can be found on the grapes you buy in the stores.

My friends, the suffering must end. So many children are dying, so many babies are born without limbs and vital organs, so many workers are dying in the fields. We have no choice, we must stop the plague of pesticides.

The growers responsible for this outrage are blinded by greed, by racism, and by power. The same inhumanity displayed at Selma, at Birmingham, in so many of Dr. King's battlegrounds, is displayed every day in the vineyards of California. The farm labor system in place today is a system of economic slavery.

My friends, even those farmworkers who do not have to bury their young children are suffering from abuse, neglect, and poverty. Our workers labor for many hours every day under the hot sun, often without safe drinking water or toilet facilities. Our workers are constantly subjected to incredible pressures and intimidation to meet excessive quotas. The women who work in the fields are routinely subjected to sexual harassment and sexual assaults by the growers' thugs. When our workers complain, or try to organize, they are fired, assaulted, and even murdered. Just as Bull Connor turned the dogs loose on nonviolent marchers in Alabama, the growers turn armed foremen on innocent farmworkers in California.

The stench of injustice in California should offend every American. Some people, especially those who just don't care, or don't understand, like to think that the government can take care of these problems. The government should, but won't. The growers used their wealth to buy good friends like Governor George Deukmajian, Ronald Reagan, and George Bush.

My friends, if we are going to end the suffering, we must use the same people power that vanquished injustice in Montgomery, Selma, and Birmingham. I have seen many boycotts succeed. Dr. King showed us the way with the bus boycott, and with our first boycott we were able to get DDT, Aldrin, and Dieldrin banned in our first contracts with grape growers. Now, even more urgently we are trying to get deadly pesticides banned. The growers and their allies have tried to stop us for years with intimidation, with character assassination, with public relations campaigns, with outright lies, and with murder. But those same tactics did not stop Dr. King, and they will not stop us.

Once social change begins, it cannot be reversed. You cannot uneducate the person who has learned to read. You cannot humiliate the person who feels pride. And you cannot oppress the people who are not afraid anymore.

In our life and death struggle for justice we have turned to the court of last resort: the American people. And the people are ruling in our favor. As a result, grape sales keep falling. We have witnessed truckloads of grapes being dumped because no one would stop to buy them. As demand drops, so do prices and profits. The growers are under tremendous economic pressure.

We are winning, but there is still much hard work ahead of us. I hope that you will join our struggle. The simple act of refusing to buy table grapes laced with pesticides is a powerful statement that the growers understand. Economic pressure is the only language the growers speak, and they are beginning to listen. Please, boycott table grapes. For your safety, for the workers, and for the children, we must act together.

My friends, Dr. King realized that the only real wealth comes from helping others. I challenge each and every one of you to be a true disciple of Dr. King, to be truly wealthy. I challenge you to carry on his work by volunteering to work for a just cause you believe in. Consider joining our movement because the farmworkers, and so many other oppressed peoples, depend on the unselfish dedication of its volunteers, people just like you.

Thousands of people have worked for our cause and have gone on to achieve success in many different fields. Our non-violent cause will give you skills that will last a lifetime. When Dr. King sounded the call for justice, the freedom riders answered the call in droves. I am giving you the same opportunity to join the same cause, to free your fellow human beings from the yoke of oppression.

I have faith that in this audience there are men and women with the same courage and the same idealism that put young Martin Luther King, Jr. on the path to social change. I challenge you to join the struggle of the United Farm Workers. And if you don't join our cause, then seek out the many organizations seeking peaceful social change. Seek out the many outstanding leaders who will speak to you this week, and make a difference.

If we fail to learn that each and every person can make a difference, then we will have betrayed Dr. King's life's work. The Reverend Martin Luther King, Jr. had more than just a dream, he had the love and the faith to act.

God bless you.

Textual Questions

1. How does Chavez use Dr. King to organize his essay, to pulls its parts together and keep them connected?

2. What crop poses the greatest danger, according to Chavez, and why?

3. Reread Chavez's speech, marking each of the places where he says "we," "us," and "my friends" (and any other friendly, inclusive terms such as these). Where does he use such terms and why? What tone do these terms set, overall?

Rhetorical Questions

4. What call to action is Chavez making, and where is he making it? How is he supporting this call, and how effective is this support?

5. How does Chavez use respect for Martin Luther King, Jr. to construct his argument? How does he use fear—and fear of what—to balance the speech?

6. If Chavez's primary argument is about pesticides and their effects, then do his introduction and conclusion adequately address this issue? Or are there too many "main" points to make the focus of this argument entirely clear?

Intertextual Questions

7. How does Chavez's argument about pesticides and their effects on human health compare and contrast with Terry Tempest Williams' argument in "The Clan of One-Breasted Women" (Chapter 4)?

8. How might Robert Hinkley, author of "How Corporate Law Inhibits Social Responsibility" (Chapter 5), respond to the topic Chavez addresses in the body of his essay?

Thinking Beyond the Text

9. Why would Cesar Chavez be regarded as an authority on the range of issues he addresses in his speech? What in his history gives him this perceived authority?

10. In the movie *American History X*, the leader of the white supremacists refers to Cesar Chavez at one point as "Cesar Commie Chavez." What in Chavez's history—or his political beliefs—would make such a slur even possible (though inaccurate)?

For Writing & Discussion

11. Searching online and/or in your school's library, locate another speech made by Cesar Chavez. In an essay, summarize this speech located in your research and explain how it argues similar/dissimilar points to the text produced here.

WILFRED M. McCLAY

Wilfred M. McClay (1951–) is a history professor at the University of Tennessee at Chattanooga, where he has held the SunTrust Bank Chair of Excellence in Humanities since 1999. He also is a Senior Scholar at the Woodrow Wilson Center for Scholars, and a Senior Fellow at the Ethics and Public Policy Center in Washington, D.C. Since 2002 he has served on the National Council on the Humanities.

McClay's 1994 book, *The Masterless: Self and Society in Modern America*, received the Merle Curti Award in Intellectual History from the Organization of American Historians. His other publications include *A Student's Guide to U.S. History* (2000), *Religion Returns to the Public Square: Faith and Policy in America* (2003), and more than 50 essays and articles. He is currently working on a biography of the sociologist David Riesman.

In "The Church of Civil Rights," originally published in 2005 in the magazine *Commentary*, McClay discusses the legacy of the American civil rights movement of the 1950s and 1960s. He counters the tendency to oversimplify the movement's issues and actions by calling attention to religion. In particular, McClay uses the roles of Southern churches, both black and white, to show how integral religion is to American social and political change.

The Church of Civil Rights

~ Prereading Question

When you think of the 1960s, especially of the civil rights movement, what images do you see on the movie screen in your mind? Whose voices do you hear? What music do you think of and why? How does the Vietnam War figure into your images of the 1960s and the civil rights movement, if it does at all?

Nearly a half-century has passed since the heyday of the early civil-rights movement, and race relations in America have grown far too complex to be reckoned by its simple compass. But the campaign to undo the system of segregation in the South seems to have lost none of its moral appeal. If my own experience as a teacher is any guide, a sizable percentage of applicants for graduate study in U.S. history are still likely to cite the civil-rights movement of the 1950's and 1960's as one of their chief inspirations. A surprising number of them set out with hopes of making the movement itself an object of their research.

One wonders what fresh discoveries these earnest young scholars expect to happen upon in such a well-sifted field. But that is beside the point. Clearly, a different kind of motivation is at work here, deeper than mere intellectual curiosity, political calculation, or professional ambition. One cannot help being impressed by it, particularly since the prospective students themselves are nearly always white and economically privileged. But neither is their choice free of self-regard. On the contrary: the felt urgency of the subject is an indication that they are, in some sense, hoping to work out their own salvation in the process of studying it. Reared in a world full of imperfect heroes and compromised ideals, in which their own wealth and ease fill them with ambivalence if not guilt, they seem to harbor a powerful need to redeem their lives through association with a cause they regard as incontrovertibly pure, simple, and noble.

By a similar process, for better or worse, the civil-rights movement has become a moral icon for American society as a whole, as well as for much of the rest of the world. For better, because it was indeed an admirable movement, in both its means and its ends, and one that clearly had the effect of improving the American nation and recalling it to its own professed ideals. For worse, because to the extent that the movement's example has come to be used mindlessly and mechanically, as a template for all social and political struggles, its exaltation has also tended to elevate social movements over institutional politics, demonstrations over deliberations, righteous theatrics over reasoned compromise.

This is not the fault of the movement itself. Nor is it the only factor contributing to the widespread tendency to reduce the multifarious patterns of history to variations upon a few easily grasped archetypes. Nevertheless, that habit is as wrongheaded as it is tempting. Not every tyrant is a Hitler, not every intervention a Vietnam, not every massacre a Holocaust—and not every aspiring social cause is analogous to the civil-rights movement or deserves to be placed on a continuum with it.

How, then, to find our way back to a truer and more precise understanding of the movement and its place in American history? One of the many virtues of David L. Chappell's new book, *A Stone of Hope: Prophetic Religion, Liberalism, and the Death of Jim Crow*, is its insistence that we look carefully at the particulars of this great undertaking and the specific reasons it succeeded. A briskly written volume by a professor of history at the University of Arkansas, feisty in tone but impressive in its scholarly documentation, *A Stone of Hope* stands back from the welter of comment accumulated over the past 50 years and asks some refreshingly direct and simple questions. How and why did this great cultural change happen? Why did the dominant liberalism of the Democratic party contribute so little, and so late, to the effort? Where did black Southerners find the inspiration to rebel against a massively entrenched social system? And why did their white Southern opponents turn out to be so surprisingly weak?

The short answer to each of these four questions can be put in a single word: religion. More specifically, Chappell argues that one cannot apprehend the movement's success without taking into account the pervasive cultural setting of Southern Protestantism within which it unfolded. He is not merely claiming religion as "a neglected factor." Instead, he is claiming it as the absolutely crucial conditioning factor, without which nothing could have occurred as it did.

In this view, the civil-rights movement was not a fundamentally political mobilization, with lots of soulful gospel songs and other colorful trappings of African-American religious culture added in on the side—a position that Chappell dismisses for the subtle condescension that it is. Instead, it was primarily a high-octane religious revival, full of prophetic utterances and messianic expectations, which had the effect, almost as a byproduct, of leading to profound political and social change.

In making this argument, Chappell gives the back of his hand to white liberal commentators like Arthur M. Schlesinger, Jr. and Gunnar Myrdal, who at the time envisioned the cause of racial justice as but one element in the great unfolding of a progressive agenda. Their untroubled confidence in the inevitable triumph of their own ideas, Chappell believes, ironically made them complacent and unwilling to act decisively. Even when they tempered their rational optimism with the gloomier outlook of the Protestant theologian Reinhold Niebuhr, as Schlesinger did repeatedly, they never really took on board the full weight of Niebuhr's pessimistic view of human nature. Whatever the setbacks of the moment, liberals knew themselves to be anointed by history as the party of the future, and so deemed the cause of black civil rights in the South to be insufficiently pressing to jeopardize the liberals' electoral chances. As Chappell puts it acidly, "opportunism on this issue dictated the same [empty] gestures as idealism."

By contrast, black Southern preachers and their followers approached life with a different anthropology, and a different view of progress. Martin Luther King, Jr.'s fundamentalist Baptist background may have been at odds with his seminary education in the liberal North, but the two meshed well in his view of human nature and the prophetic calling of the Christian leader. The doctrine of original sin, the tendency of all human endeavors to slide into corruption, the incapacity of human institutions to reform themselves without divine favor, the need for the man of God to stand outside the comfort of the status quo and speak with the boldness of Jeremiah calling the people to repentance, and the need for the faithful to experience suffering and submission to God's will as the price of their redemption: these were things that King, and his followers, all instinctively grasped.

The biblical view of man and God and sin and suffering and humility and redemption was, for those black Southerners, their chief sustenance, their spiritual meat and drink, their everyday solace and their hope for the end-times. Without the primal, driving force of their deep religious convictions, Chappell contends, the civil-rights movement would never have begun to move.

This part of Chappell's argument, though convincing, is not entirely original. Most standard accounts of the movement do give a good deal of space to its religious elements, even if they often tend (not entirely without reason) to emphasize the black church as a political and social institution rather than as a religious one. In recent years, moreover, students of the struggle have increased the attention paid to religion, as in works like Charles Marsh's *God's Long Summer: Stories of Faith and Civil Rights* (1999) and Stewart Burns's *To the Mountaintop: Martin Luther King Jr.'s Sacred Mission to Save America* (2004). Even Chappell's portrayal of King's philosophy of "hope without optimism" has been presented before, notably in an extraordinarily insightful chapter of Christopher Lasch's *The True and Only Heaven* (1991), upon which this book draws.

If Chappell is far from unique in emphasizing the depth and specific character of the movement's religious commitments, he may also be too sweeping in his condemnation of cold-war liberalism and too hard on the particular liberals he has chosen to pin to the wall. He himself has a certain prophetic impatience with the inevitable messiness and compromise of electoral politics, an impatience that is one of those ambivalent legacies of the movement itself. (Max Weber's great and gloomy lecture on "Politics as Vocation" was written with just such impatience in mind.) Similarly, he gives too little weight to the long-term legal strategy by which the NAACP sought to break the hold of segregation through a carefully calibrated succession of court cases, thereby establishing an essential (though morally far less impressive) complement to the movement's more expansive and faith-suffused impulses.

Nor does Chappell adequately stress the fact that many key players in the intellectual leadership of the movement, including Bayard Rustin and Robert Moses, espoused views that did not line up with the evangelical Protestantism of King. (It is a bit of stretch, for example, to argue that Moses's commitment to the philosophy of Albert Camus was somehow the same as a religious commitment to biblical Christianity.) This book, in short, is not without flaws, and in a number of respects may well turn out to be a corrective in need of correction.

But what makes *A Stone of Hope* a truly exciting and important intellectual breakthrough is not its claims about the religiosity of the movement itself. Rather, it is Chappell's careful and imaginative approach to *white* Southern religious convictions and the white Christian response to the movement. This has been a long time in coming. The standard image of the white South in the civil-rights struggle," Chappell rightly observes, "is a mob." In that respect, this book, although it can hardly be considered overly sympathetic to the white South, is a real advance.

It is frequently assumed, for example, that in this great cultural conflict, each side devised its own self-contained and self-confirming version of the Christian faith. King himself, in a famous line that Chappell strangely misrenders here, spoke of eleven o'clock on a Sunday morning being "the most segregated hour of Christian America." But this turns out to be far less true of the white South in the civil-rights era than King's words would suggest. As Chappell points out, even though most white Southern Protestant churches were still aligned with the same sectionalist denominations that had been created a century earlier by the Civil War, they were by and large unsupportive of the segregationist cause.

In some cases, this unsupportiveness took the form of outright and unambiguous opposition. Thus, the denominational assemblies of the Southern Baptists and Southern Presbyterians went on the record with resolutions strongly favoring desegregation. The evangelist Rev. Billy

Graham was admirably consistent in his opposition to racial segregation from the very beginning of his career, both in his public utterances and in his private and personal behavior.

Elsewhere, to be sure, the picture was different. Far from repudiating segregation, white churches characteristically adopted an attitude of quiet, passive, evasive neutrality. This naturally frustrated King, though it also fed his hopeful conviction that the majority of white Southerners could eventually be won over to his position.

In any event, as Chappell perceptively notes, the muted response of white Southern clergy also frustrated the segregationists, leaving them disabled in crucial ways. White Southern faith may not have been strong enough to overcome ingrained racial and social barriers—it was too tied to the status quo for that—but it was at least strong enough to withhold from those barriers the full mantle of legitimacy. This in turn made it necessary for segregationist politicians to fight for their cause on strictly sociological and constitutional grounds—or with undiluted demagoguery.

And that made all the difference. From the beginning, the specific dynamics of the civil-rights movement were traceable to the fact that both sides agreed on something—and that something was the truth and legitimizing force of Christianity. Though mightier than the civil-rights movement in many superficial respects, the movement's white Southern opponents were disarmed by their inability to count on the moral support of the South's most characteristic institution or to draw on the same sources of strength that animated their foes.

In Chappell's telling, the presence of this shared cultural premise was just as fundamental as anything the two sides disagreed about. It permeated the field of forces, as essential a feature of the battle as the air the antagonists breathed. And it determined the outcome: for in this struggle, as Chappell writes, the winners were those who "got strength from old-time religion," and who "used religion to inspire solidarity and self-sacrificial devotion to their cause."

If Chappell's reading of the movement is right, it ought to affect the way we assess its significance in American and world history.

For one thing, Chappell's reading should help explain to Americans why Tiananmen Square was not Selma, and why the tactics of King and Gandhi do not work against a Saddam Hussein or the Iranian mullahs. Such tactics seek to prick consciences that are shaped like one's own: but they fall pitiably short when the "other" inhabits a genuinely different moral universe. For all its shortcomings, the United States has always had such a shared moral framework, grounded not merely in abstract ideas of human rights and individual liberty but also in a longer and deeper heritage of biblical narratives, tropes, parables, and moral wisdom. This is one reason why our own struggles and triumphs are so difficult to replicate in the rest of the world.

In addition, *A Stone of Hope* reminds us that movements for change in American history are likely to succeed and endure only to the degree that they respect the country's religious heritage or are broadly congruent with it. Here one might cite not only the civil-rights movement but also the abolition of slavery, women's suffrage, and even the American Revolution itself. On all of these hard-fought issues one can find both religious and secular rationales being advanced, but the two sets of justifications are also mutually supportive and even intermingle to an extent unthinkable in other cultures.

That congruency is a key element in the genius of American politics, as of American religion. It is why Martin Luther King's finest rhetoric could with equal plausibility invoke nor only the prophetic Scriptures but also the Declaration and the Constitution and the founders, and why the historian Stewart Burns is not being fanciful in interpreting King's life's work as a "sacred mission" to "save America." We enshrine the separation of church and state, but at the same time we practice the mingling of religion and public life. It is not always logical, but it frequently makes good sense.

Of course, in each of these cases (and especially slavery and suffrage). there were also religiously grounded arguments *against* change. Sometimes, moreover, religious and secular arguments for reform may be united in their mistakenness: consider Prohibition. Nothing in life is foolproof. But there are almost no examples in the American past of successful and widely accepted reforms that have not paid their respect to Americans' religious and secular sensibilities alike. They are required to pass muster with, so to speak, a bicameral body politic.

This fact also has profound implications for the larger meanings we have allowed ourselves to derive from the civil-rights movement. In the first place, one must view with the profoundest regret the transformation of the movement by the late 1960's from an instrument of national integration and reconciliation into an instrument of what Lasch rightly called "the politics of resentment and reparations." That transformation corresponded exactly with the loss of the movement's religious core and its turn toward a rather different combination of impulses; strident social militancy on the one hand, court-imposed legalism on the other.

This purely coercive combination is still with us today, with the consequence that as the material conditions of American blacks have steadily improved, race relations remain mired in mutual suspicion—a state that has reached a kind of culmination in the astoundingly pointless and divisive debate over reparations for slavery. Whatever the outcome of that debate, it will never further the cause of reconciliation.

If, in the area of race relations, it makes no sense to abstract the movement from its relationship to its larger religious context, the same goes for its use as an analogy in other contexts. Two of the most contentious issues of recent years have been abortion and gay marriage. In both cases, not only have policy changes been imposed by courts rather than through representative institutions, but those involved have sought to challenge and override the very core of the country's prevailing religious convictions.

This tactic has been enormously costly, Even today, three decades after *Roe* v. *Wade*, the cause of unrestricted abortion rights stands largely on the acts of unelected judges and on the morally unimpressive principle of *stare decisis*. It has few if any full-throated defenders among the religiously devour—and many fervent opponents, who look increasingly to the 19th century abolitionists and the 20th-century civil-rights movement for inspiration. One can safely predict that the issue will continue to be a source of social division in the years to come.

Proponents of gay marriage, for their part, also invoke the civil-rights movement as precedent, comparing proscriptions against same-sex unions to anti-miscegenation laws and other forms of discrimination. But there is a reason why no subgroup registers more negatively on this issue in opinion surveys than blacks. It is not just that they know when their movement is being hijacked. It is that the religious sensibility that animated the civil-rights movement, and that is still very much alive in the American black community today, is bound up in a biblical world view that would no more countenance the radical redefinition of marriage than it would the reimposition of slavery. When King and his followers joyfully invoked the word "freedom," they did not mean the unlimited expressive liberty of autonomous individuals. Their conception of freedom was inseparable not only from their rootedness in their own particular place and time but in obedience to the God of Abraham, Isaac, and Jacob.

None of this is meant to imply that the religious are always right, or should have supervisory power over all social change, any more than should the federal and state judiciaries. It is merely to recognize the longstanding and indispensable place of religion in the American experiment, and the high price to be paid when it is sundered from the cause of social change. Fortunately, as David Chappell's book shows, we do not have to choose whether to call the story of the civil-rights movement a Christian story, a Southern story, or an American story, for it is all three. This is a fact for which all Americans, not only Christians or Southerners—or secularists—can be grateful, and an example to ponder with care.

Textual Questions

1. What point does McClay make in paragraph 2 about race and the study of the civil rights movement? How does this point connect with his overall argument in the remainder of the essay?

2. According to McClay's introductory section, what are the positive and negative aspects of the civil rights movement in America and beyond?

In what ways does the remainder of his essay serve to either support or refute these positives and negatives?

3. What four questions does McClay use to organize his essay? How and where does he ask each? How and where does he answer each question?

Rhetorical Questions

4. How does McClay connect Christianity with the civil rights movement? How effectively does this connection work in his essay? Why?

5. How much of McClay's essay is a rebuttal of or critique of Chappell's argument? Why is this rebuttal/critique effective or ineffective overall? Which piece of the rebuttal/critique is most persuasively argued? Why? Which is least persuasively argued and why?

6. To whom is McClay directing his argument—who would be most likely to agree with him? How do you know? Who would be least likely to agree with McClay, other than Chappell? Why?

Intertextual Questions

7. How would Martin Luther King, Jr. (see applicable reading from King in this chapter and in Chapter 1) respond to McClay? How would his response to McClay be similar to and/or different from the response of Cesar Chavez (also in this chapter)?

8. How is McClay's definition of "civil rights" similar to/different from the definition used by Hillary Rodham Clinton in "Women's Rights Are Human Rights" (Chapter 1)?

Thinking Beyond the Text

9. Near the end of his introductory section, McClay argues that "Not every tyrant is a Hitler, not every intervention a Vietnam, not every massacre a Holocaust." In your experience, how often are these exact comparisons used? Thinking of the American war in Iraq alone, Saddam Hussein was often referred to as an incarnation of Hitler, his deliberate and large-scale killing of ethnic minorities such as Kurds as a Holocaust, and the political and military situation of the United States and its allies is frequently (and unfavorably) compared to Vietnam. But what other examples can you think of?

10. Does McClay's description of the civil rights movement compare or contrast with the image you have of this same movement, which you may have described in writing or in discussion as you worked through the prereading question for this essay? Where are you and McClay in

some kind of agreement? Where do your ideas and images of the civil rights movement differ from his?

For Writing & Discussion

11. Searching online or in your library, find a review of David L. Chappell's book *A Stone of Hope*. In a single paragraph, explain how this review either supports or refutes the claims about Chappell's work made by McClay.

JONATHAN RAUCH

Jonathan Rauch (1960–) is a journalist and gay rights activist who works as a senior writer and opinion columnist for the *National Journal*. In addition to writing his biweekly *National Journal* column, "Social Studies," Rauch is a correspondent for the *Atlantic Monthly* and has written for *The Economist, Fortune, Harpers, The Jewish World Review*, the *New York Times*, the *Wall Street Journal*, and the *Washington Post*. Rauch is a writer-in-residence at the Brookings Institution, an independent think-tank in Washington, D.C., and vice president of the Independent Gay Forum, an organization that describes itself as "forging a gay mainstream." He has appeared on radio and television programs, including the PBS television show *Think Tank* where he discussed the question "What is Wrong with Congress?"

Rauch has published five books, including *Kindly Inquisitors: The New Attacks on Free Thought* (1993) and *Government's End: Why Washington Stopped Working* (1999). His work has been anthologized in *The Best American Science and Nature Writing 2004* and *The Best American Magazine Writing 2005*, and he has won the 2005 National Magazine Award and received second-place in 2000 and 2001 for the National Headliner Award for magazine columns.

"A More Perfect Union" was first published in the *Atlantic Monthly* in April 2004. Rauch also has a book on the topic, *Gay Marriage: Why It Is Good for Gays, Good for Straights, and Good for America* (2004). Although Rauch's gay rights advocacy focuses on supporting same-sex marriage and opposing hate-crimes laws, he also writes about topics ranging from campaign finance reform to living or working with introverts. The most personal information on his Web site is that he dislikes shrimp.

A More Perfect Union

How the Founding Fathers Would Have Handled Gay Marriage

∾ Prereading Question

When some cities and states began to recognize marriages between two men or two women as being legally equal to a "traditional" marriage of a man and a woman, some political and religious groups argued for a constitutional amendment that would define marriage in its man-and-woman incarnation. President George W. Bush even expressed some support for such an amendment. In your opinion, is such an amendment necessary to define marriage? Why? What are/would be the legal, social, and economic consequences of defining marriage as legally existing only between a man and a woman?

Last November the Supreme Judicial Court of Massachusetts ruled that excluding gay couples from civil marriage violated the state constitution. The court gave the legislature six months—until May—to do something about it. Some legislators mounted efforts to amend the state constitution to ban same-sex marriage, but as of this writing they have failed (and even if passed, a ban would not take effect until at least 2006). With unexpected urgency the country faces the possibility that marriage licenses might soon be issued to homosexual couples. To hear the opposing sides talk, a national culture war is unavoidable.

But same-sex marriage neither must nor should be treated as an all-or-nothing national decision. Instead individual states should be left to try gay marriage if and when they choose—no national ban, no national mandate. Not only would a decentralized approach be in keeping with the country's most venerable legal traditions; it would also improve, in three ways the odds of making same-sex marriage work for gay and straight Americans alike.

First, it would give the whole country a chance to learn. Nothing terrible—in fact, nothing even noticeable—seems to have happened to marriage since Vermont began allowing gay civil unions, in 2000. But civil unions are not marriages. The only way to find out what would happen if same-sex couples got marriage certificates is to let some of us do it. Turning marriage into a nationwide experiment might be rash, but trying it in a few states would provide test cases on a smaller scale. Would the divorce rate rise? Would the marriage rate fall? We should get some indications before long. Moreover, states are, as the saying goes, the laboratories of democracy. One state might opt for straightforward legalization. Another might add some special provisions (for instance, regarding child custody or adoption). A third might combine same-sex marriage with counseling or other assistance (not out of line with a growing movement to offer social-service support to so-called fragile families). Variety would help answer some important questions: Where would gay marriage work best? What kind of community support would it need? What would be the avoidable pitfalls? Either to forbid same-sex marriage nationwide or to legalize it nationwide would be to throw away a wealth of potential information.

Just as important is the social benefit of letting the states find their own way. Law is only part of what gives marriage its binding power, community support and social expectations are just as important. In a community that looked on same-sex marriage with bafflement or hostility, a gay couple's marriage certificate, while providing legal benefits, would confer no social support from the heterosexual majority. Both the couple and the community would be shortchanged. Letting states choose gay marriage wouldn't guarantee that everyone in the state recognized such marriages as legitimate, but it would pretty well ensure that gay married couples could find some communities in their state that did.

Finally, the political benefit of a state-by-state approach is not to be underestimated. This is the benefit of avoiding a national culture war.

The United States is not (thank goodness) a culturally homogeneous country. It consists of many distinct moral communities. On certain social issues, such as abortion and homosexuality, people don't agree and probably never will—and the signal political advantage of the federalist system is that they don't have to. Individuals and groups who find the values or laws of one state obnoxious have the right to live somewhere else.

The nationalization of abortion policy in the Supreme Court's 1973 *Roe* v. *Wade* decision created a textbook example of what can happen when this federalist principle is ignored. If the Supreme Court had not stepped in, abortion would today be legal in most states but not all; prolifers would have the comfort of knowing they could live in a state whose law was compatible with their views. Instead of endlessly confronting a cultural schism that affects every Supreme Court nomination, we would see occasional local flare-ups in state legislatures or courtrooms.

America is a stronger country for the moral diversity that federalism uniquely allows. Moral law and family law govern the most intimate and, often, the most controversial spheres of life. For the sake of domestic tranquillity, domestic law is best left to a level of government that is close to home.

So well suited is the federalist system to the gay-marriage issue that it might almost have been set up to handle it. In a new land whose citizens followed different religious traditions, it would have made no sense to centralize marriage or family law. And so marriage has been the domain of local law not just since the days of the Founders but since Colonial times, before the states were states. To my knowledge, the federal government has overruled the states on marriage only twice. The first time was when it required Utah to ban polygamy as a condition for joining the Union—and note that this ruling was issued *before* Utah became a state. The second time was in 1967, when the Supreme Court, in *Loving* v. *Virginia,* struck down sixteen states bans on interracial marriage. Here the Court said not that marriage should be defined by the federal government but only that states could not define marriage in ways that violated core constitutional rights. On the one occasion when Congress directly addressed same-sex marriage, in the 1996 Defense of Marriage Act, it decreed that the federal government would not recognize same-sex marriages but took care not to impose that role on the states.

Marriage laws (and, of course, divorce laws) continue to be established by the states. They differ on many points, from age of consent to who may marry whom. In Arizona, for example, first cousins are allowed to marry only if both are sixty-five or older or the couple can prove to a judge "that one of the cousins is unable to reproduce." (So much for the idea that marriage is about procreation.) Conventional wisdom notwithstanding the Constitution does not require states to recognize one another's marriages. The Full Faith and Credit clause (Article IV, Section 1) does require states to honor one another's public acts and judgments. But in 1939 and again in 1988 the Supreme Court ruled that the clause does not compel a state "to substitute the statutes of other states for its own statutes dealing with a subject matter concerning which it is competent to legislate." Date Carpeater, a law professor at the University of Minnesota, notes that the Full Faith and Credit clause "has never been interpreted to mean that every state must recognize every marriage performed in every other state." He writes, "Each state may refuse to recognize a marriage performed in another state if that marriage would violate the state's public policy. If Delaware, for example, decided to lower its age of consent to ten, no other state would be required to regard a ten-year-old as legally married. The public-policy exception, as it is called, is only common sense. If each state could legislate for all the rest. American-style federalism would be at an end.

Why, then, do the states all recognize one another's marriages? Because they choose to. Before the gay-marriage controversy arose, the country enjoyed a general consensus on the terms of marriage. Interstate differences were so small that states saw no need to split hairs, and mutual recognition was a big convenience. The issue of gay marriage, of course, changes the picture, by asking states to reconsider an accepted boundary of marriage. This is just the sort of controversy in which the Founders imagined that individual states could and often should go their separate ways.

Paradoxically, the gay left and the antigay right have found themselves working together against the center. They agree on little else, but where marriage is concerned, they both want the federal government to take over.

To many gay people, anything less than nationwide recognition of same-sex marriage seems both unjust and impractical. "Wait a minute," a gay person might protest. "How is this supposed to work? I get married in Maryland (say), but every time I cross the border into Virginia during my morning commute, I'm single? Am I married or not? Portability is one of the things that make marriage different from civil union. If it isn't portable, it isn't really marriage, it's second-class citizenship. Obviously, as soon as same-sex marriage is approved in any one state, we're going to sue in federal court to have it recognized in all the others."

"Exactly!" a conservative might reply. "Gay activists have no intention of settling for marriage in just one or two states. They will keep suing until they find some activist federal judge—and there are plenty—who agrees with them. Public-policy exception and Defense of Marriage Act notwithstanding, the courts, not least the Supreme Court, do as they please, and lately they have signed on to the gay cultural agenda. Besides, deciding on a state-by-state basis *is* impractical; the gay activists are right about that. The sheer inconvenience of dealing with couples who went in and out of matrimony every time they crossed state lines would drive states to the lowest common denominator, and gay marriages would wind up being recognized everywhere."

Neither of the arguments I have just sketched is without merit. But both sides are asking the country to presume that the Founders were wrong and to foreclose the possibility that seems the most likely to succeed. Both sides want something life doesn't usually offer—a guarantee. Gay-marriage supporters want a guarantee of full legal equality, and gay-marriage opponents want a guarantee that same-sex marriage will never happen at all. I can't offer any guarantees. But I can offer some reassurance.

Is a state-by-state approach impractical and unsustainable? Possibly, but the time to deal with any problems is if and when they arise. Going in, there is no reason to expect any great difficulty. There are many precedents for state-by-state action. The country currently operates under a tangle of different state banking laws. As any banker will tell you, the lack of uniformity has made interstate banking more difficult. But we do have interstate banks. Bankers long ago got used to meeting different requirements in different states. Similarly, car manufacturers have had to deal with zero-emission rules in California and a few other states. Contract law, property law, and criminal law all vary significantly from state to state. Variety is the point of federalism. Uniform national policies may be convenient, but they risk sticking us with the same wrong approach everywhere.

My guess is that if one or two states allowed gay marriage, a confusing transitional period, while state courts and legislatures worked out what to do, would quickly lead in all but a few places to routines that everyone would soon take for granted. If New Jersey adopted gay marriage, for instance, New York would have a number of options. It might refuse to recognize the marriages. It might recognize them. It might honor only certain aspects of them—say, medical power of attorney, or inheritance and tenancy rights. A state with a civil-union or domestic-partner law might automatically confer that law's benefits on any gay couple who got married in New Jersey. My fairly confident expectation is that initially most states would reject out-of-state gay marriages (as, indeed, most states have preemptively done), but a handful would fully accept them, and others would choose an intermediate option.

For married gay couples, this variation would be a real nuisance. If my partner and I got married in Maryland, we would need to be aware of differences in marriage laws and make arrangements—medical power of attorney, a will, and so on—for whenever we were out of state. Pesky and, yes unfair (or at least unequal). And outside Maryland the line between being married and not being married would be blurred. In Virginia, people who saw my wedding band would be unsure whether I was "really married" or just "Maryland married."

Even so, people in Virginia who learned that I was "Maryland married" would know I had made the strongest possible commitment in my home state and thus in the eyes of my community and its law. They would know I had gone beyond cohabitation or even domestic partnership. As a Jew, I may not recognize the spiritual authority of a Catholic priest, but I do recognize and respect the special commitment he has made to his faith and his community. In much the same way, even out-of-state gay marriages would command a significant degree of respect.

If you are starving, one or two slices of bread may not be as good as a loaf—but it is far better than no bread at all. The damage that exclusion from marriage has done to gay lives and gay culture comes not just from being unable to marry right now and right here but from knowing the law forbids us ever to marry at all. The first time a state adopted same-sex marriage, gay life would change forever. The full benefits would come only when same-sex marriage was legal everywhere. But gay people's lives would improve with the first state's announcement that in *this* community, marriage is open to everyone.

Building consensus takes time. The nationwide imposition of same-sex marriage by a federal court might discredit both gay marriage and the courts and the public rancor it unleashed might be at least as intense as that surrounding abortion. My confidence in the public's decency and in its unfailing, if sometimes slow-acting commitment to liberal principles is robust. For me personally, the pace set by a state-by-state approach would be too slow. It would be far from ideal. But it would be something much more important than ideal: it would be right.

Would a state-by-state approach inevitably lead to a nationwide court mandate anyway? Many conservatives fear that the answer is yes, and they want a federal constitutional amendment to head off the courts—an amendment banning gay marriage nationwide. These days it is a fact of life that someone will sue over anything, that some court will hear any lawsuit, and that there is no telling what a court might do. Still, I think that conservatives fears on this score are unfounded.

Remember, all precedent leaves marriage to the states. All precedent supports the public-policy exception. The Constitution gives Congress a voice in determining which of one another's laws states must recognize and Congress has spoken clearly: the Defense of Marriage Act explicitly decrees that no state most recognize any other state's same-sex marriages. In order to mandate interstate recognition of gay marriages, a court would thus need to burn through three different firewalls—a tall order, even for an activist court. The current Supreme Court, moreover, has proved particularly fierce in resisting federal incursions into states rights. We typically reserve constitutional prohibitions for imminent threats to liberty, justice, or popular sovereignty. If we are going to get into the business of constitutionally banning anything that someone imagines the Supreme Court might one day mandate, we will need a Constitution the size of the Manhattan phone book.

Social conservatives have lost one cultural battle after another in the past five decades: over divorce, abortion, pornography, gambling, school prayer, homosexuality. They have seen that every federal takeover of state and local powers comes with strings attached. They have learned all too well the power of centralization to marginalize moral dissenters—including religious ones. And yet they are willing to risk federal intervention in matrimony. Why?

Not, I suspect, because they fear gay marriage would fail. Rather, because they fear it would succeed.

One of the conservative arguments against gay marriage is particularly revealing: the contention that even if federal courts don't decide the matter on a national level, convenience will cause gay marriage to spread from state to state. As noted, I don't believe questions of convenience would force the issue either way. But let me make a deeper point here.

States recognized one another's divorce reforms in the 1960s and 1970s without giving the matter much thought (which was too bad). But the likelihood that they would recognize another state's same-sex marriages without serious debate is just about zero, especially at first: the issue is simply too controversial. As time went on, states without gay marriage might get used to the idea. They might begin to wave through other states same-sex marriages as a convenience for all concerned. If that happened, however, it could only be because gay marriage had not turned out to be a disaster. It might even be because gay marriage was working pretty well. This would not be contagion. It would be evolution—a sensible response to a successful experiment. Try something here or there. If it works, let it spread. If it fails, let it fade.

The opponents of gay marriage want to prevent the experiment altogether. If you care about finding the best way forward for gay people and for society in a changing world, that posture is hard to justify. One rationale goes something like this: "Gay marriage is so certain to be a calamity that even the smallest trial anywhere should be banned." To me, that line of argument smacks more of hysteria than of rational thought. In the 1980s and early 1990s some liberals were sure that reforming the welfare system to emphasize work would put millions of children out on the street. Even trying welfare reform, they said, was irresponsible. Fortunately, the states didn't listen. They experimented—responsibly. The results were positive enough to spark a successful national reform.

Another objection cites not certain catastrophe but insidious decay. A conservative once said to me, "Changes in complicated institutions like marriage take years to work their way through society. They are often subtle. Social scientists will argue until the cows come home about the positive and negative effects of gay marriage. So states might adopt it before they fully understood the harm it did."

Actually, you can usually tell pretty quickly what effects a major policy change is having—at least you can get a general idea. States knew quite soon that welfare reforms were working better than the old program. That's why the idea caught on. If same-sex marriage is going to cause problems, some of them should be apparent within a few years of its legalization.

And notice how the terms of the discussion have shifted. Now the anticipated problem is not sudden, catastrophic social harm but subtle, slow damage. Well there might be subtle and slow social benefits, too. But more important, there would be one large and immediate benefit: *the benefit for gay people of being able to get married.* If we are going to exclude a segment of the population from arguably the most important of all civic institutions, we need to be certain that the group's participation would cause severe disruptions. If we are going to put the burden on gay people to prove that same-sex marriage would never cause even any minor difficulty, then we are assuming that *any* cost to heterosexuals, however small, outweighs *every* benefit to homosexuals, however large. That gay people's welfare counts should of course, be obvious and inarguable; but to some it is not.

I expect same-sex marriage to have many subtle ramifications—many of them good not just for gay people but for marriage. Same-sex marriage would dramatically reaffirm the country's preference for marriage as the gold standard for committed relationships. Of course there might be harmful and neutral effects as well. I don't expect that social science would be able to sort them all out. But the fact that the world is complicated is the very reason to run the experiment. We can never know for sure what the effects of any public policy will be, so we conduct a limited experiment if possible and then decide how to proceed on the basis of necessarily imperfect information.

If conservatives genuinely oppose same-sex marriage because they fear it would harm straight marriage they should be willing to let states that want to try gay marriage do so. If, on the other hand, conservatives oppose same-sex marriage because they believe that it is immoral and wrong by definition, fine—but let them have the honesty to acknowledge that they are nor fighting for the good of marriage so much as they are using marriage as a weapon in their fight against gays.

Textual Questions

1. How is the title—"A More Perfect Union"—a play on words in two ways, one concerning marriage and one concerning the Founding Fathers?

2. How is the issue of gay marriage an example of the "culture war" in America? What are other examples?

3. According to Rauch's argument, what groups have "paradoxically" found themselves working together against legalization of gay marriage? How can their immediate goals be the same when the long-term goals of these groups are completely at odds?

Rhetorical Questions

4. Rauch divides his argument into five sections. Section one is only two paragraphs long, while section four is seven times longer. Does such uneven development strengthen or weaken the essay? Why? What effect does this uneven development have on a reader? Does it cause some points to stand out/not stand out more than others for readers?

5. In section two of his essay, Rauch argues that "The United States is not (thank goodness) a culturally homogenous country." Why, in Rauch's opinion, is this a good thing—good enough for him to add the parenthetical "thank goodness"? Wouldn't there be an upside to living in a culture that is homogenous?

6. According to Rauch's argument, what "guarantee" is being sought by each of the groups involved in the fight over gay marriage? Why is any guarantee unlikely, if not impossible?

Intertextual Questions

7. Thinking of social and economic issues only, how is Rauch's argument about gay marriage similar to/different from Timothy Sandefur's argument about eminent domain in "They're Coming for Your Land" (this chapter)?

8. In what ways can the fight over gay marriage, as described by Rauch, be compared to and contrasted with the fight for equality before the law as represented by Frederick Douglass in "Appeal to Congress for Impartial Suffrage" and Hillary Rodham Clinton in "Women's Rights Are Human Rights" (both in Chapter 1)?

Thinking Beyond the Text

9. Why is the issue of gay marriage such a divisive one for Americans? How do history, religion, and economics fuel the fires of controversy that burn around this issue?

10. What city and state governments currently respect gay marriages and offer gay couples who are married the same rights and benefits offered to male–female couples that are married?

For Writing & Discussion

11. How does your school or local city/county government recognize or not recognize gay marriages? For example, do the partners of gay students or employees receive health benefits? Are they barred from receiving such benefits, either formally or informally? What other benefits and rights affect gay couples?

MATTHEW BRZEZINSKI

Matthew Brzezinski (1965–) is an investigative reporter who writes regularly for *Mother Jones* and *The New York Times Magazine*. In the 1990s Brzezinski lived in and wrote articles on Eastern Europe for *The Economist*, *The Guardian*, the *New York Times*, and the *Toronto Globe and Mail*. From 1996–1998 he was the Moscow correspondent for the *Wall Street Journal*.

Brzezinski's 2002 book *Casino Moscow: A Tale of Greed and Adventure on Capitalism's Wildest Frontier* describes post-Communist Russia. Following his return to the United States and the September 11, 2001, attacks, Brzezinski began writing about the American government's response to terrorism. Articles on the fear-mongering and reduction and civil rights that followed 9/11 led to his 2004 book, *Fortress America: On the Frontlines of Homeland Security—An Inside Look at the Coming Surveillance State*.

In addition to writing articles on American homeland security, Brzezinski also has examined other challenges in America today ranging from heroin dealers in Baltimore to the FBI's torture of a legal immigrant from Egypt. In "Hillbangers," published in *The New York Times Magazine* in August 2004, Brzezinski writes about the dispersal of urban gangs into rural areas.

Returning to his interest in Soviet Russia, Brzezinski is currently working on a book about Sputnik, *Red Moon Rising: The Story of a Little Satellite that Started the Space-Race and Gave Birth to the Modern Wireless World.* Times Books will publish *Red Moon Rising* in 2007, Sputnik's 50th anniversary.

Hillbangers

∽ Prereading Question

Gangs, as criminal organizations, have always existed in America, yet they were not perceived as a major, terrifying threat to social order until the 1980s. Books such as The Outsiders *and movies such as* The Warriors *portrayed gangs as negative, certainly, but not in a way that was dangerous to anyone beyond gang members. (Note: The film version of* The Warriors *is very different—and much less dark—than the novel by the same name.) Why did this largely benevolent, harmless image of gangs in America change? How are gangs viewed in your home community now?*

The area around the crime scene was as picturesque as a postcard. A lazy river ran through it, the lush green mountains of Shenandoah County, Va., formed a rustic backdrop and an old wooden covered bridge and sun-bleached hayfields completed the tableau.

The crime scene itself was another story. The body was found on July 17, 2003, by a fisherman and his son. It was badly decomposed, lying contorted in the underbrush near a brier patch on the west bank of the Shenandoah River. The age, sex and race of the victim were difficult to determine, but the body appeared to be that of a young woman. Her throat had been slashed so violently that her head was almost completely severed.

The Shenandoah County chief deputy sheriff, Tim Carter, who was overseeing the investigators on the case, shipped the corpse to the nearest state forensic lab, about an hour's drive away, in Fairfax, Va. It turned out that the victim had indeed been young, probably in her late teens, and had suffered multiple stab wounds. The lack of water in her lungs confirmed that there was no possibility that she had been drowned and mutilated and floated downriver: she had been murdered, or at least dumped, on the spot.

The killing shook Shenandoah in ways that can be hard for urbanites to comprehend. For weeks following the discovery of Jane Doe, her murder was the talk of the towns along Route 11 in Virginia—from the dairy cooperative in Strasburg, to the C.E. Thompson & Son hardware store in Edinburg, to the old-fashioned lunch counter at the Walton & Smoot pharmacy in Woodstock, across Main Street from the sheriff's office. This sort of thing simply did not happen in a place where many families trace their ancestries in the region to before the Civil War, where people still take the time to stop in on their neighbors, where few people say they feel the need to lock their front doors. This was not Washington, 80 miles and a world away to the east. Folks here tended to worry more about copperheads and rattlesnakes than about knife-wielding murderers.

The sheriff's office had one promising clue to the victim's identity: an extensive collection of tattoos on her arms, legs and torso. Carter asked a colleague to sketch some of the images—a pair of comedy and tragedy masks, a clown smoking a marijuana cigarette, letters rendered in three-inch-high Gothic script—and began circulating them to the media in neighboring areas with the hope that somebody would recognize them. The sketches went out to Winchester and Front Royal, and then farther afield to Fauquier, Warren and Prince William Counties, but there was no response. Soon, Carter was sending them all the way to Loudoun County, Va., and the suburbs of Washington.

Finally, one day, Carter got a call from an investigator in the Washington metropolitan area. "He recognized the sketches instantly," Carter recalls. "They were gang tattoos."

The tattoos signaled the victim's membership in Mara Salvatrucha, or MS-13, a large street gang with ties to El Salvador that has long been a violent presence in the Hispanic neighborhoods of Washington, New York and Los Angeles. Forensic investigators were able to identify the victim as Brenda Paz, known as Smiley to her street friends, a 17-year-old member of MS-13 who had dated Denis (Rabbit) Rivera, one of the more vicious gang leaders in the Washington area. Paz, who had been a key witness in half a dozen federal cases against MS-13, had gone missing from suburban Virginia shortly before she was to testify against some of her former friends.

At first, Carter, like the rest of the community, considered the incident to be an aberration. Paz's murder was tragic and puzzling—what was a dead member of MS-13 doing in the Shenandoah Valley?—but not something that threatened the well-being of people in Edinburg, Woodstock or Strasburg. A few months later, though, after Carter was elected sheriff, an informant casually mentioned to one of his investigators that it was possible to buy drugs from gang members in the county. The way Carter tells it, the passing reference floored his investigator: " 'You can?' my guy asks. 'We have gang members living here?' "

They did indeed. Before long you could spot gang-related graffiti on local barns and buildings—and at the foot of the covered bridge in Meem's Bottom, near where Paz's body had been found.

Carter's job, and the life of his small rural community, had suddenly become a lot more complicated.

Gangs have been a fixture of urban life in the United States for more than 150 years, making their presence known in inner-city ghettos and poor immigrant neighborhoods ever since the Irish settled the Five Points district of New York. But as Carter and other small-town cops in America have discovered over the past few years, gangs are no longer just a big-city problem.

Gang activity has traditionally been a function of immigration and labor-migration patterns. Today, with those patterns changing—with unskilled jobs shifting from cities to rural regions, with sprawl pushing suburbs and exurbs deeper into the countryside—gangs are cropping up in unexpected places: tiny counties and quaint villages, farming communities and cookie-cutter developments, small towns and tourist resorts. In Toombs County, Ga., for instance, 10 Hispanic gangs roam an area marked by cotton, tobacco and onion fields, according to Art Villegas, who tracks gang activity there for the sheriff's office.

The blue-collar jobs that do not require much training or fluency in English are increasingly found in the countryside. Thanks in part to the explosive growth of the fast-food industry and the huge agro-conglomerates that service it, giant food factories now dot pastoral America. The plants actively recruit south of the border and in poor Hispanic neighborhoods on both coasts of the United States, drawing legions of immigrants to places barely big enough to register on state maps.

Not long ago, I met Fermin, a 25-year-old Guatemalan immigrant who moved to Woodstock from Delaware, four years ago. (Uncomfortable with being mentioned in an article about local gangs, he would be identified by only his first name.) Fermin had heard from a fellow immigrant that the poultry plants in the area were hiring and landed one of the better-paying jobs, as a crane operator, at a plant in nearby Edinburg. He moved into the Valley Vista apartments, Shenandoah County's equivalent of an inner-city barrio. "It seemed like a good place to start a family," he says.

Set at a distance from the lovingly preserved 200-year-old log homes that line Woodstock's historic district, Valley Vista's dozen or so three-story brown-brick buildings sit on the more recently developed edge of town near a car wash and a strip mall. A Hispanic grocery store sells phone cards, money orders to Mexico and Goya food products. Clean and well kept, the courtyards at Valley Vista are a far cry from the projects. The parking lot is filled with modest late-model cars, and a van from a local Pentecostal church regularly makes rounds, picking up parishioners and those enrolled in the church's free English classes.

But beneath the surface tranquillity is a dark side to this immigrant community, as illustrated by a drunken brawl and stabbing that took place at the Valley Vista a few days before my visit. Labor migration to areas like Shenandoah has created a work force of often illegal, itinerant industrial workers who migrate from factory to factory much as California's seasonal fruit pickers move from orchard to orchard. Alienated and isolated in what are effectively rural ghettos, many immigrant workers find solace in alcohol and are easy prey for drug dealers.

Del Hendrixson, who tours food-factory towns like Woodstock as the head of a nonprofit gang-outreach organization called Bajito Onda, or the Underground Scene, sees firsthand evidence of the disillusionment that can set in among the workers. "When you're stuck in the middle of nowhere slaughtering beef for six or seven dollars an hour, 60 hours a week," she says, "the American dream can pretty quickly turn into a nightmare."

As far as law enforcement can tell, MS-13 gang members arrived on the scene in Shenandoah early last year. For them, the Hispanic communities springing up around food-processing facilities across the country present an opportunity to expand their business interests—in particular, dealing methamphetamine—and to attract new members. (For now, the rise of rural gangs does not include African-American gangs, which remain based in large and midsize urban areas.) In addition to drug trafficking, MS-13 cells across the country engage in a range of criminal activities. In Houston, for instance, MS-13 is involved in the large-scale theft of baby formula. Some groups steal cars for chop shops or resale south of the border; others are into extortion or run prostitution rackets.

Many rural gang members, however, are not so much drawn to the opportunities of the countryside as they are pushed out of the city. In the crowded and carved-up inner cities, competition among gangs is fierce. One block that I recently visited in the Columbia Heights neighborhood of Washington was being contested by four different groups. In big-city barrios, trespassing on another gang's turf can get you killed. But in the countryside, the territory is wide open. Gangs operate on a franchise model, and as with fast-food outlets, the closer you get to crowded city centers, the smaller the individual turf. (Think how many McDonald's restaurants there are every few blocks downtown.) In less-populated outlying areas, by contrast, a single gang can service an entire neighborhood, town or county. For an ambitious young gang member, it is easiest to move up the ranks by moving to the countryside.

"You recruit a couple of farm kids, and you're an instant *jefe*," or boss, says Jessie (Chuco) Chavez, a gang leader in Dallas whom Hendrixson arranged for me to interview. Of course, not every gang member in the countryside is an amateur: according to Villegas, hard-core ex-cons from California gangs, eager to avoid the consequences of that state's "three strikes" law, are also moving to the heartland.

The countryside has another appealing feature: weak law enforcement. "In small towns, the police are punks," says Chicocano, a former gang member and a friend of Chavez's who agreed to be identified by only his street name. "You can have your way with them." The statistics seem to bear this out. Murder rates, according to the F.B.I.'s latest annual survey, have remained stable in big cities. But they have jumped in the smallest cities (those with fewer than 10,000 residents), where the police do not have the means to pursue violent offenders with the same intensity as the L.A.P.D. and N.Y.P.D. And by jumping from county to county, state to state, gang members can usually stay one step ahead of the understaffed local authorities.

One measure of the range of jurisdictions spanned by gangs is that Brenda Paz, before her death, was helping federal prosecutors with MS-13 shootings, stabbings and armed robberies across the country. According to a recent F.B.I. report, MS-13 is thought to be active in 31 states in the United States, from Alaska to Oklahoma, the Carolinas to Colorado, and has tens of thousands of members in Honduras and El Salvador.

Consider, too, the picture of a farflung criminal network that emerges from the details disclosed in law-enforcement documents about Paz's murder. Jailhouse recordings of her ex-boyfriend (against whom she was expected to testify) include calls from the detention facility in Virginia where he was held, in which he said that she needed to be "planted so hard, she would never get up." MS-13 members called her in Kansas City, Mo., where United States marshals from the Witness Protection Program had her stashed away in a Marriott hotel, and were presumably able to persuade her to leave the program voluntarily. The white S.U.V. that drove her to the site of her death in Virginia had license plates from Georgia.

"This isn't just a local issue," says Frank Wolf, a congressman from Virginia who has backed a number of antigang measures. "It must be treated as a national problem."

Like 19th-century Irish-American gangs, which arose from an immigrant community that had fled famine, MS-13 has its origins in turmoil abroad. As the brutal civil war in El Salvador was waged in the 80's, pitting leftist guerrillas against the American-backed government, more than a million Salvadorans sought refuge in the United States. Thousands literally walked much of the way to America, initially settling in the Rampart neighborhood of Los Angeles, where they were not warmly welcomed by the established Hispanic community. "Mexican gangs picked on them mercilessly," says Al Valdez, a veteran gang investigator in the district attorney's office in Orange Country, Calif.

Like the Irish before them, the Salvadorans banded together to protect themselves. Salvadoran teenagers were particularly susceptible to the lure of gang life, argues Juan Romagoza, a Salvadoran community leader in Washington who runs a health clinic, because the United States government viewed

Salvadoran refugees as suspect guerrilla sympathizers and made it difficult for them to get green cards. "These kids suffer from a severe identity crisis," he says. "They don't see themselves as fully American because the country is not making room for them. El Salvador is closed to them as well. They can't relate to their parents, who still think in the old ways and often don't speak English."

Following the end of civil war, in 1992, a second wave of immigration from El Salvador transformed MS-13. The new arrivals included veterans from both sides of the conflict. "These people had weapons training and had seen and done terrible things," Valdez says. Almost immediately the level of violence escalated. While gangs typically confine themselves to fighting one another and knocking off rivals, MS-13 killed wantonly, shooting police officers and even civilians, simply to gain street cred.

"It was no longer about self-protection," Valdez says, "but about the bragging rights of who was the biggest and baddest in town."

Today, what brings MS-13 to the Shenandoah is the lucrative rural market for methamphetamine, or crank. Made in trailer-park labs and the backs of barns, crank is the drug of choice in rural America. It is what you will find kids in Iowa or Idaho smoking in convenience-store parking lots on Friday nights. It is also sometimes used by Hispanic assembly-line workers in the food-processing industry, where the pressure to keep up with the line leads some to look for a chemical edge. "Supervisors have been known to sell crank to their workers or to supply it for free in return for certain favors, such as working a second shift," Eric Schlosser writes in "Fast Food Nation," his exposé about the fast-food industry.

Hispanic gangs do not manufacture crank, but with their national and international networks they have a natural advantage in distribution. Over the past five years, according to Valdez, they have supplanted the biker gangs that dominated the methamphetamine trade since World War II. In the Shenandoah Valley, crank has been moved by a biker gang called the Warlocks. But MS-13 is simply outhustling the competition with its immigrant work ethic.

"The Warlocks got high on their own supply and loafed around," says Carter, the sheriff. "What amazed me was that a lot of these guys"—MS-13 members—"had jobs. They'd put in 50 hours at the poultry plant and then on weekends drive down to the Carolinas to pick up loads of meth. They certainly weren't lazy."

When Carter discovered that gangs were moving into Shenandoah, he did a quick survey of the resources at his disposal. As sheriff, he had 56 people on his payroll. Nineteen of them manned the county jail and could not be deployed elsewhere. Of his remaining employees, many were support staff members who performed administrative work or were officers on highway and road patrol who could not be easily removed from their assigned duties. His captains were often tied up with paperwork and court proceedings. Rotating shifts winnowed his forces further still. The numbers alone were troubling, and the odds against him rose further still when the lack of Spanish speakers on his staff, extra money in his budget or firsthand experience dealing with gangs were factored in. "We had to learn about gang history and culture virtually from scratch," he says.

Carter didn't need to dig too deep to see what he was up against. MS-13's explosive growth and violent activity in the suburbs of northern Virginia was well documented. According to a Department of Justice memorandum to Attorney General John Ashcroft, in Fairfax County alone, MS-13 was responsible for most of the 700 gang-related incidents reported by the police department in 2003. In one Fairfax case, a 14-year-old stabbed a stranger to death simply to impress fellow MS-13 members. In another case, in May, MS-13 members attacked a teenager with a machete. All told, the gang's various local cliques—there are about 30 in northern Virginia, with nearly 1,500 members—are reportedly linked to at least half a dozen deaths in the state.

Faced with such a dangerous adversary, Carter did something other small-town sheriffs in America tend to resist: he went public and sought outside help. Community leaders are often loath to acknowledge the presence of gangs, much less to call for reinforcements. "They don't want to scare away tourists, risk property values or getting themselves re-elected," says an F.B.I. analyst in Washington, who in accordance with bureau policy, spoke on condition of anonymity. "It's part of the reason why gang activity is underreported."

But Carter realized that there was institutional knowledge out there for him to tap. "I started sending my officers for outside training," he says, "and had gang intel experts come in to instruct us." Instruction covered the basics, including a primer on how to spot gang members. In MS-13's case, that meant getting to know its colors (blue and white), brand preferences (Nike) and local enemies (the South Side Locos). The group's hand sign (the thumb holding the two middle fingers pressed to the palm), initiation rites and the significance and placement of various identifying tattoos had to be mastered. In addition to gaining some facility with Spanish, Carter's men had to familiarize themselves with street and gang slang.

Carter also needed to grapple with the issue of which police tactics he should adopt for fighting back. Unlike parts of Central America, the United States doesn't have laws forbidding gang membership. (In El Salvador and Honduras, by contrast, draconian new measures make gang membership punishable by up to 12 years in prison, prompting fears in Washington that thousands of Central American members of MS-13 will head north to avoid the crackdown.) And Carter could not simply conduct a mass roundup of Hispanic immigrants. Aside from being discriminatory, it would be impractical and counterproductive. In the late 90's, officials in Toombs County, Ga., tried that strategy, with poor results. "The I.N.S.

arrested hundreds of people," recalls Lance Hamilton, a municipal court judge in rural Georgia. "But there was a huge outcry from assemblymen and the business community." Without workers, the Vidalia onions for which Toombs is best known rotted in the fields. Processing plants stood idle. The local economy sputtered. "In the end, they allowed the workers to return to the fields to pick the crop," Hamilton says.

Carter was going to have to walk the same fine line, balancing his constituents' economic interests, their expectations of safety and the rights of the local Hispanic community. The odds, he realized, were stacked against him. But he wasn't going to sit by and watch thugs take over his county.

In early May, Carter decided that it was time to send MS-13 a message. He had learned that the group's members were implicated in a drug investigation that his officers conducted in the fall of 2003, and he decided to call in the cavalry—federal and other agencies—for a crackdown. "We had reached a point in that investigation," he says, "where, as a small department, we had exhausted all our resources." It was important, he stressed, to continue to deal with MS-13 in the context of a narcotics investigation to avoid the perception that he was initiating raids on the Hispanic community more generally. He contacted a friend of his at the Bureau of Alcohol, Tobacco, Firearms and Explosives. "In my experience," he says, "whenever the A.T.F. gets involved, people go to jail."

The message was delivered to MS-13 at 2 a.m. on a brisk Monday morning, as more than 130 law-enforcement officers from a dozen state, local and federal agencies started kicking down doors at 10 Shenandoah locations, including the Valley Vista apartments, in what was one of the largest drug raids in county history. The raids lasted most of the day, and when the dust settled, crank and cocaine with a street value of half a million dollars had been seized. There were 47 people in custody (some for immigration violations), some defiantly flashing MS-13 hand signs as they were paraded in a long, manacled procession to the county jail.

Emergency funds to finance Carter's antigang effort followed from state and federal coffers. This spring, Gov. Mark Warner of Virginia created a state task force on gangs, and thanks in part to the lobbying efforts of Frank Wolf, the Virginia congressman, the Shenandoah Valley received $500,000 from the Justice Department to create a regional gang unit.

Since then, no new graffiti have appeared in Woodstock. Fermin, the Guatemalan crane operator, says he thinks gang members are lying low in another town, farther up the valley, where there is a large apple-juice bottling plant. But the crackdown, in the meantime, is continuing. In late June, four MS-13 members, including Denis Rivera, were indicted in the United States District Court in Alexandria, Va., for Brenda Paz's murder.

Carter says he is relieved that Paz's killers will finally be brought to justice but harbors no illusions about seeing the last of gangs like MS-13. "This problem," he says, "is still in its infancy."

Textual Questions

1. According to Brzezinski's argument, why is the killing he describes in his introduction more shocking to residents of Shenandoah County than it would be to "urbanites"? Do you agree or disagree with this piece of his argument?

2. Where and how does Brzezinski describe the history of gangs in America? Does his description seem fair and accurate to you, based upon your knowledge of history?

3. How does Brzezinski use Carter's story to organize his essay? Is this organization effective or ineffective?

Rhetorical Questions

4. How does Brzezinski describe the history and activities of MS-13? How does his description support his conclusion that the problem represented by this gang is only in its early stages of development?

5. Where and how does Brzezinski argue that the problem of gangs as criminal organizations is related to issues of social and economic status, race, and ethnicity? How persuasive are these aspects of his argument?

6. Brzezinski's argument is divided into five sections. How does he connect these sections with previous/subsequent sections, directly and indirectly, and how effective is this organization, overall? Which section is most compelling and/or convincing to a reader? Which section is the weakest? Why?

Intertextual Questions

7. Consider the actions of men such as Martin Luther King, Jr. that can be (and sometimes have been) considered by some Americans to be acts of civil disobedience, deliberate violation of a law perceived to be unjust. Is there ever a situation in which gang activity—even violent activity or other criminal activity—can be considered civil disobedience?

8. In "No Country Left Behind" (Chapter 7), Colin L. Powell discusses factors that affect the security of the American nation. Based on his discussions, is a group such as MS-13 a potential threat to national security?

Thinking Beyond the Text

9. Based on Brzezinski's argument and your own knowledge and experience, how are social, economic, and political issues related to the development of gangs as criminal organizations? What part do issues of race, ethnicity, and social class play in the development of gangs?

10. As Brzezinski describes the history and criminal activity of MS-13, would you define this group as a terrorist organization? Why or why not?

For Writing & Discussion

11. In an essay, describe gang activity in either the place you live now or a place you once lived for an extended period of time. What gangs exist? What activities do they engage in? Are there positive aspects to these gangs, even if members also engage in criminal activity? If there are no gangs, then consider why not. What forces are at work in the community that you describe that cause gangs to exist/not to exist?

TIMOTHY SANDEFUR

Timothy Sandefur (1976–) is an attorney who leads the Economic Liberty Project at the Pacific Legal Foundation where he works on issues having to do with eminent domain and the Fourteenth Amendment. He has worked as a legal clerk for the libertarian Institute of Justice, and in 2002 he served as a Lincoln Fellow at the Claremont Institute. Sandefur writes for publications including *The American Enterprise*, *The Claremont Review of Books*, *The Humanist*, *Ideas on Liberty*, *The Independent Review*, *The Orange County Register*, and the *Washington Times*. He has won the George Washington Honor Medal from The Freedoms Foundation, the Felix Morley Journalism Competition from the Institute for Humane Studies, the Madison-Maibach Award from the Center for the Study of the Presidency, and a Ronald Reagan Medal from Claremont Institute.

Sandefur is a contributing editor for *Liberty* magazine, where "They're Coming for Your Land" was published in March, 2005. In this article, Sandefur explains how eminent domain laws, created to allow governments to forcibly buy private lands for public use, have been gradually redefined until they are extremely susceptible to eminent domain abuse.

In addition to his published writing, Sandefur maintains a personal blog called "Freespace" and a blog on evolution and creationism called "Panda's Thumb."

They're Coming for Your Land

∞ **Prereading Question**

Who should have the right to take land away from individual property owners, when, why, and with what compensation?

"With no power, of which they are possessed, do [legislatures] seem to be less familiar, or to handle less awkwardly, than that of eminent domain. . . . At times they fail, or seem to fail, to distinguish accurately between public and private ends, and if their terms and language be alone consulted, to pervert the power to uses to which it cannot lawfully be applied."

—Sherman v. Buick (California Supreme Court, 1867)

Frank Bugryn and his three elderly siblings owned two houses and a Christmas tree farm in Bristol, Conn. The 32-acre family homestead had been in the family for over 60 years when city officials decided the land would produce more tax revenue if it were transferred to industrial use. Specifically, the city wanted to give the land to the Yarde Metals Corporation, which hoped the state highway frontage area would allow them to construct a large sign and entranceway. When the Bugryn family turned down the city's offers to buy the property, the city began eminent domain proceedings.

In May 1998, Bugryn and his family asked a state court to bar the condemnation of his property. "I don't want to go anywhere," he told the court. "My parents built the family house in 1939, and I built my own house on the property 42 years ago. I'm almost 78. Where am I going to go now?" But Mayor Frank Nicastro testified that the industrial park was "in the best interest of the future growth of the city," because it would "build up the tax base." The court denied the injunction, holding that the condemnations of the Bugryns' homes "do not . . . constitute serious or material injuries." In the face of unremitting pressure from the community, and particularly from the Hartford Courant, which editorialized repeatedly against them, the Bugryns appealed. But the Court of Appeals also refused to stop the taking, and the city continued its plans even when Yarde Metals chose to relocate due to the legal delays.

Finally, in 2004, when the family refused to leave their homes, the city initiated proceedings to evict them. Once again, the Courant decried them in an editorial, calling their resistance a "public farce," and a "melodrama," and denouncing the family for "stall[ing] and draw[ing] upon the public's sympathy." Meanwhile, 76-year-old Michael Dudko, husband of one of the Bugryn sisters, and a Polish immigrant who at the age of 15 had been taken from his home by the Nazis and forced into farm labor, suffered a relapse of cancer and died. After a nearby radio station ran a story about the Bugryns' plight, an anonymous, irate telephone call forced the police to post a guard in the mayor's office. Relations within the Bugryn family itself became strained; when one sister failed to leave her house in time, her nephew took the city's side, telling reporters "people are pointing the finger at the mayor and the council and city officials, but all they're really doing in taking the property is using an eminent domain system that was given to them by the legislature." The reverberating effects of eminent domain not only disrupted the family and community, it also bred a sense of disillusionment best expressed by Frank Bugryn himself, who told a reporter, "I'm a veteran of World War II, I fought for our freedom, democracy. But it seems 60 years later it doesn't work."

Eminent domain—the government's power to force a person to sell real estate against his will, at a price the government deems "just compensation"— is one of the most extreme forms of government coercion, and today, among the most common. Used for centuries for building railroads, highways, and post offices, eminent domain is now a multibillion dollar industry, and a classic example of rent-seeking run amok. Governments throughout America routinely seize property to transfer it to private companies to "create jobs" and increase the tax base in a community. In 1999, the city of Merriam, Kan., condemned a Toyota dealership to sell the land to the BMW dealership next door. That same year, Bremerton, Wash., condemned 22 homes to resell the land to private developers. In one especially notorious case, billionaire Donald Trump convinced the government of Atlantic City, N.J., to condemn the home of an elderly widow so that he could build a limousine parking lot. As attorney Jennifer Kruckeberg puts it, "Whether you know it or not, your house is for sale. Corporations, using cities as their personal real estate agents, are proposing the following assignment: 'Find me your most prominent location, get rid of what is on it, help me pay for it, and maybe you will be lucky enough to have me move to your city.' Such is the state of the current eminent domain power."

The exploitation of eminent domain by such private interests is a relatively new phenomenon, and is explicitly prohibited by the U.S. Constitution, which holds that "private property" may be taken only "for public use." But a series of court decisions beginning in the first years of the 20th century, and culminating in the 1954 decision *Berman* v. *Parker,* eroded the "public use" limitation to such a degree that, as Richard Epstein once noted, some law professors have taken to replacing that clause with an ellipsis when writing out the text of the 5th Amendment.

In *Berman,* the Supreme Court held that eliminating slums was a public use because once the legislature deems a project worthy of its attention, that project is necessarily a public one: "[W]hen the legislature has spoken, the public interest has been declared in terms well-nigh conclusive," wrote Justice William O. Douglas for a unanimous Court. "In such cases the legislature, not the judiciary, is the main guardian of the public needs to be served by social legislation."

This level of deference from the Court had become standard fare for property rights and economic liberty by 1954. With the coming of the New Deal, the Supreme Court had decided to take a hands-off approach to regulations of economic rights, which it decided—without the slightest constitutional basis—were "lesser" rights, deserving only "rational basis scrutiny." Under "rational basis," a law regulating economic or property rights is presumed to be constitutional unless it is shown to lack a "rational relationship to a legitimate government interest"—a standard so advantageous to the government that laws hardly ever violate it. But if government's decisions regarding property rights are supposed to be related to a "legitimate government interest," what interests are not legitimate? Are there goals that are off-limits to the state, or beyond the acceptable use of eminent domain? *Berman* was followed by the Michigan Supreme Court's 1981 decision of *Poletown Neighborhood Council* v. *Detroit,* which held that the state could seize an entire working-class neighborhood and transfer it to the General Motors Corporation to build an automobile factory. Since the factory would "create jobs," and creating jobs is a legitimate government interest, the public use clause was satisfied. A few years later, the United States Supreme Court came to a similar conclusion in *Hawaii Housing* v. *Midkiff,* holding that the Hawaii legislature was within its constitutional limits when it wrote a law allowing renters to buy their landlords' property at a fraction of the actual value. Decisions like this rendered so little protection to property owners that the Ninth Circuit Court of Appeals once declared that "the whole scheme is for a public agency to take one man's property away from him and sell it to another. The Founding Fathers may have never thought of this, but the process has been upheld uniformly by latter-day judicial decision. . . . Our hands are tied—if the book on the procedure is followed."

By failing to define, let alone limit, the scope of "legitimate government interests," the courts sparked an explosion of condemnations in the service of any interest that the legislature decided to pursue. "The 'legitimate state interest' test in vogue today," wrote Epstein shortly after *Midkiff,* "is a bare conclusion, tantamount to asserting that the action is legitimate because it is lawful. . . . As such, it functions, at best, as a convenient label for serious inquiry, without defining the set of permissible ends of government action."

With the eminent domain power thus unmoored, the result was predictable to public choice theorists: the power to redistribute property fell into the hands, not of the most deserving, but of the most politically adept. As government became capable of transferring unlimited amounts of land between private parties, the business community began investing an ever-increasing amount in lobbying to persuade it to give the land to them. These companies portray the redistribution of land as a benefit to the community, in the form of job creation and increased funding for public services, as well as an eradication of "economic blight," a vague term attached to any neighborhood that is less than affluent but not an actual slum. Meanwhile, government officials have come to see their roles, not as defenders of the public's safety and welfare, but as sculptors of neighborhoods, for whom citizens and land are raw materials to be formed into the ideal community.

Boynton Beach, Fla., for example, is gradually implementing the "Heart of Boynton Redevelopment Plan," an immense redesign involving potentially hundreds of condemnations. After an attorney from the Pacific Legal Foundation attended a community meeting to challenge officials about the plan, City Redevelopment Director Quintus Greene gave a presentation to the city council entitled "Why We Are Doing This." Greene told the council that although the cities of Boynton Beach and Delray Beach have almost the same population, "when comparing median household incomes, Boynton Beach ranks lower at $39,845 than Delray at $43,371. Boynton Beach ranks higher in median household income than West Palm Beach at $36,774. . . . The purpose of this redevelopment, is to compensate for the loss of one of the City's major taxpayers. Our property tax values are meager compared to other cities and this redevelopment is our attempt to enhance property values within this City. Our choices are to expand our tax base, raise property taxes or reduce services to our citizens. . . . In Boynton Beach, there is a significant amount of property that pays little or no taxes. Given that reality, we must do other things to compensate for that loss of tax dollars."

In plain English: throw poor folks out of their homes, and the city's median income will be higher. Well, that is undeniably true.

But this marriage of government and private industry doesn't just benefit bureaucrats eager to be seen as "creating jobs" and "cleaning up the community." It also yields enormous boons for companies that are adept at political persuasion. Recent articles in the *Wall Street Journal* and *Mother Jones* have detailed the enormous pressure that Home Depot, Bed Bath & Beyond, Wal-Mart, Target, and especially Costco, exert on governments to give them somebody else's real estate. These efforts can be extremely enticing to government officials pursuing "the vision thing," not to mention local residents desperate for new jobs. The plans are presented with a smooth and authoritative style—with sophisticated PowerPoint presentations including lovely artist's renditions of gleaming new streets and bustling pedestrian malls—that is hard for bureaucrats to resist. There's even a website, www.eminentdomainonline.com, which bills itself as "an internet based business to government (b2g) clearinghouse for professionals in the eminent domain, right of way, and infrastructure development fields." If the lobbying efforts should include donations to mayoral election campaigns, and promises to fund giant public works projects on the side, so much the better. As one city planner told *Mother Jones*, "The reality is that you need to rely on developer interest in order to facilitate projects. We're not paying for this party." (Conveniently enough, the Internal Revenue Code allows money expended by a company seeking to persuade a city official to exert eminent domain to be deducted from the company's gross income when determining income tax liability.)

Industry uses sticks as well as carrots when prodding officials to use eminent domain on its behalf. The *Poletown* case is a prime example: GM presented its plan to the city in July of 1980. On Sept. 30, the city's Economic Development Corporation approved it. Eight days later, GM chairman Thomas Murphy wrote the mayor and the chairman of the Detroit Economic Development Corporation, strongly urging them to adopt the plan: "I firmly believe the prospect of retaining some 6,000 jobs, and the attendant revitalization of these communities is a tremendous challenge," he wrote, adding ominously, "it also is an opportunity and a responsibility which none of us can ignore." This letter and GM's other maneuvers, Michigan Supreme Court Justice James Ryan later said, "suggest the withering economic clout of the country's largest auto firm," and indeed Detroit was more than eager to do GM's bidding. Preliminary paperwork was finished within days, and the city council and mayor approved the final documents less than a month after Murphy's letter. Action in the courts moved with the same rare speed, culminating in oral arguments before the state Supreme Court on March 3, 1981, and a decision only ten days later. Meanwhile, wrote Justice Ryan, an "overwhelming psychological pressure . . . was brought to bear upon property owners in the affected area," as a "crescendo of supportive applause sustained the city and General Motors. . . . The promise of new tax revenues, retention of a mighty GM manufacturing facility in the heart of Detroit, new opportunities for satellite businesses, retention of 6,000 or more jobs . . . all fostered a community-wide chorus of support for the project."

Other cases present similar David-and-Goliath scenarios. In 2001, Mississippi redevelopment officials gave the Nissan Corporation 1,300 acres of state-owned land to construct an auto factory. When Nissan hesitated, the state condemned a middle-class black neighborhood to give Nissan another 23 acres. James Burns, Jr., executive director of the state's development authority, told the *New York Times* that the property was not actually a part of the project: "It's not that Nissan is going to leave if we don't get that land. What's important is the message it would send to other companies if we are unable to do what we said we would do. If you make a promise to a company like Nissan, you have to be able to follow through." Attorneys from the Institute for Justice, a Washington, D.C.-based libertarian law firm, managed to fight off the state, and the residents kept their homes. Less fortunate were the residents of the Toledo, Ohio, neighborhood that was taken to build a Jeep factory, which received the blessing of Ohio courts in the fall of 2004, or the property owners in Redwood City, Calif., where the city condemned land to build a movie theater. Knowing that a theater is probably not a "public use," the city declared it was really building a parking lot—and it just happened to include a theater above the parking lot.

The precise amount of money involved in the eminent domain industry is impossible to assess, but *Mother Jones'* Gary Greenberg notes that one project in Ohio—an attempt to condemn 13 acres for the benefit of a shopping mall called Rockwood Pavilion—involves about $125 million in planning and construction costs, and promises the local city some $1.5 million per year in tax revenue once completed. Multiplied by countless cases, as well as the legal expenses and the detriment to property values caused by a city's unpredictable tendency to exert eminent domain, the costs are incalculable.

Eminent domain abuse can have perverse social consequences, too. One of the most commonly voiced justifications for eminent domain is that it is necessary for cleaning up unsightly neighborhoods, which include "adult" businesses or other low-class uses. But in 1997, a consortium of Las Vegas casinos persuaded the city to take the retail property owned by Greek immigrants John and Carol Pappas to build a parking lot for the "Fremont Street Experience," a pedestrian mall including such adult attractions as the "Topless Girls of Glitter Gulch." Moreover, the concept of "blight" is so elastic that economic interest groups can easily exploit it. A mall in St. Louis was recently determined to be blighted, despite the fact that it was 100% occupied and had $100 million in annual sales. And a prep school in Wisconsin was declared blighted despite its elite $10,000 tuition price (which conveniently enough qualified it for a $5.6 million tax-exempt bond issue).

Costco, the nation's leading corporate abuser of eminent domain, has persuaded cities across the nation to engage in such transfers. Lancaster, Calif., tried to condemn a 99 Cents store to transfer it to Costco, even though Costco already had a store in the same mini-mall with the 99 Cents store. The city did so, not on the grounds that the property was blighted—it wasn't; in fact, it's probably the cleanest 99 Cents store in America—but on the grounds that the neighborhood might be blighted in the future, if the government did not act now. A federal court struck down this condemnation (an extremely rare occurrence) after noting that "by Lancaster's own admissions, it was willing to go to any lengths—even so far as condemning commercially viable, unblighted real property—simply to keep Costco within the city's boundaries. In short, the very reason that Lancaster decided to condemn 99 Cents' leasehold interest was to appease Costco. . . ." It is impossible to tell how many properties Costco has taken through eminent domain because the company hasn't released exact figures and has tried to stifle shareholder attempts to reverse the company's policies. But the cases abound. Institute for Justice lawyer Dana Berliner, who recently published a catalogue of some 10,000 instances of eminent domain abuse, reports that "of the big-box retailers, Costco shows up the most." But the company is unrepentant. Asked for an explanation, Costco senior vice president Joel Benoliel told investors that if they didn't exploit eminent domain, "our competitors . . . would . . . and our shareholders would be the losers."

It's hard to deny that assertion. So long as the power is available to the highest bidder, Costco executives would violate their duty to investors to withdraw from the scramble for other people's land. Although it is easy to damn powerful companies so insensitive to homeowners unable to afford a legal defense—a Costco attorney once told the city council of Lenexa, Kan., that the property he wanted condemned was "not much of a neighborhood, anyway"—the blame rightfully rests on the courts that have gradually erased the public use clause.

But in confronting this problem, the courts suffer from a serious intellectual handicap, which dates back to the Progressive Era at the opening of the 20th century. During this period, leading intellectuals came to reject the individualistic natural rights premises of the American founding. As Michael McGerr writes, the Progressives "wanted not only to use the state to regulate the economy; strikingly, they intended nothing less than to transform other Americans." But remaking Americans meant inverting the premise that the state was a tool of the people. John Dewey, philosophical champion of the Progressives, denounced "the notion that there are two different 'spheres' of action and of rightful claims; that of political society and that of the individual, and that in the interest of the latter the former must be as contracted as possible." Such a notion, he said, would be replaced with "that form of social organization, extending to all the areas and ways of living, in which the powers of individuals shall not be merely released from mechanical external constraint but shall be fed, sustained and directed."

The Progressives thought society should mold individuals in a manner best suited for the survival and flourishing of the state. It was during this period that various devices for controlling citizens—everything from the Pledge of Allegiance to eugenics and forced sterilization—were introduced. In his great book on this era, *The Metaphysical Club*, Louis Menand explains just how opposite the Progressive idea was to the views of the Founding Fathers. To the Progressives, "Coercion is natural; freedom is artificial. Freedoms are socially engineered spaces where parties engaged in specified pursuits enjoy protection from parties who would otherwise naturally seek to interfere in those pursuits . . . We . . . think of rights as privileges retained by individuals against the rest of society, but rights are created not for the good of individuals, but for the good of society. Individual freedoms are manufactured to achieve group ends. This way of thinking about freedoms helps explain why the . . . [Progressives] were indifferent to the notion of individual rights."

The Progressive Era began to dissolve the public-private boundary by holding that the things we think of as rights are really just permissions granted by society and revocable whenever society decides. Understandably, this period brought a corresponding explosion in the use of eminent domain. In 1923, for the first time, the Supreme Court held that government could condemn land not just for necessities, but for mere recreational facilities like scenic highways. A California court held in 1911 that "[g]enerally speaking, anything calculated to promote the education, the recreation or the pleasure of the public is to be included within the legitimate domain of public purposes" served by eminent domain.

In short, the Progressive goal of "remaking Americans" meant breaking down the limits on state power. The difference between "legitimate" and "illegitimate" government interests was accordingly dissolved. Since government would "extend to all the areas and ways of living," it would now be free to do "anything calculated to promote . . . the pleasure of the public."

It is no coincidence that the Progressive Era was the first time the word "blight" was applied to economic stagnation. The Progressives saw society as an organic whole, with each person a cell. Thus the term "blight," originally a term for a plant disease, was applied to neighborhoods that failed to perform to the standard the society desired. Private businesses were no longer private, they were a tool by which society produced a certain standard of living, and if they failed to do so, society could simply revoke the permission (formerly called property rights) and give that land to someone else.

With the boundaries of "legitimate government interests" erased, New Dealers built on the Progressives' work by establishing the concept of judicial deference. In previous decades, courts had been willing to block the more extreme Progressive social experiments, but in the 1930s they took a more deferential view. Louis Brandeis, a Progressive attorney who had once coined the term "right of privacy," was appointed to the Supreme Court, where he would instead declare that "in the interest of the public and in order to preserve the liberty and the property of the great majority of the citizens of a state, rights of property and the liberty of the individual must be remolded, from time to time, to meet the changing needs of society."

President Roosevelt's other appointees (including Justice Douglas, who would later write the *Berman* decision) agreed not only that government could "remold" the "liberty of the individual," but that courts should not stand in the way. The result was the creation of "rational basis scrutiny."

Today, courts are unable to decide whether an asserted "government interest" is legitimate or illegitimate. Indeed, the Supreme Court has confessed that "our cases have not elaborated on the standards for determining what constitutes a 'legitimate state interest.'" But without such an elaboration, it is impossible to determine whether a law is "rationally related to a legitimate state interest." Since anything at all might qualify as a "legitimate interest," anything subject to this test will receive a pass from the Court. The result is that government's power to manipulate individuals, and their property, is limited only in the rarest possible circumstances.

There is reason for optimism, however. The severest abuses of eminent domain have already forced many people to reexamine their views about the lesser stature of property rights. When the Michigan Supreme Court indicated its willingness to reconsider its *Poletown* decision, the ACLU joined forces with the Pacific Legal Foundation urging the court to declare eminent domain abuse unconstitutional. The court agreed, unanimously overruling its decades-old decision. To permit the condemnation of land "solely on the basis of the fact that use of that property by a private entity seeking its own profit might contribute to the economy's health" would "render impotent our constitutional limitations on the government's power of eminent domain," said the court. "*Poletown*'s 'economic benefit' rationale would validate practically any exercise of the power of eminent domain on behalf of a private entity. After all, if one's ownership of private property is forever subject to the government's determination that another private party would put one's land to better use, then the ownership of real property is perpetually threatened by the expansion plans of any large discount retailer, 'megastore,' or the like."

Only months later, the United States Supreme Court agreed to hear *Kelo v. New London,* a case challenging Connecticut's attempt to seize a neighborhood for the benefit of Pfizer. Although it is impossible to predict what the court will do, there are three main possibilities. The first is that the court may allow government to redistribute private land of New London residents to a private company on the grounds that any benefit to the public is good enough. Second, it might hold, on very narrow grounds, that in some cases, the private benefit is just too extreme to be labeled public. This seems the most likely outcome, but it is an unsatisfying one, because it would leave the important question unanswered. The third and least likely option is that the court could invest serious thought into the difference between what is public and what is private, and could declare that attenuated social effects of private behavior aren't enough to make it into a public concern. Just because a private business affects the public in some way doesn't make it the government's business. If the court embraced this view, the answer to the *Kelo* case would be obvious: of course a private company is not a public use, even if the public likes to purchase its products.

It is not impossible that this will happen. In *Lawrence* v. *Texas,* the Supreme Court declared that alleged harm to society by private, adult, consensual sexual activity is not enough to allow the state to pry into people's private bedrooms. It would be refreshing indeed if it also said that alleged social effects of private business interests are not enough to make a private business into a public use. But, again, I think it unlikely. Such a decision would require the court to reexamine old and politically volatile assumptions which trace back to the Progressive abandonment of America's founding principles. To city planners, your neighborhood is theirs to shape as they please. The fact that a business uses condemned land for its own profit is irrelevant to them because private businesses are public uses, in their minds. They are the tools by which society creates jobs and provides people with goods. President Eisenhower once warned the nation about the military-industrial complex, but today local governments are wrapped up in the Costco-WalMart-Home Depot complex. They believe in what they call "partnerships" between government and private industry in which government and corporations decide the shape and layout of whole neighborhoods, with no regard for the rights of the landowners who stand in their way.

But even a favorable outcome in *Kelo* might come too late to help Curtis Blanc of Liberty, Mo. Through his company, Mid-America Car, Inc., Blanc owns a well-maintained brick warehouse which he leases for $1 per year to two charities: In As Much Ministries, and Love, Inc. These ministries feed more than 400 families per month—despite one city council member's statement during a council meeting that "there are no poor people in Liberty," But the council has other plans for Blanc's land: it wants to construct a business district on "Liberty Triangle," which consists of 88 acres of land, including Blanc's warehouse. The first phase of the Triangle project has already begun, and a 160,000-square-foot Lowe's home improvement store recently opened. Steve Hansen, the city's public works director, recently told businesses that those which generate high sales tax income for the city will be allowed to remain in the area, but that "most of the businesses that are there now are not high sales producers" and will be condemned to make way for companies that will raise tax revenue for the city. Blanc has received a final notice from the city requiring him to sell his property, or face condemnation. Still, Blanc is hopeful. Along with the Bugryn and Pappas families, he agreed to be represented by the Pacific Legal Foundation in a friend of the court brief in the *Kelo* case which urges the court to breathe new life into the "public use" clause.

It is very sad that we have come this far. For the Supreme Court of the United States to declare that "our cases have not elaborated on the standards for determining what constitutes a 'legitimate state interest' " is a shocking statement. Two hundred years after the founding, with the Declaration of

Independence and the Federalist Papers at hand, and with the experiences of the Revolution, the Civil War, the World Wars, and the civil-rights movement behind us, we ought to know what a legitimate state interest is. As Hadley Arkes has put it, "this late in the seasons of our experience, federal judges should not be in need of this kind of instruction, on the rudiments of constitutional government. . . . [The Founders] did not expect that the main instruction would have to be offered to the lawyers and the judges themselves, and to the resident wits in the schools of law. . . . But that project has become, in our own day, steady work."

Textual Questions

1. According to Sandefur's argument, what are the immediate and long-term effects of current interpretations of eminent domain?

2. How did the legal principle of eminent domain become "unmoored" and to who did it finally become attached? How? With what results—for developers and individual property owners?

3. Sandefur's argument is divided into four sections. What major point does he make in each section? How does he support each of these major points—with what examples?

Rhetorical Questions

4. Examine Sandefur's examples. Based upon your analysis, with whom is he most sympathetic? How does he want his readers to feel about this issue, and how can you tell?

5. Given that his argument is about America in the twenty-first century, how effective is it for Sandefur to open his essay with a quotation from a California Supreme Court decision in 1867? Why is this effective or ineffective?

6. According to Sandefur's conclusion, there is cause "for optimism." Given the grim nature of his argument in the preceding sections, how does he make this turn in his essay? How well does it work, given the comparatively short nature of this section?

Intertextual Questions

7. Sandefur opens with a description of a homeowner. Why? How does Matthew Brzezinski use this same strategy in "Hillbangers" (this chapter)?

8. Consider the arguments about civil disobedience made by Martin Luther King, Jr. (this chapter). Based on his definition, is an individual property owner's refusal to sell his/her land to a developer an act of civil disobedience? Why or why not?

Thinking Beyond the Text

9. While Sandefur quotes a California Supreme Court decision from 1867 in the opening of his article, there are many decisions—by state and federal courts—that affect the legal interpretation of eminent domain. Locate the most recent decision made in your current state of residence and explain how that decision affects individual property owners.

10. Sandefur speaks of abuses of eminent domain, but under what conditions is the greater good best served by abridging the rights of individual property owners? Won't someone—the local/state/federal government, a private developer, or others—always benefit from seizing land and putting it to another use? Won't someone always lose?

For Writing & Discussion

11. Talk to either a city planner or land developer. What does he/she think about recent controversies over eminent domain? In a short essay, explain how this person's opinions and experiences either support or refute the claims made by Sandefur.

JACK HITT

Jack Hitt is a contributing editor with *GQ*, *Harpers*, *Lingua Franca*, and the National Public Radio series "This American Life" where he has appeared more than 20 times. He also has written for *American Prospect*, the *Los Angeles Times*, *Mother Jones*, the *New York Times*, and *Outside* magazine. In 1991 he received a Livingston Award for Young Journalists for his article on hackers breaking into the New York phone system, and in 2006 he received an MFK Fisher Distinguished Writing Award for an article in *Gourmet Magazine*. His "This American Life" episode about a production of Peter Pan is anthologized on the CD collection, "Lies, Sissies & Fiascoes: The Best of This American Life."

In "The Newest Indians," published in the *New York Times* in August 2005, Hitt explores how approaches to ethnic identity, especially for Native Americans, have changed over time and discusses the importance of language in Native American communities today. Some of Hitt's other recent publications include a 2006 *New York Times* article about abortion in El Salvador, "Pro-Life Nation"; a 2006 *Los Angeles Times* article, "Jesus Was No GOP Lobbyist"; and a 2006 *New York Times* article on a bird thought until recently to be extinct, "13 Ways of Looking at an Ivory-Billed Woodpecker."

The Newest Indians

❧ Prereading Question

In The Redneck Manifesto, *Jim Goad argues that impoverished whites, particularly those who live in southern states of the U.S., are the most disenfranchised Americans to exist in modern times. Aside from their poverty and political disenfranchisement, they are also the last minority about whom anyone can joke at will. Jokes about Jews and Blacks are, in modern America, absolutely unacceptable; jokes about rednecks, he argues, are not. Would you agree or disagree with some/all of his argument, as summarized here? Why?*

On a crisp morning in March at the Jaycee Fairgrounds near Jasper, Ala., the powwow was stirring. Amid pickups with bumper stickers reading "Native Pride" and "The earth does not belong to us. We belong to the earth," small groups gathered to check out the booths selling Indian rugs, dancing sticks, homemade knives and genealogy books. On one side, under her camper's tarp, sat Wynona Morgan, a middle-aged woman wearing a modestly embroidered Indian smock and some jewelry. Morgan had only recently discovered her Indian heritage, but, she said, in some ways she had known who she was for years. "My grandmother always told me that she came from Indians," Morgan told me. She is now a member of one of the groups meeting here in Jasper, the Cherokee Tribe of Northeast Alabama, which itself is new, having organized under that name in 1997. The tribe is committed to telling its story, in part through an R.V. campground named Cedar Winds that will eventually expand to include an "authentic, working Cherokee Indian Village."

"The only real proof we had that we were Indian was this stub," Morgan went on to say. She had brought along a copy of a century-old receipt entitling an ancestor to receive some money from the United States government for being an Indian. With the help of an amateur genealogist named Bryan Hickman, Morgan was able to connect her line to its Indian roots, and she began to raise her son, Jo-Jo, as a Native American. She was particularly proud of Jo-Jo; only a teenager, Jo-Jo had been chosen to serve as honorary headman and lead the grand entry just after the grass dancers performed later that afternoon.

"Sometimes Jo-Jo gets teased for being an Indian at school, but he doesn't care," Morgan said. What she didn't say was that the teasing is connected to the fact that neither she nor Jo-Jo look as much like Indians as they do regular Alabama white folks. In fact, every Indian at the powwow looked white. More than half my time with this tribe was spent dealing with their anxiety that I might make this observation.

This ethnic apprehension can be found even among the older tribes, where outmarriage, or exogamy, has created a contemporary population that doesn't look nearly as "Indian" as the characters of our movies and HBO westerns. What results from this can get funky. For example, among coastal Indian tribes, who depend upon tourism, it is not uncommon to see them dressed as Plains Indians with full feathered headdresses and other outfits that were never their custom. It is a practice known as "chiefing," and in some tribes it is as regulated as jewelry sales. This is the market force, ethnic-wise: coastal Indians know that they have to look like an outsider's vision of an Indian in order to be accepted by tourists as Indian.

Among the newer tribes, this anxiety can get especially intense. All weekend at the Jaycee Fairgrounds, the Cherokees of Northeast Alabama whom I spoke to were quite nervous that I might pronounce them, as some put it, "ethnic frauds." Hickman, the genealogist, insisted upon knowing if I was "going to make fun of them." In the days leading up to the powwow, he called me repeatedly, his voice filled with panic. Hardly an hour went by over the weekend that the event's spokeswoman, Karen Cooper, didn't sidle up to ask me if there was anything she could do.

Morgan, though, was happy to talk about her relatively new status as an American Indian. She had been attending powwows for years as a white woman, but became official two years ago after her genealogical work was done. "I hate to put it this way, but I'm a completely new Indian," she said. "I have had to learn everything from the ground up, and I'm learning every day."

Morgan's sincerity and her profound pleasure at all these discoveries in her ancestral line now influences every waking moment of her life, she said. She confided that she knows that there are fake Indians—so-called wannabes—and she says she feels sorry for them. "I hear some people say that they have a 'Cherokee princess' up the line," Morgan said with a laugh. "I just love that one, because of course the Cherokees didn't have a princess." This joke—about the white person claiming a Cherokee princess—is heard pretty often these days from any Indian, coast to coast. In the same way that blacks poke fun at white men who can't jump or Jews mock goyim mispronunciations of Yiddish words, it is not meant as much to put down others as to enunciate the authenticity and insider status of the person telling the joke. It is a way to assuage a new kind of ethnic unease that can be felt throughout Indian Country.

The Cherokee Tribe of Northeast Alabama is, according to the University of Oklahoma anthropologist Circe Sturm, one of more than 65 state-recognized tribes, most of which have emerged in the last few decades in the Southeast. State recognition is merely one of many legal mechanisms used to legitimate a Native American tribe. They range from the most difficult—federal recognition, which is required for running a casino—to state and local designations and on to unrecognized groups. (The Chero-kees alone account for more than 200 of these recently formed unaffiliated tribes.) All of these tribes have emerged at a moment when Native Ameri-cans have experienced skyrocketing growth in population. I had traveled to Jasper, among other places, to find out what kind of growing pains this population surge is causing Native Americans.

Soon enough, the shed at the fairgrounds was all commotion as the grass dance began. Jo-Jo was dressed in full regalia, and like all the dancers here, he had made his bustle and other ornaments. The grass dancers were pouring their hearts into it. The crowd was mostly other tribal members, as well as what are called "hobbyists," non-Indian enthusiasts who like to attend public powwows. All of them were thrilled with the performance, and it was hard not to be impressed by the difficult moves and the elabo-rate costumes. I meant to keep my eye on Jo-Jo, but I was distracted by another handsome teenage boy with light brown hair, the head grass dancer, who didn't seem to have made the full transition to Indian yet. His outfit was a painstaking interplay of beads and feathers and a series of striking variations of white and red shapes sewn onto his vest, which for some reason caught my eye and seduced me into leaving the bleacher seats in order to wander closer to the rail, elbowing my way out in front of even small children to peer more carefully and to make absolutely sure that the tiny red rectangles were—yes, indeed, no doubt about it—little Confeder-ate battle flags.

A century ago, Native Americans were down to a few hundred thousand people, and the prevailing concern was not about overpopulation but about extinction. Some observers comfortably predicted that America would close the book on its "vanishing race" by 1935. But Native Americans didn't disap-pear, and after the birth of civil rights, when the Red Power movement asserted itself in the 1960's, something unexpected happened in the Indian population count. In four consecutive censuses, which showed other groups growing by 7 to 10 percent, Native American populations soared, growing by more than 50 percent in 1970, by more than 70 percent in 1980 and another third in 1990. The 2000 census reveals an overall doubling, to more than four million. Jack D. Forbes, an emeritus professor of Native American studies at the University of California at Davis, argues that undercounts and other cen-sus quirks may mean that the total number of Indians in the United States today is in fact closer to 15 or even 30 million. Using the 2000 census data, Indians can be called America's fastest-growing minority.

The assumption many people make when they hear these huge numbers is that the new Indians are just cashing in on casino money. But tribes with casinos or even casino potential have very restrictive enrollment policies. (If anything, when casinos are involved, the story usually goes heartbreak-ingly in the other direction. Take the case of Kathy Lewis, whose grandfather was the chief of the Chukchansi tribe, which now runs a casino with another tribe outside Fresno, Calif. Her father worked out a deal with the tribal council that placed him on the lucrative tribe's rolls but cut out his own children. He no longer speaks to his daughter. Impoverished, she lives in a two-room trailer just outside the reservation.)

Instead, the demographic spike in population is a symptom of what sociologists call "ethnic shifting" or "ethnic shopping." This phenomenon reflects the way more and more Americans have come to feel comfortable changing out of the identities they were born into and donning new ethnicities in which they feel more at home. There is almost no group in this hemisphere immune to the dramas accompanying so much ethnic innovation. Last year in Montreal, for example, the selection of Tara Hecksher as Irish-Canadian parade queen seemed to many to be inspired. While the young woman's father is Irish, her mother is Nigerian. To look at her face and hair, most people would instinctively categorize her as "black." Certainly the thug that interrupted the parade by tossing a white liquid at her seemed to think that way.

Such agonies of identity abound, but nowhere are they felt more keenly than among Native Americans. There, many of the markers of being Indian—the personal adornments, the spiritual life, daily tribal culture— are the subject of intense debate, in some cases even federal regulation. Much of what has defined Indianness has been appropriated by everyone from Hollywood to charlatan spiritual guides and ground into unappealing cliche. As a result, many Indians are trying to define the new modern Native American in terms that can't be so easily commodified. Some argue that this ethnic mobility in and out of Indian Country is connected to a separate phenomenon—a rush to revitalize native languages. Many tribes have hired linguists or sent members to any of several institutes now devoted to helping Indians retain or recreate some form of their tribal languages.

In the past, ethnicity and race seemed like fixed categories, inherent qualities of self that were not only unchanging but could also be measured, quantified and reduced to small checkable boxes on bureaucratic forms. But American diversity and intermarriage (as well as the perfect match between the Internet and deep genealogical research) have changed this singular certainty into a multiple-choice question. For most of American history, identity was centrally controlled: the census taker decided your identity by quietly writing it down while asking questions at your door. But in 1960, the census was changed to permit Americans to declare their own race or ethnicity. The most significant shift, though, came as recently as the 2000 census. Americans were permitted to declare more than one race or identity. As a result, the old categories become even more fluid.

How much easier (though scarier) life might be if we all got ethnic identification cards so that when encountering a very light-skinned person claiming to be black, you could reply, "O.K., show me your federal identification card guaranteeing the proper amount of African blood to qualify you as an African-American." Here's the thing: you could ask an Indian that question. Some Native Americans carry what is called, awkwardly, a white card, officially known as a C.D.I.B., a Certificate of Degree of Indian Blood. This card certifies a Native American's "blood quantum" and can be issued only after a tribe has been cleared by a federal subagency.

The practice of measuring Indian blood dates to the period just after the Civil War when the American government decided to shift its genocide policy against the Indians from elimination at gunpoint to the gentler idea of breeding them out of existence. It wasn't a new plan. Regarding Indians, Thomas Jefferson wrote that "the ultimate point of rest and happiness for them is to let our settlements and theirs meet and blend together, to intermix, and become one people." When this idea was pursued bureaucratically under President Ulysses S. Grant, Americans were introduced to such phrases as "half breed" and "full blood" as scientific terms. In a diabolical stroke, the government granted more rewards and privileges the less Indian you were. For instance, when reservation lands were being broken up into individual land grants, full-blooded Indians were ruled "incompetent" because they didn't have enough civilized blood in them and their lands were administered for them by proxy agents. On the other hand, the land was given outright to Indians who were half white or three-quarters white. Here was the long-term catch: as Indians married among whites and gained more privileges, their blood fraction would get smaller, so that in time Indians would reproduce themselves out of existence.

Compounding this federal reward for intermarriage was the generally amicable tradition most tribes had of welcoming in outsiders. From the earliest days of European settlement, whites were amicably embraced by Indian tribes. For instance, the leader of the Cherokee Nation during the forced exile of 1838–39—the Trail of Tears—was John Ross, often described as being seven-eighths Scottish.

A lot of Indians haven't looked "Indian" for quite a while, especially in the eastern half of the country, where there is a longer history of contact with Europeans. That fact might not have been the source of much anxiety in the past, but in the post-Civil Rights era, the connotations of the word "white" began to shift at the same time that the cultural conversation progressed from the plight of "Negroes" to the civil rights of "blacks."

Suddenly "white" acquired a whiff of racism. This association may well account for the rise of more respectable ethnic descriptions like "Irish-American" or "Norwegian-American," terms that neatly leapfrog your identity from Old World to New without any hint of the Civil War in between. According to the work of Ruth Frankenberg and other scholars, some white people associate whiteness with "mayonnaise" and "paleness" and "spiritual emptiness." So whatever is happening in Indian Country is being aggravated by an unexpected ethnic pressure next door: people who could be considered white but who can legitimately (or illegitimately) find an Indian ancestor now prefer to fashion their claim of identity around a different description of self.

And in a nation defined by ethnic anxiety, what greater salve is there than to become a member of the one people who have been here all along?

The reaction from lifelong Indians runs the gamut. It is easy to find Native Americans who denounce many of these new Indians as members of the wannabe tribe. But it is also easy to find Indians like Clem Iron Wing, an elder among the Sioux, who sees this flood of new ethnic claims as magnificent, a surge of Indians "trying to come home." Those Indians who ridicule Iron Wing's lax sense of tribal membership have retrofitted the old genocidal system of blood quantum—measuring racial purity by blood—into the new standard for real Indianness, a choice rich with paradox. The Native American scholar C. Matthew Snipp has written that the relationship between Native Americans and the agency that issues the C.D.I.B. card is "not too different than the relationship that exists for championship collies and the American Kennel Club."

Out on Chicaugon Lake on a warm afternoon in Michigan, dozens of families splashed around in the water, having good summer fun. Inside the nearby picnic shed, a few dozen folks assembled for an Ojibwe language camp. The camp was off to an awkward start. The adults stood at uncomfortable attention. The teenagers, off to one side, smoked and lobbed withering looks everywhere. The little ones raced about, crazed that they couldn't join the children in the lake.

The leader was Wendy Geniusz, a young blonde whose cute cheeky smile seemed to reflect her father's Polish background (as did that killer surname). She has been raised among the Ojibwe all her life. Her mother, Mary, is the granddaughter of a Canadian Indian who gave up her native claim after marrying a Presbyterian Scot. But Mary knew this grandmother, and about 25 years ago, when she started having her children, she decided that she could no longer indulge what she saw as the luxury of her multiple backgrounds. She needed to create a coherent environment for her children.

After finding a spiritual guide to lead her back to the world of her grandmother, Mary raised her children among the Ojibwe. Wendy Geniusz was born an Indian. She is known by her birth name, Makoons, and she has attended local powwows since she can remember. Geniusz's days begin, as they have for the past five years, with a tobacco offering and prayer. She is married to an Ojibwe man, Errol Geniusz (having taken her last name), and she intends to raise her children speaking Ojibwe in her home; she mastered the language at the University of Minnesota, where her Ph.D. topic is "Decolonization of Ojibwe Plant Knowledge." She teaches the language to other members of the tribe.

One of the exercises this morning was to get people to ask one another basic questions in Ojibwe. About 10 kids, all around 11 or 12, were horsing around as Geniusz struggled to guide them through the paces. It was rough going. Two kids in particular were jumping on each other. One looked classically Indian; the other was a blond. The black-haired boy teasingly referred to the other as "whitey." There were a few anxious looks among the adults, yet here on the Upper Peninsula, no one corrected the black-haired boy, in part because he is the great grandson of the tribal elder who was in attendance to lend the language camp a sense of history (and to resolve the occasional grammar stumper). Later that morning, when the teasing continued, the blond kid broke into a rap from "Scary Movie 3": "I'm a white boy, but my neck is red/I put Miracle Whip on my Wonder Bread." The anxiety that was a constant at the Alabama powwow was present here, too, but it was acknowledged not with panic but with jokes and stories.

"People usually think I'm white," Geniusz explained. "Like recently, my sister and I took a bunch of clothing to an Indian rummage sale, and they thought we were just some white kids bringing clothes down." On the other hand, she recalled attending a recent national Indian conference at which each tribe was asked to stand up and say hello. "I was with the Chicaguan Chippewa, and they said I should get up and say hello because I spoke more Ojibwe. So I got up and said something very simple, like 'Boozhoo giinawaa,' or 'Hello, all of you.' And afterward, I had all these people coming up and hugging me and telling me that they had thought I was just some little white girl. When I speak, people get a little startled, and then they accept me."

Circe Sturm, whose book on new Indian tribes, "Claiming Redness," is due next year, suggests that "one big difference between older recognized tribes and the newer tribes is that the newer groups are marked by a nervous disavowal of whiteness. You will often hear them talk about their 'Indian hair' or their 'Indian cheekbones.' They often solemnly conclude their conversations by saying, 'For all purposes, I consider myself Indian.' The older tribes acknowledge their whiteness. Oklahoma Cherokees talk about 'white Cherokees' and often make a joke about it."

Ethnicity is a tricky thing because it is commonly understood as something fixed and essential rather than what it more likely is: an unarticulated negotiation between what you call yourself and what other people are willing to call you back. Geniusz has lived her life culturally among the Ojibwe and is recognized by them as an Indian. Her easy comfort at calling herself an Indian comes in part because everyone in her area recognizes the essential Indian life she has led. Her physically European features are, in this part of Michigan at least, understood as only marginally curious.

The way the ethnic negotiation works depends on what part of the country you are located in. Native Americans recognize that there exists a kind of spectrum. At one end there are Indians living on a well-established Western reservation in a tribe that is branded as seriously authentic—Hopi, say— where many in the tribe retain the classic Indian physical characteristics. Moving along, you encounter various tribes that have intermarried a lot—like the Ojibwe—yet whose members still feel a powerful sense of authenticity. But once you visit tribes of newcomers, where few members knew their Indian ancestors personally, you begin to sense a clawing anxiety of identity. At the far end are hobbyists, those Indian groupies who hang around powwows, hoping to find a native branch in their family tree. They enjoy wearing the traditional tribal garb and are, as the University of Michigan history professor Philip Deloria titled his book, "Playing Indian." Most hobbyists do it for fun, although some are just criminals, like Ronald A. Roberts, who pleaded guilty to federal charges after trying to establish a casino with his forged genealogical documents, or David Smith, who was jailed for holding a "healing ceremony" for a 12-year-old girl that included fondling her.

Just where in that spectrum, between land-based tribes in the West and playful hobbyists, you might locate a bright dividing line of authenticity is an open question. It is territory that is currently being remapped. It is why the population of Indians is surging and why there is such fervent debate among Indians as to just who should be able to make the claim. It becomes a kind of nature-versus-nurture argument. Do genetics make you Indian or does culture? Or can either one?

It is in the context of such continued questions that the renewed interest in language takes on more urgent meaning. According to Laura Redish, the director of a resource clearinghouse for language revival called Native Languages of the Americas, there are roughly 150 native languages that are currently spoken in North America or that have disappeared recently enough that they could still be revived. She estimates that in the last 10 years, some 80 to 90 percent of the tribes associated with these languages have put together some kind of program of revival.

"Language has a different kind of importance now than it did only 20 or 30 years ago," says Ofelia Zepeda, the director of the American Indian Language Development Institute in Arizona, whose program in revitalizing languages works with about 20 tribes each year. "Language is one of those things that you take for granted, but now it has a different dimension. It is a conscious act."

As the sun angled down over Lake Chicaugon, Wendy Geniusz's language camp magically came together. The sullen teenagers were still smoking, but like the little kids were now tuned in. Everyone gathered around separate picnic tables set for a meal, and they were calling out the names of table utensils in Ojibwe. One of Geniusz's assistants, a very handsome native speaker with a long black ponytail named James Vukelich, stood up and announced: "If you want to learn how to pick people up in Ojibwe, come over here. If you don't know what that means, stay where you are." Suddenly, the teenagers were all scrambling over to Vukelich's corner. Once the teenagers had decided that talking the ancestral language was as cool a thing as mastering smoke rings, the next three days of Ojibwe Language Camp were smooth sailing.

Geniusz is a proselytizer for language revival. She has interviewed tribal elders, put together CD-ROMs of language basics and created coloring books for kids. She attends Indian language revival conferences and exchanges tips with other tribal members, like Lone Wolf Jackson, an officer with one of the Mohegan tribes in Connecticut who is pushing his tribe to revive its language.

"I don't think we'll ever see the day when Mohegans are walking down the street speaking Mohegan to each other," Jackson told me when I met up with him at a conference on language revitalization. "But I do think we can learn enough to conduct a religious service or a funeral in our own language. And that would be profoundly important."

If you passed Jackson on the street, you would think he was black. And he is, on his father's side. But he was raised by the other side of his family, his mother and grandmother, who are Mohegan Indians.

"One of the motives behind the assimilation program was to get Indians to act like everyone else and not retain any cultural distinctiveness," philip Deloria says. The revival of Indian language may be the new front in resisting total assimilation. "For Indians to make a new argument of sovereignty, it will rely on a renewal of Indian distinctiveness."

Laura Redish sees language revival at the heart of the new anxiety of identity: "It also takes a commitment to learn a language. I've noticed that urban mixed bloods, especially, want to learn—to not be wannabes. And language shows they are serious about connecting to who they are."

From a small country lane in Connecticut, Stephanie Fielding rambled down a few dirt roads to a small clearing beside a rushing river. Her great-great-great-aunt Fidelia Fielding died in 1908, and a memorial stone dominates the sloping cemetery here. Fidelia was the last speaker of Mohegan. Today, Stephanie Fielding is devoted to reviving the language that Fidelia Fielding spoke. She travels from library to library scouring books and ancient missionary letters and documents. She is putting together her ancestral language, brick by brick, word by word.

You might mistake Stephanie Fielding for just another nice-looking lady with reddish hair and, judging from that name, British extraction. But she is a member of the wealthiest Indian tribe in America—the Connecticut Mohegans, whose members divide the revenue from two lucrative casinos. Fielding is 59, and she has devoted the rest of her life to reviving her great-great-great-aunt's language. This June, she received her master's degree in linguistics from M.I.T. Like so many people devoted to language restoration, she admires the example of Hebrew, a language that essentially died more than two millennia ago, surviving only as a sacred text. It wasn't until the 19th century that a Zionist linguist took on the painstaking work of confecting a modern, slangy, day-to-day tongue out of the hallowed idiom of Moses. Fielding is trying to do the same, and then some. She doesn't begin with a body of Scripture, like the revivers of Hebrew had, but with not much more than some missionaries' notes and transcripts of long-dead speakers. Most of Fielding's work at M.I.T. has focused on creating a kind of linguistic algorithm that will permit her to take many of the accepted proto Algonquian words and generate an authentic Mohegan vocabulary. Her tribe has commissioned her to put together a dictionary and a grammar to give the next generation a voice from the past.

Because it is time-consuming and difficult to learn any language, the commitment it takes to attend one of Wendy Geniusz's camps or to sign on with Fielding's work or to participate in any of the widespread Native American language revivals weeds out the easy hobbyists and leaves a cohort of Indians whose authenticity—regardless of genealogy or blood quantum—may one day be hard to question.

"Language is an important vehicle of transmission of culture," says Angela Gonzales, a Hopi Indian and an assistant professor of sociology at Cornell University. "Some tribes resist letting any outsiders even speak their language. But that's why language is important. It's a great vehicle for the storage of important inaccessible cultural material." Since it is no longer enough for a man passing you on the street to look Indian, maybe the next generation will note in passing that that guy certainly sounded Indian. In 50 years, many of the tribes now being dissed as wannabes will have age, tradition and solemnity on their side. Who will be around to question their authenticity? Far more likely is the possibility that the reshaping of American identity, among Indians as well as other ethnicities, will simply be accepted as the way it always was and always was meant to be.

Kathleen Hinckley, the executive director of the Association of Professional Genealogists, explains that she constantly gets calls from people asking her to "find an Indian" in the family tree. But she also says that such requests were part of a much larger surge of genealogical interest. Her membership of professional genealogists has leapt from 1,000 to 1,700 in the last five years. Genealogists will tell you the phone always rings most on Monday, the day after a Sunday family reunion when some aging great aunt finally confesses that her grandmother was a Chippewa or a Jew or from one of the noble clans of Scots, sending another anxious young American into the domains of ancestry.com or Hinckley's organization or into city-hall records to find the answer to the question What is my true past?

As an academic term, ethnic identity has long been associated with images of immigrant neighborhoods and ghettos—dense collections of Jews or Italians, Irish or Germans who maintained the old ways, married among themselves and maybe even kept up the old language. But today's scattered, more mobile generations have less access to such stable reservoirs of ethnic identity, which may account for this rise in ethnic shopping and the need to lay claim through participation in ethnic festivals or religious conversion or powwows to an identity that better suits the itch of our increasingly intermarried, interracial, intertribal America.

Textual Questions

1. Where and how does Hitt argue that the expectations of outsiders are causing modern tribes of Native Americans to lose touch with their true cultural roots?

2. What descriptive details does Hitt use in each paragraph to bring his subject to life for a reader? Which of these details are most effective? Which are least effective? Why?

3. Who are the "newest Indians" that Hitt describes? How are they defined by others? How do they define themselves?

Rhetorical Questions

4. What point does Hitt make about Native American casinos and their effects on various tribes? How effectively does he support this portion of his argument? How does this aspect of his argument connect with his overall argument?

5. In what ways is being a Native American an issue of race or ethnicity? How is it a legal and linguistic issue? How is it a construct, based upon such things as cultural expectations? How and where does Hitt discuss each of these definitions of Native American-ness? How effectively does he bring all of them together?

6. How does Hitt describe the past and present conditions under which Native Americans live/lived in America? Based on these descriptions of the past and present, what future for Native Americans does Hitt posit?

Intertextual Questions

7. How does Hitt's description of the modern plight of Native Americans compare and contrast with Martin Luther King, Jr.'s description of the lives of blacks in "I Have a Dream" (Chapter 1)?

8. How might President Lyndon Baines Johnson (see "The Great Society," Chapter 1) respond to Hitt's argument about Native Americans?

Thinking Beyond the Text

9. With what other groups—religious, ethnic, racial, cultural, and so on—can the struggle of Native Americans most legitimately be compared? Why?

10. How is language a part of Native American culture and identity? What role does language play in the past of Native Americans, their present, and their future? In what other groups is language a similar/dissimilar feature?

For Writing & Discussion

11. What tribes of Native Americans were/are native to the area in which you now live? How is their modern culture affected by the factors Hitt describes in his essay?

ANNA QUINDLEN

Anna Quindlen (1952–) is a contributing editor at *Newsweek*, a former *New York Times* Op-Ed columnist, and author of four novels, four nonfiction books, and two children's books. Quindlen has won many awards, including a 1992 Pulitzer Prize for Commentary for her *New York Times* column, "Public and Private," and two awards from the Association for Women in Communications: the Clarion Award for Best Opinion Column in 2002 and the Clarion Award for Best Regular Opinion Column in 2006. In 1995, the Child Welfare League of America created the Anna Quindlen Awards for Excellence in Journalism in Behalf of Children and Families.

In her back-page *Newsweek* column, "Final Words," Quindlen writes on a range of controversial topics such as immigration, the government's treatment of Iraq war veterans, privacy in an age of wiretapping, and women's rights. "We're Missing Some Senators," published in *Newsweek* in March 2005, takes a historical look at women's rights in the United States and at our current failure to ratify CEDAW, an international treaty of women's rights that has been signed by every other industrialized nation.

Quindlen's nonfiction books include *Being Perfect* (2005) and *A Short Guide to a Happy Life* (2000).

We're Missing Some Senators

✑ Prereading Question

Consider every level of government, from the local mayor and/or city council to state senators to the governor to members of Congress to the president. At each level, to what degree are women fairly represented, would you estimate? Why does this inequity exist when women make up more than 50 percent of the population—both nationally and globally?

A question in honor of Women's History Month: what does the United States have in common with Brunei, Somalia, Sudan and Oman? The answer: we are among only a handful of nations on earth that have refused to ratify the United Nations Convention on the Elimination of All Forms of Discrimination Against Women, a mouthful commonly called CEDAW. Jimmy Carter signed the treaty in 1980, and ever since it has languished in legislative limbo, waiting for the Senate to take action. While country after country, including such feminist strongholds as Iraq and Afghanistan, has at least paid lip service to the idea of an egalitarian society by supporting the treaty, we now stand alone as the sole industrialized nation that has not done so. "We've abdicated a leadership role in the single most important ongoing international women's-rights process," says Jessica Neuwirth, president of Equality Now.

Of course, we can boast that we're right up there with Somalia.

If only this were an aberration. I remember the halcyon days of the early '70s, when the Equal Rights Amendment was first introduced. Instead of focusing on the legal need—this was, after all, at a time when husbands could not be charged with raping their wives, and teachers could be dismissed from their jobs if their pregnant state began to show— the attention focused on the lunatic fringe. This resulted in an endless digression about unisex bathrooms, and no amendment. Score one for the protectors of the bad old days, when men were men and women were powerless.

And the same distraction tactics emerged recently as thousands of women leaders gathered at the United Nations to affirm a program for progress first developed a decade ago at a historic meeting in Beijing. Around the world women are being sold into sexual slavery, raped as spoils of war, even murdered in so-called honor killings. But the Bush adminis- tration held up the conference for days with a demand, unsupported by any other country, that a broad statement of principle include narrow and irrelevant language against abortion, a demand that was dropped after it garnered enough publicity to score points with the right wing. While con- sidering the great panorama of gender injustices in the world, the United States also managed to register its support for abstinence.

There was no similar support for international family planning. Progress in America in the last three decades can be linked directly to the increased participation of women and the increased participation of women can be linked directly to their ability to control their fertility. (Or perhaps American women have miraculously developed an innate ability to have only two children.) This president likes to talk about fight- ing for the freedom of women in the world, but he has a cynically selec- tive definition of what freedom means. Burqas, bad. Ballots, good. Birth control? Huh?

It's true that the women's movement has led to opportunities for many Americans that outstrip those elsewhere in the world. (One of the more ironic spectacles is listening as conservative women trash the women's movement, the movement that made their lives as activist lawyers, lobbyists and pundits possible.) Longtime opponents of CEDAW argue that we've come far enough on our own. They also insist incorrectly that the treaty would require the United States to provide paid maternity leave (horrors!) and to allow women in combat. Of course, women have been serving in combat since the gulf war, but it is convenient to pretend otherwise. Some conservatives also argue that if we ratify CEDAW we will have to prohibit Mother's Day. Score one for Hallmark.

Perhaps only Jesse Helms, who for years fought the treaty, was honest about the real impulse behind the obstruction. "I do not intend to be pushed around by discourteous, demanding women," he said on the Senate floor. There's the ubiquitous subtext: women are expected to ask nicely for human rights, and to say "please." A little lipstick doesn't hurt either. Score one for the protectors of the bad old days, when men were men and women were servile.

Like other international treaties, CEDAW amounts to a bill of rights, rights that may too often be honored in the breach, not so very different from "life, liberty and the pursuit of happiness." We may not need those rights in exactly the same way as women facing honor killings or genital mutilation. But, as we are so quick to note on other fronts, when the United States stands up for a principle it sends a message to the world about how that principle ought to be valued. Yet while America signs off on trade treaties and refugee treaties, it refuses to join the world community in standing up for the rights of women. Today some nations in Africa and Asia far outstrip us in female political representation. Even Iraq, under our tutelage, has written into its Constitution a guarantee that 25 percent of its legislators will be women. By my count, that means someone owes me 11 senators.

Textual Questions

1. With what nations does Quindlen compare America in her introduction and why?

2. Where does Quindlen use her own experiences to make points? Why? When does she refer to facts not related to her own experience and why?

3. How does Quindlen's essay focus—directly or indirectly—in every paragraph on the United Nations Convention on the Elimination of All Forms of Discrimination Against Women?

Rhetorical Questions

4. What tone does Quindlen take toward her subject? Why? How effective or ineffective is this tone?

5. How does Quindlen describe the situation in the 1970s that led to initial debates on the Equal Rights Amendment? How does she compare/contrast this increasingly distant time with the present and why?

6. In paragraph 5 Quindlen argues that progress in America since ca. 1970 is "linked directly to the increased participation of women and the increased participation of women can be linked directly to their ability to control their fertility." Two separate claims are being made here in this chain of causation: (1) women are the source of American progress in recent decades and (2) women are the source of American progress in recent decades because only in recent decades have women had the legal right to control their biological destiny—with everything from legal protection from marital rape to the legal right to have an abortion. Would you agree that either/both of these claims is/are valid? Why does Quindlen link them?

Intertextual Questions

7. How does Quindlen's characterization of the 1970s compare with the description of this same time offered by President Jimmy Carter (in the Introduction)?

8. How does Quindlen's argument compare/contrast with that made by Hillary Rodham Clinton in "Women's Rights Are Human Rights" (Chapter 1)?

Thinking Beyond the Text

9. At the end of her opening paragraph, Quindlen quotes Jessica Neuwirth, then president of Equality Now. What, aside from the United Nations Convention on the Elimination of All Forms of Discrimination Against Women, does this group believe in/support? Why? Does your opinion of either Quindlen or Equality Now change once you know more?

10. Internationally, which nations have the best/worst record of equal treatment for women? Where does the United States rank in relation to these other nations? Why?

For Writing & Discussion

11. Locate, either online or in your library, the full text of the United Nations Convention on the Elimination of All Forms of Discrimination Against Women. In a short essay, explain exactly what CEDAW argues. Which nations have/have not ratified this document?

FOCAL POINT

Exploring Images of The Promise of Equality and Civil Liberty

FOCAL POINT

Exploring Images of The Promise of Equality and Civil Liberty

Questions

1. Based on this photograph (page 634, top), what are your thoughts on segregation in America? How do you think Americans of all racial backgrounds felt when they encountered symbols of segregation such as the

one depicted in this photo? Would your interpretation be different if either the Caucasian or African-American were removed? How does the message compare and contrast with the message of the photograph of Martin Luther King, Jr., on page 118 in chapter 1?

2. In this photograph (page 634, bottom), new condominiums tower over a small neighborhood. How does this photograph support the arguments made in the selections "They're Coming for Your Land" Explain in detail.

3. If the photograph on page 635 (top) appeared within the selection "A More Perfect Union" by Jonathan Rauch, would it support or refute Rauch's argument? What do the facial expressions of the people say about their views on same-sex marriage? Does the fact that this couple—Hillary and Julie Goodrich—divorced in 2006 change your interpretation?

4. On the left side of this photograph (page 635, bottom), an unnamed opponent of same-sex marriage argues with Larry Kessler, in the jacket on the right, a supporter of same-sex marriage. What images in the background support/refute the positions of each person? How is your reaction to this photograph similar to or different from your reaction to the photograph of a same-sex couple on page 635?

5. What elements in this cartoon (page 636) indicate that it is responding to the terrorist attacks of 9/11? Does the time and place matter, ultimately, or could it make its argument as well at any time in American history? Name three other traumatic events from American history and explain how the message of this cartoon could apply to each.

⌒ 7 ⌒

AMERICA'S PROMISES

In the six preceding chapters, we asked that you consider the promises of America to the American people: the promise that all Constitutional rights, especially the right to vote and thus have a voice, are denied to no citizens based upon gender, race, and so forth; the promise that access to information that is not censored by a governmental agency will allow those same citizens to exercise their right to vote in an informed way; the promise that education serves as a leveler, giving everyone access to power, comfort, and some measure of stability and safety; the promise that health care, a basic, fundamental requirement of human happiness, will be available to all, citizens and noncitizens, the well-to-do and the welfare recipients alike; the promise that work, like education, provides a path to a future better than the past; the promise that all laws apply in the same measure to all Americans. In the end, these six promises come to the same conclusion: America's Promise is, at least in part, a promise of equality for all people—a promise built upon the fundamental belief that "all men are created equal" and are endowed with the same inalienable rights.

But the promise of America is not—and never was—meant to be limited to American citizens.

American republican democracy has its roots in ancient Greece, in the social experiment that the city of Athens embarked upon when the time of tyrants came to an end—for the first time, any way, and not forever. But Athenian democracy, with its every-man-has-a-voice-and-a-vote core, was anything but democratic in the modern sense. Athenians denied most rights, and even legal protections, to *metics,* the foreign barbarians that formed the vast majority of the population of the polis. Slaves were, of course, denied any and every right; in fact, in courts of law their testimony could only be admitted as evidence, if it was taken under torture. And there was no effort on the part of Athenian citizens to spread democracy beyond Athens. As their sphere of influence was pulled outward by the centrifugal force of empire, the centripetal force of Athenian democracy pulled inward. The people of her empire—beyond Athens—served to make Athenian democracy great, just as slaves would later serve to build the glory of republican Rome; the people of her empire did not exist as citizens—not in the way the Athenian citizens defined themselves and their legal rights and responsibilities. The value of the individual—politically and otherwise—inherent in modern conceptions of democracy was completely denied to all but the smallest group of men.

American republican democracy's roots can be traced to this ancient soil, but the idea (the ideal) of democracy has changed radically in the past two thousand (and more) years. The promise of America is a promise to its citizens, but it is a promise to the citizens of the world as well—a promise that the rights articulated in America's founding documents, especially the Declaration of Independence and the U.S. Constitution (see Chapter 1 and the appendix, respectively), are the rights that belong to the citizens of all nations. America does not exist to *give* anyone their rights; America exists to protect and to ensure the rights that belong to all people simply as their birthright, the rights discussed directly and indirectly in the preceding six chapters. Unlike its ancient progenitor, Athens, when the centrifugal force of American "empire" pulls outward, its ideal of representative democracy rides along.

In this chapter, we ask you to consider America's promises beyond America's shores, and many of the readings that follow discuss—directly or indirectly—the ongoing War on Terror, especially in Iraq. As you read the selections that follow, don't lose sight of the readings that came before: If America truly makes and attempts to fulfill the promises discussed in Chapters 1 through 6, then how do those promises become reality as they are pulled outward? Can we look forward to a future in which everyone on earth will share in America's Promise—in whatever way—or will that promise recede as Athens's promise did? Based upon the readings in Chapter 7, which of these futures is being set out now?

RICK WAGONER

Rick Wagoner (1953–), is the chairman and chief executive officer of General Motors Corporation, the world's largest automaker, where he has worked since receiving his MBA in 1977. In 2001 he was named Executive of the Year by *Automotive Industries.*

"Keep America Rolling" is a speech Wagoner gave to The Executives Club of Chicago on September 27, 2001. In it, Wagoner describes industry's role in responding to the September 11 attacks as making sure America stays economically strong, and details what he sees as GM's role in this effort.

As he mentions in this 2001 speech, one of Wagoner's goals as GM's top executive has been to improve the corporation's relationship with the Union of Auto Workers (UAW). After a rocky start during which he pressed hard for production at the cost of labor relations, Wagoner began working more closely with labor leaders. However, his 2005 announcement that several North American GM plants would be closing provoked criticism from union leaders. Wagoner defended the decision in a *Wall Street Journal* online article, "A Portrait of My Industry: GM Wants a Level Playing Field, Not a Bailout."

Keep America Rolling
Emerging Better, Stronger, and More Confident

∞ Prereading Question

When people speak of the events of September 11, 2001, they often speak of the human costs and the human consequences—from the loss of life in the terrorist attacks to the continuing loss of life in the War on Terror. Such considerations are, of course, important. But they are not the only considerations. Step away from the human costs and consequences and consider this: Economically speaking, what price did America pay—and is America still paying—for the attacks of 9/11? What price are other nations paying?

Delivered to The Executives' Club of Chicago, Chicago, Illinois, September 27, 2001

Thanks. Floyd. It's a pleasure to be here. I had planned to talk today on the subject of alliances. Specifically, about the growth and consolidation of the global auto industry, about GM's far-reaching alliance strategy, and about the pros and cons—especially the pros—of an alliance strategy in an age of instant communications, sophisticated consumers, and global markets.

As I say, that's what I had planned to talk about. Of course the events that have overtaken our nation and our world in the past several weeks have changed that focus.

Not GM's focus on alliances. Frankly, we have a terrific story to tell about this subject and what I believe could be an exciting new model for growth in a global economy. I hope that one day, under different circumstances. I'll have the chance to talk with you on that subject.

Today, though, I want to step back from "business as usual" and talk about how we—as business executives in a suddenly off-balance world—can continue to manage, and win, not only for our shareholders and customers and employees, but also for our country and, really, our way of life.

September 11, 2001, is one of those rare dates that splits history into a "before" and an "after." We've heard it a hundred times in the last 16 days, but I do believe it is true—our world has changed forever. It's this change, and our reaction to it, that I want to talk about this afternoon.

Of course, each of us will always remember where we were, and what we were doing, when we first heard about the terrorist attacks. I'll never forget. I was at the opening day of the Frankfurt Motor Show in Germany, where it was mid-afternoon, and I was giving a series of media interviews following a press conference in which GM and our subsidiaries unveiled several new vehicles.

The mood, as is almost always the case at major auto shows, was upbeat. We were excited about our products, and eager to talk about them and our plans for the future. Then we heard the first cryptic report about the first "accident" in New York and, of course, that gave us pause. But we continued—there seemed no reason not to. Slowly, though, the details began to trickle in, between interviews and then, as the reports grew more urgent, during the interviews themselves.

Suddenly, the collective mood of this enormous show turned completely around. The focus changed from new models and flashy concept vehicles to the events unfolding in New York, and Washington, and Pennsylvania. Like people all over the world, we left what we were doing to crowd around television sets and try to comprehend what it was we were seeing and hearing.

As it turned out, we couldn't get back into the U.S. for a few days—until late Friday. One of the things that really struck me while we worked and waited in Europe for our chance to return to the States was how swiftly and how intently the world reached out to us, as Americans. The outpouring of support from our colleagues in Germany, and throughout Europe, was simply incredible.

Then, after arriving home, I was again moved by the many personal messages of sympathy, support, and solidarity I had received from our many GM business partners—dealers, suppliers, joint-venture partners, and even competitors—from all around the globe.

It was extraordinary for me to realize that an act of terrorism that was so purposely aimed at breaking our spirit apart, had actually served to draw us closer together—and I'm not just talking about America. I mean virtually the whole world.

But the world truly had changed—and that meant we were all operating in uncharted territory. As individuals and as business executives—and in concert with our government—we're each now trying to find the right path through this territory.

As leaders within our own organizations, we're accustomed to wrestling every day with change. A month ago, I might have told you about some of the big changes facing the auto industry—changes that I suspect many of you are dealing with in your businesses, as well. Things such as:

- globalization
- excess industry capacity
- tougher competition
- or unprecedented industry consolidation.

The specific changes in my industry may be different from the changes in yours, but the consequences are the same—in today's fast-paced global economy, each of us is coping with forces that have the potential to completely transform our companies and our industries.

Many of us have undergone, or even led, crisis-management training to prepare for these forces of change. A month ago, I imagine that most of us felt fairly confident and prepared to deal with what we saw, at that time, as the potential threats facing our companies. But nothing prepared us for the shock of September 11. They certainly didn't teach that when I went to business school.

Today, each of us faces a common threat much greater than any we faced a month ago—a threat that packs the power to challenge—almost overnight—our economy, our industries, and of course our companies. That threat, boiled down to its most basic element, is really about confidence—confidence in our jobs, in the U.S. economy, in our national and personal security—in short, confidence in our future.

What can we do about it?

Last week, GM was asked by the Administration to host a meeting in one of our Detroit-area assembly plants. At this meeting were a group of business, labor, and government leaders, led by the Secretary of Commerce. Don Evans, and the Secretary of Labor, Elaine Chao.

Our purpose was to discuss what we—business, labor, and government—could do, together, to help America in the wake of the September 11 tragedy. And our overriding and unanimous conclusion was that the best way we can respond to the acts of terrorism on our soil is to keep the American economy strong—to keep our employees working, our factories humming, our economy growing, and our nation thriving.

This is a challenge with which GM is well acquainted. During World War II, GM supported the war effort by converting its factories to war production—tanks, planes, engines, trucks, and weapons—and quickly emerged as the backbone of what was called America's "Arsenal of Democracy."

Today, of course, we're dealing with an entirely different set of circumstances from those we faced 60 years ago—and different circumstances call for business to take a different role in the conflict. Our country, and all free countries, is facing a crisis that strikes at the very foundation of our open societies—from free expression to the free market. Business has a big role to play in safeguarding those freedoms, in what President Bush has called "the first war of the 21st century."

The bottom line from our meeting with Secretary Chao and Secretary Evans was that—in effect—we all need to "invest" now in America by working to support the American economy.

In fact, one of the politicians at the meeting commented that, when asked by her constituents what they personally could do to help America at this time, her advice was this: "after you give blood and make a donation, you should buy a car, buy a house, buy whatever you were planning to buy before the September 11 tragedy."

At GM, we couldn't agree more. And to help make that possible, we've introduced what we're calling our "Keep America Rolling" campaign.

The U.S. auto industry, as you know, is one of the key drivers of our economy. It accounts for 6.5 percent of U.S. manufacturing output, and nearly 4 percent of U.S. Gross Domestic Product, U.S. auto manufacturers and our first-tier suppliers employ about 1.2 million people, with another 2.6 million employed downstream in auto sales and servicing. Related automotive industries—everything from interstate trucking to car rentals—add another 3.2 million jobs. All told, the nation's automotive transportation sector accounts for a total of some 7 million jobs, or about 5.4 percent of the total civilian workforce.

At GM, we believe we have a special responsibility, as the largest U.S. automaker, to help stimulate the economy by making it easier, and more affordable, for Americans to purchase vehicles. That, in turn, supports the factory workers and parts suppliers and hometown auto dealers and others who depend on a healthy auto industry for their own livelihood.

That's one reason we're now offering 0-percent financing on every single GM car and truck—for a minimum of 36 months and, in some cases, for as long as 60 months. The scope of this incentive is unprecedented for GM—covering every vehicle we produce—but we believe it's the right thing for us to do to help keep the economy moving. Our primary goal is to help rebuild consumer confidence by demonstrating our own confidence in America and the American economy.

That's one way we at GM feel we can help. It's a start. But it's just a start. We will do more—all of us will—but frankly it's difficult to know exactly what to do. We're traveling unfamiliar ground—and the fact is that whatever we do is likely to be a delicate balancing act for corporate leaders and government officials alike.

Times of crisis require leadership. President Bush is providing strong leadership for our country. Our business community needs strong leadership now, as well—and as business executives, we have a responsibility to answer that call.

Let me repeat that: as business executives, in this time of crisis, we have a responsibility to answer the call for leadership.

How do we do it? How do we lead, through uncharted territory, to help get America rolling again?

There are three critical aspects of leadership we've been concentrating on at GM in the last two-and-a-half weeks—areas where I think we can make a difference right now.

Number one: we're engaging.

While we never can forget the horrible tragedy of September 11, I believe that it's time to engage—both ourselves and our company—in the new challenges that lie ahead of us. We must have a bias toward action. We want to get in the game, and make a difference—right now—in how our country responds economically to this crisis.

One of America's defining traits is our incredible resilience—our ability to absorb adversity and bounce back stronger than before. Through history, adversaries have underestimated our resolve and our strength. From Lexington and Concord to the Persian Gulf, from the Louisiana Purchase to the Apollo space program, we, as Americans, know how to set goals and see them through.

Well, we haven't forged that kind of history by sitting on the sidelines, or letting a few people carry the load, or letting our government solve all our problems. We've done it by chipping in, each and every one of us, to the best of our ability, and working hard until the job is done.

We've seen countless examples of that in the past two weeks—from heroic rescue efforts in New York and Washington, to the inspiring efforts of passengers to resist the hijackers on flight 93 over Pennsylvania.

We don't sit by in America and wait for things to get better—we find solutions, we work with one another to find a better way, and we help both our neighbors and ourselves. In short, we lead.

At GM, I've been telling our executives that we need to lead in two ways right now—we need to engage our employees by helping them regain their balance and, following that, we need to engage our company in the economic turnaround of the U.S.

With regard to our employees, we know they're back at work, determined to do their part, to make sacrifices—but like all Americans, they're grieving, they're angry, they're nervous, and they're distracted. And they're looking for leadership more than ever. That's why we're working overtime to reassure them that our facilities are secure, that our foremost priority is their safety, and that we understand that everyone is dealing with this tragedy, both at home and at work.

We're working to provide whatever means we can to help our people deal with the emotional side of the tragedy, from counseling, to communication, to personal example. We've asked our senior management to be highly visible right now, whether that means touring plants, or eating in the company cafeteria, or simply communicating with employees through e-mail and meetings.

As our nation and the world prepare for whatever comes next, we're working to demonstrate to our people that the company stands behind them and our nation. One concrete example: at GM we've told our people who are members of the National Guard or the Reserves, if they are called to active duty, we'll protect their incomes, and we'll assist their families while they're answering the call of duty.

In short, our approach at GM has been to take care of our people first, then to focus on ensuring that our company is fully engaged in keeping the economy moving—working with our employees, our suppliers, and our government to keep our plants running.

In ways that we never could have, or would have, predicted, this tragedy has reminded all of us of the importance of our work to the workings of the world economy. As leaders in America's business community, we have a critical role in keeping that economy strong—by keeping our companies strong.

We've absorbed a huge blow—now we must show the resilience and the resolve that America is known for, by working to break the inertia of the last several weeks and get our companies and our economy back in the game.

How do we do that? That's our second aspect of leadership focus at GM right now: we're prioritizing.

There's a lot of reassessment in our country right now. As a nation, we're trying to figure out who we are as a people, what our generation stands for, how we will respond to the crisis at hand. As business leaders, we must ensure that our companies undertake similar self-assessments—whether that means a short-term correction in reaction to immediate concerns, or a long-term change in strategy based on the new realities of the marketplace.

Clearly our first priority is the commitment to our people. Part of that commitment is a promise to keep our company healthy and strong. And that leads us to ask some tough questions—to re-evaluate virtually everything we do. Is it important? Is it critical? Can we do it better? Can we do without it?

We need to reevaluate our priorities throughout the company, and shelve—temporarily or permanently—the projects and initiatives that are not essential to the success of the business. Not only does this cause us to focus on what is most important to the success of our companies, it also helps our employees streamline their jobs at a time when many of them continue to struggle with the emotional affects of the crisis.

In short, we're stepping back from business as usual, prioritizing our needs, and working to make sure we take care of the big issues first—because those are the issues critical to the success of our businesses, and our nation's economy.

Dealing with those issues is, of course, a huge job. One of the ways we'll do it at GM right now is through our third aspect of leadership: we're renewing our commitment to innovation.

One of the qualities that has made America the most productive nation on earth is our ability to innovate. To take risks. Our inclination in uncertain times is often to hunker down and avoid risk—but we need to resist that urge, and do what we do best: innovate and improve.

At GM, for example, we've built our reputation—and our continuing 70-year run atop the global auto industry because, first and foremost, of our commitment to innovation. We're proud of that history—but, of course, we can't operate in the past. As Thomas Jefferson put it, "The past is a good place to visit, but I wouldn't want to live there."

My point is simply this: just as innovation got GM to the number one position in the global auto business—innovation has propelled the U.S. to be the most productive nation on earth. And it's innovation that will enable us to maintain that position in the years to come.

I spoke earlier of the changes we each face in our respective businesses and industries. In most cases, these forces of change still exist. They were overtaken by recent events—not necessarily overruled. One of our responsibilities is to address them—probably differently now—but to address them all the same. And at GM, we've found over the years that the best way to address change is to stay ahead of it through innovation.

Quite frankly, I feel strongly that it's innovation—technological innovation—that will help America defeat the terrorist threat that now faces us. And I believe it is also innovation—business innovation—that will help us keep our companies and our economy strong in the days to come.

In conclusion, I want to point out that—during these extraordinary times—many of the ordinary things we do have suddenly become "firsts." The first time you travel on an airplane since September 11. The first time you visit New York or Washington since September 11. The first meeting of the Executives' Club of Chicago since September 11.

We're living in a time of firsts—and that makes this a very uncertain period.

Gradually, those "firsts" will disappear. We'll tick them off as surely as we will get up every morning and do the work we need to do. Slowly, the uncertainty will fade, and the quiet strength that was America before September 11 will return to our nation and our lives.

When that time comes, we'll look back on these days and our strong resolve—as citizens, and as business leaders—to get America back on its feet—to keep America rolling—and we will be proud.

Let's start today. Let's, as business leaders, be proactive. Let's recognize our opportunity and, yes, our responsibility to help America confront the current challenge by keeping the American economy rolling, and emerging better, stronger, and more confident of our future.

Thank you.

Textual Questions

1. How does Wagoner, speaking only weeks after the terrorist attacks of 9/11, use the events of that September day as a focus for his speech?

2. According to Wagoner, what has changed in the post-9/11 world? How does he explain each of these changes?

3. In Wagoner's view, what can the auto industry as a whole—and GM in particular—do (in terms of leadership) in the wake of 9/11?

Rhetorical Questions

4. Wagoner speaks, not long after the attacks of 9/11, of the leadership that can be provided by the auto industry. Which of his ideas seems good for America? Which seem good for other nations? Which of them seem good for GM's business?

5. How does Wagoner use his own experiences—as an individual American and as a specific corporate CEO—to organize his text? Is his use of narrative effective or ineffective, given the time of his speech and its audience?

6. According to Wagoner's assessment of the situation, what must be done, in general, in order for America to return to its position of strength in the world? What does he call upon his audience members, specifically, to do? What makes his call to action particularly effective or ineffective?

Intertextual Questions

7. Compare and contrast Wagoner's vision of America's future to that of John Kerry, in "The Hope Is There" (this chapter). What similarities and differences do you see? How do both of these visions compare and contrast with that offered by President John F. Kennedy in "Ask Not What Your Country Can Do for You" (Chapter 1)?

8. How is Wagoner's argument similar to and different from that made by Robert Hinkley in "How Corporate Law Inhibits Social Responsibility" (Chapter 5)?

Thinking Beyond the Text

9. According to Wagoner, "the quiet strength that was America before September 11 will return to our nation and our lives" in the years to

come. In your opinion, what does "quiet strength" mean? Has it returned? How do you know? If it hasn't returned, then will it?

10. Is Wagoner's argument an example of American patriotism on display? Or is it an example of self-serving corporate rhetoric in a time of crisis? Why?

For Writing & Discussion

11. Near the beginning of his text, Wagoner argues that "our world has changed forever." He is speaking only 16 days after the terrorist attacks of 9/11, while you are reading his words at a date much further down the timeline. Was he right or wrong? Did 9/11 change everything? Or did the world eventually return to "normal"—and what does "normal" mean?

JIMMY CARTER

Jimmy Carter (1924–) was president of the United States from 1977–1981, and prior to that was governor of Georgia from 1971–1975. Since leaving office, he has served as a diplomat and done national and international humanitarian work, along with his wife Rosalyn, through the Carter Center. He and Rosalyn also work closely with Habitat for Humanity. Carter received a United Nations Human Rights Award in 1998, the Presidential Medal of Freedom in 1999, and won the Nobel Peace Prize in 2002. He also has been recognized by the International Institute for Human Rights, the American Arbitration Association, and the U.S. Institute of Peace.

Carter's op-ed article "Just War—or a Just War?" was published in the *New York Times* in March 2003. In it he draws on his experience as president and the international work he has done since to provide a perspective on American foreign policy and when going to war is a justifiable action. Other *New York Times* articles written since that time include "Principles Defeat Politics at the U.N." (2006), "Voting Reform Is in the Cards" (2005), and "Casting a Vote for Peace" (2004).

Carter writes for many other publications, including *Christian Century*, *National Geographic*, *Smithsonian*, and the *Washington Post* and has written 20 books. His most recent book, published in 2005, is *Our Endangered Values: America's Moral Crisis*.

Just War—or a Just War?

∾ Prereading Question

According to traditional Christian doctrines of the "just war theory," by Thomas Aquinas, the violence of a war must be proportional to the injury suffered that precipitates the war. Given Aquinas' argument about proportionality is the War on Terror a just war?

Profound changes have been taking place in American foreign policy, reversing consistent bipartisan commitments that for more than two centuries have earned our nation greatness. These commitments have been predicated on basic religious principles, respect for international law, and alliances that resulted in wise decisions and mutual restraint. Our apparent determination to launch a war against Iraq, without international support, is a violation of these premises.

As a Christian and as a president who was severely provoked by international crises, I became thoroughly familiar with the principles of a just war, and it is clear that a substantially unilateral attack on Iraq does not meet these standards. This is an almost universal conviction of religious leaders, with the most notable exception of a few spokesmen of the Southern Baptist Convention who are greatly influenced by their commitment to Israel based on eschatological, or final days, theology.

For a war to be just, it must meet several clearly defined criteria.

The war can be waged only as a last resort, with all nonviolent options exhausted. In the case of Iraq, it is obvious that clear alternatives to war exist. These options—previously proposed by our own leaders and approved by the United Nations—were outlined again by the Security Council on Friday. But now, with our own national security not directly threatened and despite the overwhelming opposition of most people and governments in the world, the United States seems determined to carry out military and diplomatic action that is almost unprecedented in the history of civilized nations. The first stage of our widely publicized war plan is to launch 3,000 bombs and missiles on a relatively defenseless Iraqi population within the first few hours of an invasion, with the purpose of so damaging and demoralizing the people that they will change their obnoxious leader, who will most likely be hidden and safe during the bombardment.

The war's weapons must discriminate between combatants and noncombatants. Extensive aerial bombardment, even with precise accuracy, inevitably results in "collateral damage." Gen. Tommy R. Franks, commander of American forces in the Persian Gulf, has expressed concern about many of the military targets being near hospitals, schools, mosques and private homes.

Its violence must be proportional to the injury we have suffered. Despite Saddam Hussein's other serious crimes, American efforts to tie Iraq to the 9/11 terrorist attacks have been unconvincing.

The attackers must have legitimate authority sanctioned by the society they profess to represent. The unanimous vote of approval in the Security Council to eliminate Iraq's weapons of mass destruction can still be honored, but our announced goals are now to achieve regime change and to establish a Pax Americana in the region, perhaps occupying the ethnically divided country for as long as a decade. For these objectives, we do not have international authority. Other members of the Security Council have so far resisted the enormous economic and political influence that is being exerted from Washington, and we are faced with the possibility of either a failure to get the necessary votes or else a veto from Russia, France and China. Although Turkey may still be enticed into helping us by enormous financial rewards and partial future control of the Kurds and oil in northern Iraq, its democratic Parliament has at least added its voice to the worldwide expressions of concern.

The peace it establishes must be a clear improvement over what exists. Although there are visions of peace and democracy in Iraq, it is quite possible that the aftermath of a military invasion will destabilize the region and prompt terrorists to further jeopardize our security at home. Also, by defying overwhelming world opposition, the United States will undermine the United Nations as a viable institution for world peace.

What about America's world standing if we don't go to war after such a great deployment of military forces in the region? The heartfelt sympathy and friendship offered to America after the 9/11 attacks, even from formerly antagonistic regimes, has been largely dissipated; increasingly unilateral and domineering policies have brought international trust in our country to its lowest level in memory. American stature will surely decline further if we launch a war in clear defiance of the United Nations. But to use the presence and threat of our military power to force Iraq's compliance with all United Nations resolutions—with war as a final option—will enhance our status as a champion of peace and justice.

Textual Questions

1. As a statesman, prolific writer on foreign policy, and former president of the United States, how does Jimmy Carter establish his authority to argue his interpretation of a then-looming attack on Iraq by the United States and its allies?

2. In the body of his essay, Carter develops five points, each in relation to one of the doctrines of the Just War theory, but he does not develop each of them evenly. Is this uneven development of points a strength or weakness of this text?

3. How does Carter build to his final argument about *not* using U.S. military power as a way to gain credibility internationally?

Rhetorical Questions

4. Who would be most likely to be persuaded by Jimmy Carter's argument? Why? What must audience members know and believe in order to be persuaded by this argument?

5. In the sixth paragraph, Carter seems to suggest that if the attacks of 9/11 could be linked to the government of Saddam Hussein in Iraq, then the war might be just. In your view, would such a link, if established, justify the U.S. war to liberate Iraq as a just war?

6. One of the principles of a just war is that its weapons must discriminate between enemy combatants and noncombatants. Is this ever truly the case in a war, however, or is this only an ideal—a standard not applicable to any actual war ever fought?

Intertextual Questions

7. In what ways does Carter's argument here compare with the argument of Martin Luther King, Jr. in "Letter from Birmingham Jail" (Chapter 6)?

8. In "Torture: Thinking About the Unthinkable," Andrew C. McCarthy (next in this chapter) makes an argument that could easily be based upon moral, ethical, or religious grounds but isn't. Is its religious foundation a strength or weakness of Carter's argument, ultimately, with the general American public? As a reader, does the fact that this essay rests firmly on a foundation of Christian doctrine make you more or less likely to be persuaded by the argument? Why?

Thinking Beyond the Text

9. Carter suggests that the United States will lose face worldwide if it goes to war in Iraq, which it did shortly after publication of this opinion piece. Did the United States, in fact, suffer the fate outlined briefly

by Carter, or was his warning about the consequences of war ultimately off base?

10. In paragraph 2, Carter states that his was a presidency "severely provoked by international crises." To what does he refer? How do the events he references in this way build his authority to speak on the issue of war with Iraq?

For Writing & Discussion

11. Consider the points Carter discusses about the Just War theory. Select one war from history—whether the United States was involved or not—and explain why, based upon Carter's summary of Aquinas's theory, the war you chose was/was not just.

A N D R E W   C .   M C C A R T H Y

Andrew C. McCarthy is an attorney and senior counterterrorism consultant at the Investigative Project, an anti-terrorist research organization in Washington, D.C. McCarthy was a federal prosecutor from 1986–2003, and from 2003–2006 he led the prosecution against the Islamic militants who were convicted of crimes including the 1993 World Trade Center bombing. He also helped convict four al-Qaida members who bombed the American embassies in Kenya and Tanzania in 1998. McCarthy received the U.S. Attorney General's Exceptional Service Award in 1996 and the U.S. Justice Department's Distinguished Service Award in 1988, and he is a former adjunct professor at the Fordham University School of Law and New York Law School.

McCarthy writes regularly for *Commentary* and *The National Review.* "Torture: Thinking About the Unthinkable" was published in *Commentary* magazine's July–August issue, 2004. In it McCarthy contextualizes the current debate about torture within the history of international law regarding prisoners of war, a particularly useful review given some claims, after the September 11 attacks, that old rules do not necessarily apply to the current situation.

McCarthy's other publications relating to terrorism, American actions, and Iraq include a June 2004 article in *The National Review,* "Iraq & al Qaeda: The 9/11 Commission Raises More Questions Than It Answers" and an April 2004 article in *Commentary* on "The Intelligence Mess: How It Happened, What to Do About It."

Torture: Thinking About the Unthinkable

∽ **Prereading Question**

Is there any situation you can imagine in which it is acceptable for the United States to allow torture, the deliberate, intentional infliction of physical and/or mental harm on an individual? When? Why?

The mortification of Iraqi prisoners by American military personnel at the Abu Ghraib prison in Baghdad has been discomfiting far beyond the impact of the now-infamous images. Coupled with other reports about harsh post-9/11 tactics to garner information from captured terrorists, and with ongoing investigations into deaths alleged to have occurred in connection with interrogations. Abu Ghraib and the reaction to it have forced front and center a profound national evasion: the propriety of torture.

As one would expect, the scandal has produced no small amount of righteous indignation. The civil-libertarian lobby, operating in overdrive, has issued ringing declarations that torture is unacceptable under any circumstances: accused the Bush administration of giving a green light to the humiliation of captives; and demanded the jettisoning of established international norms in favor of protocols codifying new rights for mass murderers. The financier George Soros, who has thrown millions of his billions behind various left-wing causes, recently proclaimed that Abu Ghraib was the functional equivalent of the 9/11 attack, only committed this time by the United States.

On the other side, deep disapproval of the abuse has been joined to brave talk about how we must make allowances for a "new kind of war," and to reminders that Abu Ghraib under American malefactors was a day at the beach compared with Abu Ghraib under Saddam and his ghouls and that our terrorist enemies, instead of stripping their captives naked and leashing them like dogs, tend to behead them instead. This is all true, as far as it goes, but it has been largely unaccompanied by any examination of the key question—namely, what are, and what are not, appropriate methods of interrogation? Appropriate, that is, according to American values and not the values of humanity's basest elements.

Finally, there are the centrists, who well understand that our enemies are covert operatives bent on killing us in sneak attacks, and that the only way to foil them is to get information about who they are and when and where they will strike next. Unfortunately, zealots inspired by Islamic militancy and willing to immolate themselves in suicide assaults are not likely to share their secrets under the comparatively mild duress of humane captivity. Thus, the centrists figure, there is probably some necessary torture afoot—which they think wrong, or at the very least unsavory, but from which they would prefer to avert their gaze.

This is all, as I say, to be expected, If the spectacle of ruthless mass murder à la 9/11 evokes blind vengefulness in some, in others it triggers deep-seated habits of denial or self-blame. In the meantime, the mere mention of torture is enough to engender disquieting thoughts of the dark brutality of which men (and women!) have historically shown themselves capable. Under the circumstances, rationality is not a good bet to rule the day. Nevertheless, it is where any discussion of the terrorist threat and how to deal with it must begin and end.

Terrorism in general is not a new phenomenon, but today's global and systematic menace is plainly not the threat that was contemplated when international humanitarian law, in the form of the Hague Convention, the Geneva Conventions, and the United Nations Convention Against Torture, took root. Those agreements were designed to institutionalize the laws of war, to promote the humane treatment of captured combatants, and to reduce civilian casualties in times of armed conflict. They were written for wars among readily identified forces—nation-states and, to some extent, intra-state liberation movements and organized insurgencies—in which conflict-appropriate tactics were well established and victory (or defeat) was easily visualized. They did not anticipate militant Islam: a sub-national force of international scope, with access to weapons of unfathomed destructive power. They did not contemplate a core methodology—targeting civilians, randomly torturing and killing prisoners—that grossly and willfully violates the very premises of humanitarian law. They did not take account of a situation in which our highest priority would be to obtain not territory or treasure but *intelligence,* and in which victory would be exceedingly difficult to define.

Does this mean that the time has come to upend the entire structure of the law of armed conflict? Hardly, The impulse for making law is driven by a firm grasp of what kinds of conduct are condemnable. The fact that militant Islam has organized itself precisely within the parameters of the *universally* condemnable—that the terrorists, to adapt Daniel P. Moynihan's famous phrase, have defined deviancy right down to the bottom—is not a reason to reshape norms in order to license execrable behavior. Rather, it compels us to weigh the overriding imperative of our national security, without which our own civil liberties would be nonexistent, against the sanctity and dignity of human life, even when that life belongs to a captured terrorist. In the end, it compels us to ask rationally whether torture is ever permissible.

Before coming to that central issue, it would be helpful to clear away some underbrush surrounding the question of who may lawfully be held for questioning. This is necessary because humanitarian-law activists, many of whom seem more preoccupied with the treatment of terrorists than with the carnage wrought *by* terrorists, have been working feverishly to convince us that the government's denial of prisoner-of-war (POW) status to al Qaeda terrorists captured in Afghanistan and held in Guantanamo Bay, Cuba, somehow caused the abuse of actual POW's in Iraq.

As it happens, however, whether one is or is not a POW is a matter not of a moment's intuition but of long-settled principle—of, one might even say, merit. "POW" is an honorable legal status. In order to earn that status, and its protections, one is expected to conduct oneself honorably. Granting it to combatants who do not do so would only offer a further incentive to belligerents to act dishonorably. Granting it to terrorists, in particular, would gravely endanger the lives of countless civilians—which, in the greater scheme of things, would lead to far worse evil than the deplorable treatment of a relative handful of prisoners.

It may well be that the failure adequately to regulate and monitor interrogation practices led to a culture that made Abu Ghraib more likely. That, however, has little to do with the legal *status* of those being interrogated. And it is incongruous, to say the least, to assail the Bush administration for the alleged consequence of a perfectly appropriate decision concerning the status of terrorists while ignoring the foreseeable (in truth, inevitable) consequence of abolishing the very distinctions on which that status rests. The whole rationale for having POW rules in the first place is to encourage civilized warfare and to protect civilians.

Where, then, do those distinctions come from? The relevant principles, developed over centuries, have been passed down to us primarily as codified in the Hague Convention IV of October 18, 1907 and the Geneva Conventions of August 12, 1949, particularly the Third, which addresses the "Treatment of Prisoners of War." It is crucial to remember that these are laws of war, and that the primary object in wartime is forcibly to defeat the enemy. In that sense, they constitute a practical effort to limit abuse and suffering while remaining ever cognizant of the martial context, which is to say of each side's drive to win. Moreover, these laws do not purport to prevent all discomfort to captives or all collateral damage to civilians and non-combatants. Rather, they seek to establish normative guidelines in which legitimate military objectives are pursued without causing disproportionate harm, fully understanding that harm is, to some extent, unavoidable.

The Hague Convention conveys the honorable notion of "lawful" or "privileged" combatant. During wartime, combatants are privileged to employ military force if they are members of a national army or of a militia that is part of such an army and that conducts itself accordingly, meaning that its members are subject to a formal chain of command; wear uniforms (i.e., "have a fixed distinctive emblem recognizable at a distance"); carry their weapons openly; and conduct their operations in accordance with "the laws and customs of war."

And what are those laws and customs? By the early 20th century, they comprised a well-founded balance of military necessity with humanitarian considerations based on the principles of "proportionality" and "distinction." The first called for factoring the likely damage to civilian infrastructure into the calculus for identifying proper military objectives: the second, for limiting acceptable targets to those objectives. The legal scholars David B. Rivkin, Jr. and Lee A. Casey have usefully summarized the resultant set of rules, which were long ago accepted "by all civilized states":

> (1) only sovereign states have the right to make war; (2) civilians cannot be deliberately attacked; (3) combatants can be attacked either en masse or individually; (4) quarter is to be granted when sought; (5) lawful combatants, when taken prisoner or otherwise incapacitated by wounds, are to be accorded the respect and privileges due prisoners of war (POW's); and (6) while all forms of force can be deployed in combat, certain weapons designed to cause unnecessary suffering are proscribed.[1]

Two other laws are likewise important for our purposes here, and are logically antecedent to rule (5) above: captured combatants may be held until the conclusion of hostilities, and they may be interrogated. Lately there has been much caterwauling over these points, particularly as they relate to captured members of al Qaeda. Leaving aside for the moment whether such persons may be classified as lawful combatants, their detention is routinely decried as unacceptable because it is "indefinite"—as if there has ever been a war in which captives could be assured that hostilities would end on a date certain.

In fact, the theory behind these laws is simple and irrefutable. Captives may be held "indefinitely" because if they are released they are likely to rejoin the battle, thus prolonging the war and its attendant suffering. By contrast, imposing a maximum and arbitrarily chosen period of detention (say, three years) would defeat the logical purpose of the detention. Similarly, captives may be questioned because they are likely to have information which, if learned by the captor state, will protect its forces, make it easier to pinpoint legitimate military targets of strategic importance, and secure victory more promptly—all of which saves lives.

The Geneva Conventions, promulgated in the middle of the last century, offered additional humanitarian protections. What impelled their drafting were the widespread atrocities visited upon captured prisoners of war during World War I and the savagery of World War II, in which civilians were broadly targeted, exterminated, and subjected to sundry lesser horrors. These 1949 accords are generally applicable only between and among national powers that have entered into them.

The Third Geneva Convention affords specific protections to prisoners of war: that is, lawful or privileged combatants who have been captured while taking part in hostilities. POW status is generally limited to two categories: members of the armed forces of nations that are parties to the conflict, and members of militias and organized resistance movements that

[1]"Unleashing the Dogs of War," the *National Interest,* Fall 2005.

belong to a nation that is a party to the conflict, provided they fulfill the conditions mentioned above (being part of a formal chain of command, wearing uniforms, etc.).

Those who satisfy these criteria are entitled "in all circumstances to respect for their persons and their honor." POW's, moreover, "must at all times be protected, particularly against acts of violence or intimidation and against insults and public curiosity." Similarly prohibited are "measures of reprisal against" them. The detaining power, in addition, is required to provide all POW's with health care and maintenance and to show no preference based "on race, nationality, religious belief, or political opinions, or any other distinction founded on similar criteria." Furthermore, while POW's may be questioned broadly, they are obligated to reveal—in the time-honored formulation—only their name, rank, and serial number. Finally, "prisoners of war who refuse to answer may not be threatened, insulted, or exposed to unpleasant or disadvantageous treatment of any kind."

Militant Islamic terrorists like those belonging to al Qaeda manifestly do not qualify for POW status because they are not lawful combatants: they are not part of a nation state, they are not signatories of the Geneva Conventions, they do not wear uniforms, they do not as a rule carry their weapons openly, they hide among (and thus gravely imperil) civilian population and infrastructure, and they intentionally target civilians for indiscriminate mass homicide in order to extort concessions from governments they oppose. As a result, they do not enjoy the special privileges of POW's, such as entitlements during interrogation to limit their answers to "pedigree" information and to refuse to answer other questions.

But there is a complication. It is true that the 1949 protocols do not apply to al Qaeda. Nevertheless, even those who rightly maintain that the general protections of the Conventions are unavailing to terrorist organizations have found in them a high-minded proscription against torture that extends to everyone including terrorists. As best I can tell, this interpretation is rooted in a pertinent passage of Article 3 (common to all four Conventions):

> Persons taking no active part in the hostilities, including members of the armed forces who have laid down their arms and *these placed bors de combat by* ... *detention* ... shall in all circumstances be treated humanely[.] [and not subjected to] violence to life and person, in particular, murder of all kinds, mutilation, cruel treatment and torture[,] [nor to] outrages upon personal dignity, in particular humiliating and degrading treatment. [Emphasis added.]

This provision, it should be noted, does not literally compel the construction that has sometimes been placed on it. Indeed, it seems plausible that the phrase, "those placed hors de combat by ... detention," was intended only to modify "members of the armed forces"—i.e., lawful combatants belonging to the signatories' armies, some of whom may have been rendered hors de combat by detention. The fact that the provision is widely interpreted as extending anti-torture protection to nonsignatories almost certainly owes more to the general disrepute in which murder and torture are held by the civilized world than to any putative desire of the framers to create an entirely new category, otherwise left virtually unmentioned in the four Conventions.

But the bottom line is that, arguably, captured terrorists may not be lawfully subjected to torture. Is that the end of the matter?

To answer that question requires a look at more law; specifically, a convention developed more than a quarter-century after the 1940 Geneva Conventions took effect. This was a protocol to the Conventions, known as Protocol I Additional, dated June 8, 1977 and relating to the "Protection of Victims of International Armed Conflicts."

The late 70's one should recall, was the heyday of home-grown insurgencies and "national liberation" movements. These groups, in collusion with Western human-rights activists, pushed to extend Geneva protections to members of nonstate militias—often, guerrillas engaged in fighting colonial powers or other regimes backed by the West (especially the United States). Protocol I, as Rivkin and Casey have observed, was the fruit of that effort.

Not only does the accord grant POW status to such guerrillas, but it actually gives them a number of significant advantages over traditional nation-state armies. It allows them to maintain their privileged combatant status even if they have concealed their arms until very shortly before attacking, and it makes it unlawful to use force against them unless they are in the act of preparing an attack or attacking—thus permitting them to dictate the time and place of battle. Protocol I tips the scales even further by its rule of nonreciprocity, under which combatants in nonstate militias do not forfeit their privileged status even if they routinely violate international humanitarian law, which they are of course far more likely to do than are national armies.

It will come as no surprise that most of Europe—including England—signed on to Protocol I. The United States, however, did not, precisely because the protocol's loosening of traditional just-war strictures would have the effect of protecting, and thus encouraging, irregular forces like terrorist organizations that pose a lethal threat to civilian populations. This disagreement between the U.S. and its key allies on so rudimentary a matter as what rules should apply to the treatment of non-state combatants has caused no small number of problems in recent conflicts, including NATO's operations in the Balkans and coalition activities in Afghanistan and Iraq. The strains have induced Washington to fudge its opposition to Protocol I—formally opposing it but, for example, suggesting in such authoritative publications as the 2002 edition of the Army's *Operational Law Handbook* that much of its substance is "either legally binding as customary international law or acceptable practice though not legally binding."

Unfortunately, this purposeful ambiguity has not only fostered uncertainty about what the law requires but has created a platform for domestic activists whose interventions have redounded to the benefit of terrorists at the very time we are most threatened. Thus, Kenneth Roth, the executive director of Human Rights Watch, warned in a December 2002 letter to President Bush that our treatment of al Qaeda detainees held at Guantanamo Bay could place the U.S. in violation of Protocol I. Skirting the inconvenient fact that the U.S. is not a signatory to the protocol. Roth deftly observed that the document "is recognized as restating customary international law"—which makes his position sound materially similar to the American Army's.

Still, ambiguity aside. Protocol I has never been ratified and as such is not binding on the United States. I hasten to add that this is immaterial as far as the Iraqis held at Abu Ghraib are concerned. Iraq is a party to the Geneva Conventions; its military personnel, apprehended in wartime, were POW's; and the U.S. conceded as much at the beginning of hostilities. Thus, even mild forms of abuse, much less the nightmarish indignities that occurred at Abu Ghraib, are violations of international law.

As for captured al Qaeda terrorists, however, none of this should be taken to suggest that it was, or is, improper to subject them to far more aggressive techniques of interrogation than can be applied to POW's. But torture? That is another matter.

Let me spell it out. It is illegal in the United States, under any circumstances, to torture *anyone*—even unlawful combatant terrorists who may have information about ongoing plots that, if revealed, could save thousands of lives. Period.[2]

There are two reasons for this, neither of them having to do with how one chooses to interpret the murky language of Article 3 of the 1949 Geneva Conventions (the one proscribing torture of some, or all, detainees). The first reason is that the United States is a signatory to an international treaty barring torture: this is the United Nations Convention Against Torture and Other Cruel, Inhuman, or Degrading Treatment or Punishment. The treaty is dated December 10, 1984 and was ratified in 1994, thus earning the force of binding law. The second reason is that federal law also categorically prohibits torture.

What constitutes torture under these laws? In Article 1 of the UN convention, torture is expressly and very broadly defined as any act, done at the direction or with the knowing acquiescence of a public official, by which

---

[2]The very clarity of the proscription is what prompted controversy earlier this month when reports emerged that government lawyers had struggled unconvincingly in 2005 to craft ways around these laws.

severe pain or suffering, whether physical or memal, is intentionally inflicted on a person for such purposes as obtaining from him or a third person information or a confession, punishing him for an act he or a third person has committed or is suspected of having committed, or intimidating or coercing him or a third person, or for any reason based on discrimination of any kind.

What about exigent circumstances? What about a state of active combat in which causing severe "physical or mental" discomfort to a captive might elicit intelligence that will save the lives of troops? What about a war against a terrorist network in which nonlethal torture against a known mass murderer might induce him to reveal plans, say, to detonate a nuclear device in New York Harbor? The treaty turns a deaf ear. In Article 2, it states flatly: "No exceptional circumstances whatsoever, whether a state of war or a threat of war, internal political instability or any other public emergency, may be invoked as a justification of torture." Not content with that, the convention dictates (in Article 16) that each signatory state must "undertake to prevent in any territory under its jurisdiction other acts of cruel, inhuman, or degrading treatment or punishment" even if they are not so severe as to "amount to torture as defined in Article 1."

Pertinent questions arise here for Americans. What about the death penalty? What about when the police cause severe physical harm to a suspect during a disputed arrest? Well, such matters are indeed exempted from the treaty its definition of torture excludes "pain or suffering arising only from, inherent in, or incidental to lawful sanctions." More importantly for our purposes, the U.S. Senate, in ratifying the treaty, registered some stringent caveats, insisting on the preservation of capital punishment and limiting our acceptance of the proscription of "cruel, inhuman, or degrading treatment or punishment" to the relevant understandings enshrined in the "Fifth, Eighth, and/or Fourteenth Amendments to the Constitution."

This was critical. As is well known, the Eighth Amendment bars "cruel and unusual punishments." But, as Alan M. Dershowitz reminds us in his 2002 book, *Why Terrorism Works.* American courts, including the Supreme Court, have held that its protection extends only to those already convicted of crimes; that is, the "punishments" it regulates are those meted out *after* guilty verdicts. Similarly with the government's mandate under the Fifth and Fourteenth Amendments to provide "due process of law": again, that term pertains almost exclusively to judicial proceedings and its substantive content is, to put it mildly, highly debatable.

Let us assume, for example, that the Abu Ghraib abuses were deemed to fall short of the "severe pain or suffering" needed to qualify as "torture." Could a humiliated prisoner find recourse in the "cruel, inhuman, or degrading treatment" provision of the UN treaty? No, according to Dershowitz his plight has nothing to do with judicial proceedings—he is being held by the military in wartime. Indeed, Dershowitz contends that the Senate's caveats limit the applicability not only of the treaty's "cruel, inhuman, or degrading" clause but even of its proscription against torture itself.[3]

Whatever qualifications may attach to the treaty, however, it cannot credibly be argued that torture is permissible—that is, beyond the reach of U.S. law—as long as it occurs outside the parameters of a judicial proceeding. That is because, fulfilling an aspiration expressed in the torture convention, the U.S. in 1994 enacted stringent anti-torture laws of its own.[4] In some ways, these laws define torture even more broadly than the UN convention. They proscribe any act (other than those incident to lawful sanctions like the death penalty) that is "specifically intended to inflict severe physical or mental pain or suffering." In other words, and contrary to the UN treaty's own slightly narrower definition, an act need not be motivated by a purpose to obtain information, to punish, or to intimidate for it to be considered torture in American law.

Nor is that all. Federal law also makes "severe mental pain or suffering" actionable with respect to a wide variety of menacing behavior. As long as mental harm is "prolonged," it is grounds for torture charges if the harm results from the intentional or threatened infliction of severe physical pain or suffering; from the administration or threatened administration of "mind-altering substances or other procedures calculated to disrupt profoundly the senses or the personality"; from a "threat of imminent death"; or from threats that another person will imminently be subjected to such abuses. Not only those who engage in such behavior but those who conspire to engage in it, even if they are unsuccessful, are subject to prosecution.

If such behavior results in death, it may itself be punished by the death penalty; in other cases, it may be punished with up to twenty years' imprisonment. Nor does it matter where in the world the offense takes place; an American citizen may be prosecuted, and so may a foreign torturer who happens to be found on U.S. soil.[5] As a matter of law, then, torture in this very expansive understanding is absolutely prohibited. The only question remaining is: should it be?

Just imagine, in this culture, having the temerity to say out loud: "I am in favor of torture." One might as well declare oneself in favor of child molestation (or tobacco). In point of fact, however, many people—probably most people—who claim to be opposed to torture are not against it in all

---

[3] *Why Terrorism Works,* p 136 I respectfully disagree: the Senate's caveats apply only to the "cruel, inhuman, or degrading" clause, not to torture. See, for example, *Senate's Advice and Consent* (www.umn.edu/humanrts/usdocs/tortue.html), and sell also Douglass Cassel, "The United States and the Torture Convention. A Useful Dialogue," *Center for Human Rights Commentators* (May 24, 2000).

[4] Codified under Title 18, U.S. Code. Sections 2340, 2340A & 2340B.

[5] The 1991 Torture Victim Protection Act, codified under Title 28, U.S. Code, Section 1350, note.

cases or in every form. Many, indeed, are no doubt secretly relieved that it goes on regardless of what the laws and the regnant pieties may dictate.

Seventy percent of Americans, all of whom presumably oppose killing, favor the death penalty. A comparably sizable number who oppose abortion favor its availability in cases of rape, incest, or where the life of the mother is at risk. All sensible people oppose the slaughter of innocent civilians, but an overwhelming number favor war if the evil it seeks to defeat is worth fighting against, even if war will ineluctably lead to the slaughter of innocent civilians.

Torture is not meaningfully different. Considered in a vacuum, it is a palpable moral evil. Moral evils, however, do not exist in a vacuum; they exist in collision with other evils, and sometimes we are forced to choose. Ask the average person if he opposes torture and the answer will surely be yes. But present him with a real-world scenario and the answer may well change.

Let us posit a terrorist, credibly believed to have murdered thousands of people. Suppose this terrorist is aware that a radiological bomb will be detonated momentarily in the heart of a major metropolis, but is refusing to impart the details to interrogators. Now, suddenly, black and white becomes gray: perhaps there are worse evils than some forms of torture. That does not mean our average person "favors" torture, but he may well be amenable to keeping it on the table as an option, and henceforth not so disposed to declare confidently that he opposes it in any form under all circumstances.

The obverse goes for the *proponent* of torture. As Dershowitz notes, arguments for torture are often crudely cast in terms of raw numbers: e.g., the torture of one guilty person would surely be justified to prevent the torture or death of a hundred innocent persons. But would it, without qualification? Are there lengths to which proponents might be unprepared to go? Of course there are. The vast majority of people who would favor torture in this case would oppose it if the form of abuse were inhumanly grisly; most would probably oppose a method that might lead to death (although that too might change if the situation were dire enough and especially if the person to be tortured were already facing execution). Moreover, most if not all people open to the rare application of torture in order to prevent terrorist acts would be immovably opposed if the torture involved abusing moral innocents—like harming a terrorist's children to induce him to talk—or in the absence of persuasive grounds for believing a terrorist attack was imminent.

All of which is to suggest that a significant gap exists between our wishes and reality. This is hardly unusual, either in life or in law. Take the canons of ethics that govern the behavior of attorneys. They are divided into two sections: ethical considerations and disciplinary rules. The former are the high principles that lawyers are enjoined to emulate; the latter are threshold commands of which they must not fall short on pain of sanction. So it is with torture. Even as we sincerely aspire never to resort to it, we are required to acknowledge that there are some instances in which it might be employed: therefore, it is incumbent upon us to regulate how and under what circumstances that could permissibly be done, and to prosecute aggressively those who step outside the parameters we undertake to define.

This conclusion, however reluctantly arrived at, is informed in part by the unpersuasiveness of the tactical and moral arguments parroted ubiquitously by the opponents of torture in the wake of Abu Ghraib. On the tactical level, it has been repeatedly asserted that torture simply does not work. The victim, it is said, has such a powerful incentive to tell the torturer what the torturer wants to hear that anything he says is by definition unreliable.

This claim might be made about countless other human endeavors in which inducements to act for ignoble reasons are similarly rampant, from politics to business to police work. It is thoroughly spacious. A witness tempted to cooperate by the promise of a lenient sentence has a powerful motive to testify falsely to a version of events that he thinks might improve the prosecutor's case. A defendant who testifies in his own behalf has a different but no less strong incentive—namely, avoiding jail or perhaps death—to give a false exculpatory account. In neither situation is it necessarily the case that the witness will lie, or that, if he does, the lie will escape notice. Information from witnesses beset by intense pressure inherently suspect but far from intrinsically unreliable.

Torture is no different. The victim may have been given an incentive to say what he thinks his torturer wants to hear, but that does not mean his compelled words are untrue. Nor does the victim necessarily even know what his torturer wants to hear. Nor can he know that he will not be tortured further if he intentionally misleads his tormentor. In fact, it could just as plausibly be asserted that torture is an ironclad guarantee of honesty as of misinformation. Neither statement holds water as an absolute, and, on the level of tactics, neither offers a sound reason either to permit or prohibit torture. As Dershowitz documents in detail, torture has been known to be a very effective method to get at truth; that it is not foolproof is hardly a reason to prohibit its selective use.

Then there is the moral argument: torture is an abomination so profound that permitting it, even if limited to rare and dire emergencies, constitutes an indelible blight on a society and its laws. So stated, the proposition has undeniable appeal. But "torture" is a loaded word. No one, it is fair to say, favors a policy of complete laissez-faire. What is envisioned instead is the administration of pressure that is capable of causing extreme pain—Dershowitz gives the example of sterile needles forced under the fingernails—but is nonlethal.

To be sure, even reading or thinking about such practices may make the teeth clench and the stomach churn. But consider: when sufficiently provoked, we already permit far worse. Capital punishment may be more humane than it used to be, thanks to lethal injection, but unlike torture it is forever. If we were to offer a choice—severe pain or execution—to convicts on death row, can there be any doubt which most of them would elect? Our weapons of war are "smarter" than they used to be, with precision targeting and the rest, but they still kill, mutilate, and maim with much less discrimination than we comfort ourselves to imagine. Is torture, with just cause and creating far less devastation, morally worse just because it is inflicted in a room looking the victim in the eye rather than from thousands of feet in the air where victims are unseen?

Equally significant from the moral point of view, one should think, are the consequences of the *current* system, in which we mouth our opposition to all torture while knowing full well that forms of it are occurring, with greater frequency than should be acceptable to anyone, inside many officially civilized countries that are signatories to the UN convention. It is here that Dershowitz is at his most trenchant: true civil libertarians are required to concern themselves with real-world outcomes rather than with proclaimed intentions, whether cynical or pure-hearted. By imposing an absolute ban on something we know is occurring, we promote disrespect for the rule of law in general and abdicate our duty to enact tailored and meaningful regulations. Both of these failings have the juggernaut effect of increasing the total amount of unjustifiable and otherwise preventable torture.

The task, then is to create controlled, highly regulated, and responsibly accountable conditions. Toward this end. Dershowitz has proposed the notion of torture warrants. Under such a system, the government would have to apply to a federal court for permission to administer a predetermined form of nonlethal torture. The warrant would be issued only on a showing of reasonable grounds for believing that a catastrophe was impending, that the person to be subjected to torture had information about this event, that he had been given immunity (meaning, his statements could not be used against him in court and therefore he could not invoke the Fifth Amendment privilege against self-incrimination as a basis for refusing to answer), and that he had nevertheless remained silent.

Other conditions might be added. There could be limitations on who would be eligible for such treatment: for example, convicted terrorists or those who, even if not previously convicted, could be demonstrated to be terrorists according to some rigorous standard of proof. Application would have to be made with the approval of a high-ranking government official—the decision could not be entrusted to a twenty-three-year-old reservist assigned as custodian of a brig for mass murderers. Since torture would now be permitted, under stricture and with scrupulous judicial monitoring, no excuse would exist for engaging in torture outside the process, and those shown to have done so would be vigorously prosecuted.

In my estimation, this is a worthy proposal, far superior to the current hypocrisy that turns a blind eye to that which it purports to forbid. But my own approach, although based on the same underlying aims—minimizing the instances of actual torture and making its application more forthright, more transparent, and more accountable—is somewhat different. The struggle against militant Islamic terrorism, I believe, calls for an across-the-board rethinking of our current system as it relates not only to interrogations but also to the detention of unlawful combatants and to the trials of members of international terrorist networks, which our judicial system and its due-process standards are not designed to accommodate.

Elsewhere I have proposed the establishment of a national-security court, structured along the lines of the current Foreign Intelligence Surveillance Court. This would be a tribunal, drawn from the national pool of federal judges, that would have jurisdiction over, and develop an expertise in, matters of national security. It would monitor the detention of terrorist captives (deferring to the executive branch's decision to detain in the first place), and it would conduct trials of terrorists whom the government elected to charge under special rules that would apply only in national-security cases. This would replace the current paradigm in which the enlightened procedures of our criminal-justice system, designed to protect Americans accused of crimes and presumed innocent until proved otherwise, has been warped as we strain to apply them to terrorists in whose hands those same procedures imperil public safety.

Refining our consideration of torture would be of a piece with this proposed overhaul. With torture strictly limited to national-security matters, and unavoidably involving highly classified information about terrorist networks, the new national-security court would be the place to consider, and monitor the execution of, torture warrants. These could be sought, in turn, only by the Attorney General or by a high-ranking Justice Department official designated for this purpose by the Attorney General.

Centralizing this sensitive matter in a single court would ensure that the standards developed for warrants win rigorous adherence rather than (as in Dershowitz's proposal) being subject to tinkering by hundreds of federal judges in scores of districts throughout the country. It would also ensure speedy determinations—a critical point since torture would be permitted only under circumstances of imminent peril. Warrants would undoubtedly be rarely sought and rarely granted, but a judge who had previously dealt with even one would be in a far better position to decide quickly than a judge for whom this was uncharted territory. To bolster the new system's integrity and effectiveness, periodic reports would be made to the appropriate committees of Congress.

It goes without saying that amending our laws to permit limited, regulated torture would unleash torrents of obloquy throughout the world, not least in the Islamic countries and in Europe—two places, it must be observed, with shameful legacies of ruthless prisoner abuse. Nevertheless, our cause would be just: to demonstrate our seriousness about dealing with torture, to reduce its incidence, to make its practitioners accountable, and to ensure that in this new kind of war that is almost entirely about intelligence, we are not unduly deprived of information that may save thousands of lives.

Abu Ghraib presents an opportunity to deal with this wrenching issue in a practical, responsible, and honorable way. The wrong would lie in failing the summons.

6"Abu Ghraib and Enemy Combatants," *National Review Online*, May 11, 2004.

Textual Questions

1. How does McCarthy use a specific example—the abuse of prisoners by U.S. military personnel at Abu Ghraib prison in Iraq—to lead into the larger issue of torture? How effective is this move from specific to general?

2. McCarthy divides his argument into eight sections. Briefly summarize each in three sentences. Given the shift in topic from section to section (which is easier to see in your summation than in the original text), how does McCarthy build his overall argument as he moves from Abu Ghraib to his conclusion, where he very briefly returns to this same topic?

3. At its heart this is an essay about definitions. What are the key terms that must be defined in each section in order for McCarthy to make his argument? How is each term defined?

Rhetorical Questions

4. According to McCarthy, how and why is an enemy who is taken into custody classified as a POW? What are the implications of this specific classification?

5. How does McCarthy describe the Geneva Convention and Protocol I? How does his description of both connect with his argument about torture and the War on Terror? Are the connections he makes ultimately persuasive to you or unpersuasive?

6. While the use of torture is a legal issue, it is also a moral and ethical issue, one that touches upon the value a society places upon all life—even

the life of a sworn enemy. Why might such an issue be so difficult to handle in the American context—legally, politically, and socially?

Intertextual Questions

7. McCarthy argues about torture in its historical and legal senses, while Michael Levin makes a very different argument in "The Case for Torture" (Chapter 6). Ultimately, how is each argument a product of its time? Which argument do you find most persuasive? Why?

8. In the history of American justice, the death penalty has sometimes been outlawed—or specific methods of execution have been outlawed—because of concerns that the practice violates the rights of individuals to be free from cruel and unusual punishment (see the U.S. Constitution and Bill of Rights in the appendix). Is such an interpretation simply no longer viable in the War on Terror? Did the events of 9/11 fundamentally change American ideas about cruelty to prisoners? Was such a change inevitable post-9/11, if there was any change at all?

Thinking Beyond the Text

9. McCarthy opens and closes his argument with references to the abuse of prisoners by U.S. military personnel at Abu Ghraib prison. Given this, would you say that his argument about torture is rooted in this exact moment in time? Or is it an argument that transcends time, given its focus on honorable and just behavior in the face or terrorism?

10. During the Vietnam War, the communist government of North Vietnam refused to classify American prisoners, including Senator John McCain, as POWs, arguing, instead, that these men were criminals captured during the commission of their crimes. Because they were not considered POWs, these American prisoners were not protected by such international agreements as the Geneva Conventions. In what ways might this situation be similar to or different from the American refusal to consider prisoners taken during the War on Terror POWs?

For Writing & Discussion

11. Searching online or in your library, locate a speech by Secretary of Defense Donald Rumsfeld in which he discusses the situation at Abu Ghraib prison or the issue of torture, one made during the years of the Bush administration (2001–2008). In a short essay, explain how the assertions Secretary Rumsfeld makes in his speech are supported or refuted by McCarthy's analysis.

JOHN MCCAIN

John McCain (1936–) is a U.S. senator from Arizona and was a Republican candidate in the 2000 presidential primaries. Prior to joining the Senate in 1987, McCain was a U.S. congressman from Arizona. McCain is a Vietnam veteran, and during his military service spent five and a half years as a prisoner of war. He has received several medals, including a Silver Star, Bronze Star, Legion of Merit, Purple Heart, and Distinguished Flying Cross. McCain has long been opposed to torture, and also was instrumental in passing legislation addressing POW-MIA issues.

McCain gave his speech, "United States and Europe," to the University Philosophical Society of Trinity University in Dublin, Ireland, while on a congressional delegation to Western Europe in 2004. The speech addresses changes in the U.S. relationship with Europe, and proposes a return to greater cross-Atlantic closeness. McCain's views on this and other topics can be found in his books, including *Why Courage Matters: The Way to a Braver Life* (2004), and *Worth the Fighting For: A Memoir.*

McCain serves on three senate committees, including the Committee on Armed Services, and has been simultaneously critical and supportive of the Iraq War.

United States and Europe
Standing Together Against Common Enemies

✎ Prereading Question

Consider a map of Europe. With which nations has the United States fought as an ally in one or more wars? Which nations has the United States fought against in one or more wars? With which nations does America currently seem to enjoy the best relationships and why? Are these the same nations that, historically, have been most closely aligned with America? What might account for the discrepancies between past and present "friendships"?

Delivered while on a Congressional Delegation (CODEL) to Western Europe, the University Philosophical Society, Trinity College, Dublin, Ireland, December 1, 2004.

Thank you. It is a privilege to be here tonight and to address the University Philosophical Society, or "the Phil," as I believe I am supposed to call it. The Society was founded in 1684, so that makes this its 320th year in operation, and I guess it proves the old adage about seeing everything if you live long enough. Before my arrival here the Irish Examiner newspaper ran a story with the headline "Former White House hopeful to address students," reminding me that I "ran a spirited but ultimately unsuccessful campaign" in 2000. It then went on to list some of the illustrious guests of years past, including the voice of Bart Simpson.

I also received a press inquiry asking how I felt about speaking here this year, when adult film star Ron Jeremy was also on the term card. Despite my reputation for candor, I declined to comment. But I guess after 320 years, you really can see everyone and everything here.

I would like to talk tonight about the future of the transatlantic relationship. With the elections behind us in the United States, and President Bush beginning his second term, pundits have spilled gallons of ink speculating on where things go from here for Europe and America. Is it possible to recapture the commonality of spirit that has eroded over the past few years? Should we even try? Are the bonds that held together the transatlantic partnership so weakened that we could not put things together again even if we so desire? Is the world moving inexorably toward a multipolar system, one in which the Europe and the United States are just two of several powers, with each serving as a counterweight to the other?

To begin answering these questions, we must first take into account the changed nature of Europe and how it views itself—bigger, with the EU and NATO's new entrants, more diverse, with eastward expansion and new immigration, and more dynamic. Ireland in many ways captures the bright promise of this new era. With a dynamic economy posting growth in excess of 8 percent from 1995 to 2002, and with positive growth since then, with a per capita GDP exceeding that of Europe's so-called "Big Four," with economic reform policies in place, and with its embrace of international trade and foreign investment, Ireland illustrates the best promise of globalization. New, non-European immigration to Ireland is producing an increasingly diverse population, with all of the social and political implications that this entails. There is a heightened sense here, as throughout Europe and throughout the world, that events in faraway places have a direct impact on daily life, whether economically or politically. And of course, there are few countries that enjoy warmer and closer ties than those that exist between the United States and Ireland. And yet, despite these close relations, when the President came to Ireland for the EU summit in June, he drew thousands of protesters. Anti-Americanism has risen dramatically throughout Europe. Something has changed.

It is also worth reflecting for a moment on how the United States has changed since September 11, 2001. The catastrophic terrorists attacks on our country produced a shift in perception that I believe is ill-understood in Europe. We saw this changed perspective evident in the recent presidential campaign. For all of the talk of "red states" and "blue states," there was a remarkable consensus in America about the urgent need to defeat international terrorism. While Republicans and Democrats may have differed on the exact combination of instruments required to do this, all shared a resolve to prevent future attacks on our homeland or those of our friends. In Europe, the choice between President Bush and Senator Kerry was often portrayed as one between vastly different foreign policies, chiefly with respect to our European allies. Yet both President Bush and Senator Kerry promised to fight terrorists wherever they are found. Both President Bush and Senator Kerry promised to prosecute the war in Iraq. And both promised to work with our friends and willing allies to enhance our security and prosperity. Don't misunderstand me—there were important differences in both style and substance between the two candidates' approaches—but these differences were not as vast as many in Europe have been led to believe.

It is important to understand this, because if you listen to many of the columnists and television chat shows, you see two Americas, bitterly at odds with one another. And yet most Americans still reside, as they always have, squarely in the political center. While the image of a divided America may make for interesting conversation, it is simply wrong. On many issues, including our core political values, Americans are unified, and we need to be—we have real enemies in this world that seek our destruction.

As I believe the gulf between red and blue in the United States has been overstated, so too do I believe that the issues that divide the United States and Europe—issues of great consequence—are manageable. I have heard an argument on both sides of the Atlantic that goes something like this: The Cold War bound the United States and Europe together in the face of a shared threat. After 1991, the U.S. and Europe began drifting apart, but the two sides remained embraced due to geopolitical inertia and an uncommonly tranquil period in international affairs. But as Europe continued to integrate and grow more powerful, it relied less and less on the United States, while the aftermath of September 11 and the war in Iraq exposed fault lines that already existed. America and the countries of Europe inevitably began down separate paths. It is only natural, I have heard, that the United States emerge as one of several power centers in the world, and the EU as another. The two powers would have occasionally overlapping goals, but our so-called "transatlantic values" are not enough to counteract the centrifugal tendencies in the relationship.

Nonsense. Surely there is some truth to the explanation that the demise of the Soviet Union has prompted us to look at other issues in the U.S.-Europe relationship with a more critical eye. And certainly the war in Iraq strained our relations beyond anything we have experienced in recent years. But there always has been, and there will continue to be, much more that binds us together than divides us. Celebrating the values that the United States and Europe share is not simply nostalgia for the more fraternal relationship of earlier times. These ideals—democracy, the rule of law, human and civil rights, freedom from tyranny and oppression, and individual liberty—are the essence of our identity as nations, cultures and friends. And they are the essence of our importance to history. We confide in our foreign policies not narrowly calculated national interests, but rather our best hopes for the progress of humanity. Our duty to fortify our common purpose in service to these ideals—a continuing duty for the leaders of both the United States and Europe—makes the relationship more than a collective response to a once imposing and now finished threat. Together, Europe and America constitute a fraternal, if occasionally fractious, order of liberal democracies with the will and the means to protect our shared ideals from outside threats, and to help advance them where they have too long been denied to others.

That is why it is so urgently important to begin putting the divisiveness of the past two years behind us. For so much that we seek to achieve in the world, a shared transatlantic commitment and a shared transatlantic effort is indispensable. Americans not only welcome European leadership, we believe it is necessary to make the world a safer, better place. This means true leadership—not a group of countries that merely follows American directives, as some fear, nor a coalition that opposes American power simply because of its country of origin, as others suggest. Even the most willfully uninformed of us knows the world suffers persecution, insecurity, danger, and oppression. If it is true, as Winston Churchill said that, 'an optimist sees opportunity in every difficulty,' we certainly do not lack for opportunities in the world today. To pay real tribute to our shared history and values, we must enhance and update the transatlantic partnership, transforming challenges into opportunities for cooperation.

The first challenge we all face is ensuring success in Iraq. It is beyond doubt that good people in both of our lands disagreed about the wisdom of toppling Saddam Hussein and liberating the people of Iraq. I choose the word "liberate" purposefully, because I firmly believed—and continue to believe—that intervening in Iraq was the right choice, and I believe that we are engaged in a just war against tyranny and danger. Americans and Iraqis are grateful to all who have participated in this struggle, and we include Ireland and its courageous Prime Minister in this group. Nevertheless, we have made mistakes throughout this conflict, and the situation in Iraq remains precarious today. Notwithstanding the position of some European governments against the war, one fact must be clear to all: failure in Iraq would have catastrophic implications for America and Europe.

Withdrawing coalition forces from Iraq in the absence of a secure, representative government there is likely to result in terrible violence, warlordism, and a failed state that would inevitably become a terrorist sanctuary. Failure in Iraq would embolden and further radicalize extremists throughout the Muslim world, including in Western Europe's Muslim communities, and strengthen the hand of al-Qaeda. None of us can afford failure, and the only acceptable exit strategy is victory. This presents a historic opportunity for European countries to support and encourage positive change in Iraq—which many are already doing. All members of the Euro-Atlantic community stand to gain—or lose—as much as America from the outcome of this mission. Success is difficult but still possible. If realized, success in Iraq would set that country on a new course, in which democratic expression and economic opportunity could provide a compelling example for other societies in that troubled region.

While Iraq remains our paramount challenge, other important issues provide great opportunity for collaboration. Iran seeks to develop nuclear weapons and divide the U.S. and its European friends in our attempts to dissuade the Iranians from continuing. Europe can lead here. But the mullahs running Iran's repressive regime should hear one unified message from all of us: the development of nuclear weapons constitutes a grave breach of the Nuclear Non-proliferation Treaty, to which Iran is a signatory, and a threat to international peace and stability, and it will be punished by multilateral sanctions imposed by the United Nations Security Council. At the same time, the reformers and the millions of Iranians who aspire to self-determination must hear that we support their natural desires for freedom and democracy. Oppression in that great land must not forever endure.

Both Iran and Iraq are elements in the emerging consensus that the United States and Europe must support and encourage positive change in the broader Middle East. At their June summit, the G-8 countries launched an initiative designed to focus the power of our shared values on the democratic transformation of that region of tyranny and violence. Doing so does not imply a program of violent regime change, but rather requires the transatlantic partners to use our economic, political, and diplomatic resources to promote fundamental reform in these countries. We have all become painfully aware that there is a stagnating status quo in many Middle Eastern countries. The lack of political participation and economic opportunity: engenders despair and even extremism in the hearts of many who live under these regimes. There are no more natural partners to work together to support a progressive agenda of freedom in the broader Middle East than Europe and the United States. The recent free elections in Afghanistan, which were overseen by a force of Europeans and Americans, constitute just a sample of what is possible in the broader region.

While the Middle East cries out for change, the neighbors to the EU's east illustrate some of the rockier soil on which the seeds of democracy have fallen, and they call for a cooperative attempt to support the forces of freedom there. From the great success stories, in the Baltics, Georgia, and elsewhere, to the countries in which democracy has struggled, like Ukraine, and where it no longer exists, in Belarus, the United States and Europe must work together to promote democratic rule. For countries like Belarus and Ukraine, the effect of our firm messages are greatly enhanced when they are coordinated and supported by all of the transatlantic democracies. Recent events in Ukraine illustrate the power of a common approach. Reacting to Russian interference and blatant electoral fraud, both the U.S. and Europe refused to recognize the declared victory of Viktor Yanukovich as President. The world—and Ukraine—took notice. Only when these types of governments see that it is impossible to split the United States and Europe do they look inward at their own actions and consider change.

Nowhere on the continent is this as important today as in Russia, where President Vladimir Putin rules as an autocrat. I have described as a "creeping coup" his efforts to use the Chechen war to roll back the democratic gains Russia won in the 1990s. In recent months I've had to start calling this a 'galloping coup.' Mr. Putin has moved to eliminate the popular election of Russia's 89 regional governors, and instead appoint them himself, and to eliminate independent members of parliament, so that Russians would vote not for specific candidates but rather for political parties-the candidates of which would be chosen by party heads, like Mr. Putin. His crackdowns on independent media continue, as does the repression of business executives who oppose the President. Mr. Putin is reasserting the Kremlin's old-style central control. Russia continues to interfere in so-called "frozen conflicts" in regions of Georgia, Moldova, and Azerbaijan, and maintains troops deployed in two of these countries, without their consent. Mr. Putin is pursuing autocracy at home and exporting autocracy abroad. And yet in the face of these outrages, Europe and the United States have remained too acquiescent, preferring to deal with Mr. Putin as an equal. We have the power to hold Russia to a higher standard, both at home and in Europe's backyard. A strong, unified *message is necessary:* reversing democracy in Russia will inevitably cause our relations with Russia to suffer, however much we value its cooperation in other areas.

"For those skeptical about what a cooperative transatlantic relationship can achieve, I would point out the progress in the western Balkans. By deploying peacekeepers in 1995, we staunched the bloodshed in Bosnia. Working together, we averted further killing in Kosovo by waging NATO's only war, and then together averted a civil war in Macedonia. A look at this region today shows just how far it has come. Albania, Croatia, and Macedonia are on track for NATO candidacy, perhaps as soon as 2006, and are on the path toward eventual EU membership. There are remaining challenges in Serbia and in resolving the final status of Kosovo, but, overall, the transformation of the western Balkans has been a significant transatlantic success.

While we focus on Europe's borders, we need not neglect the continent of Africa, where Europe has a special responsibility to assist in the development of post-colonial lands. Nowhere is this more relevant today than in Sudan, where the world's largest humanitarian crisis unfolds before our eyes. As the Sudanese government and its allied Arab militias rampage through the region of Darfur, leaving death and refugee columns in their wake, we must act now. Targeted, coordinated penalties against Sudanese government officials and militia leaders are long overdue. We should put into place a broad visa ban, an arms embargo, and freeze assets, and then increase the international armed presence in Darfur, to protect refugees in their camps and ultimately help them return home.

But the opportunities to improve our ties do not stem from country-specific challenges alone. The specter of climate change, for example, presents a real and present danger to all of countries and, indeed the world, and yet this issue hardly registers on the U.S.-European agenda. Despite broad scientific consensus that global warming is occurring, that human activity is contributing to it, and that *its consequences are extremely serious,* we remained mired in disagreement about the Kyoto Protocol. While the policy positions, especially on the American side, remain stagnant, the concentration level of greenhouse gases continues to rise and the environment suffers. Scientists observe an increased melting of the polar ice caps, the shifting and destruction of many species, the destruction of coral reefs, unprecedented heat waves and extreme weather, and new outbreaks of health problems linked to climate change. We need to reopen, immediately, U.S.–European talks on climate change and work out a solution that each side can live with. I have introduced in the U.S. Senate legislation that would require a reduction in greenhouse gas emissions, but this is just a modest start. What we need is a successor to Kyoto, a cap-and-trade system that delivers the necessary environmental impact in a financially responsible manner, and one that includes developing countries like China and India. New technologies hold great promise. We need to revise our innovation systems, so that we have policies in place that will encourage the marketplace to embrace more ideas originating in research labs. Together we can rekindle the spirit of creativity to find affordable solutions to the looming climate problem.

Many other issues—from the dangers of proliferation to trade issues to the role of an international criminal court—deserve serious consideration and discussion on both sides. With issues such as the ICC, which the U.S. administration opposes, as do I, we need to recognize that, if they are important to our European friends, so too they are important to America. We need to emphasize our areas of agreement and manage our disagreements. Only bad blood results when one side disengages completely, whether it is the Americans over the ICC or the French over Iraq.

This brings me to another point, one that concerns the importance of style in the transatlantic relationship. Behind the substantive policy debate lies a perception on the European side that I think is poorly understood in Washington. Europeans quite rightly wish to be heard and respected by the United States, while Americans, perhaps true to our nature, often let our certainty and self-regard override our impulse toward consultation and deference. For the American side, I believe we should heed Teddy Roosevelt's famous dictum to "speak softly and carry a big stick." We have carried—and used—a big stick in recent years, and now perhaps it is time to speak more softly. Our exuberance, when perceived as arrogance, is rarely successful, and we should listen to the advice of friends. But our European friends should also note America's real determination to work toward a freer, more secure world—for our sake and for yours. We intend to continue, whether our efforts are appreciated in our time or must wait for the judgment of later generations.

I would like to close with a few remarks about what I consider the true generational challenge facing the United States and Europe today. I have long believed that the means to real happiness and the true worth of a person is measured by how faithfully we serve a cause greater than our self-interest. The same holds true for the conduct of nations, particularly in this unique era, during which the traditional balance of power has faded and America, along with its democratic allies, stands astride the world with unmatched power. Political scientists refer to this time as the "unipolar moment," and I'd emphasize the "moment" part of that formulation. None of us knows for how long the United States will dominate international affairs, but we do know that history has handed us a unique opportunity. The U.S. and its democratic friends could choose to pursue narrowly defined national interests—internal and external security, economic prosperity at the cost of others, perhaps even territorial domination. And yet we choose—we must choose—a very different path.

We choose to infuse our foreign policy with values, the ones common to the world's democracies and are, I would argue, the natural rights of all mankind. We orient our national ambitions toward these ends, so that our interests and our values converge. Americans' love of country is based not in some ill-considered desire for empire, any more than is Irish love of their country or other Europeans' love of theirs. Rather, America's patriotism is based on a kinship of ideals, a shared dedication to the proposition that all men are created equal, and possess certain inalienable rights. So, too, with Europe, the continent to which Americans owe so many of its liberal conceptions. Whether we are speaking of America, or Ireland, or Germany, or Latvia, one thing binds us—we rightly believe our core values to be universal, the birthright of all people.

And so it is natural to work together to promote these rights in lands where they are lacking. We must use our power and influence not only for security and prosperity, but to promote the concepts we hold dear: democracy, the panoply of human and civil rights, strong and legitimate international institutions, a world of recognized international norms and rules. If we are successful in creating this lasting liberal order, we will have established a set of expectations for international and domestic behavior that will endure long after the unipolar moment is passed. That is the great project that lies before the transatlantic democracies today. The American historian Charles Beard once said that "the supreme challenge to intelligence is that of making the noblest and best in our curious heritage prevail." If we are to do this, it will require the brightest and most visionary minds in our respective societies, and will require that we think proactively about how our foreign policies shape the world. Above all it will require leadership— European leadership and American leadership.

But I can think of no more appropriate project for the United States and Europe, in which the Enlightenment was born and took root, where the social contract saw its great fulfillment, and where the oppressed people of the world naturally look for solace and inspiration. President Harry Truman observed that, "Men make history, not the other way around. In periods where there is no leadership, society stands still. Progress occurs when courageous, skillful leaders seize the opportunity to change things for the better." I believe that we have in both the United States and Europe the skillful leaders, and the opportunity for change now presents itself. What writer Tod Lindberg calls the "Atlanticist Community" is a community unlike any other on the globe. Built on shared values, possessing bountiful resources and democratic legitimacy, it inspires the world. There are other democracies, other military powers, other economically prosperous countries. But when the United States and the countries of Europe stand together, it creates a moral and political force that gives no ground to the enemies of freedom. The world needs us together, and we need each other.

Thank you for your gracious invitation and for your attention this evening.

Textual Questions

1. How does McCain use humor—including humor at his own expense—to ease his listeners/readers into his argument?

2. How does McCain describe the mistaken view that President George W. Bush and presidential hopeful John Kerry hold vastly different ideas and beliefs? How does this description connect with his argument about the United States and Europe?

3. While he argues that the war in Iraq is an important issue between America and European nations, what other issues confront the West, according to McCain?

Rhetorical Questions

4. How effectively does McCain link his comparison of President Bush and Senator Kerry to his comparison of the nations of Europe and the United States? Does the linking of these two comparisons strengthen or weaken his overall argument?

5. How does McCain describe the ongoing situation in the former Soviet Union—the traditional enemy of Europe and America during the Cold War? How does this description of Russia compare/contrast with McCain's description of tensions between the West and the Middle Eastern nations of Iran and Iraq?

6. Near the end of his text, McCain refers to Teddy Roosevelt's statement about walking softly and wielding a big stick. How does he use this well-known maxim for how the United States ought to behave in the world as a way to both admit that the United States has acted rashly at times and that it is now time for change?

Intertextual Questions

7. How does McCain's characterization of the relationship between the United States and the nations of Europe compare with that argued by T. R. Reid in "The Atlantic Widens" (this chapter)?

8. How does McCain's vision of the future relationship between America and the world compare with the vision of America presented by President Ronald Reagan in "We Have Made a Difference" (Chapter 1)?

Thinking Beyond the Text

9. For one week, watch the nightly news on one of the major networks—CBS, NBC, ABC, or FOX (if, in your local area, FOX runs nightly news). As you watch, make a list of the stories that discuss some aspect of the relationship between the United States and one or more of the nations of Europe. Does the relationship between the United States and Europe, in general, seem better than when McCain spoke in 2004? Or is the situation, again speaking in generalizations, somehow worse?

10. McCain speaks of the central importance of the nations of Iraq, Iran, and Afghanistan to future relations between the United States and Europe. Why? What is the current situation in each of these nations in relation to the United States and the nations of Europe? How is the situation in each affecting the "Atlanticist Community"?

For Writing & Discussion

11. McCain argues that the differences between President George W. Bush and his 2004 challenger Senator John Kerry are not as great as Europeans may believe. From your perspective, is this argument about similarities between these two men accurate? Or is it an argument crafted specifically to persuade the audience (while still telling a version of the truth)?

JOHN   KERRY

John Kerry (1943–) is a U.S. senator from Massachusetts and a 2004 Democratic candidate for president. Prior to being elected to the Senate in 1985, Kerry was lieutenant governor of Massachusetts between 1979 and 1984, during which time he worked on a precursor to the Clean Air Act of 1990. Kerry also is a veteran, having done two tours of duty in Vietnam for which he was awarded a bronze star, a silver star, and three purple hearts. After returning from his second tour of duty, Kerry became an outspoken critic of the U.S. involvement in Vietnam. He has never stopped advocating for awareness of POW-MIA issues and was instrumental in passing legislation that brought about increased cooperation on these issues between the United States and Vietnam.

Kerry gave his speech, "The Hope Is There," to the 2004 Democratic National Convention in Boston, July 2004. An acceptance speech for the presidential nomination, it lays out Kerry's plans and commitments should he win, but it also describes his perspectives on issues including safety, health care, family values, and energy independence. Kerry also talks about these and other points in his 2003 book, *A Call to Service: My Vision for a Better America.*

One of the four senate committees in which Kerry serves is the Committee on Foreign Relations, and he has many years' experience working on issues of national security. He also leads the political action committee, "Keeping America's Promises."

The Hope Is There
Looking Toward the Next Horizon

❧ Prereading Question

When people speak of the future, they often speak of a "new horizon," meaning, among other things, a new world that is coming into being as the future becomes the present. Yet "horizon," on a literal level, refers to a thing that does not exist but only appears to—a place where the sky and the earth come together. When speaking of the future, then, "horizon" has the same literal meaning as "utopia"—which, again speaking literally, means "nowhere." So is the future, literally, always a new horizon, whether the future being posited is generally positive or negative?

Delivered at the 2004 Democratic National Convention, Boston, Massachusetts, July 29, 2004

My fellow Americans: we are here tonight united in one simple purpose: to make America stronger at home and respected in the world.

A great American novelist wrote that you can't go home again. He could not have imagined this evening. Tonight, I am home. Home where my public life began and those who made it possible live. Home where our nation's history was written in blood, idealism, and hope. Home where my parents showed me the values of family, faith, and country.

Thank you, all of you, for a welcome home I will never forget.

I wish my parents could share this moment. They went to their rest in the last few years, but their example, their inspiration, their gift of open eyes, open mind, and endless world are bigger and more lasting than any words.

I was born in Colorado, in Fitzsimmons Army Hospital, when my dad was a pilot in World War II. Now, I'm not one to read into things, but guess which wing of the hospital the maternity ward was in? I'm not making this up. I was born in the West Wing!

My mother was the rock of our family as so many mothers are. She stayed up late to help me do my homework. She sat by my bed when I was sick, and she answered the questions of a child who, like all children, found the world full of wonders and mysteries.

She was my den mother when I was a Cub Scout and she was so proud of her fifty year pin as a Girl Scout leader. She gave me her passion for the environment. She taught me to see trees as the cathedrals of nature. And by the power of her example, she showed me that we can and must finish the march toward full equality for all women in our country.

My dad did the things that a boy remembers. He gave me my first model airplane, my first baseball mitt and my first bicycle. He also taught me that we are here for something bigger than ourselves, he lived out the responsibilities and sacrifices of the greatest generation to whom we owe so much.

When I was a young man, he was in the State Department, stationed in Berlin when it and the world were divided between democracy and communism. I have unforgettable memories of being a kid mesmerized by the British, French, and American troops, each of them guarding their own part of the city, and Russians standing guard on the stark line separating East from West. On one occasion, I rode my bike into Soviet East Berlin. And when I proudly told my dad, he promptly grounded me.

But what I learned has stayed with me for a lifetime. I saw how different life was on different sides of the same city. I saw the fear in the eyes of people who were not free. I saw the gratitude of people toward the United States for all that we had done. I felt goose bumps as I got off a military train and heard the Army band strike up "Stars and Stripes Forever." I learned what it meant to be America at our best. I learned the pride of our freedom. And I am determined now to restore that pride to all who look to America.

Mine were greatest generation parents. And as I thank them, we all join together to thank that whole generation for making America strong, for winning World War II, winning the Cold War, and for the great gift of service which brought America fifty years of peace and prosperity.

My parents inspired me to serve, and when I was a junior in high school, John Kennedy called my generation to service. It was the beginning of a great journey—a time to march for civil rights, for voting rights, for the environment, for women, and for peace. We believed we could change the world. And you know what? We did.

But we're not finished. The journey isn't complete. The march isn't over. The promise isn't perfected. Tonight, we're setting out again. And together, we're going to write the next great chapter of America's story.

We have it in our power to change the world again. But only if we're true to our ideals—and that starts by telling the truth to the American people. That is my first pledge to you tonight. As President, I will restore trust and credibility to the White House.

I ask you to judge me by my record: As a young prosecutor, I fought for victim's rights and made prosecuting violence against women a priority. When I came to the Senate, I broke with many in my own party to vote for a balanced budget, because I thought it was the right thing to do. I fought to put a 100,000 cops on the street.

And then I reached across the aisle to work with John McCain, to find the truth about our POW's and missing in action, and to finally make peace with Vietnam.

I will be a commander in chief who will never mislead us into war. I will have a Vice President who will not conduct secret meetings with polluters to rewrite our environmental laws. I will have a Secretary of Defense who will listen to the best advice of our military leaders. And I will appoint an Attorney General who actually upholds the Constitution of the United States.

My fellow Americans, this is the most important election of our lifetime. The stakes are high. We are a nation at war—a global war on terror against an enemy unlike any we have ever known before. And here at home, wages are falling, health care costs are rising, and our great middle class is shrinking. People are working weekends; they're working two jobs, three jobs, and they're still not getting ahead.

We're told that outsourcing jobs is good for America. We're told that new jobs that pay $9,000 less than the jobs that have been lost is the best we can do. They say this is the best economy we've ever had. And they say that anyone who thinks otherwise is a pessimist. Well, here is our answer: There is nothing more pessimistic than saying America can't do better.

We can do better and we will. We're the optimists. For us, this is a country of the future. We're the can do people. And let's not forget what we did in the 1990s. We balanced the budget. We paid down the debt. We created 23 million new jobs. We lifted millions out of poverty and we lifted the standard of living for the middle class. We just need to believe in ourselves—and we can do it again.

So tonight, in the city where America's freedom began, only a few blocks from where the sons and daughters of liberty gave birth to our nation—here tonight, on behalf of a new birth of freedom—on behalf of the middle class who deserve a champion, and those struggling to join it who deserve a fair shot—for the brave men and women in uniform who risk their lives every day and the families who pray for their return—for all those who believe our best days are ahead of us—for all of you—with great faith in the American people, I accept your nomination for President of the United States.

I am proud that at my side will be a running mate whose life is the story of the American dream and who's worked every day to make that dream real for all Americans—Senator John Edwards of North Carolina. And his wonderful wife Elizabeth and their family. This son of a mill worker is ready to lead—and next January, Americans will be proud to have a fighter for the middle class to succeed Dick Cheney as Vice President of the United States.

And what can I say about Teresa? She has the strongest moral compass of anyone I know. She's down to earth, nurturing, courageous, wise and smart. She speaks her mind and she speaks the truth, and I love her for that, too. And that's why America will embrace her as the next First Lady of the United States.

For Teresa and me, no matter what the future holds or the past has given us, nothing will ever mean as much as our children. We love them not just for who they are and what they've become, but for being themselves, making us laugh, holding our feet to the fire, and never letting me get away with anything. Thank you, Andre, Alex, Chris, Vanessa, and John.

And in this journey, I am accompanied by an extraordinary band of brothers led by that American hero, a patriot named Max Cleland. Our band of brothers doesn't march together because of who we are as veterans, but because of what we learned as soldiers. We fought for this nation because we loved it and we came back with the deep belief that every day is extra. We may be a little older now, we may be a little grayer, but we still know how to fight for our country.

And standing with us in that fight are those who shared with me the long season of the primary campaign: Carol Moseley Braun, General Wesley Clark. Howard Dean, Dick Gephardt, Bob Graham, Dennis Kucinich, Joe Lieberman and Al Sharpton.

To all of you, I say thank you for teaching me and testing me—but mostly, we say thank you for standing up for our country and giving us the unity to move America forward.

My fellow Americans, the world tonight is very different from the world of four years ago. But I believe the American people are more than equal to the challenge.

Remember the hours after September 11th, when we came together as one to answer the attack against our homeland. We drew strength when our firefighters ran up the stairs and risked their lives, so that others might live. When rescuers rushed into smoke and fire at the Pentagon. When the men and women of Flight 93 sacrificed themselves to save our nation's Capitol. When flags were hanging from front porches all across America, and strangers became friends. It was the worst day we have ever seen, but it brought out the best in all of us.

I am proud that after September 11th all our people rallied to President Bush's call for unity to meet the danger. There were no Democrats. There were no Republicans. There were only Americans. How we wish it had stayed that way.

Now I know there are those who criticize me for seeing complexities—and I do—because some issues just aren't all that simple. Saying there are weapons of mass destruction in Iraq doesn't make it so. Saying we can fight a war on the cheap doesn't make it so. And proclaiming mission accomplished certainly doesn't make it so.

As President, I will ask hard questions and demand hard evidence. I will immediately reform the intelligence system—so policy is guided by facts, and facts are never distorted by politics. And as President, I will bring back this nation's time-honored tradition: the United States of America never goes to war because we want to, we only go to war because we have to.

I know what kids go through when they are carrying an M-16 in a dangerous place and they can't tell friend from foe. I know what they go through when they're out on patrol at night and they don't know what's coming around the next bend. I know what it's like to write letters home telling your family that everything's all right when you're not sure that's true.

As President, I will wage this war with the lessons I learned in war. Before you go to battle, you have to be able to look a parent in the eye and truthfully say: "I tried everything possible to avoid sending your son or daughter into harm's way. But we had no choice. We had to protect the American people, fundamental American values from a threat that was real and imminent." So lesson one, this is the only justification for going to war.

And on my first day in office, I will send a message to every man and woman in our armed forces: You will never be asked to fight a war without a plan to win the peace.

I know what we have to do in Iraq. We need a President who has the credibility to bring our allies to our side and share the burden, reduce the cost to American taxpayers, and reduce the risk to American soldiers. That's the right way to get the job done and bring our troops home.

Here is the reality: that won't happen until we have a president who restores America's respect and leadership—so we don't have to go it alone in the world.

And we need to rebuild our alliances, so we can get the terrorists before they get us.

I defended this country as a young man and I will defend it as President. Let there be no mistake: I will never hesitate to use force when it is required. Any attack will be met with a swift and certain response. I will never give any nation or international institution a veto over our national security. And I will build a stronger American military.

We will add 40,000 active duty troops—not in Iraq, but to strengthen American forces that are now overstretched, overextended, and under pressure. We will double our special forces to conduct anti-terrorist operations. We will provide our troops with the newest weapons and technology to save their lives—and win the battle. And we will end the backdoor draft of National Guard and reservists.

To all who serve in our armed forces today, I say, help is on the way.

As President, I will fight a smarter, more effective war on terror. We will deploy every tool in our arsenal: our economic as well as our military might; our principles as well as our firepower.

In these dangerous days there is a right way and a wrong way to be strong. Strength is more than tough words. After decades of experience in national security, I know the reach of our power and I know the power of our ideals.

We need to make America once again a beacon in the world. We need to be looked up to and not just feared.

We need to lead a global effort against nuclear proliferation—to keep the most dangerous weapons in the world out of the most dangerous hands in the world.

We need a strong military and we need to lead strong alliances. And then, with confidence and determination, we will be able to tell the terrorists: You will lose and we will win. The future doesn't belong to fear; it belongs to freedom.

And the front lines of this battle are not just far away—they're right here on our shores, at our airports, and potentially in any town or city. Today, our national security begins with homeland security. The 9/11 Commission has given us a path to follow, endorsed by Democrats, Republicans, and the 9/11 families. As President, I will not evade or equivocate; I will immediately implement the recommendations of that commission. We shouldn't be letting ninety-five percent of container ships come into our ports without ever being physically inspected. We shouldn't be leaving our nuclear and chemical plants without enough protection. And we shouldn't be opening firehouses in Baghdad and closing them down in the United States of America.

And tonight, we have an important message for those who question the patriotism of Americans who offer a better direction for our country. Before wrapping themselves in the flag and shutting their eyes and ears to the truth, they should remember what America is really all about. They should remember the great idea of freedom for which so many have given their lives. Our purpose now is to reclaim democracy itself. We are here to affirm that when Americans stand up and speak their minds and say America can do better, that is not a challenge to patriotism; it is the heart and soul of patriotism.

You see that flag up there. We call her Old Glory. The stars and stripes forever. I fought under that flag, as did so many of you here and all across our country. That flag flew from the gun turret right behind my head. It was shot through and through and tattered, but it never ceased to wave in the wind. It draped the caskets of men I served with and friends I grew up with. For us, that flag is the most powerful symbol of who we are and what we believe in. Our strength. Our diversity. Our love of country. All that makes America both great and good.

That flag doesn't belong to any president. It doesn't belong to any ideology and it doesn't belong to any political party. It belongs to all the American people.

My fellow citizens, elections are about choices. And choices are about values. In the end, it's not just policies and programs that matter; the president who sits at that desk must be guided by principle.

For four years, we've heard a lot of talk about values. But values spoken without actions taken are just slogans. Values are not just words. They're what we live by. They're about the causes we champion and the people we fight for. And it is time for those who talk about family values to start valuing families.

You don't value families by kicking kids out of after school programs and taking cops off our streets, so that Enron can get another tax break.

We believe in the family value of caring for our children and protecting the neighborhoods where they walk and play.

And that is the choice in this election.

You don't value families by denying real prescription drug coverage to seniors, so big drug companies can get another windfall.

We believe in the family value expressed in one of the oldest Commandments: "Honor thy father and thy mother." As President, I will not privatize Social Security. I will not cut benefits. And together, we will make sure that senior citizens never have to cut their pills in half because they can't afford life-saving medicine.

And that is the choice in this election.

You don't value families if you force them to take up a collection to buy body armor for a son or daughter in the service, if you deny veterans health care, or if you tell middle class families to wait for a tax cut, so that the wealthiest among us can get even more.

We believe in the value of doing what's right for everyone in the American family.

And that is the choice in this election.

We believe that what matters most is not narrow appeals masquerading as values, but the shared values that show the true face of America. Not narrow appeals that divide us, but shared values that unite us. Family and faith. Hard work and responsibility. Opportunity for all—so that every child, every parent, every worker has an equal shot at living up to their God-given potential.

What does it mean in America today when Dave McCune, a steel worker I met in Canton, Ohio, saw his job sent overseas and the equipment in his factory literally unbolted, crated up, and shipped thousands of miles away along with that job? What does it mean when workers I've met had to train their foreign replacements?

America can do better. So tonight we say: help is on the way.

What does it mean when Mary Ann Knowles, a woman with breast cancer I met in New Hampshire, had to keep working day after day right through her chemotherapy, no matter how sick she felt, because she was terrified of losing her family's health insurance.

America can do better. And help is on the way.

What does it mean when Deborah Kromins from Philadelphia, Pennsylvania works and saves all her life only to find out that her pension has disappeared into thin air—and the executive who looted it has bailed out on a golden parachute?

America can do better. And help is on the way.

What does it mean when twenty five percent of the children in Harlem have asthma because of air pollution?

America can do better. And help is on the way.

What does it mean when people are huddled in blankets in the cold, sleeping in Lafayette Park on the doorstep of the White House itself—and the number of families living in poverty has risen by three million in the last four years?

America can do better. And help is on the way.

And so we come here tonight to ask: Where is the conscience of our country?

I'll tell you where it is: it's in rural and small town America; it's in urban neighborhoods and suburban main streets; it's alive in the people I've met in every part of this land. It's bursting in the hearts of Americans who are determined to give our country back its values and its truth.

We value jobs that pay you more not less than you earned before. We value jobs where, when you put in a week's work, you can actually pay your bills, provide for your children, and lift up the quality of your life. We value an America where the middle class is not being squeezed, but doing better.

So here is our economic plan to build a stronger America:

First, new incentives to revitalize manufacturing.

Second, investment in technology and innovation that will create the good-paying jobs of the future.

Third, close the tax loopholes that reward companies for shipping our jobs overseas. Instead, we will reward companies that create and keep good paying jobs where they belong—in the good old U.S.A.

We value an America that exports products, not jobs—and we believe American workers should never have to subsidize the loss of their own job.

Next, we will trade and compete in the world. But our plan calls for a fair playing field—because if you give the American worker a fair playing field, there's nobody in the world the American worker can't compete against.

And we're going to return to fiscal responsibility because it is the foundation of our economic strength. Our plan will cut the deficit in half in four years by ending tax giveaways that are nothing more than corporate welfare—and will make government live by the rule that every family has to follow: pay as you go.

And let me tell you what we won't do: we won't raise taxes on the middle class. You've heard a lot of false charges about this in recent months. So let me say straight out what I will do as President: I will cut middle class taxes. I will reduce the tax burden on small business. And I will roll back the tax cuts for the wealthiest individuals who make over $200,000 a year, so we can invest in job creation, health care and education.

Our education plan for a stronger America sets high standards and demands accountability from parents, teachers, and schools. It provides for smaller class sizes and treats teachers like the professionals they are. And it gives a tax credit to families for each and every year of college.

When I was a prosecutor, I met young kids who were in trouble, abandoned by adults. And as President, I am determined that we stop being a nation content to spend $50,000 a year to keep a young person in prison for the rest of their life—when we could invest $10,000 to give them Head Start, Early Start, Smart Start, the best possible start in life.

And we value health care that's affordable and accessible for all Americans.

Since 2000, four million people have lost their health insurance. Millions more are struggling to afford it.

You know what's happening. Your premiums, your copayments, your deductibles have all gone through the roof.

Our health care plan for a stronger America cracks down on the waste, greed, and abuse in our health care system and will save families up to $1,000 a year on their premiums. You'll get to pick your own doctor—and patients and doctors, not insurance company bureaucrats, will make medical decisions. Under our plan, Medicare will negotiate lower drug prices for seniors. And all Americans will be able to buy less expensive prescription drugs from countries like Canada.

The story of people struggling for health care is the story of so many Americans. But you know what, it's not the story of senators and members of Congress. Because we give ourselves great health care and you get the bill. Well, I'm here to say, your family's health care is just as important as any politician's in Washington, D.C.

And when I'm President, America will stop being the only advanced nation in the world which fails to understand that health care is not a privilege for the wealthy, the connected, and the elected-it is a right for all Americans.

We value an America that controls its own destiny because it's finally and forever independent of Mideast oil. What does it mean for our economy and our national security when we only have three percent of the world's oil reserves, yet we rely on foreign countries for fifty-three percent of what we consume?

I want an America that relies on its own ingenuity and innovation—not the Saudi royal family.

And our energy plan for a stronger America will invest in new technologies and alternative fuels and the cars of the future—so that no young American in uniform will ever be held hostage to our dependence on oil from the Middle East.

I've told you about our plans for the economy, for education, for health care, for energy independence. I want you to know more about them. So now I'm going to say something that Franklin Roosevelt could never have said in his acceptance speech: go to johnkerry.com.

I want to address these next words directly to President George W. Bush: In the weeks ahead, let's be optimists, not just opponents. Let's build unity in the American family, not angry division. Let's honor this nation's diversity, let's respect one another; and let's never misuse for political purposes the most precious document in American history, the Constitution of the United States.

My friends, the high road may be harder, but it leads to a better place. And that's why Republicans and Democrats must make this election a contest of big ideas, not small-minded attacks. This is our time to reject the kind of politics calculated to divide race from race, group from group, region from region. Maybe some just see us divided into red states and blue states, but I see us as one America—red, white, and blue. And when I am President, the government I lead will enlist people of talent, Republicans as well as Democrats, to find the common ground—so that no one who has something to contribute will be left on the sidelines.

And let me say it plainly: in that cause, and in this campaign, we welcome people of faith. America is not us and them. I think of what Ron Reagan said of his father a few weeks ago, and I want to say this to you tonight: I don't wear my own faith on my sleeve. But faith has given me values and hope to live by, from Vietnam to this day, from Sunday to Sunday. I don't want to claim that God is on our side. As Abraham Lincoln told us, I want to pray humbly that we are on God's side. And whatever our faith, one belief should bind us all: The measure of our character is our willingness to give of ourselves for others and for our country.

These aren't Democratic values. These aren't Republican values. They're American values. We believe in them. They're who we are. And if we honor them, if we believe in ourselves, we can build an America that's stronger at home and respected in the world.

So much promise stretches before us. Americans have always reached for the impossible, looked to the next horizon, and asked: What if?

Two young bicycle mechanics from Dayton asked what if this airplane could take off at Kitty Hawk? It did that and changed the world forever. A young president asked what if we could go to the moon in ten years? And now we're exploring the solar system and the stars themselves. A young generation of entrepreneurs asked, what if we could take all the information in a library and put it on a little chip the size of a fingernail? We did and that too changed the world forever.

And now it's our time to ask: What if?

What if we find a breakthrough to cure Parkinson's, diabetes, Alzheimer's and AIDs? What if we have a president who believes in science, so we can unleash the wonders of discovery like stem cell research to treat illness and save millions of lives?

What if we do what adults should do—and make sure all our children are safe in the afternoons after school? And what if we have a leadership that's as good as the American dream—so that bigotry and hatred never again steal the hope and future of any American?

I learned a lot about these values on that gunboat patrolling the Mekong Delta with young Americans who came from places as different as Iowa and Oregon, Arkansas, Florida and California. No one cared where we went to school. No one cared about our race or our backgrounds. We were literally all in the same boat. We looked out, one for the other—and we still do.

That is the kind of America I will lead as President—an America where we are all in the same boat.

Never has there been a more urgent moment for Americans to step up and define ourselves. I will work my heart out. But, my fellow citizens, the outcome is in your hands more than mine.

It is time to reach for the next dream. It is time to look to the next horizon. For America, the hope is there. The sun is rising. Our best days are still to come.

Goodnight, God bless you, and God bless America.

Textual Questions

1. Kerry opens with a simple statement of fact: He and his audience are united in a single, two-sided purpose: making America "stronger at home and respected in the world." How well does this basic forecast cover/include all of the topics Kerry addresses in the body and conclusion of his speech?

2. How does Kerry build to his arguments that "The journey isn't complete. The march isn't over. The promise isn't perfected"? And to what journey, march, promise do these metaphors refer?

3. According to Kerry, how is the "world tonight . . . very different from the world of four years ago"? And why would he make a better president, ultimately, in this very different world?

Rhetorical Questions

4. Reread Kerry's address, marking the places where he uses *I, you,* and *we*. Why does he seem to choose to use each of these pronouns in each separate situation? That is, what effect does the use of first-, second-,

or first-person plural have (a) for Kerry's argument and (b) on Kerry's audience?

5. How does Kerry use repetition to strengthen his argument? What does he repeat and how effective are these repetitions?

6. What are the features of the "next horizon" referred to in the subtitle of Kerry's speech? How does he describe each in a way that is persuasive or unpersuasive?

Intertextual Questions

7. In what ways does Kerry's view of America's future compare and contrast with President Lyndon Johnson's view of America presented in "The Great Society" (Chapter 1)? How does it compare and contrast with President Ronald Reagan's view of America in "We Have Made a Difference" (also in Chapter 1)?

8. How do Kerry's arguments about health care compare with those made by Terry Tempest Williams in "The Clan of One-Breasted Women" and in the editorial "America's Promises" (both in Chapter 4)?

Thinking Beyond the Text

9. Reread Kerry's text, watching specifically for those places where he appeals to patriotism—either his own or that of his audience. How does he construct each of these appeals in his argument and how effective are they? Are such appeals simply a normal, common feature of this genre of speech, or are they rooted more in the time and place of the speech?

10. Searching online or in your library, locate an archive of campaign television commercials from the 2004 presidential election. Examine one add from the Democratic Party and explain how it elaborates on an example, idea, or general appeal made by Kerry in his address to the Democratic National Convention.

For Writing & Discussion

11. In this address, Kerry is speaking to his political party after being selected as its nominee to run for president of the United States. Searching online or in your library, find the speech made by then President George W. Bush when his own party formally nominated him as its candidate for president. Compare and contrast the two speeches and, in an essay, explain three similarities and three differences between the two—from examples used to tone and so on.

T . R .   R E I D

T. R. Reid is the Rocky Mountain bureau chief for the *Washington Post* and was formerly their bureau chief in London and Tokyo. He co-authors (with Brit Hume) a weekly column on computers, The Reid-Hume Report, which is syndicated in over 60 newspapers, and he is a regular commentator on NPR's *Morning Edition*. Prior to becoming a journalist at the *Washington Post* in 1977, Reid taught Latin and Greek, served as an officer in the U.S. Navy during the Vietnam War, was a professor in Japan, and worked as a lawyer.

"The Atlantic Widens" is an excerpt from his 2004 book, *The United States of Europe: The New Superpower and the End of American Supremacy.* Reid has published six other books, two of them in Japanese, which he speaks and writes fluently. His 2001 book, *The Chip: How Two Americans Invented the Microchip and Launched a Revolution,* won the Booklist Editor's Choice for Young Adults.

As an American who has spent many years abroad, Reid provides a unique perspective, showing how the United States is viewed in other countries and speculating about the possible consequences of what he dubs "pancontinental America-bashing."

The Atlantic Widens

∾ Prereading Question

Throughout much of the twentieth century, the world was dominated politically, culturally, and militarily by various superpowers, especially the Union of Soviet Socialist Republics and the United States of America, although nations such as China and India exerted great (and growing) influence in their own spheres. The twenty-first century, it seems now, will be very different. Instead of being wielded solely by single-nation superpowers such as America, China, and Russia, power will also be wielded by nations rich in oil but comparatively weak militarily, by nations willing to support small-scale military operations such as terrorism, and by economic unions banded together to serve their collective good. Given this evolving global situation, what place will the United States continue to play on the international stage over the next twenty years—politically, militarily, and culturally?

The Lardburgers were going at it again. "Ah got no gas in mah SUV," Stacey Lardburger screamed at her husband. "And you spent all our money buyin' ammo for your stoooo-pid rifles. So how'm ah goin' to git to the welfare office? Will you tell me that?" Jeff Lardburger was in no mood to take that kind of grief from a mere woman, even the woman who happened to be his fourth wife. "Button it, you slut," he roared, hurling his beer can in the general direction of Stacey's huge head of bleached hair. "You shet that big mouth of your'n, or ah'll sendya to Texas and puttya in the chair." Stacey had heard warnings like that dozens of times before, but this time she had a comeback. "You gonna be one sorry asshole when ah get finished witya," she shouted back. "Got me a lawyer now. He says, next time you threaten me like 'at, we's gonna sue your ass bigtime."

And thus passed another interlude of domestic bliss in the typical American home depicted on "The Lardburgers," a regular segment on the satirical British TV show *Big Breakfast*. Jeff and Stacey, both so obese they resemble the Michelin Man, are presented for the enjoyment of the British public as the kind of couple Britons like to conjure up when they think about Americans. The Lardburgers are fat, loud, and ignorant. At the end of the first act the Ku Klux Klan dances onto the stage, complete with white hoods and pointed caps, and burns a cross. Despite my long experience watching Europeans make fun of my country, I found *Jerry Springer—The Opera* to be debilitating. "Really, we're not like that," I said defensively during the intermission to the kind British woman sitting next to me. She noticed that I was disturbed, and did her best to cheer me up. "Don't worry, dahling," she said. "We have daft chat shows over here as well. And look on the bright side: at least this play is providing employment for a lot of really fat opera singers."

And the play—so popular it was the toughest ticket to land in London for more than a year—provided Europeans with a basic entertainment staple they have been enjoying for two centuries. Almost as long as there has been a United States of America, the people of Europe have found a certain delicious pleasure in deploring American ways and making fun of them. Much has been made of the sharp decline in mutual respect and admiration between the United States and Europe in the first few years of the twenty-first century. All over Europe, west and east, opinion surveys show a steep plunge in positive feelings toward the United States, a trend that became even more obvious following the war in Iraq. (And Americans have returned the favor, from "liberty fries" in the congressional cafeteria to learned seminars where thinkers like Robert Kagan, argue that Europe is a pitiful weakling that can safely be ignored.)

This pancontinental America-bashing can be funny (for a while), and it can be exasperating. But it is an important mindset for Americans to understand, because the sheer pleasure that Europeans take in denigrating America has become another bond unifying the continent. Widespread anti-Americanism has strengthened Europeans' belief that an integrated European Union should stand up as a counterweight to the American brute. Until the early years of the twenty-first century, a majority of Europeans reacted warily to the suggestion that the European Union should become a "superpower." Today, Europeans have broadly embraced the notion that their united continent should be the superpower that stands up to super America. Surveys taken in the summer of 2003, after the intensely unpopular military action in Iraq, showed that more than 70 percent of Europeans want the EU to become a superpower—and more than 70 percent expect that this will happen.

To a large extent, the zeal for America-bashing stems from opposition to U.S. foreign policy—and particularly the foreign policy of George W. Bush, the most unpopular American president in a century among Europeans. But the sour feeling toward America among the people of Europe goes well beyond foreign policy issues. Across the continent today, there are all sorts of things about the United States that people can't stand, or can't understand, or both.

As with the rest of the world. Europe's attitude toward the behemoth across the Atlantic is not purely negative; it's a love-hate kind of thing. American products, and American pop culture, are pervasive in Europe and immensely popular. U.S. exports like *Beverly Hills 90210, Dawson's Creek, The West Wing, Sex and the City*, and, yes, *Jerry Springer*, fill the airwaves, often on the prestigious public networks. (*Seinfeld* has not been as successful, apparently because the jokes don't translate to a continental setting.) Belgium is one of the countries where U.S. global policies are most bitterly condemned by the general public, but Belgium's home-grown version of McDonald's, the burger-and-*frites* chain called Quick, uses the characters from *Friends* as its drawing card, with Phoebe serving Ross a Quickburger in the ads. On European MTV, more than half of the videos feature American bands; no translation is provided, on the theory that Generation E can understand the lyrics as well as an American audience. The only time MTV Europe changes this pattern is each May 9, when the network celebrates Europe Day by playing only European bands. (Actually, the producers tend to cheat by claiming Madonna as a European, on the grounds that she now lives in London with her British husband. Thus May 9 is the day to see videos of "Papa Don't Preach" or "Miss American Pie" on European TV sets.) All over the continent, fashionable people gather at predawn parties each April to watch the Oscar broadcast from Los Angeles. Most years, this is followed the next day with a series of angry newspaper columns complaining that, once again, the Oscar voters showed a disgraceful bias against all European movies. The one time when the voters proved they were not biased—that was 1999, when Roberto Benigni won the Best Actor award for his performance in *La Vita e Bella* (*Life Is Beautiful*)—all of Italy celebrated for a week.

To the consternation of the great continental fashion houses, American labels—Levi's, Gap, Tommy Hilfiger, Abercrombie—are de rigueur for

Generation E. For Europe's youth movement, any article of clothing genuinely "from the States" has innate value. Walking past a trendy boot store in London's Camden Town neighborhood one day, I was offered 200 pounds on the spot for the cowboy boots I was wearing. That was $370 more than twice what I had paid for the boots, new, back home in Colorado. When I hesitated, the shopkeeper threw in a cheap pair of trainers (that's British for "gym shoes") to get me home. I laughed all the way to the bank to cash my cheque.

American fast food is ubiquitous on the continent; that explains why the standard for price transparency is the "Big Mac Index," as we will see in chapter 3 of this book. The sheep farmer José Bové became a national hero, of sorts, in France by wrecking a McDonald's outlet and defending himself on the grounds that "it's American, from the country that promotes globalization and industrial food production and unfairly penalizes the small French farmer." (Bové was sentenced to twenty days in jail for vandalism, which only increased the size of his following.) Still, France has more than 1,000 McDonald's outlets that do quite nicely, thank you, even when situated right next to a traditional *boulangerie*. No matter what the Bové-istes might say, it is hard to call this an American "invasion," since every one of the French outlets belongs to a French franchisee. Nobody is forcing the Belgians, the Spaniards, or the Danes to drink Coca-Cola or wear Nikes; the fact is, Europeans like American stuff. The novelist Arthur Koestler, a prominent America-basher in his day, had the intellectual honesty to admit this point in a 1951 essay: "Who coerced us into buying all this? The United States do not rule Europe as the British rule India; they waged no Opium War to force the revolting 'Coke' down our throats. Europe bought the whole package because Europe wanted it."

Almost despite themselves, Europeans visiting "the States" often find themselves charmed by American ways. Even a lefty columnist like John Sutherland, of London's *Guardian* newspaper, was so taken by the little things of life in the United States that he made a list of "fifty-two things they do better in America." Among the items that caught his eye—none of them common in Europe—were:

- Free refills of coffee (without asking)
- Newspaper vendomats on street corners
- "Paper or plastic?" (what the bagger says in your friendly 24-hour supermarket)
- Drive-through banking
- High school graduation ceremonies, and regular class reunions
- Free or cut-price parking at cinemas and restaurants
- Ubiquitous 24-hour convenience stores
- Fridges big enough for a 30-pound turkey

There is a whole genre of contemporary European literature involving people who have moved to, or spent some time in, the United States and are surprised to find themselves adopting American habits. The English novelist Zoe Heller, in an essay titled "Help! I'm Turning into an American Parent," described how she was at first appalled at the way American parents constantly praise their children: "To an English sensibility, these anthologies of praise seem mawkish. Unseemly. Deleterious to an appropriate sense of modesty." But gradually, Heller wrote, she began to see her own daughter responding positively to the endless encouragement she got at preschool in Santa Monica. "One of the things most admired about Americans is their can-do spirit, their optimism and self-belief and so on," Heller concluded. "It occurs to me that their child-rearing techniques might have something to do with that sunny outlook . . . What, indeed, if the Americans' cosseting methods are the real reason they are a superpower?"

Europeans also appreciate some of the larger virtues of American life: the nation's youthful vigor, its open-armed acceptance of new ideas, its great universities, and the classlessness that means the American dream really works. Even the staunchest European leftists admire America's willingness to take in refugees by the millions, accept them as American, and then hold a fancy ceremony, with a judge or a senator presiding, to make their citizenship official. (In Europe, in contrast, becoming a new citizen generally involves nothing more than a bureaucrat stamping a form in a cluttered office, and payment of the required fee.) Almost every European— particularly east of the former iron curtain—has a neighbor or cousin or grandchild who has emigrated to Milwaukee or Portland or Tallahassee. These relatives recognize the symbolic power of the Statue of Liberty and the generosity of a rich, powerful nation that embraces poor, powerless newcomers from anywhere on earth. In the beautiful old city of Riga, Latvia, I got to talking with Marie Rabinovich, whose daughter had emigrated to Denver a decade earlier. Marie told me proudly that her daughter had become an American citizen, and was about to cast her first vote in the 2000 election between George W. Bush and Al Gore. "It is amazing thing," Marie told me, in decent English, "that my daughter, a peasant, is allowed to choosing the most powerful man in the world." No matter how fashionable America-bashing has become, people all over the continent still get letters every month from their cousins in Chicago urging them to emigrate to the U.S.A.

But the Europeans also know what they don't like about the United States. These views tend to be set forth in a series of best-selling books, one after another, with titles like *Dangereuse Amerique* or *The Eagle's Shadow* or *Pourquoi le monde deteste-t-il l'Amerique?* The depiction of the United States in these popular volumes has been summarized neatly by the American scholar Anthony Jude: "The U.S. is a selfish, individualistic society devoted to commerce, profit, and the despoliation of the planet. It is uncaring of the poor and sick and it is indifferent to the rest of humankind. The U.S. rides roughshod over international laws and treaties and threatens the moral, environmental, and physical future of humanity. It is inconsistent and hypocritical in its foreign dealings, and it wields unparalleled military clout. It is, in short, a bull in the global china shop."

As we will discuss in chapter 6 of this book, most Europeans are appalled by the death penalty. And because each American execution tends to get big play in the French, German, Spanish, and British media, Europeans think American electric chairs are used much more frequently than is actually the case. The constitutional "right to keep and bear arms," and the gun lobby that defends it, also tend to mystify the people of Europe, even those who are strongly pro-American on most issues. In September of 1999, I was watching the TV news in Norway, reporting on Hurricane Floyd, which swept up the east coast of the United States and wreaked considerable destruction. The Norwegian correspondent on the scene was deeply impressed by the fact that some 2.6 million people—equivalent to half the population of Norway!—had been successfully evacuated from coastal areas to escape danger. On the same day, though, one of those tragic gun massacres had left seven Americans dead and a dozen badly wounded in a church (1) in Texas. "What kind of society is it," the reporter asked plaintively, "that can move millions of people overnight in the name of safety, but then expose them to crazy men wielding guns on every street?"

I was surprised to find that the open display of patriotism—something I had taken to be a universal human impulse—is widely sneered at in Europe. After all, it was a European who turned that impulse into deathless verse:

> *Breathes there the man with soul so dead*
> *Who never to himself hath said,*
> *"This is my own, my native land!"*

But when the great Scot Sir Walter Scott wrote that in 1805, it was still an acceptable, even admirable, point of view for Europeans. Today, the way of thinking that says. "This is my native land, and I love it," is considered an American peculiarity. The Europeans, of course, are working hard to move away from their nationalistic tendencies and toward a supranational union that eviscerates borders and traditional national rivalries, and this perhaps explains the exasperation with old-style love of country in the United States. Ian Buruma, a Dutchman living in Britain, caught this mood perfectly after seeing the American flag everywhere during a visit to New York:

> To most Europeans born after the second world war, it is a somewhat bewildering sight, this massive outpouring of patriotism. . . . Those of us who pride

ourselves on a certain degree of sophistication view flag-waving with lofty disdain. It is embarrassing, mawkish, potentially bellicose. I must confess that I find the sight of grown men touching their hearts at the sound of the national anthem a little ridiculous, too. And the ubiquitous incantations of "God Bless America" seem absurdly over the top. Mawkishness and a beady eye on commercial opportunity go together in the land of the free in a way that can be quite disconcerting.

The place where American patriotism seems to annoy Europeans the most is at international sporting events. Chants of "USA! USA!" and "We're number one!" may seem like normal fan behavior to Americans, but they drive Europe crazy. When Russian competitors lost gold medals due to disputed calls by referees in hockey, figure skating, and Nordic skiing in the 2002 Winter Olympics, President Vladimir Putin condemned the International Olympic Committee for "biased decisions and pro-American judgements at the Winter Games." Most Americans put this down as sour grapes; almost all Europeans, however, agreed with Putin that the noisy home fans in Salt Lake City—where 93 percent of all tickets were sold to Americans—had put impossible pressure on the officials. "What the Russians are upset about," wrote Simon Barnes, the sports columnist for the *Times* of London, when the Salt Lake games ended, "is the transformation of the Olympic Games into yet another American Festival of Victory. The world has been treated to 17 days of whooping crowds and American athletes hysterical with their adrenalin-stoned patriotism. I've had many wonderful times in the States and have many good American friends. But whooping, en masse, up-yours patriotism is not endearing. . . . And so the world watched the Winter Games . . . hoping that the American in the race would fall over."

I don't think Barnes is overstating the case here. The Europeans really do want to see American competitors fall over and lose—and thus give the "whooping, up-yours patriots" in the American cheering section their due comeuppance. Even the ever-so-proper world of golf erupts in rage again and again at the conduct of U.S. players and fans. There was the infamous (in Europe, at least) "Battle of Brookline" during the 1999 Ryder Cup, the biennial competition where a team of European pro golfers takes on an American all-star team. With the match all even on the last hole in Brookline, Massachusetts, an American sank a long birdie putt that put the U.S. team ahead by one stroke. The fans erupted—"USA! USA!"—and swarmed onto the green in glee to applaud their heroes. The problem was, the match wasn't over. A European player still had a putt to make that could have tied the score; after all the hoopla, and the crowd's footprints covering the green, he missed. "Evidently, they care more about an American victory than they do about sportsmanship," declared an angry European player, José Maria Olazabal of Spain. A year later, when the

Solheim Cup competition—the female version of the Ryder Cup—was played in Scotland, the American team caused a pan-European furor. The Swedish star Annika Sorenstam sunk a long chip shot from off the green that seemed to sew up a European victory. But then the American captain, Pat Bradley, approached the referee and said Sorenstam's great birdie should be disallowed, because the Swede had shot out of turn. It was a technicality—indeed, a tiny technicality—but the judges decided, once the issue had been raised, that they had to enforce the rule. In a scene played over and over on European TV news, Sorenstam broke into tears and denounced American competitiveness. "I was shocked that they took my shot away," she said. "The entire European team is disgusted with America. We all ask ourselves, 'Is this how badly they need to win?'"

Another common grievance among Europeans is the sense—it is, indeed, conventional wisdom almost everywhere—that Americans are insular people, ignorant of and indifferent to the rest of the planet. This has been a standard European complaint for more than a century. In her 1852 best-seller *Domestic Manners of the Americans,* the British traveler Frances Trollope—aunt of the great Victorian novelist—established the theme with her conclusion about the American worldview. "If the citizens of the United States were indeed the devoted patriots they call themselves, they would surely not thus encrust themselves in the hard, dry, scubborn persuasion that they are the first and best of the human race, that nothing is to be learnt, but what they are able to teach, and that nothing is worth having, which they do not possess." In the contemporary version of this stereotype, the paradigm American is that Texan tourist on the French comedy shows who walks into a Paris café and orders "two wor wabns." Brian Reade, a columnist for the London tabloid the *Mirror,* summarizes this widespread European belief.

> They are wonderfully courteous to strangers, yet indiscriminately shoot kids in schools. They believe they are masters of the world, yet know nothing about what goes on outside their shores. Yanks . . . the people whose IQ is smaller than their waist size. People who believe the world stretches from California to Boston and everything outside is the bit they have to bomb to keep the price of oil down. When I first visited America in 1976, teenagers asked if we had cars, and, if so, how we could drive them on our cobbled streets. Two months ago, a man from Chicago asked me how often we vote for a new Queen. Only one in five Americans hold a passport and the only foreign stories that make their news are floods, famine, and wars, because it makes them feel good to be an American. Feeling good to be American is what they live for. It's why they call their baseball leagues The World Series, why they can't take our football because they didn't invent it.

As I often argued in Europe, the charge that Americans are insular is absurdly off-base. No country on earth has a broader distribution of races, creeds, and nationalities than the United States, and each of the ethnic groups in America maintains a close interest in developments back in the old country. One day on the BBC's excellent *Dateline* program, Gavin Esler, the presenter—that's the British word for "anchorman"—was haranguing me about Americans' ignorance of the outside world, and their inability to master foreign languages. "You know, the way Americans speak French is just to say the word in English, only louder," he said, laughing. I know Gavin loves a good debate, so I took him on. I said that the citizenry of the United States is the world's largest repository of language skills. "We have a couple of million Polish speakers," I said. "We have more Estonian speakers than there are in Tallinn. We have 100,000 people in America who read a Cambodian newspaper every week. I'll bet there aren't 100 people in all of Britain who can read Cambodian." Esler was undeterred by this line of argument. He responded, in essence, that America shouldn't get credit for its formidable body of Cambodian linguistic talent because we imported it rather than teaching the language in our schools.

What really annoys the Europeans is that this nation perceived to be ignorant of the rest of the world has the wealth and power to dominate much of it. The French parliamentarian Noel Mamere racked up strong sales with a book—title: *No Thanks, Uncle Sam*—arguing that "it is appropriate to be downright anti-American" because of this combination of strength and stupidity. "Ominipotence and ignorace," he wrote, "is a questionable cocktail. It would be great if they saw what they looked like from over here. But they are not interested. They think they are the best in the world, that they are way ahead of everyone, and everyone needs to learn from them."

This mix of experience, attitudes, and urban myths, some dating back many decades, meant that ordinary Europeans' view of the United States was fairly critical even before the earth-shaking developments at the start of the twenty-first century. The French polling firm Groupe CSA regularly surveys opinon across France about contemporary issues, and periodically takes a poll titled "L'Image des Etars-Unis." Almost every French citizen feels knowledgeable enough to answer the questions—only a tiny minority say they aren't familiar with the details of American life—and the results are generally unflattering. The image of the United States tends to vary slightly in these polls depending on recent events—predictably, esteem for America dropped during and after the Iraq war of 2003—but the general pattern is fairly constant over the years. A survey taken in the fall of 2000 gives a baseline reading on French attitudes toward life in the United States. Asked the question, "As far as you're concerned, what kind of country is the United States?" the French public gave the following answers:

1. A nation of violence   50%

2. A nation that uses the death penalty   48%

3. A nation of great social inequality   45%

4. A nation of innovation   37%

5. A racist nation   33%

6. A nation where anything goes   27%

7. A nation where anyone can get rich   24%

8. A nation that welcomes immigrants   15%

9. A society where religion is pervasive   15%

(No opinion about America)   3%

Given those broad impressions, it's not surprising that only 12 percent of French people surveyed said they felt "admiration" for the United States. Another 14 percent reported a generally "positive" view. In contrast to the 26 percent who held a favorable view of America, 12 percent said the United States makes them worried, and 34 percent of those polled said their view of the United States was "critical."

Other European populations were perhaps not so critical as the French, but the general pattern across the continent in the year 2000 would have been roughly similar to what that CSA survey found. And then came the Bush presidency, the horrific events of 9/11, and Iraq. As George W. Bush geared up for his reelection campaign at home, the gap in understanding, respect, and friendship was arguably wider than it had ever been before.

At first, September 11, 2001, seemed to shrink the Atlantic. Just hours after the buildings toppled in New York and Washington, British prime minister Tony Blair assured Americans that Europe "stands shoulder to shoulder with you." In a unanimous vote on September 12, NATO invoked—for the first time in its fifty-year history—Article 5 of its founding treaty, the clause that says an attack on one member is considered an attack on all NATO nations. Even that venerable organ of Euro-left anti-Americanism, France's *Le Monde,* declared "Nous sommes tous Americains"—"We are all Americans." On September 13, Queen Elizabeth II broke all precedent by ordering the Royal Marine Band to play "The Star-Spangled Banner" during the changing of the guard at Buckingham Palace. A survey two weeks after the attack by the Swiss polling company Isopublic found that the peace-minded Europeans were ready to go to war against the perpetrators of the attack, or their host nation. Asked if their own countries should support a U.S. military assault, 80 percent of Danish respondents backed the idea, as did 79 percent in Britain, 73 percent in France, 58 percent in Spain and Norway, and about 53 percent in Germany. The only European nation that resisted the idea of fighting alongside the Americans was Greece, where only 29 percent supported military action.

To be an American in Europe in those troubled, frightening days after 9/11 was to be surrounded by support, sympathy, and unsolicited words of encouragement. When people realized an American was present—usually from hearing an American accent—they would go out of their way to express consolation and friendship. On a nondescript traffic island near Grosvenor Square in London, somebody tied an American flag around an old oak tree early on September 12. Over the next few days, a mountain grew beside the tree—a mountain of flowers, flags, cards, candles, tear-stained notes, pictures, paintings, and a New York Yankees cap. This was the British people's spontaneous tribute to the Americans who were murdered on 9/11. There were no instructions about this, no coordination. These were simply ordinary people who felt a need to send America a message—people like Rob Anderson of London, who left a big spray of roses with a handwritten card: "Dear America, You supported us in two world wars. We stand with you now." Similar floral mountains went up outside the U.S. embassies in Moscow, Copenhagen. Lisbon, and Madrid. London's largest cathedral, St. Paul's, invited every Yank in town to a memorial service on September 14. The local paper in Ipswich devoted its entire front page on September 12 to a banner headline: "God Bless America." Across the continent, there was an over-whelming sense that the whole of the West was under attack. We were all Americans now. We were all in this thing together.

This initial rush of good feeling was accompanied by action. The first arrests of conspirators charged with planning the 9/11 attacks were made in Germany. European intelligence agencies basically opened their files on suspected Muslim militants to investigators from the CIA and the FBI. When the United States went to war in Afghanistan a month after the attacks, European public opinion strongly supported the move; more important, nearly every NATO member sent troops, weapons, and money to help topple the Taliban. The vaunted "Atlantic Alliance" was working together more closely than at any time since the depths of the cold war.

But over the next three years, that moment of transatlantic togetherness in the fall of 2001 came to look like a momentary blip, an aberration caused more by the sudden shock of those burning buildings than by common bonds of interest and policy. Within a year of 9/11, European government ministers, columnists, and academics were once again depicting the United States as a selfish, gun-happy "hyperpower" that had shifted into "unilateralist overdrive," to borrow a term from Chris Patten, the European Union's commissioner for external affairs, a man who was supposed to be diplomatic about such things. "The whole concept of the 'West' feels out of date now," said Dominique Moisi, of the Institut Français des Relations Inter-nationales in Paris, about eighteen months after the attacks. "September 11 brought us together, but only temporarily. We have to realize that major differences exist across the Atlantic, and will not go away. Europe and the U.S. will have to live with them." The transatlantic chill stemmed in part from one man; President George W. Bush has been highly unpopular among the people of Europe. "Almost everyone on the European side agrees that the relationship is far worse since George W. Bush was elected," Moisi said. The war in Iraq, opposed by large popular majorities in every EU country— even nations like Britain, Spain, and Poland, which the United States counted as allies in the war—exacerbated the split. Spain's José Maria Aznar, who supported Bush in Iraq, paid a high price for his prowar stance. In the spring of 2004, in the wake of a terrorist bombing, the voters of Spain dumped Aznar's Popular Party and handed the government in Madrid to the strongly antiwar Socialists.

The process of "continental drift" driving the United States and Europe apart was also propelled by venerable European complaints about America, feelings dating back at least to Mrs. Trollope. The Bush adminis-tration strengthened all the old prejudices, and tended to confirm the old stereotypes. The new president, a pro-death-penalty oil man swaggering into the White House despite winning half a million fewer votes than his opponent, was "a walking gift to every European anti-American caricaturist." It was repeatedly reported in the European press that America's new leader had never been to Europe. This claim was false— Bush had made half a dozen trips to across the Atlantic before he entered the White House—but it neatly fit the common perception of an American president who didn't know the first thing about Europe. Bush fueled this European view with some unfortunate policy blunders. As we'll see in chapter 4 of this book, the Bush administration's ham-handed effort to intervene in the General Electric dispute between Jack Welch and Mario Monti damaged the new president's stature among European leaders just months after he took office. Two years later, President Bush personally phoned European prime ministers to urge them to admit Turkey to the European Union. This lobbying mission was doomed to fail, and it did. Worse than that, the president angered the leaders on the receiving end of his calls. "How could the White House possibly think that they could play in a role in determining who joins the EU?" Chris Patten commented later.

Opinion polls demonstrate how far the image of the U.S. has fallen since that brief moment of post-9/11 togetherness. A U.S. State Depart-ment poll in 1998 found that 78 percent of Germans had a favorable view of the United States. In 2002, a survey by the Pew Research Center in Washington, D.C., found that 61 percent of Germans were favorable. Two years later, in the wake of the war in Iraq, only 38 percent of Germans had a positive feeling toward the United States, the nation that had been Ger-many's strongest ally, and military defender, for fifty-nine years. In France, positive feelings toward America fell from 62 percent in 1999 to 37 percent in the spring of 2004. "If anything, fear and loathing of the U.S. has increased," wrote the Pew Center's pollster, Andrew Kohut, a few months after the fall of Baghdad. "Even in the United Kingdom, the United States' most trusted European ally, 55% see the U.S. as a threat to global peace. And in four EU countries—Greece, Spain, Finland, and Sweden—the United States is viewed as the greatest threat to world peace, more menacing than Iran or North Korea."

In a geopolitical application of Newton's third law, the actions tending to divide the old Atlantic Alliance have sparked an equal and opposite reaction in Europe: divisions with America have prompted the Europeans to draw closer together, to look even harder for unity among themselves. The growing sense that the United States is no longer the continent's protector, but rather a potential threat—or even, perhaps, the "greatest threat"—has strengthened the movement toward "ever closer union" among the members of the EU. Since the Europeans can no longer trust or align themselves with the world's only superpower, they have no choice but to build a superpower of their own. That, at least, is the reasoning of many EU leaders, including the most recent president of the European Commission, Romano Prodi. "There is a rhythm of global dominance," Prodi observed a couple of years after 9/11. "No country remains the first player forever. Maybe this American hour will not last. And who will be the next leading player? Maybe next will be China. But more probably, before China, it will be the united Europe. Europe's time is almost here. In fact, there are many areas of world affairs where the objective conclusion would have to be that Europe is already the superpower, and the United States must follow our lead."

While this deeply felt need to be the un-America, to be different from the much-mocked nation across the sea, has been a key force in building European unity, it was not the motivation that sparked the creation of a unified New Europe in the first place. The initial steps toward a United States of Europe were propelled by a different dream. Amid the misery and ruin left behind by the twentieth century's two lethal world wars, a group of Europeans set out to create a lasting peace on the continent and a shared economy. They did not aim low. Their dream was to produce, once and for all, an end to war on the continent, and an end to poverty.

Textual Questions

1. How does Reid's opening paragraph both establish the tone of his article and summarize his overall argument?

2. Reid's article is divided into 12 separate sections. What major point does Reid make in each section? How does he connect the point in each section with those made in previous and subsequent sections?

3. According to Reid, how are sporting events a major part of European disgust, dislike, and/or disdain for Americans?

Rhetorical Questions

4. Consider the examples Reid uses to support his argument in each of the 12 sections of his argument. Based upon these examples, how does Reid seem to want his readers to feel about the European Union? About America?

5. What role does the denigration of America, Americans, and the American president play in Europe's emerging cultural identity? Why? What might the effects of this negative attitude toward America be?

6. In Reid's assessment, the nations of the European Union—like many nations across the globe—are in a love-hate relationship with America. How does he support this contention, and is his support persuasive? Where is America more hated than loved? More loved than hated? And which aspects of America and American culture are loved/hated, specifically?

Intertextual Questions

7. What connections do you see between Reid's argument and that made by former President Jimmy Carter in "Just War—or a Just War?" (this chapter)?

8. How do you think Virgil Scudder, author of "The Importance of Communication in a Global World" (Chapter 3), would respond to Reid's argument? Why?

Thinking Beyond the Text

9. According to Reid, how do most Europeans view Americans and why? Based upon your own experience, is this view of European attitudes accurate or inaccurate? Why?

10. Based upon your own experiences and observations, how (thinking in broad generalizations) do Americans feel about Europeans in general? Are there specific groups or nationalities within the classification "Europeans" of whom Americans think especially favorably or poorly? Who and why?

For Writing & Discussion

11. Watch the nightly news on one of the major broadcast networks— CBS, NBC, or ABC—and make notes on the stories that discuss the relationship between America and one or more nations in Europe. In a short essay, explain how the stories you observed either confirm or refute the claims made by Reid.

JEHANGIR POCHA

Jehangir Pocha (1968–) is a China correspondent for the *Boston Globe* and the Asia correspondent for the independent political magazine *In These Times*.

Pocha's writing has appeared in many other publications, including the *San Francisco Chronicle*, the *International Herald Tribune*, and the Indian business magazine *Businessworld*. He has lived and worked in India, the United States, Singapore, and Iran, and has written about events in Mongolia, Cambodia, Taiwan, North Korea, and Malaysia. Pocha's essay "The Sub-Continent's Opportunity" was published in the book *Dispatches from a Wounded World* in 2002, and he also has written about information technology for *LAN Times* and *IT Asia*. Before becoming a journalist, Pocha worked for nine years in global marketing and business development.

"The Axis of Oil" was first published in February 2005 in *In These Times*. It discusses possible global consequences of China's and India's decisions to move into the international oil market and the alliances these fast-growing countries are making in the process. The article draws on Pocha's familiarity with international affairs and also his two masters' degrees, one in Business Administration from the University of Bombay and one in Public Administration from Harvard.

The Axis of Oil

∾ Prereading Question

In the late 1970s, the price for a gallon of gasoline in the United States peaked, depending on the region, around $1.70. In 2006 the price has risen over $3.00 per gallon virtually nationwide. What effects does a sudden, large increase in the price of gasoline have on individual Americans? What effect does the same increase have on the price of various goods and services? Why?

China and India are locked in an increasingly aggressive wrangle with the United States over the world's most critical economic commodity: oil. More than any other issue, this tussle will shape the economic, environmental and geopolitical future of these three countries, and the world.

Ensuring a steady flow of cheap oil has always been one of the central goals of U.S. foreign and economic policy, and Washington's preeminent position in the world is based in large measure on its ability to do this. But China and India are increasingly competing with the United States to secure oil exploration rights in Africa, Southeast Asia, Central Asia and Latin America.

India has-invested more than $3 billion in global exploration ventures and has said it will continue to spend $1 billion a year on more acquisitions. China, which has already invested about $15 billion in foreign oil fields, is expected to spend 10 times more over the next decade.

The motive, says Zheng Hongfei, an energy researcher at the Beijing Institute of Technology, is that "there is just not enough oil in the world" to cover China's and India's growing energy needs.

By 2010 India will have 36-times more cars than it did in 1990. China will have 90 times more, and by 2030 it will have more cars than the United States, according to the Energy Research Institute of Beijing.

More than 4.5 million new vehicles are expected to hit Chinese roads this year alone, a far cry from the time when families saved for months to buy a Flying Pigeon bicycle. The country is now the world's largest oil importer after the United States, guzzling about 6.5 million barrels of oil a day; this figure will double by 2020, says Stephen Roach, chief economist at Morgan Stanley.

India, the world's second-fastest growing economy after China, now consumes about 2.2 million barrels a day—about the same as South Korea—and this is expected to rise to 5.3 million barrels a day by 2025, according to the U.S. Energy Information Administration.

With global oil production barely 1 million barrels over the global consumption rate of 81 million barrels a day, the surge in demand from China and India could eventually lead global demand to outstrip supply, causing fuel prices to shoot up beyond their recent highs of around $56 a barrel, says Roach.

The impact of this on the global economy, particularly in developing countries that import most of their fuel, would be severe. The International Energy Agency says that for every $1 increase in oil price, the global economy loses $25 billion.

Anxiety over this is already throwing the nervous oil market into further disequilibrium. In September, Michael Rothman, a senior energy analyst at Merrill Lynch, said rising oil prices were not so much a result of the Iraq war or political instability in Venezuela and Sudan, but of extensive "hoarding" by China.

According to Rothman's analysis, China and India are roiling oil markets by creating oil reserves, which are designed to provide the minimum cache the country needs to ride out a crisis, along the lines of the United States' Strategic Petroleum Reserve (SPR).

With both countries flush with foreign exchange reserves that are threatening to infect their economies with inflation, creating an oil stock seems a sensible solution. But critics say Beijing's and New Delhi's timing is unfortunate, coming just as the global economy seemed to be recovering and the United States was questioning the value of its own reserve.

At 175 million barrels and 25 million barrels respectively, China's and India's estimated oil reserves are just a small fraction of the 700 million barrels held by the United States in its SPR.

China and India, which are both nuclear states, are also taking advantage of the United States' strained ties with Iran, Vietnam and Myanmar by extending these countries military and political support in exchange for energy supplies. And a Washington pre-occupied with Iraq, the war on terror and nuclear crises in Iran and North Korea has been unable to checkmate either country as successfully as it did earlier.

For example, U.S. nervousness over China's intentions in Latin America had led it to use its leverage with Panama to impede China's access to the all-important canal connecting the Pacific and Atlantic. But in December, Beijing signed a landmark deal with Venezuela and its neighbor Colombia, under whose terms a pipeline would be constructed linking Venezuelan oil fields to ports along Colombia's Pacific coastline. This will allow Venezuelan oil to bypass the Panama Canal and create a new and direct route to China.

There are also signs that China is warming to the idea of a Russia–China–India axis, which, in cooperation with Iran, would turn the oil-rich Central Asian region into their domain. This proposal would put in place extensive military agreements and pipeline networks. Originally put forward by Russia's Asia-centric ex-Prime Minister Yevgeny Primakov, the proposal seems to be gaining ground with all four nations. China and India have already signed multibillion-dollar gas and energy deals with Russia, which is the largest arms supplier to both countries, and with ex-Soviet Central Asian republics such as Kazakhstan.

What worries Western powers most are China's and India's growing ties with Iran, a country Washington is trying to isolate. Both Beijing and New Delhi have recently signed 25-year gas and oil deals with Iran that are collectively valued at between $150 and $200 billion, and both countries are also deepening their military cooperation with Tehran. Iran and India conducted their first-ever joint naval exercises last September, and India has agreed to modernize Iran's aging Russian-built Kilo-class submarines and MiG fighters.

Both China and India have also tried to thwart Western attempts to curtail Iran's nuclear program, which has largely been built with Russian assistance. In a departure from China's traditional neutrality on international issues that do not involve its own interests, Chinese Foreign Minister Li Zhaoxing flew to Tehran last November when the United States threatened to haul Iran before the U.N. Security Council and announced that China would oppose any such effort. And in January, the State Department imposed penalties against some of China's largest weapons manufacturers for their support of Iran's ballistic missile program.

The potential volatility from such aggressive oil politics could bring China and India into conflict with Western, Japanese and other regional interests, says Robert Karniol, the Asia-Pacific editor of *Jane's Defence Weekly*.

"Even if China's oil consumption doubles by 2020, it will still only be half that of the U.S.," ' says Zheng, the energy researcher at Beijing Institute of Technology.

Yet the sheer size of the Asian juggernauts and the prospect that they might indiscriminately swallow global resources scare economic planners.

State-owned Indian and Chinese oil companies are investing heavily in local energy fields, such as the 200,000-square-mile Ordos Basin that stretches across the provinces of Shaanxi, Shanxi, Gansu, Ningxia and Inner Mongolia in northwestern China, and is reported to have oil reserves of up to 60 billion barrels.

To defray the substantial costs of exploration, both China and India are privatizing state-owned oil companies, and using the billions raised to restructure and modernize their operations. Other public sector oil units are also undergoing massive recapitalization and restructuring, including the retrenchment of thousands of workers.

Sharon Hurst, a Beijing-based executive with ConocoPhillips, the largest refiner in the United States, says, "Western investment is helping Chinese oil companies morph into world-class players."

Significantly, both nations are also opening up their domestic oil industries—previously considered strategic and therefore off limits to foreign and private investors. Companies such as ExxonMobil, which owns a 19 percent stake in China's giant Sinopec company, are being wooed not just for their capital but also for their refining and marketing capabilities. For example, ExxonMobil is helping Sinopec establish more than 500 gas stations across the country and build at least two refineries in southern China.

Optimists—mostly people from the corporate world such as Warren Buffet—say such common opportunity will lead to greater cooperation rather than competition between the West and China and India. But pessimists—mostly people from the security establishment—fear that China and India, two energy-hungry giants seeking access to limited world resources, will inevitably clash with the West.

Textual Questions

1. According to Pocha, with whom is the United States in direct competition for a cheap supply of oil? What are the possible implications of this competition?

2. How does Pocha describe the oil needs of India and China? What details support these descriptions most effectively?

3. What sources does Pocha paraphrase and/or quote? How are these quotations and paraphrases integrated into the argument persuasively?

Rhetorical Questions

4. While describing the current and future oil needs of China and India, Pocha barely mentions American needs. Why? Would a more detailed comparison and contrast of the United States, India, and China's needs be more or less effective? Why?

5. Who is Pocha's ideal reader for this essay? That is, who is most likely to (a) know enough to understand the argument and (b) be persuaded by it? Would this argument be persuasive to those who disagree with Pocha? Why or why not?

6. Pocha's title is a reference to a statement made by President George W. Bush early in his first term, a statement in which he referred to Iran, Iraq, and North Korea as the Axis of Evil. Why might Pocha use an allusion to this statement to construct an argument about the supply and demand for oil?

Intertextual Questions

7. How does Pocha's argument about the demand for oil and its (mostly implied) effects on U.S. relations with the world compare/contrast with Condoleezza Rice's arguments about security issues in "Transformational Democracy" (this chapter)?

8. Consider the speech by President Jimmy Carter in the introduction to this text, "Energy Problems: Erosion of Confidence." Based upon that text, how might Carter respond to Pocha's argument about oil, supply and demand, and (ultimately) America's future?

Thinking Beyond the Text

9. How much do you spend weekly for gasoline? Or, if you don't drive, then interview someone who does commute regularly to work and ask him/her about the weekly cost for gasoline. What percentage of your (his/her) monthly income is spent on gasoline? What do you (or does he/she) do to balance the cost of fuel with other ongoing expenses? That is, what sacrifices, big and small, must be made to make regular commuting possible, from not eating at restaurants to carpooling?

10. What effects does a rising gasoline price have on the U.S. economy? Why? If gasoline supplies are limited, why has there, traditionally, been a relatively limited push to develop other sources of fuel?

For Writing & Discussion

11. Searching online, find out how much a gallon of gasoline cost when you were born. How does that compare with the price of gasoline now? On a graph, chart the yearly rise (or possibly fall) in gasoline prices over your lifetime. Based upon the change between the day you were born and now, what might the price of gasoline be in ten years? Twenty?

COLIN L. POWELL

Colin L. Powell (1937–) is a retired U.S. Army general and former secretary of state (2001–2005) under President George W. Bush. From 1987–1989 he was National Security Advisor under President George H.W. Bush, and then was chairman of the Joint Chiefs of Staff from 1989–1993, resigning a few months after President Clinton took office. Powell was in the Army from 1957 to 1989 and has received numerous awards including a Bronze Star and a Purple Heart. His civilian awards include two Presidential Medals of Freedom.

"No Country Left Behind" was published in the January/February 2005 issue of *Foreign Policy* magazine shortly after President Bush began his second term. In the article, Powell describes the interplay of poverty and security around the world while explaining the Bush administration's goals for globalization and economic development.

Since officially leaving the government in 2005, Powell has spoken out on various political issues, including criticizing the Bush administration's response to Hurricane Katrina and opposing John Bolton's nomination as the U.S. ambassador to the United Nations. Powell is currently a "strategic limited partner" with a venture capital firm in Silicon Valley. He is on the Boards of Trustees of Howard University and of the United Negro College Fund, and recently became chairman of the Eisenhower Fellowship Program.

No Country Left Behind

∾ Prereading Question

The basic implication of Colin Powell's title, "No Country Left Behind," is clear: Nations "progress" at different rates, otherwise there could be no "third world." Which are the less developed nations in each region of the globe, and how do their different levels of development impact their relationships with their neighbors? Why?

> *Development is not a "soft" policy goal, but a core national security issue, says Colin Powell, as he draws the main lessons of his four years as U.S. secretary of state. However, contrary to what critics say, the best way to lift millions out of poverty is not to increase levels of foreign aid. Instead, the United States must engage in tough love and demand that corrupt, autocratic regimes change their ways.*

As the first George W. Bush administration moved toward its conclusion, many people asked me to sum up the president's foreign-policy record of the last four years. Almost invariably, their questions focused on September 11 and the war on terrorism, developments in Iraq and Afghanistan, the state of trans-Atlantic relations, or the difficulties of the intelligence craft. Almost invariably, my answers have keyed on distinguishing between issues such as these that tend to dominate the headlines, and issues of equal or greater long-term strategic significance that rarely generate as much interest.

Among these latter issues, none is more important than economic development in the world's poorest societies. As the president wrote in the National Security Strategy in September 2002, "A world where some live in comfort and plenty, while half of the human race lives on less than $2 a day, is neither just nor stable." No issue has consumed more of the administration's concern and energy. And now that George W. Bush has a mandate for a second term, he intends to pursue his goals for economic development with the same determination that made possible the liberation of Iraq and Afghanistan. The president has said that he intends to spend the political capital he earned in winning the trust of the American people, and the world can be assured that much of that capital will be spent helping the poorest of its citizens.

In doing so, the president is building upon the legacy of President John F. Kennedy, who established the U.S. Agency for International Development (USAID) in 1961. Helping poor societies to prosper has long been part of our international goals. Achieving broad and sustained success, however, has proven more difficult than most diplomats and economists envisioned at the time.

We have come to understand that development assistance does not work well when it is conceived and pursued as a narrow economic exercise. It has become ever clearer that political attitudes and cultural predispositions affect the economic behavior of individuals, and that history has shaped the economic institutions of societies. External factors, including security conditions, also play a role in determining economic progress, especially as globalization weaves together the fate of nations.

The first George W. Bush administration took these lessons to heart. We see development, democracy, and security as inextricably linked. We recognize that poverty alleviation cannot succeed without sustained economic growth, which requires that policymakers take seriously the challenge of good governance. At the same time, new and often fragile democracies cannot be reliably sustained, and democratic values cannot be spread further, unless we work hard and wisely at economic development. And no nation, no matter how powerful, can assure the safety of its people as long as economic desperation and injustice can mingle with tyranny and fanaticism.

Development is not a "soft" policy issue, but a core national security issue. Although we see a link between terrorism and poverty, we do not believe that poverty directly causes terrorism. Few terrorists are poor. The leaders of the September 11 group were all well-educated men, far from the bottom rungs of their societies. Poverty breeds frustration and resentment, which ideological entrepreneurs can turn into support for—or acquiescence to—terrorism, particularly in those countries in which poverty is coupled with a lack of political rights and basic freedoms.

The connection between poverty and the absence of freedom is not an incidental one. Although resource endowments shape development, poverty is not inevitable in countries that possess few natural resources. After all, Holland and Venice in days gone by, and Singapore and Israel today, are small territories without significant natural resources—but they have not suffered from poverty and powerlessness.

The root cause of poverty is social injustice and the bad government that abets it. Poverty arises and persists where corruption is endemic and enterprise is stifled, where basic fairness provided by the rule of law is absent. In such circumstances, poverty is an assault against human dignity, and in that assault lies the natural seed of human anger.

The United States cannot win the war on terrorism unless we confront the social and political roots of poverty. We want to bring people to justice if they commit acts of terrorism, but we also want to bring justice to people. We want to help others achieve representative government that provides opportunity and fairness. We want to unshackle the human spirit so that entrepreneurship, investment, and trade can flourish. This goal is the indispensable social and political precondition for sustainable development; it is the means by which we will uproot the social support structures of terrorism.

Development is not only a difficult and complex job; it is also a very big one. Half the people on this planet, about 3 billion human beings, live in destitute poverty. More than a billion people lack clean water. Two billion lack adequate sanitation and electrical power. However complex and massive it is, we have embraced the challenge head-on, and to do so, we have joined with other countries in reshaping development policy worldwide. The Financing for Development Summit held in Monterrey, Mexico, in 2002 reached a new consensus on development. It is a consensus we fully share, one with three central pillars: a shared commitment to private sector-led economic growth; social development; and the sound stewardship of natural resources, built on a foundation of good governance and the rule of law.

Market Incentives

Economic systems work best when access to opportunity is fair, when free people can use their talents to help themselves and others to prosper. Aid can be a catalyst for development, but the real engines of growth are entrepreneurship, investment, and trade. They are what produce jobs, and a job is the most important social safety net for any family. If economic aid to developing countries is to succeed, it must be part of an incentive system for good governance. Foreign aid that succeeds is foreign aid that makes itself obsolete. If a country needs aid year after year, decade after decade, it will develop a dependency on outside assistance.

Indeed, foreign aid to undemocratic regimes can be counterproductive in that it increases the longevity of the ruling autocracy by making it easier for despots to keep their small clique of supporters happy. Foreign aid will not make a real difference if markets are manipulated by autocrats who control access to credit, licenses, and jobs. Foreign aid will not generate growth if sound banking institutions cannot arise, because transparency exposes nepotism and other forms of corruption. Foreign aid does not work if the heavy hand of authoritarianism crushes individual initiative.

Ultimately, it is not possible to separate economics from politics. We should not expect democracy to work in places where there is blatant economic injustice. We should not expect sustained economic success in places where political life remains shackled. This symbiosis between political and economic freedom is the basis for the Millennium Challenge Account (MCA), which offers a contract modeled on the free market itself—that is its genius. Recipients of MCA money have to meet a set of eligibility requirements before they get a nickel. Governments must already have in place effective policies to rule justly, invest in their people, and promote economic freedom. They must also agree to achieve measurable results from aid assistance in terms of reducing poverty and generating broad economic growth.

Put a little differently, the MCA is an incentive system to reward the spread of freedom of speech and assembly; broader access to credit so that people can start new businesses; adherence to the rule of law to protect private property and enforce the sanctity of contracts. It is an incentive system for countries to provide their people with the basic tools for their own prosperity.

The power of the MCA was evident even before it became law. For example, one country passed and enforced four pieces of anticorruption legislation in order to become eligible for MCA funds. Now that the MCA is up and running with 17 countries eligible for funding, its influence will spread rapidly as funds for the program grow. The U.S. Congress appropriated $1 billion for the first year. The administration asked for $2.5 billion this fiscal year, and we hope funding levels will increase to $5 billion a year by fiscal year 2006.

Of course, not every country will be eligible for the MCA soon. Not every autocratic government will risk its grip on power to help their people. And the persistence of bad governance will continue to generate political instability and the humanitarian crises that usually go with it. We will continue to help alleviate those crises when we can. We will not punish people for the actions of bad governments over which they have little or no control. The work of USAID is critical in this regard. But humanitarian assistance is a stopgap measure. Our true aim is to eradicate poverty by challenging the leaderships of developing countries to take their nations' futures into their own hands. They are ultimately responsible for the success or failure of their own development efforts.

We believe that no country is excluded from this responsibility, and the benign possibilities that arise from it. Just as the president believes that no child should be left behind in education, that every child can learn, he believes that no nation should be left behind in development, that every nation can prosper. Phase by phase, one country at a time, for as long as it takes, the president aims to bring every poor society along—with USAID pushing from one end as the MCA pulls from the other.

In the meantime, we can help empower individual men and women worldwide. The international community needs to do better at matching people who want to work with markets that need their labor. At least 180 million people worldwide do not reside in their countries of birth. Some are political refugees, but the vast majority are migrants, legal and illegal. People want a better life, and they are often willing to take daunting risks to achieve it for the sake of their families' future.

Those risks are yielding rewards. Remittances sent home by migrant laborers have become a financial lifeline for developing countries, totaling around $93 billion dollars in 2003, compared to total official development aid of $77 billion. More people would migrate toward hospitable labor markets if the barriers to doing so legally were reduced. Remittances could double, or even triple. Yet there is no effective multilateral mechanism in the world today to handle these issues, nor any effective international regime to reduce the human costs of illegal migration.

The president's global initiatives on trafficking in persons—which seek to end forced prostitution, forced labor, and child soldiers—is a part of our effort to deal with illegal migration. The administration is also acting to reduce the costs of sending remittances from the United States. Most important in this regard, however, was President Bush's proposal last year of a new partnership with Mexico, calling for a temporary worker program that can match labor with markets. The president proposed a way to transform a process that is too often illegal, inefficient, and inhumane into one that respects the law, works economically, and understands that laborers are, above all, human beings.

These principles need not be limited to our own borders. Wherever it occurs, illegal migration undermines the rule of law, poses public health and security risks, and ruins lives. Illegal migration also sustains organized criminals, who peddle people with no more scruples than they peddle drugs and weapons. The deaths of desperate people suffocated in cargo containers, in the back of unventilated trucks, and in the filthy holds of cargo ships tell us what is at stake here. Illegal migration is a global challenge, so it must be dealt with on a global scale. We must redouble our efforts to form international partnerships to deal with this pressing issue.

∽

The Health of Nations

Sound economic and political institutions cannot work unless people are healthy and educated enough to take advantage of them. So we fight hunger and malnutrition through the Food for Peace program, which makes commodity donations and emergency food assistance available for developing countries facing food crises. We support poorer countries that invest in their own people, especially in education.

We also try to spur business development through programs such as the Digital Freedom Initiative, which helps make new information and communications technologies accessible to entrepreneurs and small businesses throughout the developing world. We are conducting pilot information technology-development projects in Senegal, Indonesia, Peru, and Jordan. If these projects work as we hope, we aim to involve at least 16 more countries over the next four years.

Above all, we see the achievement of basic health and sanitation as the key prerequisite for development, and we see clean water as central to this task. Growing populations and increased economic activity in many parts of the world have made access to clean water harder for millions of people. The United Nations Children's Fund estimates that 6,000 children die each day from water-related diseases, such as diarrhea, which are a consequence of poor sanitation. Our Water for the Poor Initiative, which helps partnering countries better manage their water supply and prevent the pollution of precious fresh water supplies, will help ensure that every person, particularly every child, can look forward to a world where the simple act of drinking a glass of water is not a life-threatening risk. With $970 million as seed capital, we are trying to leverage at least $1.6 billion worldwide for this purpose.

We are fighting disease on many other fronts. Along with the Group of Eight industrialized countries (G-8), we are determined to eradicate polio once and for all. To this end, the G-8—with public and private partners—has pledged $3.48 billion. We are also combating malaria and drug-resistant tuberculosis. And we are dedicated to improving the global public health system, because, as the SARS epidemic revealed, infectious diseases know no borders.

Above all, we are fighting the scourge of HIV/AIDS. President Bush sees the struggle against this pandemic as a moral imperative, but he also sees the ravages that HIV imposes on development. Its victims include not just those who become ill but whole societies held hostage by this tragedy. The president's emergency AIDS fund devotes $15 billion over five years to prevent new infections, to treat millions already infected, and to care for the orphans the dead leave behind. Under President Bush's leadership, the United States spends nearly twice as much as the rest of the world's donor governments on fighting AIDS.

Here, too, fighting disease as a part of our development strategy cannot be separated from its political and security dimensions. AIDS is more than a medical problem, and money alone won't cure it. It is a problem with social roots, and political obstacles still loom large in some countries. Our world will be less secure if we fail this test before us.

ॐ

Compassionate Conservationism

To be sustainable, development must be a process that invests and pays dividends, plants as well as harvests. We believe deeply in the sound stewardship of natural resources, as the organic connection between the words "conservation" and "conservative" suggest. It was, after all, a Republican president, Theodore Roosevelt, who pioneered the modern concept of conservation nearly a century ago. No one should be surprised, therefore, that the first George W. Bush administration initiated or joined 20 major programs promoting sustainable development.

For example, in 2002, during the World Summit on Sustainable Development in Johannesburg, I launched the Congo Basin Forest Partnership. That program is a coalition of 13 governments, 3 international organizations, and 10 civil society groups united to protect the world's second largest tropical forest. We want to protect it because it is beautiful and irreplaceable, but also because it provides a livelihood to millions of people by being a key source of natural resources and tourism. In 2003, the president presented his initiative against illegal logging worldwide. Poachers who chop down and sell timber harm the environment, the legal lumber business, and consumers by making the sound use of scarce resources far more difficult. We are organizing ourselves and others to put a stop to this form of environmental desecration and theft.

Also at the 2002 World Summit on Sustainable Development, the United States joined the Global Village Energy Partnership. This public-private partnership that started with just over 70 entities now encompasses more than 300 governments, international organizations, and business and civil society groups. It is devoted to shaping national and regional energy strategies that balance development needs with resources, and it is starting to yield results. In the first six months of 2004, for example, USAID spent upward of $7.2 million to provide more than half a million people with access to clean, efficient, and healthy forms of energy in areas either not served or underserved by current energy delivery systems.

We also need to better husband ocean resources for sustainable development, and to that end the Bush administration helped launch the White Water to Blue Water program. This project has already mobilized more than $3 million to create or support over a hundred partnerships for watershed and marine ecosystem management in the wider Caribbean area.

We live in a world in which our own self-interest depends on advancing the interests of others. Key environmental goals, such as ensuring biodiversity, affect all people in all nations. So we have shared our experience and our technology, and we have used our wealth to help others grow and develop. By helping others, we help ourselves.

&

A Mandate for Hope

Our goal is to eradicate poverty. The president has a vision of how to achieve that goal: enabling the spread of political systems where access to opportunity is fair, and where democracy and the rule of law enable free people to use their God-given talents to prosper. And we have a strategy that sees economics, politics, and security as three parts of a whole— a strategy that combines growth methods that work with social development and sound environmental stewardship.

We have a goal, a vision, and a strategy, but we also have something else of supreme importance: faith in the capacity of human beings to care about one another. After all, most people do not work to get rich; their labor is an act of love. They work to provide for spouses, children, and grandchildren, sometimes parents, grandparents, and other family members and dear friends. When we realize this underlying truth, then the all important moral dimension of what we're striving for stands out—and that provides both our highest motivation and our greatest hope.

As President Bush begins his second term in office, the United States now has an unprecedented opportunity to translate our hopes into lasting achievements. Americans have been telling people around the world for many years that representative government and market systems are the best means to unleash the energy that produces prosperity. Through our words and deeds, we have demonstrated that respect for human dignity empowers people, motivating them to dream and to work toward those dreams.

Today, just a dozen or so years after the Cold War, more people who believe in these principles can act on their beliefs. More national leaders accept these tenets. More societies are embracing freedom. But this task is not easy; results do not spring up overnight. The path to reform and development has many obstacles. The United States has a particular moral obligation to help overcome those difficulties, and we are doing so through the most creative development policies since the birth of USAID and that will be, if fully funded by congress, the most generous since the Marshall Plan. By 2006, U.S. government assistance will have doubled since 2000, and its trajectory remains upward. If one combines official development assistance, U.S. imports from poorer countries, and voluntary philanthropic grants from private citizens and foundations, the United States alone accounts for more than 65 percent of all Group of Seven economic development activities.

Yes, development is a big job, but it is a crucial one. What is at stake is whether globalization can be made to work for enough people, in enough ways, to produce a world that is both stable and prosperous. We believe it can, and we are determined to ensure that outcome, for ourselves and for others.

Textual Questions

1. Consider the first four paragraphs of Powell's essay. How do they connect with one another to make a single, well-focused line of argument?

2. How does Powell define "development" and support his argument that it is a "core national security issue"?

3. How does Powell build to the argument he makes in the final section of his essay? What details in each of the preceding sections of the essay lead directly to his final assertions?

Rhetorical Questions

4. According to Powell, the central issue confronting U.S. national security is poverty. How does he support this contention? How persuasive is his support?

5. How does Powell describe America's past? Present? Future course of action? Why? How is his description of the past/present/future part of his overall argument?

6. Consider the arguments Powell makes in each section of his essay. Which of these sections is argued most persuasively or least persuasively and why?

Intertextual Questions

7. How does Powell's characterization of the United States under President George W. Bush compare and contrast with that offered by T. R. Reid in "The Atlantic Widens" (this chapter)?

8. How might Michael Ignatieff, author of "Who Are Americans to Think That Freedom Is Theirs to Spread?" (this chapter), respond to Powell's arguments?

Thinking Beyond the Text

9. Why is Colin L. Powell considered a credible person to make this argument? What aspects of his past give him particular authority to write on all of the issues he addresses? Does his public stature give his words more authority and credibility than they would have if made by someone else? Does his public stature give his words more authority and credibility than they deserve?

10. Powell made his argument early in 2005. From your perspective years down-the-line, which aspects of Powell's argument seem most accurate? Which seem least accurate? Why?

For Writing & Discussion

11. In the final section of his essay, Powell argues that "Our goal is to eradicate poverty." Is this the same essential goal of President Lyndon Johnson, offered in "The Great Society" (Chapter 1)? How are their arguments about poverty, separated by 41 years, similar and different?

꩜

ROBERT CONQUEST

Robert Conquest (1917–) is a British historian and a Fellow at Stanford's Hoover Institution. A Russian history specialist and former member of the British Communist Party, Conquest served as an intelligence officer in the British army during World War II. Following the war he was a press officer in the diplomatic service, then a member of the Foreign Office's Information Research Department, an anti-Communist organization that worked with journalists and others to spread anti-Communist ideas. In 1956 he left government work to give more time to writing.

Conquest has received numerous awards, including the Richard Weaver Award for Scholarly Letters and the Alexis de Tocqueville Award. He also has been made a Companion of the Order of St. Michael and St. George in the United Kingdom, and he received the Presidential Medal of Freedom from President Bush in 2005.

"Downloading Democracy" is an excerpt from Conquest's most recent book, *The Dragons of Expectation: Reality and Delusion in the Course of History* (2004) and was published in the Winter 2004/2005 issue of *The National Interest*. He has published several other scholarly books, and six volumes of poetry.

Conquest's early involvement in the British Communist Party, and his later involvement in international diplomacy, give him particular insight into the strength of words, ideals, and ideologies.

Downloading Democracy

꩜ **Prereading Question**

Listen to a single broadcast of a radio call-in program—the type of show where listeners phone either the host of the show or his/her guest(s) to discuss the issues of the day. As you listen, make a list of the topics discussed. What are three key terms used by the callers and/or the host—"freedom" or "immigration," for example? Are these terms ever defined by anyone taking part in the discussion? How do the callers/host seem to be defining these terms, based on the things they say? How would you define them?

The common addiction to general words or concepts tends to produce mind blockers or reality distorters. As Clive James has put it, "verbal cleverness, unless its limitations are clearly and continuously seen by its possessors, is an unbeatable way of blurring reality until nothing can be seen at all."

"Democracy" is high on the list of blur-begetters—not a weasel word so much as a huge rampaging Kodiak bear of a word. The conception is, of course, Greek. It was a matter of the free vote by the public (though confined to males and citizens). Pericles, praising the Athenian system, is especially proud of the fact that policies are argued about and debated before being put into action, thus, he says, "avoiding the worst thing in the world," which is to rush into action without considering the consequences. And, indeed, the Athenians did discuss and debate, often sensibly.

Its faults are almost as obvious as its virtues. And examples are many—for instance, the sentencing of Socrates, who lost votes because of his politically incorrect speech in his own defense. Or the Athenian assembly voting for the death of all the adult males and the enslavement of all the women and children of Mytilene, then regretting the decision and sending a second boat to intercept, just in time, the boat carrying the order. Democracy had the even more grievous result of procuring the ruin of Athens, by voting for the disastrous and pointless expedition to Syracuse against the advice of the more sensible, on being bamboozled by the attractive promises of the destructive demagogue Alcibiades.

Even in failure, the thought-fires it set off went on burning. But the views it posed did not really return to Europe and elsewhere until a quarter of a millennium ago. Thus it was not its example but its theory that hit the inexperienced thinkers of the European Enlightenment. Unfortunately, the inheritance was less about the Periclean need for debate than about the need to harness the people (to a succession of rulers). And though the broader forces of real consensual rule began to penetrate, from England and elsewhere (such as the early New England town meetings or those of Swiss rural cantons), they had to compete in the struggle for the vote with inexperienced populations and "philosophical" elites.

The revival of the *concept* of democracy on the European continent saw this huge stress on the *demos,* the people. They could not in fact match the direct participation of the Athenian *demos,* but they could be "represented" by any revolutionary regime claiming to do so—often concerned, above all, to repress "enemies of the people." Also, the people, or those of military age, could be conscripted in bulk—the *levée en masse* that long defeated more conventional armies. As the 19th century continued, the people could be polled in plebiscites and thus democratically authenticated. Napoleon III, of course, relied on this, and it is clear that he actually had high majority support. In any case, the new orders, democratic or not, had to seek or claim authentication by the people, the masses, the population.

Another aspect of premature "democracy" is the adulation of what used to be and might still be called "the city mob" (noted by Aristotle as *ochlocracy*). In France, of course, in the 1790s, a spate of ideologues turned to the Paris mob, in riot after riot, until the 18th Brumaire, Napoleon's coup of 1799. The ploy was that, as A. E. Housman put it, a capital city with far fewer inhabitants could decide the fate of the country's millions.

That democracy is not the only, or inevitable, criterion of social progress is obvious. If free elections give power to a repression of consensuality, they are worse than useless. We will presumably not forget that Hitler came to power in 1933 by election, with mass and militant support. The communist coup in Czechoslovakia in 1948 was effected by constitutional intrigues backed by "mass demonstrations." We need hardly mention the "peoples' democracies" and the 90 percent votes they always received. As to later elections, a few years ago there was a fairly authentic one in Algeria. If its results had been honored, it would have replaced the established military rulers with an Islamist political order. This was something like the choice facing Pakistan in 2002. At any rate it is not a matter on which the simple concepts of democracy and free elections provide us with clear criteria.

"Democracy" is often given as the essential definition of Western political culture. At the same time, it is applied to other areas of the world in a formal and misleading way. So we are told to regard more or less uncritically the legitimacy of any regime in which a majority has thus won an election. But "democracy" did not develop or become viable in the West until quite a time after a law-and-liberty polity had emerged. Habeas corpus, the jury system and the rule of law were not products of "democracy," but of a long effort, from medieval times, to curb the power of the English executive. And democracy can only be seen in any positive or laudable sense if it emerges from and is an aspect of the law-and-liberty tradition.

Institutions that differ in the United States and the United Kingdom have worked (though forms created in other countries that were theoretically much the same have often collapsed). That is to say, at least two formally different sets of institutions have generally flourished. It seems that the main thing they share is not so much the institutions as the habits of mind, which are far more crucial, and, above all, the acceptance of the traditional rules of the political game.

More broadly, in the West it has been *tradition* that has been generally determinant of public policy. Habituation is more central to a viable constitution than any other factor. Even the Western "democracies" are not exactly models of societies generated by the word, the abstract idea. Still they, or some of them, roughly embody the concept, as we know it, and at least are basically consensual and plural—the product of at best a long evolution.

The countries without at least a particle of that background or evolution cannot be expected to become instant democracies; and if they do not live up to it, they will unavoidably be, with their Western sponsors, denounced as failures. Democracy in any Western sense is not easily constructed or imposed. The experience of Haiti should be enough comment.

What we can hope for and work for is the emergence, in former rogue or ideomaniac states, of a beginning, a minimum. The new orders must be non-militant, non-expansionist, non-fanatical. And that goes with, or tends to go with, some level of internal tolerance, of plural order, with some real prospect of settling into habit or tradition.

Democracy cannot work without a fair level of political and social stability. This implies a certain amount of political apathy. Anything resembling fanaticism, a domination of the normal internal debate by "activists" is plainly to be deplored. And democracy must accept anomalies. As John Paul Jones, the American naval hero, sensibly put it in 1775, "True as may be the political principles for which we are now contending, . . . the ships themselves must be ruled under a system of absolute despotism." The navy, indeed, is an extreme case; no democratization in any real degree makes sense, any more than it does in, say, a university, at the other end of the spectrum.

Democratization of undemocratizable institutions is sometimes doubtless the expression of a genuine utopian ideal, as when the Jacobins by these means destroyed the French navy. But more often it is (in the minds of the leading activists, at least) a conscious attempt to ruin the institutions in question, as when the Bolsheviks used the idea to destroy the old Russian army. When this, among other things, enabled them to take power themselves, they were the first to insist on a discipline even more vigorous.

In its most important aspect, civic order is that which has created a strong state while still maintaining the principle of consensus that existed in primitive society. Such an aim involves the articulation of a complex political and social order. The strains cannot be eliminated but can be continually adjusted. Political civilization is thus not primarily a matter of the goodwill of leadership or of ideal constitutions. It is, above all, a matter of time in custom.

All the major troubles we have had in the last half century have been caused by people who have let politics become a mania. The politician should be a servant and should play a limited role. For what our political culture has stood for (as against the principles of total theorists and abstractionists) is the view of society as a developing and broadening of established liberties and responsibilities, and the belief, founded on experience, that in political and social matters, long-term predictions, however exciting and visionary, seldom work out.

Democracy is almost invariably criticized by revolutionaries for the blemishes found in any real example, as compared with the grand abstraction of the mere word. Real politics is full of what it would be charitable to call imperfections. And there are those who, often without knowing it, become apologists and finally accomplices of the closing of society. As Alexander Hamilton wrote in *The Federalist* (No. 1),

> A dangerous ambition more often lurks behind the specious mask of zeal for the rights of the people, than under the forbidding appearance of zeal for the firmness and efficiency of government. History will teach us, that the former has been found a much more certain road to the introduction of despotism, than the latter.

But with a civic culture it is more clearly a matter of a basis on which improvements can be made. For a civic society is a society in which the various elements can express themselves politically, in which an articulation exists between those elements at the political level: not a perfect social order, which is in any case unobtainable, but a society that hears, considers and reforms grievances. It is not necessarily democratic, but it contains the possibility of democracy.

We cannot predict. The near future teems with urgent problems, with as yet irresoluble balances of force and thought. The law-and-liberty cultures may flourish, and as yet unpromising regions may over a period bring not merely the forms but the habits of consensuality to their populations. Let us hope.

Everywhere we always find the human urges to preserve at least a measure of personal autonomy, on the one hand, and to form communal relationships, on the other. It is the latter that tends to get out of hand. To form a national or other such grouping without forfeiting liberties and without generating venom against other such groupings—such is the problem before the world. To cope with it, we need careful thinking, balanced understanding, open yet unservile minds.

And this is also why we still need to be careful about the signing of international treaties and the acceptance of international tribunals that appeal to a certain internationalist idealism, but one that needs to be carefully deployed. It is surely right to note that the acceptance of international obligations, and nowadays especially those affecting the policies, interests and traditional rights and powers of the states of established law and liberty, must be preceded by, at the least, negotiation that is careful, skeptical and unaffected by superficial generalities, however attractive at first sight. Permitting international bodies to intrude into the law-and-liberty countries also involves the institutionalization, on purely abstract grounds, of an as yet primitive *apparat.*

A very important trouble with international arrangements of all types has also been that Western governments sign on to policies that have not been properly (or at all) argued or debated by their publics or legislatures. Thus these arrangements are a means of giving more power to their own executive branches and, of course, more power to the international bureaucracies and permanent staff.

In particular, the UN, like the EU, approaches "human rights" on the basis of the general high-mindedness of the Continental Enlightenment. Declarations are made, agreements are reached. It is taken for granted that many states—about half the membership of the UN—will not in fact conform. And in the regions where liberty largely prevails, the signatories find their own countries denounced, often by their own citizens. The result is that under abstract human rights definitions, every state in the West that submits to treaties of the human rights sort lays itself open to aggressive litigation. As the late Raymond Aron, who spent so much of his life trying to educate the French intelligentsia, put it, "every known regime is blame-worthy if one holds it to an abstract idea of equality over liberty."

> *From the west I saw fly*
> *the dragons of expectation*
> *and open the way of the fire-powerful;*
> *they beat their wings,*
> *so that everywhere it appeared to me*
> *the earth and heaven burst.*
>
> —*translation by Thomas Wright of the* Poetic (or Elder) Edda

Textual Questions

1. How does Conquest use the first two paragraphs of his essay to set up the argument he makes about democracy in the remainder of the essay?

2. How is a discussion of language central to Conquest's argument? Does this focus help keep the argument organized, or does it ultimately, only confuse readers?

3. Conquest divides his argument into four sections. What is the focus of each—what is the central point in each? How does Conquest relate each section to the section that follows? How does section one connect with section four? Why does Conquest divide his argument in this way, rather than simply writing a single-section essay that runs in an unbroken stream from introduction to conclusion?

Rhetorical Questions

4. Why does Conquest open his discussion with references to Pericles, Socrates, and Alcibiades? What image of himself—as a writer and an authority on the issues at hand—do such references create?

5. Why does Conquest refer to history throughout his essay but only refer to the present and the future at the end? What historical references does he make in each of the four sections of his essay?

6. What does Conquest assume about his readers? Put another way, who are Conquest's ideal readers? What do they think, know, believe? What view of the past do they share? How do they think about the present? What future do they see as likely to come to pass?

Intertextual Questions

7. How does Conquest's discussion of democracy compare and contrast with the assertions made by President Franklin D. Roosevelt in "The Four Freedoms" (Chapter 1)? Do both men seem to share the same

beliefs and assumptions about the meaning of "democracy"? How are their definitions similar/different?

8. How do Conquest's arguments about democracy and the future compare to those of Mike Rose in "Our Schools and Our Children" (chapter two)?

Thinking Beyond the Text

9. List the historical references Conquest makes throughout his essay. Pick three of them and write a brief paragraph in which you explain who/what he is referencing and why each reference is appropriate to his argument. To do this well, you will need to do some minimal library/Internet research.

10. Consider the final paragraph of Conquest's argument. What image of the United Nations is he creating here? How does it compare with your own ideas about the role of the UN and its effectiveness in the world?

For Writing & Discussion

11. Searching online, visit the homepage of the United Nations. How does the UN describe itself, its history, its current work, and its ultimate purposes for existence? In a short essay, consider this: How does this "official" image of the UN compare and contrast with the image of the UN presented by Conquest? Which aspects of each description are, in your opinion, most closely aligned with reality?

MICHAEL IGNATIEFF

Michael Ignatieff (1947–) is a member of Parliament in the Canadian House of Commons and a recognized author of both fiction and nonfiction books. A former professor of history at the University of British Columbia and Kings College at Cambridge, Ignatieff also taught as the Carr Professor of the Practice of Human Rights and Director of the Carr Center for Human Rights Policy at Harvard's John F. Kennedy School of Government. Ignatieff received the Governor General's Award for Nonfiction in 1987 and in 2000 won the Orwell Prize for political nonfiction for his 2000 book, *Virtual War: Kosovo and Beyond.* He also has won the Gordon Montador Award for Best Canadian Book on Social Issues and the Lionel Gelber Award.

"Who Are Americans to Think That Freedom Is Theirs to Spread?" was a 2005 op-ed article in *The New York Times Magazine*. Beginning with Thomas Jefferson, the slave-owning proponent of freedom, it explores the historical tension between American ideals of freedom and American actions. Ignatieff's other work examines American and global political issues. His two most recent books are *Empire Lite: Nation-Building in Bosnia, Kosovo and Afghanistan* (2003) and *The Lesser Evil: Political Ethics in an Age of Terror* (2004), and in 2005 he edited a collection, *American Exceptionalism and Human Rights* (2005).

Who Are Americans to Think That Freedom Is Theirs to Spread?

✑ Prereading Question

Is "democracy" synonymous with "freedom"? Can an individual be "free" even if he or she lives in a nation ruled by a tyrant? Is it possible to be "free" only in a democracy, or is "freedom" even possible in a theocracy, oligarchy, monarchy, and meritocracy?

✑

I

As, Thomas Jefferson lay dying at his hilltop estate, Monticello, in late June 1826, he wrote a letter telling the citizens of the city of Washington that he was too ill to join them for the 50th-anniversary celebrations of the Declaration of Independence. Wanting his letter to inspire the gathering, he told them that one day the experiment he and the founders started would spread to the whole world. "To some parts sooner, to others later, but finally to all," he wrote, the American form of republican self-government would become every nation's birthright. Democracy's worldwide triumph was assured, he went on to say, because "the unbounded exercise of reason and freedom of opinion" would soon convince all men that they were born not to be ruled but to rule themselves in freedom.

It was the last letter he ever wrote. The slave-owning apostle of liberty, that incomparable genius and moral scandal, died 10 days later on July 4, 1826, on the same day as his old friend and fellow founder, John Adams.

It's impossible to untangle the contradictions of American freedom without thinking about Jefferson and the spiritual abyss that separates his pronouncement that "all men are created equal" from the reality of the human beings he owned, slept with and never imagined as fellow citizens. American freedom aspires to be universal, but it has always been exceptional because America is the only modern democratic experiment that began in slavery. From the Emancipation Proclamation of 1863 to the Civil Rights Act of 1964, it took a century for the promise of American freedom to even begin to be kept.

Despite the exceptional character of American liberty, every American president has proclaimed America's duty to defend it abroad as the universal birthright of mankind. John F. Kennedy echoed Jefferson when, in a speech in 1961, he said that the spread of freedom abroad was powered by "the force of right and reason"; but, he went on, in a sober and pragmatic vein, "reason does not always appeal to unreasonable men." The contrast between Kennedy and the current incumbent of the White House is striking. Until George W. Bush, no American president—not even Franklin Roosevelt or Woodrow Wilson—actually risked his presidency on the premise that Jefferson might be right. But this gambler from Texas has bet his place in history on the proposition, as he stated in a speech in March, that decades of American presidents' "excusing and accommodating tyranny, in the pursuit of stability" in the Middle East inflamed the hatred of the fanatics who piloted the planes into the twin towers on Sept. 11.

If democracy plants itself in Iraq and spreads throughout the Middle East, Bush will be remembered as a plain-speaking visionary. If Iraq fails, it will be his Vietnam, and nothing else will matter much about his time in office. For any president, it must be daunting to know already that his reputation depends on what Jefferson once called "so inscrutable [an] arrangement of causes and consequences in this world."

The consequences are more likely to be positive if the president begins to show some concern about the gap between his words and his administration's performance. For he runs an administration with the least care for consistency between what it says and does of any administration in modern times. The real money committed to the promotion of democracy in the Middle East is trifling. The president may have doubled the National Endowment for Democracy's budget, but it is still only $80 million a year. But even if there were more money, there is such doubt in the Middle East that the president actually means what he says—in the wake of 60 years of American presidents cozying up to tyrants in the region—that every dollar spent on democracy in the Middle East runs the risk of undermining the cause it supports. Actual Arab democrats recoil from the embrace of American good intentions. Just ask a community-affairs officer trying to give American dollars away for the promotion of democracy in Mosul, in northern Iraq, how easy it is to get anyone to even take the money, let alone spend it honestly.

And then there are the prisoners, the hooded man with the wires hanging from his body, the universal icon of the gap between the ideals of American freedom and the sordid—and criminal—realities of American detention and interrogation practice. The fetid example of these abuses makes American talk of democracy sound hollow. It will not be possible to encourage the rule of law in Egypt if America is sending Hosni Mubarak shackled prisoners to torture. It will be impossible to secure democratic change in Morocco or Afghanistan or anywhere else if Muslims believe that American guards desecrated the Koran. The failure to convict anybody higher than a sergeant for these crimes leaves many Americans and a lot of the world wondering whether Jefferson's vision of America hasn't degenerated into an ideology of self-congratulation, whose function is no longer to inspire but to lie.

∾

II

And yet . . . and yet. . . .

If Jefferson's vision were only an ideology of self-congratulation, it would never have inspired Americans to do the hard work of reducing the gap between dream and reality. Think about the explosive force of Jefferson's self-evident truth. First white working men, then women, then blacks, then the disabled, then gay Americans—all have used his words to demand that the withheld promise be delivered to them. Without Jefferson, no Lincoln, no Emancipation Proclamation. Without the slave-owning Jefferson, no Martin Luther King, Jr. and the dream of white and black citizens together reaching the Promised Land.

Jefferson's words have had the same explosive force abroad. American men and women in two world wars died believing that they had fought to save the freedom of strangers. And they were not deceived. Bill Clinton saluted the men who died at Omaha Beach with the words, "They gave us our world." That seems literally true: a democratic Germany, an unimaginably prosperous Europe at peace with itself. The men who died at Iwo Jima bequeathed their children a democratic Japan and 60 years of stability throughout Asia.

These achievements have left Americans claiming credit for everything good that has happened since, especially the fact that there are more democracies in the world than at any time in history. Jefferson's vaunting language makes appropriate historical modesty particularly hard, yet modesty is called for. Freedom's global dispersion owes less to America and more to a contagion of local civic courage, beginning with the people of Portugal and Spain who threw off dictatorship in the 1970's, the Eastern Europeans who threw off Communism in the 90's and the Georgians,

Serbs, Kyrgyz and Ukrainians who have thrown off post-Soviet autocratic governments since. The direct American role in these revolutions was often slight, but American officials, spies and activists were there, too, giving a benign green light to regime change from the streets.

This democratic turn in American foreign policy has been recent. Latin Americans remember when the American presence meant backing death squads and military juntas. Now in the Middle East and elsewhere, when the crowds wave Lebanese flags in Beirut and clamor for the Syrians to go, when Iraqi housewives proudly hold up their purple fingers on exiting the polling stations, when Afghans quietly line up to vote in their villages, when Egyptians chant "Enough!" and demand that Mubarak leave power, few Islamic democrats believe they owe their free voice to America. But many know that they have not been silenced, at least not yet, because the United States actually seems, for the first time, to be betting on them and not on the autocrats.

In the cold war, most presidents opted for stability at the price of liberty when they had to choose. This president, as his second Inaugural Address made clear, has soldered stability and liberty together: "America's vital interests and our deepest beliefs are now one." As he has said, "Sixty years of Western nations excusing and accommodating the lack of freedom in the Middle East did nothing to make us safe—because in the long run stability cannot be purchased at the expense of liberty."

It is terrorism that has joined together the freedom of strangers and the national interest of the United States. But not everyone believes that democracy in the Middle East will actually make America safer, even in the medium term. Thomas Carothers of the Carnegie Endowment for International Peace, for one, has questioned the "facile assumption that a straight line exists between progress on democratization and the elimination of the roots of Islamic terrorism." In the short term, democratization in Egypt, for example, might only bring the radical Muslim Brotherhood to power. Even in the medium term, becoming a democracy does not immunize a society from terrorism. Just look at democratic Spain, menaced by Basque terrorism.

Moreover, proclaiming freedom to be God's plan for mankind, as the president has done, does not make it so. There is, as yet, no evidence of a sweeping tide of freedom and democracy through the Middle East. Lebanon could pitch from Syrian occupation into civil strife; Egypt might well re-elect Mubarak after a fraudulent exercise in pseudodemocracy; little Jordan hopes nobody will notice that government remains the family monopoly of the Hashemite dynasty; Tunisia remains a good place for tourists but a lousy place for democrats; democratic hopes are most alive in Palestine, but here the bullet is still competing with the ballot box. Over it all hangs Iraq, poised between democratic transition and anarchy.

And yet . . . and yet . . . More than one world leader has been heard to ask his advisers recently, "What if Bush is right?"

∾

III

Other democratic leaders may suspect Bush is right, but that doesn't mean they are joining his crusade. Never have there been more democracies. Never has America been more alone in spreading democracy's promise.

The reticence extends even to those nations that owe their democracy to American force of arms. Freedom in Germany was an American imperial imposition, from the cashiering of ex-Nazi officials and the expunging of anti-Semitic nonsense from school textbooks to the drafting of a new federal constitution. Yet Chancellor Gerhard Schroder can still intone that democracy cannot be "forced upon these societies from the outside." This is not the only oddity. As Thomas Kleine-Brockhoff of the German weekly Die Zeit points out, the '68-ers now in power in Germany all spent their radical youth denouncing American support for tyrannies around the world: "Across the Atlantic they shouted: Pinochet! Somoza! Mubarak! Shah Pahlevi! King Faisal! Now it seems as though an American president has finally heard their complaints. . . . But what is coming out of Germany? . . . Nothing but deafening silence!"

The deafening silence extends beyond Germany. Like Germany, Canada sat out the war in Iraq. Ask the Canadians why they aren't joining the American crusade to spread democracy, and you get this from their government's recent foreign-policy review: "Canadians hold their values dear, but are not keen to see them imposed on others. This is not the Canadian way." One reason it is not the Canadian way is that when American presidents speak of liberty as God's plan for mankind, even God-fearing Canadians wonder when God began disclosing his plan to presidents.

The same discomfort with the American project extends to the nation that, in the splendid form of the Marquis de Lafayette, once joined the American fight for freedom. The French used to talk about exporting Liberte, Egalite et Fraternite, but nowadays they don't seem to mind standing by and watching Iraqi democrats struggling to keep chaos and anarchy at bay. Even America's best friend, Tony Blair, is circumspect about defining the Iraq project as anything more than managing the chaos. The strategy unit at 10Downing Street recently conducted a study on how to prevent future international crises: debt relief, overseas aid and humanitarian intervention were all featured, but the promotion of democracy and freedom barely got a mention. European political foundations and overseas development organizations do promote free elections and rule of law, but they bundle up these good works in the parlance of "governance" rather than in the language of spreading freedom and democracy. So America presides over a loose alliance of democracies, most of whose leaders think that promoting freedom and democracy is better left to the zealous imperialists in Washington.

The charge that promoting democracy is imperialism by another name is baffling to many Americans. How can it be imperialist to help people throw off the shackles of tyranny?

It may be that other nations just have longer memories of their own failed imperial projects. From Napoleon onward, France sought to export French political virtues, though not freedom itself, to its colonies. The British Empire was sustained by the conceit that the British had a special talent for government that entitled them to spread the rule of law to Kipling's "lesser breeds." In the 20th century, the Soviet Union advanced missionary claims about the superiority of Soviet rule, backed by Marxist pseudoscience.

What is exceptional about the Jefferson dream is that it is the last imperial ideology left standing in the world, the sole survivor of national claims to universal significance. All the others—the Soviet, the French and the British—have been consigned to the ash heap of history. This may explain why what so many Americans regard as simply an exercise in good intentions strikes even their allies as a delusive piece of hubris.

The problem here is that while no one wants imperialism to win, no one in his right mind can want liberty to fail either. If the American project of encouraging freedom fails, there may be no one else available with the resourcefulness and energy, even the self-deception, necessary for the task. Very few countries can achieve and maintain freedom without outside help. Big imperial allies are often necessary to the establishment of liberty. As the Harvard ethicist Arthur Applbaum likes to put it, "All foundings are forced." Just remember how much America itself needed the assistance of France to free itself of the British. Who else is available to sponsor liberty in the Middle East but America? Certainly the Europeans themselves have not done a very distinguished job defending freedom close to home.

During the cold war, while most Western Europeans tacitly accepted the division of their continent, American presidents stood up and called for the walls to come tumbling down. When an anonymous graffiti artist in Berlin sprayed the wall with a message— "This wall will fall. Beliefs become reality"—it was President Reagan, not a European politician, who seized on those words and declared that the wall "cannot withstand faith; it cannot withstand truth. The wall cannot withstand freedom."

This is why much of the European support for Bush in Iraq came from the people who had grown up behind that wall. It wasn't just the promise of bases and money and strategic partnerships that tipped Poles, Romanians, Czechs and Hungarians into sending troops; it was the memory that when the chips were down, in the dying years of Soviet tyranny, American presidents were there, and Western European politicians looked the other way.

It is true that Western Europe has had a democracy-promotion project of its own since the wall came down: bringing the fledgling regimes of Eastern Europe into the brave new world of the European Union. This very real achievement has now been delayed by the "no" votes in France and the Netherlands. Sponsoring the promotion of democracy in the East and preparing an Islamic giant, Turkey, for a later entry is precisely what the referendum votes want to stop. So who will be there to prevent Islamic fundamentalism or military authoritarianism breaking through in Turkey now that the Europeans have told the Turks to remain in the waiting room forever? If democracy within requires patrons without, the only patron left is the United States.

IV

While Americans characteristically oversell and exaggerate the world's desire to live as they do, it is actually reasonable to suppose, as Americans believe, that most human beings, if given the chance, would like to rule themselves. It is not imperialistic to believe this. It might even be condescending to believe anything else.

If Europeans are embarrassed to admit this universal yearning or to assist it, Americans have difficulty understanding that there are many different forms that this yearning can take, Islamic democracy among them. Democracy may be a universal value, but democracies differ—mightily— on ultimate questions. One reason the American promotion of democracy conjures up so little support from other democrats is that American democracy, once a model to emulate, has become an exception to avoid.

Consider America's neighbor to the north. Canadians look south and ask themselves why access to health care remains a privilege of income in the United States and not a right of citizenship. They like hunting and shooting, but can't understand why anyone would regard a right to bear arms as a constitutional right. They can't understand why the American love of limited government does not extend to a ban on the government's ultimate power—capital punishment. The Canadian government seems poised to extend full marriage rights to gays.

Some American liberals wistfully wish their own country were more like Canada, while for American conservatives, "Soviet Canuckistan"—as Pat Buchanan calls it—is the liberal hell they are seeking to avoid. But if American liberals can't persuade their own society to be more like other democracies and American conservatives don't want to, both of them are acknowledging, the first with sorrow, the other with joy, that America is an exception.

This is not how it used to be. From the era of F.D.R. to the era of John Kennedy, liberal and progressive foreigners used to look to America for inspiration. For conservatives like Margaret Thatcher, Ronald Reagan was a lodestar. The grand boulevards in foreign capitals were once named after these large figures of American legend. For a complex set of reasons, American democracy has ceased to be the inspiration it was. This is partly because of the religious turn in American conservatism, which awakens incomprehension in the largely secular politics of America's democratic allies. It is partly because of the chaos of the contested presidential election in 2000, which left the impression, worldwide, that closure had been achieved at the expense of justice. And partly because of the phenomenal influence of money on American elections.

But the differences between America and its democratic allies run deeper than that. When American policy makers occasionally muse out loud about creating a "community of democracies" to become a kind of alternative to the United Nations, they forget that America and its democratic friends continue to disagree about what fundamental rights a democracy should protect and the limits to power government should observe. As Europeans and Canadians head leftward on issues like gay marriage, capital punishment and abortion, and as American politics head rightward, the possibility of America leading in the promotion of a common core of beliefs recedes ever further. Hence the paradox of Jefferson's dream: American liberty as a moral universal seems less and less recognizable to the very democracies once inspired by that dream. In the cold war, America was accepted as the leader of "the free world." The free world—the West—has fractured, leaving a fierce and growing argument about democracy in its place.

V

The fact that many foreigners do not happen to buy into the American version of promoting democracy may not be much of a surprise. What is significant is how many American liberals don't share the vision, either.

On this issue, there has been a huge reversal of roles in American politics. Once upon a time, liberal Democrats were the custodians of the Jeffersonian message that American democracy should be exported to the world, and conservative Republicans were its realist opponents. Beginning in the late 1940's, as the political commentator Peter Beinart has rediscovered, liberals like Eleanor Roosevelt, Arthur Schlesinger Jr. and Adlai Stevenson realized that liberals would have to reinvent themselves. This was partly a matter of principle—they detested Soviet tyranny—and partly a matter of pragmatism. They wanted to avoid being tarred as fellow travelers, the fate that had met Franklin Roosevelt's former running mate, the radical reformer Henry Wallace. The liberals who founded Americans for Democratic Action refounded liberalism as an anti-Communist internationalism, dedicated to defending freedom and democracy abroad from Communist threat. The missionary Jeffersonianism in this reinvention worried many people—for example, George Kennan, the diplomat and foreign-policy analyst who argued that containment of the Communist menace was all that prudent politics could accomplish.

The leading Republicans of the 1950's—Robert Taft, for example— were isolationist realists, doubtful that America should impose its way on the world. Eisenhower, that wise old veteran of European carnage, was in that vein, too: prudent, risk-avoiding, letting the Soviets walk into Hungary because he thought war was simply out of the question, too horrible to contemplate. In the 1960's and 70's, Richard Nixon and Henry Kissinger remained in the realist mode. Since stability mattered more to them than freedom, they propped up the shah of Iran, despite his odious secret police, and helped to depose Salvador Allende in Chile. Kissinger's guiding star was not Jefferson but Bismarck. Kissinger contended that people who wanted freedom and democracy in Eastern Europe were lamentable sentimentalists, unable to look at the map and accommodate themselves to the eternal reality of Soviet power.

It was Reagan who began the realignment of American politics, making the Republicans into internationalist Jeffersonians with his speech in London at the Palace of Westminster in 1982, which led to the creation of the National Endowment for Democracy and the emergence of democracy promotion as a central goal of United States foreign policy. At the time, many conservative realists argued for detente, risk avoidance and placation of the Soviet bear. Faced with the Republican embrace of Jeffersonian ambitions for America abroad, liberals chose retreat or scorn. Bill Clinton—who took reluctant risks to defend freedom in Bosnia and Kosovo—partly arrested this retreat, yet since his administration, the withdrawal of American liberalism from the defense and promotion of freedom overseas has been startling. The Michael Moore-style left conquered the Democratic Party's heart; now the view was that America's only guiding interest overseas was furthering the interests of Halliburton and Exxon. The relentless emphasis on the hidden role of oil makes the promotion of democracy seem like a devious cover or lame excuse. The unseen cost of this pseudo-Marxist realism is that it disconnected the Democratic Party from the patriotic idealism of the very electorate it sought to persuade.

John Kerry's presidential campaign could not overcome liberal America's fatal incapacity to connect to the common faith of the American electorate in the Jeffersonian ideal. Instead he ran as the prudent, risk-avoiding realist in 2004—despite, or perhaps because of, the fact that he had fought in Vietnam. Kerry's caution was bred in the Mekong. The danger and death he encountered gave him some good reasons to prefer realism to idealism, and risk avoidance to hubris. Faced with a rival who proclaimed that freedom was not just America's gift to mankind but God's gift to the world, it was understandable that Kerry would seek to emphasize how complex reality was, how resistant to American purposes it might be and how high the price of American dreams could prove. As it turned out, the American electorate seemed to know only too well how high the price was in Iraq, and it still chose the gambler over the realist. In 2004, the Jefferson dream won decisively over American prudence.

But this is more than just a difference between risk taking and prudence. It is also a disagreement about whether American values properly deserve to be called universal at all. The contemporary liberal attitude toward the promotion of democratic freedom—we like what we have, but we have no right to promote it to others—sounds to many conservative Americans like complacent and timorous relativism, timorous because it won't lift a finger to help those who want an escape from tyranny, relativist because it seems to have abandoned the idea that all people do want to be free. Judging from the results of the election in 2004, a majority of Americans do not want to be told that Jefferson was wrong.

∽

VI

A relativist America is properly inconceivable. Leave relativism, complexity and realism to other nations. America is the last nation left whose citizens don't laugh out loud when their leader asks God to bless the country and further its mighty work of freedom. It is the last country with a mission, a mandate and a dream, as old as its founders.

All of this may be dangerous, even delusional, but it is also unavoidable. It is impossible to think of America without these properties of self-belief.

Of course, American self-belief is not an eternal quantity. Jefferson airily assumed that democracy would be carried on the wings of enlightenment, reason and science. No one argues that now. Not even Bush. He does speak of liberty as "the plan of heaven for humanity and the best hope for progress here on Earth," but in more sober moments, he will concede that the promotion of freedom is hard work, stretching out for generations and with no certain end in sight.

The activists, experts and bureaucrats who do the work of promoting democracy talk sometimes as if democracy were just a piece of technology, like a water pump, that needs only the right installation to work in foreign climes. Others suggest that the promotion of democracy requires anthropological sensitivity, a deep understanding of the infinitely complex board game of foreign (in this case Iraqi) politics.

But Iraqi freedom also depends on something whose measurement is equally complex: what price, in soldiers' bodies and lives, the American people are prepared to pay. The members of the American public are ceaselessly told that stabilizing Iraq will make them more secure. They are told that fighting the terrorists there is better than fighting them at home. They are told that victory in Iraq will spread democracy and stability in the arc from Algeria to Afghanistan. They are told that when this happens, "they" won't hate Americans, or hate them as much as they do now. It's hard to know what the American people believe about these claims, but one vital test of whether the claims are believed is the number of adolescent men and women prepared to show up at the recruiting posts in the suburban shopping malls and how many already in the service or Guard choose to re-enlist and sign up for another tour in Ramadi or Falluja. The current word is that recruitment is down, and this is a serious sign that someone at least thinks America is paying too high a price for its ideals.

Of all human activities, fighting for your country is the one that requires most elaborate justification. Oliver Wendell Holmes Jr. once said that "to fight out a war, you must believe something and want something with all your might." He had survived Antietam and the annihilating horror of the Battle of the Wilderness, so he knew of what he spoke. The test that Jefferson's dream has to pass is whether it gives members of a new generation something they want to fight for with all their might.

Two years from now is the earliest any senior United States commander says that Americans can begin to come home from Iraq in any significant numbers. Already the steady drip of casualties is the faintly heard, offstage noise of contemporary American politics. As this noise grows louder, it may soon drown out everything else. Flag-draped caskets are slid down the ramps of cargo planes at Dover Air Force Base and readied for their last ride home to the graveyards of America. In some region of every American's mind, those caskets raise a simple question: Is Iraqi freedom worth this?

It would be a noble thing if one day 26 million Iraqis could live their lives without fear in a country of their own. But it would also have been a noble dream if the South Vietnamese had been able to resist the armored divisions of North Vietnam and to maintain such freedom as they had. Lyndon Johnson said the reason Americans were there was the "principle for which our ancestors fought in the valleys of Pennsylvania," the right of people to choose their own path to change. Noble dream or not, the price turned out to be just too high.

There is nothing worse than believing your son or daughter, brother or sister, father or mother died in vain. Even those who have opposed the Iraq war all along, who believe that the hope of planting democracy has lured America into a criminal folly, do not want to tell those who have died that they have given their lives for nothing. This is where Jefferson's dream must work. Its ultimate task in American life is to redeem loss, to rescue sacrifice from oblivion and futility and to give it shining purpose. The real truth about Iraq is that we just don't know—yet—whether the dream will do its work this time. This is the somber question that hangs unanswered as Americans approach this Fourth of July.

Textual Questions

1. How does Ignatieff build to the argument he makes about America and contradictions in the opening of paragraph 3? From this paragraph, how and where does he forecast the overall argument that he makes?

2. How does Ignatieff use Thomas Jefferson to summarize his overall argument? How does he connect back to Jefferson, implicitly if not explicitly, in his conclusion? Why?

3. What argument does Ignatieff make about the United States and its stated goal of shepherding Iraq into being as a free nation? How does Ignatieff seem to feel about this work? How does he seem to want his audience to feel?

Rhetorical Questions

4. How effectively do the opening fragments of section two—"And yet . . . and yet . . ."—transition between the end of section one and the points made in section two? What makes this transition particularly effective or ineffective?

5. Divided into six sections, Ignatieff's essay uses many examples from American history (including recent history). Which of these six sections makes its argument most/least effectively and why?

6. At the beginning of section three, Ignatieff refers to President's George W. Bush's "crusade." What, literally, is Ignatieff referring to? Metaphorically, what is he referring to? Why?

Intertextual Questions

7. How is Ignatieff's characterization of the relationship between America and the other nations of the world—especially the nations of the West—similar to/different from the same relationships as described by Colin L. Powell in "No Country Left Behind" and John McCain in "United States and Europe" (both in this chapter)?

8. Does Ignatieff seem to be using the same definition of "freedom" as Martin Luther King, Jr. in "I Have a Dream" (Chapter 1)? How are the definitions used by these two men similar/different from one another?

Thinking Beyond the Text

9. Is Ignatieff's use of Thomas Jefferson in the opening section of his argument fair, or is it a deliberate simplification and decontextualization of historical complexities? Or is it something else entirely?

10. Consider the imagery and comparisons Ignatieff deploys in the final section of his essay, including the image of flag-draped coffins and an extended reference to the American war in Vietnam. How effective are these images/comparisons? Why? What makes them effective or ineffective? Do they have a cumulative effect that is greater than the sum of the individual parts?

For Writing & Discussion

11. In paragraph 4, Ignatieff states that "every American president has proclaimed America's duty to defend [liberty] abroad as the universal birthright of mankind." Assuming that the first piece of this assertion (about "every" president) is correct, is the second piece of the declaration also true? That is, is liberty—defined in its American context—the ultimate destiny of all nations? Is there a downside to the good intention of spreading liberty? What?

CONDOLEEZZA RICE

Condoleezza Rice (1954–) is the U.S. Secretary of State, a position she has held since 2005, and prior to that she was President George W. Bush's national security advisor (2001–2005). Before joining the Bush administration Rice was a political science professor and then a provost at Stanford University. She also was a Senior Fellow at Stanford's Institute for International Studies with a special focus on the Soviet Union. Under President George H. W. Bush she acted as the National Security Council's Director of Soviet and East European Affairs, and she was a special assistant to the president for National Security Affairs. Forbes named her the world's Most Powerful Woman in 2005.

In addition to her scholarly books on the Soviet Union and the unification of Germany, Rice has written articles for publications including the *Washington Post* and *Foreign Affairs* magazine. Rice's experience with international affairs is reflected in "Transformational Diplomacy," a speech she gave at Georgetown University's School of Foreign Service in January, 2006. The speech details the Bush administration's approach to international relations and how it departs from those of previous administrations.

Transformational Diplomacy

Prereading Question

In your opinion of the modern War on Terror, how effective is international diplomacy as a weapon to fight against terrorism? How and when is diplomacy effective? How and when is it ineffective?

Thank you very much. Thank you President DeGioia for that wonderful introduction. Thank you. Happy for that great start to this session. I'd like to thank the Board of Trustees and say how pleased I am to be here at Georgetown University's distinguished School of Foreign Service. I just have to recognize my friend, Andrew Natsios, who's sitting in the front row, even if he did leave us to come to Georgetown. He said he was doing it because this is an institution that he loves dearly. You've got a fine man and you're going to have a fine professor in Andrew Natsios. Thank you for your service to the country.

I want to thank members of the diplomatic corps who are here and several members of the Administration. I also want you to know that I do know a good deal about Georgetown and it is because this is a fine school of foreign service for which we all owe a debt of gratitude for the people that you have trained, for the people who have come to us in government, for the people from whom I have learned as an academic. This is also a fine university in general, a university that is well known for its dedication to learning, but also its dedication to values and to social justice. And it's also a university that is recovering its heritage in basketball and I look very much forward to this year.

Almost a year ago today in his second Inaugural Address, President Bush laid out a vision that now leads America into the world. "It is the policy of the United States," the President said, "to seek and support the growth of democratic movements and institutions in every nation and culture with the ultimate goal of ending tyranny in our world." To achieve this bold mission, America needs equally bold diplomacy, a diplomacy that not only reports about the world as it is, but seeks to change the world itself. I and others have called this mission "transformational diplomacy." And today I want to explain what it is in principle and how we are advancing it in practice.

We are living in an extraordinary time, one in which centuries of international precedent are being overturned. The prospect of violent conflict among great powers is more remote than ever. States are increasingly competing and cooperating in peace, not preparing for war. Peoples in China and India, in South Africa and Indonesia and Brazil are lifting their countries into new prominence. Reform—democratic reform—has begun and is spreading in the Middle East. And the United States is working with our many partners, particularly our partners who share our values in Europe and in Asia and in other parts of the world to build a true form of global stability, a balance of power that favors freedom.

At the same time, other challenges have assumed a new urgency. Since its creation more than 350 years ago, the modern state system has rested on the concept of sovereignty. It was always assumed that every state could control and direct the threats emerging from its territory. It was also assumed that weak and poorly governed states were merely a burden to their people, or at most, an international humanitarian concern but never a true security threat.

Today, however, these old assumptions no longer hold. Technology is collapsing the distance that once clearly separated right here from over there. And the greatest threats now emerge more within states than between them. The fundamental character of regimes now matters more than the international distribution of power. In this world it is impossible to draw neat, clear lines between our security interests, our development efforts and our democratic ideals. American diplomacy must integrate and advance all of these goals together.

So, I would define the objective of transformational diplomacy this way: to work with our many partners around the world, to build and sustain democratic, well-governed states that will respond to the needs of their people and conduct themselves responsibly in the international system. Let me be clear, transformational diplomacy is rooted in partnership; not in paternalism. In doing things with people, not for them; we seek to use America's diplomatic power to help foreign citizens better their own lives and to build their own nations and to transform their own futures.

In extraordinary times like those of today, when the very terrain of history is shifting beneath our feet, we must transform old diplomatic institutions to serve new diplomatic purposes. This kind of challenge is sweeping and difficult but it is not unprecedented; America has done this kind of work before. In the aftermath of World War II, as the Cold War hardened into place, we turned our diplomatic focus to Europe and parts of Asia. We hired new people. We taught them new languages, we gave them new training. We partnered with old adversaries in Germany and Japan and helped them to rebuild their countries. Our diplomacy was instrumental in transforming devastated countries into thriving democratic allies, allies who joined with us for decades in the struggle to defend freedom from communism.

With the end of the Cold War, America again rose to new challenges. We opened 14 new embassies in the countries of Central and Eastern Europe and we repositioned over 100 of our diplomats to staff them. Our efforts helped newly liberated peoples to transform the character of their countries and now many of them, too, have become partners in liberty and freedom, members of NATO, members of the European Union, something unthought of just a few years ago. And during the last decade, we finally realized a historic dream of the 20th century therefore, a vision of a Europe whole and free and at peace.

In the past five years, it was my friend and predecessor Colin Powell who led the men and women of American diplomacy into the 21st century. He modernized the State Department's technology and transformed dozens of our facilities abroad. Most importantly, Secretary Powell invested in our people. He created over 2,000 new positions and hired thousands of new employees and trained them all to be diplomatic leaders of tomorrow.

Now, today, to advance transformational diplomacy all around the world, we in the State Department must again answer a new calling of our time. We must begin to lay the diplomatic foundations to secure a future of freedom for all people. Like the great changes of the past, the new efforts we undertake today will not be completed quickly. Transforming our diplomacy and transforming the State Department is the work of a generation, but it is urgent work that must begin.

To advance transformational diplomacy, we are and we must change our diplomatic posture. In the 21st century, emerging nations like India and China and Brazil and Egypt and Indonesia and South Africa are increasingly shaping the course of history. At the same time, the new front lines of our diplomacy are appearing more clearly, in transitional countries of Africa and of Latin America and of the Middle East. Our current global posture does not really reflect that fact. For instance, we have nearly the same number of State Department personnel in Germany, a country of 82 million people that we have in India, a country of one billion people. It is clear today that America must begin to reposition our diplomatic forces around the world, so over the next few years the United States will begin to shift several hundred of our diplomatic positions to new critical posts for the 21st century. We will begin this year with a down payment of moving 100 positions from Europe and, yes, from here in Washington, D.C., to countries like China and India and Nigeria and Lebanon, where additional staffing will make an essential difference.

We are making these changes by shifting existing resources to meet our new priorities, but we are also eager to work more closely with Congress to enhance our global strategy with new resources and new positions.

We will also put new emphasis on our regional and transnational strategies. In the 21st century, geographic regions are growing ever more integrated economically, politically and culturally. This creates new opportunities but it also presents new challenges, especially from transnational threats like terrorism and weapons proliferation and drug smuggling and trafficking in persons and disease.

Building regional partnerships is one foundation today of our counter-terrorism strategy. We are empowering countries that have the will to fight terror but need help with the means. And we are joining with key regional countries like Indonesia and Nigeria and Morocco and Pakistan, working together not only to take the fight to the enemy but also to combat the ideology of hatred that uses terror as a weapon.

We will use a regional approach to tackle disease as well. Rather than station many experts in every embassy, we will now deploy small, agile transnational networks of our diplomats. These rapid response teams will monitor and combat the spread of pandemics across entire continents. We are adopting a more regional strategy in our public diplomacy as well.

In the Middle East, for example, as you well know, a vast majority of people get their news from a regional media network like Al Jazeera, not from a local newspaper. So our diplomats must tell America's story not just in translated op-eds, but live on TV in Arabic for a regional audience. To make this happen, we are creating a regional public diplomacy center. We are forward deploying our best Arabic-speaking diplomats and we are broadly coordinating our public diplomacy strategy both for the region and from the region.

Our third goal is to localize our diplomatic posture. Transformational diplomacy requires us to move our diplomatic presence out of foreign capitals and to spread it more widely across countries. We must work on the front lines of domestic reform as well as in the back rooms of foreign ministries. There are nearly 200 cities worldwide with over one million people in which the United States has no formal diplomatic presence. This is where the action is today and this is where we must be. To reach citizens in bustling new population centers, we cannot always build new consulates beyond a nation's capital.

A newer, more economical idea is what we call an American Presence Post. This idea is simple. One of our best diplomats moves outside the embassy to live and work and represent America in an emerging community of change. We currently operate American Presence Posts in places like Egypt and Indonesia and we are eager to expand both the size and the scope of this new approach.

Perhaps the newest and most cost effective way to adopt a more local posture is through a Virtual Presence Post. Here one or more of our young officers creates and manages an internet site that is focused on key population centers. This digital meeting room enables foreign citizens, young people most of all, to engage online with American diplomats who could be hundreds of miles away. This is a great way to connect with millions of new people across Europe and Asia and Latin America.

In today's world, our diplomats will not only work in different places, they will work in different communities and they will serve in different kinds of conditions, like reconstruction and stabilization missions, where they must partner more directly with the military.

So to advance transformational diplomacy we are empowering our diplomats to work more jointly with our men and women in uniform.

Over the past 15 years, as violent state failure has become a greater global threat, our military has borne a disproportionate share of post-conflict responsibilities because we have not had the standing civilian capability to play our part fully. This was true in Somalia and Haiti, in Bosnia, in Kosovo, and it is still partially true in Iraq and Afghanistan.

These experiences have shown us the need to enhance our ability to work more effectively at the critical intersections of diplomacy, democracy promotion, economic reconstruction and military security. That is why President Bush created within the State Department the Office of Reconstruction and Stabilization. Recently, President Bush broadened the authority and mandate for this office and Congress authorized the Pentagon to transfer up to $100 million to State in the event of a post-conflict operation, funds that would empower our reconstruction and stabilization efforts. We have an expansive vision for this new office, and let there be no doubt, we are committed to realizing it. Should a state fail in the future, we want the men and the women of this office to be able to spring into action quickly. We will look to them to partner immediately with our military, with other federal agencies and with our international allies, and eventually we envision this office assembling and deploying the kinds of civilians who are essential in post-conflict operations: police officers and judges and electricians and engineers, bankers and economists and legal experts and election monitors.

Our Reconstruction and Stabilization Office must be able to help a failed state to exercise responsible sovereignty and to prevent its territory from becoming a source of global instability, as Afghanistan was in 2001.

The diplomacy of the 21st century requires better "jointness" too between our soldiers and our civilians, and we are taking additional steps to achieve it. We for decades have positions in our Foreign Service called Political Advisors to Military Forces, affectionately called POLADS, in our business. We station these diplomats where the world of diplomacy intersects the world of military force, but increasingly this intersection is seen in the dusty streets of Fallujah or the tsunami-wrecked coasts of Indonesia. I want American diplomats to eagerly seek our assignments working side-by-side with our men and women in uniform, whether it is in disaster relief in Pakistan or in stabilization missions in Liberia or fighting the illegal drug trade in Latin America.

Finally, to advance transformational diplomacy, we are preparing our people with new expertise and challenging them with new expectations. I've been Secretary of State for almost exactly one year now, and in that time I have become more convinced than ever that we have the finest diplomatic service in the world. I've seen the noble spirit of that service, a service that defines the men and women of our Foreign Service and Civil Service and our Foreign Service Nationals, many of whom are serving in dangerous places far away from their families.

I see in them the desire and the ability to adapt to a changing world and to our changing diplomatic mission. More and more often, over the course of this new century, we will ask the men and women of the State Department to be active in the field. We will need them to engage with private citizens in emerging regional centers, not just with government officials in their nations' capitals. We must train record numbers of people to master difficult languages like Arabic and Chinese and Farsi and Urdu.

In addition, to advance in their careers, our Foreign Service Officers must now serve in what we call hardship posts. These are challenging jobs in critical countries like Iraq and Afghanistan and Sudan and Angola, countries where we are working with foreign citizens in difficult conditions to maintain security and fight poverty and make democratic reforms. To succeed in these kinds of posts, we will train our diplomats not only as expert analysts of policy but as first-rate administrators of programs, capable of helping foreign citizens to strengthen the rule of law, to start businesses, to improve health and to reform education.

Ladies and gentlemen, President Bush has outlined the historic calling of our time. We on the right side of freedom's divide have a responsibility to help all people who find themselves on the wrong side of that divide. The men and women of American diplomacy are being summoned to advance an exciting new mission. But there is one other great asset that America will bring to this challenge. No, in a day and a time when difference is still a license to kill, America stands as a tremendous example of what can happen with people of diverse backgrounds, ethnic groups, religions all call themselves American. Because it does not matter whether you are Italian American or African American or Korean American. It does not matter whether you are Muslim or Presbyterian or Jewish or Catholic. What matters is that you are American and you are devoted to an ideal and to a set of beliefs that unites us.

Ladies and gentlemen, in order for America to fully play its role in the world, it must send out into the world a diplomatic force, a diplomatic corps that reflects that great diversity. It cannot be that the last three Secretaries of State—the daughter of European immigrants, the son of Jamaican immigrants and a daughter of the American segregated South—would be more diverse than the Foreign Service with which they work. And so I want to make a special appeal to each and every one of you. It's exciting to be a diplomat these days because it is not just about reporting on countries. It's not just influencing governments. It's being a part of changing people's lives, whether in our AIDS programs abroad or in our efforts to educate girls in Afghanistan or to help with extremism in the Middle East with good partners like Pakistan and Jordan. Imagine the excitement of the people who are going to work in Liberia now with the first woman president on the African continent to try and build a Liberia where people can reach their dreams and their future.

But we cannot do it without America's best and brightest, and America's best and brightest come in all colors, they come in all religions, they come in all heritages. Our Foreign Service has got to be that way, too.

I sit in an office when I meet with foreign secretaries and foreign ministers from around the world that is a grand office that looks like it's actually out of the 19th century although it was actually built in 1947, but that's very American, too. And there's a portrait of Thomas Jefferson that looks directly at me when I am speaking to those foreign ministers, and I wonder sometimes, "What would Mr. Jefferson have thought?" What would he have thought about America's reach and influence in the world? What would he have thought about America's pursuit of the democratic enterprise on behalf of the peoples of the world? What would he have thought that an ancestor—that my ancestors, who were three-fifths of a man in his constitution—would produce a Secretary of State who would carry out that mission?

Ladies and gentlemen, America has come a long way and America stands as a symbol but also a reality for all of those who have a long way to go, that democracy is hard and democracy takes time, but democracy is always worth it.

Thank you very much.

Textual Questions

1. In her third paragraph, Rice quotes President Bush. Why? What purpose does the quotation serve as she makes her own argument about diplomacy?

2. How and where does Rice describe the past, particularly America's relationship with other nations? Where and how does she describe the ways in which the present is creating a future very different from this past? How is the future to be different than the past, in her opinion?

3. How does Rice define "transformational diplomacy"? What examples does she offer to support her definition? How would her ideas about "transformational diplomacy" change America's relationships with other nations of the world?

Rhetorical Questions

4. Where does Rice refer to other nations, either in the past or present? To what purpose does she put these references? How effective are they? Why?

5. What is the United States doing to advance the cause of transformational diplomacy, according to Rice? Which part of her argument about these advances is most persuasive and why? Which is least persuasive and why?

6. How does Rice build to the points she makes in her second-to-last paragraph? How effective are those points, both logically and emotionally, in relation to her entire argument? What makes them effective or ineffective?

Intertextual Questions

7. How does the vision of America in the past, present, and future that Rice offers here compare/contrast with that advanced by John Kerry in "The Hope Is There" (this chapter)?

8. How does Rice's description of America compare compare/contrast with that offered by President George W. Bush in "We Have Seen the State of Our Union" (Introduction)?

Thinking Beyond the Text

9. Consider the argument Rice makes near the end of her address, in the paragraph beginning with "Ladies and gentlemen, President Bush has outlined the historic calling of our time" and ending with "What matters is that you are American and you are devoted to an ideal and to a set of beliefs that unites us." In your experience and opinion, how accurate is Rice's description of America in this paragraph—and how much of the description she offers is the ideal rather than the actual?

10. How is Rice especially able to speak on all of the topics she addresses in her speech? What, in her history and experience, gives her the authority to be viewed as, unquestionably, an expert on all these issues? What other, external, sources of authority boost her credibility?

For Writing & Discussion

11. In an essay, explain how Rice's speech on the subject of diplomacy represents the same set of core values about America expressed in three of these texts: "The Gettysburg Address" (Chapter 1), "Our Schools and Our Children" (Chapter 2), "Common Media for an Uncommon Nation" (Chapter 3), "America's Promises" (Chapter 4), "Success" (Chapter 5), and/or "America's Best Days are Yet to Come" (Chapter 6).

FOCAL POINT
Exploring America's Promises

DOONESBURY
by G.B. Trudeau

OPERATION IRAQI FREEDOM

IN MEMORIAM SINCE 4/23/05 · PART II

OPERATION ENDURING FREEDOM (AFGHANISTAN) SINCE 4/23/05

GB Trudeau 6-4

FOCAL POINT

Exploring America's Promises

Questions

1. When this image of an Iraqi prisoner being menaced by an attack dog (748, top) first appeared in the media, it ignited controversy over the definition of (and use of) torture in the War on Terror. How might someone who supports the war in Iraq interpret this photograph? How might someone who is against the war interpret it? What emotions does this image invoke in you? Explain.

2. In this 2003 photograph on page 748 (bottom), a United States soldier distributes books to schoolgirls in Iraq. What message about the ongoing United States occupation of Iraq does this image give? What details support this message? Why might this picture be less likely to appear in a news story than an image like that on page 748 (top)?

3. In what city would you guess the photograph on page 750 was taken? Why? What visual cues suggest a specific time and place to you? How much is your "reading" of this photograph based upon your own experience in the world and how much of your "reading" is based upon movies and television programs?

4. The comic strip Doonesbury is, traditionally, thought to espouse liberal opinions on American politics. In its first two panels, the cartoon on page 749 (bottom) shows a flag-draped coffin and a ceremonial gun salute. The next six panels are dominated by the names of soldiers killed during Operation Iraqi Freedom. Is this cartoon a tribute to the fallen? A protest against the war? Both? Something else entirely? Explain.

5. The picture on page 749 (top) shows an Iraqi woman who just voted in the nation's first post-Hussein election. What does the gesture she is making mean? How does the gesture influence your "reading" of this image's meaning?

APPENDIX

The Constitution of the United States of America

Preamble

We the People of the United States, in Order to form a more perfect Union, establish Justice, insure domestic Tranquility, provide for the common defence, promote the general Welfare, and secure the Blessings of Liberty to ourselves and our Posterity, do ordain and establish this Constitution for the United States of America.

Article I

Section 1

All legislative Powers herein granted shall be vested in a Congress of the United States, which shall consist of a Senate and House of Representatives.

Section 2

The House of Representatives shall be composed of Members chosen every second Year by the People of the several States, and the Electors in each State shall have the Qualifications requisite for Electors of the most numerous Branch of the State Legislature.

No Person shall be a Representative who shall not have attained to the Age of twenty five Years, and been seven Years a Citizen of the United States, and who shall not, when elected, be an inhabitant of that State in which he shall be chosen.

Representatives and direct Taxes shall be apportioned among the several States which may be included within this Union, according to their respective Numbers, *which shall be determined by adding to the whole Number of free Persons, including those bound to Service for a Term of Years, and excluding Indians not taxed, three fifths of all other Persons.* [*] The actual Enumeration shall be made within three Years after the first Meeting of the Congress of the United States, and within every subsequent Term of ten Years, in such Manner as they shall by Law direct. The Number of Representatives shall not exceed one for every thirty Thousand, but each State shall have at Least one Representative; *and until such enumeration shall be made, the State of New Hampshire shall be entitled to chuse three, Massachusetts eight, Rhode-Island and Providence Plantations one, Connecticut five, New York six, New Jersey four, Pennsylvania eight, Delaware one, Maryland six, Virginia ten, North Carolina five, South Carolina five, and Georgia three.*

When vacancies happen in the Representation from any State, the Executive Authority thereof shall issue Writs of Election to fill such Vacancies.

The House of Representatives shall chuse their Speaker and other Officers; and shall have the sole Power of Impeachment.

[*] Passages no longer in effect are printed in italic type.

Section 3

The Senate of the United States shall be composed of two Senators from each State, *chosen by the Legislature thereof,* for six Years; and each Senator shall have one Vote.

Immediately after they shall be assembled in Consequence of the first Election, they shall be divided as equally as may be into three Classes. The Seats of the Senators of the first Class shall be vacated at the Expiration of the second Year, of the second Class at the Expiration of the fourth Year, and of the third Class at the Expiration of the sixth Year so that one third may be chosen every second Year; and if Vacancies happen by Resignation, or otherwise, during the Recess of the Legislature of any state, the Executive thereof may make temporary Appointments until the next Meeting of the Legislature, which shall then fill such Vacancies.

No Person shall be a Senator who shall not have attained to the Age of thirty Years, and been nine Years a Citizen of the United States, and who shall not, when elected, be an Inhabitant of that State for which he shall be chosen.

The Vice President of the United States shall be President of the Senate, but shall have no Vote, unless they be equally divided.

The Senate shall chuse their other Officers, and also a President *pro tempore,* in the Absence of the Vice President, or when he shall exercise the Office of President of the United States.

The Senate shall have the sole Power to try all Impeachments. When sitting for that Purpose, they shall be on Oath or Affirmation. When the President of the United States is tried the Chief Justice shall preside: And no Person shall be convicted without the Concurrence of two thirds of the Members present.

Judgment in Cases of Impeachment shall not extend further than to removal from Office, and disqualification to hold and enjoy any Office of honor, Trust or Profit under the United States: but the Party convicted shall nevertheless be liable and subject to Indictment, Trial, Judgment and Punishment, according to Law.

Section 4

The Times, Places and Manner of holding Elections for Senators and Representatives, shall be prescribed in each State by the Legislature thereof; but the Congress may at any time by Law make or alter such Regulations, except as to the Places of chusing Senators.

The Congress shall assemble at least once in every Year, *and such Meeting shall be on the first Monday in December, unless they shall by Law appoint a different Day.*

Section 5

Each House shall be the Judge of the Elections, Returns and Qualifications of its own Members, and a Majority of each shall constitute a Quorum to do Business; but a smaller Number may adjourn from day to day, and may be authorized to compel the Attendance of absent Members, in such Manner, and under such Penalties as each House may provide.

Each House may determine the Rules of its Proceedings, punish its Members for disorderly Behaviour, and, with the Concurrence of two thirds, expel a Member.

Each House shall keep a Journal of its Proceedings, and from/time to time publish the same, excepting such Parts as may in their Judgment require Secrecy; and the Yeas and Nays of the Members of either House on any question shall, at the Desire of one fifth of those Present, be entered on the Journal.

Neither House, during the Session of Congress, shall, without the Consent of the other, adjourn for more than three days, nor to any other Place than that in which the two Houses shall be sitting.

Section 6

The Senators and Representatives shall receive a Compensation for their Services, to be ascertained by Law, and paid out of the Treasury of the United States. They shall in all Cases, except Treason, Felony and Breach of the Peace, be privileged from Arrest during their Attendance at the Session of their respective Houses, and in going to and returning from the same; and for any Speech or Debate in either House, they shall not be questioned in any other Place.

No Senator or Representative shall, during the Time for which he was elected, be appointed to any civil Office under the Authority of the United States, which shall have been created, or the Emoluments whereof shall have been encreased during such time, and no Person holding any Office under the United States, shall be a Member of either House during his Continuance in Office.

Section 7

All Bills for raising Revenue shall originate in the House of Representatives; but the Senate may propose or concur with Amendments as on other Bills.

Every Bill which shall have passed the House of Representatives and the Senate, shall, before it become a Law, be presented to the President of the United States; If he approve he shall sign it, but if not he shall return it, with his Objections to the House in which it shall have originated, who shall enter the Objections at large on their Journal, and proceed to reconsider it. If after such Reconsideration two thirds of that House shall agree to pass the Bill, it shall be sent, together with the Objections, to the other House, by which it shall likewise be reconsidered, and if approved by two thirds of that House, it shall become a Law. But in all such Cases the Votes of both Houses shall be determined by yeas and Nays, and the Names of the Persons voting for and against the Bill shall be entered on the Journal of each House respectively. If any Bill shall not be returned by the President within ten Days (Sundays excepted) after it shall have been presented to him, the Same shall be a Law, in like Manner as if he had signed it, unless the Congress by their Adjournment prevent its Return, in which Case it shall not be a Law.

Every Order, Resolution, or Vote to which the Concurrence of the Senate and House of Representatives may be necessary (except on a question of Adjournment) shall be presented to the President of the United States; and before the Same shall take Effect, shall be approved by him, or being disapproved by him, shall be repassed by two thirds of the Senate and House of Representatives, according to the Rules and Limitations prescribed in the Case of a Bill.

Section 8

The Congress shall have Power To lay and collect Taxes, Duties, Imposts and Excises, to pay the Debts and provide for the common Defence and general Welfare of the United States; but all Duties, Imposts and Excises shall be uniform throughout the United States;

To borrow Money on the credit of the United States;

To regulate Commerce with foreign Nations, and among the several States, and with the Indian Tribes;

To establish an uniform Rule of Naturalization, and uniform Laws on the subject of Bankruptcies throughout the United States;

To coin Money, regulate the Value thereof, and of foreign Coin, and fix the Standard of Weights and Measures;

To provide for the Punishment of counterfeiting the Securities and current Coin of the United States;

To establish Post Offices and post Roads;

To promote the Progress of Science and useful Arts, by securing for limited Times to Authors and Inventors the exclusive Right to their respective Writings and Discoveries;

To constitute Tribunals inferior to the supreme Court;

To define and punish Piracies and Felonies committed on the high Seas, and Offences against the Law of Nations;

To declare War, grant Letters of Marque and Reprisal, and make Rules concerning Captures on Land and Water;

To raise and support Armies, but no Appropriation of Money to that Use shall be for a longer Term than two Years;

To provide and maintain a Navy;

To make Rules for the Government and Regulation of the land and naval Forces;

To provide for calling forth the Militia to execute the Laws of the Union, suppress Insurrections and repel Invasions;

To provide for organizing, arming, and disciplining, the Militia, and for governing such Part of them as may be employed in the Service of the United States, reserving to the States respectively, the Appointment of the Officers, and the Authority of training the Militia according to the discipline prescribed by Congress;

To exercise exclusive Legislation in all Cases whatsoever, over such District (not exceeding ten Miles square) as may, by Cession of particular States, and the Acceptance of Congress, become the Seat of the Government of the United States, and to exercise like Authority over all Places purchased by the Consent of the Legislature of the State in which the Same shall be, for the Erection of Forts, Magazines, Arsenals, dock-Yards, and other needful Buildings;—And

To make all Laws which shall be necessary and proper for carrying into Execution the foregoing Powers, and all other Powers vested by this Constitution in the Government of the United States, or in any Department of Officer thereof.

Section 9

The Migration or Importation of such Persons as any of the States now existing shall think proper to admit, shall not be prohibited by the Congress prior to the Year one thousand eight hundred and eight, but a Tax or duty may be imposed on such Importation, not exceeding ten dollars for each Person.

The Privilege of the Writ of Habeas Corpus shall not be suspended, unless when in Cases of Rebellion or Invasion the public Safety may require it.

No Bill of Attainder or ex post facto Law shall be passed.

No Capitation, or other direct, Tax shall be laid, unless in Proportion to the Census or Enumeration herein before directed to be taken.

No Tax or Duty shall be laid on Articles exported from any State.

No Preference shall be given by any Regulation of Commerce or Revenue to the Ports of one State over those of another: nor shall Vessels bound to, or from, one State, be obliged to enter, clear, or pay Duties in another.

No Money shall be drawn from the Treasury, but in Consequence of Appropriations made by Law; and a regular Statement and Account of the Receipts and Expenditures of all public Money shall be published from time to time.

No Title of Nobility shall be granted by the United States: And no Person holding any Office of Profit or Trust under them, shall, without the Consent of the Congress, accept of any present, Emolument, Office, or Title, of any kind whatever, from any King, Prince, or foreign State.

Section 10

No State shall enter into any Treaty, Alliance, or Confederation; grant Letters of Marque and Reprisal; coin Money; emit Bills of Credit; make any Thing but gold and silver Coin a Tender in Payment of Debts; pass any Bill of Attainder, ex post facto Law, or Law impairing the obligation of Contracts, or grant any Title of Nobility.

No State shall, without the Consent of the Congress, lay any Imposts or Duties on Imports or Exports, except what may be absolutely necessary for executing its inspection Laws: and the net Produce of all Duties and Imposts, laid by any State on Imports or Exports, shall be for the Use of the Treasury of the United States; and all such Laws shall be subject to the Revision and Controul of the Congress.

No State shall, without the Consent of Congress, lay any Duty of Tonnage, keep Troops, or Ships of War in time of Peace, enter into any Agreement or Compact with another State, or with a foreign Power, or engage in War, unless actually invaded, or in such imminent Danger as will not admit of delay.

Article II

Section 1

The executive Power shall be vested in a President of the United States of America. He shall hold his Office during the Term of four Years, and, together with the Vice President, chosen for the same Term, be elected, as follows:

Each State shall appoint, in such Manner as the Legislature thereof may direct, a Number of Electors, equal to the whole Number of Senators and Representatives to which the State may be entitled in the Congress: but no Senator or Representative, or Person holding an Office of Trust or Profit under the United States, shall be appointed an Elector.

The Electors shall meet in their respective States, and vote by Ballot for two Persons, of whom one at least shall not be an Inhabitant of the same State with themselves. And they shall make a List of all the Persons voted for, and of the Number of Votes for each; which List they shall sign and certify, and transmit sealed to the Seat of the Government of the United States, directed to the President of the Senate. The President of the Senate shall, in the Presence of the Senate and House of Representatives, open all the Certificates, and the Votes shall then be counted. The Person having the greatest Number of Votes shall be the President, if such Number be a Majority of the whole number of Electors appointed; and if there be more than one who have such Majority, and have an equal Number of Votes, then the House of Representatives shall immediately chuse by Ballot one of them for President; and if no Person have a Majority, then from the five highest on the List the said House shall in like Manner chuse the President. But in chusing the President, the Votes shall be taken by States, the Representation from each State having one Vote; A quorum for this Purpose shall consist of a Member or Members from two thirds of the States, and a Majority of all the States shall be necessary to a Choice. In every Case, after the Choice of the President, the Person having the greatest Number of Votes of the Electors shall be the Vice President. But if there should remain two or more who have equal Votes, the Senate shall chuse from them by Ballot the Vice President.

The Congress may determine the time of chusing the Electors, and the Day on which they shall give their Votes; which Day shall be the same throughout the United States.

No person except a natural born Citizen, *or a Citizen of the United States, at the time of the Adoption of this Constitution,* shall be eligible to the Office of President; neither shall any Person be eligible to that Office who shall not have attained to the Age of thirty five Years, and been fourteen Years a Resident within the United States.

In Case of the Removal of the President from Office, or of his Death, Resignation, or Inability to discharge the Powers and Duties of the said Office, the Same shall devolve on the Vice President, and the Congress may by Law provide for the Case of Removal, Death, Resignation or Inability, both of the President and Vice President, declaring what Officer shall then act as President, and such Officer shall act accordingly, until the Disability be removed, or a President shall be elected.

The President shall, at stated Times, receive for his Services, a Compensation, which shall neither be encreased nor diminished during the Period for which he shall have been elected, and he shall not receive within that period any other Emolument from the United States, or any of them.

Before he enter on the Execution of his Office, he shall take the following Oath or Affirmation:—"I do solemnly swear (or affirm) that I will faithfully execute the Office of President of the United States, and will to the best of my Ability, preserve, protect and defend the Constitution of the United States."

Section 2

The President shall be Commander in Chief of the Army and Navy of the United States, and of the Militia of the several States, when called into the actual Service of the United States; he may require the Opinion, in writing, of the principal Officer in each of the executive Departments, upon any Subject relating to the Duties of their respective Offices, and he shall have Power to grant Reprieves and Pardons for Offences against the United States, except in Cases of Impeachment.

He shall have Power, by and with the Advice and Consent of the Senate, to make Treaties, provided two thirds of the Senators present concur; and he shall nominate, and by and with the Advice and Consent of the Senate, shall appoint Ambassadors, other public Ministers and Consuls, Judges of the supreme Court, and all other Officers of the United States, whose Appointments are not herein otherwise provided for, and which shall be established by Law: but the Congress may by Law vest the Appointment of such inferior Officers, as they think proper in the President alone, in the Courts of Law, or in the Heads of Departments.

The President shall have Power to fill up all Vacancies that may happen during the Recess of the Senate, by granting Commissions which shall expire at the End of their next Session.

Section 3

He shall from time to time give to the Congress Information of the State of the Union, and recommend to their Consideration such Measures as he shall judge necessary and expedient; he may, on extraordinary Occasions, convene both Houses, or either of them, and in Case of disagreement between them, with Respect to the Time of Adjournment, he may adjourn them to such Time as he shall think proper; he shall receive Ambassadors and other public Ministers; he shall take Care that the Laws be faithfully executed, and shall Commission all the officers of the United States.

Section 4

The President, Vice President and all civil Officers of the United States, shall be removed from Office on Impeachment for, and Conviction of, Treason, Bribery or other high Crimes and Misdemeanors.

Article III
Section 1

The judicial Power of the United States, shall be vested in one supreme Court, and in such inferior Courts as the Congress may from time to time ordain and establish. The Judges, both of the supreme and inferior Courts, shall hold their offices during good Behaviour, and shall, at stated Times, receive for their Services, a Compensation, which shall not be diminished during their Continuance in Office.

Section 2

The judicial Power shall extend to all Cases, in Law and Equity, arising under this Constitution, the Laws of the United States, and Treaties made, or which shall be made, under their Authority;—to all Cases affecting Ambassadors, other public Ministers and Consuls;—to all Cases of admiralty and maritime Jurisdiction;—to Controversies to which the United States shall be a Party;—to Controversies between two or more States;—*between a State and Citizens of another State;*—between Citizens of different States;—between Citizens of the same State claiming Lands under Grants of different States, and between a State, or the Citizens thereof, and foreign States, Citizens or Subjects.

　　In all Cases affecting Ambassadors, other public Ministers and Consuls, and those in which a State shall be Party, the supreme Court shall have original Jurisdiction. In all the other Cases before mentioned, the supreme Court shall have appellate Jurisdiction, both as to Law and Fact, with such Exceptions, and under such Regulations as the Congress shall make.

　　The Trial of all Crimes, except in Cases of Impeachment, shall be by Jury; and such Trial shall be held in the State where the said Crimes shall have been committed, but when not committed within any State, the Trial shall be at such Place or Places as the Congress may by Law have directed.

Section 3

Treason against the United States, shall consist only in levying War against them, or in adhering to their Enemies, giving them Aid and Comfort. No person shall be convicted of Treason unless on the Testimony of two Witnesses to the same overt Act, or on Confession in open Court.

The Congress shall have Power to declare the Punishment of Treason, but no Attainder of Treason shall work Corruption of Blood, or Forfeiture except during the Life of the Person attainted.

Article IV
Section 1

Full Faith and Credit shall be given in each State to the public Acts, Records, and judicial Proceedings of every other State. And the Congress may by general Laws prescribe the Manner in which such Acts, Records and Proceedings shall be proved, and the Effect thereof.

Section 2

The Citizens of each State shall be entitled to all Privileges and Immunities of Citizens in the several States.

A Person charged in any State with Treason, Felony, or other Crime, who shall flee from Justice, and be found in another State, shall on Demand of the executive Authority of the State from which he fled, be delivered up, to be removed to the State having Jurisdiction of the Crime.

No Person held to Service or Labour in one State, under the Laws thereof, escaping into another, shall, in Consequence of any Law or Regulation therein, be discharged from such Service or Labour, but shall be delivered up on Claim of the Party to whom such Service or Labour may be due.

Section 3

New States may be admitted by the Congress into this Union; but no new State shall be formed or erected within the Jurisdiction of any other State; nor any State be formed by the Junction of two or more States, or Parts of States, without the Consent of the Legislatures of the States concerned as well as of the Congress.

The Congress shall have Power to dispose of and make all needful Rules and Regulations respecting the Territory or other Property belonging to the United States; and nothing in this Constitution shall be so construed as to Prejudice any Claims of the United States, or of any particular States.

Section 4

The United States shall guarantee to every State in this Union a Republican Form of Government, and shall protect each of them against Invasion; and on Application of the Legislature, or of the Executive (when the Legislature cannot be convened) against domestic violence.

Article V

The Congress, whenever two thirds of both Houses shall deem it necessary, shall propose Amendments to this Constitution, or, on the Application of the Legislatures of two thirds of the several States, shall call a Convention for proposing Amendments, which, in either Case, shall be valid to all Intents and Purposes, as Part of this Constitution, when ratified by the Legislatures of three fourths of the several States, or by Conventions in three fourths thereof, as the one or the other Mode of Ratification may be proposed by the Congress; Provided *that no Amendment which may be made prior to the Year One thousand eight hundred and eight shall in any Manner affect the first and fourth Clauses in the Ninth Section of the first Article;* and that no State, without its Consent, shall be deprived of its equal Suffrage in the Senate.

Article VI

All Debts contracted and Engagements entered into, before the Adoption of this Constitution, shall be as valid against the United States under this Constitution, as under the Confederation.

This Constitution, and Laws of the United States which shall be made in Pursuance thereof; and all Treaties made, or which shall be made, under the Authority of the United States, shall be the supreme Law of the Land; and the Judges in every State shall be bound thereby, any Thing in the Constitution or Laws of any State to the Contrary notwithstanding.

The Senators and Representatives before mentioned, and the Members of the several State Legislatures, and all executive and Judicial Officers, both of the United States and of the several States, shall be bound by Oath or Affirmation, to support this Constitution; but no religious Test shall ever be required as a Qualification to any Office of public Trust under the United States.

Article VII

The Ratification of the Conventions of nine States, shall be sufficient for the Establishment of this Constitution between the States so ratifying the Same.

Done in Convention by the Unanimous Consent of the States present the Seventeenth Day of September in the Year of our Lord one thousand seven hundred and Eighty seven and of the Independence of the United States of America the Twelfth* IN WITNESS whereof We have hereunto subscribed our Names,

George Washington
President and Deputy from Virginia

Delaware
George Read
Gunning Bedford, Jr.
John Dickinson
Richard Bassett
Jacob Broom

Maryland
James McHenry
Daniel of St. Thomas Jenifer
Daniel Carroll

South Carolina
John Rutledge
Charles Cotesworth Pinckney
Charles Pinckney
Pierce Butler

Georgia
William Few
Abraham Baldwin

New York
Alexander Hamilton

New Jersey
William Livingston
David Brearley
William Paterson
Jonathan Dayton

---

*The Constitution was submitted on September 17, 1787, by the Constitutional Convention, was ratified by conventions of the several states at various dates up to May 29, 1790, and became effective on March 4, 1789.

Virginia	*New Hampshire*	*Pennsylvania*
John Blair	John Langdon	Benjamin Franklin
James Madison, Jr.	Nicholas Gilman	Thomas Mifflin
		Robert Morris
North Carolina	*Massachusetts*	George Clymer
William Blount	Nathaniel Gorham	Thomas FitzSimons
Richard Dobbs Spraight	Rufus King	Jared Ingersoll
Hugh Williamson		James Wilson
	Connecticut	Gouverneur Morris
	William Samuel Johnson	
	Roger Sherman	

Amendments to the Constitution

Amendment I

Congress shall make no law respecting an establishment of religion, or prohibiting the free exercise thereof; or abridging the freedom of speech, or of the press; or the right of the people peaceably to assemble, and to petition the Government for a redress of grievances.

Amendment II

A well regulated Militia being necessary to the security of a free State, the right of the people to keep and bear Arms, shall not be infringed.

Amendment III

No Soldier shall, in time of peace be quartered in any house, without the consent of the Owner, nor in time of war, but in a manner to be prescribed by law.

Amendment IV

The right of the people to be secure in their persons, houses, papers, and effects, against unreasonable searches and seizures, shall not be violated, and no Warrants shall issue, but upon probable cause, supported by Oath or affirmation, and particularly describing the place to be searched, and the persons or things to be seized.

Amendment V

No person shall be held to answer for a capital, or otherwise infamous crime, unless on a presentment or indictment of a Grand Jury, except in cases arising in the land or naval forces, or in the Militia, when in actual service in time of War or public danger; nor shall any person be subject for the same offense to be twice put in jeopardy of life or limb; nor shall be compelled in any criminal case to be a witness against himself, nor be deprived of life, liberty, or property, without due process of law; nor shall private property be taken for public use, without just compensation.

Amendment VI

In all criminal prosecutions, the accused shall enjoy the right to a speedy and public trial, by an impartial jury of the State and district wherein the crime shall have been committed, which district shall have been previously ascertained by law, and to be informed of the nature and cause of the accusation; to be confronted with the witnesses against him; to have compulsory process for obtaining witnesses in his favor, and to have the Assistance of Counsel for his defence.

Amendment VII

In Suits at common law, where the value in controversy shall exceed twenty dollars, the right of trial by jury shall be preserved, and no fact tried by a jury, shall be otherwise re-examined in any Court of the United States, than according to the rules of the common law.

Amendment VIII

Excessive bail shall not be required, nor excessive fines imposed, nor cruel and unusual punishments inflicted.

Amendment IX

The enumeration in the Constitution, of certain rights, shall not be construed to deny or disparage others retained by the people.

Amendment X*

The powers not delegated to the United States by the Constitution, nor prohibited by it to the States, are reserved to the States respectively, or to the people.

Amendment XI [Adopted 1798]

The Judicial power of the United States shall not be construed to extend to any suit in law or equity, commenced or prosecuted against one of the United States by Citizens of another State, or by Citizens or Subjects of any Foreign State.

Amendment XII [Adopted 1804]

The Electors shall meet in their respective states, and vote by ballot for President and Vice President, one of whom, at least, shall not be an inhabitant of the same state with themselves; they shall name in their ballots the person voted for as President, and in distinct ballots the person voted for as Vice President, and they shall make distinct lists of all persons voted for as President, and of all persons voted for as Vice President, and of the number of votes for each, which lists they shall sign and certify, and transmit sealed to the seat of the government of the United States, directed to the President of the Senate;— The President of the Senate shall, in the presence of the Senate and House of Representatives, open all the certificates and the votes shall then be counted;—The person having

---

*The first ten amendments (the Bill of Rights) were ratified and their adoption was certified on December 15, 1791.

the greatest number of votes for president, shall be the President, if such number be a majority of the whole number of Electors appointed; and if no person have such majority, then from the persons having the highest numbers not exceeding three on the list of those voted for as President, the House of Representatives shall choose immediately, by ballot, the President. But in choosing the President, the votes shall be taken by states, the representation from each state having one vote; a quorum for this purpose shall consist of a member or members from two-thirds of the states, and a majority of all the states shall be necessary to a choice. And if the House of Representatives shall not choose a President whenever the right of choice shall devolve upon them, before *the fourth day of March* next following, then the Vice President shall act as President, as in the case of the death or other constitutional disability of the President.—The person having the greatest number of votes as Vice President, shall be the Vice President, if such number be a majority of the whole number of Electors appointed, and if no person have a majority, then from the two highest numbers on the list, the Senate shall choose the Vice President; a quorum for the purpose shall consist of two-thirds of the whole number of Senators, and a majority of the whole number shall be necessary to a choice. But no person constitutionally ineligible to the office of President shall be eligible to that of Vice President of the United States.

Amendment XIII [Adopted 1865]

Section 1

Neither slavery nor involuntary servitude, except as a punishment for crime whereof the party shall have been duly convicted, shall exist within the United States, or any place subject to their jurisdiction.

Section 2

Congress shall have power to enforce this article by appropriate legislation.

Amendment XIV [Adopted 1868]

Section 1

All persons born or naturalized in the United States, and subject to the jurisdiction thereof, are citizens of the United States and of the State wherein they reside. No State shall make or enforce any law which shall abridge the privileges or immunities of citizens of the United States; nor shall any State deprive any person of life, liberty, or property, without due process of law; nor deny to any person within its jurisdiction the equal protection of the laws.

Section 2

Representatives shall be apportioned among the several States according to their respective numbers, counting the whole number of persons in each State, excluding Indians not taxed. But when the right to vote at any election for the choice of electors for President and Vice President of the United States, Representatives in Congress, the Executive and Judicial officers of a State, or the members of the Legislature thereof, is denied to any of the male inhabitants of such State, being twenty-one years of age, and citizens of the United States, or in any way abridged, except for participation in rebellion, or other crime, the basis of representation therein shall be reduced in the proportion which the number of such male citizens shall bear to the whole number of male citizens twenty-one years of age in such State.

Section 3

No person shall be a Senator or Representative in Congress, or elector of President and Vice President, or hold any office, civil or military, under the United States, or under any State, who, having previously taken an oath, as a member of Congress, or as an officer of the United States, or as a member of any State legislature, or as an executive or judicial officer of any State, to support the Constitution of the United States, shall have engaged in insurrection or rebellion against the same, or given aid or comfort to the enemies thereof. But Congress may by a vote of two-thirds of each House, remove such disability.

Section 4

The validity of the public debt of the United States, authorized by law, including debts incurred for payment of pensions and bounties for services in suppressing insurrection or rebellion, shall not be questioned. But neither the United States nor any State shall assume or pay any debt or obligation incurred in aid of insurrection or rebellion against the United States, or any claim for the loss or emancipation of any slave; but all such debts, obligations and claims shall be held illegal and void.

Section 5

The Congress shall have power to enforce, by appropriate legislation, the provisions of this article.

Amendment XV [Adopted 1870]
Section 1

The right of citizens of the United States to vote shall not be denied or abridged by the United States or by any State on account of race, color, or previous condition of servitude.

Section 2

The Congress shall have power to enforce this article by appropriate legislation.

Amendment XVI [Adopted 1913]

The Congress shall have power to lay and collect taxes on incomes, from whatever source derived, without apportionment among the several States, and without regard to any census or enumeration.

Amendment XVII [Adopted 1913]

The Senate of the United States shall be composed of two Senators from each State, elected by the people thereof, for six years; and each Senator shall have one vote. The electors in each State shall have the qualifications requisite for electors of the most numerous branch of the State legislatures.

When vacancies happen in the representation of any State in the Senate, the executive authority of such State shall issue writs of election to fill such vacancies: *Provided,* That the legislature of any State may empower the executive thereof to make temporary appointments until the people fill the vacancies by election as the legislature may direct.

This amendment shall not be so construed as to affect the election or term of any Senator chosen before it becomes valid as part of the Constitution.

Amendment XVIII [Adopted 1919, repealed 1933]
Section 1

After one year from the ratification of this article the manufacture, sale, or transportation of intoxicating liquors within, the importation thereof into, or the exportation thereof from the United States and all territory subject to the jurisdiction thereof for beverage purposes is hereby prohibited.

Section 2

The Congress and the several States shall have concurrent power to enforce this article by appropriate legislation.

Section 3

This article shall be inoperative unless it shall have been ratified as an amendment to the Constitution by the legislatures of the several States, as provided in the Constitution, within seven years from the date of the submission hereof to the States by the Congress.

Amendment XIX [Adopted 1920]

The right of citizens of the United States to vote shall not be denied or abridged by the United States or by any State on account of sex.

Congress shall have power to enforce this article by appropriate legislation.

Amendment XX [Adopted 1933]
Section 1

The terms of the President and Vice President shall end at noon on the 20th day of January, and the terms of Senators and Representatives at noon on the 3d day of January, of the years in which such terms would have ended if this article had not been ratified and the terms of their successors shall then begin.

Section 2

The Congress shall assemble at least once in every year, and such meeting shall begin at noon on the 3d day of January, unless they shall by law appoint a different day.

Section 3

If, at the time fixed for the beginning of the President, the President elect shall have died, the Vice President elect shall become President. If a President shall not have been chosen before the time fixed for the beginning of his term, or if the President elect shall have failed to qualify, then the Vice President elect shall act as President until a President shall have qualified; and the Congress may by law provide for the case wherein neither a President elect nor a Vice President elect shall have qualified, declaring who shall then act as President, or the manner in which one who is to act shall be selected, and such person shall act accordingly until a President or Vice President shall have qualified.

Section 4

The Congress may by law provide for the case of the death of any of the persons from whom the House of Representatives may choose a President whenever the right of choice shall have devolved upon them, and for the case of the death of any of the persons from whom the Senate may choose a Vice President whenever the right of choice shall have devolved upon them.

Section 5

Sections 1 and 2 shall take effect on the 15th day of October following the ratification of this article.

Section 6

This article shall be inoperative unless it shall have been ratified as an amendment to the Constitution by the legislatures of three fourths of the several States within seven years from the date of its submission.

Amendment XXI [Adopted 1933]
Section 1

The eighteenth article of amendment to the Constitution of the United States is hereby repealed.

Section 2

The transportation or importation into any State, Territory, or possession of the United States for delivery or use therein of intoxicating liquors in violation of the laws thereof, is hereby prohibited.

Section 3

This article shall be inoperative unless it shall have been ratified as an amendment to the Constitution by conventions in the several States, as provided in the Constitution, within seven years from the date of the submission hereof to the States by the Congress.

Amendment XXII [Adopted 1951]
Section 1

No person shall be elected to the office of the President more than twice, and no person who has held the office of President, or acted as President, for more than two years of a term to which some other person was elected President shall be elected to the office of the President more than once. But this Article shall not apply to any person holding the office of President when this Article was proposed by the Congress, and shall not prevent any person who may be holding the office of President, or acting as President, during the term within which this Article becomes operative from holding the office of President or acting as President during the remainder of such term.

Section 2

This article shall be inoperative unless it shall have been ratified as an amendment to the Constitution by the legislatures of three-fourths of the several States within seven years from the date of its submission to the States by the Congress.

Amendment X.XIII [Adopted 1961]
Section 1

The District constituting the seat of Government of the United States shall appoint in such manner as the Congress shall direct:

A number of electors of President and Vice President equal to the whole number of Senators and Representatives in Congress to which the District would be entitled if it were a State, but in no event more than the least populous State; they shall be in addition to those appointed by the States, but they shall be considered, for the purposes of the election of President and Vice President, to be electors appointed by a State; and they shall meet in the District and perform such duties as provided by the twelfth article of amendment.

Section 2

The Congress shall have power to enforce this article by appropriate legislation.

Amendment XXIV [Adopted 1964]
Section 1

The right of citizens of the United States to vote in any primary or other election for President or Vice President, for electors for President or Vice President, or for Senator or Representative in Congress, shall not be denied or abridged by the United States or any state by reason of failure to pay any poll tax or other tax.

Section 2

The Congress shall have the power to enforce this article by appropriate legislation.

Amendment XXV [Adopted 1967]
Section 1

In case of the removal of the President from office or his death or resignation, the Vice President shall become President.

Section 2

Whenever there is a vacancy in the office of the Vice President, the President shall nominate a Vice President who shall take the office upon confirmation by a majority vote of both houses of Congress.

Section 3

Whenever the President transmits to the President pro tempore of the Senate and the Speaker of the House of Representatives his written declaration that he is unable to discharge the powers and duties of his office, and until he transmits to them a written declaration to the contrary, such powers and duties shall be discharged by the Vice President as Acting President.ssssss

Section 4

Whenever the Vice President and a majority of either the principal officers of the executive departments or of such other body as Congress may be law provide, transmit to the President pro tempore of the Senate and the Speaker of the House of Representatives their written declaration that the President is unable to discharge the powers and duties of his office, the Vice President shall immediately assume the powers and duties of the office as Acting President.

Thereafter, when the President transmits to the President pro tempore of the Senate and the Speaker of the House of Representatives his written declaration that no inability exists, he shall resume the powers and duties of his office unless the Vice President and a majority of either the principal officers of the executive department or of such other body as Congress may by law provide, transmit within four days to the President pro tempore of the Senate and the Speaker of the House of Representatives their written declaration that the President is unable to discharge the powers and duties of his office. Thereupon Congress shall decide the issue, assembling within 48 hours for that purpose if not in session. If the Congress, within 21 days after receipt of the latter written declaration, or, if Congress is not in session, within 21 days after Congress is required to assemble, determines by two-thirds vote of both houses that the President is unable to discharge the powers and duties of his office, the Vice President shall continue to discharge the same as Acting President; otherwise, the President shall resume the powers and duties of his office.

Amendment XXVI [Adopted 1971]
Section 1

The right of citizens of the United States, who are 18 years of age or older, to vote shall not be denied or abridged by the United States or any state on account of age.

Section 2

The Congress shall have the power to enforce this article by appropriate legislation.

Amendment XXVII [Adopted 1992]

No law, varying the compensation for the services of the Senators and Representatives shall take effect, until an election of Representatives shall have intervened.

CREDITS

Chapter 1

Martin Luther King, Jr.: "I Have a Dream" speech, copyright © 1963 by Martin Luther King, Jr., copyright renewed 1991 by Coretta Scott King. Reprinted by arrangement with the Estate of Martin Luther King, Jr., c/o Writers House as agent for the proprietor New York, NY.

Chapter 2

Gerald W. Bracey: "The Perfect Law: No Child Left Behind and the Assault on Public Schools" by Gerald W. Bracey from *Dissent*, Fall, 2004. Reprinted with permission.

Blouke Carus: "Education Reform: Teachers and Schools" (2004). Reprinted by permission.

Dacia Charlesworth: "Which Number Will You Be?" by Dacia Charlesworth (2004). Reprinted by permission.

Ross Douthat: "The Truth About Harvard" by Ross Douthat from *The Atlantic Monthly*, March 2005. Reprinted by permission of the author.

Stanley Fish: "Reverse Racism, or How the Pot Got to Call the Kettle Black" by Stanley Fish from *Crisis* (1993). Copyright the Crisis Publishing Company, Inc. Reprinted by permission of the author.

bell hooks: "Pedagogy and Political Commitment: A Comment" by bell hooks from *Talking Back: Thinking Feminist, Thinking Black*. Boston: South End Press, 1989. Reprinted by permission.

David Leonhardt: "The College Dropout Boom" by David Leonhardt from *New York Times*, May 24, 2005. Copyright © 2005 by The New York Times Company. Reprinted with permission.

Kenyatta Matthews: "Black College in (White) America" by Kenyatta Matthews from *Ms. Magazine*, Aug/Sept 2001. Reprinted by permission of the author.

Victoria Murphey: "Where Everyone Can Overachieve" by Victoria Murphy from *Forbes* 10/11/04. Reprinted by permission of Forbes Magazine © 2006 Forbes Inc.

Mike Rose: "Our Schools and Our Children" from *Lives on the Boundary: The Struggles and Achievements of America's Underprepared* by Mike Rose. Copyright © 1989 by Mike Rose. Reprinted with the permission of The Free Press, a Division of Simon & Schuster Adult Publishing Group. All rights reserved.

Michael J. Sandel: "Marketers are Storming the Schoolhouse" from *Ad Nauseam* by Michael J. Sandel, from *The New Republic*, September 1, 1997. Reprinted by permission of *The New Republic*, © 1997, *The New Republic*, LLC.

James Traub: "The Moral Imperative" by James Traub from *Education Next*, Winter 2005. Reprinted with permission.

Chapter 3

Eric Alterman: "You're Only as Liberal as the Man Who Owns You," from *What Liberal Media?*. Copyright © 2003 by Eric Alterman. Reprinted by permission of Basic Books, a member of Perseus Book, L.L.C.

Ben H. Bagdikian: "Common Media for an Uncommon Nation" by Ben H. Bagdikian from *The New Media Monopoly*, copyright © 2004 by Ben Bagdikian. Reprinted by permission of Beacon Press.

Daniel W. Drezner and Henry Farrell: "Web of Influence" by Daniel W. Drezner and Henry Farrell from *Foreign Policy*, Nov/Dec. 2004. Reprinted by permission of Foreign Policy, http://www.foreignpolicy.com.

Bernard Goldberg: From the book *Bias* by Bernard Goldberg. Copyright © 2002. Published by Regnery Publishing, Inc. All right reserved. Reprinted by special permission of Regnery Publishing, Inc., Washington, D.C.

Edward S. Herman and Noam Chomsky: "The Propaganda Mill" by E. S. Herman and N. Chomsky, 1988 from *The Progressive* 52(6): 14–17. Reprinted by permission from *The Progressive*, 409 E. Main St., Madison, WI 53703. http://www.progressive.org.

Neil Postman and Steve Powers: "The Bias of Language, The Bias of Pictures" from *How to Watch TV News* by Neil Postman and Steve Powers, copyright © 1992 by Neil Postman and Steve Powers. Used by permission of Viking Penguin, a division of Penguin Group (USA) Inc.

Frank Rich: "All The News That's Fit to Bully" by Frank Rich from *New York Times*, July 9, 2006. Copyright © 2006 by The New York Times Company. Reprinted by permission.

Virgil Scudder: "The Importance of Communication in a Global World: Not 'Me to Me to Me'" by Virgil Scudder (2004). Reprinted with permission.

Bob Wright: "Technology and the Rule of Law in the Digital Age: Protection of Intellectual Property" address by Bob Wright delivered to the Media Institute Friends and Benefactors Awards Banquet, Washington, D.C., October 27, 2004. Reprinted with permission.

Chapter 4

Robbie E. Davis-Floyd: "Gender and Ritual: Giving Birth the American Way" by Robbie E. Davis-Floyd, 1992. Reprinted by permission of the author.

Malcolm Gladwell: "The Moral-Hazard Myth" by Malcolm Gladwell from *The New Yorker*, Aug. 29, 2005. Reprinted by permission of Malcolm Gladwell.

Chapter 5

Chapter 6

Chapter 7

Michael Ignatieff: "Who Are Americans to Think That Freedom Is Theirs to Spread?" by Michael Ignatieff, from *New York Times*, June 26, 2005. Reprinted by permission of The New York Times Company.

Andrew C. McCarthy: "Torture: Thinking About the Unthinkable" by Andrew C. McCarthy. Reprinted from *Commentary*, July–August 2004, by permission; all rights reserved.

Jehangir Pocha: "The Axis of Oil" by Jehangir Pocha from *In These Times*, Feb. 28, 2005. Reprinted with permission of *In These Times*, and is available at http://www.inthesetimes.com.

T.R. Reid: "The Atlantic Widens" from *The United States of Europe* by T. R. Reid, copyright © 2004 by T. R. Reid. Used by permission of The Penguin Press, a division of Penguin Group (USA) Inc.

Rick Wagoner: "Keep America Rolling" address by Rick Wagoner, President and Chief Executive Officer, General Motors Corporation. Delivered to The Executives' Club of Chicago, Chicago, Illinois, Sept. 27, 2001. Reprinted with permission.

Photo Credits

Page 27 (top): Eric Draper/Getty Images
Page 27 (bottom): AP/Wide World Photos
Page 28 (top): Dick Lochner Tribune Media Services, Inc. All Rights Reserved.
Page 28 (bottom): Bettmann/Corbis
Page 29: AP/Wide World Photos
Page 118 (top): AP/Wide World Photos
Page 118 (bottom): Bettmann/Corbis
Page 119 (top): Shane Borrowman
Page 119 (bottom): Bettmann/Corbis
Page 120: A 1999 Herblock cartoon, copyright by The Herb Block Foundation.
Page 226 (top): Bettmann/Corbis
Page 226 (bottom): Bettmann Corbis
Page 227 (top): Michael Newman/PhotoEdit, Inc.
Page 227 (bottom): Jana Birchum/Getty Images
Page 228: DOONESBURY© G.B. Trudeau. Reprinted with permission of Universal Press Syndicate. All Rights Reserved.
Page 331: Patrick Roberts/Corbis
Page 332 (top): Patrick Roberts/Corbis
Page 332 (bottom): Bettmann/Corbis
Page 333 (top): Bettmann/Corbis
Page 333 (bottom): Ed Stein ©The Rocky Mountain News/Dist. by Newspaper Enterprise Association/United Media
Page 424 (top): National Museum of Health & Medicine, Armed Forces Institute of Pathology, NCP 1603
Page 424 (bottom): Todd Bigelow/Aurora/Getty Images
Page 425 (top): Dennis Brack/IPN/Aurora
Page 425 (bottom): AP/Wide World Photos

Page 426: Carol Simpson Productions
Page 535 (top): Dorothea Lange/Landov
Page 535 (bottom): Andrew Lichtenstein/Corbis
Page 536 (top): Ron Zalme
Page 536 (bottom): Kim Kulish/Corbis
Page 537: © 2006 J.P. Rini from cartoonbank.com
Page 634 (top): Bettmann/Corbis
Page 634 (bottom): AP/Wide World Photos
Page 635 (top): AP/Wide World Photos
Page 635 (bottom): Jim Bourg/Reuters/Landov
Page 636: Mike Keefe/Cagle Cartoons, Inc.
Page 748 (top): AP/Wide World Photos
Page 748 (bottom): Ahmad Al-Rubaye/AFP/Getty Images
Page 749 (top): AP/Wide World Photos
Page 749 (bottom): DOONESBURY© G.B. Trudeau. Reprinted with permission of Universal Press Syndicate. All Rights Reserved.
Page 750: Robert Landau/Corbis

INDEX OF AUTHORS
AND TITLES